D0843699

The
"True Professional Ideal"
in America

For Lynne, who heals

The
"True Professional Ideal" in America

A History

BRUCE A. KIMBALL

ROWMAN & LITTLEFIELD PUBLISHERS, INC.

ROWMAN & LITTLEFIELD PUBLISHERS, INC.

Published in the United States of America
by Rowman & Littlefield Publishers, Inc.
4720 Boston Way, Lanham, Maryland 20706

3 Henrietta Street
London WC2E 8LU, England

British Cataloging in Publication Information Available

Library of Congress Cataloging-in-Publication Data

Kimball, Bruce A.
The "True Professional Ideal" in America: A History/Bruce A. Kimball.
p. cm.
Includes bibliographical references and indexes.
1. Professions—United States—History. I. Title.
HD8038.U5K56   1992   331.7'12'0973—dc20   91-25259   CIP

ISBN 0–8476–8143–2 (pbk. : alk. paper)

Printed in the United States of America

♾™ The paper used in this publication meets the minimum requirements of
American National Standard for Information Sciences—Permanence of
Paper for Printed Library Materials, ANSI Z39.48–1984.

CONTENTS

—

TABLES

___

FIGURES

PREFACE

———

Though it is difficult to say exactly when a book began, I know that this study was under way by 1983, and it would not have been completed without the help of a number of individuals and institutions. For invaluable assistance, I wish to thank the staff of the Alexander Library of Rutgers University, American Baptist Historical Society, University of Pennsylvania Archives, Harvard University Libraries and Archives, Trask Library of Andover-Newton Theological School, Swem Library of the College of William and Mary, Baker Library of Dartmouth College, Sterling Library of Yale University, Massachusetts Historical Society, University of Houston Library, and, especially, the University of Rochester Libraries. I am indebted as well to my research assistants Kim Byoung-uk, Stephen Appel, and Kathleen Mahoney. I also gratefully acknowledge a small grant from the American Philosophical Society, a Liberal Arts Fellowship from Harvard Law School, a Spencer Fellowship from the National Academy of Education, and a Small Grant from the Spencer Foundation, which provided support for this research. Permission to quote in chapters 1 and 5 from Goethe's *Faust*, translated by Walter Kaufman, was kindly granted by Bantam, Doubleday, Dell Publishing Group, Inc., (Garden City, NY).

In addition, I wish to express heartfelt gratitude to several people who read drafts of chapters over the past eight years and provided criticism that helped immensely to improve the work: Eva Brann of St. John's College, Philip Gleason of the University of Notre Dame, Wendell Harris of Pennsylvania State University, Thomas Haskell of Rice University, Thomas James of Brown University, Geraldine Jonçich Clifford of the University of California, Myron Marty of Drake University, Edmund S. Morgan of Yale University, Herman Sinaiko of the University of Chicago, David Smith of Indiana University, Steven Weiland of the University of Minnesota, Marjorie Woods of the University of Texas, and Lynn Gordon, Christopher Lasch, and Philip Wexler of the University of Rochester. In particular, I wish to thank Lawrence Cremin, now deceased, Robert Hariman, and David Riesman and who provided support and feedback over the course of the project.

Finally, I must thank Lynne, Zachary, and now Rebecca, without whom the book might have been completed sooner, or perhaps later, and, in either case, without joy.

BIBLIOGRAPHICAL NOTE

———

Full citations are given for each source the first time it is cited in a chapter. Medical, legal and other specialized conventions have been converted to the same format as other citations, although law cases and statutes are cited in a slightly expanded version of conventional legal form.

Dates of the Julian calender, in which dates were recorded ten days behind the Gregorian calender and the new year began on March 25, have been converted to the Gregorian. Thus, a seventeenth-century date of March 12, 1630, becomes March 22, 1631.

Spelling, punctuation, and capitalization in older sources have generally been preserved, although some changes have been made in order to clarify the meaning or in cases where a modern edition seemed preferable to the edition of the original source that was available to me. Ellipsis has been omitted from the beginning and end of phrases, except where the sense would be changed.

Biblical quotations are from the King James version. Translations of other non-English works are my own unless otherwise indicated.

Short titles

Acts of Massachusetts Bay
   The Acts and Resolves, Public and Private, of the Province of the Massachusetts Bay, 21 vols. (Boston, 1869–1929).

American Bibliography
   Ralph R. Shaw and Richard H. Shoemaker, comps., *American Bibliography: a Preliminary Checklist for 1801–19* (New York, 1958–66), 22 vols.; Richard H. Shoemaker, *A Checklist of American Imprints, 1820–1825* (New York, 1964–9).

Archives of Maryland
> *Archives of Maryland, Proceedings and Acts of the General Assembly*, ed.
> William H. Browne et al. (Baltimore, 1883–).

Creeds and Platforms
> Williston Walker, ed., *The Creeds and Platforms of Congregationalism* (New
> York, 1893).

Curate of Souls
> John R. Moorman, ed., *The Curate of Souls, Being a Collection of Writings on
> the Nature of and Work of a Priest from the First Century after the Restoration
> 1660–1760* (London, 1958).

Earliest Laws of Connecticut
> John D. Cushing, comp., *The Earliest Laws of the New Haven and Connecticut
> Colonies, 1639–1673* (Wilmington, DE, 1977).

Earliest Laws of Rhode Island
> John D. Cushing, comp., *The Earliest Acts and Laws of the Colony of Rhode
> Island and the Providence Plantations, 1647–1719* (Wilmington, DE, 1977).

Harvard Graduates
> John Langdon Sibley, *Biographical Sketches of Graduates of Harvard Univer-
> sity in Cambridge, Massachusetts*, 3 vols. (Cambridge, MA, 1873–85); Clifford
> K. Shipton, *Biographical Sketches of Those Who Attended Harvard
> College*, vols. 4–18 (Cambridge, MA, 1933–75).

Historical Statistics
> US Bureau of the Census, *Historical Statistics of the United States, Colonial
> Times to 1970* (Washington, DC, 1975).

Laws of the Royal Colony of New Jersey
> Bernard Bush, comp., *Laws of the Royal Colony of New Jersey, New Jersey
> Archives, 3rd Ser.*, vols. 2–5 (Trenton, NJ, 1977–86).

Legal Mind in America
> Perry Miller, ed., *The Legal Mind in America: From Independence to the Civil
> War* (Garden City, NY, 1962).

Philadelphia Baptist Association
> *Minutes of the Philadelphia Baptist Association from AD 1707 to AD 1807,
> being the First One Hundred Years of Its Existence*, ed. A. D. Gillette (Phila-
> delphia, 1851).

Princetonians
> James McLachlan, *Princetonians 1748–1768, A Biographical Dictionary*
> (Princeton, 1976), [vol. 1]; Richard A. Harrison, *Princetonians 1769–1775, A
> Biographical Dictionary* (Princeton, NJ, 1980), [vol. 2]; Richard A. Harrison,

Princetonians 1776–1783, A Biographical Dictionary (Princeton, NJ, 1981), [vol. 3].

Public Records of Connecticut
   The Public Records of the Colony of Connecticut, 1636–1776, vols. 1–3, ed. J. H. Trumbull; vols. 4–15, ed. C. J. Hoadly, 15 vols. (Hartford: 1850–90).

Records of Massachusetts Bay
   Nathaniel B. Shurtleff, ed., *Records of the Governor and Company of the Massachusetts Bay in New England (1628–86)*, 5 vols. (Boston, 1853–4).

State Records of North Carolina
   William L. Saunders, ed., *The State Records of North Carolina*, 26 vols. (Raleigh, NC, 1886–1907).

Statutes of Pennsylvania
   James T. Mitchell and Henry Flanders, comps., *The Statutes at Large of Pennsylvania, from 1682 to 1801*, 18 vols. (Harrisburg, PA, 1896–1915).

Statutes of South Carolina
   David J. McCord and Thomas Cooper, eds., *The Statutes at Large of South Carolina*, 10 vols. (Columbia, SC, 1836–41).

Statutes of Virginia
   William W. Hening, ed., *The Statutes at Large; Being a Collection of All the Laws of Virginia, from the First Session of the Legislature, in the Year 1619*, 13 vols. (Richmond, VA [imprint varies], 1809–23).

US Statutes
   Statutes at Large of the United States of America.

Yale Graduates
   Franklin B. Dexter, *Biographical Sketches of the Graduates of Yale College with Annals of the College History*, series 1–7 (New York, 1885–).

Abbreviations

ABA   American Bar Association.
AHR   *American Historical Review.*
AJLH   *American Journal of Legal History.*
AMA   American Medical Association.
HEQ   *History of Education Quarterly.*
JP   Justice of the Peace.
NEA   National Education Association, *Journal of Proceedings and Addresses.*
OED   *Oxford English Dictionary* (cited references are identical in first edition of 1908 and second edition of 1989).
USCommEd (date)   US Commissioner of Education, Department of Interior, *Annual Reports for* [date] (Washington, DC, 1868–).
WMQ   *William and Mary Quarterly.*

1
INTRODUCTION

There are certain vocations of ancient lineage which by common consent are called professions ... they are the typical professions, and we must begin with them.

A. M. Carr-Saunders and P. A. Wilson, The Professions *(1933)*

What is to be counted as a profession? More particularly, what was counted as a profession ...? Was the word used at all ...? And if so, of what groups and by what groups?

Kenneth Charlton, "The Professions in Sixteenth-Century England" (1969)

I propose to define the professions as nothing more than a series of rather random occupations that have historically been called that in our culture.

Laurence Veysey, "Higher Education as a Profession: Changes and Discontinuities"
(1988)

In 1894 the president of the American Bar Association held forth on "The True Professional Ideal" in a widely reprinted address typifying the idealization of profession occurring in the United States in the late nineteenth and early twentieth centuries.[1] Echoing the ABA president, professionals of all types, from fellow

1. John F. Dillon, "The True Professional Ideal," *Reports and Transactions of the ABA* (1894): 409; reprinted in *American Law Review,* 28 (1894): 671; *West Virginia Bar,* 1 (1894): 176; *Law Times* (London), 97 (1894): 410; *Albany Law Journal,* 50 (1895): 130; *American Lawyer,* 3 (1895): 59.

members of the bar to the editor of the *Journal of Education*, advocated making "a nearer approach to the ideal" and maintained that individuals "cannot vote themselves a profession.... It must come from an indefinable sentiment generally recognized, born of ... idealizing an occupation." Successive presidents of the Carnegie Foundation for the Advancement of Teaching, which sponsored the famous Flexner report on medical education as well notable studies of other professions, likewise commended "the dominant ideal ... of regard for the honor of the profession."[2] Although this process of idealization has scarcely been noted, the concern for professionalization that accompanied "the true professional ideal" has led most twentieth-century scholars of the professions, notwithstanding quite varied perspectives and theories, to maintain that the late nineteenth century was the formative era for professions in the United States.

This book proposes a different interpretation, comprising three basic theses. First, the meaning of "profession" changed episodically in American history. Second, those changes in meaning were directly informed by the nature of the preeminent vocation to which the term conventionally referred. Third, the conventional meaning of the term reflexively informed the nature of that preeminent vocation. By this interpretation, the late nineteenth- and early twentieth-century developments in the meaning of "profession" – even its idealization – were not *the* formative era but *a* formative era among successive ones, including the twentieth century itself. The purpose, then, of this book is to explain how those episodic changes occurred in the meaning of "profession" and its cognates, including "professed," "professor," and "professional."

Now, if one assumes *a priori* that "profession" means a middle-class occupation or a high-status occupation, or even an occupation at all, then one should turn immediately to the helpful analyses of Everett Hughes, Robert Wiebe, Burton Bledstein, Magali Sarfatti Larson, or Eliot Freidson, to name a few of the often-cited scholars addressing this topic over the last four decades. But if one believes that understanding professions has something to do with the history of what were called "professions" then one will want something more than a look at the *Shorter Oxford English Dictionary*, or even the unabridged version, as these and most scholars of the professions have tended to do.

Given the "truly tremendous literature" on the professions that has appeared in the twentieth century,[3] it is surprising how little attention has been devoted to the actual usage of "profession" and its cognates in the past. This neglect is even more surprising in light of the recent attention to historical "keywords" and the "'linguistic turn' in recent academic thought."[4] Indeed, since it is widely

2. James C. Carter, Jr., "The Ideal and the Actual in the Law," *Reports and Transactions of the ABA* (1890): 3; Albert E. Winship, *Is there a Science of Pedagogy?* (Boston, 1892), pp. 8, 10, 12; Henry Suzzallo, "The Reorganization of the Teaching Profession," *NEA* (1913): 366; Henry S. Pritchett, "Introduction," Abraham Flexner, *Medical Education in the United States and Canada* (New York, 1910), pp. xiii–xiv.

3. Wilbert E. Moore and Gerald W. Rosenblum, *The Professions: Roles and Rules* (New York, 1970), pp. 245–91.

4. John P. Diggins, "Language and History," *Reviews in American History*, 17 (1989): 1. "Profession" unfortunately is not an entry in Raymond Williams, *Keywords: A Vocabulary of Culture and Society*, rev. edn (London, 1983), or Daniel T. Rodgers, *Contested Truths: Keywords in American Politics since Independence* (New York, 1987).

recognized that "few words are so loosely used as *profession*,"[5] it might appear obvious that understanding the past usage of the term could shed light on its current ambiguities. Nevertheless, some scholars have discussed the meaning of "The Term Profession" without considering its historical usage at all.[6] Even distinguished historians have dismissed the issue because "the safest course is to study the function and not the name."[7] On the other hand, some scholars who have at least consulted the *OED* have misinterpreted it,[8] and these misinterpretations demonstrate the further problem that the *OED* is misleading or misinformed at key points, such as when and how the terms "learned profession," "liberal profession," and "professional" emerged.[9]

Other scholars have pledged to attend to historical usage but soon lost their way. Kenneth Charlton promised to answer: "What was counted as a profession in the sixteenth century? Was the word used at all in that period? And if so, of what groups and by what groups?" But three pages later, without even addressing these questions, he dismissed them, announcing that "the *lexicographical* [issue] is perhaps the least valuable."[10] In their classic work, Carr-Saunders and Wilson stated that they would look only at occupations that they knew to be professions, not occupations that claim to be professions. One is eager to learn how this can be done, and surprised to find that such knowledge comes by listening to historical claims about "certain vocations of ancient lineage which by common consent are called professions." Having contradicted themselves and promised to examine

---

5. T. M. Stinnett, *The Profession of Teaching* (New York, 1962), p. 2.

6. A. R. Brubacher, *Teaching Profession and Practice* (New York, 1927), pp. 12–3; Howard S. Becker, "The Nature of a Profession," pp. 27–46, in *Education for the Professions*, ed. Nelson B. Henry (Chicago, 1962). John S. Brubacher discusses the history but offers no evidence on behalf of his erroneous views. "The Evolution of Professional Education," in *Education for the Professions*, p. 47.

7. J. H. Baker, *The Legal Profession and the Common Law, Historical Essays* (London, 1986), p. 108.

8. See Everett C. Hughes, "Professions" (1963), reprinted in *The Professions in America*, ed. Kenneth S. Lynn (Boston, 1967), p. 2; Hughes et al., *Education for the Professions of Medicine, Theology, Law and Social Welfare* (New York, 1973), p. 1; Edgar H. Schein and Diane W. Kommers, *Professional Education: Some New Directions* (New York, 1972), p. 7; Charles R. McKirdy, "Massachusetts Lawyers on the Eve of the American Revolution: The State of the Profession," in *Law in Colonial Massachusetts, 1630–1800* (Boston, 1984), p. 313n.

9. Among those misled are: Frances P. DeLancy, *The Licensing of Professions in West Virginia* (Chicago, 1938), pp. 2, 2n.; Morris L. Cogan, "Toward a Definition of Profession," *Harvard Educational Review*, 23 (1953): 34; Anthony Russell, *The Clerical Profession* (London, 1980), p. 9.

10. Kenneth Charlton, "The Professions in Sixteenth-Century England," *University of Birmingham Historical Journal*, 12 (1969): 20, 23. Eliot Freidson spends more effort than most in analyzing the origins of "profession". But his analysis is limited to examining the *OED* and *Webster's Third New International Dictionary* and "employing [his] own ear for the contemporary language." This analysis convinces him of "the contradiction and confusion intrinsic to [the term] in the English language," and the resulting "semantic ambiguity" seems to him to make a historical investigation of the term pointless. *Professional Powers* (Chicago, 1986), pp. 21, 26–7.

historical usage, Carr-Saunders and Wilson then arbitrarily dismissed the long-standing profession of theology and relied upon anachronistic interpretations of historical testimony. In the end, they studied neither things that are somehow known to be professions, nor things that "by common consent are called pro-fessions," but simply some vocations that they chose to identify as such, while draping themselves with the appearance of historicity.[11]

Even more telling is Burton Bledstein's influential history of "professionalism", which includes a section on the use of "words" in "the culture of professionalism." While addressing the historical meaning of "middle," "middle class," "amateur," "private," and other terms, Bledstein unaccountably neglects "profession" and "professional," and assumes at the outset that professionalism is "a cultural process by which the middle class in America matured and defined itself." When he does ask the historical question about "the meaning of this professional interest," Bledstein cites the definitions of a dozen twentieth-century sociologists writing about the twentieth century and adumbrates these definitions with a description of Victorian characteristics without providing evidence that "profession" was employed particularly in connection with those characteristics.[12]

If these are examples of studies that explicitly discuss the usage of the term "profession," it is scarcely surprising that established historians employ such terms as "liberal professions" and "learned professions" as though they were commonly used in the sixteenth and seventeenth centuries, without offering a single instance

11. A. M. Carr-Saunders and P. A. Wilson, *The Professions* (Oxford, 1933), pp. 3, 284, 294–5, 309. Chief among the quotations is one that many other sources have taken from Carr-Saunders and Wilson: "I hold every man a debtor to his profession, from the which as men do of course seek to receive countenance and profit, so ought they of duty to endeavour themselves, by way of amends, to be a help and an ornament thereunto." Francis Bacon, "Maxims of the Law," in *The Works*, ed. James Spedding et al. (Boston, 1861), vol. 14, pp. 179–80. Bacon is quoted by the *OED* and many other authorities in order to demonstrate that "the term profession indicated certain vocations with peculiar characteristics, and in this sense it has been used for centuries." Carr-Saunders and Wilson, p. 1. See Pritchett, "Intro-duction," p. xiv; Stinnett, *The Profession of Teaching*, p. 14; Geoffrey Holmes, *Augustan England: Professions, State and Society, 1680–1730* (London, 1982), p. 3, ch. 3; Burton R. Clark, *The Academic Life: Small Worlds, Different Worlds* (Princeton, NJ, 1987), p. vii.

12. Burton J. Bledstein, *The Culture of Professionalism: The Middle Class and the Develop-ment of Higher Education in America* (New York, 1976), pp. ix, 1–8, 31–2, 56–79, 86–87. This approach is carried even further in Clifford Siskin's recent attempt "to historicize ... the power of language, literacy, and the institution of literature" in order to "inquire historically into how literary activity constructed the professional" in the first half of the nineteenth century. Siskin maintains that addressing "the professionalization of work" requires "historicizing the terminology itself." His approach is to presuppose that "professional" means certain attributes, to identify those same attributes in Romanticism, and to infer that the latter is the source of the former. Aside from the fact that the correlation does not imply causation, Siskin cites the *OED* but not a single usage of "profession" or "professional" from the period in question. Surely, this approach is the farthest thing from "historicizing the terminology itself." "Wordsworth's Prescriptions: Romanticism and Professional Power," in *The Romantics and Us*, ed. Gene W. Ruoff (New Brunswick, NJ, 1990), pp. 309, 321. One might also have expected Gerald Graff to address the historical terminology, but he does not. *Professing Literature: An Institutional History* (Chicago, 1987).

of this usage.[13] For example, such usage is so far beyond doubt to Geoffrey Holmes that he offers no evidence apart from quoting an eighteenth-century phrase as though it were a commonplace in the seventeenth century. Meanwhile he cites a few examples of the term "profession" in a different sense, and these are presented as *variations* on the taken-for-granted major theme of "professions" meaning three "liberal" professions. Similarly, writing about the late nineteenth century in his Pulitzer-Prize-winning volume, Alfred Chandler discusses the "professionalization of the managers of large industrial enterprises" who took on "the standard appurtenances of a profession," including "professional societies ... professional journals ... professional courses." But in all of Chandler's discussion of "professionalization" no one is ever quoted using these terms.[14]

Given this widespread neglect of historical usage, it is no wonder that a prominent new work of historical sociology maintains that "definitions, then, must follow from theoretical questions.... My central questions and my framework thus determine my definition of profession.... I have used the word 'profession' very loosely." And other distinguished scholars, such as Laurence Veysey, throw up their hands in frustration: "it is best simply to give up the effort to abstractly define the term *professional*. That is, I propose to define professions as nothing more than a series of rather random occupations that have historically been called that in our culture."[15] However, these occupations were not random precisely because they were called "professions," and this fact is why they are interesting. Hence, the initial challenge for scholars, as Veysey himself implies, is not to define the term, but to examine definitions that were employed in the past. It therefore cries out to be studied: When and how did the word "profession" come into use? What were called the "professions"? Did this usage change? If so, how did these changes lead to "the true professional ideal" of the early twentieth century?

13. Baker, *The Legal Profession and the Common Law*, p. 123; C. W. Brooks, *Pettyfoggers and Vipers of the Commonwealth: The "Lower Branch" of the Legal Profession in Early Modern England* (Cambridge, UK, 1986), pp. 270–2, passim; Wilfrid R. Prest, ed., *The Professions in Early Modern England* (London, 1987), pp. 12–14; James W. Schmotter, "The Irony of Clerical Professionalism: New England's Congregational Minsters and the Great Awakening," *American Quarterly*, 31 (1979): 149.

14. Alfred D. Chandler, Jr., *The Visible Hand: The Managerial Revolution in American Business* (Cambridge, MA, 1977), pp. 130–3, 143, 281–2, 456, 464–8; Holmes, *Augustan England: Professions, State and Society, 1680–1730*, pp. 3–21, 83, 136. Though recognizing that "Holmes is attempting to push back the vocabulary of professionalism by a whole century," W. F. Bynum himself anachronistically writes of "the traditional learned professions." "Physicians, Hospitals and Career Structures in Eighteenth-Century London," in *William Hunter and the Eighteenth-Century Medical World*, ed. W. F. Bynum and Roy Porter (Cambridge, UK, 1985), pp. 111, 110.

15. Andrew Abbott, *The System of Professions: An Essay on the Division of Expert Labor* (Chicago, 1988), pp. 8–9, 315; Laurence R. Veysey, "Higher Education as a Profession: Changes and Discontinuities," in *The Professions in American History*, ed. Nathan O. Hatch (Notre Dame, IN, 1988), p. 17. Elsewhere Veysey proposes that professions are simply "a very miscellaneous sector of the population" ("The Plural Organized Worlds of the Humanities," in *The Organization of Knowledge in Modern America, 1860–1920* (Baltimore, MD, 1979), pp. 60ff.).

These questions about the meaning, status, and function of words are questions about rhetoric, and I hope to demonstrate that we must take rhetoric seriously in order to account for important moments in cultural transformation. These questions are not only important, but also difficult because the topic is enormously broad and the evidence is, in many respects, difficult to obtain and hazardous to generalize from. Nevertheless, we do have some guidelines, because it is well established that during the eighteenth and nineteenth centuries the term "professions" commonly referred to the fields of theology, law, medicine, and education – what scholars have sometimes called "the four great traditional professions."[16]

Theology, law, medicine, and education originally became associated in the medieval universities, which provided the meeting ground of learning for the other three fields in the form of graduate faculties. Into the fifteenth century, theology was the most esteemed among these disciplines and vocations, and medicine the least. Some individuals, such as John of Paris, considered law to rival theology, while others, such as John Baldus of Florence and John of Arezzo, considered medicine to rival law. But by and large, the order of increasing status was medicine, law, and theology, with teaching masters ranked correlatively above the practitioners. Coluccio Salutati and Pietro Paolo Vergerio observed this ranking, and their opinions carry special weight because they were both Renaissance humanists and no friends of the scholastic theologians.[17]

The conventional association of these four fields was adopted by sixteenth- and seventeenth-century Englishmen, such as Richard Baxter and Cotton Mather. Hence, legislation in the American colonies, such as New Jersey, gave special exemptions from military duty to "Ministers, Physitians [*sic*], School-Masters, [and] Civil Officers" of the government and courts.[18] And in the first edition of *An*

16. William J. Goode, "The Theoretical Limits of Professionalization," in *The Semi-Professions and their Organization*, ed. Amitai Etzioni (New York, 1969), pp. 267–8. Donald O. Schneider, "Education in Colonial American Colleges, 1750–1770, and the Occupations and Political Offices of their Alumni" (PhD diss., George Peabody College for Teachers, 1965), p. 166; Earl F. Cheit, *The Useful Arts and the Liberal Tradition* (New York, 1975), pp. 1–2. Barbara J. Harris, *Beyond her Sphere: Women and the Professions in American History* (Greenwood, CT, 1978), p. 116; Cindy Sondik Aron, *Ladies and Gentlemen of the Civil Service: Middle-class Workers in Victorian America* (New York, 1987), pp. 27ff. See Jackson T. Main, *The Social Structure of Revolutionary America* (Princeton, NJ, 1965), p. 275, passim; Magali Sarfatti Larson, *The Rise of Professionalism: A Sociological Analysis* (Berkeley, CA, 1977), pp. 4–5.

17. The treatises are: John of Paris, *Tractatus de potestate regia et papali* (1302–3); Coluccio Salutati, *Tractatus de nobilitate legum et medicinae* (1399); John Baldus, *Disputatio an medicina sit legibus politicis preferenda vel econtra* (1415); John of Arezzo, *De medicina et legum prestantia* (1450–70); Pietro Paolo Vergerio, *De ingenuis moribus et liberalibus adolescentiae studiis* (c.1400). See Lynn Thorndike, "Medicine versus Law in Late Medieval and Medicean Florence," *The Romanic Review*, 17 (1926): 8–31; Jean Leclerq, ed., *Jean de Paris et l'Ecclésiologie du XIIIe Siècle* (Paris, 1942), pp. 214–25; William H. Woodward, ed. and tr., *Vittorino da Feltre and Other Humanist Educators* (Cambridge, UK, 1897), pp. 93–118.

18. Richard Baxter, *Gildas Salvianus, or The Reformed Pastor* (1656; New York, 1860), pp. 46, 102, 131, 179, 356–8; Cotton Mather, *BONIFACIUS: An Essay upon the Good* (Cambridge, MA, 1710); Rosemary O'Day, *The English Clergy: The Emergence and Consolidation of a Profession, 1558–1642* (Leicester, UK, 1982), p. 1; *Laws of the Royal Colony of*

American Dictionary of the English Language (1828) Noah Webster defined "university" to include "the four faculties of theology, medicine, law, and the sciences and arts." By that point, these four fields were conventionally known as "the learned professions," as shown by entries in subsequent editions of Webster's dictionary.[19] Whether among individuals excluded from these fields, such as Catharine Beecher, or those well established within them, "the *four* learned professions" or simply "the professions" conventionally referred to clergy, attorneys, physicians, and teachers of the other three.[20]

To be sure, there were variations in eighteenth- and nineteenth-century lists of "the professions." The well established ranks within the British medical and legal professions never made the transition to the American colonies.[21] Neither did "the profession of arms," which was frequently cited by British observers, such as Joseph Priestley in 1764, Richard Edgeworth in 1809, and Byerly Thomson in 1857.[22] The British tradition of civilian armies weakened the military vocation relative to that on the Continent, and the British army and naval officers had relatively low status and income through the first half of the eighteenth century.[23]

New Jersey, vol. 2, pp. 19, 49, 133, 289, 411. The association extended also to the Continent where, in Germany, the liberal arts faculty had become the faculty of philosophy, a development that led Goethe to refer to four fields of study: "Philosophy/Jurisprudence and medicine, too,/And ... theology" from which are graduated "the shysters/The doctors, and teachers, and ... Christers." *Faust* (1808), tr. Walter Kaufmann (Garden City, NY, 1961), pt. 1, ll. 354–5, 366–7.

19. Noah Webster, *An American Dictionary of the English Language*, 2 vols. (New Haven, CT, 1828), s.v. "university"; Webster, *An American Dictionary of the English Language ... revised and enlarged by Chauncey A. Goodrich* (Springfield, MA, 1850), s.v. "profession."

20. Edward Brooks, "Centennial Thoughts on Normal Schools," *NEA* (1876): 164; Catharine E. Beecher, *The Evils Suffered by American Women and American Children: The Causes and the Remedy* (New York, 1847), pp. 18–20; *History and Manual of the Second Congregational Church and Society ... 1847–1895* (Palmer, MA, 1895); Edwin G. Dexter, "Training for the Learned Professions," *Educational Review*, 25 (1903): 28, 38; Suzzallo, "The Reorganization of the Teaching Profession," p. 363; [Walter F. Willcox], *Census Statistics of Teachers, Bulletin 23 of the US Bureau of the Census* (Washington, DC, 1905), p. 7; Mary D. Vaughan, comp., *Historical Catalogue of Brown University, 1764–1904* (Providence, RI, 1905), p. x; Francis B. Pearson, *The Teacher* (New York, 1921), p. 84; Leonidas W. Crawford, *Vocations within the Church* (Cincinnati, OH, 1920), pp. 43–5; Robert M. Hutchins, *The Higher Learning in America* (New Haven, CT, 1936), pp. 112–5.

21. Samuel Haber, "The Professions and Higher Education in America: A Historical View," in *Higher Education and the Labor Market*, ed. Margaret S. Gordon (New York, 1974), p. 240; Maxwell Bloomfield, "Law: The Development of a Profession," in *The Professions in American History*, ed. Nathan O. Hatch (Notre Dame, IN, 1988), p. 35.

22. Joseph Priestley, *An Essay on a Course of Liberal Education for Civil and Active Life* (1764), in *Lectures on History and General Policy* (London: 1793), p. 9; Richard L. Edgeworth, *Essays on Professional Education* (London, 1809), p. vii; H. Byerly Thomson, *The Choice of a Profession* (London, 1857), p. 1.

23. Holmes, *Augustan England: Professions, State and Society, 1680–1730*, ch. 9; Ian Roy, "The Profession of Arms," in *The Professions in Early Modern England*, ed. Wilfrid R. Prest (London, 1987), pp. 181–219; G. W. Stephen Brodsky, *Gentlemen of the Blade: A Social and Literary History of the British Army since 1660* (New York, 1988), chs. 1–2.

These factors were heightened in the colonies and the young American nation, where frontier fighting and guerilla tactics obviated formal military training. More-over, republican spirit led President Jefferson, to "undertake a social and political reformation" of the military in order to ensure that military obligation would inhere in citizenship rather than a specialized elite. In the words of Daniel Calhoun: "Americans only occasionally thought of the military as one of the learned professions, the infrequency with which they included it in lists of the professions signalized the extent to which they feared it."[24]

Another potential interloper into the "professions" was business or commerce. Although the early generations of merchants in the major colonial towns expressed anxiety over "their mediocre social credentials,"[25] they climbed the social ladder quickly. By 1846 the renowned preacher Theodore Parker suggested that "Com-merce and manufactures offer the most brilliant rewards.... Accordingly, the ablest men go into the class of merchants. The strongest men in Boston, taken as a body, are not lawyers, doctors, clergymen, bookwrights, but merchants."[26] Nevertheless, from Joseph Priestley in 1764 to John Lalor in 1839, Henry Ware Jr. in 1847, and Cambridge dons at the end of the century, almost no one dignified "the business of merchandise" with the term "profession," for "the professional man" was expected to avoid "the pursuit of wealth."[27] It was only in the twentieth century that some observers, such as Louis Brandeis, began to suggest that "business should be, and to some extent already is, one of the professions."[28]

24. Theodore J. Crackel, *Mr. Jefferson's Army: Political and Social Reform of the Military Establishment, 1801–1809* (New York, 1987), p. 14; Daniel H. Calhoun, *Professional Lives in America: Structure and Aspiration* (Princeton, NJ, 1965), p. 16. See Daniel J. Boorstin, *The Americans: The Colonial Experience* (New York, 1958), pp. 363ff.; Morris Janowitz, *The Professional Soldier: A Social and Political Portrait* (Glencoe, IL, 1960), chs. 1–3; Timothy K. Nenninger, *Leavenworth Schools and the Old Army: Education, Professionalism, and the Officer Corps of the United States Army, 1881–1918* (Westport, CT, 1978), p. 6; James L. Morrison, Jr., *"The Best School in the World": West Point, the Pre-Civil War Years, 1833–1866* (Kent, OH, 1986); Edward M. Coffman, *The Old Army: A Portrait of the American Army in Peacetime, 1784–1898* (New York, 1986), chs. 1–3; John Shy, "The American Military Profession," pp. 93–106, in *The Professions in American History*, ed. Nathan O. Hatch (Notre Dame, IN, 1988).

25. Thomas M. Doerflinger, *A Vigorous Spirit of Enterprise: Merchants and Economic Development in Revolutionary Philadelphia* (Chapel Hill, NC, 1986), pp. 135–9. See Virginia D. Harrington, *The New York Merchant on the Eve of the Revolution* (New York, 1935), p. 11; Bernard Bailyn, *The New England Merchants in the Seventeenth Century* (Cambridge, MA, 1955), p. 38; Frederick B. Tolles, *Meeting House and Counting House: The Quaker Merchants of Colonial Philadelphia, 1682–1763* (1948; New York, 1963), ch. 6.

26. Theodore Parker, "The Mercantile Classes" (1846), in *Works: Social Classes in a Republic*, ed. Samuel A. Eliot (Boston, 1907), p. 9.

27. Priestley, *An Essay on a Course of Liberal Education for Civil and Active Life*, p. 9; John Lalor, "The Social Position of Educators," in *The Educator: Prize Essays on the Means and Expediency of Elevating the Profession of the Educator in Society* (London, 1839), p. 78; Henry Ware, Jr., "The Principles that Should Govern a Young Man in the Choice of a Profession," in *Works* (Boston, 1847), vol. 3, p. 258; Sheldon Rothblatt, *The Revolution of the Dons: Cambridge and Society in Victorian England* (New York, 1968), pp. 257–8.

28. Louis D. Brandeis, *Business – A Profession* (Boston, 1914), p. 12. In 1920 R. H. Tawney argued that business should become professionalized in order to curb the "acquisi-

Consequently, it is well known that theology, law, medicine, and education had a long association extending back to the thirteenth century, and that they came to have particular bearing on the meaning of "profession" at least by the eighteenth and nineteenth centuries. The following chapters therefore pay special attention to these four vocations in assessing the changes in usage and meaning of "profess," "profession," "professed," "professional" and so forth in the American colonies and United States. In addition to, on the one hand, the actual usage of "profession" and its cognates and, on the other hand, the nature and status of four vocations that preeminently came to be called "professions," this assessment will involve analysis of cultural ideals and values as time passed. These three domains – the rhetoric of profession, the nature and status of vocations, and the cultural ideals and values – were reflexively related, and the reflexive relationships were extremely complex. Indeed, it is hazardous to generalize from the mosaic of episodic historical experience in each of these domains, let alone all three together. Nevertheless, it is possible to abstract certain broad patterns that are helpful as tentative frames of interpretation, even while other frames may usefully be abstracted from the same historical eras in regard to other issues and topics.[29] I turn now to describe my

---

tive" impulse and pursuit of self-interest. (*The Acquisitive Society* (New York, 1920), ch. 7.) Talcott Parsons wrote that professions and business were fundamentally distinct due to their respective motivations of altruistic service and acquisitiveness. ("Remarks on Education and the Professions," *International Journal of Ethics*, 47 (1937): 365–9.) But, within two years, Parsons's thoroughgoing functionalism led him to argue that business was indistinguishable from a profession insofar as it was functional and rationally organized. ("The Professions and Social Structure," *Social Forces*, 17 (1939): 457–67.) Into the 1960s, however, scholars were generally still inclined to regard business as an "emerging or marginal profession." Bernard Barber, "Some Problems in the Sociology of the Professions" (1965), reprinted in *The Professions in America*, ed. Kenneth S. Lynn (Boston, 1967), p. 22. See Barber, "Is American Business Becoming Professionalized? Analysis of a Social Ideology," pp. 121–46, in *Sociological Theory, Values, and Sociocultural Changes*, ed. Edward A. Tiryakian (New York, 1963); Howard R. Bowen, "Business Management: A Profession?', *Annals of the American Academy of Political and Social Science*, 297 (1955): 112–7; Richard L. Kozelka, "Business – the Emerging Profession," pp. 168–89, in *Education for the Professions*, ed. Nelson B. Henry (Chicago, 1962). Cf. Chandler, *The Visible Hand*, pp. 464–8, 490–7.

29. During the 1960s and 1970s historians were commonly advised to pursue detailed examinations of individuals, groups, and local communities. (Kenneth A. Lockridge, *A New England Town: The First Hundred Years* (New York, 1970), pp. xi–xv; John M. Murrin, "Review Essay," *History and Theory*, 2 (1972): 226–75.) By the 1980s such studies yielded a picture that "is to a considerable extent blurred, inconsistent, and often confusing." (Richard B. Sheridan, "The Domestic Economy," in *Colonial British America*, ed. Jack P. Greene and J. R. Pole (Baltimore, MD, 1984), p. 61. See Lawrence Stone, *The Past and the Present* (Boston, 1981), pp. 81–96; Bernard Bailyn, "The Challenge of Modern Historiography," *AHR*, 87 (1982): 1–24; Thomas Bender, "Wholes and Parts: The Need for Synthesis in American History," *Journal of American History*, 73 (1986): 120–36.) In response, advocates of the "close analysis of specific historical contexts" have implied that historians must choose between modest and accurate assertions about a small topic or woefully inaccurate and arrogant generalities. (T. H. Breen, "Creative Adaptations: Peoples and Cultures," in *Colonial British America*, p. 197; Kenneth A. Lockridge, *A New England Town*, enlarged edn (New York, 1985), pp. 181–91.) Now, if such a trade-off were a true statement of the matter, then one would face the dismaying responsibility of disaggregating or avoiding every

approach to abstracting and interpreting these broad patterns, which approach also
constitutes the organization of each subsequent chapter.

Architectonic and rhetoric

In analyzing the development of the meaning of "profession" through the early
twentieth century, I have found it helpful to think in terms of three eras, each
identified with a primary source of cultural inspiration and validation, a cultural
ideal. These are: "religion" through the mid-eighteenth century, "polity" through
the mid-nineteenth century, and "science" through the 1910s. Each of these
cultural ideals has special nuances conditioned by the context of the time, and is
manifested in what I will call the "architectonic" of the era. Here a word of historiographical background is necessary to explain this term and my choice of it.

Despite the efforts of Progressive historians from the early twentieth century, of
consensus historians who reacted to the Progressive "conflict" thesis, and of the
"new social historians," who have attempted to write history "from the bottom up,"[30]
the relationship between ideation and behavior in historical experience is still
not satisfactorily understood. This problem is particularly relevant for studying
professions and professionalization, which explicitly concern the relationship
between esoteric knowledge and conduct. On this topic especially, the perilous task
of historiography remains that of navigating between "the two great sins a method
of social study can commit": the Scylla of behaviorism and causal explanation and
the Charybdis of idealism and putatively objective description.[31] The vessel that
many have felt to be most seaworthy is "ideology."

---

generalization. But the proposition that by looking at a modest topic one can say something
more accurate is just as false as the modesty. For example, what began in the 1960s as the
study of the "New England Town" in the colonial period soon developed into the study of
Connecticut towns and Massachusetts towns, which then became the study of large, commercial, Massachusetts towns and smaller, farming, Massachusetts towns, and those located near
Boston and those in the hinterlands, and those in the seventeenth century and those in the
eighteenth century. Moreover, the town histories themselves demonstrated that the historian
cannot generalize even about an individual town, but must disaggregate it into villages and
neighborhoods, not to mention family units and, finally, individuals, for every person is
somewhat different from everybody else and each day in each person's life is different from
all others. (See James T. Lemon, "Spatial Order: Households in Local Communities and
Regions," in *Colonial British America*, pp. 86–122.) On the other hand, generalizations that
do not fit every or most or even *any* particular case can be helpful and accurate as heuristic
guides. Frictionless surfaces do not exist, and projectiles never move in straight lines. But
even in the natural sciences, such generalizations help to explain and understand phenomena,
at least until more adequate generalizations can be devised to replace them.

30. Jesse Lemisch, "The American Revolution Seen from the Bottom Up," in *Towards a
New Past: Dissenting Essays in American History*, ed. Barton Bernstein (New York, 1967),
pp. 3–45.

31. Roberto M. Unger, *Law in Modern Society: Toward a Criticism of Social Theory* (New
York, 1976), p. 256.

"Ideology," however, is employed from many different academic perspectives, ranging from sociology of knowledge to symbolic anthropology, and the term has become profoundly ambiguous in recent historiography of the professions. "Ideology" sometimes refers pejoratively to the belief system of the dominant class that tries to mask its interests by gaining adherence of the underclasses to the "legitimating mystification" of that belief system. In this view, "ideology means the appropriation of the general conceptual structure of a culture for the benefit of certain groups within that culture"; and "professional ideologies are intrinsically imperialistic."[32] For other scholars, "ideology" is a neutral term that refers to the prevailing belief system in a culture at a particular time without the pejorative implication that the ideology is conspiratorially conceived. Still others employ the term to refer to the beliefs of any group of individuals. Hence, "everyone, including the least educated members of the community, has an ideology."[33] Finally, to make matters more ambiguous, these different usages sometimes appear in the same work. Due partly to this ambiguity, as well as to its generally pejorative connotations, I have avoided the word "ideology" in this book, although it occasionally appears in the third sense above. Instead, I have employed the historical concept "architectonic," by which I hope to examine the meaning of the rhetoric that mediated ideation and behavior in the past.

The term "architectonic" is derived from the Greek roots *archi-* (from "chief," "first," or "master') and *tektōn* ("one who builds'). Together, these roots formed the Greek term *architektōn* ("chief artificer" or "master builder'). Aristotle extended this meaning in his discussions of the relationship between the sciences, employing *architektōn* to refer to the "first science" or "master science" that organizes other sciences, determining and rationalizing their relationships.[34]

32. Quotations are from Peter Gabel and Jay M. Feinman, "Contract Law as Ideology," in *The Politics of Law: A Progressive Critique*, ed. David Kairys (New York, 1982), p. 176; Edward Countryman, *A People in Revolution: The American Revolution and Political Society in New York, 1760–90* (Baltimore, MD, 1981), p. 96; Eliot Freidson, "Professions and the Occupational Principle," in *The Professions and their Prospects*, ed. Freidson (London, 1971), p. 31. Laurence Shore, *Southern Capitalists: The Ideological Leadership of an Elite, 1832–1885* (Chapel Hill, NC, 1986), ch. 1; Larson, *The Rise of Professionalism*, pp. xv–xviii, ch. 12; Jan Goldstein, " 'Moral Contagion': A Professional Ideology of Medicine and Psychiatry in Eighteenth- and Nineteenth-Century France," in *Professions and the French State, 1700–1900*, ed. Gerald L. Geison (Philadelphia, 1984), pp. 181–220.

33. Gary B. Nash, *The Urban Crucible: Social Change, Political Consciousness, and the Origins of the American Revolution* (Cambridge, MA, 1979), p. 339. A. G. Roeber, *Faithful Magistrates and Republican Lawyers: Creators of Virginia Legal Culture, 1680–1810* (Chapel Hill, NC, 1981), pp. xv–xvi; Theodore Caplow, *The Sociology of Work* (Minneapolis, MN, 1954), ch. 6.

34. Aristotle, *Nicomachean Ethics* 1094a14–15, *Metaphysics* 1013a13–15; Henry G. Liddell and Robert Scott, *A Greek–English Lexicon*, rev. Henry S. Jones (Oxford, 1968), s.v. "architektōn." In the words of Richard McKeon: "Architectonic arts treat ends which order the ends of subordinate arts. The architectonic art is the most authoritative art.... At each stage of the evolution of the arts and sciences since the Renaissance, an architectonic art was sought and used." "The Uses of Rhetoric in a Technological Age: Architectonic Productive Arts" (1971), in *Rhetoric: Essays in Invention and Discovery*, ed. Mark Backman (Woodbridge, CT, 1987), pp. 3, 10.

Eventually the word passed into English with similar epistemological and meta-physical implications. In his *Apology for Poetry* (c.1580), Philip Sidney discussed the "serving sciences ... directed to the highest end of the mistress-knowledge, by the Greeks called *architectonike*." A century later Ralph Cudworth, the Master of Christ's College at Cambridge, published *The True Intellectual System of the Universe*, commenting on "an immoveable and standing *Nous* or intellect ... or architectonic framer of the whole world." This influential work was subsequently republished in England in 1706, 1733, 1743, 1820, and 1840, and had a significant American readership. Ralph Waldo Emerson owned and annotated a copy of the 1820 edition, and an American edition was published in 1837.[35] In that same year, William Whewell in his *History of the Inductive Sciences* invoked "the language of Aristotle" and noted that "Classification is the *architectonic* science."[36] In his 1851 inaugural address at the University of Michigan, President Henry Tappan observed that "the *architectonic* science of theology" had passed away, and in 1870, an American jurist, in a widely reprinted article, argued for the supremacy of jurisprudence as "the 'science of sciences'" ... just as the chief-architect and designer of an edifice is superior to the workmen."[37] Later that decade, Edward Caird maintained that "the architectonic impulse of reason ... seeks to refer all science to one principle," a point he repeated in his magisterial *The Critical Philosophy of Immanuel Kant*, which John Dewey acclaimed in1890.[38] By that point, the term was becoming outmoded, a fact that testified, ironically enough, to the supremacy of the new architectonic of the era. Alternative definitions of "science" were extinguished in deference to the new master science.

"Architectonic" thus had a long history extending to the end of the nineteenth century. The term referred to the dominant science or discipline that gave systematic formalization to the highest values and ideals of the culture, the primary source of cultural validation, which might today be discussed in terms of "cultural hegemony" or "ideological hegemony."[39] Given the implications of these latter terms, however, there are at least two reasons to prefer the construct of architectonic for understanding the relations between belief systems in American culture through the end of the nineteenth century.

35. Philip Sidney, *An Apology for Poetry* (c.1580), in *The Norton Anthology of English Literature* (New York, 1968), vol. 1, p. 481. Cudworth is quoted from the American edition: *A True Intellectual System of the Universe [1678], with an Account of the Life and Writings of R. Cudworth by Thomas Birch* (New York, 1837), vol. 1, pp. 17–23, 539. Emerson's signed and annotated copy is in the Houghton Library at Harvard University.

36. William Whewell, *History of the Inductive Sciences, from the Earliest to the Present Times* (London, 1837), vol. 3, p. 227.

37. Henry P. Tappan, *University Education* (Ann Arbor, MI, 1851), p. 31; "Lawyers and Doctors," *Albany Law Journal*, 7 (1873): 35.

38. Edward Caird, *A Critical Account of the Philosophy of Kant with an Historical Introduction* (New York, 1877), p. 575; Caird, *The Critical Philosophy of Immanuel Kant*, 2 vols. (Glasgow, 1889); John Dewey, in the *Andover Review*, 13 (1890): 325–7. See Immanuel Kant, *Critique of Pure Reason* (1787), tr. Norman K. Smith (1929; New York, 1965), I, pt. II, div. II, ch. 2, ss. 3, p. B502; II, ch. 3, p. B860.

39. See T. J. Jackson Lears, "The Concept of Cultural Hegemony: Problems and Possibilities," *AHR*, 90 (1985): 567–93.

First is that "cultural hegemony" conjures up images of jackboots and truncheons, as though competing ideas and beliefs were being rounded up and herded off to prison camp. Granted, censorship has been used to support sovereign ideologies, but the more powerful and enduring kind of intellectual sovereignty is based upon rationalization and conviction. One important advantage, then, of thinking in terms of the construct of architectonic is that it implies a coherent rationalized ordering among ideologies, rather than a hamfisted hegemony. Understanding the architectonic helps to explain the basis for rationalization and conviction within a culture and, ultimately, for the intellectual sovereignty of a belief system. The architectonic is one ideology among many in a culture, but one that happens to serve as the reference point for all others, providing their premises, structuring their relationships, and explaining human experience by ordering it systematically and comprehensively, under the assumption that all things that need explanation are included within its system.

Beyond assuming that an ideology becomes an architectonic because it "fits" what are perceived as the ultimate ends and highest values of a culture in a particular era, I do not speculate on whether the ends and values precede the ideology or vice versa, or why the cultural ends and values change.[40] In examining the meaning of "profession" in American culture, I am more concerned to propose an analytic framework that comprehends, on the one hand, sincere belief in the ultimacy of certain ends and values and in the integrity of associated kinds of knowledge, as well as, on the other hand, the evident historical experience that such kinds of knowledge and values are relative and transitory. This approach requires that one examine a profession from its own perspective, while also stepping outside that perspective in order to place it in context. This dialectic of appreciation and detachment is the second reason for preferring "architectonic" over "cultural hegemony." Because it was employed throughout the period under consideration here, "architectonic" provides a framework for detached analysis, expressed in terms that were meaningful to the historical period under consideration. Such cannot be said for "cultural hegemony."[41]

In the following chapters I therefore identify successive, though overlapping, cultural eras and ideals, analyzing them in conjunction with their architectonic sciences whose nature is conditioned by the historical context: colonial religion with Calvinist theology, early national polity with liberal jurisprudence, and late nineteenth-century science with a shift from Baconian to experimental method. Associated with each ideal and architectonic is a vocation that successively achieved preeminence: those who worked in the church, in the law, and in education.

---

40. For example, one might explain such shifts in terms of class conflict or the evolution of epistemology or social technology. See Karl Popper, *Objective Knowledge: An Evolutionary Approach* (Oxford, 1972); Arthur Stinchcombe, "Social Structure and Organizations," in *Handbook of Organizations*, ed. James G. March (New York, 1965), ch. 4.

41. This would also apply to the alternative constructs of cultural *mentalité* and "meaning." See James A. Henretta, "Families and Farms: *Mentalité* in Pre-Industrial America," *WMQ*, 3d ser., 35 (1978): 3–32; William J. Bouwsma, "Intellectual History in the 1980s: From History of Ideas to History of Meaning," *Journal of Interdisciplinary History*, 12 (1981): 279–91; David A. Hollinger, *In the American Province: Studies in the History and Historiography of Ideas* (Bloomington, IN, 1985), pp. 130–51.

I demonstrate this preeminence by looking at the authority and status of these individuals first within their professional institution and then in political, social, and economic life generally. Finally, I compare the preeminent "profession" with other vocations, particularly those other three that were conventionally known as "professions," and I examine the relative appeal of each of the "professions" to the most advantaged of the population during the era in question. Interwoven in this discussion of cultural ideals, architectonics, and institutional, political, social, and economic authority, are posited specific links to the rhetoric of "profession." I try to show how the very nature of the vocations reflexively informed and was informed by the usage of "profession." Here again, a word of explanation is in order.

The emphasis upon social history over the past three decades has resulted in a tendency to dismiss formal, documentary sources on the grounds that documents hover above the real stuff of historical experience or express the views of elites imposed upon the mute masses. Most scholars concur on the value of particular, empirical, often quantitative studies coupled with analysis of ideology, but this agreement has led to discrediting literary sources.[42] In response, it must be asked: how is the ideology to be known? When A. G. Roeber notes that the problems of explaining the relationship between "ideation and behavior ... now occupy the best scholars of the Revolution and republicanism" including "J. G. A. Pocock, John Murrin, Lance Banning, Drew McCoy, and myself,"[43] one wonders whether such scholars are groping about for the very thing they have thrown away: the rhetoric of the time. Rhetoric mediates between ideation and behavior and constitutes the vehicle of ideology. "A word ... is the skin of a living thought," Justice Holmes once observed.[44] Indeed, it can be argued that the rhetoric *is* the ideology.

This emphasis upon rhetoric appears to neglect the fact that sometimes people lie or, at least, deceive themselves and, even if speaking truly, represent only a single point of view. Due to these limitations of being deceitful or unrepresentative, formal testimony and prominent documents have been discredited in recent historiography. "Rhetoric is often a weak indicator of reality," it is said. Church sermons are held to belie the popular culture of parishioners, and the "rosy picture" of Benjamin Franklin's *Autobiography* is tossed aside because it "was written for propaganda purposes."[45] Meanwhile physicians are alleged to cloak their

42. See Peter Laslett, "The Wrong Way through the Telescope, a Note on Literary Evidence in Sociology and Historical Sociology," *British Journal of Sociology*, 27 (1976): 319–42. Joyce Appleby has noted the paradox that "social historians ... are no less dependent upon literary evidence, but in their case, the literature comes from modern sociology rather than contemporary writings." "Value and Society," in *Colonial British America*, ed. Jack P. Greene and J. R. Pole (Baltimore, MD, 1984), p. 308.
43. A. G. Roeber, "The *Mentalité* of Debt: The Virginia Paradox," *Reviews in American History*, 15 (1987): 12–3.
44. Quoted in Clinton Rossiter, *Conservatism in America: The Thankless Persuasion*, 2d edn (New York, 1962), p. 5.
45. Quotations are from David B. Danbom, *"The World of Hope": Progressives and the Struggle for an Ethical Public Life* (Philadelphia, 1987), p. viii; Richard S. Dunn, "Servants and Slaves: The Recruitment and Employment of Labor," in *Colonial British America*, ed. Jack P. Greene and J. R. Pole (Baltimore, MD, 1984), p. 181. See Cynthia S. Jordan, " 'Old Words' in 'New Circumstances': Language and Leadership in Post-Revolutionary America," *American Quarterly*, 40 (1988): 491–513.

motives by "employing the usual rhetoric about ... 'promoting medical knowledge' and protecting the public," while ministers hide behind "the coy ambiguities of ... clerical rhetoric."[46]

Yet it must be asked how the accusers know the *real* thoughts and feelings behind "the usual rhetoric." How is one to determine why Franklin wrote the *Autobiography* or why doctors seek to promote medical expertise? Knowledge about socio-economic class is not indicative of thoughts and feelings unless additional assumptions are made about how people in such-and-such circumstances feel and think. And these assumptions are certainly no less conjectural than are interpretations of the expressed rhetoric.[47] As to the objection that prominent, formal documents are unrepresentative of a culture, it may be wondered how anything could be more representative. Surely obscurity does not make testimony more representative.[48] Furthermore, this objection overlooks the reflexive nature of rhetoric. Sermons that were heard by every citizen in a small town or essays that were read by thousands of individuals shaped the way their listeners and readers thought and spoke. Tom Paine's writings both reflected and shaped "common sense." Expressing the thoughts and feelings of an individual, however imperfectly, rhetoric is itself shaped by the exchange with others' expression, and that shaping inevitably reforms the individual's thoughts and feelings and influences their future expression.

Like the construct "architectonic," this attention to rhetoric is not new. In broad terms, it extends back to Isocrates and Cicero, while in the young United States it appeared in Noah Webster's undertaking *An American Dictionary of the English Language* with the express notion that linguistic sovereignty and political sovereignty are intimately linked and that changing language can change behavior. More recently, a number of studies have appeared that analyze the historical importance of "keywords" and times "when words lose their meaning." Thus, the importance of rhetoric is longstanding and now receiving attention from scholars.[49] Even in this

46. Quotations are from: Peter D. Hall, "The Social Foundations of Professional Credibility: Linking the Medical Profession to Higher Education in Connecticut and Massachusetts, 1700–1830," in *The Authority of Experts*, ed. Thomas L. Haskell (Bloomington, IN, 1984), p. 117; Stephen Botein, "Income and Ideology: Harvard-Trained Clergymen in Eighteenth-Century New England," *Eighteenth-Century Studies*, 13 (1980): 399, 401.

47. Anticipating that someone might contend that "the 'model' professions of medicine and the law *sought* to insert themselves in the upper rungs of the status system" (Larson, *The Rise of Professionalism*, p. 159. Emphasis added.) Milton H. Friedman and Simon Kuznets noted in 1945, "An adequate judgment of this explanation would be exceedingly difficult.... It would require an analysis of the motives, acts, and influence of each group involved in controlling entry into medicine – the American Medical Association and its Council on Medical Education, the individual medical schools and their national association, the state boards of medical examiners and their national federation," not to mention every individual involved. *Income from Independent Professional Practice* (New York, 1945), p. 137.

48. See Lewis O. Saum, *The Popular Mind of Pre-Civil War America* (Westport, CT, 1980), appendix. Cf. Anne Norton, *Alternative Americas: A Reading of Antebellum Political Culture* (Chicago, 1986). It might be added that attention to published rhetoric is particularly pertinent when studying the formation of elites, such as professions.

49. Williams, *Keywords*; Rodgers, *Contested Truths*; James B. White, *When Words Lose their Meaning: Constitutions and Reconstitutions of Language, Character, and Community*

recent historical work, however, rhetoric is often regarded as a disguise and the term is used pejoratively.[50] Yet, rehabilitating the word "rhetoric" is the key to interpreting events in terms that were meaningful to the historical period under consideration. In order to attend to the rhetoric of the past – as regarding "profession" – one must begin by taking seriously the rhetoric about rhetoric. The fact that scholars of the professions generally employ the word "rhetoric" to suggest duplicity and subterfuge fits perfectly with the general lack of attention to the rhetoric of "profession."

What I have tried to do is to provide an abstracted framework of cultural ideals, of intellectual developments, and of institutional, political, social, and economic status and authority of vocations. Into this framework is woven an account of six "moments" in the rhetoric of "profession," six changes in the usage of "profession" and its cognates. First was the extension of "profession" from referring to a religious vow to denoting the group who made the vow, especially, the "secular" clergy. Second was the shift in reference from the clergy to dignified, non-religious occupations. Third was the introduction of the terms "learned professions" and "liberal professions," which identified certain dignified occupations. Fourth was the displacement of "professed" by "professional" as the adjective denoting "occupational" or "vocational." Fifth was the introduction of the noun "professional" to replace "professor," which was narrowed to the field of education. The sixth moment in the rhetoric of "profession" was the sloughing away of the terms "learned professions" and "liberal professions" in the early twentieth century, as "professions" began to refer to many vocations, just as it had in sixteenth-century English.

These changes in rhetorical usage, I try to show, are linked to episodic shifts in cultural ideals, architectonics, and the status and authority of the vocations called "professions." In fact, these vocations are informed by the meaning of "profession" they inherit, while they reflexively inform that meaning with their particular nature. Out of this episodic, reflexive historical process, "the true professional ideal" emerges by the beginning of the twentieth century. Ideally, a "profession" is a dignified occupation espousing an ethic of service, organized into an association,

---

(Chicago, 1984), ch. 9. See, too, Donald Weber, *Rhetoric and History in Revolutionary New England* (New York, 1987), ch. 1; David Simpson, *The Politics of American English, 1776–1850* (New York, 1988), chs. 1, 2. Meanwhile, in contemporary social and political theory, there have appeared works on rhetoric that are related to the explosion of recent theory on interpretation and "hermeneutics." See Richard H. Brown, *Society as Text: Essays on Rhetoric, Reason, and Reality* (Chicago, 1987); Paul Rabinow and William M. Sullivan, eds., *Interpretive Social Science: A Second Look* (Berkeley, CA, 1987); and the book series "Rhetoric of the Human Sciences" from University of Wisconsin Press, with its flagship work: *Rhetoric of the Human Sciences: Language and Argument in Scholarship and Public Affairs*, ed. John S. Nelson et al. (Madison, WI, 1987). A helpful bibliographical source and analysis is John S. Nelson, "Approaches, Opportunities and Priorities in the Rhetoric of Political Inquiry: A Critical Synthesis," *Social Epistemology*, 2 (1988): 21–42.

50. See George H. Daniels, ed., *Nineteenth-Century American Science: A Reappraisal* (Evanston, IL, 1972), p. xi; Botein, "Income and Ideology," pp. 406–8, 412; Burton J. Bledstein, "Humanistic Pieties, Historical Counterpieties," *Reviews in American History*, 15 (1987): 413–7.

and practicing functional science. These characteristics then provide the topics for most of twentieth-century discussion about professions, notwithstanding great diversity in theoretical and normative assessments of professions.

This final point is the import of the concluding chapter, where I propose that twentieth-century scholarship of the professions has largely remained in the same "groove," in Whitehead's term, even though scholars profess otherwise.[51] I argue that this scholarship is of a piece, being determined by a rhetoric, and thus a history, that it does not understand and by scholars' interest in being a "profession," which may explain the lack of understanding. My intent in this conclusion is to demonstrate again that in order to understand professions we must examine how the word was used and how that usage was transformed episodically and reflexively by the nature of its referents and the contemporaneous intellectual, political, economic, and social context.

51. Alfred N. Whitehead, *Science in the Modern World* (1925; New York, 1963), pp. 78, 275–6.

2

1600–1760s

THEOLOGY AND THE PROFESSION OF SERVICE

PROFESSION in the most frequent and familiar apprehension, signifies *the publike manifestation of our assent to the doctrine of Faith ... and our resolution to persist in the maintainance of the same.*

Thomas Hooker, A Survey of the Summe of Church Discipline *(1648)*

Divinity is the Queen of the Sciences: a Profession in itself, and in the estimation of all that are wise, the most noble.

Ebenezer Gay, The Mystery of the Seven Stars in Christ's Right Hand *(1752)*

Professors of religion are too ready to join with the men of the world, in the useless, vain, and sinful customs of it.... You profess to be people of the Lord ... consider, then, the great High Priest of your profession, who was holy, harmless, undefiled.

Samuel Jones, Philadelphia Baptist Association *(1778)*

From the early seventeenth century until the mid-eighteenth century theology was the preeminent profession in America, both in the sense expressed by Rev. Thomas Hooker and in the usage of Rev. Ebenezer Gay. The Queen of the Sciences and her ministers reigned until nearly the 1760s, when the Treaty of Paris, the "Intolerable Acts," and still another wave of inflation and economic recession made apparent new social, political, and economic conditions, as well as new kinds of intellectual authority and, with it all, new ways of speaking. The meaning of "profession" was transformed by these developments, and the new denotations became conventional by the end of the eighteenth century.

Rhetorical and Intellectual: "our holy profession"

The word in English stems directly from the classical Latin noun *professio*, which derived from the past participle *professus* of the verb *profiteri*, denoting "to declare publicly, own freely, acknowledge, avow." *Professio* in the time of Cicero and Tacitus referred primarily to an oath, vow or declaration, and this meaning continued to predominate in the monastic culture of the early and high Middle Ages. Gradually adopted into English, the forms of the verb *profiteri* retained their medieval denotations through the sixteenth century. "Profess" was used only in a religious sense. In its passive form of "to be professed," it meant "to have made one's profession of religion ... to take the vows of some religious order," while in the active voice, it denoted "to receive the profession ... to receive or admit into a religious order." By the sixteenth century "profess" was employed reflexively and intransitively and in the sense of making any vow or affirmation, including "to declare oneself expert or proficient in" some craft or art.[1] Hence, in 1611 the King James Bible clarified the phrase "to maintain good works" with the gloss: "professe honest trades," and in 1651 Thomas Hobbes referred to anyone "that professeth the study of the Law."[2]

The noun "profession" meanwhile denoted "declaration, promise or vow made by one entering a religious order." Over time, this denotation was extended in two ways, and this twofold semantic extension constitutes the first of six moments in the rhetoric of "profession," each of which marked a step in the emergence of what would become "the true professional ideal" in America. On the one hand, the meaning of "profession" was extended from referring to the vow, to denoting the act of joining and belonging, and then to signifying the group of those who made the vow. "Profession" in English thus came to refer to the group of likeminded clerics who made the profession: "a particular order of monks, nuns, or other professed persons."[3] On the other hand, the meaning of profession was extended from referring to the "regular" monastic clergy to denoting the "secular" clergy and the laity. This latter development was rooted in the sixteenth-century Protestant Reformation. Luther, Calvin, Zwingli, and the radical reformers differed on

1. *Oxford Latin Dictionary*, s.v. "professio"; *OED*, s.v. "profess." The *OED* proposes that "profess" was used "often implying insincerity," but little evidence is offered to support this point, and such usage was infrequent in the American colonies apart from Protestant attacks directed against Roman Catholics.

2. *Titus* 3: 14; Thomas Hobbes, *Leviathan* (1651), ed. C. B. Macpherson (Harmondsworth, UK, 1968), pt. II, ch. 26, sect. 8, no. 142.

3. *OED*, s.v. "profession." This extension in meaning and the resulting ambiguity appeared as well in other European languages that incorporated the Latin *professio*. Ignatius of Loyola, writing in Spanish in the second half of the sixteenth century, employed the word *prófession* to refer to the most solemn vows taken by those entering the Society of Jesus: "I, N, make profession, and I promise to Almighty God...." He also prescribed "The Procedure in Admission to Profession" and referred to "those who are admitted to the profession." Ignatius of Loyola, *The Constitutions of the Society of Jesus*, ed. and tr. George E. Ganss (St. Louis, 1970), p. 82n.; pt. 5 ch. 1 sect. 1 para. 524, sect. 3 para. 527, sect. 5 para. 531.

many points, but they were united in rejecting the medieval view that the monastic orders, who "professed" a rule (*regula*) to govern their lives, were normative for the clergy and for Christian life in general. According to the medieval norm, the "regular," monastic clergy were more religious than the laity or the "secular" priesthood, the parish clergy who lived in and of the world.[4] In contrast, Protestants maintained that the secular clergy and, indeed, the Christian laity were no less religious than the monastic clergy because no order of persons could claim to be above or apart from the sinful world. In England this belief was reflected in the application of the word "profession" to the creed or confession that any Protestant would make. Whether from a fugitive English Puritan such as William Ames in the 1620s, a prominent Anglican such as Henry Dodwell in the 1670s, or John Locke, who was pleased to tolerate either one, the word "profession" came to refer primarily to the religious oath or creed of a Protestant believer.[5]

This semantic secularization from friars to laity went hand in hand with the other kind of semantic extension from a vow to a group. As a result, "profession" began to refer ambiguously both to the religious creed or oath and to the corporate group of lay believers who made the vow. Hence, the General Court of Massachusetts Bay Colony warned in 1657 that the failure to provide for ministers "such suitable supply as theire state and condicion doe require ... tendeth ... to the scandall of our proffession."[6] This usage, in which "profession" signified the body of professors as well as what they professed, appeared subsequently in the words of English Baptist minister David Rees, who addressed "any Body of profess'd Christians" or "the Christian profession." A century later the ambiguity was still evident in discussion at the Philadelphia Baptist Association, which admonished: "Professors of religion are too ready to join with the men of the world, in the useless, vain, and sinful customs of it.... You profess to be the people of the Lord ... consider, then, the great High Priest of your profession, who was holy, harmless, undefiled."[7]

This Protestant secularizing of "profession" did not, however, completely obliterate the semantic restriction that derived from the "regular" monastic clergy. While English Protestants extended "profession" to refer to the body of Christian professors, they also applied it restrictively to the clergy, who were the group of professors charged with particular responsibility for the Christian religion. This lingering restriction of the corporate sense of "profession" appears clearly in the writings of Anglican Bishop Gilbert Burnet, who published in 1692 *A Discourse of Pastoral Care* that went through 14 editions by 1821. Burnet's language demon-

---

4. This view persisted into the Catholic Counter-reformation, as when Loyola stipulated that all candidates for the Jesuits "must be priests before [making] their profession" into the Society. Ignatius of Loyola, *The Constitutions of the Society of Jesus,* "The General Examen," pt. 1 ch. 1 sect. 8 para. 12.

5. William Ames, *The Marrow of Sacred Divinity, drawne out of the Holy Scriptures* (London, 1643), pp. 140–1; Henry Dodwell, *Two Letters of Advice* (1672), in *Curate of Souls,* pp. 40–1; John Locke, *A Second Letter Concerning Toleration* (1690), in *The Works* (1823; Aalen, Germany, 1963), vol. 6, pp. 61–2.

6. *Records of Massachusetts Bay,* vol. 4, pt. 1, p. 286.

7. David Rees, *The State of True Religion in all Ages ... Consider'd. With a Modest Plea for the Maintenance of the Christian Ministry* (London, 1726), pp. viii, 21, 32; Samuel Jones, "Circular Letter" (1778), in *Philadelphia Baptist Association,* pp. 160–1.

strates the ambiguity between referring to a creed and designating the corporate body of the clergy. He calls on ministers

> to raise the honour of our holy profession, to walk worthy of it, to perform the engagements that we came under at the altar, when we were dedicated to the service of God and the church.... [I]f we studied to honour God, and so to do honour to our profession, we might justly hope that he would raise it again to that credit which is due to it.[8]

In a letter to the clergy of his diocese, Simon Patrick, who was ordained a Presbyterian clergyman in 1648, then converted to Anglicanism and became a bishop in 1690, wrote similarly: "the pastors and guides of the church of all ranks [should] adorn their profession with a good conversation, and apply themselves seriously to the duties of their function.... [I]t is not enough for men in holy orders to be free from those crying sins.... It is a monstrous thing to see one of that holy profession give himself to the excesses of eating and drinking, or other sensual appetites."[9]

To be sure, "confession" was sometimes interchanged with "profession," as appears in the Savoy "Declaration of ... the Congregational Churches in England" (1658), a declaration that was echoed in "A Confession of Faith" issued by the Reforming Synod of New England ministers in 1680. Recalling these two statements in 1726, Cotton Mather employed the two words interchangeably.[10] Meanwhile the 1694 Yearly Meeting of Society of Friends in Philadelphia spoke of those "who are Believers, and Profess, and Confess the Truth," and the first Baptist Association in America employed "confession of faith" interchangeably with "profession of faith" from its founding in 1707.[11] Nevertheless, the English colonists most often followed the practice of Puritan Richard Baxter's influential *The Reformed Pastor* (1656) and predominantly employed "profession" in the sense of "catechisms and professions."[12] In 1643 the leading minister of Connecticut, Thomas Hooker, published a treatise that, as Increase Mather noted in 1719, "had the Approbation of all the Ministers" and, in the twentieth century, has been called "the supreme exposition" of Congregationalism.[13] Therein, Hooker gave what is

8. Gilbert Burnet, *A Discourse of the Pastoral Care*, 14th edn (London, 1821), pp. xxxvi, xxxiv–xxxv.

9. Simon Patrick, *A Letter of the Bishop of Chichester to his Clergy* (1690), in *Curate of Souls*, pp. 50–1. By "conversation" Patrick means "behavior," the conventional meaning of the term.

10. The Declaration and Confession are in *Creeds and Platforms*, pp. 354, 367–402, 439; [Cotton Mather], *RATIO DISCIPLINAE FRATRUM NOV-ANGLORUM: A Faithful Account of the Discipline Professed and Practised in the Churches of New-England* (Boston, 1726; reprint, New York: 1972), pp. 5, 12; cf. pp. 81, 88.

11. Frederick B. Tolles, *Meeting House and Counting House: The Quaker Merchants of Colonial Philadelphia, 1682–1763* (1948; New York, 1963), pp. 119–20; *Philadelphia Baptist Association* (1851), passim.

12. Richard Baxter, *Gildas Salvianus, or The Reformed Pastor* (1656; New York, 1860), p. 345.

13. Increase Mather is quoted in [Mather], *RATIO DISCIPLINAE FRATRUM NOV-ANGLORUM*, p. ii; Perry Miller and Thomas H. Johnson, eds., *The Puritans: A Sourcebook of their Writings*, rev. edn (New York, 1963), vol. 1, p. 291.

perhaps the most conscious, explicit, and apparently uncontrived definition of the word in seventeenth-century American writings: "PROFESSION in the most frequent and familiar apprehension, signifies *the publike manifestation of our assent to the doctrine of Faith ... and our resolution to persist in the maintainance of the same.*" Likewise, Edward Taylor, who served as a minister and wrote poetry from 1682 to 1725, was only echoing the conventional discourse in his verse "Profession of faith" and his meditation "Oh, that I ever felt what I profess."[14]

The first moment in the rhetoric of "profession" that would come to be associated with "the true professional ideal" in America was thus a twofold semantic extension of the term: from referring to a religious vow to denoting those who made the vow, and from referring to the monastic "regular" clergy to denoting the "secular" clergy and laity. This development, which was still occurring as Thomas Hooker and Edward Taylor wrote, reflected the highest ends and values of seventeenth-century and early eighteenth-century colonial culture. These were religious and concerned salvation of the soul as construed by Protestant Christianity, especially its Calvinist tradition. Such a generalization may be doubted today, when ideological articulation of self-interest is sometimes the marrow of historical interpretation. Nevertheless, one must be wary of the danger identified by John Demos in his classic work on daily life in seventeenth-century Plymouth: "the danger for us, from our vantage point of three centuries later, is that we may fail to appreciate ... the power of religion.... It was simply too basic, too much an assumed constant of life to be rendered fully visible and self-conscious. It registered as a kind of underlying presence, part of the very atmosphere which surrounded and suffused all aspects of experience."[15] The influence of religion was pervasive, though not monolithic, as noted by Hugh Jones in 1724:

If New England be called a receptacle of dissenters, and an Amsterdam of religion, Pennsylvania the nursery of Quakers, Maryland the retirement of Roman Catholicks, North Carolina the refuge of run-aways, and South Carolina

14. Thomas Hooker, *A Survey of the Summe of Church Discipline* (London, 1648), p. 60, ch. 6; Edward Taylor, *Poems*, ed. Donald E. Stanford (New Haven, CT, 1960) ser. 1, no. 35. The first five English dictionaries did not include an entry for "profession": Robert Cawdrey, *A Table Alphabeticall of Hard Usual English Words* (1604; Gainesville, FL, 1966); John Bullokar, *An English Expositor, or Compleat Dictionary* (1616; Menston, UK, 1967); Henry Cockeram, *The English Dictionarie* (1623; Menston, UK, 1968); Thomas Blount, *Glossographia: or a Dictionary* (1656; Menston, UK, 1969); Edward Phillips, *The New World of English Words* (1658; Menston, UK, 1969). The sixth dictionary included the entry "*Profession,* the entering into any Religious Order" and went through eleven editions by 1732. Elisha Coles, *An English Dictionary* (1676; Menston, UK, 1971). The first dictionary of the eighteenth century, and the first intended for the general reader, included the entry "*To* profess, *to declare openly, protest, acknowledge, own, &c.*" "*A* Profession." J. K. [John Kersey], *A New English Dictionary* (1702; Menston, UK, 1969). See De Witt T. Starnes and Gertrude E. Noyes, *The English Dictionary from Cawdrey to Johnson, 1604–1755* (Chapel Hill, NC, 1946).

15. John Demos, *A Little Commonwealth: Family Life in Plymouth Colony* (London, 1970), p. 12. Patricia U. Bonomi has recently reaffirmed this view in *Under the Cope of Heaven: Religion, Society, and Politics in Colonial America* (New York, 1986).

the delight of buccaneers and pyrates, Virginia may be justly esteemed the happy retreat of true Britons and true [Anglican] churchmen for the most part.[16]

New York and Pennsylvania were, indeed, outside the sphere of New England Congregationalism, but the influence of religion was readily apparent in the professions of Dutch Calvinists, Presbyterians, Quakers, and Baptists. During the seventeenth century the Dutch and English alternated in occupying New Amsterdam, or New York, and the English Governor reported in 1684 that the colony was religiously dominated by "Dutch Calvinists" although "of all sorts of opinions there are some."[17] This dominance of the Calvinist professions continued into the early eighteenth century even after several decades of nominal Anglican establishment. Meanwhile Pennsylvania was established in 1682 as a "holy experiment" for the Society of Friends and other dissident reformers. Baptists thus found refuge there, and the first and largest association of Baptist churches in colonial America was organized in Philadelphia in 1707. Each year this Philadelphia Association opened the minutes of its annual meeting with the formulaic introduction:

> The elders, ministers, and messengers of the several congregations, baptized on profession of faith, meeting at Philadelphia.... Unto the several churches, we send our loving and Christian salutation.... Dearly beloved brethren, who profess to be called out of darkness into light ...[18]

Here, too, the profession of religion was fundamental to the world view of the colonists.

In the Chesapeake region, the colonists' religiosity was tempered along the lines of Hugh Jones' observation that New Englanders were consumed by religion while Virginians adopted the moderate, genteel, and Anglican approach of "true Britons." Lionel Gatford's early treatise confirms this view, as does the complementary observation of John Winthrop that Massachusetts would not make the mistake of other plantations (like Virginia) of valuing money over religion. John Adams had much the same point in mind when he later proposed a plan "for making a New England in Virginia."[19] Even opposing critics of either colony agreed on the distinction between them. Whereas New England was often denounced for fanaticism and intolerance, "English critics often heaped special abuse" on seventeenth-century Virginians for their failure to build strong religious and educational institutions.[20]

16. Hugh Jones, *The Present State of Virginia from Whence is Inferred A Short View of Maryland and North Carolina* (1724), ed. Richard L. Morton (Chapel Hill, NC, 1956), p. 48.
17. E. B. O'Callaghan, ed., *Documents Relative to the Colonial History of the State of New York*, 15 vols. (Albany, NY, 1853–1887), vol. 3, p. 415.
18. *Philadelphia Baptist Association*, pp. 46, 59.
19. Lionel Gatford, *Publick Good Without Private Interest: or ... the Present Sad State and Condition of the English Colonie in Virginea* (London, 1657); John Winthrop, *Winthrop Papers*, ed. Samuel E. Morison et al. (Boston, 1931), vol. 2, pp. 140–9; John Adams, *The Works*, ed. Charles F. Adams (Boston, 1851), vol. 3, p. 400.
20. Carole Shammas, "English-Born and Creole Elites in Turn-of-the-Century Virginia," in *The Chesapeake in the Seventeenth Century*, ed. Thad W. Tate and David L. Ammerman (New York, 1979), p. 275.

Such testimony by Jones, Gatford, Winthrop, and Adams led nineteenth-century scholars to conclude that "[t]he settlement of Virginia ... was a mercantile adventure, a purely business proposition." In contrast, Perry Miller, the foremost colonial historian of the mid-twentieth century, argued that religion was "the compelling, or at least the pervading, force," and Miller's opinion was echoed by Sydney Ahlstrom in his magisterial history of American religious life.[21] Recently scholars have taken to attacking Miller's view,[22] although other prominent historians still affirm his generalization that, even for Virginians, religion provided "a world view that structured their daily lives."[23] Resolving such historical and historiographical contradictions may be impossible. Yet it seems reasonable to conclude, with Miller and Ahlstrom, that, relative to twentieth-century America, the culture of colonial Virginia was grounded in religion and to concede to the early observers and certain recent historians that, relative to New England, Virginia was less obsessed with that concern.

Obsessed or not, the "Councel of Virginia" in 1610 expressed the commitment that "our primarie end is to plant religion, our secondarie and subalternate ends are for the honour and profit of our nation." That commitment was manifested in legislation of 1612, 1619, 1632, and 1646, requiring various kinds of religious observance "according to the Ecclesiastical laws and orders of the Churche of Englande." After the Restoration, the House of Burgesses in 1662 enacted a series of provisions for ecclesiastical buildings, organization, liturgy, attendance, holidays, and financial support; and the code of 1705 detailed criminal penalties for heresy, blasphemy, witchcraft, and disrespect toward clergy, sacraments, and scripture.[24] It is sometimes said that Virginia, and other southern colonies, disregarded such legislation, which they nevertheless felt compelled to enact. Yet, as late as the second quarter of the eighteenth century, three of the four most numerous offenses recorded by grand juries in every county of Virginia were religious and moral offenses: absence from church, blasphemy, and fornication.[25] Meanwhile statutes of

21. Perry Miller, *Errand into the Wilderness* (Cambridge, MA, 1956), p. 101; Sydney E. Ahlstrom, *A Religious History of the American People* (New York, 1972), vol. 1, p. 244.

22. Thad W. Tate, "The Seventeenth-Century Chesapeake and its Modern Historians," in *The Chesapeake in the Seventeenth Century*, ed. Thad W. Tate and David L. Ammerman (New York, 1979), p. 24. See Darrett B. Rutman, *American Puritanism: Faith and Practice* (Philadelphia, 1970), p. 48.

23. Timothy H. Breen, *Puritans and Adventurers: Change and Persistence in Early America* (New York, 1980), p. 108. Rhys Isaac, *The Transformation of Virginia, 1740–1790* (Chapel Hill, NC, 1982), pp. 58–70; Richard Beale Davis, *The Intellectual Life in the Colonial South, 1585–1763*, 3 vols. (Knoxville, TN, 1978), pp. xxiv, ch. 5.

24. *A True Declaration of the Estate of the Colonie of Virginia ... Published by ... the Councell of Virginia* (1610), and *For the Colony in Virginia Britannia. Lawes Divine, Morall and Martiall* (1612), in *Tracts and Other Papers Relating ... to the Origin, Settlement, and Progress of the Colonies in North America*, ed. Peter Force (Washington, DC, 1844), vol. 3; Lyon G. Tyler, ed., *Narratives of Early Virginia, 1606–1625* (New York, 1907), pp. 271–3; *Statutes of Virginia*, vol. 1, pp. 157, 181–2, 311–2; vol. 2, pp. 41–52, 356; vol. 3, pp. 358–62.

25. A. G. Roeber, *Faithful Magistrates and Republican Lawyers: Creators of Virginia Legal Culture, 1680–1810* (Chapel Hill, NC, 1981), p. 141. Although JPs often dismissed these indictments, such official disregard testifies all the more strongly to the persistent sentiment among the people, who continued to present their neighbors for these religious and moral offenses.

1727 and 1748 were directed against parents who "neglect to take due care of the education of ... children, and their instruction in the principles of christianity," and these statutes were incorporated into subsequent criminal codes.[26]

In view of such evidence, one can affirm that the ends and values of seventeenth- and early eighteenth-century colonial culture were expressly religious, which is to say that people were ultimately concerned with the fate of their eternal souls. This statement does not mean that social, political, economic, and other aspects of human life were unimportant or strictly dependent on religion. Rather, it states that other matters were viewed in terms of and instrumental to those religious ends and that religion was the supreme source of legitimation and authority. Rationalizing the relationships among these various aspects of life – fitting them together in a comprehensive and comprehensible way – was the task of theology, which therefore constituted the architectonic of colonial culture through the mid-eighteenth century. Theology structured the way in which all issues were finally considered and understood, and the consideration and understanding were, in turn, reflected in the rhetoric of the culture: the way people talked about and discussed their lives. The usage of "profession" was a part of that rhetoric and closely linked with the theological architectonic and religious concerns of the culture, as we have seen.

In order to understand the particular nature of those religious ends and architectonic, one must take note of the fact that the chief profession in the American colonies was Calvinist, or Puritan, and most particularly Congregational or "Independent," as portrayed on Figure 2.1.[27]

If one assumes that the numbers of churches and congregations bear some correspondence to the relative influence of the theology of the various sects and if one notes that Anglicanism, particularly its colonial branch, was considerably influenced by Puritan thought, one can therefore say that Puritanism – the English expression of Calvinism – dominated the theology of the colonies. The truth of this generalization is ironically demonstrated by the fact that "it is almost impossible to define Puritanism accurately."[28]

26. *Statutes of Virginia*, vol. 4, pp. 208–12; vol. 6, p. 32.

27. The category "Calvinist" includes Congregationalists, Presbyterians, Baptists, and Dutch and German Reformed traditions. The chart excludes numerically smaller and more elusive groups, such as Jews, Quakers, Moravians, Huguenots, Mennonites, and Anabaptists. Since several of these sects stem from the Calvinist tradition, the ratios suggested here would probably be weighted no less heavily toward Calvinism if these groups were included. The numerical totals are:

Year	Total	Calvinist	(Congregational)	Anglican	Lutheran	Catholic
1660	154	97	(75)	41	4	12
1700	373	233	(146)	111	7	22
1740	1,176	808	(423)	246	95	27
1780	2,731	2,029	(749)	406	240	56

Source: Edwin S. Gaustad, *Historical Atlas of Religion in America*, rev. edn (New York, 1976), pp. 1–36.

28. Emil Oberholzer, Jr., *Delinquent Saints: Disciplinary Action in the Early Congregational Churches of Massachusetts* (New York, 1956), p. 6. On the lineage of Calvinism to Puritanism

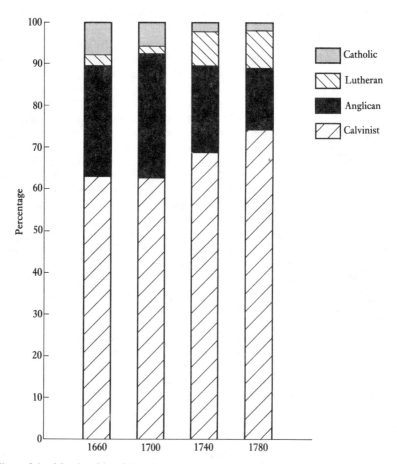

Figure 2.1   Membership of churches or congregations in the American colonies, 1660–1780

In a penetrating essay, the foremost scholar of the seventeenth-century colonial Puritan clergy, David Hall, takes up the question that has been addressed by legions of historians: "What is Puritanism?" Hall observes that Perry Miller and many subsequent scholars tried "to determine how Puritanism was socially functional," and this perspective continues to dominate much of the historiography of the Puritan clergy. Beyond their functionalist view, Miller and others tried to order Puritan thought into a systematic body of thought that, Ramist-like, delineates phenomena into categories and seeks to reconcile tensions such as that between piety and intellect. Turning away from the functionalist and categorical perspective to emphasize the creedal tenets that Miller had not, Hall maintains, "What gave

and the relations between Puritanism, Calvinism, and Anglicanism, see Miller, *Errand into the Wilderness*, pp. 48–98; Hugh Trevor-Roper, *Catholics, Anglicans, Puritans: Seventeenth-Century Essays* (Chicago, 1987).

substance to the movement was a certain inventory of ideas – the separation of grace and nature, an understanding of God and man as active forces, an eschatology."[29]

Even this helpful correction, however, tells more about the substance of Puritan theology than its nature as a profoundly dialectical worldview. The theology of the Puritans, especially the clergy, was grounded in the views of Paul and Augustine, who provided the foundation for the thought of both Luther and Calvin. The theological task, which Paul undertakes succinctly in his *Letter to the Romans* and Augustine sets in a larger context in the *City of God*, is to try to think in a disciplined way about how God sees the world, that is, to consider the perspective that regards the ultimate ends and highest values of existence as a whole. A moment's reflection will reveal both the inevitability and the necessity of this task, for a person can scarcely go through life without encountering questions of ultimate meaning and highest value. Yet it is also apparent that the enterprise is futile. One can never fully comprehend the ultimate purposes and designs of the cosmos. Thus, in the very act of theology, one undertakes something that one must and will do, but something that is bound to fail. This paradoxical character of what is to be investigated appears as well in how it is to be investigated, for the fact that one can objectify oneself and one's world is evidence that one can assume the viewpoint of God, but the finitude and limits of one's capacities become apparent at the same time. Paul and Augustine therefore conclude that people bear the responsibility for knowing and doing better, but their limited nature makes it impossible that they will achieve what they themselves understand they must do.

Here one arrives at the heart of the Pauline-Augustinian perspective that grounds Lutheran and Calvinist thought, particularly the distilled form of it in Puritanism. It is fundamentally dialectical, and the act of trying to analyze the dialectic becomes even more profoundly dialectical. All this proceeds from asking the theological question of how the world, and one's place within it, looks from the viewpoint of God. Understanding Puritanism in this way reveals that the essence of the Puritan perspective lies neither in a catechism, nor in the reconciliation of polar opposites, nor in ordering categories of dichotomous ideas, but rather in a dialectical view of the world that identifies and embraces tensions in the human situation, rather than seeking to resolve them.

The dialectic of freedom and finitude, of human beings endowed with a divine aspiration who are nevertheless not divine, is reflected in Edmund Morgan's observation: "This was the constant message of Puritan preachers: in order to be sure [of salvation] one must be unsure."[30] It is further revealed in various paradoxes that are sometimes perceived as self-contradictions on the part of the Puritans. William Kilpatrick, for example, derided the 1638 Massachusetts statute that established

29. David D. Hall, "Understanding the Puritans," pp. 31–50 in *Colonial America*, ed. Stanley N. Katz (Boston, 1971), p. 47. Perry Miller, *The New England Mind: The Seventeenth Century* (Cambridge, MA, 1939). On the other hand, some have believed that "The fundamental contribution of Perry Miller ... was to rescue from oblivion the intricate grandeur of Puritan theology." Charles E. Hambrick-Stowe, *The Practice of Piety: Puritan Devotional Disciplines in Seventeenth-Century New England* (Chapel Hill, NC, 1982), p. 3n.

30. Edmund S. Morgan, *Visible Saints: The History of a Puritan Idea* (1963; Ithaca, NY, 1965), p. 70.

compulsory voluntary contributions to maintain the churches.[31] Ridicule has also been directed at John Cotton's view from the following decade and at the provisions of the Connecticut legislature that religious toleration should be extended to all persons "Orthodox and Sound in the ... Christian Religion."[32]

Similarly, the early eighteenth-century Puritan clergy are portrayed as manipulative or self-contradictory by some recent social historians, who presuppose that there is no place for "clericalism" in Calvinist, Congregational Christianity.[33] The role of Puritan ministers is best understood dialectically, however, because "English Puritans had bent Calvin's system toward a prophetic style of ministry and a congregational, gathered understanding of the church."[34] The prophetic style elevated the role of the clergy, who derived authority directly from God; the congregational polity weakened the authority of the clergy within the church. This appreciation of Puritan thinking as profoundly dialectical goes far toward explaining historical shifts in the status of the clergy, as well as historiographical shifts between assessments of the Puritans as narrow-minded bigots and liberal freedom-fighters, as medieval theologians and proto-capitalists.

It is also important to see that certain forms and sources of knowledge were closely connected with the religious concerns of colonial culture and the theological rationalization of those concerns and, thus, with the rhetoric of "profession." This knowledge was derived not from scholastic theological systems, but from the interpretation of the Bible, a sacred text. Beyond the evaluation of "signs," prayers, and prophesies in light of Biblical verses, which fascinated Tudor and Stuart England, Christian professors were expected to ground their theological positions in the text. Calvinists were particularly noted for this appeal to Scripture. Thus, an English Presbyterian arguing against a Baptist in 1648 turned a question of ecclesiastical practice into a question of textual interpretation: "You derogate from the Scripture and endeavour to make us beleeve that there is something in Scripture that is not authentick Text. But I shall easily discover the vanity of this evasion."[35]

Such reasoning was certainly not limited to Calvinists, for the appeal to the text was a cardinal tenet of Protestantism in general. William Chillingworth, who converted from Catholicism and was ordained in the Church of England in 1638,

31. *Records of Massachusetts Bay*, vol. 1, pp. 240–1; William H. Kilpatrick, *The Dutch Schools of New Netherland and Colonial New York* (Washington, DC, 1912), pp. 162–3.

32. John Cotton ("It is not lawfull to persecute any for *Conscience* sake, *Rightly informed*"), quoted in *The Puritans*, ed. Miller and Johnson, p. 217; *Earliest Laws of Connecticut*, pp. 30, 92.

33. J. William T. Youngs, Jr., *God's Messengers: Religious Leadership in Colonial New England, 1700–1750* (Baltimore, MD, 1976), chs. 2, 3; Stephen Botein, "Income and Ideology: Harvard-Trained Clergymen in Eighteenth-Century New England," *Eighteenth-Century Studies*, 13 (1980): 396–413; James W. Schmotter, "The Irony of Clerical Professionalism: New England's Congregational Minsters and the Great Awakening," *American Quarterly*, 31 (1979): 148–68.

34. David D. Hall, *The Faithful Shepherd: A History of the New England Ministry in the Seventeenth Century* (Chapel Hill, NC, 1972), p. 75, chs. 1–4.

35. Gracious Francklin, *A Soft Answer to Captain Freeman's Passionate Book wherein ... Ministers Maintenance by Tithes [is] Justified* (London, 1648), p. 12.

emphasized the point in a famous aphorism: "The Bible, I say, the Bible only, is the religion of Protestants!" So, too, John Locke wrote in 1695 that he based *The Reasonableness of Christianity* upon "the sole reading of the scriptures.... for the understanding of the Christian Religion," and dismissed "systems of divinity" as offering "little satisfaction and consistency."[36] Meanwhile Congregational ministers were being trained in the works of the renowned Puritan divine, William Ames, who had urged that ministers should not "propound or doe any thing in the Church which they have not prescribed to them in the Scriptures."[37]

It is telling that Ames should address the ministers in this regard, for the clergy, being trained in the languages, references, and arguments of the text, had the greatest command of the forms and sources of religious knowledge while expressing the greatest devotion to the ends and values of the culture. They therefore became the exemplary professors, who professed the highest profession of the culture. In "The Propositions of the Ministers," composed by Richard Baxter for the Worcestershire Association, the clergy were explicitly put at the head of Christian professors:

> [W]e judge it very fit, if not of necessity, to desire a more expresse signification of our people's consent to our Ministry, and Ministerial actions, and in particular to submit to this Discipline.... We judge it fit withall to require an understanding profession of Assent and Consent to such fundamentals. ...

THE PROFESSION

> ... I do consent to be a Member of the Particular Church of Christ at _____ wherof [Rev] _____ [is] Teacher and Overseer and to submit to _____ [his] Teaching and Ministeriall Guidance, according to God's Word ... and hereby may the more Please and Glorifie GOD.[38]

The religious issue of salvation was the highest human concern. The knowledge of that issue was derived from the sacred text and the theological rationalization of the text, both on its own terms and with respect to the rest of human experience. And the ministers were considered the experts in that knowledge and the leaders in its practice, the masters of the architectonic. Although Luther and Calvin had supposedly overthrown clerical claims to religious authority, one would scarcely know it from many statements by Protestant ministers. A treatise that was written for English Baptists in 1689 and circulated in the middle colonies noted that ministers:

36. William Chillingworth, *The Religion of Protestants, A Safe Way to Salvation*, in *The Complete Works*, 12th edn (London, 1836), p. 465; John Locke, *The Reasonableness of Christianity as Delivered in the Scriptures* (1695), in *The Works*, vol. 7, p. 3.

37. Ames, *The Marrow of Sacred Divinity*, p. 154. The Puritans thus relied on "the infallible Bible.... It was not that they refused to accept a higher judgment than their own; they honestly believed that their own judgment had not entered into the matter at all. They were only repeating the highest judgment ever recorded." Perry Miller, *Orthodoxy in Massachusetts, 1630–1650* (1933; New York, 1970), pp. 15, 51; Harry S. Stout, *The New England Soul: Preaching and Religious Culture in Colonial New England* (New York, 1986), p. 150.

38. John T. Wilkinson, ed., *Gildas Salvianus: The Reformed Pastor by Richard Baxter 1656*, 2d edn (London, 1950), app. 1, pp. 179, 180, 185–6.

are intrusted with matters of the highest moment in the World, Christ having committed the Management of his Glorious Interests and great concerns he has on Earth into their Hands; they are sent to treat with poor Sinners about Eternal Matters, even Eternal Life, or Eternal Death and Damnation of their Precious and Immortal Souls, in and about these things. Ministers of the Gospel are Fellow Workers together with Christ.... [I]s it not, think you, a high and most sacred Place and Office thus to be imployed?[39]

This employment the leaders of Massachusetts Bay colony considered to be preeminent when they met in England in 1629 to plan for the needs of a new settlement in the wilderness. Drawing up a long list of necessities, they itemized tools and implements, foodstuffs, and seeds, raw materials and clothing. Above these were listed the necessary kinds of workers to build the new colony: artisans, craftsmen, and farmers. Higher up still were the "seale" of the corporation and the King's "Pattent": the political tools for certifying and legitimating all acts by the colonial government. But even higher than these, at the very top of the list, they wrote "Ministers," the masters of the architectonic. Similarly, the first compilation of the laws of the colony of New Haven provided: "That if any Christian (so called) shall ... behave himself contemptuously toward ... any Minister ... every such person or persons, shall be duly punished."[40]

Such legislation, like that in Virginia, indicates an important degree of social and political support, but it neither guaranteed nor delimited the preeminence of the clergy. Their "holy profession" – their religious commitment, their particular religious covenant, the corporate body of likeminded believers to which they belonged, and finally their leadership of that group – brought them institutional, political, social, and economic authority and status, which, in some respects, exceeded and, in other respects, fell short of the letter of the law. Before examining those kinds of authority in the American colonies, we turn to consider the second moment in the rhetoric of "profession." Initiated by the Reformation and completed by 1800, this second rhetorical step was the emphasizing and dignifying of the reference of "profession" to employment or occupation, a development sponsored by theological usage, which commensurately declined.

In classical and medieval Latin, *professio* had from time to time denoted "occupation," and this secondary denotation was transmitted into English. In about 1597 Francis Bacon wrote his frequently quoted and misunderstood statement: "I hold every man a debtor to his profession; from the which ... men of course do seek to receive countenance and profit." In 1656 the eminent Puritan divine Richard Baxter noted about the ministry that "this employment ... is like the profession of a physician, a soldier, or a pilot"; and Edward Randolph, the royal envoy to New England, observed in 1676 that the "chief professions are merchants ... and wealthy shopkeepers or retailers, who ... get good estates."[41] "Profession" and its

39. Hanserd Knollys, *The Gospel Minister's Maintenance Vindicated* (London, 1689), pp. 114–6.

40. *Records of Massachusetts Bay*, vol. 1, p. 24; *Earliest Laws of Connecticut*, pp. 29–30.

41. Francis Bacon, *Maxims of the Law* (1597), in *The Works*, ed. James Spedding et al. (Boston, 1861), vol. 14, pp. 158, 179–80; Baxter, *The Reformed Pastor*, p. 367; Robert N. Toppan, ed., *Edward Randolph* (Boston, 1898), vol. 2, p. 235.

variants thus applied to any trade or occupation, including the absence of one, for William Bullock complained in 1649 that indentured servants, whether in England or bound for Virginia, "have professed idelenesse, and will rather beg than work."[42]

This occupational usage of "profession" was not as prevalent as the religious usage described above. Other terms were applied at least as frequently to employment. The landmark Statute of Monopolies (1623), for example, neglected this secondary usage of the term "profession" when addressing "corporations, companies or fellowships of any art, trade, occupation or mystery."[43] Similarly, Virginia legislation concerning occupations generally neglected the term "profession." Statutes of 1646, 1648, and 1672 stipulated that youths be educated "in honest and profitable trades and manufactures," "some good and lawful calling," "useful occupations and trades," or "other necessary employments." A 1736 act addressed the colony's need for persons with "skill in trades, arts, and industries," and in 1748 penalties were enacted against parents who failed to teach their children how to earn their livelihood "in honest courses."[44] Meanwhile "mystery" had become one of the most common terms applied to occupations or trades that required extensive training. The usage of the *Boston Almanack* of 1692 was typical: "And the MASTER shall use the utmost of his endeavour, to teach ... his said Apprentice in the Trade or MYSTERY that he now followeth."[45]

In this fashion, "profession" tended to be reserved for religious matters. The early Baptist Hanserd Knollys, in a lengthy treatise describing "the Ministry of Christ" and "the Nature and Weightiness of that Sacred Work and Office," wrote about "work," "trades," "callings," "imployments," "office," and "secular Business" rather than "profession." Roger Williams did likewise when, on the one hand, he decried "the *Hireling Ministry*, that *Trade, Faculty, Calling*, and *Living*,

---

42. William Bullock, *Virginia Impartially Examined, and Left to Publick View, to be Considered by all Judicious and Honest Men* (London, 1649), p. 14.

43. Statute of Monopolies (1623), 21 James 1, ch. 3.

44. *Statutes of Virginia*, vol. 1, pp. 336–7; vol. 2, pp. 266–7, 298; vol. 4, pp. 208, 482; vol. 6, p. 32.

45. H. B. [Benjamin Harrison], *Boston Almanack for the year of our Lord God 1692* (Boston, 1692), endpages. Similar to the way in which "profession" moved from the religious sphere to the occupational sphere, so "mystery" moved from the classical Greek *mystērion* "denoting certain secret religious ceremonies," through confusion in medieval Latin between *mysterium* and *ministerium*, to the meaning of "service, occupation; office, ministry" in the late fourteenth, fifteenth, and early sixteenth centuries. This transition was hastened by confusion between "mystery" and "mastery" in English. (*OED*, s.v. "mystery.") The ancient Greek root and the medieval Latin confusion are slender pegs on which to hang the association between "mystery" as religious insight or power with "mystery" as occupational expertise. However, it appears that Anglican and Puritan clergy through the early eighteenth century persistently suggested such an association. See John Collings, *Vindiciae Ministerii Evangelici; A Vindication of ... A Gospel Ministry* (London, 1651), sigs. b3r–v; William Langley, *The Persecuted Minister, In defence of the Ministerie* (London, 1656), p. 21; Hanserd Knollys, *The Gospel Minister's Maintenance Vindicated*, p. 126; Hercules Collins, *The Temple Repair'd: or ... Ordaining Ministers duly Qualified* (London, 1702), pp. 3–4; Thomas Brett, *A Sermon of the Honour of the Christian Priesthood* (1712) and John Wesley, *An Address to the Clergy*, in *Curate of Souls*, pp. 132, 218.

by *Preaching*" and, on the other, referred to a particular sect as "a *Profession* of *Christ Jesus*."[46] Similarly, Cotton Mather sometimes referred to an occupation as a "profession," but in *Directions for a Candidate of the Ministry*, he used "profession" solely to mean a religious vow and referred to employment as "a WORK" or "Calling."[47] Meanwhile observers such as English merchant Lionel Gatford described Virginia as "a Colonie, Planted ... by Christians and those of the same Nation and Profession of faith with us."[48]

With the passage of time, however, the dignity of the theological usage of "profession" was imparted to what had been the minor denotation referring to occupation. Gradually in the seventeenth century and increasingly in the eighteenth, the meaning of the word "profession," as well as the very significance of an occupation, were transformed by the fact that the ministry was the preeminent "implyment. " The clerical preeminence informed thinking and speaking, especially the rhetoric of "profession," and this rhetorical development influenced the way people thought and talked about "profession" long after the clergy had declined. This emphasizing and dignifying of the occupational usage of "profession" – a development sponsored by theological usage, which commensurately declined – is the second of the six rhetorical moments that signify steps in the emergence of what would become "the true professional ideal" in America.

The beginnings of an explanation for this rhetorical development can be found, ironically enough, in Max Weber. The irony is twofold and lies, on the one hand, in the fact that although *The Protestant Ethic and the Spirit of Capitalism* has been disputed and debated in countless treatises regarding capitalism and work,[49] Weber's long etymological explanatory notes to his third chapter, "Luther's Conception of the Calling," have not been related to the development of the idea of "profession," which is perhaps the most significant aspect of "calling" in twentieth-century capitalism. On the other hand, it is ironic that Weber in these notes addresses primarily the words *Beruf* ("call") in German, *vocatio* and *professio* in Latin, and "vocation" in English without attending to the term "profession." Consequently, although he properly attributes the maturation of the idea of "calling" to English Puritans, Weber never links this maturation to the demonstrable semantic shift that occurred to "profession" – the English word that had come to possess most fully, by the time Weber wrote, the traditional dignity of "calling," which Weber was describing.

Weber argues that Luther was the first to employ *Beruf* in the sense of both an inner, spiritual calling and a secular, occupational calling from God, and he

46. Knollys, *The Gospel Minister's Maintenance Vindicated*, passim; Roger Williams, "The Hireling Ministry None of Christ's" (1652), in *The Complete Writings*, ed. Perry Miller (New York, 1963), vol. 7, pp. 163, 184.

47. Cotton Mather, *Manuductio ad Ministerium, Directions for a Candidate of the Ministry* (Boston, 1726), pp. 34, 76, 110; Cotton Mather, *BONIFACIUS, An Essay upon the Good* (Cambridge, MA, 1710), p. 101.

48. Gatford, *Publick Good Without Private Interest*, pp. 1–9.

49. See, for example, Robert W. Green, ed., *Protestantism, Capitalism, and Social Science: The Weber Thesis Controversy* (Lexington, MA, 1959); Christopher Hill, "Protestantism and the Rise of Capitalism," in *Essays in the Economic and Social History of Tudor and Stuart England* (Cambridge, 1961), pp. 15–39; David Little, *Religion, Order, and Law: A Study in Pre-Revolutionary England* (New York, 1969), pp. 226–37.

maintains that Thomas Cranmer's English translation of the Bible (1537) "is the source of the Puritan conception of calling in the sense of *Beruf.*" However, *Beruf,* for Luther, signified merely that a worldly occupation was not subordinate to an ascetic or religious one. It was English Puritans, in Weber's view, who then extrapolated "calling" into the idea that one's worldly vocation was the realization and fulfillment of one's spiritual vocation.[50] One need not subscribe to any of Weber's much contested theories about the "Protestant ethic" and the development of capitalism in order to see that he is on firm ground in describing these changes in the concept of "calling." The changes are reflected in the innumerable references to the distinction between "general calling" and "particular calling" that are found in writings from the seventeenth and early eighteenth centuries. The former signified one's spiritual, religious call; the latter, one's particular role, or work, in the world.[51] Nevertheless, it is curious that Weber never precisely explains how the link was made between an "internal call" and an "external vocation" – either in regard to Luther's elevation of a secular occupation to the level of an ascetic, religious role or in regard to the Calvinists' further dignification of an external vocation. Instead, he proceeds to analyze "vocation" as though there were no question of where or how the link originated.[52] But the explanation lies precisely in the rhetorical development that Weber overlooked: the rhetoric of "profession."

The Protestant Reformation wrought significant changes in clerical work by elevating the secular clergy. In fact, it "produced a new social and vocational class, that of the Protestant minister."[53] The Reformation thus invested clerical work with new status and authority that would attain even greater eminence in the American colonies. This preeminence followed from the fact that

> The *Clergy* have one great advantage, beyond all the rest of the World, in this respect ... that whereas the particular Callings of other Men prove to them great Distractions, and lay many Temptations in their way, to divert them from minding their *high and holy Calling* of being *Christians,* it is quite otherwise with the *Clergy.* The more they follow their private *Callings,* they do the more

50. Max Weber, *The Protestant Ethic and the Spirit of Capitalism,* tr. Talcott Parsons (New York, 1958), pp. 210, 79–92, 204–11.

51. See William Perkins, *A Treatise of the Vocations,* in *The Workes,* 3 vols. (Cambridge, UK, 1612), vol. 1, p. 757; John Cotton, *The Way of Life* (London, 1641), pp. 436–8, 449–50; Simon Patrick, *The Work of the Ministry* (1692), in *Curate of Souls,* p. 57; Cotton Mather, *A Christian at His Calling. Two brief Discourses. One Directing a Christian in his General Calling; Another Directing him in his Personal Calling* (Boston, 1701); Burnet, *A Discourse of the Pastoral Care,* pp. 181–2; Edmund Morgan, *The Puritan Family: Religion and Domestic Relations in Seventeenth Century England,* rev. edn (New York, 1966), pp. 69–70; Stephen Foster, *Their Solitary Way: The Puritan Social Ethic, the First Century of Settlement* (New Haven, CT, 1971), pp. 99–127. Cf. Charles L. Cohen, *God's Caress: The Psychology of Puritan Religious Experience* (New York, 1986), pp. 111–33.

52. Weber, *The Protestant Ethic,* pp. 87, 108–9, 133–54, 166.

53. Wilhelm Pauck, "The Ministry in the Time of the Continental Reformation," in *The Ministry in Historical Perspectives,* ed. H. Richard Niebuhr and Daniel D. Williams (New York, 1956), p. 143. Rosemary O'Day, *The English Clergy: The Emergence and Consolidation of a Profession, 1558–1642* (Leicester, UK, 1979), pp. 231–3; Winthrop S. Hudson, "The Ministry in the Puritan Age," in *The Ministry in Historical Perspective,* ed. H. Richard Niebuhr and Daniel D. Williams (New York, 1956), pp. 180–206.

certainly advance their general one: the better *Priests* they are, they become also the better *Christians*.[54]

Concurrent with the elevation of clerical work, "profession" gradually became the English word most prominently applied, first, to the covenantal act that defined Christians and their "general calling"; second, to the covenantal act that defined the clergy and their special commitment to that general calling; and, finally, to the corporate body of the clergy themselves. Inevitably, "profession," which already bore the secondary meaning of "occupation" derived from Latin usage, came to refer especially to that "particular calling" by which the clergy fulfilled their "general calling" and earned the greatest esteem and respect. In the words of the Oxford theologian Henry Dodwell:

> You must therefore so behave your self as to neglect no part of your duty: whether as to your *general* or your *particular Calling*; as a *Christian*, or as a *Clergieman* ... not only in omitting no duty, but in performing all the good that may be expected from your *Profession*.... How can you adorn your Profession ... by the excellency of your Conversation?[55]

The general calling and the particular calling were necessarily united in the clergy, and the term "profession," which referred primarily to the former in the seventeenth-century colonies, gradually came to refer also to the latter. As a result, the occupational sense of "profession" acquired a new dignity due to its close association both with the "general calling" and with the most esteemed of "particular callings." Subsequently, as the clerical eminence began to ebb, theological usage of the term "profession" commenced to decline, leaving the occupational usage to stand alone. This second moment in the rhetoric of profession – theological usage elevating and dignifying occupational usage and then declining – is demonstrated perfectly by an evaluation of the items in the Eighteenth-Century Short Title Catalog.[56]

The ESTC is yet incomplete, and a review of the titles is not necessarily indicative of the contents of the works. Nevertheless, the Catalog does provide a broad sample of rhetorical usage, and Figure 2.2 depicts the relative frequency of "profession" to refer to either theology or employment in the titles in the Catalog. This depiction gives a remarkably clear sense of how, during the eighteenth century, the occupational sense of "profession" supplanted the theological usage, after the latter had sponsored the emphasizing and dignifying of the former in the sixteenth and seventeenth centuries.[57]

54. Burnet, *A Discourse of the Pastoral Care*, pp. 181–2.
55. Dodwell, *Two Letters of Advice*, pp. 40–1. By "conversation" Dodwell means "behavior," the conventional meaning of the time.
56. ESTC is the international bibliographical database of more than 200,000 items printed from 1700 to 1800 in English or in England or its colonies.
57. The Catalog includes 178 items with "profession" as a word or root of a word in the title. After discounting for repeat editions, reprintings, and foreign language texts, one arrives at 101 titles of different works, and 100 of these employ "profession" by itself or its variants in reference to either theology or employment. The data for the figure are: 1700–20: total 12, theology 8; 1721–40: total 17, theology 10; 1741–60: total 11, theology 6; 1761–80: total 17, theology 5; 1781–1800: total 43, theology 8.

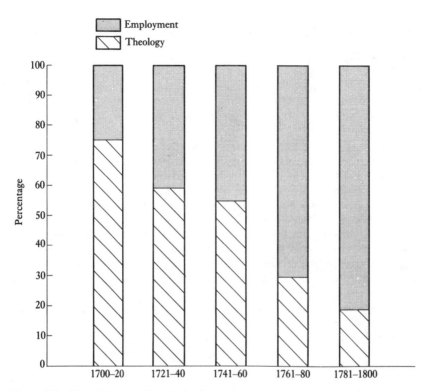

Figure 2.2   Use of the term "profession" to refer to theology or employment in the Eighteenth-Century Short Title Catalog

By the year 1800 the occupational sense of "profession" had developed from a secondary, occasional usage to the primary and highly dignified denotation of the term. In order to understand this development and its deeper implications, we turn now to examine the nature of the "particular calling" of the clergy and its institutional, political, social, and economic authority in the American colonies. Following this examination and then a comparison of the clergy with other "professions," we will have reached a vantage point from which to consider, in conclusion, how a third moment occurred in the rhetoric of "profession" and was informed by the nature of the vocation to which "profession" preeminently referred.

Institutional: "the Dignity ... and the Duty"

Governor William Bradford recorded that when the first minister of Plymouth arrived in 1624, "the Governor ... with his Assistants ... called [him] also to counsel with them in their weightiest businesses.... [H]e hath ever had a larger allowance of food out of the store for him and his than any, and clothing as his need hath required; a dwelling in one of our best houses, and a man wholly at his own command to tend his private affairs."[58] In 1630 the Massachusetts Bay Colony not only made similar arrangements, but also provided that the settlement at their best harbor "shalbe called Boston" in honor of the English town of the illustrious minister John Cotton, who would arrive at this second Boston in 1633. William Hubbard later recorded that, after John Cotton and other ministers did arrive, "such was the authority they (especially Mr. Cotton) had in the hearts of the people, that whatever he delivered in the pulpit was put into an Order of Court ... or set up as a practice in the church."[59]

It comes as no surprise that the authority of John Cotton, or any other Congregational minister, never matched William Hubbard's exaggerated account from the end of the seventeenth century, and the authority and status of clergy in other colonies often fell short of what the ministers in New England enjoyed. But the respect for and importance of ministers conveyed by these descriptions from Plymouth and Massachusetts are sincere. Even if, as some scholars maintain, such descriptions indicate the high water mark of the status of the clergy, both geographically and temporally, then the ministers – and the architectonic that legitimated their role – had a very long way to decline. In fact, their authority and status among occupations that came to be called "professions" were scarcely rivaled for more than a century.

In considering the institutional, that is, ecclesiastical, authority of the colonial ministers, one encounters immediately the paradox that, in theory, Congregational ministers should have had the least authority and Anglicans the most, while in fact the colonial situation was reversed. Part of the reason for this paradox is that, although the acrimony of debate might belie it, the major colonial sects had a common background, and at various times and places they enjoyed close and warm relations.[60] During the long reign of Queen Elizabeth beginning in 1558, the religious establishment was kept broad and flexible, and the term "Puritan" arose to characterize the party within the Church of England that wished to "purify" it of Catholic usages. When the Queen died in 1603, the establishment that served some 9,000 parishes in England and Wales included a party of about 350 Puritan clergy. Until about 1660, dissenting Puritans and conforming Anglicans moved easily back and forth between the parties. "[T]he differences were of a minor nature.... in terms of the definition of the ministerial function itself there was virtual unanimity."[61]

58. William Bradford, *Of Plymouth Plantation, 1620–1647*, ed. Samuel E. Morison (New York, 1952), bk. 2, ch. 15, pp. 148, 161.

59. *Records of Massachusetts Bay*, vol. 1, pp. 73, 75; William Hubbard, *A General History of New England from the Discovery to MDCLXXX*, 2d edn (Boston, 1848), p. 182.

60. Sidney Mead has shown that sectarian differentiation arrived with the evolution of "denominations" between about 1776 and 1850. Sidney E. Mead, "Denominationalism: the Shape of Protestantism in America," *Church History*, 23 (1954): 291–320.

61. Hudson, "The Ministry in the Puritan Age," p. 182. See A. Tindall Hart, *The Country Clergy in Elizabethan and Stuart Times, 1558–1660* (London, 1958), p. 18; A. Tindall Hart, *Clergy and Society, 1600–1800* (London, 1968), chs. 1, 2; O'Day, *The English Clergy ... 1558–1642*, ch. 1. Because they wished to avoid disloyalty, as well as un-Christian and unharmonious divisiveness, which had plagued the Reformation, most New England

The Restoration of the monarchy in 1660 brought restrictive legislation directed against the Puritans and other Dissenters, but by the 1690s a group of colonial Puritan ministers were moving back toward Anglicanism. This movement grew until in the 1720s a large number converted to the Church of England, including Timothy Cutler, rector of the college in New Haven, and Samuel Johnson, the future president of King's College in New York. Meanwhile the sparsely settled Carolinas became a royal colony in 1729 and thus nominally Anglican. Even so, the Anglican strength of the most vital community, Charleston, was matched by that of the Presbyterians,[62] and North Carolina was renowned as a haven for dissenters from the strict laws of Virginia. In the small buffer colony of Georgia, this tendency of colonial Anglicans and dissenters to converse and convert assumed a special form. John and Charles Wesley began their ministry in Georgia in 1736, initiating a schism within the Anglican fold that would yield the American Methodist church after the Revolution. This development demonstrates especially well the protean nature of colonial Anglicanism.

One should not, therefore, overemphasize the disagreements between Puritans and Anglicans, who generally tolerated and listened to each other, and not infrequently switched sides. There is nothing like a common enemy to unite feuding siblings, and the Puritans and Anglicans always reserved their real venom for Catholics and Jews. Moreover, the absence of a bishop in the American colonies vitiated the fundamental sticking point between Puritan and Anglican polity. Episcopacy, a kind of ecclesiastical polity, generated divisiveness among colonists only in the 1760s, when it began to represent a kind of political polity.[63]

If Congregationalists found common ground with Anglicans, they certainly could do so with Presbyterians, who became the second most numerous of explicitly Calvinist sects prior to the Revolution. Presbyterianism was subsumed under the term "Puritan" and scarcely distinguished from Congregationalism until about the 1640s, when the two groups commenced two decades of conflict. They again became allied following the reestablishment of the Church of England in 1660. By 1690 the leading clergyman in America, Increase Mather, was engineering a unifying agreement between the two groups, and in 1726 Cotton Mather observed that "the Differences between PRESBYTERIAN and CONGREGATIONAL seem hardly to be known in this Country."[64] The mutual influence and cooperation

---

Puritans maintained the fiction that they had not separated from the Anglican church. See the Preface to the *Cambridge Platform,* in *Creeds and Platforms,* pp. 194–202; Williston Walker, *A History of the Congregational Churches in the United States* (New York, 1894), chs. 3–4; Miller, *Orthodoxy in Massachusetts,* chs. 3–4; Morgan, *Visible Saints,* chs. 1, 2.

62. Hall, *The Faithful Shepherd,* pp. 273–5; Richard Warch, *School of the Prophets: Yale College, 1701–1740* (New Haven, CT, 1973), pp. 99–118; Ahlstrom, *A Religious History of the American People,* vol. 1, pp. 251–5; Bonomi, *Under the Cope of Heaven,* pp. 50, 92, 97–102.

63. See Carl Bridenbaugh, *Mitre and Sceptre: Transatlantic Faiths, Ideas, Personalities and Politics* (New York, 1962), pp. 171–340; Isaac, *The Transformation of Virginia, 1740–1790,* ch. 9.

64. [Mather], *RATIO DISCIPLINAE FRATRUM NOV-ANGLORUM,* p. 3. *Heads of Agreement* (1691), in *Creeds and Platforms,* pp. 455–62; Morgan, *Visible Saints,* pp. 12–3, 110–2, 142–9.

between the two groups and between different geographic areas of the colonies can be shown by the frequency with which graduates of the early colonial colleges circulated freely in these regards.[65]

The polity of the Baptists fell within the range staked out by the Congregationalists and Presbyterians. In fact, English Baptists were essentially Congregationalists who differed on matters of religious practice, and in 1718 the leading Boston ministers went so far as to join in a Baptist ordination. The Quakers, the German Lutherans, and the German Reformed Church, which stemmed from Zwingli rather than Calvin, did offer alternatives in ecclesiastical organization. But these groups, located largely in Pennsylvania, were relatively small and without ministers, either by design or by default, until the 1740s. As a result, they lacked an organized leadership to advance their views. Elsewhere, in all the colonies founded after the Act of Toleration of 1689, dissenters were in the majority.[66]

Consequently, notwithstanding the acrimonious squabbles, there existed a relatively uniform Calvinist cast to the ecclesiastical polity in the American colonies through the first half of the eighteenth century. By this is meant neither that an "oligarchy" of ministers dominated the churches, as Perry Miller claimed for New England, nor that "the Puritan oligarchy" determined "the founding of American civilization," as Thomas Wertenbaker suggested. Rather, in the words of Sidney Mead, "one institutional development stands out as having tremendous influence on the conception and practice of the [colonial] ministry, namely, the tendency in all the transported churches of whatever polity to gravitate toward an actual 'congregationalism' or localism. This development is most strikingly illustrated in the history of the Church of England in the colonies."[67] The Church of England

---

65. For example, a number of Harvard graduates went to Congregational-Presbyterian pulpits in and near Charleston, South Carolina: Benjamin Pierpont (HC 1689), Joseph Lord (HC 1691), Hugh Adams (HC 1697), Nathan Bassett (HC 1719), Josiah Smith (HC 1725), Job Parker (HC 1729), Thomas Rand (HC 1732), John Osgood (HC 1733), Samuel Fayerweather (HC 1743). Meanwhile, after graduating from Congregational Yale, Samuel Pomeroy (YC 1705) and Jonathan Dickinson (YC 1706) went to the Presbytery of Philadelphia, and, after graduating from Presbyterian Princeton, John Huntington (PC 1759), John Simpson (PC 1763), John Bacon (PC 1765), and Josiah Lewis (PC 1766) served Congregational churches throughout the colonies. Frederick L. Weiss, *The Colonial Clergy of Virginia, North Carolina and South Carolina* (Boston, 1955), pp. 71–95; *Harvard Graduates*, vol. 3, p. 429; vol. 4, pp. 101–6, 321–6; vol. 6, pp. 289–92; vol. 7, pp. 569–85; vol. 8, pp. 609–10; vol. 9, p. 188, 319–23; vol. 11, pp. 221–9; *Yale Graduates*, vol. 1, pp. 39, 46; *Princetonians*, vol. 1, pp. 259, 444, 479–81, 570–1.

66. Bonomi, *Under the Cope of Heaven*, pp. 82–90; Richard W. Pointer, *Protestant Pluralism and the New York Experience: A Study of Eighteenth-Century Religious Diversity* (Bloomington, IN, 1987); Sally Schwartz, *A Mixed Multitude: The Struggle for Toleration in Colonial Pennsylvania* (New York, 1987).

67. Sidney E. Mead, "The Rise of the Evangelical Conception of the Ministry in America: 1607–1850," in *The Ministry in Historical Perspectives*, ed. H. Richard Niebuhr and Daniel D. Williams (New York, 1956), p. 212; Miller, *Orthodoxy in Massachusetts*, ch. 6; Thomas J. Wertenbaker, *The Puritan Oligarchy: The Founding of American Civilization* (New York, 1947).

is the striking illustration because the other numerically prominent sects – Congregational, Presbyterian, Baptist – were Puritan by profession and endorsed localism, to a greater or lesser extent, as a matter of principle. But it was special circumstances in the colonies that transformed the episcopal polity into one of local lay organization.

In 1662 only ten clergymen served the 45 parishes in Virginia, and by the beginning of the eighteenth century, there were but 50 Anglican clerics in the colonies: some 25 in Virginia, about 17 in Maryland, and no more than two in any of the other colonies.[68] The shortage of Anglican clergy was compounded by the large territory of parishes resulting from the immense acreage of tobacco farms. But the fundamental problem was the absence of an episcopal presence in, or even concern for, the colonies. In the 1680s the Bishop of London had obtained jurisdiction over the colonies and began to appoint officials known as commissaries to represent him in the colonies. But these individuals had no authority, and the responsibility for many ecclesiastical matters in the most important Anglican colony, Virginia, devolved upon the Governor and the House of Burgesses, from whom it fell finally to the local vestries, which were the boards elected by and from the laity in each parish.[69]

The keystone to the authority of the vestries was an act of 1662, which, while reaffirming an earlier provision that only Anglican ministers had the right "to teach or preach publiquely or privately," made the vestries self-perpetuating. In addition, the statute provided vestries with the right of presenting a minister to the Governor for induction into the tenured office of rector. Not only did the episcopal polity thereby become "congregational" by vesting the right to choose the rector in the local laity. But many vestries hired ministers and never presented them to the Governor for permanent induction, thus maintaining them on a temporary and tenuous basis.[70] Here one finds the second circumstance that contributed to transforming and weakening the episcopal polity. The absence of a bishop was complemented by the presence of the lesser gentry in Virginia, who claimed a status and authority that they could not have demanded in England. The clergy

68. Here and below, I draw from Marcus W. Jernegan, *Laboring and Dependent Classes in Colonial America, 1607–1783* (1931; Westport, CT, 1980), chs. 9–11; Breen, *Puritans and Adventurers*, chs. 6, 9; Timothy H. Breen, "The Culture of Agriculture: The Symbolic World of the Tidewater Planter, 1760–1790," in *Saints and Revolutionaries*, ed. David D. Hall et al. (New York, 1984), pp. 252–60.; Kevin P. Kelly, " 'In dispers'd Country Plantations': Settlement Patterns in Seventeenth-Century Surry County, Virginia," pp. 183–205, and David W. Jordan, "Political Stability and the Emergence of a Native Elite in Maryland," pp. 243–73, in *The Chesapeake in the Seventeenth Century*, ed. Thad W. Tate and David L. Ammerman (New York, 1979).

69. William H. Seiler, "The Anglican Church: A Basic Institution of Local Government in Colonial Virginia," in *Town and Country: Essays on the Structure of Local Government in the American Colonies*, ed. Bruce C. Daniels (Middletown, CT, 1978), pp. 135–7; Mead, "The Rise of the Evangelical Conception of the Ministry," p. 213. James Blair served as Commissary in Virginia from 1689 to 1743.

70. *Statutes of Virginia*, vol. 2, pp. 44–7, 356; Seiler, "The Anglican Church," pp. 137–43.

were vulnerable, and found themselves subject to self-perpetuating vestries, comprising pretenders to nobility.

Several factors still worked in favor of the ministers. For one thing, everyone knew that the Anglican Church was not supposed to operate in this fashion. Compared to other Protestant sects, the Church of England was relatively sacerdotal: hierarchical, theocratic in the sense of offices in church and state being united, and sacramental in regarding the clergy's administration of the sacraments as the mediation between God and human beings. These sacerdotal tenets elevated the position of the clergy among Anglicans, even though some of the structural supports were missing.[71] Another factor was the activity of the commissaries who, at the least, had the authority to lobby for the clergy both in Virginia and in London. Finally, and most importantly, episcopacy and monarchy were closely allied. The Anglican clergy and the king's agent, the Governor, were consequently allied as well. Moreover, the Governors of Virginia, who were not necessarily religious men, needed local support against the gentry and House of Burgesses.

Due to all these factors, the governors and the commissaries made repeated efforts to revoke or curtail the vestries' right of presentation, and the system was legally changed in an act of 1748 that limited vestries to "twelve months" to determine whom to present to the Governor to fill a vacant pulpit. Failure to decide within that period entitled the Governor to choose and induct a rector. In 1749 the House of Burgesses amended the law to grant tenure to rectors immediately upon being received by the parish, whether or not they were presented by the vestry or inducted by the governor.[72] The parsons had for the moment won permanency of tenure, and could more nearly fulfill the ideal of "Pastoral Duty and Authority" which repeated printings of George Herbert's *The Country Parson* had held before them for almost a century:

> A Pastor is the Deputy of Christ for the reducing of Man to the Obedience of God.... Out of this Chartre of the Priesthood may be plainly gathered both the Dignity therof, and the Duty: The Dignity, in that a Priest may do that which Christ did, and by his Authority, and as his Vicegerent. The Duty, in that a Priest is to do that which Christ did, and after this manner, both for Doctrine and Life.[73]

While the relatively sacerdotal Anglican clergy experienced a threat to their ecclesiastical authority and status, the Puritan clergy, ironically enough, enjoyed an unrivaled position within their churches. The model for human organization in

71. Even in England, however, the landed gentry controlled the admission of clerics to many livings, because the gentry in many country parishes owned the advowson, the legal right to present someone to the bishop to be admitted to a particular church living. *The English Clergy ... 1558–1642*, pp. 210–21.

72. *Statutes of Virginia*, vol. 6, p. 90; Rhys Isaac, "Religion and Authority: Problems of the Anglican Establishment in Virginia in the Era of the Great Awakening and the Parsons' Cause," *WMQ*, 3d ser., 30 (1973): 3–36.

73. George Herbert, *A Priest to the Temple, or, The Countrey Parson, His Character, and Rule of Holy Life* (1652), in *The English Works*, ed. George H. Palmer (New York, 1945), vol. 1, pp. 225–6. First published 19 years after Herbert's death, the treatise enjoyed immense popularity and was reprinted in 1671, 1675, and 1701.

Puritan theology was the congregation: the group of elect believers freely gathering together out of the population and binding themselves by a covenant. Church members were to be accorded an equal voice in congregational affairs; it was the members who made a minister, not vice versa; and *"one* minister may not have superiority or domain over another."[74] Congregational organization would therefore appear to undercut the authority and status of the clergy, even as the theological architectonic extended the covenant among believers to an institutional covenant of the church and, ultimately, to a social covenant. Arriving in the new world to build their "Citty upon a Hill,"[75] the Puritans, whose creed soon became the predominant profession in the American colonies, sought to adhere closely to congregational polity.

This early enthusiasm for and continuing expression of the covenantal ideal are the sources for the interpretation maintaining, even today, that congregational polity meant "that in virtually every area of church governance the laity reigned supreme."[76] However, not even the early seventeenth-century Puritan colonists, who were committed to a particularly pristine form of that polity, organized their congregations democratically. The principle of the equality of all Christians before God stood in dialectical tension with an equally firm Protestant commitment to the high status of the clergy. Calvin himself had maintained that God "commended the dignity of the ministry by all possible marks of approval in order that it might be held among us in highest honor and esteem, even as the most excellent of all things." Both Luther and Calvin, while rejecting the notion of a sacerdotal priesthood, agreed on this point. They also held that only the clergy could admit new members to their group, though they added, in a characteristically dialectical fashion, that church members retained final authority and must give their assent, as well.[77]

By the mid-seventeenth century nearly all New England Congregationalists had moved away from the covenantal theory that prescribed lay authority in all church affairs. In 1636 the Massachusetts General Court required the majority of the colony's magistrates and ministers to be present at the gathering of any new church, thus preventing the laity from founding a congregation on their own.[78] In 1648 representatives of the churches in the New England colonies published

74. D. F., minister, *The Equallity of the Ministery plainly described both by Scriptures, Fathers, and Councels* (London, 1641), p. 6. The literature on the Puritan covenant is voluminous. See the classic discussion in Miller, *The New England Mind: The Seventeenth Century,* chs. 13–5.

75. John Winthrop, "A Modell of Christian Charity," in *Winthrop Papers,* vol. 2, p. 295. In the following discussion, I draw from Hall, *The Faithful Sheperd.*

76. David Harlan, *The Clergy and the Great Awakening in New England* (Ann Arbor, MI, 1980), p. 7, ch. 1.

77. John Calvin, *Institutes of the Christian Religion* (1559, 1560), ed. John T. McNeill and tr. Ford L. Battles, vol. 2 (Philadelphia, 1960), bk. 4, ch. 1, sects. 6, 22; ch. 3, sects. 1, 14–6. See Martin Luther, "Concerning the Ministry" (1523), pp. 3–44 in *Luther's Works,* vol. 40: *Church and Ministry II,* ed. Conrad Bergendoff (Philadelphia, 1958); B. A. Gerrish, "Priesthood and Ministry in the Theology of Luther," *Church History,* 34 (1965): 404–22; James L. Ainslie, *The Doctrines of Ministerial Order in the Reformed Churches of the Sixteenth and Seventeenth Centuries* (Edinburgh, 1940), pp. 148–9.

78. *Records of Massachusetts Bay,* vol. 1, pp. 142–3, 168.

the *Cambridge Platform,* which stood for decades as the normative statement of Congregational polity and, though never officially adopted by the colonial governments, was still being cited authoritatively by the Massachusetts Superior Court in 1820.[79]

Citing suitable Biblical verses for each point, the *Cambridge Platform* invested ministers with authority to call an assembly of church members and prohibited lay persons from speaking in church "before they have leave from the elders."[80] These strictures buttressed the effective control that ministers exercised over admission to membership and full communion and, thereby, to the highest sacraments of religion and culture. In fact, a new criterion for church membership introduced by the New England Puritans in the 1630s demonstrates perfectly how the rhetoric of "profession" reflected the elevated status and Calvinist stamp of religion. In addition to meeting the standard Puritan criteria of affirming the church covenant and being of upright character and behavior, a candidate for church membership was expected to make a "profession" or "confession" before the entire church, which included a "relation" of the candidate's conversion experience. The profession thus constituted the special criterion that ensured the purity of New England's congregations by signifying their commitment to the highest ideals of the culture. As the barriers to membership were eased in the course of the seventeenth century, the "profession" of one's salvation experience was reduced from a public "relation" to a personal interview with the minister, who largely determined one's fitness for full membership in the church.[81]

Overall, the guiding principle of Congregational polity was summed up in the words of the *Cambridge Platform:* "This *Government* of the Church is a mixt Government.... In respect of the body, or *Brotherhood* of the church, ... it resembles a *Democracy.* In respect of the *Presbyetry* and powr comitted to them, it is an *Aristocracy.*"[82] This formula was apparently drawn from Rev. Samuel Stone, one of the first generation of New England clergymen, who described congregational polity as "a speaking *Aristocracy* in the face of a silent *Democracy.*" After the metaphor appeared in the *Cambridge Platform,* Stone's phrase was quoted by succeeding generations of ministers and modern historians.[83] The phrase persevered because it accurately conveys both the movement of Congregational churches toward according more authority to their ministers and the impetus of the ministers toward organizing themselves together more formally.

Throughout the seventeenth century these two trends were strengthened by

79. *Baker* v. *Fales,* 16 Massachusetts 488, 504, 512, 513 (1820).

80. *Cambridge Platform,* ch. 10, in *Creeds and Platforms,* p. 219. "Elders" refers both to the clergy and to lay ruling elders, whose office was rarely instituted and finally subsumed by the clergy.

81. *Cambridge Platform,* chs. 3, 12, in *Creeds and Platforms,* pp. 205–6, 221–4; Morgan, *Visible Saints,* pp. 41–2, 62–3; Hall, *The Faithful Shepherd,* pp. 21–47, 96–100, 205–6.

82. *Cambridge Platform,* ch. 10, in *Creeds and Platforms,* pp. 217–8.

83. Cotton Mather, *Magnalia Christi Americana; or The Ecclesiastical History of New-England* (1702; Hartford, CT, 1853), vol. 1, p. 437; William Williams, *The Work of Ministers and the Duty of Hearers asserted and enforced* (Boston, 1733), pp. 1–26; Walker, *A History of the Congregational Churches,* p. 46; Miller, *Orthodoxy in Massachusetts,* p. 186; Hall, *The Faithful Shepherd,* p. 114.

statutes that required attendance at church and maintenance of ministers and meetinghouses, and prohibited disrespect toward Puritan ministers, doctrine, liturgy, and morality. Such provisions can be found in the compilations of laws published for New Haven colony in 1656, Connecticut in 1673, and Plymouth in 1685.[84] In 1691 Massachusetts received a new charter, which provided for liberty of conscience and eliminated church membership as a requirement for the franchise. Even so, the first acts passed under the new Charter stipulated "That the inhabitants of each town ... shall ... be constantly provided of an able, learned, orthodox minister" and, should the town fail in this duty, the legislature "shall ... order a competent allowance unto such minister according to the estate and ability of the town."[85]

At the turn of the century Congregational and Presbyterian churches were still committed, in theory, to the harmonious and dialectically balanced relationship between the clerical "speaking Aristocracy" and the lay "silent Democracy." But the application of this principle placed the great bulk of ecclesiastical authority in the hands of the ministers, as can be seen in the *Saybrook Platform* of 1708 and Cotton Mather's "straightforward descriptions of specific church practices" in his *A Faithful account of the Discipline Professed and Practised in the Churches of New-England* (1726).[86] In the words of Richard Bushman: "a century after settlement Congregationalism had reverted to many practices of the very [Anglican] Establishment the Puritans had once sought to escape."[87]

It is important to reemphasize that the legitimacy of these developments derived from the role of the clergy in interpreting the sacred text, to which Protestants had attributed final authority. As in the mid-seventeenth century, the ministers in the early eighteenth century "were the interpreters of the Word.... As official expounders of the law, the elders took the lead in every action and laid down the principles upon which the congregation was to make its decisions."[88] The one fundamental decision left to the laity was the choice of the interpreter: the election of their minister. Making that choice then served to reconcile the theory with the practice through the reasoning that the minister, chosen by the people, was acting on their behalf in accordance with his learned understanding of the scriptures. This was the point made by Ebenezer Gay, one of the most respected and long-serving Congregational ministers of the mid-eighteenth century. The clergy, Gay preached,

84. *Earliest Laws of Connecticut,* pp. 29–32, 47, 80–2, 92–4, 99, 123, 129; *The Book of the General Laws of ... New-Plimouth* (1685), in *The Laws of the Pilgrims,* ed. John D. Cushing (Wilmington, DE, 1977), pp. 23–6, 50–1, 57–8.

85. "An Act for the Settlement and Support of Ministers and Schoolmasters," in *Acts of Massachusetts Bay,* vol. 1, p. 62. For qualifying and elaborating legislation between 1692 and 1695, see pp. 66, 102–3, 216–7.

86. Kenneth Silverman, *The Life and Times of Cotton Mather* (New York, 1985), p. 404. *Saybrook Platform,* in *Creeds and Platforms,* pp. 502–6; [Mather], *RATIO DISCIPLINAE FRATRUM NOV-ANGLORUM.*

87. Richard L. Bushman, *From Puritan to Yankee: Character and the Social Order in Connecticut, 1690–1765* (Cambridge, MA, 1967), p. 147; Hambrick-Stowe, *The Practice of Piety,* pp. 127–9.

88. Miller, *Orthodoxy in Massachusetts,* p. 182, ch. 6; Hall, *The Faithful Shepherd,* p. 270; Stout, *The New England Soul,* p. 150.

are constituted Rulers over GOD's household, and Obedience to them is plainly required.... Waiving all Dispute about the immediate Receivers of Ecclesiastical Authority from the Head of the Church, this is without Controversy: that it belongs to the Ministers of Christ to exert it. Whoever be the first Recipient of the keys of the Kingdom of Heaven, the Stewards of Christ's family should turn 'em.[89]

Even this authority of the laity to choose their turnkey was curtailed, however, because churches could elect only individuals who had the proper credentials and approval of the local ministerial association. Formal associations were in theory prohibited to congregational clergy, who were not to look beyond their local church. But the desire for doctrinal and ecclesiastical consistency, which never seemed to emerge as cleanly from scripture as the Puritans wished, soon prompted the Congregational clergy to begin meeting in informal "consociations." The *Cambridge Platform* then provided for synods whose "directions and determinations, so far as consonant to the word of God, are to be received with reverence and submission." In this way, it came to be the practice even among Congregationalists to call a synod, or a meeting of ministers, to settle disputes among ministers, among congregations, or, most often, between a minister and a congregation. Such synods were hampered by the fact that they had no more authority than a respected group of consultants, although "most pious men and women would hesitate to back their own views above the collective wisdom of the clergy."[90]

By the 1660s it was not uncommon for one disputing party within a church to call a synod if they believed the ministers would side with them, while the opposing party would insist on the right of the congregation to decide its own affairs. Attempting to prevent the indeterminate and acrimonious free-for-alls that ensued, ministers in New England formed associations in order to help resolve disputes. For a number of reasons these associations were unsuccessful in this regard, but they did serve the function of screening candidates for congregational pulpits and thereby ensuring that new ministers had proper training and orthodox beliefs. In 1730, for example, when a group of lay Congregationalists in Rhode Island found a recent college graduate they wanted for their minister, they asked the Boston ministers to examine his theology and ordain him over them.[91] This custom became so well enshrined that Baptist Isaac Backus complained in 1768: "In fact, the right of *trying* ministers which Christ gave to his *Church* ... is now usurped by the *clergy*, and after they have thus robbed God's people of their right, they charge them with want of a *good temper* if they will not be easy under such tyranny."[92]

89. Ebenezer Gay, *Ministers' Insufficiency for their Important and Difficult Work* (Boston, 1742), p. 6.

90. Quotations are from *Cambridge Platform*, ch. 15, in *Creeds and Platforms*, p. 234; Edmund S. Morgan, *The Puritan Dilemma: The Story of John Winthrop* (Boston, 1958), p. 82; Harlan, *The Clergy and the Great Awakening in New England*, ch. 6.

91. *Creeds and Platforms*, pp. 466–72, 486–8; Hall, *The Faithful Shepherd*, pp. 219–20; Robert F. Scholz, "Clerical Consociation in Massachusetts Bay: Reassessing the New England Way and its Origins," *WMQ*, 3d ser., 29 (1972): 391–414; *Harvard Graduates*, vol. 8, pp. 500–1.

92. Isaac Backus, "A Fish Caught in His Own Net" (1768), in *Isaac Backus on Church, State, and Calvinism, Pamphlets, 1754–1789*, ed. William G. McLoughlin (Cambridge, MA,

Baptists in New England, such as Backus, had reason to complain under the yoke of the Congregational-Presbyterian establishment. Yet, in other regions, the Baptists acted no differently. After noting the importance of a person's internal call to the ministry, the early English Baptist Immanuel Knutton conceded: "a learned Synod is better able to judge of a Ministers ability and fidility for that sacred function, than a vulgar congregation." Baptist Hanserd Knollys echoed this view in 1689.[93] In 1707 the clergy and elders of the Baptist churches from Virginia, New Jersey, Pennsylvania, New York, and Connecticut met in Philadelphia to form the first association of Baptist churches in America. The very first resolution at the first meeting of that first association stipulated: "That no man shall be allowed to preach among the Associated churches, except he produce credentials of his being ... licensed to preach."[94]

Not only was a Baptist licensing procedure, more formal than anything in Congregational associations, introduced, but this flagship Baptist association assumed as well the authority to expel a minister. In 1712, for example, a committee formed for this purpose adjudged that the minister of the church of Philadelphia and Pennepek was "to be discharged from any further service in the work of the ministry; he being a person, in our judgment, not likely for the promotion of the Gospel." In 1762, six years before Isaac Backus castigated the New England clergy, a "CERTIFICATE" was authorized by "the ministers and messengers" of this leading Baptist association:

> This certifies that the bearer hereof ... was, (after due examination, whereby he appeared to have a competent share of learning and other prerequisites to the sacred office,) admitted into holy orders, according to the known and approved rites of the Baptist church, whereby he is authorized to preach the gospel, and administer the ordinances thereof.[95]

The Presbyterian ministers scarcely exceeded these strictures, and they, by definition, were supposed to form associations, or synods. As early as 1651 in England, John Collings noted approvingly that New Englanders were beginning to endorse the view that "those that are to be set apart for the work of ordinary preaching and dispensing out the mysteries of God must be set apart by the Presbytery, that is, by other ministers in Office." Collings's treatise was cited approvingly by Hercules Collins in 1702; and in 1763 George Beckwith, the minister of Lyme, Connecticut, endorsed the position in a tract entitled *The Invalidity, or Unwarrantableness of Lay-Ordination.*[96] Meanwhile Presbyterian ministerial associations did not hesitate to exercise their authority to license and examine the

---

1968), p. 232; C. C. Goen, *Revivalism and Separatism in New England, 1740–1800: Strict Congregationalists and Separate Baptists in the Great Awakening* (New Haven, CT, 1962).

93. Immanuel Knutton, *Seven Questions about the Controversie between the Church of England and the Separatists and Anabaptists briefly discussed* (London, 1644), p. 9; Knollys, *The Gospel Minister's Maintenance Vindicated.*

94. *Philadelphia Baptist Association,* p. 121.

95. *Philadelphia Baptist Association,* pp. 86–7.

96. Collings, *Vindicae Ministerii Evangelici,* b1r, c4v, p. 65; Collins, *The Temple Repair'd,* p. 9; George Beckwith, *The Invalidity, or Unwarrantableness of Lay-Ordination* (New London, 1763).

credentials of ministers. In New Jersey and Connecticut associations repeatedly summoned before them unlicensed preachers, such as John Whiting in 1727, Samuel Heaton in 1734, and Timothy Allen in 1738. These recent graduates of Yale College acknowledged their fault, then satisfied the association, and were duly licensed. Nor were the associations unwilling to revoke a license once granted, as in the case of Simon Ely, or to deny a license for insufficient preparation, as happened to Jonathan Elmer soon after he graduated from Yale in 1747.[97]

In sum, it may be said that the paradox of ecclesiastical authority in the colonies was twofold. The clergy of the theoretically sacerdotal, hierarchical, episcopal polity found their traditional authority curtailed by local lay boards of vestrymen, while the ministers in the putatively decentralized, "democratic" congregations kept the laity and each other on a fairly short leash. The preponderance of colonial churches in the latter group – nearly 70 percent in 1740 – suggests that the colonial professions of religion came from a fairly uniform mold. But this uniformity was enhanced by the twofold paradox, which indicates how both groups – almost 90 percent in 1740 – converged toward a localism that nevertheless vested significant ecclesiastical authority in the local pastor. The pastor's institutional authority then ramified into political, social, and economic life.

Political and Social: *"the real weight of clergymen"*

Even as nineteenth-century Whig historians, such as George Bancroft and John Palfrey, were portraying Puritans as early champions of religious and political freedom, other scholars had begun to argue that "in the colonial period the name "theocracy" best expressed the nature of the government."[98] By the early decades of the twentieth century, historians such as James Adams and Vernon Parrington, impressed particularly by the persecutions of the Quakers, had come to regard the Puritans as theocratic bigots.[99] Although the Whiggish view continued to echo in the works of those who regarded the colonial clergy as prophets of the Revolution and the New England towns as *seminaria* of democratic republics,[100] the dominant

97. *Yale Graduates*, vol. 1, pp. 342, 372, 552; vol. 2, pp. 38, 112.

98. Susan M. Reed, *Church and State in Massachusetts, 1691–1740* (Urbana, IL, 1914), p. 50; Herman F. Uhden, *The New England Theocracy: A History of the Congregationalists in New England to the Revivals of 1740*, tr. H. C. Conant from the 2d German edn (New York, 1859); John Fiske, *The Beginnings of New England Or, the Puritan Theocracy in its Relations to Civil and Religious Liberties* (London, 1889; Cambridge, MA, 1917).

99. See especially James T. Adams, *The Founding of New England* (Boston, 1921); Vernon L. Parrington, *Main Currents in American Thought*, vol. 1, *The Colonial Mind* (New York, 1927), pp. 5–10.

100. See Alice Baldwin, *The New England Clergy and the American Revolution* (Durham, NC, 1928); Ola E. Winslow, *Meetinghouse Hill, 1630–1783* (New York, 1952); B. Katherine Brown, "Freemanship in Puritan Massachusetts," *AHR*, 59 (1954): 865–83; Robert E. Brown, *Middle Class Democracy and the Revolution in Massachusetts, 1691–1780* (Ithaca, NY, 1955).

view from Perry Miller to Thomas Wertenbaker to Michael Walzer has dwelled upon "the Massachusetts theocracy" or "the Puritan oligarchy."[101]

The "theocratic nature of the Puritan colony"[102] may be inferred from seventeenth-century restrictions that made office-holding and the franchise conditional upon church membership in certain colonies. For example, the first provision in the first printed compilation of New Haven's laws was: "That none shall be admitted Free-men … but such Planters as are Members of some one, or other of the approved Churches of *New-England.*" Massachusetts and Connecticut colonies introduced similar restrictions, whose impact varied over time because the definition of church membership and the accompanying property requirements changed, and because distinctions were introduced in the qualifications for voting in local or colony-wide elections.[103] Nevertheless, in *The Power of Congregational Churches* John Davenport was fully justified in noting approvingly that "in these places and times … Church-fellowship is an honour, and draws after it sundry out-ward and worldly advantages."[104] This situation naturally endowed the clergy, who had much control over church membership, with a good deal of indirect political authority.

The stricture that political rights could be obtained only through "Church-fellowship" and only in "the approved churches" was not limited to Congregationalists or to New England. In Virginia, analogous privileges effectively existed for Anglicans until 1699, when the 1689 Act of Toleration was formally adopted. Even then, the Anglican clergy successfully resisted the licensing of dissenting ministers through the 1750s.[105] In colonies noted for their toleration, the right to vote or hold

101. Miller, *Orthodoxy in Massachusetts,* pp. 226, 227, ch. 7; Wertenbaker, *The Puritan Oligarchy,* p. 60, ch. 2; Michael Walzer, *Revolution of the Saints* (Cambridge, MA, 1965), p. 88. In the following, I draw from Thomas J. Curry, *The First Freedoms: Church and State in America to the Passage of the First Amendment* (New York, 1986), chs. 1–4.

102. Paul S. Reinsch, *English Common Law in the Early American Colonies* (Madison, WI, 1899), p. 13.

103. *Earliest Laws of Connecticut,* p. 9. For examples and discussion of these changes, see *Records of Massachusetts Bay,* vol. 1, pp. 79–80, 168; vol. 4, pt. 1, p. 420; Kenneth A. Lockridge, *A New England Town, The First Hundred Years: Dedham, Massachusetts, 1636–1736,* enlarged edn (New York, 1985), pp. 204–7; Morgan, *The Puritan Dilemma,* pp. 91–2; Hall, *The Faithful Shepherd,* pp. 228–34. John G. Palfrey estimated that only one-fifth of the population were church members in the year 1670. (*History of New England* (Boston, 1858), vol. 3, p. 41n.) Samuel E. Morison held that Palfrey's estimate might be correct for 1670 due to the decline in church membership by that date, but that the fraction was much higher for the first generation of New Englanders. (*Builders of the Bay Colony* (Boston, 1930), pp. 339–46.) Perry Miller thought Palfrey's estimate correct not only for the year 1670, but for the original migration as well. (Miller and Johnson, eds., *The Puritans,* p. 191.) Morgan argues that Morison's view is too high for the original migration and Miller's too low, asserting that by 1640 less than a majority of New Englanders were in full communion. (*The Puritan Family,* p. 171n.) Hall substantially agrees with Morgan. (*The Faithful Shepherd,* pp. 99–100, 201.)

104. John Davenport, *The Power of Congregational Churches Asserted and Vindicated* (London, 1672), pp. 9–10; Miller, *Orthodoxy in Massachusetts,* ch. 6.

105. Act of Toleration (1689), 1 William and Mary ch. 18; *Statutes of Virginia,* vol. 3, p. 171.

office was still limited to professors of Christianity, that is, church members, and generally those in the Protestant professions. The tolerant Rhode Island statute of 1662 declared "that all Men Professing Christianity ... (Roman Catholicks only excepted) shall be admitted Free-Men, and shall have Liberty to Chuse and be Chosen Officers in the Colony." Similarly, in New Jersey, the most religiously diverse colony, the 1677 charter for Quaker West Jersey and the proposed 1683 constitution for Puritan East Jersey allowed any person to hold office, except those "who shall not profess Faith in *Christ-Jesus.*"[106]

Notwithstanding these strictures, historians have more recently avoided the term "theocracy" as imprecise or simplistic, or redefined it as "not the rule of the priest-hood, but the harmony between minister and magistrate in church and state affairs."[107] Even of New England, where the clergy reached the zenith of their political authority, it is now said that "the Puritans drew a firmer dividing line between the two than existed anywhere in Europe.... The church had no authority in the government."[108] On behalf of this view, it is noted that the Puritans divided the Ten Commandments into two tables of law: the church to administer the ecclesiastical provisions, and the state the secular provisions. Even matters such as marriage and divorce came under the jurisdiction of civil courts, not the church meeting.[109] Although the state was to "nurture" the church and the church to preach obedience to the state, an individual Puritan was not permitted to hold office in both domains at once.

These countervailing trends in the historiography regarding the political authority of the clergy and the relationship between church and state in the colonies are similar to the contradictions noted earlier among comparisons of the religiosity in Massachusetts and Virginia. From the perspective of the twentieth century, the Puritans unconscionably, not to say unconstitutionally, expected governmental support for the church and permitted only churched people to govern. But, compared to clerics in contemporary western Europe, the colonial clergy were relatively removed from direct political authority. Moreover, the situation changed even in the seventeenth century. By the 1680s the New England ministers could no longer rely on the government to stifle religious dissent, and they became the balancing faction between the elected deputies and elite magistrates.[110]

The historiographical contradictions thus underscore the dialectical nature of the

106. *Earliest Laws of Rhode Island,* p. 139; *Fundamental Laws and Constitutions of New Jersey, 1664–1964,* ed. Julian P. Boyd (Princeton, NJ, 1964), pp. 84, 108, 120.

107. Sacvan Bercovitch, *The American Jeremiad* (Madison, WI, 1978), p. 3n.; Brian Tierney, *The Crisis of Church and State, 1050–1300* (Englewood Cliffs, NJ, 1964), p. 1; Little, *Religion, Order, and Law,* pp. 76–7; G. B. Warden, "The Rhode Island Civil Code of 1647," in *Saints and Revolutionaries,* ed. David D. Hall et al. (New York, 1984), p. 148.

108. Morgan, *The Puritan Dilemma,* pp. 163, 95–6; Hall, *The Faithful Shepherd,* p. 286; Everett C. Goodwin, *The Magistracy Rediscovered Connecticut, 1636–1818* (Ann Arbor, MI, 1981), p. 26; Lockridge, *A New England Town: The First Hundred Years,* p. 23.

109. Wilkinson, ed., *Gildas Salvianus,* p. 177; Morgan, *The Puritan Family,* pp. 31–4; Oberholzer, *Delinquent Saints,* p. 8.

110. Bernard Bailyn, *The New England Merchants in the Seventeenth Century* (Cambridge, MA, 1955), ch. 4; Hall, *The Faithful Shepherd,* chs. 6, 10; George D. Langdon, Jr., *Pilgrim Colony: A History of New Plymouth, 1620–1691* (New Haven, CT, 1966), ch. 5.

Puritan architectonic and the foundation on which it rested – the sacred text. Christ had said: "Render therefore unto Caesar the things which be Caesar's, and unto God the things which be God's." (*Luke* 20: 25). But what exactly did this mean? Separation and subordination of church to state? Jesus seemed to imply so when he claimed to be a king, but said his kingdom was not of this world (*John* 18: 36). Or did separation mean the subordination of state to church, because the spiritual realm takes precedence over the temporal? As Jesus said to Peter, "I will give unto thee the keys of the kingdom of heaven: and whatsoever thou shalt bind on earth shall be bound in heaven" (*Matthew* 16: 19). And Peter later affirmed, "Fear God. Honour the king" (1 *Peter* 2: 17), and "We ought to obey God rather than men" (*Acts* 5: 29).

Paul followed Jesus and his disciples in this paradoxical advice, and Luther and Calvin later affirmed what H. Richard Niebuhr called "the clear-cut separation of church and state." But they did so in a highly dialectical fashion that emphasized both the independence and interdependence of the two realms.[111] The tension subsequently appeared in the *Cambridge Platform*,[112] and in certain respects, it is possible to reconcile the independence and interdependence by introducing distinctions such as between the state prohibiting evil and the church compelling virtue. Nevertheless, there remains an irreducible dialectic whereby the human condition is viewed as incorporating inevitable tensions.

The paradoxes of the sacred text and the dialectics of the Calvinist architectonic are, then, the roots of the historiographical contradictions regarding the political authority of the clergy and the relationship between church and state. The question of whether and how ministers exercised such authority is not simply a matter of whether the franchise or office-holding were conditional upon the ecclesiastical authority of the clergy. Rather, the political influence of the ministers is evidenced most fundamentally in that political life was conceived as a temporary existence and a transition to religious life.[113] Even if the magistrates had supreme authority in political life, the logic that rationalized and structured the relationship among authorities was derived from the religious architectonic.

Another way in which the architectonic rationalized and shaped the political domain appeared in the organizational model of the polity. Calvinist communities were modeled upon the congregation. Puritan towns were organized through a covenant among persons who, in principle, freely gathered together and made a binding commitment to live together. On a larger scale, the 1643 "Articles of Confederation betwixt ... *Massachusets*, ... *Plimouth*, ... *Connectceut*, and ... *New Haven*" demonstrate the covenantal model in establishing a "Consotiation" among several colonies. On a smaller scale, the Puritan family, not the individual, was the

111. Cf. *Romans* 13: 1, and 1 *Corinthians* 2: 6; H. Richard Niebuhr, *The Kingdom of God in America* (New York, 1937), p. 39. See John Calvin, *Institutes of the Christian Religion*, bk. 3, ch. 19, sect. 15; Martin Luther, "The Keys" (1530), pp. 321–78, and "Concerning the Ministry" (1523), pp. 3–44, in *Luther's Works*, vol. 40: *Church and Ministry II*, ed. Conrad Bergendoff (Philadelphia, 1958).

112. *Cambridge Platform*, chs. 11, 14, 17, in *Creeds and Platforms*, pp. 221, 228, 235–7.

113. On sacred and secular time, see Abraham J. Heschel, *The Earth is the Lord's and The Sabbath* (New York, 1966), pp. 103–17; Sacvan Bercovitch *The Puritan Origins of the American Self* (New Haven, CT, 1975).

basic unit of civil society and church organization.[114] In purely Calvinist locales, the religious architectonic thereby shaped civil polity according to the congregational model.

In other parts of the colonies, the somewhat different religious polity led to a commensurately altered structure of the political domain. While local town government was more important in the northern colonies, commensurate with the smaller scale of congregational polity, the county was the most important level of government in the South. The strength of southern county government has been attributed to geography and to choice of crops. But in view of the religious ends of the culture, it is also possible that the larger organizational units of episcopal and presbyterian polities in the South had a role in promoting and legitimating the strength of county government or, at least, in not invalidating it. Indeed, in South Carolina ten Anglican parishes were established by an act of 1706, and the powers of the vestries were limited to the maintenance of churches, parsonages, and glebes. However, as in Virginia, the vestries came to exercise jurisdiction over secular affairs as well.[115] Thus, the ecclesiastical polity not only contributed to shaping the jurisdictions of political authority, but began to subsume them as well.

In addition to the ideological influence of their dialectical logic and organizational model, the ministers, especially the nearly 70 percent in the explicitly Calvinist professions, exercised a great deal of personal and indirect authority in political affairs. Through the eighteenth century in New England, on official days of thanksgiving or repentance or days when newly-elected leaders were sworn into office, a minister was chosen to preach a lengthy sermon reminding the political and social leaders of the basic principles of covenantal theology, to which the culture was dedicated. Meanwhile, throughout the countryside, echoes of the sermon would issue forth from every pulpit. In this way, ministers were formally recognized as the architects of the relationship between politics and religion.[116]

Still another influence on political affairs arose from the fact that, although ministers did not generally serve in political office, those who left the ministry or, after studying theology, decided not to enter it, were an important source of recruits for judicial and governmental posts. Joseph Dudley, for instance, trained for the ministry but entered the military and public office instead. In the 1680s he

114. *Earliest Laws of Connecticut,* pp. 4–5; Morgan, *The Puritan Family,* ch. 6; Miller, *The New England Mind: The Seventeenth Century,* pp. 365–97; Miller, *Errand into the Wilderness,* pp. 48–98.

115. *Statutes of South Carolina,* vol. 2, pp. 243–4. See Jernegan, *Laboring and Dependent Classes in Colonial America,* pp. 176–7; Hart, *Clergy and Society, 1600–1800,* p. 16; Alan Tully, *William Penn's Legacy: Politics and Social Structure in Provincial Pennsylvania, 1726–1755* (Baltimore, MD, 1977); Richard Waterhouse, "The Responsible Gentry of Colonial South Carolina: A Study in Local Government, 1670–1770," in *Town and Country,* ed. Bruce C. Daniels (Middletown, CT, 1978), pp. 160–85; Davis, *The Intellectual Life in the Colonial South, 1585–1763,* ch. 10.

116. W. DeLoss Love, Jr., *The Fast and Thanksgiving Days of New England* (Boston, 1895) is the classic authority. Hambrick-Stowe, *The Practice of Piety,* pp. 133–5; Baldwin, *The New England Clergy and the American Revolution,* pp. 5–6, passim; A. W. Plumstead, ed., *The Wall and the Garden: Selected Massachusetts Election Sermons, 1660–1775* (Minneapolis, MN, 1968).

was appointed president of the eastern part of New England and Chief Justice of the highest court in Massachusetts. William Stoughton also served as Chief Justice of that court into the early eighteenth century, after having studied divinity and entered the military and public service. In Connecticut, Gershom Bulkeley's prominence as a minister led to his appointment as Justice of the Peace and, then, election as representative to the legislature.[117] In the eighteenth century Gurdon Saltonstall, minister of New London from 1691 to 1708, became Chief Justice of the highest court in Connecticut and then Governor until his death in 1724. Subsequently Nathaniel Hubbard studied divinity, preached, entered public service, and was appointed to the highest court of Massachusetts in 1746. As late as 1783, Rev. Caleb Wallace, a Presbyterian, was appointed to the new Supreme Court of the territory of Kentucky.[118]

Apart from those trained in theology who moved into judicial and governmental posts, the settled Puritan ministers in New England were consulted informally by the magistrates concerning colony-wide political issues. Although this practice generally ceased by the end of the seventeenth century, the parish minister continued to be consulted about local affairs by town leaders through the middle of the eighteenth century.[119] In this fashion the clergy exercised political authority informally and largely as a function of their considerable social authority, which president Timothy Dwight later called "*the real weight of clergymen* ... an influence derived from their office and their conduct.... A minister ... is the common friend; the common peacemaker; the common father."[120]

This social authority, exercised outside of the political realm, was graphically portrayed by the seating in church each sabbath. In all sects, even the Quakers, church pews were occupied according to the hierarchy of social status. This arrangement stemmed from sixteenth-century England, where a "pew had become, in fact, a symbol of ... the social status of each parishioner."[121] Not only was this true of the hierarchical episcopal churches, but, as Kenneth Lockridge has indicated in his classic study of a Congregational town: "The selectmen, chief officers of the town, were also charged with arranging the seating in the meetinghouse according to the rank of the persons within the society. The local hierarchy of age, service, and estate was literally displayed before the eyes of each inhabitant as he took his seat on Sunday mornings."[122]

117. *Harvard Graduates,* vol. 1, pp. 194–203, 389–401; vol. 2, pp. 166–9.

118. *Harvard Graduates,* vol. 3, pp. 277–81; vol. 4, pp. 406–8; *Princetonians,* vol. 2, p. 119.

119. Morgan, *The Puritan Dilemma,* pp. 163–4; Hall, "Understanding the Puritans," pp. 36ff.; Hall, *The Faithful Shepherd,* pp. 127–44, 248; T. H. Breen, *The Character of the Good Ruler: Puritan Political Ideas in New England, 1630–1730* (New Haven, CT, 1970), passim; John J. Waters, "Hingham, Massachusetts, 1631–1661: An East Anglian Oligarchy in the New World," *Journal of Social History,* 1 (1968): 351–70; Robert J. Wilson III, *The Benevolent Deity: Ebenezer Gay and the Rise of Rational Religion in New England* (Philadelphia, 1984), p. 49.

120. Timothy Dwight, *Travels in New England and New York,* 4 vols. (1822; reprint, Cambridge, MA, 1969), vol. 4, pp. 295–6.

121. Hart, *The Country Clergy in Elizabethan and Stuart Times,* p. 42.

122. Lockridge, *A New England Town The First Hundred Years,* p. 16; Wilson, *The Benevolent Deity,* p. 197.

At the head of the assembly stood the minister, who spoke to the entire assembly, and here was another significant source of social authority. The standard legal requirement to attend church – for religious tolerance meant simply the choice of which church to attend – applied to everyone, not merely church members. Even where, as in the Chesapeake region, the penalties for non-attendance were gradually weakened or neglected, the great majority of colonists attended church on a regular basis through the mid-eighteenth century.[123] This practice meant that ministers had the opportunity to express themselves to most of the populace on all matters of import. Indeed, the clergy had the opportunity to lay out their best arguments for several hours each Sunday and to ground them in "the Bible ... the Religion of Protestants," as Rector Chillingworth averred. "The Country Parson preacheth constantly, the pulpit is his joy and his throne," George Herbert observed.[124] Here was the architectonic explicitly at work, and no less so for Puritans than among Anglicans. A study of "the power and the pulpit" in New England has shown how "the sermon ... provided the outlet for public expression of the deepest tensions of the society." The importance of preaching did not abate in the eighteenth century. "By 1776 Congregational ministers in New England were delivering over two thousand discourses a week and publishing them at an unprecedented rate that outnumbered secular pamphlets (from all colonies) by a ratio of more than four to one."[125]

The importance of sermons lay not only in legitimating social and political events, but also in exercising moral authority. The role of the church and the clergy in shaping social mores was acknowledged in each colony, and every legislature enacted laws prohibiting "injury to public morals and religion." No sooner had east and west Jersey merged into a royal colony in 1703 than "An Act for Suppressing of Immorality within this Province" was immediately passed, detailing fines, prison terms, and whippings for Sabbath-breaking, profanity, drunkenness, and other religious and moral transgressions, two categories that were scarcely distinguished.[126] In Virginia church wardens were charged to present those suspected moral or religious offenses to the county court, which combined the functions of the quarter session court, the ecclesiastical court, and the vestry. In fact, the Virginia county court often comprised the same individuals who sat on the vestry.[127] In Con-

123. Allan Kulikoff, *Tobacco and Slaves: The Development of Southern Cultures in the Chesapeake, 1680–1800* (Chapel Hill, NC, 1986), p. 235; Patricia U. Bonomi and Peter R. Eisenstadt, "Church Adherence in the Eighteenth-Century British American Colonies," *WMQ*, 3d ser., 39 (1982): 245–86; Davis, *The Intellectual Life in the Colonial South, 1585–1763*, ch. 6.

124. Herbert, *The Country Parson*, p. 223, ch. 7.

125. Quotations are from Emory Elliott, *The Power and the Pulpit in Puritan New England* (Princeton, NJ, 1975), p. 10; Stout, *The New England Soul*, p. 6. See Samuel E. Morison, *The Intellectual Life of Colonial New England* (Ithaca, NY, 1956), ch. 7; Daniel H. Calhoun, *The Intelligence of a People* (Princeton, NJ, 1973), pp. 210–29; Marie L. Ahearn, *The Rhetoric of War: Training Day, the Militia, and the Military Sermon* (Westport, CT, 1989).

126. Quotations are from Chief Justice Parker in *Adams v. Howe*, 14 Massachusetts 340, 344 (1817); *Laws of the Royal Colony of New Jersey*, vol. 2, pp. 21–2.

127. Edmund S. Morgan, *American Slavery and American Freedom: The Ordeal of Colonial Virginia* (New York, 1975), p. 150; Roeber, *Faithful Magistrates and Republican Lawyers*, pp. 140ff.; *Statutes of Virginia*, vol. 1, pp. 126, 156, 182, 227, 240, 309; vol. 2, pp. 51–3.

gregational churches and communities, although the ecclesiastical trials were theoretically distinct from the civil trials, the church elders effectively determined the guilt and punishment both in cases of alleged sacrilege or immorality, such as fornication, drunkenness, and profanity, and in small civil crimes, such as breach of promise, petty theft, and minor torts.[128]

Even where the degree or jurisdiction of a transgression made it incumbent upon the civil court system to adjudicate a crime, ministers not infrequently influenced the outcome of a case. The yet informal legal system welcomed the intercession and heeded the views of leading citizens, such as ministers, and the absence of regular police meant that mediation by such individuals was often crucial in resolving disputes without turning to force. Moreover, the clergy "are all agreed likewise, That where men are thus notoriously scandalous, or obstinate in known sin ... we must proceed to the forementioned publick reproof, and casting them out of our communion, else the remaining members of our Church will harden themselves, offend the godly, occasion the weak to separate, and will be a scandal to our Profession."[129]

The ministers thus exercised great social authority by preaching formally to the assembled community and by speaking informally as individuals to civil and judicial officials. But perhaps their greatest social influence derived from their formal role in counseling individual parishioners about the entire range of human problems: medical, familial, financial, and, of course, spiritual. George Herbert's handbook detailed the duty of an Anglican parson to ride the circuit of his neighbors and admonish them; and Cotton Mather advised young ministers of this obligation: "You may set upon *visiting* all the families, belonging to your flock.... And when you come unto them; you may assay ... to treat every person particularly about their everlasting interests."[130] It goes without saying that these pastoral visits about "everlasting interests" were not Rogerian. In fact, when Edward Wigglesworth was looking for a pulpit in 1722, one of his recommenders wrote on his behalf: "As for his deafness I look on it as good ministerial qualification."[131] Ministers were expected not to listen, but to instruct, admonish, and praise individuals according to the architectonic that ordered life in view of the ultimate values and goal of religious salvation. Neither were the visits cold or emotionless. Scholars have demonstrated that Puritan ministers were invited into the most intimate concerns of their parishioners, while probing their fears and anxieties in order to enhance the process of conversion and their receptivity to "God's Caress."[132]

The ministerial role, constituting the leadership of the institution charged with representing and advancing the highest human values and ends, therefore attained

128. Oberholzer, *Delinquent Saints*, chs. 3–10; William E. Nelson, *Dispute and Conflict Resolution in Plymouth County, Massachusetts, 1725–1825* (Chapel Hill, NC, 1981), pp. 10–11, chs. 2–3.

129. "The Propositions of the Ministers" of the Worcestershire Association (1653), in *Gildas Salvianus*, ed. Wilkinson, p. 178.

130. Herbert, *The Country Parson*, ch. 14; Mather, *BONIFACIUS, An Essay upon the Good*, p. 75.

131. *Harvard Graduates*, vol. 5, pp. 548–9.

132. Hambrick-Stowe, *The Practice of Piety*, chs. 5–6; Gordon S. Wakefield, *Puritan Devotion, Its Place in the Development of Christian Piety* (London, 1957), p. 111; Cohen, *God's Caress: The Psychology of Puritan Religious Experience*, passim.

great social authority and status. Not all ministers may have been able to insist, as did Rev. Josiah Winship of Woolwich, Maine, that the boys of the town doff their caps as they passed the parsonage. Nor could every minister oversee temporal affairs as did Rev. John Odlin of Exeter, New Hampshire, where the parishioners set their clocks by his grandfather clock. But all clergy were known by the title of "Mister," which was reserved for persons of wealth and social distinction. They were leaders of an institution that the social elite necessarily heeded, so that even a popular evangelist such as John Wesley maintained that "Next to *Prudence* or *Common Sense* ... a Clergyman ought certainly to have some degree of *Good-breeding*: I mean, Address, Easiness and Propriety of Behaviour ... all the *Courtesy* of a *Gentleman*, joined with the Correctness of a *Scholar*."[133]

Economic: "an *Honourable Maintenance*"

In addition to their ecclesiastical, political, and social authority, the clergy and the churches had great economic influence in early colonial society. Medieval religious conceptions of economic exchange grounded the conventional strictures that a merchant should charge no more than a "just price" and that "usury" should be avoided, and these conventions persevered among colonial Calvinists well into the second half of the seventeenth century. The prominent Boston merchant Robert Keayne, who was fined by the Massachusetts General Court and severely reprimanded by his church for charging excessive prices and practicing usury during times of scarcity in New England, devoted some nineteen pages of his will in 1653 to refuting these charges. But he never questioned either the conventions limiting the marketplace and money-lending or the shared purview of the church and state over these matters.[134]

These limitations on mercantile activity eroded by the end of the seventeenth century. But the state regulation of economic activity in line with religious goals continued in the form of statutory requirements to maintain ministers and churches. Every colony except Rhode Island, Pennsylvania, and Delaware legislated requirements of all residents to contribute financially to the established Protestant church. In the Carolinas, Virginia, Connecticut, Massachusetts, and New Hampshire, the religious establishment was more consistent than in New York, New Jersey, Maryland, and Georgia. Yet in either case the only modification of such requirements before the Revolution came in the form of allowing dissenters to make their contribution to a non-establishment church.

Such legal requirements dictated the minimum expectations of economic support for religion, standards that nevertheless made the building and maintenance of

133. Wesley, *An Address to the Clergy*, p. 216; *Harvard Graduates*, vol. 5, pp. 171–2; vol. 15, p. 339.

134. Robert Keayne, *The Apologia of Robert Keayne, The Last Will and Testament ... 1653*, ed. Bernard Bailyn (New York, 1965), pp. 45–64; Bailyn, *New England Merchants*, pp. 20–1; Oberholzer, *Delinquent Saints*, ch. 11.

the local church the largest investment of public capital[135] and the support of the minister the largest annual expenditure for most colonial communities. When Peter Thatcher became minister of Weymouth, Massachusetts, in the first decade of the eighteenth century his annual salary was one-half of the town budget. In a typical parish in Hanover County, Virginia, in the following decade the minister's salary was 68 percent of the budget, and in the 1730s, 47 percent. In the same decade Rochester, New Hampshire, settled its first minister, whose salary through 1760 was about 90 percent of the town budget. The following year the nearby town of Boscawen ordained a recent Harvard graduate at a salary of some two-thirds of the town budget. These situations typify the pattern of local allocation of financial resources that was demanded by the social authority of ministers, enforced by the state, and legitimated by the ultimacy of religious concerns within the culture.[136] As a result, the ministry through the mid-eighteenth century became the best compensated vocation, apart from merchants; and the clergy occupied a place well within the top fifth of the free, male population in financial standing.

Scholars have long underestimated the "scanty income" of the "needy minister."[137] This underestimation arises partly from a lack of appreciation for the dialectical nature of ministers" derogation of worldly wealth, on the one hand, and complaints about their financial standing, on the other. Even recent historians who stress colonial ministers" desires for "earthly rewards" and "worldly prestige" view the clergy as having modest financial resources, apparently in the effort to show that such desires are intrinsically part of "professionalization."[138] Whatever the

135. In Virginia the church occupied an architectural status on the "hierarchy in buildings" just below the "great house" of the plantation owner and above that of the courthouse or the planter's house. (Isaac, *The Transformation of Virginia, 1740–1790*, pp. 66–7.) Meanwhile, New Englanders erected over 220 meetinghouses in the seventeenth century and over 2,000 in the eighteenth. Some have claimed that early meetinghouses were not, first and foremost, religious buildings. (J. Frederick Kelly, *Early Connecticut Meetinghouses* (New York, 1948), pp. xxiii–xxiv; Winslow, *Meetinghouse Hill, 1630–1783*, pp. 50–1.) But even granting this claim for the first generation of Puritans, the meetinghouses came to be called "churches" by 1700, and "symbolically they proclaimed to all that religion was the chief business of the community and the highest priority of its people." Stout, *The New England Soul*, p. 14. Wertenbaker, *The Puritan Oligarchy*, ch. 4; Peter Benes and Philip Zimmerman, *New England Meeting House and Church, 1630–1850* (Boston, 1979); Peter I. Mallary, *New England Churches and Meetinghouses* (New York, 1985).

136. *Harvard Graduates*, vol. 4, p. 304; vol. 8, p. 601; vol. 13, pp. 629–30; Seiler, "The Anglican Church," p. 147. Since this kind of allocation was contributed "voluntarily" and not taxed (unless a community became recalcitrant), this kind of economic authority has often been undervalued in discussions of colonial taxes and levies. See, for example, Edwin J. Perkins, *The Economy of Colonial America* (New York, 1980), ch. 7.

137. Bailey B. Burritt, *Professional Distribution of College and University Graduates* (Washington, DC, 1912), p. 16. *Yale Graduates*, passim; *Harvard Graduates*, passim; Silverman, *The Life and Times of Cotton Mather*, p. 49.

138. Youngs, *God's Messengers: Religious Leadership in Colonial New England*, p. 10. Merely a few pages of discussion about ministers finances are found in Youngs, pp. 105–8; Hall, *The Faithful Sheperd*, pp. 152–3, 182–3; James W. Schmotter, "Ministerial Careers in Eighteenth-Century New England: The Social Context, 1700–1760," *Journal of Social History*, 9 (1975): 257–60; Schmotter, "The Irony of Clerical Professionalism: New

historiographical intent, the fundamental reason for this underestimation is that
financial data, ecclesiastical practices, and clerical testimony have not been analyzed
relative to other contemporary occupations so that scholars can free themselves
from twentieth-century norms of ministers' compensation and wealth.

Such an analysis is difficult. First, one must sort through the often contradictory
or paradoxical views regarding ministers' support and wealth. During the sixteenth
and seventeenth centuries, English dissenters fiercely debated the status of tithes:
"the sacred tenth" of produce or profits that was to be reserved for the church. The
purest Puritans agreed with John Milton that tithes, and all religious taxes, were
"violent and irreligious exactions," part of "the tricks and impostures of clergie
men, contriv'd with all the art and argument that thir bellies can invent or suggest."[139] But more pragmatic Puritans saw them as a means to augment the livings
of the lower clergy and to circumvent the Anglican establishment or, in any case,
agreed with Presbyterian minister Gracious Francklin that the clergy had no less of
a "Gospel warrant to ... such and such houses and lands" than any others "that are
blessed with personal estates."[140]

Rev. Francklin himself acknowledged, however, the temptation to "a *Minister* to
be more desirous of the *fleece*, then to profit the *flocke.*" This temptation raised the
more fundamental question of whether payment, even gathered from voluntary
contributions, contaminated the religious purity and role of the clergy. John Milton
again expressed the extreme view, endorsed by many Quakers, Baptists and, later,
the Sandemanians, that, if ministers did not have a private income, they should
earn their living as craftsmen or physicians, rather than from the church. Less
radical was the opinion of Roger Williams that, while an unpaid clergy might be
preferable, Biblical justification existed for "the free and willing contribution of the
Saints, according to I *Cor.* 16 *Luc.* 8. 3. etc."[141]

Baptists continued to agonize over this issue through the end of the eighteenth
century because, unlike the Quakers, they had clergy to support, and because they
rarely established themselves as the dominant profession in a colony and thus
continually assumed the position of a nonconformist sect.[142] The Congregationalists

---

England's Congregational Ministers and the Great Awakening," pp. 159–60; Harlan, *The
Clergy and the Great Awakening in New England,* ch. 2; Bonomi, *Under the Cope of Heaven,*
pp. 41–54. More information is available in Joan R. Gundersen, "The Anglican Ministry in
Virginia, 1723–1776: A Study of Social Class" (PhD diss., University of Notre Dame, 1972);
Carol Lee van Voorst, "The Anglican Clergy in Maryland, 1692–1776" (PhD diss., Prince-
ton University, 1978).

139. John Milton, "Considerations Touching the Likeliest Means" (1659), pp. 297–8, and
Austin Woolrych, "Introduction," ch. 5 in *Complete Prose Works of John Milton,* ed. Don M.
Wolfe (New Haven, CT, 1974), vol. 7.

140. Francklin, *A Soft Answer to Captain Freeman's Passionate Book,* p. 17; Christopher
Hill, *The Century of Revolution, 1603–1714,* 2d edn (London, 1980), pp. 73–4, 139.

141. Francklin, *A Soft Answer to Captain Freeman's Passionate Book,* pp. 3–4; Milton,
"Considerations Touching the Likeliest Means," p. 307; John Milton, "Aeropagitica" (1644),
in *Complete Prose Works of John Milton,* ed. Don M. Wolfe (New Haven, CT, 1969), vol. 2,
p. 531; Roger Williams, "The Bloudy Tenent of Persecution" (1644), in *The Complete
Writings of Roger Williams,* ed. Perry Miller (New York, 1963), vol. 6, pp. 304–5.

142. See the succession of Baptist discussions in Roger Williams, "The Hireling Ministry

and Presbyterians, by contrast, shifted from dissenting sects in England to colonial establishments, and embraced a position that was well expressed by Increase and Cotton Mather early in the eighteenth century. Ideally the minister should secure "an *Honourable Maintenance* ... by the *Voluntary Contribution* of those that attend on [the] ministry." But in a sinful, compromised world, required maintenance was the necessary instrument to achieve the ends of religion, although tithes, which smacked of "popery," were impermissible.[143] The ambiguity in this view demonstrates again the dialectical imprint of the religious architectonic. The colonial Calvinist ministers generally argued that "the Labourer is worthy of his Hire," according to the most frequently cited Biblical injunction in these debates. Yet, while accepting their *"Honourable Maintenance"* they felt compelled at ministerial gatherings to remind each other of *The Gaining of Souls, the Most Joyful Gain to Faithful Ministers* and to ask accusingly: "Was a *comfortable Livelihood* then your Motive for Entering into the Ministry?"[144]

Apart from the ambivalence and ambiguity in clerical opinion regarding voluntary and required maintenance and compensation in general, another reason for the difficulty in assessing ministers' financial position lies in the uncertainty of monetary value. Coin was scarce in the colonies, and payment during the seventeenth century usually came partly in the form of "country pay" in New England, wampum in New Netherlands and New York, and tobacco in Virginia. The value of such commodities was variable and often no less uncertain to colonists than to modern scholars.[145] At the turn of the century, colonial currencies had generally replaced the exchange of commodities, but this replacement merely swapped one problem for another due to the varying valuation of these currencies against each other and against the pound sterling. By the 1720s it was not uncommon to find churches somewhat lamely offering a salary "in such money as shall pass from time to time between man and man." In addition, horrendous inflation plagued the colonies during the second quarter of the eighteenth century. Not only did this

---

None of Christs" (1652); Lewis Stuckley, *A Gospel Class, representing the Miscarriages of English Professors* (n.p., 1667), ch. 32; Knollys, *The Gospel Minister's Maintenance Vindicated*; John Ryland, Jr., "Paul's Charge to the Corinthians respecting their Treatment of Timothy applied to the Conduct of Churches toward their Pastors," in *Two Discourses* (London, 1787); Isaac Backus, *The Liberal Support of Gospel Ministers Opened and Inculcated* (Boston, 1790).

143. Increase Mather, "Dedication," in *A Discourse Concerning the Maintenance due to those that Preach the Gospel* (Boston, 1706); [Mather], *RATIO DISCIPLINAE FRATRUM NOV-ANGLORUM*, p. 20.

144. *Luke* 10: 17; John Hancock, *The Gaining of Souls, the Most Joyful Gain to Faithful Ministers* (Boston, 1748); Wesley, *An Address to the Clergy*, p. 228.

145. The practice of paying the parson in kind, and the concomitant imprecision, extended back to Elizabethan England and continued into the eighteenth century. (Hart, *The Country Clergy in Elizabethan and Stuart Times*, pp. 47–8; O'Day, *The English Clergy ... 1558–1642*, passim; Hart, *Clergy and Society, 1600–1800*, p. 69, ch. 5.) See Kilpatrick, *The Dutch Schools of New Netherland and Colonial New York*, pp. 16f; Morgan, *American Slavery and American Freedom*, p. 108; Richard B. Sheridan, "The Domestic Economy," pp. 43–85, in *Colonial British America*, ed. Jack P. Greene and J. R. Pole (Baltimore, MD, 1984); Roeber, *Faithful Magistrates and Republican Lawyers*, p. 39; *Harvard Graduates*, vol. 2, pp. 150–3, 161–2, 229–33, 519–20; vol. 3, pp. 174–6; Warch, *School of the Prophets*, pp. 143–4.

Table 2.1   Estates of American colonists during the mid-eighteenth century (estimated)

Value of estate*	*Proportion of free, male population (%)*
over £800	15 (wealthy)
£500–800	10 (substantial property owners)
£200–600	35 (small property owners)
£50–200	20 (lower middle class)
Under £80	25 (dependent, landless laborers)
Total	100

* Figures are equated to pounds sterling of real and chattel property. I have presented overlapping categories in the values of the estates and percentages in order to convey points of disagreement between Hanson, Nash and Main and the actual indeterminacy in such classifications.
Sources: Gary B. Nash, *The Urban Crucible: Social Change, Political Consciousness, and the Origins of the American Revolution* (Cambridge, MA, 1976), pp. 19–20, 400–17; Jackson T. Main, *The Social Structure of Revolutionary America* (Princeton, NJ, 1965), pp. 66–7, 270–5; Main, *Society and Economy in Colonial Connecticut* (Princeton, NJ, 1985), passim; Alice Hanson Jones *American Colonial Wealth: Documents and methods*, 2d edn (New York, 1978), vol. 3; Jones, *Wealth of a Nation to Be: The American Colonies on the Eve of the Revolution* (New York, 1980), pp. 54–8.

factor compound the problem of variance in valuation, but several colonies, such as Massachusetts, introduced "New Tenor" to replace "Old Tenor" as time passed. Thus, different currencies and bills of credit were authorized by and circulated within the same colony. The situation became particularly volatile in the 1740s. After about 1750, most of the colonial currencies were revalued, and remained fairly stable until the Revolution at levels about the same as those of the early eighteenth century.[146]

These fluctuations in value naturally compound what is intrinsically a difficult task of trying to estimate the relative wealth of various occupational groups in colonial society. Fortunately, a composite sketch of the relative wealth of the colonists can be educed from the scholarship of Jackson Main, Gary Nash, and Alice Jones. These three historians from different generations have different views on the valence and fluidity of the colonial economic class structure, but their quantifications of that structure are remarkably similar, as reported on Table 2.1.

146. *Harvard Graduates*, vol. 6, p. 171. Perkins, *The Economy of Colonial America*, ch. 6; John J. McCusker, *Money and Exchange in Europe and America, 1660–1775: A Handbook* (Chapel Hill, NC, 1978), pp. 125–278. In general fractions compared to pounds sterling in the final third of the eighteenth century, "lawful money" of New England and Virginia was worth about three-quarters of face value; New York and North Carolina about one-half; Pennsylvania, Maryland, Delaware, and New Jersey about two-fifths; South Carolina and Georgia about one-seventh.

In order to correlate estates with annual income, one can find a benchmark in the range of £20 to £40 that laborers earned annually, including room or board. The lower end of the range went to unskilled and agricultural workers, mariners, and skilled laborers who worked in rural areas. The higher end was paid to artisans and craftsmen and those who worked in larger communities. In fact, a top craftsman in Boston, New York, or Philadelphia might earn as much as £50 or £60. Another benchmark may be found in the estimates that a typical bachelor could live decently on £25, a family could live comfortably on £100, and £150 would support the life of a gentleman.[147]

Of course, the specific amounts varied across time and location, and what is more meaningful than absolute figures is a *relative* comparison of where the clergy stood economically with respect to those in other vocations.[148] For example, upon arriving in 1630 and establishing the salary for a minister and his family, the Massachusetts magistrates attempted to set limits on all wages and prices, but soon had to abandon this medieval effort to make the market just. Nevertheless, the rates set in 1630 indicate the magistrates' sense of the relative levels of compensation that were intended to and did prevail: ministers received between two and three times the compensation of master craftsmen and five to six times the compensation of laborers. By 1766, when the descendants of those Puritans ordained a new minister at a salary of £100 in Concord, Massachusetts, the economic position of ministers had eroded considerably. But that salary was still two-and-a-half times a year's wages for a laborer in the town.[149]

Recent studies indicate that the clerical standard of living in England slowly rose between 1535 and 1660, that most parochial clergy were much better off than the farmers in their parish, that an effort was made to raise the minimum annual income to £100, and that "the clergy were, at least in the larger and wealthier

147. Here and below, I draw upon Bailyn, *The New England Merchants*, ch. 2; Stephen Innes, *Labor in a New Land: Economy and Society in Seventeenth-Century Springfield* (Princeton, NJ, 1983), pp. 47, 74–5; Manfred Jonas, "Wages in Early Colonial Maryland," *Maryland Historical Magazine*, 51 (1956): 27–38; Main, *The Social Structure of Revolutionary America*, pp. 73–80, 115–9; Perkins, *The Economy of Colonial America*, ch. 7; Aubrey C. Land, "Economic Base and Social Structure: The Northern Chesapeake in the Eighteenth Century," *Journal of Economic History*, 25 (1965): 641–3; Russell R. Menard, "From Servant to Freeholder: Status Mobility and Property Accumulation in Seventeenth-Century Maryland," *WMQ*, 3d ser., 30 (1973): 37–64; Nash, *The Urban Crucible*, pp. 12, 392–4, 413–4; Russell R. Menard, P. M. G. Harris, and Lois G. Carr, "Opportunity and Inequality: The Distribution of Wealth on the Lower Western Shore of Maryland, 1638–1705," *Maryland Historical Magazine*, 69 (1974): 169–84; Marcus Rediker, "The Anglo-American Seaman as Collective Worker, 1700–1750," pp. 256–7, 275–7, and Billy G. Smith, "The Vicissitudes of Fortune: The Careers of Laboring Men in Philadelphia, 1750–1800," pp. 221–51, and Paul G. E. Clemens and Lucy Simler, "Rural Labor and the Farm Household in Chester County, Pennsylvania, 1750–1820," pp. 116–42, in *Work and Labor in Early America*, ed. Stephen Innes (Chapel Hill, NC, 1988).

148. A relative comparison seems to give a better sense of economic standing than do efforts to convert colonial figures to present dollars as in Jones, *American Colonial Wealth*, table 3.5; Perkins, *The Economy of Colonial America*, ch. 8.

149. *Records of Massachusetts Bay*, vol. 1, pp. 73–7, 84, 160; Robert A. Gross, *The Minutemen and their World* (New York, 1976), pp. 11, 21.

parishes, beginning to share the more opulent life-style of the lesser gentry."[150] In subsequent decades clerical incomes continued to rise, and most country rectories in England received between £80 and £300 annually in the 1730s. Nevertheless, a number of problems arose for the established church, and the relative social and economic status of the English clergy declined from 1660 until the middle of the eighteenth century.[151]

This English background helps to explain the paradox that the Anglican clergy were well supported in the early southern colonies, especially after the founding of the Society for the Propagation of the Gospel in Foreign Parts (SPG) in 1701. Yet historians have frequently asserted that "the social position of the clergy in the South was not very good."[152] In fact, the economic and social standing of Anglican clergy ranked higher than that of most of the colonists who came to the South through the mid-eighteenth century. Since about 80 percent of white emigrants to the Chesapeake in the seventeenth century were indentured servants, a clergyman, who came to America as a free man with an education and a position, stepped off the boat in at least the top fifth of socio-economic status among new arrivals. Indeed, through 1775 nearly two-thirds of all whites who came to the colonies from Britain and Europe were servants. Even in the mid-1770s, less than 3 percent of British emigrants whose occupations are known claimed status as a 'gentle' person or a member of the liberal professions.[153] Moreover, the gentry in Virginia, as throughout the colonies, were not upper-crust, but upstart aspirants to high social status that they would not have attained in England. All colonists were tainted to some extent, for "emigration to Virginia connoted social inferiority: at best it meant one could not compete in English society and had to leave the country to be a

150. O'Day, *The English Clergy ... 1558–1642,* p. 189, ch. 13. See Hart, *The Country Clergy in Elizabethan and Stuart Times,* pp. 49–51, 166; Hart, *Clergy and Society, 1600– 1800,* ch. 2; Michael L. Zell, "Economic Problems of the Parochial Clergy in the Sixteenth Century," pp. 19–44, and Claire Cross, "The Incomes of Provincial Urban Clergy, 1520– 1645," pp. 65–90, and Joel Berlatsky, "The Elizabethan Episcopate: Patterns of Life and Expenditure," pp. 111–28, in *Princes and Paupers in the English Church, 1500–1800,* ed. Rosemary O'Day and Felicity Heal (Leicester, UK, 1981).

151. Hill, *The Century of Revolution, 1603–1714,* pp. 73–4, app. C; Hart, *Clergy and Society, 1600–1800,* pp. 65–6; Geoffrey Holmes, *Augustan England: Professions, State and Society, 1680–1730* (London, 1982), p. 97, ch. 5; D. R. Hirschberg, "Episcopal Incomes and Expenses, 1660–c.1760," in *Princes and Paupers in the English Church, 1500–1800,* ed. Rosemary O'Day and Felicity Heal (Leicester, UK, 1981), pp. 211–30; John Pruett, *The Parish Clergy under the Later Stuarts* (Urbana, IL, 1978), pp. 74–5, 100–10.

152. William W. Manross, *The Episcopal Church in the United States, 1800–1840* (New York, 1938), pp. 24–5; Morgan, *American Slavery and American Freedom,* p. 348.

153. Bernard Bailyn, *Voyagers to the West, A Passage in the Peopling of America on the Eve of the Revolution* (New York, 1986), pp. 147–51; James Horn, "Servant Emigration to the Chesapeake in the Seventeenth Century," in *The Chesapeake in the Seventeenth Century,* ed. Thad W. Tate and David L. Ammerman (New York, 1979), p. 54; Gundersen, "The Anglican Ministry in Virginia, 1723–1776," chs. 2–3; van Voorst, "The Anglican Clergy in Maryland, 1692–1776," pp. 50ff., 222–49; Morgan, *American Slavery and American Freedom,* ch. 10; Main, *The Social Structure of Revolutionary America,* pp. 96–7.

success."[154] Hence, Governor William Berkeley may have expressed the truth in 1671, when he wrote of the Virginia clergy: "But of all other commodities, so of this, *the worst are sent to us.*"[155] However, the inference often drawn from Berkeley's frequently quoted remark – that the Anglican clergy were the "worst" of the Southerners – does not follow.

The SPG established the level of "sufficient Support" for a missionary at a handsome £100 sterling, which figure was also cited by *American Husbandry* as the cost of housekeeping for a planter's family. In theory the £100 was covered by a payment of £50 from the SPG and a contribution from the local congregation of £50 plus a house and glebe, or farm. Often the congregation did not entirely fulfill its end of the arrangement, but the estimable salaries of the SPG missionaries are nevertheless confirmed by the reports of the colonial college graduates.[156] Anglican ministers in prominent or strategically significant pulpits such as William Veysey, Rector of Trinity Church in New York from 1698 to 1746; Thomas Chandler, missionary to the largest Episcopal congregation in New Jersey during the 1750s; and William Sturgeon, rector of Christ Church, Philadelphia, from 1762, received a princely salary of between £150 and £200.[157] Meanwhile Anglican clergy in the South, where the Church of England was established, earned an ample income exceeding that of most small property owners.

In 1619, at the first session of the new House of Burgesses of Virginia, the minimum living for ministers was set at £200. After the Restoration the Burgesses enacted in 1662 that clergy should be provided with a glebe and a house with furnishings and other perquisites plus a salary of "valuable and current commodities ... worth *at least* fourscore pounds per annum."[158] Although ministers did not always receive the legislative standard, which hovered between £80 and £100, there is no reason to doubt Governor Berkeley's report of 1671 that "the ministers [are] well paid." In 1748 the legislature stipulated that a ministers' maintenance was to be "a good and convenient tract of land, to contain two hundred acres at the least ... one convenient mansion house, kitchen, barn, stable, dairy, meat house, corn house, and garden ... with other such conveniences as they shall think fit,"

154. Shammas, "English-Born and Creole Elites in Turn-of-the-Century Virginia," p. 275. Morgan, *American Slavery and American Freedom*, pp. 254–5. No less in New England than in Virginia, "The migration from England ... made possible an enormous leap in social status for the ministers.... [I]n wealth and prestige they now ranked higher than any other group save the magistrates." Hall, *The Faithful Shepherd*, p. 152. Bradford, *Of Plymouth Plantation, 1620–1647*, ch. 7; Bailyn, *New England Merchants*, pp. 32ff., 155.

155. *Statutes of Virginia*, vol. 2, p. 517.

156. Main, *The Social Structure of Revolutionary America*, p. 118; Edward R. Hardy, Jr., "Priestly Ministries in the Modern Church," in *The Ministry in Historical Perspectives*, ed. H. Richard Niebuhr and Daniel D. Williams (New York, 1956), pp. 162–3; Andrew Burnaby, *Travels through the Middle Settlements in North America in the Years 1759 and 1760*, 3d edn (London, 1798), pp. 67, 81, 88; John Calam, *Parsons and Pedagogues: The S.P.G. Adventure in American Education* (New York, 1971), pp. 30–40, 105–7, 134–43, 206–7; Manross, *The Episcopal Church in the United States*, p. 24. For a sampling of the salaries, see Table A1.1 in Appendix 1.

157. *Harvard Graduates*, vol. 4, pp. 175–9; *Yale Graduates*, vol. 2, pp. 24–5, 61–2.

158. Tyler, ed., *Narratives of Early Virginia*, pp. 271–2; *Statutes of Virginia*, vol. 2, p. 45.

plus a salary of some 16,000 pounds of tobacco, the equivalent of about £100 in the subsequent years.[159] Overall, then, "income accruing from all sources in a more substantial eighteenth-century tidewater parish could have approximated as much as £150 or perhaps a total of £175.... For the Virginia Anglican clergy ... most were above the great majority of small landholders in the socioeconomic scale, but appreciably below the affluent planters who were the leading members of their vestries."[160]

Remuneration in many pulpits further south was similar to that in Virginia. The graduates of northern colonial colleges therefore gladly accepted settlements in South Carolina. Hugh Adams (HC 1697), for example, accepted a call to Wandoe River, near Charleston, at a salary of £70 in 1699. By the 1720s inflation plagued the South Carolina currency, and the Congregational church of Charleston converted the salary of Josiah Smith (HC 1725) to £100 sterling in 1743. The plague continued, but even so, a salary of £1,400 in South Carolina currency was an extraordinary offer that enticed William Tennent, Jr. (PC 1758) from his Presbyterian Church in Norwalk, Connecticut, to a pulpit in Charleston.[161] To the north, the Maryland clergy enjoyed what has been repeatedly described as the most remunerative settlements in the colonies. In the early 1700s their salaries amounted to about £75 sterling and ranged up to £200 by the 1760s.[162] Further northward, the ministers of every profession in Pennsylvania, New Jersey, Delaware, New York, and New England received a salary of £60–150 in colonial currency or country pay from 1640 to about 1720. In the subsequent three decades, salaries rose in bursts when ministers struggled to keep up with the rampant inflation, as will be described in the next chapter. Consequently, the range in salaries became fairly broad, commensurate with the fluctuation in currencies and with the range of pulpits from large wealthy churches to small frontier meetinghouses.[163] Yet, the relative income of ministers within their communities was fairly consistent: their

159. *Statutes of Virginia*, vol. 2, p. 517; vol. 6, pp. 88–90; George M. Brydon, *Virginia's Mother Church and the Political Conditions under which it Grew* (Richmond, VA, 1947), vol. 1, pp. 13–9, 238–9.

160. Seiler, "The Anglican Church," pp. 146–7; Gundersen found that most Anglican parsons in Virginia were "middle class" and about half had estates valued at more than £200 sterling. "The Anglican Ministry in Virginia, 1723–1776," ch. 3.

161. *Harvard Graduates*, vol. 4, p. 323, vol. 7, p. 576; *Princetonians*, vol. 1, p. 249.

162. William S. Perry, ed., *Historical Collections Relating to the American Colonial Church* (Hartford, CT, 1870), vol. 4, pp. 339–40; Manross, *The Episcopal Church in the United States*, p. 24; van Voorst, "The Anglican Clergy in Maryland, 1692–1776," pp. 50ff., 223–49; Burnaby *Travels through the Middle Settlements in North America in the Years 1759 and 1760*, p. 56.

163. These generalizations are based on a review of the salaries of 326 colonial college graduates who became ministers in the northern colonies. See Table A1.2 in Appendix 1. Somewhat different estimates based upon an evaluation of 152 unidentified graduates drawn from *Harvard Graduates* may be found in Stephen Botein, "Income and Ideology: Harvard-Trained Clergymen in Eighteenth-Century New England," pp. 396–413. James W. Schmotter estimated that the average salary of a New England minister was £65 in 1700, £65 in 1710, £70 in 1720, £85 in 1730, and £98 in 1740. "Provincial Professionalism: The New England Ministry, 1692–1745" (PhD diss., Northwestern University, 1973), pp. 166–9.

salary was about three times that of an unskilled laborer, about two times the earnings of a craftsman or artisan, and slightly below that of a "gentleman."

Insofar as estates were a function of income, this salary placed ministers near the third quartile in accumulated wealth, according to Table 2.1. What is important to recognize, however, is that ministers' salaries render a low estimate of their wealth because that income was augmented by two other important kinds of financial resources which have been undervalued or largely ignored in discussions of clerical income. On the one hand, ministers received perquisites that amounted to about half again the amount of their salary. For instance, while the laity paid what amounted to a religious tax to support the church, clergymen were generally exempt from taxation. These exemptions were not always the carte blanche granted by the 1671 Massachusetts provision that "henceforth the ministers of God's word ... shall be freed from all rates for the country, county, and church, and for the towne also." The exemptions varied across time and jurisdiction. Nevertheless, from the Virginia statute of 1734 to the 1780 petition presented by an itinerant preacher to the Connecticut assembly, the expectation prevailed that a minister deserved some abatement of taxes.[164]

Various kinds of gratuities for funerals and special services and other gifts also came to the clergy. Andrew Eliot, after a long ministry in Boston during the mid-eighteenth century, figured that he had received nearly 3,000 pairs of gloves as gifts at funerals, which he had sold for some £1,441. In a debate over clerical salaries in Virginia in 1696, such gratuities were figured to be worth about 10 percent of the salary.[165] Freewill offerings made by guests and visitors to church services were also frequently consigned to the minister, and parishes or wealthy parishioners sometimes bestowed a windfall upon their pastor. In 1746 the town of Nottingham-West, New Hampshire, decided to build a new meetinghouse, so they gave their old one to their minister, who sold it to the neighboring town for a tidy sum. Ministers were also favored in inheritances, both among their parishioners and within their families.[166]

But perhaps the perquisites of greatest value, particularly in the northern colonies, were the firewood and free labor that were routinely provided by the parishioners,[167] as well as the permanent tenure that a ministerial settlement implied. Notwithstanding the presentation controversy in Virginia, the relationship between a pastor and a congregation among either Anglicans or Calvinists was regarded like a marriage covenant. To divorce was a personal failure for both parties, and an affront to the profession that grounded the culture. Congregational and Presbyterian ministers who sought to leave their parish normally requested an ecclesiastical council to grant them a "dismission," that is, a divorce for irreconcilable differences that would justify the breaking of the covenant to any future congregation. A minister who sought to leave his pulpit for another church or a college

164. *Records of Massachusetts Bay*, vol. 4, pt. 2, p. 486; *Statutes of Virginia*, vol. 4, p. 433; *Harvard Graduates*, vol. 3, p. 56.

165. *Harvard Graduates*, vol. 10, p. 131; Brydon, *Virginia's Mother Church*, vol. 1, pp. 13–9, 238–9; Seiler, "The Anglican Church," pp. 145–8.

166. *Harvard Graduates*, vol. 2, pp. 136–7, 189; vol. 9, pp. 84–5; Wilson, *The Benevolent Deity*, p. 46; Keayne, *The Apologia*, pp. 41–3, 92.

167. See, for example, *Harvard Graduates*, vol. 1, pp. 492–3.

presidency had to obtain permission from his church, which sometimes, as in the case of Increase Mather and the Harvard presidency, it would not grant. If the church did consent, then it received compensation, as in the case of Rev. Edward Holyoke in 1738 when the Massachusetts legislature granted £140 to his church so that he could become president of Harvard College. Similarly, when Samuel Wales was invited to become Livingston Professor of Divinity at Yale in 1782, his congregation refused to let him go until an ecclesiastical council recommended it and the College agreed to compensate the church with a payment of £200.[168]

Such compensation was not demanded out of spite. It was required by a necessity that stemmed from the second major source of wealth that augmented clerical salaries and that scholars have frequently overlooked or undervalued.[169] As implied in the Virginia statutes of 1662 and 1748, the universal custom – indeed, obligation – was to endow a newly installed pastor with a "settlement." The typical settlement ranged from the ownership of a farm, or glebe, with a house and barn to simply the use of unimproved land that had been reserved for the ministry, although it was almost always the case that the labor to build a house and barn was included as well.

Newly established townships often possessed few commodities and less coin with which to pay their clergy, but they did have land, and as long as that lasted, they were able to supplement even modest salaries with a large settlement grant. In 1704 Josiah Torrey was settled in the poor town of Tisbury on Martha's Vineyard, with a salary of only £20. But Tisbury had set aside one-sixteenth of all its land for the minister, and the town deeded that entire fraction to the 25-year-old Rev. Torrey with some help to work it. In 1710 Mansfield, Connecticut, installed the 22-year-old Eleazer Williams into its pastorate, and paid him the modest salary of £40 plus 40 cords of wood per year. But the town provided a settlement of 1,000 acres of land, £160 cash, and assistance in building his parsonage and working his land, such that, by the minister's own report, some 40 parishioners showed up to cut his hay every year and cart it to the barn.[170]

Through the late 1700s, by law or by custom, townships generally provided a sizeable homestead and farm for their minister. In 1763 Hinsdale, New Hampshire, ordained a new minister with a salary of £50 plus 350 acres of land; and in the same year a Harvard graduate was settled with 500 acres of land in the Presbyterian pulpit in Cumberland, Nova Scotia, under the same provisions that existed in the Anglican establishment and in the American colonies. In 1768 the Presbyterian church in Cold Spring, New Jersey, called a recent graduate of Princeton and provided him with a salary of £55 plus a parsonage and glebe; and as late as 1805 Brownsfield, Maine, settled its new minister with a grant of one sixty-fourth of all the town lands. Meanwhile Nathaniel Erwin was ordained over the Presbyterian Church in Neshimany, Pennsylvania, at a salary of £100 plus the choice between a parsonage and £130 for a settlement.[171] Erwin's situation indicates the variability in financial arrangements. The settlement was sometimes equated to a lump sum

---

168. *Harvard Graduates,* vol. 8, p. 365; *Yale Graduates,* vol. 3, p. 258.

169. Main notes the existence of a settlement in one sentence. (*The Social Structure of Revolutionary America,* p. 96.) The other scholars cited here scarcely mention it.

170. *Harvard Graduates,* vol. 4, p. 419; vol. 5, p. 472.

171. *Harvard Graduates,* vol. 14, p. 606; vol. 15, p. 393; vol. 16, p. 210; *Princetonians,* vol. 1, p. 447; vol. 2, p. 89.

payment in money, or a payment was made a part of the settlement and certain perquisites were added on top of that. In 1681 Windsor, Connecticut, installed a new pastor at a salary of £100 plus an additional payment of £100 to help him settle into the land and house reserved for the minister. In 1718 North Haven, Connecticut, ordained a recent Yale graduate at a salary of £80 in country pay plus a settlement of £150 in money or grain.[172] These examples, like those above, demonstrate that a settlement was deemed to be worth about twice the amount of one year's salary, and this ratio continued to prevail as the salaries rose with inflation in the 1720s.[173]

Whether such offers were in silver, country pay, or the various colonial currencies made a great difference in the real value of the pulpit and whether it was acceptable, and the divergence in the value of such payments increased over the next two decades. Nevertheless, a fairly clear norm of about £150 in salary and £300 in settlement in colonial currency prevailed until the early 1740s, when inflation drove up salaries and settlements astronomically. In the 1750s, with the return to stability of revalued currencies, ministerial agreements returned near to the levels of the early 1700s. New ministers' salaries and settlements hovered at about £70 and £135, respectively.[174]

Despite the fluctuations in currency and the variability in arrangements from parish to parish, it is evident that the ministerial settlement through at least 1760 had considerable value. Whether or not the town deeded the ministerial lands and parsonage to the clergyman outright, as was often the case, their use-value was considerable, and it was often stipulated that a minister's heirs gained title to the land if the minister spent his life in the parish. In fact, even if a minister left after a short period, and under embarrassing circumstances, he was frequently able to capitalize on his settlement. Rev. John James was dismissed from his pulpit in Connecticut in 1706, and sold the parsonage back to the town for £90, one-and-a-half times his salary. In Massachusetts, Jonathan Mills, whose stipend was £75, saw his ministry fall apart in the difficult 1730s, and he left his church and sold the parsonage and settlement lands for the small fortune of £675. Even more boldly, 31-year-old Peter Pratt was dismissed from his pulpit in Connecticut for intemperance in 1747, merely seven years after he had been installed. He stayed on to reside in the parish as one of the largest landholders by virtue of the lands granted to him as part of his settlement.[175]

Given that the settlement amounted to about two times the minister's salary, a newly installed minister was immediately endowed with an estate worth perhaps £150–300, which placed him about at the median of the population. Surmounted upon this foundation was a salary that approximately equaled the yearly earnings of the wealthiest of the "small property owners" and that was augmented by perquisites so as to approach the income of "gentlemen," who were themselves in the top

172. *Harvard Graduates*, vol. 2, pp. 365–6; *Yale Graduates*, vol. 1, pp. 133–4.

173. In the 1720s offers of a £100 salary and a £100 settlement were rejected, while offers of a £100 salary and a £200 settlement were accepted. See Table A1.2 in Appendix 1; *Harvard Graduates*, vol. 7, pp. 77, 167, 266, 269.

174. See Table A1.2 in Appendix 1. *Harvard Graduates*, vol. 9, pp. 18–9; vol. 10, p. 189; vol. 11, p. 182. Note that many offers during this decade were stated in terms of silver, as well as Old and New Tenor.

175. *Harvard Graduates*, vol. 5, pp. 13–5; vol. 7, p. 240; *Yale Graduates*, vol. 1, p. 566.

fifth of the population. And all this was bestowed upon a clergyman at the outset of his career, usually a few years after graduating from college. Consequently, it may be inferred that the clergy throughout the colonies and through the mid-eighteenth century were not very far from David Hall's estimation of the seventeenth-century New England clergy – "the average size of their estates placed the ministers within the wealthiest 15 percent of colonists."[176]

To be sure, not all ministers were wealthy, or even comfortable. Particularly in areas where the colony or the profession forbade required maintenance of ministers, the clergy were sometimes uneducated tradesmen who preached on the side and earned little. But in other areas even dissenting ministers acquired handsome estates. Elisha Callender, minister of the first Baptist church in Boston until his death in 1738, left an estate valued at £950. Callender had studied at Harvard College, and a sample of Harvard graduates who became ministers in the early eighteenth century indicates that many others left sizeable estates, as well.[177]

More representative and comparative data can be gathered from the first 20 classes of Yale College, which included 101 graduates between 1702 and 1721. In *Yale Graduates* F. B. Dexter recorded the estates of 39 of these graduates, the proportion of whose careers are representative of the total 101 graduates.[178] As indicated on Table 2.2, the estates of these ministers, who served in Delaware, Pennsylvania, New Jersey, New York, and New England, are comparable to those of individuals in other fields. In fact, the great majority of the clerical estates rank well within the top fifth of the population in terms of wealth.

What is important to note about these figures, before we turn to examine the

176. Hall, *The Faithful Sheperd*, p. 183. Donald M. Scott, *From Office to Profession: The New England Ministry, 1750–1850* (Philadelphia, 1978), ch. 4.

177. *Harvard Graduates*, vol. 5, p. 516. In the Harvard classes from 1690 to 1712, 156 graduates devoted themselves to the ministry, and the estates of the 23 that are recorded in *Harvard Graduates* are distributed in this way:

Value of Estate	(%)
over £800	78
£500–800	9
£300–500	9
£200–300	0
below £200	4
Total	100

Source: Harvard Graduates, vol. 4, 61–2, 146–153, 233, 238–5, 254–9, 273–5, 293–4, 379–83, 388–90, 473–6, 529; vol. 5, pp. 120, 131–4, 172–4, 371–4, 402, 406–8, 444, 516, 616–21, 624–30, 647–8. The currencies of these estates and the definition of "property" are not always specified.

178. The corresponding fractions are: total graduates 39/101, theology 23/65, medicine 1/2, law 2/5, education 0/0, finance or commerce 4/5, public or military service 2/4, other 5/15, unknown 0/2, died young 2/3. Dexter rarely specifies the currencies in which these estates are valued or whether both chattel and real property are included.

Table 2.2   Representative sample of Yale graduates in the first 20 classes, 1702–1721, sorted by vocation and estate

Value of estate	Theology* (%)	Other vocations* (%)	Died young* (%)	Total (%)
Over £800	39	28	5	72
£500–800	15	0	0	15
£200–500	5	5	0	10
Below £200	0	3	0	3
Total	59	36	5	100

* See Appendix 2 for definitions of these categories and the method of categorizing individuals.
Source: *Yale Graduates,* vol. 1, pp. 9–258.

financial standing of the other "learned professions," are two things. Since the great majority of ministers were college graduates in the early eighteenth century, the cases of "theology" are fairly representative of the estates of those who entered the ministry early in the eighteenth century. And since the vast majority of those in other fields were not college graduates, the cases in the table from these vocations represent the elite of those fields. Table 2.2 therefore offers a glimpse of the economic standing of the *average* minister compared to the *elite* of other vocations. Given this, it scarcely needs to be said that "theology," on average, looks to be the most lucrative vocation, apart from commerce or finance.

Physicians and teachers were about half as well off financially as ministers. Although rampant disease and the high death rate in early seventeenth-century Virginia allowed doctors to charge high fees, the practice was soon curtailed by statute, and the competition among practitioners and the paucity of therapeutic knowledge undercut their authority and income. Meanwhile "there were not a dozen communities in New England where a physician could earn a living" during the seventeenth century, and doctors there and throughout the colonies usually combined medicine with some other work.[179] Even the few college graduates who became physicians resorted to such moonlighting, a practice that continued throughout the eighteenth century. Joshua Babcock (YC 1724), who practiced in Rhode Island, opened a country store on the side; both Adam Collson (HC 1739) and Job Parker (HC 1739) taught school while working as physicians; John Herpin (YC 1741) found that his license as a tavern-keeper was as valuable as his medical

179. Quotation is from Samuel E. Morison, *Harvard College in the Seventeenth Century* (Cambridge, MA, 1936), pt. 2, p. 558. *Statutes of Virginia,* vol. 1, p. 316; Morgan, *American Slavery and American Freedom,* pp. 163–4, 182. See Wyndham B. Blanton, *Medicine in Virginia in the Eighteenth Century* (Richmond, VA, 1931); Richard H. Shryock, *Medicine and Society in America, 1660–1860* (New York, 1960), chs. 1–3; Harold B. Gill, Jr., *The Apothecary in Colonial Virginia* (Williamsburg, VA, 1972), pp. 16–20.

Table 2.3   Representative* sample of estates of colonial college graduates in classes 1700–1740 who became physicians

Value of Estate	(%)
over £800	39
£500–800	4
£300–400	10
£200–300	4
below £200 (insolvent)	43 (18)
Total	100

*The 28 estates recorded for the 97 physicians are representative inasmuch as *Yale Graduates* and *Harvard Graduates* both record about the same percentage of such graduates: 31 percent (9/29) and 28 percent (19/68), respectively.

Sources: *Yale Graduates*, vol. 1, pp. 254–5, 269, 331–2, 355–6, 464–5, 483–4, 543, 545, 647; *Harvard Graduates*, vol. 5, pp. 188, 614; vol. 6, pp. 91, 339, 487; vol. 7, pp. 545, 592; vol. 8, pp. 18, 59, 109, 128, 599, 730, 782; vol. 9, 370, 430, 437; vol. 10, pp. 288, 356. The records of William and Mary, the only other colonial college until 1746, are few and unreliable.

practice in Connecticut.[180] Such individuals, being college graduates, were the elite among the doctors, and in the first four decades of the eighteenth century 97 alumni of colonial colleges are known to have practiced medicine as their primary vocation. A representative sample of their estates is recorded on Table 2.3.

The estates of almost half (47 percent) of this sample of physicians were in the lower half of the total population, whereas relatively few ministers who graduated early in the eighteenth century had estates that small. When one considers further that Tables 2.2 and 2.3 compare a cross-section of ministers with the top strata of physicians, the higher financial status of ministers becomes even more apparent.

With respect to schoolmasters, Lawrence Cremin has summarized well the situation for the seventeenth century: "the salary remained modest, ranging from ten pounds a year for reading and writing masters in the smaller rural communities, to an average of around twenty-five pounds, to the more generous fifty or sixty pounds received by some of the distinguished grammar schoolmasters. In addition there were all sorts of special grants and benefits: gifts of land, houses, and firewood; a share of the tuition fees; exemptions from taxation and military service."[181] This income of schoolmasters, many of whom were recent college graduates studying for the ministry, was about the same as the wages of a skilled laborer, or about half of what the clergyman earned, in the same community. The schoolmaster's perquisites were also proportionately less than those of the minister, and the settlement was virtually nil. In New Netherlands, for example, schoolmasters

180. *Yale Graduates*, vol. 1, pp. 293, 670; *Harvard Graduates*, vol. 10, pp. 356, 393.
181. Lawrence Cremin, *American Education: The Colonial Experience, 1607–1783* (New York, 1970), p. 188.

received a salary, fees from students, and often room and board; yet they generally had to augment their salary with other income. A 1644 schedule of the salaries to be paid by the (Dutch) West Indian Company to the 69 public officials in New Netherlands indicates that the schoolmaster, who also assumed minor ecclesiastical duties, was paid 360 florins. This was about three times what a common soldier received and twice the median wage of 156 florins. The clergyman received four times what the schoolmaster received and more than eleven times what a common soldier received.[182]

By the turn of the century the salaries of schoolmasters had risen generally to £40 or £50 in colonial currency, and in 1720 reached some £80 or £90, figures that are confirmed by Cremin's estimates for the 1700s.[183] These figures are also in line with the salaries set by the (Anglican) Society for the Propagation of Christian Knowledge (SPCK) in England. From the 1690s the SPCK was attempting to pay a salary of £30 sterling in London schools and £20 in the country. In the 1720s most English grammar schools aimed to provide £40, and by the middle of the century, the SPCK salaries had risen to £50–60.[184]

The colonial colleges were staffed by one or more tutors, who were recent graduates; occasionally a professor, who also was a practicing minister; and a president or rector. The tutors generally received about the same remuneration as schoolmasters, while the presidencies were worth about as much as the best pulpits. At Harvard in the seventeenth century the tutors were paid about £20 in salary, which grew to nearly £35 at the turn of century, not including modest gratuities and small fees from the students. When Yale was founded in 1701 tutors earned about £50 in total income from salaries and fees, and after 1720 the figure climbed proportionally with inflation. With the return to hard money after 1750, salaries dropped to about the levels of 1700, and then climbed slowly. At the College of New Jersey, founded at Princeton in 1746 as the fourth colonial college, the tutor during the early 1750s received a salary of £10, while in the 1760s the senior tutor earned £75; and the first tutor at the College of Rhode Island, which opened in 1766, was paid £72.[185]

At the College of William and Mary, founded in 1693, the president, masters, and tutors received the standard exemption from taxes that most colonies granted to educators and clergy. While the president during the first four decades received a handsome £200 salary, the professors were limited to £80 plus some student fees and the income from local churches in which they served.[186] This pattern was

182. Kilpatrick, *The Dutch Schools of New Netherland and Colonial New York*, pp. 26–7, 57–9, 88–93, 142.

183. See Table A1.3 in Appendix 1 for a sample of the situations and salaries of college graduates who became schoolmasters; Cremin, *American Education: The Colonial Experience*, p. 506n; Main, *The Social Structure of Revolutionary America*, pp. 91–4.

184. Holmes, *Augustan England: Professions, State and Society, 1680–1730*, ch. 3; W. A. L. Vincent, *The Grammar Schools their Continuing Tradition, 1660–1714* (London, 1969), chs. 6, 7.

185. *Harvard Graduates*, vol. 4, pp. 163–6, 202, 275, 532–4; Warch, *School of the Prophets*, p. 143; *Yale Graduates*, vol. 1, pp. 346, 378, 408, 521, 597, 663, 755; *Princetonians*, vol. 1, pp. 35, 361, 563.

186. Tyler, *Narratives of Early Virginia, 1606–1625*, p. 4; *Statutes of Virginia*, vol. 4, p. 433.

typical for the few eighteenth-century college professors, many of whom, such as Edward Wigglesworth at Harvard, complained that they had to supplement their salary. In fact, some ministers, such as Solomon Williams, declined appointments like the Yale Professorship of Divinity because, in part, the position did not offer a sufficient salary.[187]

By 1737 the newly appointed president of Harvard, Edward Holyoke, was being paid £200, and his experience demonstrates the relative financial status between college educators and ministers. In 1713 Holyoke became a Harvard tutor at a salary of £50, and left in 1715 for a much better financial situation in a pulpit. In 1737 he returned to Harvard as president at a salary of £50 plus a yearly supplement of some £150 voted by the Massachusetts legislature. Like a country parson during those inflationary times, Holyoke was periodically forced to appeal for additional supplements, arguing that his living expenses were much higher than his salary. In 1747 young Jonathan Mayhew, who had graduated in 1744 and been called to a prosperous church in Boston at a higher salary than that of Holyoke, insulted the President by offering him a petty tip when Mayhew returned to Harvard to receive his MA.[188] Meanwhile Yale had repeated difficulties in finding a minister to become rector, or president, because of "the want of an assured pecuniary support in the Presidency."[189]

If physicians and educators scarcely rivaled the clergy financially through the 1760s, neither did the law provide much competition until the second half of the eighteenth century. Although in England lawyers were the best paid "professors" by the late 1600s,[190] every colony prohibited or refused to sanction the practice of law for a fee at one time or another during the seventeenth and early eighteenth centuries. Even after colonies began to recognize statutorily a right to practice law, licensing requirements were kept low in order to provide easy access to the field, and the amount that attorneys could charge was strictly regulated by detailed tables, whose "fees, in the main, were extremely modest, if not paltry."[191]

187. *Harvard Graduates*, vol. 6, pp. 355–8; vol. 12, p. 510. For other testimony on professorial salaries, see Main, *The Social Structure of Revolutionary America*, p. 95; *Harvard Graduates*, vol. 13, p. 496; vol. 15, p. 108; *Princetonians*, vol. 1, p. 644; *Yale Graduates*, vol. 3, p. 91.

188. *Harvard Graduates*, vol. 5, pp. 265–77; vol. 11, p. 443. For other Harvard presidents, see *Harvard Graduates*, vol. 1, pp. 167, 180–1, 236, 426–7; vol. 2, pp. 22, 477; vol. 3, pp. 185–6; vol. 4, pp. 85–6; vol. 5, p. 324, vol. 13, pp. 622–4.

189. *Yale Graduates*, vol. 1, p. 539. On Yale Presidents, see *Yale Graduates*, vol. 1, pp. 17, 346, 378, 408, 521, 539, 597, 663, 755; *Harvard Graduates*, vol. 2, pp. 256–7; vol. 5, pp. 45–66.

190. Michael Landon, *The Triumph of the Lawyers: Their Role in English Politics, 1678–1689* (University, AL, 1970), pp. 21–2, 254; Holmes, *Augustan England: Professions, State and Society, 1680–1730*, p. 124; C. W. Brooks, *Pettifoggers and Vipers of the Commonwealth: The "Lower Branch" of the Legal Profession in Early Modern England* (Cambridge, UK, 1986), pp. 227–62.

191. Anton-Hermann Chroust, *The Rise of the Legal Profession in America*, 2 vols. (Norman, OK, 1965), vol. 1, p. 28. Chroust is neither balanced nor completely reliable, but in this respect correct and, in any case, remains the most informative, general history of the legal profession in America. For the following, I draw upon Ruth E. Peters, "Statutory Regulation of Lawyers' Fees in Massachusetts, New York, Pennsylvania, South Carolina,

Virginia was the oldest English colony, and, notwithstanding its later progeny of lawyer statesmen, the Old Dominion "waged against the lawyers ... a relentless war for more than a century," for "in no state do we find more hostile legislation concerning lawyers."[192] Until at least 1750 the legal system in Virginia and other southern colonies was dominated by untrained Justices of the Peace who championed "Country" virtues of simplicity, deference to social superiors, and adherence to tradition in administering "natural" justice. Moreover, these JPs in the South, as in England, "served for no fee, or at best, for next to nothing." The planters in Virginia saw themselves as the counterpart to the landed gentry of England, and carried over the Country gentry's opposition to the economic competition represented by Court lawyers, whom they viewed with fearful contempt.[193]

In the 1600s Virginia alternately prohibited pleading for another for payment, repealed those prohibitions while strictly limiting the fees of the "mercenary attorneys," repealed those limits, and then reenacted them. In 1718 attorneys' fees for arguing a case in the General Court were limited to 50s, which far exceeded the colonial norm. However, Virginia's relatively high limit was offset by the fact that fees could be paid in tobacco, which was normally worth but a fraction of the money. This act was reaffirmed in 1727, 1732, and 1742, and the fees were doubled in 1765.[194] In the Carolinas the proprietors' *Fundamental Constitutions* (1669) proclaimed that pleading a case for a fee is "a base and vile thing." Although these *Constitutions* were never adopted, anti-lawyer sentiment persevered in a 1694 act, which set a retaining fee of 5s and a "fee upon tryall", among others, of 5s. These paltry fees were approximately doubled in special courts before the Governor and Council.[195] After separate governors were appointed for the two Carolinas in 1712, South Carolina adhered to the 1694 statute until an act of 1769 stipulated that an attorney should receive no more than 10s for an appearance in court, and a counsel, or barrister, no more than 20s in colonial currency. Meanwhile North Carolina limited lawyers' fees in 1715, even though the colony established a system of courts only in 1746. Responding to complaints about incompetent lawyers and excessive fees, the assembly in 1743 enacted fees of 30s in the highest court and 15s in the county courts. These were approximately doubled in a statute of 1770.[196] Georgia

---

Tennessee and Virginia from the Mid-Seventeenth Century to the Mid-Nineteenth Century" (Third-year JD paper, Harvard Law School, 1975).

192. John B. Minor, *Institutes of Common and Statute Law*, 4th edn (Richmond, VA, 1893), vol. 4, p. 200; Reinsch, *English Common Law in the Early American Colonies*, p. 48.

193. Roeber, *Faithful Magistrates and Republican Lawyers*, p. 14, chs. 1–3; Isaac, *The Transformation of Virginia, 1740–1790*, pp. 131–3. On the English background, see Norma Landau, *Justices of the Peace: 1679–1760* (Berkeley, CA, 1984), pp. 69–145, 269–332.

194. *Statutes of Virginia*, vol. 1, pp. 275, 302, 349, 419, 482, 495; vol. 2, pp. 478–9; vol. 4, pp. 59, 187, 361; vol. 5, p. 182; vol. 8, pp. 184–5; vol. 9, p. 528.

195. *The Fundamental Constitutions*, sect. 70, in *The Earliest Printed Laws of North Carolina: 1669–1751* (Wilmington, DE, 1977), vol. 2; *Statutes of South Carolina*, vol. 2, p. 78. The *Fundamental Constitutions* "is attributed to [John] Locke, since a copy of it in his hand was found amongst his papers, but it is very unlikely that he is the author of it." Richard Aaron, *John Locke*, 3d edn (Oxford, 1971), p. 16.

196. *State Records of North Carolina*, vol. 23, pp. 86, 213, 788–9; *Statutes of South Carolina*, vol. 4, p. 306; Hoyt P. Canady, Jr., "Gentlemen of the Bar: Lawyers in Colonial South Carolina" (PhD diss., University of Tennessee, 1979), ch. 7.

was settled only in 1733, and there were neither fee statutes, nor trained lawyers, except for the Governor, until after the mid-eighteenth century.

Northward, the Marylanders in the seventeenth century and early eighteenth centuries welcomed the common law as a shield against a proprietor who had extraordinary powers. Maryland was therefore relatively receptive to lawyers and litigation, and established an elaborate system of courts in the seventeenth century and a licensing procedure for attorneys as early as 1657. Nevertheless, the view "that these Privileged Attorneys are ... the Grand Grievances of the Country" was frequently expressed, and acts regulating attorneys were successively enacted, repealed, and reenacted through 1725.[197] In that year the attempts at regulation culminated in the comprehensive and hostile legislation: "An Act to Restrain the Ill Practices of Attornies and to Prevent Their Taking Money-Fees." This act set low fees, which clients were allowed to pay either in money or tobacco according to a rate established by law. Under this arrangement, even the modest fees were sharply reduced in value because clients could pay in whichever item was cheaper, depending on the market.[198] After vociferous complaints and petitions by lawyers, the act was disallowed in 1730, and subsequent attempts to regulate fees failed, opening the way for the emergence of a large and powerful bar after 1750.

The 1677 founding charter of West New Jersey recognized the practice of law but carefully stipulated that "no person ... shall be compelled to fee any Attorney or Councellor to plead his cause" and "that all persons have free liberty to plead his own cause if he please." Six years later "The Fundamental Constitutions" for East New-Jersey prohibited pleading a case for a fee.[199] In fact, opposition was so strong that, although the royal Colony of New Jersey was established in 1703, the right to hire an attorney was sanctioned only in 1714. After a schedule of fees for "Practitioners of the Law" was disallowed by the Crown in 1733 a detailed table of 21 categories was enacted in 1743, and four years later an even more detailed schedule with some 43 categories was set forth, including an item for "Drawing every special Plea ... fifteen Lines to a Sheet, and six Words to a Line, Ten Pence per sheet." These rates remained in effect for the rest of the colonial period.[200]

New Jersey's hesitant and qualified sanctioning of lawyers reflects the influence of neighboring Pennsylvania, where Quakers avoided litigation in preference for the mediation and arbitration that characterized the Society of Friends. Indeed, the Society's founder in England, George Fox, often invoked Paul's admonition against going to law, and in *The Law of God* (1658) Fox recounted a foreboding vision of "the lawyers black, their black robe as a puddle, and like a black pit, almost covered over with blackness."[201] The aversion to litigation was such that only in

197. *Archives of Maryland*, vol. 2, p. 169; vol. 35, pp. 433, 445–7, 474–5; vol. 36, pp. 226, 233; vol. 38, pp. 372–5; vol. 41, pp. 10–1; Alan F. Day, "Lawyers in Colonial Maryland, 1660–1715," *AJLH*, 17 (1973): 144–65.

198. *Archives of Maryland*, vol. 36, pp. 586–9.

199. *Fundamental Laws and Constitutions of New Jersey*, pp. 88, 122.

200. *Laws of the Royal Colony of New Jersey*, vol. 2, pp. 157, 465; vol. 5, pp. 432–3; vol. 3, pp. 90–2.

201. Quoted in Tolles, *Meeting House and Counting House*, p. 122, ch. 4, app. B. George S. Odiorne, "Arbitration and Mediation among Early Quakers," *Arbitration Journal*, n.s., 9 (1954): 161–6; Craig W. Horle, *The Quakers and the English Legal System, 1660–1688* (Philadelphia, 1988). Paul's admonition is in 1 *Corinthians* 6: 1.

1723 was a right to practice law enacted in Philadelphia and upheld in England. This statute prescribed a short list of feeable items, the largest being 12s for pleading a case, and the same fees were reenacted in 1752. In 1777, "by reason of the high and extravagant prices of the necessaries of life," the fees were doubled.[202]

No less suspicious of lawyers were the New Englanders. Neither New Haven's 1656 compilation of laws, nor the first printed compilation of laws for Connecticut in 1673 explicitly sanctioned the use of an "Attorney to prosecute his case." Only in 1673 did Massachusetts officially sanction the practice of a "lawfull atturney." Meanwhile Rhode Island, always somewhat outside the mainstream, did provide for lawyers in its first Code of Laws of 1647. But in the very same breath the General Assembly declared a limit of "two [attorneys] in a town, to wit; discreet, honest and able men for understanding chosen by the townsmen of the same town, and solemnly engaged by the head officer thereof, not ... to beguile either court or party."[203]

By the turn of the century, attorneys' fees in Massachusetts and Maine were set at 12s for each action in the Superior Court and 10s in inferior courts, with only one lawyer to be paid per case. New Hampshire enacted the same limits in 1714.[204] Somewhat perversely, Massachusetts lowered the fees in 1765 and repeated the stricture in subsequent statutes until 1778, when the fees were finally raised.[205] Connecticut originally set fees so low that the legislature had to establish a minimum tax assessment for lawyers of £50 – the earnings of an artisan. In 1730 the colony raised fees for pressing an action in the Superior Court to 20s and in the inferior courts to 10s.[206] Meanwhile Rhode Island had enacted detailed fee tables in 1666 and 1705, and the compilation of 1719 conflated the fees into one of 12s.[207]

New York is often said to be the colony most receptive to litigation and common lawyers. But even there fees were tightly controlled. Under the Dutch, a system of mediation and arbitration and a schedule of fees for legal services had prevailed, and this arrangement continued beyond the English occupation until nearly the end of the seventeenth century. At that point, the General Assembly approved limits of 6s "For Attorneys Fees" and 6s "For Pleading each Cause," which were reaffirmed in 1709. Although that fee table was then disallowed in England, the Governor and Council ordained detailed fee tables in 1710 and 1728, which about doubled the fees in other colonies and stood until another ordinance was promulgated in 1768.[208]

202. *Statutes of Pennsylvania*, vol. 2, p. 331; vol. 3, p. 96; vol. 3, pp. 367, 376–7; vol. 5, p. 173; vol. 9, p. 229. See Tully, *William Penn's Legacy: Politics and Social Structure in Provincial Pennsylvania, 1726–1755*, passim.

203. *Records of Massachusetts Bay*, vol. 4, pt. 2, p. 563; *Earliest Laws of Connecticut*, pp. 14, 73, 90, 138; *Earliest Laws of Rhode Island*, p. 52.

204. *Acts of Massachusetts Bay*, vol. 1, pp. 287, 467; *Acts and Laws of His Majesty's Province of New-Hampshire in New-England with Sundry Acts of Parliament* (Portsmouth, NH, 1761; reprinted 1887), chs. 37, 50 (1714), pp. 78–9, 135–6. New Hampshire became a royal colony in 1679, but achieved fully separate governance from Massachusetts only in 1741. Maine was a district of Massachusetts from 1677 to 1820.

205. *Acts of Massachusetts Bay*, vol. 4, p. 743; vol. 5, pp. 240, 486, 761.

206. *Public Records of Connecticut*, vol. 6, p. 525; vol. 7, pp. 279–80.

207. *Earliest Laws of Rhode Island*, pp. 74–5, 157.

208. *The Colonial Laws of New York from the Year 1664 to the Revolution*, 5 vols. (Albany,

In sum, it may be said that in every colony during the seventeenth century payment for legal representation in court was either prohibited or barely tolerated. Near the turn of the century, colonial legislatures enacted firm statutory limits of about 15*s* per action in the superior courts and 10*s* in the lower courts. In the 1760s and 1770s these limits began to rise, but prior to that, a lawyer would have had to plead some 200 cases in the inferior courts in order to earn £100 per year. Even that number of cases is conservative because certain statutes stipulated that only the "attorney's fees ... for the party prevailing" were to be paid or taxed to the parties in the case.[209] This stipulation meant that many attorneys had not merely to plead, but to *win* about 200 cases in the inferior courts in order to earn £100 per year. If one considers further that lawyers were generally able to collect less than half of the fees due them, then the fact becomes that an attorney had to win some 400 cases in order to earn £100 in a year.[210]

The amounts earned from trial work were supplemented by fees for drafting documents and, especially, debt collection. Even so, the first full-time lawyer appeared in Massachusetts only in the first two decades of the eighteenth century.[211] In the 1730s one of the first lawyers to practice in Maine, Robert E. Gerrish, kept school to provide a steady income, and in 1760 his estate was valued at £9. In New Hampshire John Smith returned home to practice law in the 1740s after graduating from Harvard, and began farming because there was not enough legal business in the entire colony to support a full-time lawyer.[212] In New Jersey, although some

---

NY, 1894), vol. 1, pp. 351–2, 409, 841–5; Paul M. Hamlin and Charles E. Baker, *Supreme Court of Judicature of the Province of New York, 1691–1704,* 3 vols. (New York, 1959), vol. 1, pp. 265, 272–4; John R. Aiken, "Utopianism and the Emergence of the Colonial Legal Profession: New York, 1664–1710, A Test Case" (PhD diss., University of Rochester, 1967); Julius Goebel, Jr., and T. Raymond Naughton, *Law Enforcement in Colonial New York* (New York, 1944), pp. 731–48.

209. *Public Records of Connecticut,* vol. 7, pp. 279–80; *Acts of Massachusetts Bay,* vol. 5, p. 761. Other variations of this arrangement were that the losing party would pay all the fees of the victorious lawyer, or that both attorneys could tax their fees for each step of legal process, and only the amount taxed for judgment went to the winning attorney as a kind of bonus. *Statutes of Virginia,* vol. 4, p. 59 (1718).

210. A sense of the maximum caseload may be gathered from the fact that when John Adams later became the busiest lawyer in Massachusetts in the year 1768, he handled 310 cases, 200 of them in the inferior courts. John Adams, *Legal Papers,* ed. with an introduction by L. Kinvin Wroth and Hiller B. Zobel (Cambridge, MA, 1965), vol. 1, pp. lix, lxix–lxxii.

211. John M. Murrin, "The Legal Transformation: The Bench and Bar of Eighteenth-Century Massachusetts" (1971), in *Colonial America, Essays in Politics and Social Development,* ed. Stanley N. Katz and John M. Murrin, 3d edn (New York, 1983), pp. 546, 550–1. Debt collection undertaken on behalf of creditors certainly did nothing to improve the public opinion of lawyers, who commonly expanded this business by purchasing notes from creditors at a discount and then pursuing the debtors to collect the money. See Charles R. McKirdy, "Massachusetts Lawyers on the Eve of the American Revolution: The State of the Profession," *Law in Colonial Massachusetts, 1630–1800,* ed. Daniel R. Coquillette (Boston, 1984), pp. 318–28; Stephen Botein, "The Legal Profession in Colonial North America," in *Lawyers in Early Modern Europe and America,* ed. Wilfrid R. Prest (New York, 1981), p. 131; Daniel J. Boorstin, *The Americans: The Colonial Experience* (New York, 1958), ch. 32.

212. *Harvard Graduates,* vol. 8, p. 719; vol. 11, p. 579. A recent attempt to show that an

attorneys, such as Daniel I. Brown, earned as much as £400–450 per year in the 1760s, others, such as William Paterson, were unable to support themselves and became tradesmen.[213] Further south, a few lawyers such as John Rutledge in the Carolinas prospered, but not until the 1770s. Admitted to the Virginia bar in 1767, Thomas Jefferson often billed out £500, but, as was typical, he collected far less than half his billings, and his best year was in 1770, when he actually received £213.[214] In fine, it was only after 1750, even in a relatively legalistic colony such as New York, that "the business of law became profitable enough ... to attract those who might otherwise have entered trade."[215]

Comparative: "the best of employments"

One day in 1773 Dr. Marshall Spring, who had graduated from college eleven years earlier, was riding to Newton, Massachusetts, intent upon proposing marriage to Miss Ann Hammond. On the way he happened to meet an acquaintance, Rev, Joseph Pope, who had graduated in 1770 and settled in a church in western New England. In the course of their conversation, it came out that Rev. Pope was also riding to see Miss Hammond on the same errand. The competition was quickly resolved, however, because, after learning the clergyman's intentions, Dr. Spring decided to forego his proposal. After all, the young Reverend could offer the security, salary, and position of a settled minister, while he had merely the prospects of an established physician. Ann married the minister in 1777. A few years earlier, lawyer and future president John Adams (HC 1755) learned the same lesson that "bachelor ministers were much sought after."[216] When Adams was courting Abigail

early seventeenth-century Massachusetts lawyer, Thomas Lechford, earned a good living contrary to his own often quoted testimony, actually confirms the traditional view. After careful examination of the evidence, the revisionist is forced to call Lechford's nearly empty purse partly full by proposing that he should have been satisfied with his "average annual cash income of almost £29," which "was well above subsistence." That an Anglican solicitor such as Lechford would have been happy with the income of a colonial Puritan schoolmaster is, however, incredible. Thomas G. Barnes, "Thomas Lechford and the Earliest Lawyering in Massachusetts, 1638–1641," in *Law in Colonial Massachusetts, 1630–1800* (Boston, 1984), pp. 33–4.

213. Richard C. Haskett, "William Paterson, Attorney General of New Jersey: Public Office and Private Profit in the American Revolution," *WMQ*, 3d ser., 7 (1950): 26–38; *Princetonians*, vol. 1, pp. 69, 437–8.

214. Dumas Malone, *Jefferson the Virginian* (Boston, 1948), chs. 4, 9; Clement Eaton, "A Mirror of the Southern Colonial Lawyer: The Fee Books of Patrick Henry, Thomas Jefferson and Waightstill Avery," *WMQ*, 3d ser., 8 (1951): 520–34; Canady, "Gentlemen of the Bar: Lawyers in Colonial South Carolina," ch. 7; Frank L. Dewey, *Thomas Jefferson, Lawyer* (Charlottesville, VA, 1986).

215. Milton M. Klein, "From Community to Status: The Development of the Legal Profession in Colonial New York," *New York History*, 60 (1979): 148; Main, *The Social Structure of Revolutionary America*, chs. 3, 4.

216. Silverman, *The Life and Times of Cotton Mather*, p. 49; *Harvard Graduates*, vol. 17, p. 422.

Smith, her father, the local pastor, disliked lawyers so much that he would not let Adams put his horse in the barn when he came courting. Subsequently, when Abigail's sister married John Shaw, who was contemplating the ministry, Rev. Smith preached the wedding sermon from *John* 1: 6: "There was a man sent from God, whose name was John." But when Abigail married lawyer Adams, the text was *Matthew* 11: 18: "For John came neither eating nor drinking, and they say, He hath a devil."[217]

Rev. Smith's preference between his daughters' suitors was not due merely to favoring his own occupation, although clergymen, such as Robert Hale in 1697 and Cotton Mather in 1726, had long referred to the ministry as "the best of employments" and "a WORK which on these Illustrious Accounts, no other Calling may be compared unto."[218] Indeed, a Baptist contemporary of Rev. Pope and Dr. Smith warned about the worldly attractions of the sacred office:

> Let me advise you, my young Friends, seriously to reflect on your *views* in devoting yourselves to this sacred employ. Was it merely to have an opportunity of pursuing different branches of literature, to which you had perhaps a strong natural inclination? Was it that you might lead an easy and genteel life, which you might be ready to suppose a Minister's life to be? Was it to obtain popular applause and fame, which you might fondly hope your abilities would procure you?[219]

Physicians, such as Marshall Spring, recognized all these attractions, and John Adams acknowledged in a letter of 1756, when he was studying for the ministry, that it was the most eminent of vocations. Even "the richest men in New England, the merchants of Boston, agreed to frequent marriages between their daughters and young parsons, while often marrying themselves into ministerial families."[220]

In some respects, this continued preeminence of the ministry into the second half of the eighteenth century is surprising. Already in 1673 New England ministers, such as Samuel Willard, were warning: "Look into Congregations and there you shall see ... Ministers despised, their Office questioned, their Authority cast off, and trampled upon, their persons undervalued and vilified, their comfortable Supply and Maintenance neglected." This experience of "declension" whereby the third- and fourth-generation New England Puritans, especially the clergy, viewed their religious commitment and institutions as declining was emphasized by Perry Miller and has become a standard theme in the historiography of colonial religion.[221]

Recent analysis, however, suggests that Miller overemphasized the theme, for it

217. *Harvard Graduates*, vol. 7, pp. 590–1.

218. *Harvard Graduates*, vol. 3, pp. 362–3; Cotton Mather, *Manuductio ad Ministerium, Directions for a Candidate of the Ministry*, p. 76.

219. C. Evans, *Advice to Students Having in View Christian Ministry* (Bristol, 1770), p. 1.

220. Hall, *Faithful Sheperd*, p. 183; Adams, *Legal Papers*, vol. 1, p. lii. On the lineal descendance of church membership within certain families of high socio-economic status, see Morgan, *The Puritan Family*, ch. 7.

221. Samuel Willard, *Useful Instructions for a professing People in Times of Great Security and Degeneracy* (Cambridge, MA, 1673), p. 75. Declension is a major theme in Perry Miller, *The New England Mind: From Colony to Province* (Cambridge, MA, 1953); Hall, *Faithful Sheperd*, chs. 8–12.

was not until the 1730s that "the century-long movement to strengthen the Congregational Establishment had come to a halt." Insofar as declension occurred among New England churches, it was counterbalanced by "an enlarged view of the minister's functions and authority" within New England and "the rising level of religious intensity in the Middle Colonies and the backcountry South."[222] It is perhaps going too far to suggest that the ministers" status was still rising, but certainly the clergy had not declined to outcasts by the year 1700, which is the impression left by Perry Miller and David Hall. One factor bolstering the pastors" position was that the educational level, economic standing, and social status of the clergy in England were beginning to rise. Reaching a high point early in the 1600s, the position of the clergy had fallen dramatically after about 1610, moving inversely to that of the colonial ministers. Then, in the course of the eighteenth century, it reversed and rose until "the country clergyman ... had by the time of the Napoleonic wars in some cases at least become accepted by the gentry as almost their social equal."[223] This development in England, along with the reluctance of the gentry to move to the colonies, contributed to elevating the social position of the colonial Anglican clergy, which has often been undervalued.[224]

Not only did the ministry enjoy elevated status generally in society. But among the four fields of theology, law, medicine, and education, which had long been dignified through their association together in the university, the ministry was regarded as the most demanding and preferred vocation. As John Wesley observed:

> A Blockhead ... may do well enough ... in the Capacity of a Lawyer or Physician.... But O! think not of his being a Minister, unless you would bring a Blot upon your Family, a Scandal upon our Church, and a Reproach on the Gospel, which he may murder, but cannot teach.[225]

However perversely, Wesley spoke truly, for the expectations were higher for a Reverend than for others.

Intemperance would end a ministry, as it did for Jared Harrison (YC 1736) in Connecticut and Jonathan Elmer (YC 1747) in New Jersey. Sexual transgressions would not only end a ministry, but prevent one from ever securing another call, as Harvard graduate Joseph Manning (1751) and Princeton graduate Nathaniel Potter (1753) discovered.[226] Poor health could also force one out of the pulpit, where two

---

222. Quotations are from, respectively: Bushman, *From Puritan to Yankee*, p. 163; Morgan, *Visible Saints*, p. 141; Bonomi, *Under the Cope of Heaven*, pp. 7–8. See Hambrick-Stowe, *The Practice of Piety*, p. viii.

223. Hart, *Clergy and Society, 1600–1800*, pp. 70–1, chs. 1–4. See Hart, *The Country Clergy in Elizabethan and Stuart Times*, p. 67; Hudson, "The Ministry in the Puritan Age," pp. 180–206; O'Day, *The English Clergy ... 1558–1642*, p. 23; Anthony Russell, *The Clerical Profession* (London, 1980), ch. 3; Holmes, *Augustan England: Professions, State and Society, 1680–1730*, p. 87.

224. Gundersen, "The Anglican Ministry in Virginia, 1723–1776," ch. 3; van Voorst, "The Anglican Clergy in Maryland, 1692–1776," pp. 50ff., 222–49; Bonomi, *Under the Cope of Heaven*, chs. 3, 5.

225. Wesley, *An Address to the Clergy*, p. 223; William Staughton, "What are the Qualifications of a Gospel Minister?" (1807), in *Philadelphia Baptist Association*, pp. 440–6.

226. *Yale Graduates*, vol. 1, p. 563; vol. 2, p. 113; *Harvard Graduates*, vol. 13, pp. 114, 347–9.

to three hours of preaching every Sunday was required, and into commerce, medicine, or law. This happened to Jonathan Hunting (YC 1735), Josiah Wolcott (YC 1742), Eneas Munson (YC 1753), and Simeon Strong (YC 1756).[227] Or, worst of all, one could be reduced to a schoolmaster by poor eyesight or fits of insanity, as happened to David Mitchell (HC 1751) and Caleb Billings (YC 1766).[228]

More than simply the stamina for preaching throughout the year, a minister needed to have something to say and to be able to express it. Though the requirements of knowledge and education eroded in the Great Awakening, it was still the case in the late 1740s that the ministerial associations would reject even a college graduate on the grounds of insufficient preparation. After John Archer graduated from the College of New Jersey, the Presbytery of New Castle examined him in 1764 and concluded that: "Mr. Archer through the whole course of his tryals discovers such a want of knowledge ... as well as such an incapacity to communicate his ideas on any subject, that we cannot encourage him to prosecute his tryals for the Gospel ministry any further." Archer then turned to medicine and earned a medical degree from the College of Philadelphia in 1768.[229]

That college graduates could be refused a license to preach or be unable to find a settlement, once licensed, suggests that the ministry was the vocation most often chosen by college graduates through 1750. Figure 2.3 demonstrates this fact, which is highly significant given that college graduates were among the most advantaged of the population and could choose most freely among employments.[230]

Notwithstanding some fluctuations, particularly after the Restoration of 1660, a large majority of the colonial college graduates entered "the best of employments" until about 1720. At that point, the percentage dropped to a norm of about 40 percent, which held steady through the mid-1750s. Even during the latter period, the percentage of graduates entering the ministry was about three times higher than the next highest percentage entering another vocation: either medicine, which had always attracted a handful of graduates from the very first classes, or law and commerce, both of which had begun to attract graduates for the first time in the late seventeenth century. The fact that far more college graduates went into the ministry indicates a preference for that field on the part of the most advantaged of the population. This preference then further elevated the prestige of the clergy because ministers became the mostly highly educated vocational group.

The interest in education among Calvinists in the sixteenth and seventeenth centuries derived from a reaction against the "Confusion, Ignourance, Errour or Prophaneness" of the established clergy.[231] This interest in education was, however, dialectically balanced by revulsion at the intimations of human self-reliance and pride that accompanied advanced study. Reforming enthusiasts, such as Samuel

---

227. *Yale Graduates*, vol. 1, pp. 538, 722; vol. 2, p. 311, 437.

228. *Harvard Graduates*, vol. 13, pp. 116–7; *Yale Graduates*, vol. 3, p. 174.

229. *Princetonians*, vol. 1, pp. 300–1. See, too, *Yale Graduates*, vol. 2, p. 113.

230. Figure 2.3 is based on Table A2.5 in Appendix 2, which explains the sources, categories, and method of sorting the graduates.

231. "The Preface [to] The Profession of the Associated Churches in Worcestershire" (1653), in *Gildas Salvianus*, ed. Wilkinson, p. 184. See Hart, *The Country Clergy in Elizabethan and Stuart Times*, pp. 17–26; O'Day, *The English Clergy ... 1558–1642*, passim.

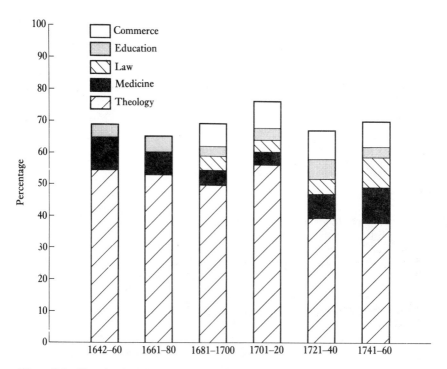

Figure 2.3 Vocational choices of colonial college graduates in classes 1642–1760

How, wrote treatises "Tending to Prove Humane Learning to be No Help to the Spirituall Understanding of the Word of God." And they sent countless letters, like that of 1683 "from the Quakers at Pensilvania to the *Protestant Reconciler*," observing: "Thy Humane Learning, thy Greek and Latine, thy Fathers and Counsels, thy *Prolegomena*'s and Propositions, thy Problemes and thy corollaries, make thee look like a Conjurer.... all this is offensive to us, yea, and very abominable."[232]

Though sensitive to the danger, moderate reformers responded harshly to the "company of unlettered, unskillful Laicks," the "Coblers and Howists and other Shameless Mechanicks, worthie to be chastised rather with a Cudgell than a Quill, who ... do miserably rack the word of God."[233] This establishment view largely prevailed through the early eighteenth century in the colonies, where Charles Chauncy, in his first commencement sermon as president of Harvard in 1655,

232. Samuel How, *The Sufficiencie of the Spirits Teaching without Humane Learning* (London, 1640), p. 1; "A Letter of Thanks from the Quakers at Pensilvania to the *Protestant Reconciler*," in *Three Letters of Thanks to the PROTESTANT RECONCILER* (London, 1683), p. 25; Mary L. Gambrell, *Ministerial Training in Eighteenth-Century New England* (New York, 1937), pp. 15–6.

233. Henry Denne, *A Den of Thieves Discovered. Or Certaine Errours and False Doctrines* (London, 1643), p. 16; *The Clergyes Bill of Complaint, or Submissive Suite of one in the behalf of ... Church-men throughout England* (Oxford, 1643), p. 5.

forcefully defended the learned ministry while warning the graduates that "neither your own study or parts, nor the teaching and instruction of others" suffice to make a minister. Even the earliest associations of Baptist churches founded in America – Philadelphia in 1707, Charleston in 1751, Leyden, Massachusetts, in 1763, and Ketocton, Virginia, in 1766 – endorsed advanced education. In South Carolina, for example, the newly founded Charleston Association organized societies in 1755 and 1757 to provide funding for the education of Baptist ministers.[234]

The resulting pattern of ministerial training was neither formal nor consistent. In the colonial colleges a few recent graduates read divinity with the president while serving as tutors. Most, however, studied with a parish minister for a year or two while keeping school. Even when the first professorships of divinity were established at Harvard in 1722 and at Yale in 1755, the appointees served more as college chaplain than graduate instructor. The tutors and few resident graduates, who remained at the college after graduation, read informally on their own, while attending chapel and some undergraduate lectures and conversing now and then with the college president or professor of divinity. Not until 1784 did the second professor of divinity at Harvard propose a formal course of training for ministerial candidates.[235] Advanced theological training was therefore brief and informal, and varied considerably. Nevertheless, within any given colony, the clergy were better educated than the members of any other vocation. Overall, about half of the colonial clergy through 1776 held degrees, a fraction far greater than for any other vocation.[236]

That college graduates preferred the ministry to schoolteaching was preordained, so to speak. According to the architectonic of culture, schoolmasters were semi-clergy, who taught temporal lessons preparatory to universal and eternal truths. This ideological relationship was manifested in the occupational relationship whereby schoolteachers were normally recent college graduates who were preparing for the ministry by reading theology under the direction of the local minister. John Eliot, for example, after graduating from Harvard, entered "in the too *difficult* and *unthankful,* but very *necessary* employment of a *schoolmaster....* [and] reckoned the calling of a schoolmaster ... *a dusty and disagreeable vocation.*" This instrumental

---

234. Charles Chauncy, *Gods Mercy, Shewed to his people in giving them a Faithful Ministry and Schooles of Learning for the Continual Supplyes Therof* (Cambridge, MA, 1655), p. 23; Wood Furman, comp., *A History of the Charleston Association of Baptist Churches in the State of South Carolina* (Charleston, SC, 1811), pp. 11–2.

235. Gambrell, *Ministerial Training in Eighteenth-Century New England,* chs. 4, 5. See *Harvard Graduates,* vol. 12, pp. 512–5; Samuel Simpson, "Early Ministerial Training in America," *Papers of the American Society of Church History,* 2d ser., 2 (1917): 117–29; William O. Shewmaker, "The Training of the Protestant Ministry in the US of America before the Establishment of Theological Seminaries," *Papers of the American Society of Church History,* 2d ser., 5, 6 (1921): 73–202; Albea Godbold, *The Church College of the Old South* (Durham, NC, 1944), ch. 2; Roland H. Bainton, *Yale and the Ministry: A History of Education for the Christian Ministry at Yale from the Founding in 1701* (New Haven, CT, 1957), chs. 1, 2.

236. The number of clergy holding degrees in the various colonies and during various periods and the percentages of degree-holders for the entire colonial period can be estimated as follows:

relationship between the schoolhouse and the pulpit was most clearly instanced on those occasions when a young schoolmaster, upon receiving the MA, was sometimes asked by the very same town "that he would return unto them, and instruct, not their children as a *school-master*, but themselves as a *minister*."[237] In terms of ideology, career path, social status, and remuneration, schoolmasters were thus semi-clergy. Schoolmasters who tried and could not make the leap to the pulpit, such as Josiah Cotton (HC 1698) or Samuel Angier (HC 1748), were regarded as lacking talent, energy, or ambition. Clergymen who failed at preaching or a settled ministry and slid back down to schoolteaching were regarded as damaged goods, as happened to Grindall Rawson in New Hampshire and Flint Dwight in New York.[238] In either case, such persons were relegated to "The Miserable Life of a

Colony	Cergy holding degrees				Total	(%)
	1600–99	*1700–50*	*1750–76*	*1600–1776*	*clergy*	
Massachusetts, Maine, Connecticut, New Hampshire	287	762	1,138	1,624	1,978	82.1
Rhode Island	5	32	21	48	154	31.1
New York	33	142	175	292	501	58.3
Pennsylvania	3	33	184	199	769	25.9
New Jersey	8	42	92	125	318	39.3
Delaware	8	8	26	36	127	28.3
Maryland	28	45	57	111	428	25.9
Virginia	49	52	66	141	648	21.7
North Carolina	–	3	15	18	155	11.6
South Carolina	6	53	55	105	276	38.0
Georgia	–	9	5	12	45	26.6
Totals	418	1,149	1,798	2,711	5,399	50.2

Figures are computed from an analysis of the lists in Frederick L. Weiss, *The Colonial Clergy and the Colonial Churches of New England* (Lancaster, MA, 1936); Weiss, *The Colonial Clergy of Maryland, Delaware and Georgia* (Lancaster, MA, 1950); Weiss, *The Colonial Clergy of Virginia, North Carolina and South Carolina* (Boston, 1955); Weiss, *The Colonial Clergy of the Middle Colonies: New York, New Jersey, and Pennsylvania, 1628–1776* (Worcester, MA, 1957). Weiss's lists are not entirely reliable, but they remain the best comprehensive source. These numbers include those who received degrees from British and American colleges and universities, those who attended Continental universities (for which Weiss did not list degrees), and members of Catholic orders. The "Totals" are always less than the sum of the figures in the corresponding column or row because I have counted in each period those ministers who straddled two periods and in each colony those who served more than one colony. Van Voorst indicates that more than half of the Anglican clergy in Maryland held BA degrees and a quarter held MA degrees. "The Anglican Clergy in Maryland, 1692–1776," pp. 130–44.

237. Mather, *Magnalia Christi Americana*, vol. 1, pp. 530, 446.

238. *Harvard Graduates*, vol. 4, pp. 398–401; vol. 12, pp. 234–5; vol. 7, pp. 333–4; Wilson, *The Benevolent Deity*, p. 162.

Pedagogue," described by Philip Freneau (PC 1771), who lasted thirteen days as a teacher on Long Island.[239]

Although some schoolmasters in large communities earned decent incomes and status, college tutors generally enjoyed somewhat higher status due to their association with an educational institution of greater prestige. But a tutor's compensation was about the same as a schoolmaster's, and there existed less prospect of the position becoming permanent, should the tutor desire it. Jabez Fitch in 1697 left a Harvard tutorship to become the minister of a nearby town for a £100 raise in salary, and John Whiting did the same in 1710 for a raise of £50. Meanwhile Samuel Whitman in 1705 chose a pulpit in Connecticut over a tutorship at Yale, and in 1760 Benjamin Trumbull did likewise. Even Henry Flynt, the noted Harvard tutor who served from 1699 to 1754, assumed his position after an unsuccessful search for a pulpit.[240]

The professorships and presidencies of colleges were no easier to fill with ministers from the best pulpits. The early heads of Harvard College were merely recent graduates, and, although the Harvard presidency was a coveted post by the end of the century, a leading clergyman, such as Increase Mather, was unwilling to resign his pulpit in Boston for the position. In the 1720s two prominent Boston ministers, Joseph Sewall and Benjamin Colman, turned down the Harvard presidency, and it was repeatedly refused after Edward Holyoke died in 1768 and again in 1780 after Samuel Langdon's brief tenure. Meanwhile Yale's repeated difficulties in finding a leader were demonstrated by the fact that Henry Flynt, the Harvard tutor who could not find a pulpit, declined the rectorship of Yale in 1718.[241]

Newly established colleges had difficulties attracting clergymen even at the end of the eighteenth century. In the 1780s Theodore Romeyn (PC 1765) repeatedly turned down the presidency of Queen's College in New Jersey because the salary was too low compared to his pastorate in Bergen County. Rev. John Blair Smith (PC 1773) had meanwhile become the first president of Hampden-Sydney College in 1783, but he left for a Presbyterian pulpit in Philadelphia in 1791. Smith tried a college presidency once again when Union College called him as its first president in 1795, but in 1799 he resigned and returned to his former pulpit. Meanwhile Rev. Charles Backus of Connecticut declined positions of Professor of Theology at Dartmouth and Professor of Divinity at Yale.[242]

Physicians, like educators, were another order of semi-clergy. According to the architectonic, they healed half – the lesser half – of the human being, and did not even heal that lesser half very well. "As precarious ... as our lives are in the hands of the physicians," they are naturally held in contempt, noted John Mallory. Even

239. Philip M. Freneau, "The Miserable Life of a Pedagogue" (1772), in *The Poems of Philip Freneau,* ed. F. L. Pattee (Princeton, NJ, 1906), vol. 3, pp. 396–9; Lewis G. Leary, *That Rascal Freneau, A Study in Literary Failure* (New Brunswick, NJ, 1941), ch. 3.
240. *Harvard Graduates,* vol. 4, pp. 202, 315–6, 532–4; *Yale Graduates,* vol. 2, p. 622; Edward T. Dunn, "Henry Flynt and The Great Awakening at Harvard College (1741–1744)," *History of Higher Education Annual,* 3 (1983): 3.
241. Samuel E. Morison, *The Founding of Harvard College* (Cambridge, MA, 1935), p. 203; *Harvard Graduates,* vol. 1, pp. 426–7; vol. 2, p. 22; vol. 4, pp. 85–6, 163–6; vol. 5, pp. 324, 385–6; vol. 9, pp. 255–6; vol. 10, pp. 140, 516–23.
242. *Princetonians,* vol. 1, pp. 523–4; vol. 2, pp. 343–5; *Yale Graduates,* vol. 3, pp. 311–3.

in the 1730s, by which point British doctors are said to have developed some effective therapies, the greatest developments came in surgery, which stood on the bottom rung of the medical hierarchy and remained there throughout the eighteenth century.[243]

This paucity of therapeutic knowledge made it "easie for any Scholer to attaine such a measure of Physick, as may be of much use to him both for himself, and others," noted George Herbert, who therefore recommended that the country parson acquire some medical knowledge. Meanwhile "all manner of people took up medicine in the colonies and appropriated the title of doctor."[244] Abiel Abbot left Harvard after six months of cutting classes and playing cards, then entered a medical apprenticeship, and by 1757 had set himself up in practice in Massachusetts. And Abbot was one of the better prepared. Only in 1768 did the College and Academy of Philadelphia graduate the first medical school class "on a regular Collegiate Plan." And only in 1772 did a neighboring colony such as New Jersey – persuaded that "many ignorant and unskilful Persons ... do take upon themselves to administer Physick, and practise Surgery ... to the endangering of the lives and limbs of their Patients" – enact a law requiring some demonstration of medical knowledge in order to practice.[245]

Given this encroachment on medicine, distinguished physicians who had gone to great lengths for their training not infrequently left the field. Samuel Cutler (HC 1765), who traveled to North Carolina and then to London in order to study medicine, gave it up soon after returning to New York in 1781. Ezra Green (HC 1765) of New Hampshire and Samuel Darling (YC 1769) of Connecticut helped to found the medical society in their respective colonies and then relinquished practice shortly thereafter. After graduating from Princeton in 1762 Nathaniel Manning studied medicine at the College of Philadelphia and became an early member of the New Jersey Medical Society. Nevertheless, he traveled to England to be ordained in 1772 and returned to Virginia to become an Anglican rector.[246]

243. John Mallory, *Modern Entries in English* (London, 1735), vol. 2, p. 367; Holmes, *Augustan England: Professions, State and Society, 1680–1730,* chs. 6–7. Surgeons understood this paradox, as indicated by the anonymous treatise *The State of Surgery: but more particularly, the disadvantages its professors lie under considered* (London, 1752). Notwithstanding the innovation of hospital-based training, surgeons generally had merely a grammar school education. Irvine Loudon, *Medical Care and the General Practitioner, 1750–1850* (Oxford, 1986), chs. 3, 4, 7, 8.

244. Herbert, *The Country Parson,* p. 276; Paul Starr, *The Social Transformation of American Medicine* (New York, 1982), p. 39; Joseph F. Kett, *The Formation of the American Medical Profession: The Role of Institutions, 1780–1860* (New Haven, CT, 1968), ch. 1; Richard H. Shryock, *Medical Licensing in America, 1650–1965* (Baltimore, MD, 1967), ch. 1; Eric H. Christianson, "The Medical Practitioners of Massachusetts, 1630–1800: Patterns of Change and Continuity," in *Medicine in Colonial Massachusetts, 1620–1820* (Boston, 1980), p. 54.

245. *Harvard Graduates,* vol. 14, p. 244; *Minutes of the Trustees of the College, Academy and Charitable Schools, University of Pennsylvania ... 1749–1768* (Wilmington, DE, 1974), pp. 336–7; *Laws of the Royal Colony of New Jersey,* vol. 5, pp. 129–31.

246. *Harvard Graduates,* vol. 16, pp. 154–5, 163; *Yale Graduates,* vol. 3, p. 320; *Princetonians,* vol. 1, pp. 393–4.

"Physic" was therefore a second-choice or fall-back vocation, slightly preferable to teaching. Nicholas Webster (HC 1695), for example, did supply preaching until about age 38 without receiving a call and then opted for physic. In 1718 Daniel Witham graduated from Harvard and began teaching school for the next 12 years, before switching to medicine. Joseph Baxter (HC 1724) looked unsuccessfully for a pulpit for several years, turned to teaching, and gave it up in 1731 to become a physician. Joseph Marsh (HC 1728) tried and failed first at preaching, then at physic, and finally taught school outside Boston for his life work.[247] The pattern of such cases demonstrates that physicians were accorded far less than the clergy's compensation and status, and merely a fraction more than a schoolmaster's.

Comparative: *"between a Legal and an Evangelical Justification"*

If educators and doctors were semi-clergy, then lawyers were anti-clergy, and their field was generally more competitive than and preferable to either teaching or medicine after about 1690. John Sparhawk (HC 1723), for example, kept school in Plymouth and subsequently worked as a merchant and lawyer in the 1730s. Repeatedly admonished for drunkenness by his church, Sparhawk was prohibited from legal practice in 1740; and until his death in 1747 practiced physic, for which one did not need to obtain a license or survive extensive public scrutiny.[248] On the other hand, law ranked far below theology. Elisha Williams (HC 1711) embarked on the typical path of teaching school and studying theology, but in 1714 gave it up to read law. In 1716 he returned to theology, and became pastor of a church in Connecticut and later the rector of Yale. Ezra Stiles (HC 1746) began studying theology but, fearing that he could not satisfy the Connecticut clerical associations, turned to law. Admitted to the bar in 1753, he found the social standing of a lawyer to be less than a minister, and soon accepted a call to a church in Rhode Island, eventually becoming president of Yale. Timothy Dwight followed nearly the same route to the Yale presidency in the 1770s and 1780s.[249]

Williams', Stiles', and Dwight's flirtation and abandonment of law – duplicated by John Henry Livingston, Isaac Hunt, and James Sayre in New York and Pennsylvania during the 1760s – illustrate the lesson of Figure 2.3 that relatively few graduates of the colonial colleges found law a worthy occupation.[250] Due to this fact and the absence of law books and case reports in the colonies,[251] the licensing of attorneys developed slowly, initially with a requirement merely of swearing an

247. *Harvard Graduates*, vol. 4, p. 287; vol. 6, p. 288; vol. 7, p. 305; vol. 8, p. 448.

248. *Harvard Graduates*, vol. 7, pp. 258–9.

249. Warch, *School of the Prophets*, pp. 131–3; *Harvard Graduates*, vol. 12, p. 70; *Yale Graduates*, vol. 3, pp. 322–4.

250. *Yale Graduates*, vol. 2, pp. 755–60; [Persifor Frazier et al.], *University of Pennsylvania Biographical Catalogue of the Matriculates of the College ... of Philadelphia ... 1749–1857* (New York, 1894), pp. 10, 12.

251. Morris L. Cohen, "Legal Literature in Colonial Massachusetts," in *Law in Colonial Massachusetts, 1630–1800* (Boston, 1984), p. 243.

oath, followed later by a modest requirement of legal expertise usually tested by the governor or a justice of the court in which the attorney wished to practice. Even when an examination of legal knowledge was added to the licensing procedure, as in South Carolina in 1721 and Virginia in 1732, the governors and justices, who were themselves often not trained in the law, generally received their fees only upon granting the license. Hence, they had no incentive to be strict and, in fact, regarded such fees as an important perquisite of their position. In cases where an examiner was to receive the fee regardless of the decision about the license, as prescribed in Virginia in 1745, there was still an incentive for the examiner to be lenient so as to attract more licensing business, or, at least, not to be so strict as to lose a fair share of the business to other examiners.[252]

Maryland in 1707 introduced a licensing requirement that attorneys had to demonstrate some legal knowledge, either by having attended the Inns of Court or Chancery in London or by undergoing an examination by members of the bench. However, the colony did not require any specific training of lawyers until 1776, by which time attorneys were complaining that "none of the Judges were lawyers by profession."[253] Neighboring Delaware established its own system of courts in 1721 and merely required its citizens to swear an oath in order to be licensed by the Governor. In New Jersey the Assembly enacted in 1733 one of the most stringent colonial licensing statutes, but the act was disallowed by the Crown in 1735. No educational requirements were subsequently established during the colonial period, and David Ogden (YC 1728), who moved to Newark in the 1730s, became "perhaps the first thoroughly educated lawyer" in New Jersey.[254]

Massachusetts probably had more individuals trained in English law than any other colony early in the seventeenth century. But nearly all disdained to practice, and John Adams still sensed this disdain among the college-educated a century later.[255] Meanwhile in New Hampshire the first college graduate joined the bar only in 1731, while the first Chief Justice with any legal training was appointed only in 1754. As late as the 1740s Rhode Island apparently had only one college graduate practicing law. Under Connecticut's first licensing requirements, established in 1708, attorneys had merely to register with the Court and take an oath, and in 1730 the colony limited the number of lawyers to eleven.[256]

---

252. *Statutes of Virginia*, vol. 2, pp. 478–9; vol. 4, pp. 360–1; vol. 5, pp. 345–50; *Statutes of South Carolina*, vol. 2, pp. 173, 447.

253. *West* v. *Stigar*, 1 Harris & McHenry 247, 247 (Maryland 1767). *Archives of Maryland*, vol. 25, p. 224; Day, "Lawyers in Colonial Maryland, 1660–1715," pp. 149–65.

254. *Yale Graduates*, vol. 1, p. 373. *Laws of the State of Delaware, 1700–1797* (Wilmington, DE, 1797), vol. 1, p. 133; *Laws of the Royal Colony of New Jersey*, vol. 2, p. 471; vol. 5, p. 469.

255. Adams, *Legal Papers*, vol. 1, pp. xcv–cxiv; George L. Haskins, "Lay Judges: Magistrates and Justices in Early Massachusetts," in *Law in Colonial Massachusetts: 1630–1800* (Boston, 1984), pp. 39–55; Charles R. McKirdy, "The Lawyer as Apprentice: Legal Education in Eighteenth Century Massachusetts," *Journal of Legal Education*, 28 (1976): 124–36.

256. *Harvard Graduates*, vol. 7, p. 88; vol. 9, p. 363; *Public Records of Connecticut*, vol. 7, pp. 279–80 (1730); Goodwin, *The Magistracy Rediscovered: Connecticut, 1636–1818*, pp. 65–8.

Overall, then, few lawyers were educated or trained through 1750, and few college graduates chose to enter the field. Even New York, sometimes cited as exceptional due to the findings of historian Paul Hamlin, turns out to be the exception that proves the rule. Hamlin inflated his figures in order to prove that "one-third" of the bar was composed of college graduates in colonial New York. Actually, at the very end of the colonial period when more lawyers were educated, no more than one-quarter graduated from college even in New York.[257] This fraction therefore represents the high point in educational standards that lawyers attained in the colonies, as compared to one half for the ministry over the entire colonial period and the apex of 85–90 percent that was reached in Massachusetts and Connecticut.

The lesser standards and opportunities in law stemmed, at least in part, from theological opposition to litigation. Paul had admonished his followers: "Dare any of you, having a matter against another, go to law before the unjust, and not before the saints?" Augustine had maintained that "lawsuits both civil and criminal" evidence the sin in the City of Man.[258] During the seventeenth century these views were repeated by many Anglican clergymen, such as Bishop Jeremy Taylor: "Let no minister be litigious in any thing … not insisting upon little things, or quarrelling for, or exacting of, every minute portion of his dues." Puritans were even more insistent, as portrayed in the famous allegory *Pilgrim's Progress*, in which Evangelist tells Christian, "This Legality therefore is not able to set thee free from thy burden…. ye cannot be justified by the works of the law; for by the deeds of the law no man living can be rid of his burden."[259]

When a clergymen such as Cotton Mather conceded law to be potentially "a noble and useful profession," he was normally thinking of "a *lawyer* [who]…. when any of his neighbors, desirous to sue one another, addressed him for *counsel,* it was his manner … to endeavor a *reconciliation* between both parties; preferring the *consolations* of a *peacemaker,* before all the *fees* that he might have got, by blowing up of *differences*…. O excellent imitation of our glorious ADVOCATE in the heavens!" In other words, a good lawyer acted like a minister. Even this kind of concession was usually forgotten if a minister happened to become entangled in law-suits, as Mather later did. Then the opinion became the more typical one recorded in the diary of evangelist George Whitefield: "As for the *Business* of an

257. Paul M. Hamlin, *Legal Education in Colonial New York* (New York, 1939), p. 117, chs. 4, 8, app. 4. Hamlin (i) counted all lawyers who ever appeared in a New York court, regardless of whether or how long they lived or practiced in the colony; (ii) used 1784 as a cutoff date for the colonial period, rather than the more conventional 1776; and, most telling, (iii) counted ten college graduates who were clerks in 1784 and would only later join the bar. By these devices, he was able to inflate the number of New York colonial lawyers who were college graduates by about 25. Cf. McKirdy, "The Lawyer as Apprentice: Legal Education in Eighteenth Century Massachusetts," pp. 124–36; Charles E. Consalus, "Legal Education during the Colonial Period, 1663–1776," *Journal of Legal Education,* 29 (1978): 295–310; Klein, "From Community to Status: The Development of the Legal Profession in Colonial New York," pp. 146–7.

258. 1 *Corinthians* 6: 1; Augustine, *De civitate dei,* bk. 19, ch. 5.

259. Jeremy Taylor, *Rules and Advices to the Clergy* (1661), in *Curate of Souls,* p. 6; John Bunyan, *The Pilgrim's Progress,* ed. Roger Sharrock (1678; New York, 1965), pp. 54–5.

Attorney, I think it *unlawful* for a Christian, at least *exceeding Dangerous: Avoid it therefore,* and glorify God in some *other Station.*"[260]

This opposition to law may be partly construed as an expression of the self-interest of an age-old competing vocation, and that competition may have been reinforced by the analogous nature of law and theology. Both are hermeneutical disciplines, whose essential project is to abstract underlying principles from an authoritative, textual tradition, to rationalize those principles, and to apply them systematically to specific situations in life.[261] Nevertheless, the opposition is more deeply rooted in the Puritan and Protestant doctrine elevating "faith" above "law." It is impossible here to explicate fully the doctrine of "justification by faith" announced by Paul, elaborated by Augustine, Luther, and Calvin, and repeated in countless colonial tracts such as Nathaniel Appleton's *The Difference between a Legal and an Evangelical Justification* (1749). Suffice it to say that the doctrine proposes, in part, that one should freely resign all claims to what one believes one is owed or has somehow earned. In terms of social life, this position therefore finds repugnant the adversarial model of law, in which disagreeing parties resolve disputes by "joining issue" and arguing on behalf of their own self-interest. The doctrine envisions instead a harmonious community held together by bonds of cooperation and mutual self-criticism.[262]

The complaints against the adversarial nature of jurisprudence were legion. Prominent among the sins of New Englanders, the ministers at the 1679 Reforming Synod listed the fact that "Law suits are frequent, Brother going to Law with Brother, and provoking and abusing one another in publick Courts of Judicature, to the scandal of their holy Profession."[263] Statutes penalizing "troublesome and Litigious Persons" for bringing "vexatious suits" were enacted and reenacted in every colony: Connecticut in 1672, Plymouth in 1685, South Carolina in 1694,

---

260. Mather, *BONIFACIUS, An Essay Upon the Good,* pp. 126, 129, 130; Silverman, *The Life and Times of Cotton Mather,* pp. 312–9; Whitefield is quoted from Alan Heimert, *Religion and the American Mind from the Great Awakening to the Revolution* (Cambridge, MA, 1966), p. 180.

261. This hermeneutical congruence strikes me as more significant than efforts to find substantive, doctrinal links between theology and law, as by Roscoe Pound (*Law and Religion* (Houston, TX, 1940)) or Harold J. Berman ("Religious Foundations of Law in the West: An Historical Perspective," *Journal of Law and Religion,* 1 (1983): 3–44). See Linell E. Cady, "Hermeneutics and Tradition: The Role of the Past in Jurisprudence and Theology," *Harvard Theological Review,* 79 (1986): 439–63; Howard J. Vogel, "A Survey and Commentary on the New Literature in Law and Religion," *Journal of Law and Religion,* 1 (1983): 79–169.

262. Nathaniel Appleton, *The Difference between a Legal and an Evangelical Justification* (Boston, 1749). I thus disagree with interpretations that construe the "long-existing split in the American mind between ... the evangelical and the legal scheme" as, most fundamentally, a tension between personal, moral reform, and reform through social policy. Gordon S. Wood, *The Creation of the American Republic, 1776–1787* (Chapel Hill, NC, 1969), pp. 428, 471–99. See Heimert, *Religion and the American Mind,* passim; Richard E. Ellis, *The Jeffersonian Crisis: Courts and Politics in the Young Republic* (New York, 1971), pp. 253ff.

263. *The Necessity of Reformation,* in *Creeds and Platforms,* p. 430.

Rhode Island in 1718, New Jersey in 1722, Maryland in 1725, Virginia in 1732.[264] Meanwhile many a clergyman, in evaluating a call to a parish, applied the criterion that Lyman Beecher did in 1798 to East Hampton, Long Island: "The people are peaceable. Not a lawyer in the whole county. Industrious, hospitable. In the habit of being influenced by their minister."[265]

True to form, the analysis was dialectical, for, while the architectonic demoted law, it also proscribed lawlessness and disrespect of authority. Faith therefore trumped law, but one had to be faithful in a lawful way. Thus, New England ministers in the 1630s were quick to declare as heretical a position that provided for individual autonomy in matters of faith. This position they labeled "Antinomian," meaning literally "against law." Antinomians, such as the brilliant Anne Hutchinson, responded by labeling the ministers as "legal," or lacking grace; and the religious descendants of Hutchinson, such as Isaac Backus, continued to attack the clerical establishment as "legal teachers" of the gospel.[266] "Antinomian" and "legal" thus described poles of yet another dialectic that the Calvinist tradition sought to balance. Even so, there was no room within the dialectic for enthusiasm about conventional legal institutions.

The historiography of those institutions in the colonies is as confusing and contradictory as a series of opposing briefs written in Law French by common lawyers. The traditional view asserts that early colonial law was based on religious and customary injunctions, and considerable evidence indicates that throughout the colonies a relatively informal system of handling disputes built on local custom gradually gave way by the 1790s to a sophisticated adversarial legal system required by a more complex, commercial society. In short, colonists moved "from the authority of custom to the rule of law."[267] Although traditional Whiggish historians,

---

264. Quotation is from "An Act for preventing Multiplicity of Law-Suits," in *Laws of the Royal Colony of New Jersey*, vol. 2, pp. 292–3. *Earliest Laws of Connecticut*, pp. 64–5; *The Book of the General Laws of … New-Plimouth* (1685), pp. 4–5; *Earliest Laws of Rhode Island*, pp. 232–3; *Statutes of South Carolina*, vol. 2, p. 78; *Archives of Maryland*, vol. 36, pp. 586–93; *Statutes of Virginia*, vol. 4, pp. 360–1.

265. Lyman Beecher, *Autobiography* (1864), ed. Barbara M. Cross (Cambridge, MA, 1961), vol. 1, p. 70. See David Punter, "Fictional Representation of the Law in the Eighteenth Century," *Eighteenth-Century Studies*, 16 (1982): 47–74.

266. David D. Hall, ed., *The Antinomian Controversy, 1636–1638: A Documentary History* (Middletown, CT, 1968), p. 347, passim; Isaac Backus, *All True Ministers of the Gospel, are called into that Work by the Special Influences of the Holy Spirit* (1754), in *Isaac Backus on Church, State, and Calvinism: Pamphlets, 1754–1789*, ed. William G. McLoughlin (Cambridge, MA, 1968), p. 93; Morgan, *The Puritan Dilemma*, ch. 10.

267. Jerold S. Auerbach, *Justice Without Law?* (New York, 1983), p. 42. Here and below, I draw from George A. Billias, ed., *Law and Authority in Colonial America: Selected Essays* (Barre, MA, 1965); Stanley N. Katz, "Looking Backward: The Early History of American Law," *University of Chicago Law Review*, 33 (1966): 867–84; Stephen Botein, "Professional History Reconsidered," *AJLH*, 21 (1977): 60–79; Daniel R. Coquillette, "Introduction: The 'Countenance of Authoritie'," in *Law in Colonial Massachusetts, 1630–1800* (Boston, 1984), pp. xxi–lxiv; Richard Weisman, *Witchcraft, Magic, and Religion in 17th-Century Massachusetts* (Amherst, MA, 1984), pp. 134, 148–59; Paul Boyer and Stephen Nissenbaum, *Salem Possessed: The Social Origins of Witchcraft* (Cambridge, MA, 1974), pp. 9–21.

such as Paul Reinsch, had little good to say about the colonial clergy who irrationally opposed the supposedly inevitable evolution from "rude, untechnical popular law" to "complex" social, economic and legal systems, they did occasionally concede that the lay magistrates were "characterized not so much by profound legal learning or judicial distinction, as by plain sense, a rugged idea of justice."[268]

This portrayal of a development out of "the dark ages of American law" has often been repeated[269] even by prominent legal historians who revise the traditional view while writing about later periods.[270] Nevertheless, one major thrust of revisionism has appeared in the efforts of some legal historians to locate a sophisticated legal system and profession earlier in the colonial period. Some discover it "by the middle of the eighteenth century,"[271] while more ambitious revisionists have dated the appearance of a legal system even earlier, citing the criminal court system of North Carolina in the early 1700s, "an orgy of code making that occurred in New England before 1680" or the presence of the English common law in the first two decades of the settlement of Massachusetts.[272] A number of paradoxes appear in such efforts because some of the very same evidence, such as statutory restrictions on legal practice, cited by the traditional historians to show an animus *against* legal practice is now invoked by revisionists to show how vital legal practice must have been in order for it to be regulated. Moreover, these revisers of the traditional view are often strange bedfellows, for they include lawyer historians looking for earlier evidence of the dignity of their profession and, more recently, social historians looking for earlier evidence of social and economic conflict underlying the simple cooperative harmony in early colonial society posited by the traditional view.

A second kind of revisionism makes many of the same assumptions as the

---

268. Quotations are from Reinsch, *English Common Law in the Early American Colonies,* p. 8; John Noble, comp., *Records of the Courts of Assistants of the Colony of the Massachusetts Bay, 1630–1692* (Boston, 1901), p. x.

269. Lawrence M. Friedman, *A History of American Law* (New York, 1973), p. 29. See Charles Warren, *A History of the American Bar* (Boston, 1911); Roscoe Pound, *The Lawyer from Antiquity to Modern Times* (St. Paul, MN, 1953); Chroust, *The Rise of the Legal Profession in America,* vol. 1; Goodwin, *The Magistracy Rediscovered: Connecticut, 1636–1818,* pp. 13–32, 118–21.

270. See, for example, Wood, *The Creation of the American Republic, 1776–1787,* pp. 297–9; Morton J. Horwitz, *The Transformation of American Law, 1780–1860* (Cambridge, MA, 1977). Cf. Stanley N. Katz, "The Problem of a Colonial Legal History," in *Colonial British America,* ed. Jack P. Greene and J. R. Pole (Baltimore, MD, 1984), p. 471.

271. Botein, "The Legal Profession in Colonial North America," p. 129. See Murrin, "The Legal Transformation: The Bench and Bar of Eighteenth-Century Massachusetts," pp. 540–72; Gerard W. Gawalt, *The Promise of Power: The Emergence of the Legal Profession in Massachusetts, 1760–1840* (Westport, CT, 1979), pp. 7–35; David H. Flaherty, "Criminal Practice in Provincial Massachusetts," in *Law in Colonial Massachusetts, 1630–1800* (Boston, 1984), pp. 191–242.

272. Warden, "The Rhode Island Civil Code of 1647," p. 139; George L. Haskins, *Law and Authority in Early Massachusetts,* pp. 35, 117; Donna J. Spindel, *Crime and Society in North Carolina, 1663–1776* (Baton Rouge, LA, 1989), pp. ix–x; Herbert A. Johnson, *Essays in New York Colonial Legal History* (New York, 1981), pp. 3–34. See, too, *Essays in the History of Early American Law,* ed. David H. Flaherty (Chapel Hill, NC, 1969).

traditional view in denying the existence of a sophisticated legal system and profession through at least the 1750s. But rather than regarding the antecedent, customary and irregular legal system as crude and unsophisticated, this view emphasizes the beneficial effectiveness of the local, communal, informal system of dispute resolution that was rooted in a harmonious and well ordered community. The recent profusion of histories of New England towns has contributed to this line of revisionism by portraying their social system as "a Christian Utopian Closed Corporate Community."[273] According to this view, colonial systems of mediation were founded in "a strong communitarian impulse.... The nature of community varied: Most often religious, especially in the seventeenth century, it might also be geographical, ethnic, or commercial. The tighter the communal bonds the less need there was for lawyers or courts."[274] A variant of this second revisionist view simply puts a different valence on the communal order. Rather than viewing colonial communities as harmonious cooperatives built on shared values, these revisers propose that the disputes were mediated by a hierarchical and authoritative system, which stifled a great deal of conflict and dissent that had no place for expression precisely because legal institutions were absent, inoperative, or controlled by elites. According to this view, not only did social discord and dissent exist in these communities, but it was suppressed by a rigid hierarchy disguised as a communitarian system whereby lesser folk were included as voters but essentially co-opted.[275]

Finally, a third kind of revisionism attempts to argue all sides of the case at once. Looking at seventeenth-century Massachusetts, these historians argue that the Puritans were contentious but maintained a veneer of order and harmony by relying on formal legal and judicial systems. Thus, "legal institutions were to a large degree responsible for that stability" of New England communities, because "a system of justices of the peace and quarterly courts was an indispensable support for the Puritan ideal of communalism." The key point in this analysis is that such courts were not staffed by trained lawyers because they relied on local, English custom rather than the common law. This most recent revisionism has been welcomed particularly by those who wish to divorce the history of the law from the

273. Lockridge, *A New England Town, The First Hundred Years,* pp. 16, 193–209.

274. Auerbach, *Justice Without Law?,* p. 19. See Gross, *The Minutemen and their World,* p. 14; Christine A. Young, *From "Good Order" to Glorious Revolution: Salem, Massachusetts, 1628–1689* (Ann Arbor, MI, 1980), p. 1; Nelson, *Dispute and Conflict Resolution in Plymouth County, Massachusetts, 1725–1825,* pp. 10–1, chs. 2–3; James A. Henretta, "Families and Farms: *Mentalité* in Pre-Industrial America," *WMQ,* 3d ser., 35 (1978): 3–32; Bruce H. Mann, *Neighbors and Strangers: Law and Community in Early Connecticut* (Chapel Hill, NC, 1987), pp. 9–10, 93–100.

275. Innes, *Labor in a New Land ... Seventeenth-Century Springfield,* p. 171; Darrett B. Rutman, *Winthrop's Boston: Portrait of a Puritan Town, 1630–1649* (Chapel Hill, NC, 1965); Michael Zuckerman, *Peaceable Kingdoms: New England Towns in the Eighteenth Century* (New York, 1970), pp. 47–50, 147–8; L. Kinvin Wroth, "Possible Kingdoms: The New England Town from the Perspective of Legal History," *AJLH,* 15 (1971): 318–20; John M. Murrin, "Review Essay," *History and Theory,* 2 (1972): 248–51; David G. Allen, "The Zuckerman Thesis and the Process of Legal Rationalization in Provincial Massachusetts," *WMQ,* 3d ser., 29 (1972): 443–60; Hiller B. Zobel, "Some Agonies and Misuses of Legal History," *New England Quarterly,* 50 (1977): 138–48.

history of the bar.[276] However, in their eagerness to deny Whiggish assertions of modern jurists that "there is no law without lawyers,"[277] as well as to overturn the traditional historiography, these revisionists and their supporters say everything and nothing. No one has ever denied that courts existed and rendered verdicts from the early seventeenth century. The question has always been whether the courts were operated according to the common law by "professors" of the law. Indeed, for all of their illuminating and detailed research about specific communities, it is not clear that any of the revisionists have really disproved the traditional view, or even contradicted it. In fact, the revisionism has in certain respects come full circle.[278]

When all is considered, it seems fair to conclude that the colonial legal system through the mid-eighteenth century was not, in Weber's terms, a formally rational legal system. It did not primarily emphasize adherence to formal principles of legal logic of the kind that Edward Coke envisioned. Rather, the process of adjudication was substantively rational inasmuch as it resolved disputes by reference to an external and explicitly authoritative belief system. That system was grounded in the Bible, and it is manifest that colonial dispute resolution, whether in churches, town meetings, or courts, was more concerned with substantive results than with adherence to formal procedure. This concern was precisely the point of the trial described in *Pilgrim's Progress*. Christian and his companion, Faithful, are unjustly convicted even though the formalities of legal process are observed, and Faithful is sentenced to be tortured to death.[279]

But what precisely were the substantive results desired from a "faithful" rather than a "legal" trial? Two somewhat irreconcilable ends were sought. On the one

276. David T. Konig, *Law and Society in Puritan Massachusetts: Essex County, 1629–1692* (Chapel Hill, NC, 1979), pp. xii–xiii. See David G. Allen, *In English Ways: The Movement of Societies and the Transferal of English Local Law and Custom to Massachusetts Bay in the Seventeenth Century* (1981; New York, 1982), pp. 226ff.; Auerbach, *Justice Without Law?*, p. 153n.; Katz, "The Problem of a Colonial Legal History," pp. 457–89. On divorcing the history of law from that of the bar, see Katz, pp. 471f.; Coquillette, "Introduction: The 'Countenance of Authoritie'," pp. xxv, xxxiiiff.

277. Roscoe Pound, "A Hundred Years of American Law," in *Law, A Century of Progress, 1835–1935* (New York, 1937), vol. 1, p. 8; Chroust, *The Rise of the Legal Profession in America*, vol. 1, p. 3.

278. Relying on the insights of Clifford Geertz and Lawrence Stone, A. G. Roeber has announced himself to be employing state-of-the-art colonial historiography in an interpretation of the Virginia situation that reads very much like a subtle elaboration of Paul Reinsch. *Faithful Magistrates and Republican Lawyers*, p. 260. Similarly, a recent, sophisticated study of New Haven courts in the mid-seventeenth century concludes that "while the floor plan of New Haven's criminal justice system may have been English, the furnishings were designed according to scriptural specifications, and they had a distinctly Puritan style," including "its nonadversary character." Gail Sussman Marcus, " 'Due Execution of the Generall Rules of Righteousness': Criminal Procedure in New Haven Town and County, 1638–1658," in *Saints and Revolutionaries*, ed. David D. Hall et al. (New York, 1984), pp. 109, 136.

279. Bunyan, *Pilgrim's Progress*, pp. 129–34. Max Weber, *Economy and Society: An Outline of Interpretive Sociology*, ed. Guenther Roth and Claus Wittich and tr. Ephraim Fischoff et al. (New York, 1968), vol. 2, ch. 8, sects. v, viii.

hand stood the goal of substantive justice. "You will abhor, Sir, to appear in a *dirty cause*," Cotton Mather advised the future lawyer, "If you discern, that your *client* has an *unjust cause*, you will faithfully advise him of it." And the chief justice of the highest court in Massachusetts during the 1760s wrote: "I never presumed to call myself a Lawyer.... The most I could pretend to was when I heard the Law laid on both sides to judge which was right."[280] In this way, "New England courts paid only limited heed to the right against self-incrimination," and the legislatures entertained "appeals from almost anyone dissatisfied with a verdict in a lower tribunal."[281] No less in the county courts of Virginia; through the early eighteenth century, "justice was personal.... Regardless of the final decision, there are constant reminders in the statutes that the main issue in any deliberation was to decide who was right. Therefore, judgments were not to be postponed or information rejected because the proper form had not been followed."[282]

On the other hand, there existed the desire for peace and harmony as a substantive result of legal process. Through the seventeenth century, Anglican JPs "continued to advocate that the law be considered a species of activity very much like that carried on by the church – both were designed to keep the peace."

---

280. Mather, *BONIFACIUS, An Essay Upon the Good*, p. 127; Adams, *Legal Papers*, vol. 1, p. xli. The tension between adherence to procedure and attention to substantive results had long been recognized in England. The fifteenth-century establishment of "equity was a reaction to the morally obnoxious common law maxim that a 'mischief' (a failure of substantial justice in a particular case) was to be tolerated rather than an 'inconvenience' (a breach of legal principle). The chancellor [of equity] operated on the opposite principle." Ironically, courts of equity became bogged down with slow, expensive and arcane procedure that outstripped even that of the common law. For this reason and because the concern for substantive justice was intrinsically part of the religiously based systems of adjudication, courts of equity never took root in the seventeenth-century colonies. Stanley N. Katz, "The Politics of Law in Colonial America: Controversies over Chancery Courts and Equity Law in the Eighteenth Century," in *Colonial America*, ed. Stanley N. Katz, 2d edn (Boston, 1976), pp. 404–7.

281. John M. Murrin, "Magistrates, Sinners, and a Precarious Liberty: Trial by Jury in Seventeenth-Century New England," in *Saints and Revolutionaries*, ed. David D. Hall et al. (New York, 1984), pp. 194, 198; Goodwin, *The Magistracy Rediscovered: Connecticut, 1636–1818*, ch. 2; Bruce C. Daniels, "The Political Structure of Local Government in Colonial Connecticut," in *Town and Country*, ed. Daniels (Middletown, CT, 1978), p. 51.

282. Robert Wheeler, "The County Court in Colonial Virginia," in *Town and Country*, ed. Bruce C. Daniels (Middletown, CT, 1978), pp. 114, 119. Appropriately, it is said that the model for pre-1776 lawyers was the Roman orator, who persuaded fellow citizens to pursue virtue: Cicero in New England and Cato in Virginia. Stephen Botein, "Cicero as Role Model for Early American Lawyers: A Case Study in Classical 'Influence'," *Classical Journal*, 73 (1977–8): 313–21; Jack P. Greene, "Society, Ideology, and Politics: An Analysis of the Political Culture of Mid-Eighteenth-Century Virginia," in *Society, Freedom, and Conscience: The American Revolution in Virginia, Massachusetts, and New York*, ed. Richard M. Jellison (New York, 1976), pp. 54–5; Frederic M. Litto, "Addison's *Cato* in the Colonies," *WMQ*, 3d ser., 23 (1966): 431–49; Kenneth Silverman, *A Cultural History of the American Revolution: Painting, Music, Literature and the Theatre ... 1763–1789* (1976; New York, 1987), pp. 83ff.

In eighteenth-century South Carolina, JPs were evenly drawn from untrained merchants and planters and from artisans and workmen, who generally endorsed the "Country" virtues compatible with a consensual, harmonious approach to politics and adjudication.[283] Similarly, Pennsylvania Quakers and New York Dutch Calvinists sought to resolve disputes by means that would promote harmony.[284]

Both the desire for substantive justice and the emphasis on mediation and arbitration necessarily placed personal discretion above adherence to formal procedure. "[D]o justice between the parties not by any quirks of the law ... but by common sense and common honesty as between man and man," a justice of the highest court of New Hampshire charged a jury in the 1760s. Since "common sense" carried more weight than jurisprudence, the JPs, who adjudicated the cases that most affected people's daily lives, were generally untrained in the law. In Maryland, for example, some JPs, even in the 1690s, were illiterate, and a number were former indentured servants. From 1660 to 1692 in one Maryland county "25 percent of the justices were ex-servants, and 62.5 percent arrived in the colony without claim to the title of Mr., much less gentleman." If such folk could adjudicate disputes, then naturally "gentlemen sitting on the benches of the courts of law in the Colonies ... are not and cannot be expected to be lawyers or learned in the law," affirmed Thomas Pownall, who served as a royal functionary in New York and New Jersey and governor of South Carolina and Massachusetts.[285]

Despite this common ground in devaluing sophisticated legal formality, the emphasis on mediation and arbitration stood in dialectical tension with the commitment to substantive justice. The former implied that the resolution of a dispute was negotiable and subject to the mutual satisfaction of the parties involved, so that harmony and consensus would be preserved. The latter implied that absolute moral standards existed and that the community had an obligation to fulfill them. This dialectic, reflecting the architectonic of culture, has scarcely been noticed amid the avalanche of revisionist legal historiography, though John Murrin has astutely linked it to the seemingly paradoxical use of juries in early New England. In

283. Roeber, *Faithful Magistrates and Republican Lawyers*, p. 6. Waterhouse, "The Responsible Gentry of Colonial South Carolina," pp. 162–4; Robert M. Weir, "'The Harmony we were Famous for': An Interpretation of Pre-Revolutionary South Carolina Politics," *WMQ*, 3d ser., 26 (1969): 473–501; Canady, "Gentlemen of the Bar: Lawyers in Colonial South Carolina," chs. 1–4.

284. John R. Aiken, "New Netherlands Arbitration in the Seventeenth Century," *Arbitration Journal*, n.s., 29 (1974): 145–60; Wayne E. Bockelman, "Local Government in Colonial Pennsylvania," in *Town and Country*, ed. Bruce C. Daniels (Middletown, CT, 1978), pp. 216–38; Odiorne, "Arbitration and Mediation Among Early Quakers," pp. 161–6; Horle, *The Quakers and the English Legal System, 1660–1688*, passim; Thomas E. Carbonneau, *Alternative Dispute Resolution: Melting the Lances and Dismounting the Steeds* (Urbana, IL, 1989), ch. 1.

285. Quotations are, respectively, from: William Plumer, Jr., *Life of William Plumer* (Boston, 1857), p. 154; Lois Green Carr, "The Foundations of Social Order: Local Government in Colonial Maryland," in *Town and Country*, ed. Bruce C. Daniels (Middletown, CT, 1978), p. 89; Thomas Pownall, *The Administration of the American Colonies; wherein Their Rights and Constitution are Discussed*, 4th edn (1768; New York, 1971), p. 107. Pownall's book went through six editions by 1777.

criminal trials before 1660 New England courts rarely employed juries, relying on magistrates to determine the substantively just resolution for the crime. But in civil suits, juries were used extensively, much more than in England, because the verdict had to reflect the consensus of the neighbors who would help to mediate between the disputing parties.[286]

Consequently, formal legal process and learned jurisprudence were not highly valued in the colonies through the mid-eighteenth century. Whether in courts, churches, town meetings, or informal settings, disputes were more often resolved by appeal, on the one hand, to some notion of substantive justice or, on the other hand, to a vision of harmony, cooperation, and consensus that founded a well ordered community. It is important to see that neither of these two poles of the dialectic implies a sense of democracy or liberty and more than did Moses' covenant with Yahweh. In fact, it has been held that the mechanisms of mediation and arbitration relied upon a hierarchical and coercive social system. That coercion is said to reside in the ethic of "deference": "the term employed to describe the unquestioning acceptance of an eighteenth-century moral order which consigned laboring people to economic, social, and political subordination ... From deference it is only a step to speaking of cultural hegemony."[287]

More meaningful than the idea of "cultural hegemony" to the colonists, however, would have been the fact that in the Bible they found the model of a covenant to be an all-powerful superior generously extending to an undeserving inferior the opportunity to live in peace and relative dignity in return for the acknowledgement of the superior's status. Scriptural authority seemed to warrant the order that John Winthrop prescribed for civil society: "the riche and mighty should not eate upp the poore, nor the poore and despised rise upp against theire superiours, and shake off theire yoake." Even in Rhode Island, which included the disaffected rebels who had left Massachusetts and Plymouth, the deferential social customs were enacted at the very first meeting of the colonial assembly in 1647: "It is agreed and enacted ... that no inferior shall rise up or rebel against his superior ... it being altogether unsuitable to civil order." In 1672 the Connecticut legislature included a similar provision in the first printed compilation of their laws, and 50 years later Rev. William Burnham preached before that same legislature on *God's Providence in Placing Men in Their Respective Stations & Conditions.*[288]

Whether described explicitly in Calvinist terms by Congregationalists, Presbyterians, Baptists, and Quakers or in terms of "country ideology" among Anglicans, "the essence of the social order lay in the superiority of husband over wife, parents

---

286. Murrin, "Magistrates, Sinners, and a Precarious Liberty: Trial by Jury in Seventeenth-Century New England," pp. 153, 186–97.

287. Gary B. Nash, *Race, Class and Politics: Essays on American Colonial and Revolutionary Society* (Urbana, IL, 1986), p. 250. See J. G. A. Pocock, "The Classical Theory of Deference," *AHR,* 81 (1976): 516–23; John B. Kirby, "Early American Politics – The Search for Ideology: An Historical Analysis and Critique of the Concept of 'Deference'," *Journal of Politics,* 32 (1970): 808–38.

288. John Winthrop, *Winthrop Papers,* vol. 2, p. 283; *Earliest Laws of Rhode Island,* p. 18; *Earliest Laws of Connecticut,* pp. 10, 14; Bushman, *From Puritan to Yankee,* chs. 1–2; William Burnham, *God's Providence in Placing Men in Their Respective Stations & Conditions* (New London, 1722).

over children, and master over servants in the family, ministers and elders over congregation in the church, rulers over subjects in the state."[289] This order was rooted in the theological architectonic that rejected an adversarial model of resolving disputes. Instead, it advocated social harmony and consensus, on the one hand, and substantive justice truly ascertained from an authoritative text, on the other.

Comparative: "The Parson's Compleatnesse"

Not only was theology preferred to the other "professions," but it also encroached on them, a phenomenon that recent scholars have sometimes regarded as an imperialistic invention of modern professionals in industrial society.[290] Yet already in the seventeenth century George Herbert was warning the Country Parson "not to encroach on others' Professions, but to live on his own."[291] Since the colonial ministry was preferable to other learned vocations, this preeminent vocation encroached upon those others insofar as it seemed worthwhile to do. Notwithstanding his warning, even George Herbert apparently endorsed both the ideological and functional encroachment so long as it was not overtly self-interested. This endorsement is perfectly expressed in Herbert's chapter "The Parson's Compleatnesse," which opens: "The Country Parson desires to be all to his Parish, and not only a Pastor, but a Lawyer also, and a Physician." Similarly, Gilbert Burnet's *A Discourse of the Pastoral Care* noted that many pastors, whether or not they needed supplemental income, took up "the farming of grounds," "the teaching of schools," and "the study and practice of *Physick.*"[292] These popular, pastoral handbooks were intended for Anglicans, but "The Parson's Compleatnesse" applied no less to the Congregational, Presbyterian, Baptist, and other explicitly Calvinist professions.

Although most ministers were not trained in the law, they often encroached on the work of the anti-clergy by drawing up legal documents. Especially in rural towns, where they were usually the best educated persons, ministers drafted deeds, wills, and agreements. Many clergymen, in effect, also encroached on trial work because "the Country Parson ... endures not that any of his Flock should go to Law, but in any Controversie, that they should resort to him as their Judge."[293]

289. Morgan, *The Puritan Family,* p. 19.

290. Cf. William J. Goode, "Encroachment, Charlatanism, and the Emerging Profession: Psychology, Sociology, and Medicine," *American Sociological Review,* 25 (1960): 902–14; Carol L. Kraus, "The Evolution of Occupational Power: A Historical Study of Task Boundaries between Physicians and Pharmacists," *Sociology of Work and Occupations,* 3 (1976): 3–37; Robert A. Rothman, "Deprofessionalization: The Case of Law in America," *Work and Occupations,* 11 (1984): 195–9. Andrew Abbott, *The System of Professions: An Essay on the Division of Expert Labor* (Chicago, 1988) has proposed that "the history of jurisdictional disputes" is "the real, the determining history of the professions" (p. 2, passim).

291. Herbert, *The Country Parson,* p. 278.

292. Herbert, *The Country Parson,* p. 274, ch. 23; Burnet, *A Discourse of the Pastoral Care,* pp. 183–6.

293. Herbert, *The Country Parson,* p. 274. See Russell, *The Clerical Profession,* ch. 11; Hart, *Clergy and Society, 1600–1800,* ch. 5.

Such dispute resolution usually amounted to informal mediation, but the role was occasionally formalized when ministers were appointed JPs, such as James Scales (HC 1733) in New Hampshire, William Woodhull (PC 1764) in New Jersey, and John Bacon (PC 1765) in Maryland and Massachusetts.[294] Although those efforts had the fortuitous result of putting the anti-clergy out of business, although such encroachment on legal work was distasteful to the ministers. Following Bishop Burnet's suggestion, the divines found it more congenial to displace the two kinds of semi-clergy. As Richard Baxter avowed:

> I know not of any simile that doth more aptly express the ministerial power and duty, and the people's duty, than these two conjunct – viz., a physician in an hospital, that hath taken charge of it, and a schoolmaster in his school.... Such are ministers in the Church, and such is their work, and their authority to do it, and the duty of the people to submit thereto.[295]

The encroachment on education had a long tradition, evidenced by the fact that educational institutions had generally been founded by churches. This institutional relationship was reflected in the rhetorical practice of seventeenth-century Congregational churches to apply the term "teacher" to the ministerial office of the preacher or sermonizer. Although this new office had largely disappeared by the beginning of the eighteenth century, the scriptural text *Ephesians* 4: 11–12 was still being cited to justify the office in the early nineteenth century. Indeed, the term "public religious teacher," "Christian teacher," or "public teacher of religion" was commonly employed instead of "minister" through the mid-nineteenth century.[296] In the words of an early eighteenth-century Baptist minister: "This word [teacher] is not anywhere used ... but for a Publick Teacher, Preacher or Instructor of Disciplines in the Knowledge of God. And this word Teachers is the word whereby the writers of the New Testament express Rabbi, which was the usual Name of the Publick Teachers of the Law among the Jews."[297]

The rhetoric concerning "teacher" reflects well the occupational and ideological relationship between ministers and schoolmasters, "from which latter ... there has been a frequent *ascent* into the former; as well as a step [down] now and then from the former to the latter." For, "certainly, "tis a nobler work, to make the little ones know their *Saviour*, than to know their *letters.*" These words were Cotton Mather's, and precisely the same logic appeared in the order of the founding purposes for the College of William and Mary: "the advance of learning, education of youth, supply of the ministry, and promotion of piety."[298] Since the local clergyman generally selected and supervised the local schoolteacher and since anyone who

---

294. For these and other examples, see *Harvard Graduates,* vol. 7, p. 92; vol. 9, pp. 110–1, 324–6; vol. 13, p. 225; *Princetonians,* vol. 1, pp. 475–6, 479–81.

295. Baxter, *The Reformed Pastor,* pp. 357–8.

296. "Letter to Rev. Mr. Jonathan Boucher [by] A Consistent Protestant," *Maryland Gazette,* no. 1458 (August 19, 1773): 2; *Acts and Laws of the Commonwealth of Massachusetts* (Boston, 1786), p. 23 (1786 ch. 10); John Jeffrey, *The Importance, Difficulties, Encouragements, and Duties of the Christian Ministry* (London, 1809); Wilbur Fisk, *A Sermon delivered ... on the day of General Election* (Boston, 1829); George B. Ide, *The Ministry Demanded by the Present Crisis* (Philadelphia, 1845), passim.

297. Collins, *The Temple Repair'd,* p. 4.

298. *Statutes of Virginia,* vol. 2, p. 56 (1662); Mather, *BONIFACIUS: An Essay upon the*

taught from a pulpit necessarily could teach in a schoolhouse, ministers encroached on schoolteaching as it seemed expedient or interesting to do. Most, such as Benjamin Tallmadge (YC 1747) in New York and New Jersey and David Caldwell (PC 1761) in North Carolina, were simply augmenting their income and serving the needs of a small town that could not afford both a minister and a schoolmaster. But others, such as James Hunt (PC 1759) in Maryland and Virginia and John Springer (PC 1775) and Samuel Doak (PC 1775) in Georgia, the Carolinas, and Tennessee, were deeply interested in education and founded a series of schools and academies.[299] By either rationale, ministers subsumed the role of teachers, as they saw fit.

The encroachment upon medicine had, in a sense, an even longer tradition. The medical metaphor of philosophy or theology as "care for the soul" (*psychēs therapeia*) extended back to Socrates. The idea was endorsed by subsequent philosophers and early leaders of the Greek Church, such as John Chrysostom (345–407), who likened the church to a hospital and portrayed himself as a curer of souls in a treatise that was translated into English in 1728, 1759, 1837, 1844, and 1866.[300] The Latin Church also adopted the idea in the phrase *cura animarum*, which was subsequently employed by medieval Catholics and Protestant reformers, leading finally to the term "curate of souls" appearing in English and referring to the clerical office. In the meantime, acerbic Puritans, such as John Milton, and devout Anglicans, such as Henry Dodwell, employed the medical metaphors for ministry. By 1711 it was far more typical than innovative that Peter Thatcher entitled his election sermon: *The Alsufficient Physician Tendering to Heal the Political and Spiritual Wounds & Sickness of a Distressed Province.*[301]

Meanwhile, colonial ministers practiced physic actually as well as metaphorically. The foremost colonial authority on medicine early in the eighteenth century was Cotton Mather, and his renowned *Magnalia Christi Americana* is filled with instances of ministers practicing medicine. As he elsewhere wrote:

> Nor has it been a rare thing in latter ages for *clergymen* to be *physicians*.... And we have known many a *country minister* prove a vast blessing to his flock by being so. If a *minister* do anything this way, let him forever make it an engine, to address the *souls* of his people, and oblige them unto piety.[302]

Good, pp. 83–4; Tyler, ed., *Narratives of Early Virginia, 1606–1625*, p. 114; *The History of the College of William and Mary (including the General Catalogue) from its Foundation, 1660, to 1874* (Richmond, VA, 1874), ch. 1.

299. *Princetonians*, vol. 1, pp. 268–9, 341–2; vol. 2, pp. 474–5, 525–6; *Yale Graduates*, vol. 2, pp. 134–5.

300. Plato, *Apology* 29d, 30b; John Chrysostom, *On the Priesthood* (387), tr. R. Harris Cowper (London, 1866), p. vii.

301. John T. McNeill, *A History of the Cure of Souls* (London, 1952), chs. 2, 5–13; John Milton, *Complete Prose Works of John Milton*, ed. Don M. Wolfe (New Haven, CT, 1953), vol. 3, pp. 222n., 227, 514; vol. 4, p. 658; Herbert, *The Country Parson*, pp. 278–9; Dodwell, *Two Letters of Advice*, p. 29; Peter Thatcher, *The Alsufficient Physician Tendering to Heal the Political and Spiritual Wounds & Sickness of a Distressed Province* (Boston, 1711).

302. Mather, *BONIFACIUS: An Essay upon the Good*, p. 82; Otho T. Beall, Jr., and Richard H. Shryock, *Cotton Mather: First Significant Figure in American Medicine* (Baltimore, MD, 1954).

The encroachment upon medical work was thus a commonplace and a logical outgrowth of the greater intellectual authority of ministers, a fact that reflected the ideological relationship between medicine and theology prescribed by the architectonic.

In fine, it is evident that the colonial clergy occupied the foremost position among the four vocations that had been closely associated for centuries due to their common origin and home in the seats of learning, the medieval universities. Although the "estates," or legally defined "orders," had been abolished in England after the Reformation, the clergy – being the only learned vocation among the three major orders in England: aristocracy, peasantry, clergy – had both the lineage and the actual statutory privileges and protections that made them the closest approximation to a legally defined "order" in colonial society.[303] The colonial ministers enjoyed high social status and profited from the comfortable material conditions of those in the top fifth of the population. They therefore stood foremost among the learned vocations due to their institutional, political, social, and economic standing and authority, all of which was justified by the fact that they exemplified the true "professors" who most fully professed the ultimate ends and values of the culture. Here is where the rhetoric of "profession" helps in understanding events.

However proud or grasping they may or may not have been, the clergy in the seventeenth and early eighteenth centuries did not have in mind some alluring concept of an occupation, or "profession," to which they aspired. They were not engaged in "professionalization," a term that imposes a twentieth-century perspective upon the past. Instead, it is nearer the truth to say that the meaning of occupation and of the word "profession" were transformed by the fact that the clergy, shaping and being shaped by a certain constellation of human values and beliefs, became preeminent at a particular time. Their preeminence informed thinking and speaking, especially the rhetoric of "profession," and this rhetorical development influenced the way people thought and talked about "profession" long after the clergy had declined.

We have already examined the initial two moments in the rhetoric of "profession," which marked steps in the emergence of what would become "the true professional ideal" in America. First, there was a twofold extension in the meaning of the term: from referring to a religious vow to denoting the group who made the vow and from referring to the monastic, "regular" clergy to denoting the "secular" clergy and laity. In this way, "profession" in English came to signify, above all, the group of likeminded clergy who made the same religious vow and who lived and worked in the world among the laity. Subsequently, a second moment in the rhetoric of "profession" took place: theological usage emphasized and dignified occupational usage and then declined. This second step resulted because "profession," which already bore the secondary meaning of "occupation" derived from Latin usage, came to refer especially to that "particular calling" by which the clergy fulfilled their "general calling" and earned the greatest esteem and respect.

303. Rosemary O'Day, "The Anatomy of a Profession: the Clergy of the Church of England," in *The Professions in Early Modern England,* ed. Wilfrid Prest (London, 1987), pp. 28–31. The four major estates in continental Europe had meanwhile persevered: nobility, bourgeoisie, peasantry, clergy. See the succinct discussion in Franklin L. Ford, *Europe, 1780–1830* (London, 1970), pp. 21–9.

Notwithstanding this second step, the generalized usage of "profession" that derived from the Latin *professio* and applied to any occupation from "cookery" to "villainy" to "writing" was never extinguished and lingered on.[304] However, the increasing usage of "profession" in reference to occupations during the eighteenth century was accompanied by a significant narrowing of the number of employments that the term primarily denoted. Over time, "profession" began to refer primarily to theology, law, medicine, and learning, four fields that originally became associated when the medieval university provided the meeting ground for the other three fields in the form of graduate faculties. This semantic narrowing is demonstrated by the introduction of the terms "learned professions" and "liberal professions," which became commonplace over the middle third of the eighteenth century. This semantic narrowing of "profession" to the learned fields and the introduction of these two new terms constitute the third moment in the rhetoric of profession. Here again, the preeminence of theology was responsible for the fact and the nature of this development.

Scholars have often assumed that in the Middle Ages or, at least by the fifteenth or sixteenth centuries, the term "professions" denoted primarily theology, law, and medicine, which were also called the "three learned professions" or "three liberal professions." Many are the scholarly discussions treating the "learned professions" in this way without citing a single instance of such usage.[305] Surely it is not semantic quibbling to point out the danger in such discussions. The application of "profession" or "learned professions" to three or four fields signifies two important ideas: first, the introduction of a specially dignified conception of employment; second, the application of that conception to a small set of specific occupations. The appearance and use of the terms is the best way, indeed the only way, to determine that the two ideas consciously existed. Consequently, it is misleading to employ such terms, and therefore the ideas, as though they existed centuries before they can be shown to exist.

The anachronistic assumption about the three, or four, "professions" has apparently arisen from misinterpreting the entry in the *OED*,[306] which is itself both ambiguous and misleading and has contributed to misunderstanding on these points. In the *OED* "profession" is defined as

---

304. See, for example, [B. Clermont], *The Professed Cook, or the modern art of cookery …
adapted to the London markets by the editor*, 2d edn (London, 1769), 10th edn (London, 1812);
James Caulfield, *Blackguardiana: or, a dictionary of rogues, bawds, pimps, whores, pickpockets,
shoplifters … the most remarkable professors of villainy* ([London, 1793?]); James Ralph, *The
Case of Authors by Profession or Trade* (London, 1758; reprinted Gainesville, FL, 1966),
pp. 6–7; David Ramsay, *The History of the American Revolution*, 2 vols. (New York, 1789),
vol. 1, pp. 61–2; vol. 2, pp. 314–6.

305. See, for example, Geoffrey Holmes, *Augustan England: Professions, State and Society,
1680–1730*, pp. 3–21, 83, 136; J. H. Baker, *The Legal Profession and the Common Law,
Historical Essays* (London, 1986), p. 123; Brooks, *Pettyfoggers and Vipers of the Commonwealth*, pp. 270–2, passim; Wilfrid R. Prest, ed., *The Professions in Early Modern England*
(London, 1987), "Preface" and pp. 12–4.

306. See, for example, Frances P. DeLancy, *The Licensing of Professions in West Virginia*
(Chicago, 1938), pp. 2, 2n.; McKirdy, "Massachusetts Lawyers on the Eve of the American
Revolution," p. 313n.; Eliot Freidson, *Professional Powers: A Study of the Institutionalization
of Formal Knowledge* (Chicago, IL, 1986), pp. 21–7.

a vocation in which a professed knowledge of some department of learning or science is used in its application to the affairs of others ... Applied *spec.* to the three learned professions of divinity, law and medicine; also to the military profession.

This entry is followed by twelve examples, none instancing the term "three learned professions" before 1888. The sixteenth- and seventeenth-century examples portray theology, law, or medicine *individually*, not collectively, being called a "profession." But, because virtually any occupation could have been called a "profession" during the sixteenth and seventeenth centuries, these examples do not demonstrate that "profession" attached to theology, law, medicine, and learning in some special way. Such examples carry weight only if one *presupposes* that the conception and the terms "three professions," "three learned professions," or "three liberal professions" already existed, which is precisely what the citations are intended to prove. Conversely, numerous examples exist in the late seventeenth and early eighteenth centuries when authors discuss divinity, law, medicine, and learning, and never employ these terms where it would be natural to do so, had they been conventional.[307]

The original instance of what became the conventional term – "the three learned professions" – may well be from Joseph Addison in *The Spectator*, which is quoted by the *OED*. But even in the 1711 issue cited by the *OED*, Addison writes of "the three great professions" rather than "the learned professions," while he employs varying terminology in subsequent issues during 1711 and early 1712. He does, however, observe that these three professions are dependent "upon a learned education." This observation evidences the emerging set of ideas that would come to be denoted by the conventional term: the association of the three fields; the special dignity attributed to them and, therefore, to a "profession"; and the importance of learning and education to all three. Then, in late 1712, Addison employs the term for the first time in *The Spectator*: "I come now to that Point of Precedency which is settled among the three Learned Professions."[308] That the term first appeared about this time, whether in *The Spectator* or elsewhere, is confirmed by the fact that contemporaries who employ "the three learned professions" consciously define it. Writing in 1724, Isaac Watts noted: "There are three learned professions among us, *viz.*, divinity, law, and medicine," before he proceeded to use the term. This phrasing obviously suggests that it was not yet a commonplace.[309]

---

307. See, for example, Herbert, *The Country Parson*, chs. 10, 23; Mather, *BONI-FACIUS, An Essay upon the Good*, passim; [Mather], *RATIO DISCIPLINAE FRATRUM NOV-ANGLORUM*, pp. 81, 117.

308. Joseph Addison and Richard Steele, *The Spectator*, ed. Donald F. Bond, 5 vols. (Oxford, 1965), nos. 21 (1711), 499 (1712), 529 (1712). This modern critical edition exemplifies the anachronism referred to above by lumping all these and other instances under the index heading "The Three Learned Professions."

309. Isaac Watts, "Logick: Or, the Right Use of Reason in the Inquiry after Truth" (1724), in *The Works ... Selected by the Rev. Dr. Jennings and the Rev. Dr. Doddridge, in 1753*, 6 vols. (London, 1810), vol. 5, p. 303. Watt's usage was subsequently cited as pathbreaking by Baptist minister Dan Taylor. *The Nature and Importance of Preparatory Studies prior to Entering on the Christian Ministry* (London, 1807), p. 30n.

By mid-century Dr. William Douglass wrote matter-of-factly in the *Present State of the British Settlement in North America* of "the three learned professions of divinity, law, and medicine." In 1762 Rev. James Maury in an often cited letter on the education proper for a Virginia gentleman referred to "Divinity, Medicine, or Law" as "the Learned Professions," which require a foundation in "the liberal sciences and politer Arts." Six years later, upon assuming the presidency of Princeton, John Witherspoon anticipated that prospective students reading the College's advertisements in New Jersey newspapers would be aiming for "those called learned Professions, Divinity, Law and Physic or such liberal accomplishments in general."[310] By 1773 when the fourth edition of Samuel Johnson's dictionary appeared, it was felt necessary to add a sentence to the entry under "profession" that had not appeared in the first edition of 1755: "The term *profession* is particularly used of divinity, physick and law."[311] The semantic narrowing of the term had thus consciously and unmistakably occurred.

As suggested by Maury and Witherspoon, the term "liberal" was also becoming associated with the three professions, and gradually "liberal professions" was employed interchangeably with "learned professions." The reasons for this association are informative about the third rhetorical moment and its connections with theology. In a general sense, the term "learned professions" reflected the legacy of theology, law, and medicine being graduate faculties at the medieval universities. This legacy established the norm that a minister, lawyer, or physician should have had a liberal education, and that norm was specifically strengthened by the Protestant desire for a learned ministry, which had become the preeminent profession. By the mid-1700s essayists writing on liberal education, such as Benjamin Rush and Joseph Priestley, were guided in their recommendations by what "a lawyer, a physician, or a divine" ought to know because "liberal education ... was almost

---

310. William Douglass, *A Summary, Historical and Political, of the First Planting, Progressive Improvements, and Present State of the British Settlements in North America*, 2 vols. (London, 1755), vol. 1, p. 256; James Maury, "A Dissertation on Education in the Form of a Letter from James Maury to Robert Jackson, July 17, 1762," ed. Helen D. Bullock, *Papers of the Albemarle County Historical Society*, 2 (April 1942): 36–60. Witherspoon's advertisement is quoted from Darrell L. Guder, "The Belles Lettres at Princeton: An Investigation of the Expansion and Secularization of Curriculum at the College of New Jersey" (PhD diss., University of Hamburg, 1965), p. 161.

311. Samuel Johnson, *A Dictionary of the English Language* (London, 1755), s.v. "profession"; Samuel Johnson, *A Dictionary of the English Language*, 4th edn (London, 1773), s.v. "profession." In other ways, Johnson's first edition of 1755 already recognized "these three professions above all others." (Robert DeMaria, Jr., *Johnson's DICTIONARY and the Language of Learning* (Chapel Hill, NC, 1986), p. 221.) No previous dictionary associated these three vocations particularly with "profession." The first to list any examples of "profession" was apparently Nathan Bailey's *Dictionariam Britannicum: Or a more Compleat Universal Etymological English Dictionary than any Extant* (1730; Menston, UK, 1969), which included the entries: "*To Profess* ... to declare and make one's self known to be a such a Religion, Sect, or Party; to protest or declare solemnly; also to exercise some particular Study or Calling publickly.... *Profession*, a Condition of Life, Trade, Calling, or any Art or Mystery that one has chosen; as Law, Physick, &c. also publick Confession, Protestation."

entirely adapted to *the learned professions.*"[312] The fact that liberal education was the mark of learning suggests one reason why "learned profession" and "liberal profession" would appear concurrently and be used interchangeably. An additional reason can be found in the implications of status and class that "liberal" had long implied.

The Latin adjective *liberalis* originally referred to a citizen who was "free" by virtue of having political freedom as well as the free time, or leisure, afforded by possessing some degree of wealth. The connotation that the *artes liberales* constituted the education for a citizen with the freedom, or leisure, to study was carried over to the liberal arts in English universities and the American colonial colleges. Through the eighteenth century, the adjective "liberal" signified generosity in mind and in material possessions, the latter presupposing some access to wealth. Liberality and learning were conjoined in a liberal education, on the one hand, because college education required some access to extraordinary resources and conferred a degree of social status and, on the other hand, because the education was thought to convey some breadth, or generosity, of thought and character. Learning and liberality were therefore entailed in a liberal education, which a "learned profession" presupposed.

Princeton President John Witherspoon consequently regarded the studies that aimed at the "learned Professions, Divinity, Law, and Physic" to be "liberal accomplishments." The Yale faculty later expressed this thinking quintessentially in the equation that "liberal education" produces a "liberal character" that fits one for a "liberal profession." Meanwhile Adam Smith was less impressed with appeals to "character" and "taste" than with the expense of education, when he analyzed why the "liberal professions" were able to demand higher remuneration than other employments.[313] The equivalence between "learned professions" and "liberal professions" thus signified that education, wealth, character, and status met in these "professors."

The introduction of these two interchangeable terms, the specially dignified conception of employment that they signified, and the application of that conception to a small set of specific occupations constituted the third moment in the rhetoric of profession. The new terms and meanings began to appear early in the 1700s and became widespread by the end of the century, when Americans spoke matter-of-factly about "the Gentlemen of learning and liberal professions."[314]

312. Joseph Priestley, *An Essay on a Course of Liberal Education for Civil and Active Life* (1764), in *Lectures on History and General Policy* (London: 1793), pp. 1, 22, 28–9; Benjamin Rush, "Observations upon the Study of the Latin and Greek Languages as a Branch of Liberal Education, with Hints of a Plan of Liberal Instruction without them" (1789), in *Essays, Literary, Moral, and Philosophical* (Philadelphia, 1798), pp. 21–56.

313. *Reports on the Course of Instruction in Yale College by a Committee of the Corporation and the Academical Faculty* (New Haven, CT, 1928), pp. 35–7; Adam Smith, *An Inquiry into the Nature and Causes of the Wealth of Nations* (1776), ed. Edwin Cannan (1904; Chicago, 1976), bk. 1, ch. 10, pt. 1.

314. Barnabas Bidwell, Letter of June 16, 1787, in *American Antiquarian Society Proceedings*, n.s., 4 (1887): 368.

Rhetorical: "servant unto all"

Theology was the most learned and liberal profession in the seventeenth- and early eighteenth-century American colonies, and the contemporaneous second and third moments in the rhetoric of professions reflect this preeminence. "PROFESSION in the most familiar and frequent apprehension" signified the Christian's "general calling"; the "general calling" was most fully realized in the minister's "particular calling," and the weight and dignity of the religious denotation was thereby extended to the occupational denotation. Since theology was linked with law, medicine, and education through their historical association in the graduate faculties of the medieval university, the newly dignified sense of "profession" was gradually applied to these other fields as well, initially by means of the qualifying adjectives "learned" and "liberal" and later by "profession" alone. Meanwhile the application of "profession" to lesser trades and callings was slowly, though never completely, sloughed away. By the early nineteenth century the shift in usage from theology to employment had proceeded to the point that one had to explain which "profession" was meant. For example, the adjective "religious" might be added to distinguish the theological profession from the employment, as did Baptist minister Robert Hall in 1811, whose work went through ten editions by 1850.[315] How people conceived and spoke of "profession" was therefore shaped by the nature of the preeminent "profession." But the influence of theology was not limited to the first three moments in the rhetoric of the term. The emphasizing and dignifying of the occupational sense of "profession" also informed the term with specifically religious import. Most important in this regard was an ethic of selfless service.

This ethic was, of course, a central tenet of Christian doctrine; and, in keeping with the influence of Pauline theology, selfless service was understood dialectically. The sacred text commanded Christians to give in order to receive, to love in order to be loved, to be selfless for the sake of self:

> So the last shall be first, and the first last.... For whosoever will save his life shall lose it; and whosoever will lose his life for my sake shall find it.... [W]hosoever will be great among you, shall be your minister; and whosoever will be your chiefest, shall be servant of all.[316]

Appropriately, the word "minister" here in the King James Version was translated from the Greek *diakonos* ("deacon"), which could also be rendered "servant," as it was in later translations. The ministers, being the exemplary professors, stretched the dialectic as tautly as possible. Clergy, above all others, were to follow Paul, who said, "I made myself servant unto all, that I might gain the more." Hence, John Cotton wrote: "We live by faith in our vocations, in that faith, *in serving God, serves men, and in serving men, serves God.*" And Cotton Mather proclaimed that the

---

315. Robert Hall, "On the Discouragements and Supports of the Christian Minister" (1811), in *Works*, 10th edn (London, 1850), vol. 1, pp. 229–30, 260.
316. *Matthew* 20: 16, 16: 25; *Mark* 10: 43–4.

purpose of the ministry is "TO SERVE GOD," which is accomplished by serving others; while John Wesley echoed Paul: a clergymen *"is the Servant of all."*[317]

To contend that the ministers were insincere in these pronouncements is as simplistic as to think that they were oblivious to earthly rewards. Only a dialectical conception comprehends the subtle tension bound into the self-abasing service ethic. The tension is expressed in the journal of a young college graduate contemplating a call to a pulpit in 1718: "Oh my insufficiency! Oh my great unworthiness, to be employed in the sacred and solemn work." The tension echoes in countless sermons, such as *The Greatness and Difficulty of the Work of the Ministry* (1732), *Ministers' Insufficiency for their Important and Difficult Work* (1742), *Ministers Insufficient of Themselves Rightly to Discharge the Duties of their Sacred Calling* (1742), and *The Ministerial Work Great and Important, Arduous and Difficult: Yet Pleasant Noble and Honorable* (1766).[318]

Into the early nineteenth century, as Baptist, Methodist and Presbyterian clergy itinerated further south and west, the message was the same: "The ablest preacher is but an earthen vessel.... If he must be the greatest, he will acquire the elevation by becoming the servant of all." For, "when you are engaged in the work of the Lord ... you learned what the Apostle Paul meant by the expression, *when I am weak then I am strong.*"[319] To interpret such statements as "the coy ambiguities of ... clerical rhetoric" or "the irony of clerical professionalism" is to project late twentieth-century ideology upon the colonial ministers.[320] It is also to misunderstand the dialectical subtlety of the service ethic, the commitment to which became a constituent aspect of a "profession" while the rhetorical transformation of the term was occurring under the influence of theology.[321]

317. I *Corinthians* 9: 19; Cotton, *The Way of Life,* pp. 442–3; Mather, *BONIFACIUS, An Essay upon the Good,* ch. 4; Mather, *Manuductio ad Ministerium, Directions for a Candidate of the Ministry,* pp. 120–45; Wesley, *An Address to the Clergy,* p. 216.

318. John Barnard, *Memoranda,* in S. J. Spaulding, "John Barnard: An Autobiographical Fragment," *Congregational Quarterly,* 4 (1862): 381–2; Thomas Clap, *The Greatness and Difficulty of the Work of the Ministry* (Boston, 1732); Israel Loring, *Ministers Insufficient of Themselves Rightly to Discharge the Duties of their Sacred Calling* (Boston, 1742); Gay, *Ministers' Insufficiency for their Important and Difficult Work*; Theophilus Hall, *The Ministerial Work Great and Important, Arduous and Difficult; yet Pleasant Noble, and Honorable* (Portsmouth, 1766).

319. Staughton, "What are the Qualifications of a Gospel Minister?', pp. 445–6; Thomas Baldwin, *The Christian Ministry, A Sermon* (Boston, 1814), pp. 14, 42; Gardinar Spring, *Memoirs of the Rev. Samuel J. Mills, Late Missionary to the South Western Section of the United States* (New York, 1820), pp. 234–5.

320. Botein, "Income and Ideology: Harvard-Trained Clergymen in Eighteenth-Century New England," p. 401; Schmotter, "The Irony of Clerical Professionalism: New England's Congregational Ministers and the Great Awakening," pp. 148–68; Youngs, *God's Messengers: Religious Leadership in Colonial New England,* pp. 1–2, 137–40.

321. Harold Laski's explanation that law and medicine by "a subtle alchemy in historic tradition" elevated the ethic of service among vocations is, I believe, historiographical alchemy. ("The Decline of the Professions," *Harper's Magazine,* 171 (1935): 676.) No more satisfactory is the view of Magali Sarfatti Larson who excludes theology from the professions and considers "the ideal of service" (which, in her view, disguises professional motives to control the market) to be an artifact of a nebulous "traditional moral law." *The Rise of*

In conclusion, it may be said that the preeminence of the colonial clergy resulted in the special weight and dignity of "profession" in its religious sense being extended to the occupational sense. The fact that "profession" came to refer to a corporate body of people; the fact that it began to denote the work, or "particular calling," which those people did; the fact that "profession" began to signify the most dignified kind of work undertaken by such groups of people; and the fact that a dialectical ethic of selfless service came to be associated with a "profession" – these developments are explained by the preeminence of theology as an architectonic and an occupation in the seventeenth and eighteenth centuries.

By the middle of the eighteenth century, a "profession" was becoming a very special kind of "particular calling" or work; and the introduction of the interchangeable terms "learned professions" and "liberal professions" reflected and extended this semantic transformation. At the same time, the particular nature of the clerical office informed the meaning of "profession" with an ethic of selfless service that was dialectically related to the high status and authority implied by the special weight and dignity. Henceforth, any learned and liberal professor would have to say with Paul: "I made myself servant unto all, that I might gain the more." None, however, could say it quite as firmly as a minister, so long as the highest ends and values of the culture were religious. For who then could disagree with Rev. Robert Hall: "In our *profession,* the full force and vigour of the mind may be exerted on that which will employ it forever; on *religion,* the final centre of repose; the goal to which all things tend."[322] And what college senior contemplating a career could fail to ponder the valedictory of Princeton President John Witherspoon:

> Some of you, I know, and more, I hope, are intended for the service of Christ in the ministry…. But I wish those who are destined for other employments may not sometimes make a comparison…. [A]t the close of life, it will be little comfort to a man that he must go to the place of torments, not as a minister, but as a lawyer, physician, soldier or merchant.[323]

Contemporaneous with President Witherspoon's valedictory, President Timothy Dwight at Yale warned his graduating seniors against the dangers of legal practice: "that meanness, that infernal knavery, which multiplies needless litigations, which retards the operation of justice, which, from court to court, upon the most trifling pretences, postpones trial to glean the last emptyings of a client's pocket, for unjust fees."[324] Notwithstanding such sentiments, the Reverends Witherspoon and Dwight were, in fact, making their own valedictory. Among the signers of the Declaration of Independence, which proclaimed a new architectonic in a new rhetoric, Witherspoon was the only clergyman amid the company of 25 lawyers.

Professionalism: A Sociological Analysis (Berkeley, CA, 1977), pp. 222–3. See, too, Edward T. Silva and Sheila A. Slaughter, *Serving Power: The Making of the Social Science Expert, 1860–1920* (Westport, CT, 1984), pp. 4, 9.

322. Hall, "On the Discouragements and Supports of the Christian Minister," p. 263.

323. John Witherspoon, "An Address to the Students of the Senior Class on the Lord's Day Preceding Commencement, September 23, 1775," in *Sermons* (Edinburgh, 1798), p. 278.

324. Timothy Dwight, "A Valedictory Address to the Young Gentlemen, Who Commenced Bachelors of Arts, at Yale College, July 25th, 1776," reprinted in *American Magazine*, 1 (January 1788): 101.

3

1720s – 1870s

LAW AND THE
PROFESSIONAL POLITY

The next fair young lady for whom I conceived an affection was *Miss Theology* ... yet we both saw the necessity of ceasing to indulge my fond thought of a union.... The present object of my soft attentions is a Miss Law, a grave and comely young lady, a little pitted with the small pox.... This young lady is of a prudent industrious turn, and though she does not possess at present any very great fortune, yet what she has in expectancy is considerable.

Hugh Henry Brackenridge, The United States Magazine: A Repository of History, Politics, and Literature *(1779)*

Lawyers are so numerous in all our populous towns.... They are here what the clergy were in past centuries with you; the reformation which clipped the clerical wings is the boast of that age, and the happiest event that could possibly happen; a reformation equally useful is now wanted to relieve us.

J. Hector St. John de Crèvecoeur, Letters from an American Farmer *(1782)*

To be eminent in *our* profession is to hold a place among the great ones of the earth, and ... leads to the highest objects of honorable ambition.... The history of our country is full of proof that the bar is the road to eminence.

Nathaniel Beverly Tucker, "A Lecture on the Study of the Law; Being an Introduction to a Course of Lectures on that Subject in the College of William and Mary" (1834)

The clergy in the early 1700s had not declined to a shadow of their seventeenth-century profession, as might be inferred from scholarly discussions of declension.

Nor were they modest parsons suddenly infected by the contagion of "professionalization," which gave rise to the Great Awakening, as some recent historians have suggested. Rather, the ministers, still the indisputably preeminent profession, gradually began to recognize and lament the fact that, due to a constellation of forces they could not control or even fully understand, they were losing authority, income, and status. By the end of the eighteenth century it was manifest that the "Holy Profession" had been eclipsed by "professional" lawyers. The stock of these attorneys enjoyed a bullish run from the mid-eighteenth century through the 1860s, despite periodic reverses in the post-Revolutionary, Jeffersonian, and Jacksonian periods. Indeed, if the noteworthy fortunes in the market of professions are made by starting in low and exiting high, then lawyers did better over this period than any other profession.

Cultural: "Polity eateth up Religion, and the Common wealth devours the Church"

The proposition that polity, jurisprudence, and lawyers eclipsed religion, theology and the clergy between the mid-eighteenth and the mid-nineteenth century is, from one historiographical perspective, entirely conventional. Distinguished authorities, such as Perry Miller and Edmund Morgan, have long testified to lawyers" "amazing rise ... to a position of political and intellectual domination" over this period.[1] However, while this longstanding view is still endorsed,[2] historians have come to criticize Miller's analysis of the legal profession between the Revolution and the Civil War.[3] This criticism comports with the alternative proposition that it was following the Civil War, particularly after the reformation of Harvard Law School

1. Perry Miller, *The Life of the Mind in America: From the Revolution to the Civil War* (Cambridge, MA, 1965), p. 109. Edmund Morgan, "The American Revolution Considered as an Intellectual Movement," in *Paths of American Thought*, ed. Arthur M. Schlesinger, Jr., and Morton White (Boston, 1963), pp. 11–33; Alan Heimert, *Religion and the American Mind from the Great Awakening to the Revolution* (Cambridge, MA, 1966), pp. 182–3, 451.

2. Jackson T. Main, *The Social Structure of Revolutionary America* (Princeton, NJ, 1965), pp. 203–6; David C. Humphrey, *From King's College to Columbia, 1746–1800* (New York, 1976), p. 225; Herbert A. Johnson, "John Jay: Lawyer in a Time of Transition," *University of Pennsylvania Law Review*, 124 (1976): 1260–92; William R. Johnson, *Schooled Lawyers: A Study in the Clash of Professional Cultures* (New York, 1978), p. 173; A. G. Roeber, *Faithful Magistrates and Republican Lawyers: Creators of Virginia Legal Culture, 1680–1810* (Chapel Hill, NC, 1981), pp. xix, 257, chs. 4–6.

3. Miller, *The Life of the Mind in America: From the Revolution to the Civil War*, pp. 99–265. See Richard M. Cover, *Justice Accused: Antislavery and the Judicial Process* (New Haven, CT, 1975), p. 292 (n. 33); Wythe Holt, "Now and Then: The Uncertain State of Nineteenth-Century American Legal History," *Indiana Law Review*, 7 (1974): 635; Stephen Botein, "Professional History Reconsidered," *AJLH*, 21 (1977): 61–2; Maxwell Bloomfield, *American Lawyers in a Changing Society, 1776–1876* (Cambridge, MA, 1976), pp. 137, 151, 239–65, 360n. Some scholars emphasize early eighteenth-century developments in the legal profession of Massachusetts: Gerard W. Gawalt, "Sources of Anti-Lawyer Sentiment in Massachusetts, 1740–1840," *AJLH*, 14 (1970): 285–6; John M. Murrin, "The Legal

in the 1870s, that attorneys became "the new high priests" displacing the clergy. Indeed, it is said that lawyers were "without a profession ... until the end of the nineteenth century."[4]

This historiographical disagreement must be interpreted in light of the testimony from yet other eminent scholars that, somewhere in some fashion, law surpassed theology during every half century between the death of Thomas Aquinas and the ascension of Roscoe Pound to be dean of Harvard Law School in 1916. It has been said that jurists displaced clerics in the early fourteenth-century common law of England, the late fourteenth-century civil law of Switzerland, the mid-fifteenth century civil law of Germany, and the late fifteenth-century Court of the Exchequer in England.[5] Other scholars contend that the displacement occurred in England only in the mid-sixteenth century[6] or the early seventeenth century.[7] Thus, in 1656 William Langley observed:

Transformation: The Bench and Bar of Eighteenth-Century Massachusetts" (1971), in *Colonial America,* ed. Stanley M. Katz and John M. Murrin, 3d edn (New York, 1983), pp. 540–72; David H. Flaherty, "Criminal Practice in Provincial Massachusetts," in *Law in Colonial Massachusetts, 1630–1800* (Boston, 1984), pp. 191–242.

4. Gerard W. Gawalt, ed., *The New High Priests: Lawyers in Post-Civil War America* (Westport, CT, 1984), passim; Richard L. Abel, *American Lawyers* (New York, 1978), p. 40. See Jerold S. Auerbach, *Unequal Justice: Lawyers and Social Change in Modern America* (New York, 1976), ch. 3; Kermit L. Hall, *The Magic Mirror: Law in American History* (New York, 1989), p. 211. The literature associating professionalization with university-based professional schools naturally emphasizes the period after 1860. See Josef Redlich, *The Common Law and the Case Method in American University Law Schools* (New York, 1914); Alfred Z. Reed, *Training for the Public Profession of the Law* (New York, 1921); Arthur E. Sutherland, *The Law at Harvard: A History of Ideas and Men, 1817–1967* (Cambridge, MA, 1967), pts. 4–7; Robert Stevens, *Law School: Legal Education in America from the 1850s to the 1980s* (Chapel Hill, NC, 1983). In fact, recent works on legal education in the nineteenth century have been criticized for "excessive nostalgia" about the "unprofessionalized" pre-Civil War bar "which allegedly served the egalitarian impulses of the early republic." Frederic C. Jaher, "The Education of American Lawyers," *HEQ*, 21 (1981): 105–13.

5. J. H. Baker, *An Introduction to English Legal History,* 2d edn (London, 1979), ch. 10; Sven Stelling-Michaud, *"La Diffusion du droit romain en Suisse, étudiants Suisses à l'étranger et leur activité professionelle ultérieure juridique, manuscrits et bibliothèques," IUS ROMANUM MEDII AEVI* (1977), pars V, no. 12, pp. 13–4; Helmut Coing, "Römisches Recht in Deutschland," *IUS ROMANUM MEDII AEVI* (1964), pars V, no. 8, pp. 77–90; J. H. Baker, "The English Legal Profession, 1450–1550," in *Lawyers in Early Modern Europe and America,* ed. Wilfrid R. Prest (New York, 1981), p. 20.

6. Wilfrid R. Prest, *The Inns of Court under Elizabeth I and the Early Stuarts, 1590–1640* (London, 1972), pp. 21–2. See Joan Simon, *Education and Society in Tudor England* (Cambridge, UK, 1966), pp. 247–9; Rosemary O'Day, *The English Clergy: The Emergence and Consolidation of a Profession, 1558–1642* (Leicester, UK, 1979), p. 244; Wilfrid R. Prest, "The English Bar, 1550–1700," in *Lawyers in Early Modern Europe and America,* ed. Prest (New York, 1981), pp. 69, 73.

7. C. W. Brooks, "The Common Lawyers in England, c.1558–1642," in *Lawyers in Early Modern Europe and America,* ed. Wilfred R. Prest (New York, 1981), p. 42; Michael Landon, *The Triumph of the Lawyers: Their Role in English Politics, 1678–1689* (University, AL, 1970), p. 15; Wilfrid R. Prest, *The Rise of the Barristers: A Social History of the English Bar, 1590–1640* (London, 1987).

Time was that Religion did eat up Poli[t]y, and the Church devoured the
Common wealth, but now Poli[t]y eateth up Religion, and the Common wealth
devours the Church.[8]

Nevertheless, the ensuing decline of legal education at the Inns of Court supports
the claim that in the eighteenth century "the Church ... offered greater security
and surer prospects of advancement than did the highly competitive and crowded
bar."[9] Then, too, there is evidence that American lawyers had not yet eclipsed the
clergy at the end of the nineteenth century. As late as 1900, for example, the aggregate endowment of divinity schools in the United States was nine times the endowment of law schools, and admissions standards for the former were uniformly
higher than for the latter.[10] Hence, it was not clear that law "eateth up Religion"
even at the beginning of the twentieth century.

These conflicting opinions reflect, in part, the different criteria and purposes
adopted by scholars. With respect to the historiographical disagreements regarding
American lawyers, one should note that historians who emphasize the revolutionary
and antebellum rise of attorneys over ministers, such as Morgan and Miller, tend to
be those who have looked closely at the colonial period, particularly the clergy. In
contrast, scholars who emphasize the postbellum ascension, such as Robert Stevens,
tend to assume that after the Revolution "with little by way of competing professions, the new nation was almost inevitably bound to rely on lawyers to perform
a wide range of functions.... These facts suggest that the legal profession was
virtually indestructible, or at least that Karl Llewellyn was right in postulating that
every society has certain 'lawyer-jobs'.... In American society, there was virtually
no profession competing for such 'jobs'."[11]

But the legal profession was very much destructible, as we have seen. The clergy
had long been fulfilling "lawyer-jobs" and were still competitive at the end of the
eighteenth century. It is more accurate to say that lawyers began to fill "clergy-
jobs," and even more accurate to say that attorneys turned "clergy-jobs" into
"lawyer-jobs." Consequently, one can concede to Stevens, Llewellyn, and others
that lawyers would become the "new high priests" after the Civil War, while
affirming with Morgan and Miller that law had already surpassed theology and,
indeed, attained preeminence well before 1860. Certainly, the legal profession was
not challenged either by "the profession of educators" – "the *dernier ressort*" for
aspiring youths, according to a prize-winning essay of 1839 – or by medicine – "the

8. William Langley, *The Persecuted Minister, In defence of the Ministerie* (London, 1656),
p. 159. See Edward Coke, *The Reports ... in English in Thirteen Chapters Compleat* (London,
1738), no. 2, Pref., pp. x–xi.

9. Daniel Duman, "The English Bar in the Georgian Era," in *Lawyers in Early Modern
Europe and America*, ed. Wilfrid R. Prest (New York, 1981), p. 95. Cf. Prest, *The Inns of
Court under Elizabeth I and the Early Stuarts, 1590–1640*, chs. 4, 6; Prest, "The English Bar,
1550–1700," pp. 78–81; Anthony Russell, *The Clerical Profession* (London, 1980), ch. 3;
Geoffrey Holmes, *Augustan England: Professions, State, and Society, 1680–1730* (London,
1982), p. 115; Daniel Duman, *The English and Colonial Bars in the Nineteenth Century*
(London, 1983), ch. 7.

10. Henry L. Taylor and James R. Parsons, Jr., *Professional Education in the United States*
(Albany, NY, 1900), pp. 10–2, 19–21.

11. Stevens, *Law School ... from the 1850s to the 1980s*, pp. 7–9.

dernier resort of all Blockheads" according to the son of a prominent North Carolina lawyer in 1828.[12]

This is not to say that hostility toward lawyers disappeared during or after the Revolution.[13] In the late 1760s and 1770s lawyers and courts were the target of riots in New Jersey, South Carolina, and North Carolina. More than a few of the increasing minority of college graduates who ventured into the bench or bar, such as William Tisdale (HC 1755), Alexander Martin (PC 1756), and Edmund Fanning (YC 1757), were beaten in these uprisings.[14] Lawyers and courts were also targeted in the 1780s in Shays's Rebellion in Massachusetts and the Camden court protest in South Carolina, as well as in the Whiskey Rebellion in western Pennsylvania in 1794.[15] There were special reasons for the anti-lawyer animus following the Revolution. Many leading attorneys had been loyalists, and the dislike of England naturally extended to things English, such as the common law. In addition, Revolutionary thinking led easily to attacking elites, including the bench and bar. But the most significant factor was that lawyers and courts were involved in the collection of debts and taxes, leading them to be associated with the oppressive economic conditions of the post-war recession. This association was strengthened in states such as North Carolina, where most attorneys belonged to the political opposition to the party of debtors and farmers.[16]

Even after the fervor and perturbation of the Revolution had subsided, lawyers continued to be satirized and criticized. In Pittsburgh in 1808 George Watterston published *The Lawyer, or, Man as He Ought Not To Be.* In Boston in 1819 the previously printed essays of "Honestus" were collected and reissued in *Observations on the Pernicious Practice of the Law.* Meanwhile, as Jeffersonian Republicans

---

12. John A. Heraud, "Expediency and Means of Elevating the Profession of the Educator in the Public Estimation," in *The Educator. Prize Essays on the Means and Expediency of Elevating the Profession of the Educator in Society* (London, 1839), p. 143; Anton-Hermann Chroust, *The Rise of the Legal Profession in America* (Norman, OK, 1965), vol. 2, p. 112.

13. On the continuing animus, see Charles Warren, *A History of the American Bar* (Boston, 1911), pp. 211–32; Erwin N. Griswold, *Law and Lawyers in the United States* (Cambridge, MA, 1964), pp. 12–25; Heimert, *Religion and the American Mind from the Great Awakening to the Revolution*, pp. 180–2; Lawrence M. Friedman, *A History of American Law*, 2d edn (New York, 1985), pp. 94ff., 303ff.; Bloomfield, *American Lawyers in a Changing Society, 1776–1876,* ch. 2.

14. *Princetonians,* vol. 1, pp. 157–8; *Harvard Graduates,* vol. 13, p. 648; vol. 14, pp. 162–5.

15. Michael S. Hindus, *Prison and Plantation: Crime, Justice, and Authority in Massachusetts and South Carolina, 1767–1878* (Chapel Hill, NC, 1980), p. 5; David R. Chesnutt, " 'Greedy Party Work': The South Carolina Election of 1768," in *Party and Political Opposition in Revolutionary America,* ed. Patricia U. Bonomi (Tarrytown, NY, 1980), pp. 70–86.

16. Norman K. Risjord, *Chesapeake Politics, 1781–1800* (New York, 1978), p. 92, ch. 6. For descriptions of post-revolutionary animus, see Roscoe Pound, *The Lawyer from Antiquity to Modern Times* (St. Paul, MN, 1953), p. 233; Chroust, *The Rise of the Legal Profession in America,* vol. 2, ch. 1; Richard E. Ellis, *The Jeffersonian Crisis: Courts and Politics in the Young Republic* (New York, 1971), ch. 8. For views challenging the strength of that animus, see Gerard W. Gawalt, *The Promise of Power: The Emergence of the Legal Profession in Massachusetts, 1760–1840* (Westport, CT, 1979), ch. 2; Dennis R. Nolan, "The Effect of the Revolution on the Bar: The Maryland Experience," *Virginia Law Review,* 62 (1976): 969–90.

championed the agrarian and debtor classes against the Federalist judiciary in the first decade of the nineteenth century, a Delaware landowner published the most influential anti-lawyer treatise in the middle states: *The Reformation of Lawsuits, ... Justice Made Cheap, Speedy and Brought Home to Every Man's Door.*[17] Similar sentiments in subsequent decades were expressed by or portrayed in classic American literature: James Fenimore Cooper's *The Pioneers* (1823, 1832), Nathaniel Hawthorne's *The House of the Seven Gables* (1851), and Herman Melville's "Bartleby the Scrivener" (1856).

No less did children's literature adopt the theme. Throughout American schoolbooks of the early nineteenth century, "lawyers as a class are looked on with suspicion. The law is regarded generally as a parasitic occupation." For example, the only attorney portrayed in Noah Webster's immensely popular *American Spelling Book* is depicted as a hypocrite protecting his self-interest against a farmer.[18] Meanwhile the clergy continued to express reservations about the bar. After surveying Oneida County for the state of New York, a Presbyterian minister noted in his census report of 1795: "Thank God we have no lawyers." On behalf of the Mormons, Brigham Young stated in the second quarter of the nineteenth century, "I swear by the God of Heaven that we will not spend money in feeing Lawyers.... I had rather have a six shooter than all the lawyers in Illinois."[19]

In all these complaints there appeared certain recurring themes, which had persisted from the English Revolution (1640–60), if not Thomas More's *Utopia.*[20] Apart from being associated with privileged elites, the bar was blamed for "the expence and difficulty of obtaining the decision of courts," which David Ramsay of South Carolina noted in 1789. This financial complaint was compounded by the laity's faith in native intuition and common sense, because jurists seemed intent on transforming words "obvious and plain" into "unintelligible jargon," as Robert Coram observed in Delaware in 1791.[21] In addition, the adversarial nature of

---

17. George Watterston, *The Lawyer, or, Man as He Ought Not To Be. A Tale* (Pittsburgh, PA, 1808); Honestus [Benjamin Austin], *Observations on the Pernicious Practice of the Law* (1786, 1819), reprinted in *AJLH,* 13 (1969): 241–302; [Jesse Higgins], *Sampson against the Philistines; or, The Reformation of Lawsuits, ... Justice Made Cheap, Speedy and Brought Home to Every Man's Door* (Philadelphia, 1805); Bloomfield, *American Lawyers in a Changing Society, 1776–1876,* p. 46.

18. Quotation is from Ruth M. Elson, *Guardians of Tradition: American Schoolbooks of the Nineteenth Century* (Lincoln, NE, 1964), p. 26. Noah Webster, *The American Spelling Book, containing the Rudiments of the English Language* (Middletown, CT, 1831), fable 8; Richard M. Rollins, *The Long Journey of Noah Webster* (Philadelphia, 1980), pp. 19–22, 34–5. First published in 1783, the speller sold 20 million copies by 1829.

19. Quotations are from *Princetonians,* vol. 2, p. 85; Orma Linford, "The Mormons, the Law, and the Territory of Utah," *AJLH,* 23 (1979): 223–4.

20. Thomas More, *Utopia* (1515, tr. 1551), ed. Edward Surtz (New Haven, CT, 1964), p. 114; Prest, *The Inns of Court ... 1590–1640,* p. 75. O'Day, *The English Clergy ... 1558–1642,* chs. 14–5; G. B. Warden, "The Rhode Island Civil Code of 1647," in *Saints and Revolutionaries,* ed. David D. Hall et al. (New York, 1984), pp. 138–51; David Punter, "Fictional Representation of the Law in the Eighteenth Century," *Eighteenth-Century Studies,* 16 (1982): 47.

21. David Ramsay, *The History of the American Revolution* (Philadelphia, 1789), vol. 2,

Anglo-American jurisprudence attracted criticism. The ancillary complaint that lawyers manufactured disputes was also voiced, although it was no less true that lawyers simply provided the vehicle for people to act on existing grievances. Venturing into the newly opened lands of Alabama and Mississippi, attorney Joseph Baldwin described the "Old Southwest" of 1836 as "that sunny land of fussing, quarrelling, murdering, violation of contracts, and the whole catalogue of … litigation … a legal Utopia, peopled by a race of eager litigants."[22]

If the hostility toward law was longstanding, the novel development near the turn of the century was the counterbalancing approbation. Directed first to the revolutionary polity and political institutions, respect and admiration were increasingly accorded to legal institutions and the individuals who led them. By the 1830s the public was avidly reading about attorneys climbing from rags to riches while defending the right and vanquishing injustice, exploits recounted in popular literature such as *Clinton Bradshaw; or, The Adventures of a Lawyer* (1835) by Frederick W. Thomas, *Jonas A Judge; or, A Law Among the Boys* (1840) by Jacob Abbott, and *Biographical Sketches of Eminent American Lawyers Now Living* (1852) by John Livingston. The genre culminated in Emma Southworth's *Ishmael* (1864), which was based loosely on the life of William Wirt, the exemplar of the poor orphan who rose to honor, fame, and wealth through the law. Wirt himself was the first clarion of the law as the route to both success and virtue for the young American, proclaiming the theme in *Sketches of the Life and Character of Patrick Henry* (1817), which went through 25 editions by 1871.[23]

In sum, "the antiprofessional movement … was simply overwhelmed by a professional countermovement"[24] on the part of the bench and bar between the 1750s and the 1850s. To fathom how and why this happened, as well as the meaning of the new term "professional," we must first examine the decline of the clergy and the accompanying shift to a new architectonic of culture. With this understanding, we will be able to evaluate the fourth moment in the rhetoric of "profession" and, finally, the overwhelming rise of "professional" lawyers in comparison to the other liberal and learned professions.

Comparative: "liberal warfare against the clergy"

The displacement of religion and the clergy culminated in the disestablishment of state churches, and it is significant that the disestablishment occurred largely

---

pp. 312–3; Robert Coram, "Political Inquiries" (1791), reprinted in *Essays on Education in the Early Republic*, ed. Frederick Rudolph (Cambridge, 1965), p. 95.

22. Joseph G. Baldwin, *The Flush Times of Alabama and Mississippi, A Series of Sketches* (1853; Baton Rouge, LA, 1987), pp. 47–8.

23. For a discussion and list of this literature, see Bloomfield, *American Lawyers in a Changing Society, 1776–1876*, pp. 163–90. Brook Thomas has argued that prominent antebellum literature in which attorneys are ostensibly condemned draws upon the dominant jurisprudence enshrining "rule of law." *Cross-examinations of Law and Literature: Cooper, Hawthorne, Stowe, and Melville* (Cambridge, UK, 1987).

24. William E. Nelson, *Americanization of the Common Law: The Impact of Legal Change on Massachusetts Society, 1760–1830* (Cambridge, MA, 1975), p. 70.

during the Revolution. To be sure, certain colonies, notably Rhode Island and Pennsylvania, had always prohibited such establishments in the form of state-mandated support for one sect, and the privileges of the religious establishments even in Massachusetts and Virginia had been eroding for some time.[25] Moreover, the separation from England would have meant the disestablishment of the Anglican church regardless of other changes in cultural values. Nevertheless, only revolutionary conceptions of polity could have sustained the view that "our civil rights have no dependence on our religious opinions, any more than our opinions in physics or geometry," as stated Virginia's renowned "Act for Establishing Religious Freedom" (1786).[26] With this in mind, most jurisdictions eliminated required maintenance of churches and clergy in the late 1770s, either by legislation, as in Virginia, or with the passage of a new state constitution, as in Maryland.[27] The stiff-necked New Englanders followed more slowly: Connecticut in 1818, New Hampshire in 1819, and, last of all, Massachusetts in 1833.

Sometimes attorneys led the movement to separate church and state, especially in New York in the 1750s, where a "'triumvirate' of antiprelatic lawyers" vociferously attacked the "little Popes."[28] But such activities by members of the chief competing profession were not the root cause of the decline of the clergy. The erosion of ministers' status and authority had been evidenced for some time by a growing number of disputes with parishioners. Needless to say, pastoral quarrels were as old as Christianity and had long exhibited the frailties that eternally beset human beings. But early in the eighteenth century quarrels that ought to have been settled amicably, such as over the location of a new meetinghouse, began to result in the dissolution of ministries, as happened to Rev. Timothy Woodbridge in Connecticut and Rev. George Daman in Vermont.[29]

The reasons for this erosion are multiple and complex, yet three stand out prominently: the egalitarian enthusiasm of the Great Awakening, the changing economic conditions, and the "enlightened" shift toward "liberal" thinking that

---

25. For example, in the late 1720s and 1730s exemptions or "pay overs" were allowed to non-Congregationalists in Massachusetts, while in Virginia the 1744 penal code omitted many of the religious and moral offenses of the 1705 code. *Acts of Massachusetts Bay*, vol. 2, p. 459 (1727); vol. 2, p. 494 (1728); *Statutes of Virginia*, vol. 3, pp. 358–62 (1705), vol. 5, pp. 225–6 (1744).

26. *Statutes of Virginia*, vol. 12, p. 85. See Carl Bridenbaugh, *Mitre and Sceptre: Trans-atlantic Faiths, Ideas, Personalities and Politics* (New York, 1962), pp. 171–340; Rhys Isaac, *The Transformation of Virginia, 1740–1790* (Chapel Hill, NC, 1982), ch. 9.

27. *Statutes of Virginia*, vol. 9, pp. 164–6; vol. 10, pp. 197–8; "The Declaration of Rights," art. 33, in *Proceedings of the Convention of the Province of Maryland of Maryland Held at Annapolis, in 1774, 1775, & 1776* (Annapolis, 1836), pp. 314–5; Thomas O. Hanley, *The American Revolution and Religion, Maryland, 1770–1800* (Washington, DC, 1971), ch. 3; Thomas J. Curry, *The First Freedoms: Church and State in America to the Passage of the First Amendment* (New York, 1986), chs. 5, 6, 7.

28. Quotations are respectively from George Bancroft, *History of the United States of America from the Discovery of the Continent* (New York, 1890), vol. 3, p. 283; [William Livingston], *Independent Reflector* (January 4, 1753): 93.

29. *Yale Graduates*, vol. 1, pp. 57–8; *Harvard Graduates*, vol. 14, pp. 7–8.

was partly sponsored by "liberal Christians." Each factor by itself would have constituted a severe trial for the clergy, but over the second and third quarters of the eighteenth century they arrived as successive shocks or, worse, combined together to shake the strongest pastorate. By the end of the eighteenth century, clergymen felt less secure and often unappreciated. Looking back on his troubled ministry in Massachusetts from 1763 to 1783, Rev. Archibald Campbell remarked, "I used to preach there, but they were cruel and drove me away and ruined me." The same sentiment was doubtlessly on the mind of Lewis Beebe, who was dismissed from his Vermont parish in 1791. The bitter congregation voted that every mention of his name should be struck from the church records, while Rev. Beebe gave up the ministry, moved to New York, and opened a liquor store. Observing such events, Rev. Moses Hemmenway, who served a church in Maine from 1759 to 1810, suggested that ordaining a new minister had become like inviting a cat into a household where "come pretty kitty" soon became "scat, you bitch."[30]

The Great Awakening has traditionally been regarded as an eruption of religious enthusiasm anticipated by Solomon Stoddard and Theodorus Frelinghuysen in the 1720s, ignited by Jonathan Edwards in the mid-1730s, and fueled by George Whitefield in the early 1740s. Recently, the Awakening has been re-interpreted as a protest against social and economic elites aligned with the established clergy, analogous to the revivalism during the Salem witchcraft trials.[31] Another revisionist view construes the Awakening as a veiled attempt to elevate clerical status by stimulating religious enthusiasm. "[I]nstead of fulfilling the purpose of the ministerial profession, the Great Awakening actually undermined the position of the clergy," according to this view. The moral lesson clearly intended here is that those who attempt to "professionalize" end up losing whatever status and authority they enjoyed before the attempt.[32] These interpretations of the Great Awakening have been criticized[33] amid a large scholarly literature that addresses the complex events and debates of the 1730s and 1740s.[34] Without reviewing all these arguments,

30. *Harvard Graduates,* vol. 13, p. 615; vol. 15, p. 28; *Yale Graduates,* vol. 3, p. 404.

31. Paul Boyer and Stephen Nissenbaum, *Salem Possessed: The Social Origins of Witchcraft* (Cambridge, MA, 1974), pp. 25–30; Gary B. Nash, *The Urban Crucible: Social Change, Political Consciousness, and the Origins of the American Revolution* (New York, 1979), ch. 8.

32. J. William T. Youngs, Jr., *God's Messengers: Religious Leadership in Colonial New England, 1700–1750* (Baltimore, MD, 1976), p. 121. See, too, Heimert, *Religion and the American Mind from the Great Awakening to the Revolution,* pp. 165–6; James W. Schmotter, "Ministerial Careers in Eighteenth-Century New England: The Social Context, 1700–1750," *Journal of Social History,* 9 (1975): 263; Schmotter, "The Irony of Clerical Professionalism: New England's Congregational Minsters and the Great Awakening," *American Quarterly,* 31 (1979): 148–68.

33. See Richard D. Birdsall, "The Second Great Awakening and the New England Social Order," *Church History,* 39 (1970): 345–65; Harry S. Stout, "The Great Awakening in New England Reconsidered: The New England Clergy," *Journal of Social History,* 8 (1974): 21–47. David Harlan, *Clergy and the Great Awakening in New England* (Ann Arbor, MI, 1980), pp. 11–6, 39.

34. Here and below, I draw from Wesley M. Gewehr, *The Great Awakening in Virginia, 1740–1790* (Durham, NC, 1930); William L. Lumpkin, *Baptist Foundations in the South:*

suffice it to say that the traditional view fits most closely with the theological architectonic of colonial culture posited here. From this perspective the Great Awakening must be considered fundamentally a religious revival that profoundly unbalanced the Protestant idea of clerical authority.

That idea asserted "a high conception both of the ministry and of the power of the congregation over the ministry," and produced "two conflicting images" of the clergy – "a gentleman, exalted and elevated through character, erudition, and professional status" and "a man embodying the religious sentiments of the common folk."[35] This dialectical view of authority – the "Achilles' heel of Protestantism" – is exemplified in Richard Baxter's assertions that ultimate authority lies in the sacred text, although the laity are not to use this fact as a reason to disobey ministers, unless the ministers err in their interpretation of the text.[36] With this in mind, the Calvinist clergy translated the text into the language of the laity, and began publishing in 1560 a small, portable edition with numbered verses. Moreover, they urged – required when they could – that all laymen learn to read the sacred text and study it closely. While faithful to their "profession," these ministers were nevertheless, in the terms of modern scholarship, breaking down "the tyranny of the experts."[37] For, armed with a numerically versified translation, any Christian could "try the Preachers ... and see whether those things are so, that such preachers say."[38]

No cleric intended, of course, that *his* reading of scripture should be challenged by "a Cobler, Robine, a Sadler, Sammon, a Sho-maker, Barde, a Smith" or any of the "unlettered, unskillful Laicks" who possessed a numerically versified, pocketbook translation.[39] The colonial ministers for a long period were able to check the

---

Tracing through the Separates the Influence of the Great Awakening, 1754–1787 (Nashville, TN, 1961); C. C. Goen, *Revivalism and Separatism in New England, 1740–1800: Strict Congregationalists and Separate Baptists in the Great Awakening* (New Haven, CT, 1962); Douglas Sloan, *The Scottish Enlightenment and the American College Ideal* (New York, 1971), chs. 2, 3; Patricia U. Bonomi, *Under the Cope of Heaven: Religion, Society, and Politics in Colonial America* (New York, 1986), ch. 5.

35. Quotations are from Wilhelm Pauck, "The Ministry in the Time of the Continental Reformation," in *The Ministry in Historical Perspectives*, ed. H. Richard Niebuhr and Daniel D. Williams (New York, 1956), p. 113; E. Brooks Holifield, *The Gentleman Theologians: American Theology in Southern Culture 1795–1860* (Durham, NC, 1978), p. 24.

36. Robert M. Brown, *The Spirit of Protestantism* (New York, 1961), ch. 14; Richard Baxter, "The Propositions of the Ministers" of the Worcestershire Association, 1653, no. XV, in *Gildas Salvianus: The Reformed Pastor by Richard Baxter 1656*, ed. John T. Wilkinson, 2d edn (London, 1950), app. 1, p. 178. See H. Richard Niebuhr, *The Kingdom of God in America* (New York, 1937), pp. 34–6; Gillian R. Evans, *The Language and Logic of the Bible: The Road to Reformation* (Cambridge, UK, 1986).

37. Jethro K. Liebermann, *The Tyranny of the Experts: How Professionals are Closing the Open Society* (New York, 1970); Magali Sarfatti Larson, "The Production of Expertise and the Constitution of Expert Power," in *The Authority of Experts: Studies in History and Theory*, ed. Thomas L. Haskell (Bloomington, IN, 1984), pp. 28–80.

38. *The Anabaptists Late Protestation. Or, their Resolution to Depart the City of London* (n.p., 1647), p. 3.

39. *Tub-Preachers overturn'd. Or, Independency to be abandon'd and abhor'd as destructive to the Majestracy and Ministery of the Church and Commonwealth of England* (London, 1647),

latent threat to their authority arising from the intractable problem of establishing a correct and consistent interpretation of scripture. But the challenge to religious leadership inevitably surfaced with the burst of religious enthusiasm in the 1720s, 1730s, and 1740s. Believers within and without the parishes challenged the settled ministers for their shortcomings in piety, character, and doctrine. Most ministers were put on the defensive, and more than a few were forced out of their pulpits, as happened to Isaac Burr in 1745, after twenty years in his Worcester parish.[40]

The established clergy responded by emphasizing the opposite pole of the dialectic of authority: the eminence of learned clergy. Sermons in the second quarter of the eighteenth century increasingly proclaimed this theme. The prominent minister Ebenezer Gay, for example, moved from equalitarian pronouncements, such as *Ministers are Men of Like Passions with Others* in 1725, to qualified aggrandizements, such as *Ministers' Insufficiency for their Important and Difficult Work* in 1742, and finally to grand claims for the clerical office in the 1750s.[41] Such responses led to a debate over the need for a "learned minister," a controversy that has frequently been examined and involves many of the perennial tensions in subsequent United States' culture: intellect versus sentiment, sophisticated learning versus common sense, merited privilege versus the essential equality of all human beings. These tensions were no more reconcilable than the clergy's responses were effective in bringing back the unquestioning acceptance of ministerial authority. By 1750 the Awakening had ebbed, leaving "institutions shattered, authority weakened, traditions challenged, a social landscape fundamentally changed."[42]

This change would not have been so dramatic apart from contemporaneous economic developments. By the early eighteenth century most of the desirable and easily accessible land in New England and the Chesapeake region had been claimed or exhausted by overuse. As a result, there was limited good land to grant to new ministers, whose settlements were commensurately reduced in value.[43] Trouble-

---

title page; Henry Denne, *A Den of Thieves Discovered, Or Certain Errours and False Doctrines* (London, 1643), p. 16.

40. *Yale Graduates,* vol. 1, p. 164. See Youngs, *God's Messengers: Religious Leadership in Colonial New England,* p. 135, appendix.

41. Ebenezer Gay, *Ministers are Men of Like Passions with Others* (Boston, 1725); *Ministers' Insufficiency for their Important and Difficult Work* (Boston, 1742); *The Mystery of the Seven Stars in Christ's Right Hand* (Boston, 1752); Robert J. Wilson, III, *The Benevolent Deity: Ebenezer Gay and the Rise of Rational Religion in New England* (Philadelphia, 1984), pp. 132, 155; Youngs, *God's Messengers: Religious Leadership in Colonial New England,* pp. 9–10, 35–6.

42. Howard Miller, *The Revolutionary College: American Presbyterian Higher Education, 1707–1837* (New York, 1976), p. 55.

43. Richard L. Bushman, *From Puritan to Yankee: Character and the Social Order in Connecticut, 1690–1765* (Cambridge, MA, 1967), chs. 3, 6; Robert A. Gross, *The Minutemen and their World* (New York, 1976), pp. 78–9; Richard B. Sheridan, "The Domestic Economy," in *Colonial British America,* ed. Jack P. Greene and J. R. Pole (Baltimore, MD, 1984), pp. 56–8. By 1816, former President of Yale Timothy Dwight noted: "I wish every minister in New England had a farm.... I presume, however, that scarcely one in fifty can boast of such a possession." *Travels in New England and New York* (1822; Cambridge, MA, 1969), vol. 4, p. 317.

some enough, that problem was soon overshadowed by the horrendous inflation that occurred in the second quarter of the eighteenth century. The first twinges were felt in the second decade of the 1700s. David Parsons, for example, was ordained in Massachusetts in 1709, and by 1720 he complained that his salary was "not so Good by A third as it was when he first settled heer." Although Parsons' parish did not respond, others, such as Charlestown, nearly doubled their minister's salary over the same decade.[44]

It is important to recognize the novelty of raising a salary in this way. The ministerial contracts of young college graduates had occasionally included automatic raises that were triggered when the young man was formally ordained, married, or had children. But apart from those extraordinary circumstances, the minister was expected to be satisfied with a fixed income. Such was still the case when Newark, New Jersey, installed Jabez Wakeman in 1700.[45] But early in the eighteenth century a shortage of labor and commodities, particularly in the middle colonies and New England, inflated wages and prices, and new kinds of escalator clauses began to appear in ministerial contracts. In 1713, for example, the new minister of Medford, Massachusetts, included a provision that his salary of £55 was to be raised £2 per year.

By the 1720s it was not uncommon for clergy to state an equivalency of their salary in specie or commodities, as well as in the rapidly inflating paper currencies. Most prudent and fortunate were those ministers who stipulated an equivalency in ounces of silver, such as Benjamin Bass and Theophilus Pickering. Negotiating with his prospective church in Connecticut, John Wadsworth summed up the situation in 1729: "As touching the annual salary, I look upon an hundred and ten pounds as the stated sum, but not unalterable. Times are changeable, and we in time. If for my comfortable maintenance, £150, £200, or £300 per annum is necessary, as is requisite in Carolina, I shall expect it to be freely offered; on the contrary, if ten be sufficient, I remit the hundred."[46] Through the 1730s the inflation continued, and then reached crisis proportions by the late 1740s. Ordained in Connecticut in 1725 at a salary of £100, Peter Reynolds negotiated raises to £600 over these decades. In 1740 Abner Bayley was ordained in New Hampshire at a salary of £150, which was raised to £1,000 in 1762. The currency in New Hampshire, like the Carolinas, was particularly inflated, and most colonies had already returned to specie by 1760. Ministerial salaries then dropped to between £60 and £100, where they generally remained until the Revolution.[47]

Despite the stupendous raises, the ministers lost in a number of respects over these decades. For one thing, the raises generally fell far short of the decline in real value. When Isaiah Dunster stated in 1747 that an offer of a £350 salary and a

---

44. *Harvard Graduates*, vol. 5, pp. 240–3, 283–6, 293.

45. *Harvard Graduates*, vol. 4, pp. 391–2.

46. *Harvard Graduates*, vol. 5, p. 441; vol. 6, pp. 73, 331. Quotation is from vol. 7, p. 266.

47. *Harvard Graduates*, vol. 6, p. 398; vol. 10; pp. 11–3; vol. 13, p. 227. See, too, Appendix 1; Stephen Botein, "Income and Ideology: Harvard-Trained Clergymen in Eighteenth-Century New England," *Eighteenth-Century Studies*, 13 (1980): 400–3; John J. McCusker, *Money and Exchange in Europe and America, 1660–1775: A Handbook* (Chapel Hill, NC, 1978), pp. 125–278.

£600 settlement was not enough, his prospective church replied that it was more than the neighboring ministers were receiving, to which Dunster responded that it was less than the value of the initial salary of those same ministers. Indeed, the salary offered Dunster was the amount being paid in 1748 to Rev. William Burnham, who had been ordained in his Connecticut parish in 1712 at salary of £50. When Burnham died in 1750, his son computed that, based on the amount and currency expressed in the original contract, the town owed his father about £4,000 for unpaid and depreciated salary.[48]

What could Rev. Burnham have done? Most ministers had to request more from their congregations, and this, in itself, constituted a significant shift in ecclesiastical authority. Previously, a congregation – often flushed with charitable and hopeful feelings, as at a wedding – had bestowed a relatively handsome fixed income upon a young man. After that point, the congregation had little chance to reconsider the decision. But inflation and the need to adjust the income introduced a periodic, even annual, opportunity for the parish to hold the parson financially accountable for his ministry. Moreover, the insidious inflation meant that parishioners had to take a positive action in order to prevent the minister's income from declining. Those who wished to express disapproval or who did not care enough to express approval simply had to abstain from supporting a "raise." Even the idea of "raising" the salary was a psychological barrier to maintaining the value of the minister's income in difficult economic times. In the face of such barriers, which continued into the 1760s when many commercial centers became economically depressed after the end of the Seven Year's War, ministers occasionally requested from their association or presbytery a "dismission" from their pulpit for lack of support. This happened in the 1760s to Rev. Joseph Montgomery of Georgetown, Maryland, and to Moses Tuttle, who wandered among Presbyterian churches in Delaware, Maryland, New Jersey, and New York, while collecting a small sum from the Corporation for the Relief of Poor and Distressed Ministers.[49]

The shift in authority resulting from the economic changes was compounded by the Great Awakening. The former provided the mechanism by which the clergy could be held accountable; the latter supplied the reason. For, just as the inflation was accelerating, the fabric of religious culture was torn apart in the revival. In parish after parish, upstart enthusiasts led by itinerant preachers, on the one side, and traditionalists often drawn from the social elite, on the other, pulled the minister to endorse their views. More often than not, the settled clergy sided against the revivalists, but they paid a price no matter which side they failed to support. Rev. Samuel Brown opposed the Great Awakening in the 1740s, and his Massachusetts town punished him by voting to pay his salary in depreciated currency. In contrast, Rev. Henry Messinger, who supported the revival, was denied a raise from 1719 until his death in 1750. Even the conversion to specie in the 1750s and consequent refiguring of the remuneration offered the opportunity for disenchanted parishioners to cut the value of a salary, as Rev. Nathaniel Hancock discovered in 1756.[50]

48. *Harvard Graduates*, vol. 5, pp. 137–41; vol. 11, p. 27.

49. *Princetonians*, vol. 1, p. 145; *Yale Graduates*, vol. 2, pp. 67–8.

50. *Harvard Graduates*, vol. 5, p. 481; vol. 6, pp. 199, 488–9. Messinger's salary was occasionally augmented by special contributions.

If the minister's position on the revival did not suit his congregation or if the Christian charity of the good townspeople weakened in the face of their sinful self-interest, then the raises would not keep pace with the rampant inflation. Should the minister, in response, begin criticizing and demanding? However softly or stridently, many resorted to this approach, though it was discomfiting for several reasons. Continuing remonstrances would sour any working relationship, but the pastoral relationship was particularly at risk because it was based, in theory, upon kindness and charity. Dunning for an "honourable maintenance" implicitly undermined both the fact and the theory of the pastor's position. According to one tenet of the architectonic, the Protestant minister was to turn the other cheek to his parish's neglect. But, in so doing, he would begin to lose the high status and authority that he was expected to maintain according to the opposite pole of the dialectic of clerical authority.

Clergymen could only lose, and most balanced a gradual decline in income with occasional lapses in Christian forbearance as they cajoled their churches into making a financial accommodation. Some, however, due to either genuine need or their own sense of pride or justice, appealed to ecclesiastical councils, colonial legislatures, or, finally, the courts in order to collect the fair value of their salaries.[51] Rev. David Parsons, for example, successively petitioned in all three forums in order not only to coerce his town into raising his salary with inflation, but even to obtain the devalued salary that he was owed.[52] The resort to law, of course, is the clearest evidence of the erosion of ministers' status and authority, ecclesiastically and culturally. The leaders of the institution devoted to conciliatory mediation of human problems were being forced to petition the chief competing profession for relief.

The relief they received was small. Some, such as Rev. John Rogers, died before the case was settled in court. Others, such as Rev. Joseph Metcalf, lost their suit because there was nothing technically illegal in the town paying the contracted salary in depreciated currency. Still others, such as a minister in Salem, Massachusetts, won a significant award, which the town refused to pay. Even that insult was exceeded by Warner, New Hampshire. When it was sued by its minister after falling several years behind in paying his salary in the 1790s, the town sold the land that had been reserved "for the use of the ministry forever" in order to pay the legal fees for its defense.[53]

The most renowned suit of this kind – and the most famous defeat of the

---

51. In a study of ministers in New England and Long Island between 1680 and 1740, Shipton found that 12 percent were involved in serious financial disputes with their congregations, and about 5 percent left their pulpits on this account. Bushman cites this point to show that there were *many* disputes, indicating widespread deterioration in clerical authority and finances. Youngs cites Shipton's study in order to show how ambitiously disputatious the ministers were; Bonomi cites Shipton's study to show how *few* disputes there were. Clifford K. Shipton, "The New England Clergy of the 'Glacial Age'," *Publications of the Colonial Society of Massachusetts*, 32 (1933–7): 24–54; Bushman, *From Puritan to Yankee*, p. 157; Youngs, *God's Messengers: Religious Leadership in Colonial New England*, p. 107; Bonomi, *Under the Cope of Heaven*, pp. 71, 238.

52. *Harvard Graduates*, vol. 5, pp. 283–8.

53. *Harvard Graduates*, vol. 5, pp. 221–3, 293, 485–8; vol. 16, p. 490.

clergy – was the Parsons' Cause in Virginia in the 1760s. In 1749 the colony had enacted a generous annual salary for establishment clergy "of sixteen thousand pounds of tobacco." When the crop failed, the legislature in 1755, and again in 1759, allowed debts in tobacco to be paid at the undervalued rate of two pence per pound in order to prevent inflation. The clergy, whose real income had declined during previous years of bountiful crops, were outraged at the lost opportunity to compensate for those losses. When the two-pence rate was eventually disallowed by the Privy Council in England, clergymen seeking to recover their unrealized gains entered four suits in four different courts, which collectively came to be known as the Parsons' Cause. In the most memorable case, argued in 1763, Patrick Henry defended the rate and portrayed the Anglican clergy as selfish and grasping supporters of royal tyranny. Those charges fit with the opinion of the many Virginians who had been enthused by Baptist revivalism in the previous two decades, and the parsons lost every suit.[54]

Small wonder that some ministers began to study law and join the bar. After seeking a dismission due to insufficient support and being charged with immorality, Cyrus Marsh left his Connecticut parish in 1755, entered the law, and never returned to the pulpit. Rev. Thomas Paine progressed through an even more telling sequence. In 1734 he obtained a dismission from his Massachusetts church after it failed to raise his salary. Entering commerce in the hopes of securing an honorable estate, he became tangled in lawsuits with English merchants. Seeking to free himself from the legal tangles of the marketplace, he finally took up the law and applied to join the bar. No less significant is the example of Rev. Timothy Fuller, who read law and joined the bar in order to defend himself after his parish tried to dismiss him for his political views during the Revolution.[55]

That Rev. Fuller was driven into the arms of the legal profession for the sake of the right to express his politics exemplifies perfectly the third factor that weakened the clerical profession. The combined impact of the changing economic conditions and the egalitarian enthusiasm of the Great Awakening was further exacerbated by the contemporaneous rise of "liberal" thought that was partly sponsored by "liberal Christians." Needless to say, liberalism is an elusive, not to say chimerical, phenomenon that has many meanings and interpretations, which continue to grow in number.[56] One wonders, indeed, whether anything determinate can be said about it. Yet the protean nature of liberalism suggests the importance of trying to assay it.

Among analyses of the historical meaning of "liberal" ideas, several approaches

---

54. *Statutes of Virginia,* vol. 6, pp. 88–90; Isaac, *The Transformation of Virginia, 1740–1790,* chs. 7, 8; David W. Robson, *Educating Republicans: the College in the Era of the American Revolution, 1750–1800* (Westport, CT, 1985), pp. 42–4.

55. *Yale Graduates,* vol. 1, pp. 624–5; *Harvard Graduates,* vol. 6, pp. 202–7; vol. 14, pp. 603–4.

56. See Michael J. Sandel, *Liberalism and the Limits of Justice* (Cambridge, UK, 1982); Larry G. Gerber, *The Limits of Liberalism … and the Development of Modern Political Economy* (New York, 1984); John P. Diggins, *The Lost Soul of American Politics: Virtue, Self-Interest, and the Foundations of Liberalism* (New York, 1984); Nancy L. Rosenblum, *Another Liberalism: Romanticism and the Reconstruction of Liberal Thought* (Cambridge, MA, 1987); D. A. Lloyd Thomas, *In Defence of Liberalism* (New York, 1988); Benjamin Barber, *The Conquest of Politics: Liberal Philosophy in Democratic Times* (Princeton, NJ, 1988).

are prominent. Progressive historians of the early twentieth century maintained that "liberalism has been ordinarily the movement on the part of the other sections of society to restrain the power of the business community. This was the tradition of Jefferson and Jackson, and it has been the basic meaning of American liberalism."[57] For "Consensus" historians who dominated the period after World War II, "liberalism" referred to the consensus supposedly shared by most United States citizens through history: that the government's task is to promote commerce and prosperity within the framework of Lockean rights to personal liberty and personal property.[58] Subsequently the social and critical historiography that has emerged since the 1960s tends to speak in one breath of "liberal capitalism" or "corporate liberalism," affirming that "what was dearest to the heart of the historical, living liberal was individualism of a possessive and acquisitive sort." For this third historical interpretation, liberalism represents not a consensus but the view of one privileged class in American society. In fact, liberalism is said to require and promote industrial capitalism and, consequently, "brings degradation to labor."[59]

Liberalism has therefore been interpreted in various ways, but underlying this variety is a common disregard for the historical term "liberal."[60] Through the eighteenth and well into the nineteenth century, the word "liberal" meant, first and foremost, "generous." When President John Quincy Adams promised Daniel Webster in 1823 that he would be "liberal" in his appointment of Federalists to public office, he was not addressing himself to avaricious capitalists, but describing how he would dispense political patronage.[61] This denotation of "generous," derived from *liberalis* in Latin, had two primary aspects: openminded and openhanded, that is, generosity of mind and generosity in material things. Thus, Benjamin Rush urged the appropriation of public funds "to allow [teachers] liberal salaries," and a writer in *The [Virginia] Evangelical and Literary Magazine*

57. Arthur M. Schlesinger, Jr., *The Age of Jackson* (Boston, 1945), p. 505.

58. Richard Hofstadter, *The American Political Tradition and the Men who Made it* (New York, 1948); Daniel J. Boorstin, *The Genius of American Politics* (Chicago, 1953); Louis Hartz, *The Liberal Tradition in America: An Interpretation of American Political Thought since the Revolution* (New York, 1955).

59. Quotations are, respectively, from Steven Watts, *The Republic Reborn: War and the Making of Liberal America, 1790–1820* (Baltimore, MD, 1987), pp. xvii, 6; R. Jeffrey Lustig, *Corporate Liberalism: The Origins of Modern American Political Theory, 1890–1920* (Berkeley, CA, 1982), p. 36; Allen Kaufman, *Capitalism, Slavery, and Republican Values: American Political Economists, 1819–1848* (Austin, 1982), p. xxx. James Weinstein, *The Corporate Ideal in the Liberal State, 1900–1918* (Boston, 1968).

60. Benson described the "liberal" consensus in Jacksonian America without quoting anyone employing "liberal" in his senses. Watts neglects and contradicts the historical usage with the justification that "rhetoric" is deceptive, and "the power of these rhetorical fictions ... flowed from a deeper psychological source." Hence, "a close penetrating reading" reveals to the historian "myriad deeper meanings" of what people really felt and believed. Lee Benson, *The Concept of Jacksonian Democracy: New York as a Test Case* (Princeton, NJ, 1961), ch. 5; Watts, *The Republic Reborn: War and the Making of Liberal America, 1790–1820*, pp. xix, xviii, 64, 165–6, 274.

61. Shaw Livermore, Jr., *The Twilight of Federalism: The Disintegration of the Federalist Party, 1815–1830* (Princeton, NJ, 1962), pp. 174–5, 184.

appealed to "men of enlarged and liberal minds," as did a proposal in 1830 to establish a university in New York city.[62]

This twofold, "liberal" idea of generosity of mind and of material possessions was not only longstanding and conventional, but also happened to fit remarkably well with two primary tenets of "enlightened" eighteenth-century thought: free-thinking and the free market, the free exchange of ideas and the free exchange of properties. Via its twofold denotation of generosity, the term "liberal" thus came to denote the intellectual movement associated with these two primary points. And it was these two "liberal" conceptions that stood at the core of a new architectonic of culture that was manifested, above all, in the polity and the law at the turn of the century. These rhetorical and conceptual developments and the consequent challenge to the clergy and to the religious architectonic unfolded in the following way.

In the course of the eighteenth century, the most prominent sense in which "liberal" meant openminded appeared in religion. A group of Protestants, while denying themselves to be Arminians or deists, began calling themselves "liberal" to mean "broadminded" and "tolerant." In the view of these "liberal Christians," this tolerant attitude was a necessary and generous response to the increasing sectarianism of Protestantism which had, ever since the Reformation, put in doubt the idea that one sect had the only truth while all others were in error. Treatises expressing this toleration continued to appear early in the nineteenth century, as in *The Little Apostle of Gospel Liberality* (1812) and *Female Liberality Acceptable to Jesus Christ* (1818).[63]

Toleration was "a new virtue" when it appeared at the end of the seventeenth century. Tolerance had previously implied cowardice or lack of commitment to one's professed beliefs, and the word "liberal," when applied to doctrinal matters, had pejoratively connoted licentiousness.[64] But this "new virtue" and the new usage of "liberal" gained acceptance, and from toleration it was only a step to "Free-Thinking," which Anthony Collins celebrated in a notorious treatise of 1713. To be sure, the liberal Christians for a long time opposed "the rise and growth of a sect call'd Free-Thinkers." Yet they could not forever deny the connection between tolerance and free-thinking. Both were founded in skepticism. John Locke had expressed the skeptical foundation of tolerance in his famous argument that, since one cannot finally know which Protestant theological system is correct, then one must tolerate the different systems.[65] Meanwhile vociferous critics were eager to

62. Benjamin Rush, "A Plan for the Establishment of Public Schools and the Diffusion of Knowledge in Pennsylvania" (1786), reprinted in *Essays on Education in the Early Republic*, ed. Frederick Rudolph (Cambridge, MA, 1965), p. 21; Holem, "Remarks on Missionary Journals," *The [Virginia] Evangelical and Literary Magazine*, 6 (1823): 424; [anon.], *Considerations upon the Expediency and the Means of Establishing a University in The City of New York* (New York, 1830), p. 22.

63. Thomas Hershey, *The Little Apostle of Gospel Liberality* (Pittsburgh, PA, 1812); John H. Church, *Female Liberality Acceptable to Jesus Christ* (Concord, NH, 1818). See C. Conrad Wright, *The Liberal Christians: Essays on American Unitarian History* (Boston, 1970), chs. 1–2.

64. Paul Hazard, *The European Mind, 1680–1715*, tr. J. Lewis May (1953; Harmondsworth, UK, 1964), pp. 343–4; *OED*, s.v. "liberal."

65. Anthony Collins, *A Discourse of Free-Thinking Occasion'd by the Rise and Growth of a Sect call'd Free-Thinkers* (London, 1713); John Locke, *A Second Letter Concerning Toleration* (1690), in *The Works* (1823; Aalen, W. Germany, 1963), vol. 6, pp. 61–137.

point out the skeptical foundation of free-thinking in warnings to the young that the "arrogance and vanity of the Scepticks" means that "no beneficial Consequences can result from the modern Free-thinking."⁶⁶

Through the Trojan horse of generous toleration, free-thinking gradually became associated with "liberal Christians" and with the term "liberal" over the course of the eighteenth century. By the early nineteenth century the religious and semantic implications were manifest in tracts that contrasted "the death-bed of a free-thinker, and the death-bed of a Christian" or attacked the "absurdity and danger of that Liberality which looks with complacency on all opinions advocated by those calling themselves Christians."⁶⁷ Some opponents tried to reverse these implications by defining "true liberality" to fit with the mission of "educating pious youths for the gospel ministry." However, by 1834 it was clear to religious partisans that "*Free Enquirers* ... who, under the mask of *Free Enquiry,* are ... trampling on the most sacred of all truths" were precisely those who "style themselves Liberals, or the Liberal Party: and how have these Liberals proved their liberality? ... they commenced their liberal warfare against the clergy."⁶⁸

The second tenet of eighteenth-century enlightened thought gradually subtended by the term "liberal" was that the marketplace should be free. This idea slowly gained acceptance between the time of John Locke's assertions about "the preservation of property being the end of government" and Adam Smith's observation that "freedom of trade" is essential to being "really free in our present sense of the word Freedom."⁶⁹ This freedom of the market gradually eclipsed the view that financial transactions should be based upon the substantive justice or fairness of the exchange. The older view stemmed from the covenantal model of human relations that was founded in the religious architectonic of colonial culture. The idea of covenant, implying a promise to maintain a just and lifelong reciprocal relationship, was commensurately superseded by the idea of contract, which implied a transaction within a specified term based on what the market would bear.⁷⁰

---

66. [Samuel Richardson], *The Apprentice's VADE MECUM: or, Young Man's Pocket Companion* (London, 1734), pp. 57, 71.

67. [anon.] *The Contrast: or, the death-bed of a free-thinker, and the death-bed of a Christian* (Middlebury, VT, 1807); Clark Brown, *Absurdity and Danger of that Liberality which looks with complacency on all Opinions Advocated by Those Calling Themselves Christians* (Concord, NH, 1814).

68. Samuel Worcester, *True Liberality. A Sermon preached in Boston on the first Anniversary of the American Society for Educating Pious Youths for the Gospel Ministry* (Andover, MA, 1816); Sherlock, *Letter Addressed to Thomas Herttell, Member of the House of Assembly* (New York, 1834), pp. 14, 22.

69. John Locke, *Two Treatises of Government ... 1689,* ed. Peter Laslett, rev. edn (Cambridge, UK, 1967), II, ch. 6, ss. 138; Adam Smith, *An Inquiry into the Nature and Causes of the Wealth of Nations* (1776), ed. Edwin Cannan (1904; Chicago, 1976), bk. 3, ch. 3, ss. 5.

70. Contracts had existed throughout the colonial period, but until the last quarter of the eighteenth century they were adjudicated in the courts according to an "objective theory of value" rather than a subjective "meeting of the minds," Even then, "contracts" was not a recognized field of law until well into the nineteenth century, when non-real property and negotiable instruments became a significant source of wealth. Morton J. Horwitz, *The*

The contractual free-market ethic was strengthened by the developing complexity of commerce. Over the seventeenth and eighteenth centuries, commercial transactions came to involve more markets, commodities, currencies, and time. These complicating factors introduced variability that undermined notions of stable value on which a "just price" could be based. Moreover, the greater distances, duration, and number of parties involved meant such transactions could no longer be made on a personal basis or through familial ties. Trade was conducted by strangers, and binding contracts were therefore demanded. By 1826 American courts explicitly denied that a promise made out of moral obligation was enforceable as a contract in the marketplace.[71] The semantic link between the free-market ethic and the term "liberal" lay in the generosity in material things that the term had long denoted. A free person, a liberal person, was generous with property, and such generosity presupposed that one had property to share, that is, one had wealth.[72] The semantic connection, then, between "liberal" and the emerging devotion to the free market was, on the one hand, the concern for freedom and, on the other hand, the application of that freedom to property and wealth.

Both aspects of emergent liberalism weakened the position of the clergy. The free market was, in fact, the root of the financial problems of the clergy, because the scarcity of labor and commodities and the instability of prices produced the conditions that undermined colonial ministers' fixed income. In addition, the free market, wherein individuals pursued wealth unrestrained by mores of just and fair exchange, eroded the traditional ethics of deference and corporate responsibility to the community. As "freedom of trade" expanded, ministers therefore lamented the self-interest, the money-getting, and "the dangerous tendency to ignore distinctions of rank in existing society."[73] But their repeated pronouncements about just price, deference to authority, and community harmony were ineffective. As a result, congregations were less responsive to pleas for voluntary support for their ministers,

---

Transformation of American Law, 1780–1860 (Cambridge, MA, 1977), p. 196, chs. 2, 4; Grant Gilmore, *The Death of Contract* (Columbus, OH, 1974), ch. 1; A. W. B. Simpson, "The Horwitz Thesis and the History of Contracts," *University of Chicago Law Review*, 46 (1979): 533–601.

71. *Mills* v. *Wyman*, 3 Pickering 207 (Massachusetts 1826). Here and below, I draw upon: Bushman, *From Puritan to Yankee*, chs. 7–9; Wesley F. Craven, *The Colonies in Transition, 1660–1713* (New York, 1968); E. P. Thompson, "The Moral Economy of the English Crowd in the Eighteenth Century," *Past and Present*, 50 (1971): 76–136; Holmes, *Augustan England: Professions, State and Society, 1680–1730* (1982), ch. 5; Roeber, *Faithful Magistrates and Republican Lawyers ... 1680–1810*, chs. 3–5; Thomas M. Doerflinger, *A Vigorous Spirit of Enterprise: Merchants and Economic Development in Revolutionary Philadelphia* (Chapel Hill, NC, 1986).

72. *Oxford Latin Dictionary*, s.v. "liber," "liberalis."

73. Alice Baldwin, *The New England Clergy and the American Revolution* (Durham, NC, 1928), p. 49. Max Weber, of course, proposed the much-debated thesis that Calvinism contributed to the development of free-market capitalism via "the earning of more and more money, combined with the strict avoidance of all spontaneous enjoyment of life" (*The Protestant Ethic and the Spirit of Capitalism*, tr. Talcott Parsons (New York, 1958), p. 53.) I propose here that the clergy could not countenance the liberal free market, however much their theology may have contributed to capitalism.

and their indifference accompanied a trend toward contractualization between parsons and congregations. By 1790, when Rev. Joshua Knapp was installed in a Connecticut church, it was not uncommon for the parties to stipulate that the life-long covenant between minister and congregation was, in fact, a contract: "it being understood that this Installation or Settlement shall continue as a Covenant only during the pleasure of the Parties, or Either of them, and no longer."[74]

The freedom and expansion of the market also led parishioners into disputes with each other and, for the first time, with distant individuals. The mediation and informal arbitration of conflicts thus began to break down as people went to law to resolve their differences. For example, although churches in mid-eighteenth-century rural New England continued to adjudicate most disputes between citizens of the same town, courts began adjudicating most disputes between citizens of different towns. In the final quarter of the century, intra-town disputes also began to appear in courts, until by the 1810s "the courts had become ... the only institution that was available to adjudicate a dispute." A similar development occurred in Quaker Pennsylvania, while in Virginia during the third quarter of the eighteenth century the commercial offenses of failing to keep up roads or to list taxable property began to displace religious and moral offenses as the most numerous presentments made by grand juries to JPs.[75] In these ways, the contractual, free-market ethic challenged the working conditions, the doctrine and the responsibilities of the "Holy Profession."

Free-thinking, the complementary side of emergent liberalism, also posed an inherent challenge to religious belief and thus to the clergy. The story about the challenge of "liberal," "enlightened," and Arminian Christianity has been told many times,[76] to the point that it is sometimes considered to be an exaggerated minor theme in the history of American religion.[77] Yet the threat of "vapid

74. *Yale Graduates,* vol. 3, p. 384. This trend toward contractualization has been dated at various points between the late seventeenth century and the early nineteenth century. Cf. David D. Hall, *The Faithful Shepherd: A History of the New England Ministry in the Seventeenth Century* (Chapel Hill, NC, 1972), pp. 185–96; Youngs, *God's Messengers: Religious Leadership in Colonial New England,* passim; Wilson, *The Benevolent Deity,* p. 54; Donald M. Scott, *From Office to Profession: The New England Ministry, 1750–1850* (Philadelphia, 1978), pp. 120–2. Accompanying this contractualization was the decline in tenure of clergy in parts of New England, modestly from 1790 to about 1812 and then steadily through mid-century. Daniel H. Calhoun, *Professional Lives in America: Structure and Aspiration* (Cambridge, MA, 1965), pp. 120, 126–7.

75. William E. Nelson, *Dispute and Conflict Resolution in Plymouth Colony, Massachusetts, 1725–1825* (Chapel Hill, NC, 1981), p. 76, passim. See Bushman, *From Puritan to Yankee,* pt. 4; Bruce C. Daniels, "The Political Structure of Local Government in Colonial Connecticut," in *Town and Country,* ed. Daniels (Middletown, CT, 1978), p. 50; Roeber, *Faithful Magistrates and Republican Lawyers ... 1680–1810,* pp. 142, 180.

76. See C. Conrad Wright, *The Beginnings of Unitarianism in America* (Boston, 1955); James W. Jones, *The Shattered Synthesis: New England Puritanism before the Great Awakening* (New Haven, CT, 1973); James Turner, *Without God, Without Creed: The Origins of Unbelief in America* (Baltimore, MD, 1985), ch. 2.

77. Holifield, *The Gentleman Theologians ... in Southern Culture, 1795–1860,* pp. ix–24; Bruce Kuklick, *Churchmen and Philosophers: From Jonathan Edwards to John Dewey* (New Haven, CT, 1985), pp. xvi–xx.

liberalism" appeared menacing enough to evangelists through the mid-nineteenth century;[78] and even if scholars have exaggerated the theme, the exaggeration only goes to show that a minor movement in theology bulked large in American thought. In other words, to emphasize the marginal view in American religion is simply to suggest that the theological architectonic was gradually moving to the margin of intellectual life.

Free-thinking also compounded the problems for the clergy created by the Great Awakening. For one thing, the revivalists demanded strict attention to the sacred text, and free-thinking exacerbated the hermeneutical problem of determining the meaning of the text. In addition, free-thinking raised a thicket of thorny doctrinal issues that became points of contention among the established clergy themselves. While holding the revivalists at bay, the clergy therefore began quarreling among themselves, behavior that only worsened their public image. As one layman noted: "The treatment which the Clergy give to one another, makes it the less to be wondered ... that the laity use them with disrespect."[79]

Overall, it may be said that the egalitarian enthusiasm of the Great Awakening, the changing economic conditions, and the two tenets of "liberality" – free-thinking and the free market – contributed individually and in concert to weaken the clerical profession over the second and third quarters of the eighteenth century. The ministers' situation was not helped by the fact that a long time competing vocation was ready to assume the preeminent role among professions, a vocation whose field of endeavor fit closely the new cultural ideal and architectonic.

Intellectual: "the 'science of sciences'"

As suggested by James Madison's "architectonic calculations" in the *Federalist Papers*, reflection upon the polity and the law gradually acquired intellectual sovereignty in the final quarter of the eighteenth century. This displacement of religion and theology by the liberal polity and law was evident even among Kentucky Baptists who were "wildly excited on the subject of politics ... The country had been agitated with the most exciting political questions almost constantly from the first settlement at Boonesborough.... But in religious affairs, the land was enveloped in the deepest gloom.... It was openly asserted by leading politicians that christianity was inconsistent with liberal and enlightened statesmanship."[80] By the

78. Horace Bushnell, *Barbarism the First Danger: A Discourse for Home Missions* (New York, 1847), p. 31.

79. Samuel Richardson, *A Collection of the Moral and Instructive Sentiments ... Contained in the Histories of Pamela, Clarissa, and Sir Charles Grandison* (London, 1755), p. 14. On the interaction of "liberal" toleration and religious enthusiasm, see Richard W. Pointer, *Protestant Pluralism and the New York Experience: A Study of Eighteenth Century Religious Diversity* (Bloomington, IN, 1988); Sally Schwartz, *A Mixed Multitude: The Struggle for Toleration in Colonial Pennsylvania* (New York, 1987).

80. Quotations are, respectively, from: Glen E. Thurow, *Abraham Lincoln and American Political Religion* (Albany, NY, 1976), p. x; J. H. Spencer, *A History of Kentucky Baptists* (Cincinnati, OH, 1885), vol. 1, pp. 367, 452.

centennial of 1776 it had therefore become commonplace for jurists to invoke for law the conception and image of an architectonic:

> [L]aw, which is the "science of sciences," must have the best and latest results of every other science before it can reach its ideal perfection. But, just as the chief-architect and designer of an edifice is superior to the workmen ... and just as the science of the former is grander and broader, more general and more elevated than that of the latter, so is the statesman or the jurist who devises laws for the government of a great humanity ... superior to the mere observer of physical phenomena, the scientist or the physicist, and so is the science of the former greater and more complex than that of the latter.[81]

This new architectonic, in the most general sense, amounted to reflection upon the polity: the organization of human beings living together in the *polis.* Whether the rise of a political architectonic and jurisprudence is shaped more by historical circumstance, as Edmund Burke suggested in *Reflections on the Revolution in France* (1790), or by intrinsic principles of legal rationality, as Friedrich Karl von Savigny implied in *The Vocation of Our Time for Legislation and Jurisprudence* (1814, Eng. tr. 1831), is probably unanswerable. By either explanation, however, the Revolution was the transforming and crystallizing event in America. In the words of Gordon Wood:

> This revolution marked ... the beginning of what might be called a romantic view of politics.... The result was phenomenal: an outpouring of political writings ... that has never been equaled in the nation's history.... It was as if every American agreed ... that establishing new governments "on wise and lasting principles, is the greatest work the mind of man can undertake".[82]

The Revolution was proclaimed in the music, theater, literature, and painting that flourished contemporaneously in America for the first time. In the colleges, commencement orators, who had begun to discuss politics in the mid-1760s, when difficulties with Britain escalated, made politics their chief topic, as did the students. "By 1810 America possessed more political journals in proportion to its population than had ever been known anywhere in the world."[83]

The success of the polity thus became the cultural ideal, the primary source of cultural validation and legitimation, and this fact was expressed in the rhetoric of the time. The adjective "political" denoted not "of politics" as we think of it today, but rather "of the polity," as appeared in school textbooks.[84] The noun "politician"

81. "Lawyers and Doctors," *Albany Law Journal,* 7 (1873): 35; reprinted in *[London] Law Journal,* 8 (1873): 308.

82. Gordon S. Wood, *The Creation of the American Republic, 1776–1787* (Chapel Hill, NC, 1969), pp. 6, 127–8, 606.

83. Donald H. Stewart, "Jeffersonian Journalism: Newspaper Propaganda and the Development of the Democratic-Republican Party, 1789–1801" (PhD diss., Columbia University, 1950), p. 26. Kenneth Silverman, *A Cultural History of the American Revolution: Painting, Music, Literature and the Theatre ... 1763–1789* (1976; New York, 1987); Robson, *Educating Republicans: the College in the Era of the American Revolution,* p. 67.

84. See William Sullivan, *The Political Class Book; Intended to Instruct the Higher Classes in School* (Boston, 1830); Alexander Maitland, *The Political Instructor and Guide to General Knowledge; Being a Compendium of Political Information* (Philadelphia, 1833).

did not carry a negative connotation, but denoted someone who attends to the polity. Thus, "it is the duty of every intelligent man to be a politician," William Leggett maintained; and a successor to the portable Bible of the past was entitled: *The Politician's Pocket Companion: Containing the Declaration of Independence, the Constitution of the United States, with the Amendments.*[85] Meanwhile political interest was demonstrated by the high and increasing participation of eligible voters. More than 80 percent of the eligible voters participated in state elections in 1804 in Delaware, 1812 in Vermont, 1814 in New Hampshire, 1817 in Tennessee, 1819 in Alabama, 1823 in Mississippi, and 1828 in Ohio. In presidential elections, the turnout grew in two jumps – from 27 to 58 percent between 1824 and 1828 and from 58 to 80 percent between 1836 and 1840.[86]

The shift from a religious to a political architectonic over the last half of the eighteenth century inevitably raises the issue of the relationship between the two. It seems inconceivable that revolutionary concern for the polity could have developed without direct influence by the environing religiosity. Yet there is substantial disagreement about the existence and nature of such influence.[87] Some scholars have attended to the denominational and geographical divisions among the clergy who supported, opposed, or merely watched the Revolution.[88] Others have proposed that the theologically conservative but enthusiastic revivalists of the Great Awakening became supporters of the Revolution, whereas the theologically liberal but unenthused opponents of the revival became political conservatives. However, while such interpretations still receive support,[89] the notion of correlating particular religious parties with particular political groups has generally been discredited.[90]

85. William Leggett, "The Morals of Politics," in *Plaindealer* (June 3, 1837), reprinted in *Democratick Editorials, Essays in Jacksonian Political Economy*, ed. Lawrence H. White (Indianapolis, IN, 1984), p. 56; Jeremiah Chapin, *Sermon delivered at the Ordination of the Rev. Stephen Chapin* (Portland, ME, 1819), p. 6; [Henry P. Russell, printer], *The Politician's Pocket Companion: Containing the Declaration of Independence, the Constitution of the United States, with the Amendments, and the Constitution of New-Jersey* (Morristown, NJ, 1804).

86. Richard P. McCormick, "New Perspectives on Jacksonian Politics," *AHR*, 65 (1960): 292; Arthur M. Schlesinger, Jr., "Introduction," in *History of US Political Parties*, ed. Schlesinger (New York, 1973), vol. 1, p. xxxvii; Robert H. Wiebe, *The Opening of American Society from the Adoption of the Constitution to the Eve of Disunion* (New York, 1984), pp. 154, 348.

87. See Ruth Bloch, "The Social and Political Base of Millennial Literature in late Eighteenth-Century America," *American Quarterly*, 40 (1988): 378–9; Stephen Botein, "Religious Dimensions of the Early American State," in *Beyond Confederation*, ed. Richard Beeman et al. (Chapel Hill, NC, 1987), pp. 315–30.

88. Baldwin, *The New England Clergy and the American Revolution*; Mark A. Noll, *Christians in the American Revolution* (Washington, DC, 1977); Lester D. Joyce, *Church and Clergy in the American Revolution: A Study in Group Behavior* (New York, 1966).

89. Heimert, *Religion and the American Mind from the Great Awakening to the Revolution*; William G. McLoughlin, "'Enthusiasm for Liberty': The Great Awakening as the Key to the Revolution," in *Preachers and Politicians*, ed. Jack P. Greene and William G. McLoughlin (Worcester, MA, 1977), pp. 47–73; Stanley N. Katz, "The Legal and Religious Context of Natural Rights Theory: A Comment," in *Party and Political Opposition in Revolutionary America*, ed. Patricia U. Bonomi (Tarrytown, NY, 1980), p. 37.

90. Sidney E. Mead, "Through and Beyond the Lines," *Journal of Religion*, 48 (1968):

Nevertheless, influences from the religious architectonic can be identified at a more abstract level. The most renowned example is perhaps American "civil religion." The recent interest in this topic was stimulated by Robert Bellah in 1967, although other scholars had anticipated the idea and Bellah later acknowledged "a certain ambiguity" in his own expression. In any case, the tenets of civil religion can best be drawn from what has to be the earliest statement so far as America concerned: Governor John Winthrop's sermon of 1630. Winthrop preached that the colonists were a chosen people in a chosen land, embarking on a divinely appointed mission and therefore accountable to God and history for the outcome. Fulfillment would bring great reward and happiness; failure would mean infamy.[91] These themes not only persevered in the new nation, but were adumbrated by millennialism, which contributed to establishing the faith in a visionary future for the republic.[92] In addition, revivalism seems to have encouraged public partisanship and the willingness to challenge established authority, two factors that strengthened the revolutionary spirit.[93]

More significant than any other architectonical influence, however, is the model of "congregationalism" that the religious polity provided for the new civil polity. Observing in 1789 that "the presbyterians and independents were almost universally" in favor of the Continental Congress, David Ramsay noted that: "Their religious societies are governed on the republican plan." Baptist pastor G. B. Perry of Philadelphia associated the polity of congregational Protestants, in contrast to that

---

274–88; Bernard Bailyn, "Religion and Revolution: Three Biographical Studies," *Perspectives in American History*, 4 (1970): 83–169; Nathan O. Hatch, "The Origins of Civil Millennialism in America: New England Clergymen, War with France and the Revolution," *WMQ*, 3d ser., 31 (1974): 407–30. Some argue for continuity between the economic and social conflicts and groups of the Great Awakening and those of the American Revolution. See Gregory H. Nobles, *Divisions Throughout the Whole: Politics and Society in Hampshire County, Massachusetts, 1740–1775* (Cambridge, UK, 1983); Kenneth A. Lockridge, *Settlement and Unsettlement in Early America: The Crisis of Political Legitimacy before the Revolution* (New York, 1981).

91. John Winthrop, "A Modell of Christian Charity," in *Winthrop Papers*, ed. Samuel E. Morison et al. (Boston, 1931), vol. 2, p. 295; Robert N. Bellah, "The Revolution and the Civil Religion," in *Religion and the American Revolution*, ed. Jerald C. Brauer (Philadelphia, 1976), p. 56. Frequently reprinted, Bellah's "Civil Religion in America" was originally published in *Daedalus*, 96 (1967): 1–19. See Russell E. Richey and D. G. Jones, eds., *American Civil Religion* (New York, 1974); Sacvan Bercovitch, *The American Jeremiad* (Madison, WI, 1978), ch. 1. Anticipatory statements include: John R. Bodo, *The Protestant Clergy and Public Issues, 1812–1848* (Princeton, NJ, 1954), pp. 5–6; Sidney E. Mead, *The Lively Experiment: The Shaping of Christianity in America* (New York, 1963), chs. 2–4; Loren Baritz, *City on a Hill: A History of Ideas and Myths in America* (New York, 1964).

92. Nathan O. Hatch, *The Sacred Cause of Liberty: Republican Thought and the Millennium in Revolutionary New England* (New Haven, CT, 1977); Ruth Bloch, *Millennial Themes in American Thought, 1756–1800* (New York, 1985).

93. Rhys Isaac, "Evangelical Revolt: The Nature of the Baptists' Challenge to the Traditional Order in Virginia, 1765 to 1775," *WMQ*, 3d ser., 31 (1974): 345–68; Jerald C. Brauer, "Puritanism, Revivalism, and the Revolution," in *Religion and the American Revolution*, ed. Brauer (Philadelphia, 1976), pp. 1–27; Bonomi, *Under the Cope of Heaven*, chs. 6, 7.

of Roman Catholics, with "the science of *our* national jurisprudence." Likewise, Michael Chevalier, who toured the United States on behalf of the French Minister of the Interior, observed, "Protestantism is republican; puritanism is absolute self-government in religion, and begets it in politics ...; protestantism, republicanism, and individuality are all one." In this respect, "a Christian Church was the model of our republicanism," affirmed Carroll Bitting at Union University in Tennessee in 1855.[94]

In these ways the colonial religious tradition influenced the emerging attention to the polity, but it is equally significant that after the Revolution clergymen began to preach the political architectonic. This fact is perhaps the strongest evidence for the shift in worldview. Whereas the religious ideal had formerly prompted ministers to look beyond death to "Another and Better Country," as Rev. Joseph Stevens preached in 1723, now the clergy extolled "The United States Elevated to Glory and Honor," as did Ezra Stiles in a famous sermon of 1783. If colonial children were formerly taught that their lives belonged to God, now an American youth "must be taught that this life 'is not his own' when the safety of his country requires it," as Benjamin Rush affirmed, quoting scripture.[95]

Rev. Asa Messer, president of the College of Rhode Island, demonstrated the shift perfectly in an 1803 oration. After recalling Revolutionary War battles, Messer employed Jefferson's language in linking the polity to education: "a general diffusion of knowledge among our citizens is essential to the preservation of our freedom and ... our invaluable civil privileges." However, Messer continued, "the general diffusion of virtue among our citizens, not less than the general diffusion of knowledge, is essential to the security of our freedom and independence." Therefore, "as virtue is dependent on religion, a prime pillar in our political edifice must rest on the encouragement given to religious principle." In this fashion, Messer reduced religion from an ultimate end to an instrument of polity, a tool analogous to education. Other prominent divines and college presidents, from Thomas Reese of South Carolina in 1788 to Timothy Dwight of Connecticut in the 1820s, likewise endorsed "the utility ... of religion, to the well being ... of civil society."[96]

---

94. David Ramsey, *History of the American Revolution* (1789), vol. 2, pp. 312–3; G. B. Perry, "To The Reader," in *An Examination of the Seven Sacraments of the Church of Rome,* by John Thomas (Philadelphia, 1834), p. 3; Michael Chevalier, *Society, Manners and Politics in the United States, Being a Series of Letters on North America* (1839; New York, 1969), p. 368; C. Carroll Bitting, *Liberty and Literature, or Moral, Political and Intellectual Freedom. An Oration* (Nashville, TN, 1855), p. 20. Frederick V. Mills, Sr., has argued the opposite case, that republicanism reshaped the polity of the Protestant Episcopal Church. *Bishops by Ballot: An Eighteenth-Century Ecclesiastical Revolution* (New York, 1978).

95. Joseph Stevens, *Another and Better Country.... Being the Last Sermons of ... Mr. Joseph Stevens* (Boston, 1723); Ezra Stiles, "The United States Elevated to Glory and Honor: A Sermon" (1783), in *The Pulpit of the American Revolution,* ed. John W. Thornton (Boston, 1860), p. 403; Rush, "Plan for the Establishment of Public Schools and the Diffusion of Knowledge in Pennsylvania," pp. 14–5.

96. Asa Messer, *An Oration delivered at Providence ... on the Fourth of July, 1803* (Providence, RI, 1803), pp. 6–8, 11–2; Thomas Reese, *An Essay on the Influence of Religion on Civil Society* (Charleston, SC, 1788), p. 5; Dwight, *Travels in New England and New York,* vol. 4, p. 403.

If leading clergymen were declaring religion to be an instrument of polity, rather than vice versa, then the cultural architectonic had unmistakably shifted on the fulcrum of the Revolution. But what was the precise meaning of this revolutionary polity? Historians have debated the question intensely. During the nineteenth century, interpretations of the Revolution and ensuing decades were dominated by the Nationalist school, which described how "a favoring Providence, calling our institutions into being, has conducted the country to its present happiness and glory."[97] This Nationalist view was challenged in the early twentieth century by Progressive historians, such as Charles Beard and J. Franklin Jameson, who argued that the revolutionary, Constitutional and early national periods of the United States could be understood in terms of economic self-interest, whether of individuals, groups, or classes. Such self-interest was said to have inspired the formation of political parties at the beginning of the nineteenth century.[98] In the 1950s the "Consensus" historiography emerged. According to this interpretation the United States" polity was "exceptional," compared to Europe, inasmuch as Americans reached consensus on the framework of the polity, which was defined in terms of certain "rights" held by individual citizens. From this perspective the cantankerous debate between the political parties that emerged in the early nineteenth century is explained by religious and ethnic differences rather than economic ones.[99]

The emphasis on rights, derived either from nature or from the British constitutional tradition, was actually shared by most historians ranging from the Nationalist historians to those with varying allegiance to the Progressive school, such as Carl Becker and Charles McIlwain.[100] This overarching emphasis on what is often called "liberal, Lockean rights," prevailed among historians until Bernard Bailyn's reinterpretation of the American revolution in 1967. Drawing upon Caroline Robbins and turning away from the emphasis on Lockean natural rights of the individual, Bailyn focused upon the "ideology" of the American revolutionary generation, deriving from the Commonwealth Whig or republican tradition. This tradition warned against the erosion of citizens' freedom by tyrannical

---

97. George Bancroft, *A History of the United States* (Boston, 1834), vol. 1, p. 4. Bancroft published this work in ten volumes between 1834 and 1874, and issued new editions until 1890.

98. See, for example, Charles A. Beard, *An Economic Interpretation of the Constitution of the United States* (New York, 1913); J. Franklin Jameson, *The American Revolution Considered as a Social Movement* (Princeton, NJ, 1926); Roger W. Shugg, *Origins of Class Struggle in Louisiana: A Social History of White Farmers and Laborers during Slavery and After, 1840–1875* (Baton Rouge, LA, 1939); Schlesinger, *The Age of Jackson*, pp. 306–7.

99. The "Consensus" school was identified and discussed critically by John Higham, "The Cult of the 'American Consensus'," *Commentary*, 27 (1959): 93–100. Significant exponents of the consensus view include: Hofstadter, *The American Political Tradition*; Boorstin, *The Genius of American Politics*; Hartz, *The Liberal Tradition in America*; Michael F. Holt, *Forging a Majority: The Formation of the Republican Party in Pittsburgh, 1848–1860* (New Haven, CT, 1969). Recently, Robert H. Wiebe appears to restate the consensus view. *The Opening of American Society*, p. xiii.

100. Carl L. Becker, *History of Political Parties in the Province of New York, 1760–1776* (Madison, WI, 1909); Charles H. McIlwain, *The American Revolution: A Constitutional Interpretation* (New York, 1923).

governments and emphasized the virtuous responsibility that each citizen owed to the corporate community and state, the *res publica*. Only gradually in the decades after the Revolution did "liberal Lockean" rights of the individual displace the republican tradition, according to this view.

Since the late 1960s, many scholars have embraced Bailyn's interpretation, and the subliminal influence of the continuing republican tradition has been traced in many dimensions of American culture throughout the nineteenth century.[101] Part of the reason for the widespread enthusiasm for this interpretation is that the republican tradition offers support for those, particularly recent social historians, who argue that a Lockean "consensus" never existed in American history. These scholars maintain instead that Consensus history expressed and legitimated the political conservatism of the 1950s.[102] Consequently, they regard the appearance of political parties in the 1790s as evidence of class divisions and conflict in American life. More recently, certain scholars have begun to reemphasize the centrality of Locke and natural rights to colonial and revolutionary America.[103] At the same time, advocates of the "new political history" have accounted for political partisanship by employing "the methods and speculations of the social sciences" and concluded that "ethnocultural conflict," rather than economic inequities, gave rise to American political parties.[104]

101. Caroline Robbins, *The Eighteenth-Century Commonwealthman* (Cambridge, MA, 1959); Bernard Bailyn, *The Ideological Origins of the American Revolution* (Cambridge, MA, 1967). See J. G. A. Pocock, *The Machiavellian Moment: Florentine Political Thought and the Atlantic Republican Tradition* (Princeton, NJ, 1975); Robert E. Shalhope, "Toward a Republican Synthesis: The Emergence of an Understanding of Republicanism in American Historiography," *WMQ*, 3d ser., 29 (1972): 49–80; Shalhope, "Republicanism and Early American Historiography," *WMQ*, 3d ser., 39 (1982): 334–56; Joyce Appleby, ed., "Republicanism in the History and Historiography of the United States," a special issue of the *American Quarterly*, 37 (Fall 1985).

102. To this, Richard Hofstadter responded that "the consensus idea" was neither necessarily "*prescriptive*" nor "intrinsically linked to ideological conservatism." *The Progressive Historians: Turner, Beard, Parrington* (New York, 1968), pp. 451–2.

103. Stuart Bruchey, "Law and Economic Change in the Early American Republic," in *American Industrialization, Economic Expansion, and the Law*, ed. Joseph R. Frese and Jacob Judd (Tarrytown, NY, 1981), p. 96; John P. Reid, *Constitutional History of the American Revolution: The Authority of Rights* (Madison, WI, 1986); Stanley N. Katz, "The American Constitution: A Revolutionary Interpretation," in *Beyond Confederation*, ed. Richard Beeman et al. (Chapel Hill, NC, 1987), pp. 23–37; Thomas L. Pangle, *The Spirit of Modern Republicanism: The Moral Vision of the American Founders and the Philosophy of Locke* (Chicago, 1988); Stephen Macedo, *Liberal Virtues: Citizenship, Virtue, and Community in Liberal Constitutionalism* (Oxford, 1990).

104. Joel H. Silbey, *The Partisan Imperative: The Dynamics of American Politics before the Civil War* (New York, 1985), pp. xiii, xvii; Richard L. McCormick, *The Party Period and Public Policy: American Politics from the Age of Jackson to the Progressive Era* (New York, 1986), pp. 89–140; Harry L. Watson, *Jacksonian Politics and Community Conflict: The Emergence of the Second Party System in Cumberland County North Carolina* (Baton Rouge, LA, 1981), pp. 1–16; John Ashworth, *"Agrarians" and "Aristocrats": Party Political Ideology in the United States, 1837–1846* (London, 1983).

Although it is hazardous to generalize from this tortuous historiography, one may safely conclude that Lockean natural rights became predominant by the beginning of the nineteenth century. One can therefore infer that the new political architectonic was given a "liberal" cast by eighteenth-century "enlightened" thought extending from Locke to Adam Smith. At the center of this liberal viewpoint were free-thinking and the free market, the free exchange of ideas and the free exchange of properties. And the connection between these two points was more intrinsic than their semantic association in the twofold denotation of "liberal" discussed above. The connection between free-thinking and the free market appears in the point demonstrated brilliantly by Charles Reich: ideas are properties and property is an idea.[105] In his analysis, Reich focused upon "the new property" of the twentieth century, including privileges and benefits that have become legally cognizable as properties, such as driver's licenses or welfare payments. But the insight is valid as well for the late eighteenth and early nineteenth centuries, the period when the newly invented abstractions of negotiable instruments and fungible commodities became properties that displaced real property in importance, as will be seen below.

The new cultural architectonic therefore constituted, in general terms, a concern for polity. That political concern implied, specifically, the two tenets of free-thinking and the free market, which stemmed from Locke, Smith, and eighteenth-century enlightened thought and came to be known as "liberal" due to the longstanding twofold denotation of generosity of mind and generosity in material possessions. That "liberal" viewpoint was then manifested in the law, the enactment of the political vision. The federal Constitution consequently enshrined rights to property and contract, while establishing in the First Amendment rights designed to ensure what Oliver Wendell Holmes, Jr., later called "free trade in ideas – that the best test of truth is the power of the thought to get itself accepted in the competition of the market."[106] Meanwhile the twofold liberal viewpoint informed the adoption and interpretation of the inherited, common law jurisprudence, which was well suited to express the liberal polity of the young American nation. As the Constitutional Court of South Carolina noted in 1821, one "who has been bred a lawyer" is one "whose mind has been thereby liberalized."[107]

105. Charles A. Reich, "The New Property," *Yale Law Journal,* 73 (1964): 733–87.

106. *US Constitution,* art. 1, sect. 10, para. 1; amendments 1, 5. Joined by Justice Louis D. Brandeis, Holmes expressed this view in a famous dissent in *Adams* v. *United States,* 250 US 616, 624, 634–5 (1919).

107. *Duncan* v. *Breithaupt,* 1 McCord 149, 154 (South Carolina 1821). Seven of the 11 exemplary "liberals" identified by Steven Watts were trained in the law and another intended to do so. (*The Republic Reborn: War and the Making of Liberal America, 1790–1820,* passim.) It is also noteworthy that Francis Lieber, the paradigmatic "nineteenth-century liberal," is the "one figure of specific importance" for political science in the antebellum period, and Lieber's *Manual of Political Ethics designed Chiefly for the Use of Colleges and Students at Law,* 2 vols. (Boston, 1838–9), 2d edn (Philadelphia, 1875) was "the first systematic treatise on political science to appear in America." Bernard Crick, *The American Science of Politics: Its Origins and Conditions* (Berkeley, CA, 1959), p. 15; Anna Haddow, *Political Science in American Colleges and Universities, 1636–1900,* ed. William Anderson (New York, 1939), pp. 94–7; Charles E. Merriam, *American Political Theories* (New York, 1928), p. 305; Frank Freidel, *Francis Lieber: Nineteenth-Century Liberal* (Baton Rouge, LA, 1947).

The Court meant not that lawyers were educated to be avaricious capitalists, but that the "liberalized" legal mind was trained to challenge *a priori* truths and to inquire about other points of view and take account of them. This capacity was necessary to defend one's client in the adversary model of jurisprudence, which constituted a marketplace of ideas. In contrast to systems of mediation and arbitration, the adversary system cast lawyers in the role of single-minded advocates devoted to their clients' interests. The "Common Law image of man" was "one of self-interest, of pressing one's legal rights against any individual or against society ... regardless of the morality of one's cause."[108] At first glance, the adversary system may appear to identify justice with the will of the strong or the lucky. But it fundamentally rests on the principle that the just resolution of a dispute must be approximated in a marketplace of ideas, where all views are presented competitively and duly considered. From this perspective, an "adversary presentation seems the only effective means for combatting this natural tendency to judge too swiftly in terms of the familiar that which is not yet fully known."[109] That principle derives, in turn, from an epistemology of skepticism maintaining that justice is too uncertain and elusive to be known definitively. "The advocate's prime loyalty is to his client, not to truth as such," for "in the end who really knows what is truth?"[110]

The difficult point in this argument comes in determining the degree to which advocates, being amoral skeptical technicians, are free to ignore their personal sense of justice in order that the marketplace of ideas may work uninhibited. It has long been agreed that lawyers may not commit illegal acts, but there is a great deal of disagreement over whether lawyers have a responsibility not to employ some patently unfair tactic in advancing a client's interest or whether they have an affirmative duty to report an illegal act admitted by a client, thus breaking the client's confidence. The difficulty of arguing on behalf of such a responsibility or duty lies in reconciling them with the paradox, which lies at the heart of Anglo-American jurisprudence, that justice is most closely approximated when the marketplace of ideas works freely and the adversarial advocates argue on behalf of their clients' interests without preconceptions about the justice of the causes represented.[111]

108. John R. Aiken, "Utopianism and the Emergence of the Colonial Legal Profession: New York, 1664–1710, A Test Case" (PhD diss., University of Rochester, 1967), pp. vii–viii.

109. "Professional Responsibility: Report of the Joint Conference on Professional Responsibility of the Association of American Law Schools and the American Bar Association," *ABA Journal,* 44 (1958): 1162. This language was incorporated into the ABA Model Code of Professional Responsibility (1969) under EC 7-19 "Duty of the Lawyer to the Adversary System of Justice," reprinted in *1985 Selected Standards on Professional Responsibility,* ed. T. D. Morgan and R. D. Rotunda (Mineola, NY, 1985).

110. Marvin Frankel, "The Search for Truth: An Umpireal View," *University of Pennsylvania Law Review* (1975): 1035, 1038–9.

111. John T. Noonan, Jr., "The Purposes of Advocacy and the Limits of Confidentiality," *Michigan Law Review,* 64 (1966): 1485–92; Monroe H. Freedman, *Lawyers' Ethics in an Adversary System* (Indianapolis, IN, 1975); Charles Fried, "The Lawyer as Friend: The Moral Foundations of the Lawyer–Client Relation," *Yale Law Journal,* 85 (1976): 1080–7; Henry D. Levine, "Self-Interest or Self-Defense: Lawyer Disregard of the Attorney–Client Privilege for Profit and Protection," *Hofstra Law Review,* 5 (1977): 783–829; William H. Simon, "The Ideology of Advocacy: Procedural Justice and Professional Ethics," *Wisconsin*

Like the liberal marketplace of ideas, the liberal free market of properties also inhered in the jurisprudence of the new nation, especially in the rule of law. Described in different ways, the rule of law is generally said to include at least the tenets that laws must be clear, publicized, prospective, general, and applied equally.[112] These "general conditions of legal formalism" were precisely those demanded by commercial transactions in the free market. Such transactions required the assurance that disputes would be settled by consistent adherence to substantively neutral and impersonal rules agreed upon in advance. Without this assurance, the market could not work freely. Thus, merchants in North Carolina, Virginia, and Maryland called for courts where cases would be heard not by JPs guided by a personal sense of justice, but "by trained judges, under standardized procedures, and governed by known precedents."[113]

Though implied in several provisions of the new state and federal Constitutions, such as prohibitions against any "Bill of Attainder or ex post facto Law," the rule of law developed gradually in the early decades of the United States. In particular, adherence to the rule of law varied according to whether the new commercial culture was well established, as in Massachusetts, or incipient, as in South Carolina.[114] Nevertheless, courts gradually affirmed the rule of law. In 1798 and again in 1810 the US Supreme Court warned against "retrospective laws" and invoked the Constitutional prohibitions against *ex post facto* laws and bills of attainder. In 1818 the New Hampshire Supreme Court held that statutes must be general and applied equally; hence, a legislature cannot act in a "judicial" capacity and resolve by statute a dispute between individuals.[115] This principle was explicitly endorsed in 1819 in Massachusetts, 1833 in North Carolina, and 1845 in Tennessee.[116]

Consequently, the very nature of Anglo-American law, as well as the new federal Constitution, provided, through the adversary system and the rule of law, for the

---

Law Review (1978): 29–144; Erwin Chemerinsky, "Protecting Lawyers from their Profession: Redefining the Lawyer's Role," *Journal of the Legal Profession*, 5 (1980): 31–43; Deborah L. Rhode, "Ethical Perspectives on Legal Practice," *Stanford Law Review*, 37 (1985): 589–652.

112. Lon Fuller, *The Morality of Law* (New Haven, CT, 1964), ch. 2; Friedrich A. Hayek, *The Political Ideal of the Rule of Law* (Cairo, 1955), lect. 3, ss. 14–5; Robert P. Wolff, ed., *The Rule of Law* (New York, 1971); Joseph Raz, *The Authority of Law: Essays on Law and Morality* (New York, 1979), ch. 11.

113. Quotations are from Max Weber, *Economy and Society: An Outline of Interpretive Sociology*, ed. Guenther Roth and Claus Wittich, tr. Ephraim Fischoff et al. (New York, 1968), vol. 2, ch. 8, sect. v; Risjord, *Chesapeake Politics, 1781–1800*, p. 182. See Roeber, *Faithful Magistrates and Republican Lawyers ... 1680–1910*, chs. 5–6; John R. Nelson, Jr., *Liberty and Property: Political Economy and Policymaking in the New Nation, 1789–1812* (Baltimore, MD, 1987).

114. *US Constitution*, art. 1, sect. 9, para. 3; Noble E. Cunningham, Jr., *The Jeffersonian Republicans: The Formation of Party Organization, 1789–1901* (Chapel Hill, NC, 1957), ch. 8; Hindus, *Prison and Plantation: Crime, Justice, and Authority in Massachusetts and South Carolina, 1767–1878*, ch. 1.

115. *Calder* v. *Bull*, 3 Dallas (3 US) 386, 390–1 (1798); *Fletcher* v. *Peck*, 6 Cranch (10 US) 87, 136–9 (1810); *Merrill* v. *Sherburne*, 1 New Hampshire 199, 212–7 (1818).

116. *Foster* v. *Essex Bank*, 16 Massachusetts 245 (1819); *Hoke* v. *Henderson*, 15 North Carolina 1 (1833); *Mayor and Aldermen* v. *Maberry*, 6 Humphreys 368 (Tennessee 1845).

twofold "liberal" viewpoint of free-thinking and the free market, the free exchange of ideas and of properties unhindered by moral absolutes. The concern for building a polity dominated culture and turned "every citizen" into "a political architect," as Samuel Goodrich observed in a popular textbook. Notwithstanding this espoused egalitarianism, the leading "political architects" came from the bench and bar. This was so not merely because law was the instrument by which any political vision was necessarily enacted but, more fundamentally, because the nature of the inherited jurisprudence fit remarkably well with the envisioned political architecture. "To this profession," Edward Hazen observed, "the American people may confidently look for the maintenance of correct political principles."[117] This ideological fit between law and the "liberal" polity then translated into, while it was reflexively strengthened by, juridical, political, social, and economic authority for lawyers. Before examining those issues, we turn to describe the fourth moment in the rhetoric of "profession," which was informed by the nature of the new preeminent profession in America.

Rhetorical: "now professional with the bar"

Through the middle of the nineteenth century, "profession" was still being employed in the sense of religious vow, as in the 1824 tract *Profession is not Principle; or, The Name of Christian is not Christianity.* Nevertheless, theological usage continued to decline as occupational usage was emphasized and dignified. This development is the second moment in the rhetoric of "profession." Thus, the terms "confession" and "denomination" more and more crowded out the religious usage of "profession," while Rev. Henry Ware, for example, asked the Harvard graduating class of 1847 to advance Christianity "by a faithful life and a consistent profession," by which he meant their jobs, not their religious vow or sect.[118] In addition, following from the third moment in the rhetoric of "profession," the

117. Samuel G. Goodrich, *The Young American: or Book of Government and Law* (New York, 1845), p. 1; Edward Hazen, *The Panorama of Professions and Trades* (Philadelphia, 1837), p. 126.

118. [Grace Kennedy], *Profession is not Principle; or, The Name of Christian is not Christianity*, 2d edn (New York, 1824); Henry Ware, Jr., "The Principles that Should Govern a Young Man in the Choice of a Profession," *Works* (Boston, 1847), vol. 3, p. 269. This judgment is based on a review of the 76,000+ titles in *American Bibliography, 1801–1825.* See, for example, Reformed Dutch Church in North America, *The Psalms of David, with ... confession of faith and liturgy of the Reformed Church in the Netherlands* (New York, 1805); Presbytery of Springfield, *An Apology ... To which is Added ... a Few Remarks on the Confession of Faith* (Lexington, KY, 1805); Mennonite Church, *The Christian Confession of the faith [of those] ... known by the name of Mennonists* (New Market, VA, 1810); Congregational Churches of Vermont, *A Shorter Confession of Faith with Scripture Proofs* (Middlebury, VT, 1812); David Simpson, *A Plea for Religion ... Addressed ... to Wavering Christians of Every Denomination* (Baltimore, MD, 1807); David Rise, *A Second Epistle to the Citizens of Kentucky Professing the Cs. religion, Especially Those Who are or have been Denominated Presbyterians* (Lexington, KY, 1808); [anon.] *A Concise View of the Principal Religious Denominations in the US of America* (Philadelphia, 1811).

terms "liberal professions" and "learned professions" were popularly employed, and "professions" was used synonymously with them. Such discourse was found in the 1830 call for "establishing a university in the City of New York" and the 1840 pronouncement of a faculty member at Pennsylvania College that "a more elevated and liberal education" is "principally designed to prepare young men for what are termed the learned professions."[119] Theodore Parker, Francis Wayland, and various jurists from New York to South Carolina employed similar language while distinguishing "a professional person" from those who "carry on any handicraft, trade, or calling."[120]

To be sure, the terminological distinction among vocations was not precise. The older, broader usage of "profession" in the sense of any calling still appeared, particularly in British publications reprinted in the United States, such as the popular *Book of Trades, or Library of the Useful Arts.* Even members of college faculties were not consistent in confining their usage of "profession" to divinity, law, physic, and education.[121] In addition, some individuals, particularly engineers, who desired to elevate their vocation and associate it with the learned professions, self-consciously employed the term "profession."[122] This desire appeared as well in the declared need of "having more of the children of wealthy citizens educated for the profession of farming," expressed by the Surveyor General of New York in 1819. This broader usage, however, merely testified to the dignified sense that had been conveyed to the term "profession" in the second rhetorical moment. The popular *Panorama of Professions and Trades* (1837), which described nearly one hundred vocations, applied the term "profession" only to ministers, lawyers, and doctors, denominating the rest as "trade," "art," "employment," or "business."[123]

119. [anon.], *Considerations upon ... Establishing a University in The City of New York,* p. 7; H. I. Smith, *Education* (New York, 1842), pp. 248–9.

120. Theodore Parker, "Thoughts on Labor" (1841), in *Works: Social Classes in a Republic,* ed. Samuel A. Eliot (Boston, 1907), pp. 76, 91; Francis Wayland, *The Education demanded by the People of the U. States, A Discourse Delivered at Union College* (1854; reprint, Schenectady, NY, 1973), pp. 36–7; David D. Field, David Graham, and Aphraxed Loomis, *First Report of the New York Commissioners on Practice and Pleadings* (New York, 1848), p. 207; *Snee* v. *Trice,* 2 Bay 345, 346–7 (South Carolina 1802).

121. *The Book of Trades, or Library of the Useful Arts* (London, 1806; Philadelphia, 1807; Richmond, VA, 1807), pp. 30, 103; *Reports on the Course of Instruction in Yale College by a Committee of the Corporation and the Academical Faculty* (New Haven, CT, 1828), p. 32; Theodore Parker, "The American Scholar" (1849), in *Works: The American Scholar,* ed. Samuel A. Eliot (Boston, 1907), p. 10.

122. Nathan Reingold, "Definitions and Speculations: The Professionalization of Science in America in the Nineteenth Century," in *The Pursuit of Knowledge in the Early Republic,* ed. Alexandra Oleson and Sanborn C. Brown (Baltimore, MD, 1976), p. 49; Monte A. Calvert, *The Mechanical Engineer in America, 1830–1910* (Baltimore, MD, 1967), p. 109; Daniel H. Calhoun, *The American Civil Engineer: Origins and Conflict* (Cambridge, MA, 1960), ch. 8; Bruce Sinclair, "Episodes in the History of the American Engineering Profession," in *The Professions in American History,* ed. Nathan O. Hatch (Notre Dame, IN, 1988), p. 129.

123. Simeon De Witt, *Considerations on the Necessity of Establishing an Agricultural College, and Having More of the Children of Wealthy Citizens Educated for the Profession of Farming* (New York, 1819). In *The Panorama of Professions and Trades,* Hazen calls architecture a "profession" once in passing (p. 205).

This conventional, restrictive usage of "professions" appeared particularly in comparative statements where "professors" of these fields constituted a separate social category analogous to other, much larger categories.[124] In his 1753 plan for a college William Smith proposed to "divide the whole Body of People into two grand Classes. The First consists of those designed for the learn'd Professions ... *Divinity, Law, Physic, Agriculture,* and the Chief Offices of the State. The Second Class of those design'd for Mechanic Professions, and all the remaining People of the Country." In *The Federalist* Alexander Hamilton divided society among "the manufacturing and trading interests," "the learned professions," and "the landed interest." Subsequently Byerly Thomson proposed: "Mind, body, and capital, being the three elements of production, point to the three divisions of classes who employ these for the purposes of a living – namely, into professional men, handworkers, and merchants."[125] Similarly, those in the agricultural education movement, such as Jonathan Turner in Illinois and Justin Morrill of Vermont, asserted that society was divided "into two, distinct, cooperative, not antagonistic, classes." The small minority was the "Professional" – those professing "religion, medicine, law, science, art, and literature" – and the great majority was the "Industrial" which included farmers, artisans, merchants, and mechanics.[126] In these classifica-

124. The "professions" comprised but a small percentage of the population during this period. In New York City, for example, about 4 percent of free adult males were ministers, lawyers, or doctors in 1796 and 1855, whereas in Virginia, Georgia, Alabama, and Mississippi in 1850 less than 1 percent of the population were lawyers, physicians, editors, and teachers. Census figures from 1840, 1850, and 1860 indicate that ministers, lawyers, and physicians were less than one-half of 1 percent of the entire population and less than 1 percent of the free male population. Notwithstanding the difficulty in comparing such data, it may be said that these "professors" comprised no more than 2 percent of the total labor force between the mid-eighteenth and mid-nineteenth century. J. D. B. DeBow, *Statistical View of the United States ... Being a Compendium of ... the Results of Every Previous Census, Beginning with 1790* (Washington, DC, 1854), tables 128, 130, 131, pp. 125, 128–9; Taylor and Parsons, *Professional Education in the United States,* p. 9; P. K. Whelpton, "Occupational Groups in the United States, 1820–1920," *Journal of the American Statistical Association,* 21 (1926): 339–40; Frances P. DeLancy, *The Licensing of Professions in West Virginia* (Chicago, 1938), p. 44; Sidney H. Aronson, *Status and Kinship in the Higher Civil Service: Standards of Selection in the Administrations of John Adams, Thomas Jefferson, and Andrew Jackson* (Cambridge, MA, 1964), pp. 45ff.; Carl F. Kaestle, *The Evolution of an Urban School Systems, New York City, 1750–1850* (Cambridge, MA, 1973), tables 1, 15, pp. 31, 102; Holifield, *The Gentleman Theologians ... in Southern Culture, 1795–1860,* p. 32.

125. William Smith, *A General Idea of the College of Mirania* (New York, 1753), pp. 13–4; [Alexander Hamilton], *Federalist No. 35,* in *The Federalist, A Commentary on the Constitution of the United States* (1788; reprint, New York, 1964); H. Byerly Thomson, *The Choice of a Profession* (London, 1857), p. 3; William J. Barber, "Political Economy from the Top Down: Brown University," in *Breaking the Academic Mould: Economists and American Higher Learning in the Nineteenth Century,* ed. Barber (Middletown, CT, 1988), pp. 73–8.

126. Jonathan B. Turner, "A Plan for an Industrial University for the State of Illinois" (1851), reprinted in *Proceedings of the Society for the Promotion of Agricultural Science,* 28 (1914): 54. Justin S. Morrill, *The Land-Grant Colleges, An Address* (Burlington, VT, 1893), p. 10; Edward D. Eddy, Jr., *Colleges for our Land and Time: The Land-Grant Idea in American Education* (New York, 1957), pp. 36–7.

tions, one finds evidence of the fourth moment in the rhetoric of "profession." Marking another step in the emergence of "the true professional ideal" in America, this fourth rhetorical moment is the appearance of the adjective "professional," which was sponsored and informed by the rise of the legal profession.

It is striking that this semantic development has been neglected despite the abundant attention given to language both contemporaneously and in recent time. The period between the Revolution and the Civil War saw "the coming into being of an American language and an American literature," and the revolution in the polity was explicitly connected to rebellion in the republic of letters. Noah Webster was the chief rebel of language, compiling his *American Dictionary of the English Language* (1828) and arguing that "A *national language* is a brand of *national union*.... Let us then seize the present moment and establish a *national language*, as well as a national government."[127] Nor was this attention to political language confined to the new nation. Books on "political fallacies" by Jeremy Bentham, on "definitions in political economy" by Thomas Malthus, "on the Use and Abuse of Some Political terms" by George C. Lewis, "on certain terms which are peculiarly liable to be used ambiguously in Political Economy" by Nassau Senior appeared in Britain and circulated in the United States in the second quarter of the nineteenth century.[128]

Recent scholars have likewise studied the "language of politics" generally, the "paradigms of judicial rhetoric" in the antebellum period, and "keywords in American politics since independence."[129] In addition, scholars have examined the

127. Quotations are from David Simpson, *The Politics of American English, 1776–1850* (New York, 1986), p. 28, chs. 1–2; Noah Webster, *Dissertations on the English Language: with Notes Historical and Critical* (Boston, 1789), p. 397. See Joseph J. Ellis, *After the Revolution: Profiles of Early American Culture* (New York, 1979), pp. 172–3, ch. 4; Rollins, *The Long Journey of Noah Webster,* ch. 8.

128. Jeremy Bentham, *The Handbook of Political Fallacies* (1824), rev. and ed. H. A. Larrabee (New York, 1952); Thomas R. Malthus, *Definitions in Political Economy ... preceded by Rules which Ought to Guide Political Economists in the Definitions and Use of their Terms* (London, 1827); George C. Lewis, *Remarks on the Use and Abuse of some Political Terms* (1832; Columbia, MO, 1970); Nassau W. Senior, *Outline of the Science of Political Economy* (London, 1836), appendix. Meanwhile, for the foreign visitor to the United States early in the nineteenth century, "the greatest curiosities ... were the changes in the pronunciation and in the use of words." Jane L. Mesick, *The English Traveller in America, 1785–1835* (New York, 1922), p. 241. See John M. Duncan, *Travels through Part of the United States and Canada 1818 and 1819* (New York, 1823), vol. 1, p. 306; Isaac Candler, *A Summary View of America* (London, 1824), p. 331; Godfrey T. Vigne, *Six Months in America* (London, 1832), vol. 2, p. 75; Thomas Hamilton, *Men and Manners in America* (Edinburgh, 1823), vol. 1, p. 227; Edward S. Abdy, *Journal of a Residence and Tour in the United States* (London, 1835), vol. 1, p. 186.

129. Harold Lasswell, Nathan Leites, et al., *Language of Politics: Studies in Quantitative Semantics* (New York, 1949); Cover, *Justice Accused: Antislavery and the Judicial Process,* pp. 119–30; Daniel T. Rodgers, *Contested Truths: Keywords in American Politics since Independence* (New York, 1987). Mark Olsen and Louis-George Harvey show that Rodgers's selection of "keywords" in the first half of the nineteenth century is based not on the quantitative frequency of the appearance of the "keyword," but "on the ideological importance of those words." ("Contested Methods: Daniel T. Rodgers's *Contested Truths," Journal of the*

sermonic rhetoric of clergymen responding to the Revolution, as well as the language of partisan politics in speeches, periodicals, and pamphlets of the 1830s and 1840s.[130] They have also treated "literary texts" that "help define the legal ideology" of the antebellum period, and considered "the complex links between language and authority, and language and power, that came to exist in the minds of the men who first shaped this country."[131] In fact scholars have specifically addressed "the rhetoric of vocation and work" and "how literary activity constructed the professional" in the early decades of the United States.[132] Scholars have accomplished all this, however, without attending to the appearance of the term "professional" or its link to the rise of the legal profession, which is the fourth moment in the rhetoric of "profession" in America.

The term "professional" extends back at least to the fifteenth century as an adjective meaning "avowed" and referring to religious professions. Characterizing this usage as "obsolete, rare" the *OED* cites only one example, dated from 1420, and recent scholars have generally neglected the religious sense of the term.[133] Yet in the second half of the eighteenth century when "professional" began to gain

History of Ideas, 49 (1988): 654.) Rodgers replies astutely that "a keyword is characterized not by its frequency in discourse but by the intensity of contest over its use and possession." ("Keywords: A Reply," *Journal of the History of Ideas*, 49 (1988): 674.) Even this astute reply, however, begs the question of how "intensity of contest" is determined.

130. Donald Weber, *Rhetoric and History in Revolutionary New England* (New York, 1988); Lawrence F. Kohl, *The Politics of Individualism: Parties and the American Character in the Jacksonian Era* (New York, 1989); Marie L. Ahearn, *The Rhetoric of War: Training Day, the Militia, and the Military Sermon* (Westport, CT, 1989).

131. Thomas, *Cross-examinations of Law and Literature: Cooper, Hawthorne, Stowe, and Melville*, p. 4; Cynthia S. Jordan, "'Old Words' in 'New Circumstances': Language and Leadership in Post-Revolutionary America," *American Quarterly*, 40 (1988): 503; Robert A. Ferguson, *Law and Letters in American Culture* (Cambridge, MA, 1984). Thomas dismisses "reflection theory" (pp. 3ff.), which is employed by Mark R. Patterson in an effort to show that major literary figures in the first half of the nineteenth century dwelled on the issues of political authority, autonomy, and representation in order to enhance their own social authority. On the other hand, both Thomas and Patterson employ the analogy between law and literature, which is dismissed by Richard A. Posner. Patterson, *Authority, Autonomy, and Representation in American Literature, 1776–1865* (Princeton, NJ, 1988); Posner, *Law and Literature: A Misunderstood Relation* (Cambridge, MA, 1988).

132. Marie L. Ahearn, "The Rhetoric of Work and Vocation in some Popular Northern Writings before 1860" (PhD diss., Brown University, 1965); Clifford Siskin, "Wordsworth's Prescriptions: Romanticism and Professional Power," in *The Romantics and Us*, ed. Gene W. Ruoff (New Brunswick, NJ, 1990), pp. 303–21.

133. *OED*, s.v. "professional." Eminent sociologists, such as Everett C. Hughes, have tended to ignore the religious usage altogether while citing the *OED*. ("Professions," in *The Professions in America*, ed. Kenneth S. Lynn (1963; Boston, 1967), pp. 2, 4.) Discussing the clergy's use of the term "professional" in the early nineteenth century, Holifield ironically neglects its religious significance. (*The Gentleman Theologians ... in Southern Culture, 1795–1860*, p. 34.) Other scholars anachronistically put the term in quotation marks as though it were used in their period with a modern meaning. Schmotter, "The Irony of Clerical Professionalism," p. 149; Holmes, *Augustan England: Professions, State and Society, 1680–1730*, p. 5.

wider usage the religious sense of the word appeared prominently. In 1788 a notable Baptist in Pennsylvania defended his denomination on the grounds that: "Baptism washeth away the defilements of sin professionally. Every subject of this ordinance professeth faith in Christ." In 1794 Thomas Paine published *Age of Reason,* which went through more than seventeen editions, and in the very first chapter entitled "The Author's Profession of Faith," Paine wrote: "I do not believe in the creed professed ... by any church.... When a man has ... subscribe[d] *his professional belief* to things he does not believe, he has prepared himself for the commission of every other crime."[134] This adjectival meaning of "avowed" was not confined to religion, but extended to matters of law and polity. In 1805 a Republican ally warned Thomas Jefferson against "verbal professional Republicans ... on whom no dependence can, or ought to be placed."[135] Neglecting this sense of "professional" as "archaic usage" of the fifteenth century, the *OED* cites 27 examples of "professional" pertaining to vocation or employment. Two of these instances antedate 1800, one from 1793 and the earliest from 1747–8.

Now, it appears to be true that "professional" in the sense of "occupational" gradually entered into common usage in the late eighteenth and early nineteenth centuries. In the Eighteenth-Century Short Title Catalog, the term appears first in 1772, then four times in the 1780s and three times in the 1790s – all in publications printed in England. It does not appear in *American Bibliography* until 1811. But scholars have been misled into thinking that the "occupational" reference was the exclusive meaning of the term or even its original meaning, given that the *OED* presents the reference to a religious "profession" as a long-forgotten artifact of the 1400s. This misrepresentation is epitomized in the 1747–8 instance of "professional," which the *OED* offers as the earliest instance of the "occupational" sense: "Professional, as well as national, reflections are to be avoided." The 1747–8 example is quoted from Samuel Johnson's dictionary of 1755, which attributed it to Samuel Richardson's famous novel *Clarissa,* first published in the winter of 1747–8.[136] One point to note immediately about the quotation is that "professional" is contrasted with "national." Since this contrast would be more fitting if "professional" meant "sectarian," rather than "occupational," the quotation on its face appears to favor reading "professional" in its religious sense. An examination of the source of the example supports this reading in a surprising way.

Samuel Johnson cited Richardson frequently in his *Dictionary.* In fact he had to answer criticism that such novelists "were beneath the dignity" of his work because

134. C. Whitfield, "Ananias's Reprehension and Exhortation to Saul," in *Two Discourses* (Philadelphia, 1788), p. 43; Spencer, *A History of Kentucky Baptists,* vol. 1, p. 500; Thomas Paine, *The Age of Reason* (1794), in *The Writings of Thomas Paine,* ed. Moncure D. Conway (New York, 1899), vol. 4, pt. 1, ch. 1. Emphasis added.

135. Warning to Jefferson quoted in Ellis, *The Jeffersonian Crisis: Courts and Politics in the Young Republic,* p. 212. The semantic shift in "professional" is demonstrated perfectly by an 1873 editorial against "A Professional 'Republican'" who earned money lecturing on his political views. "A Professional 'Republican'," *New-York Times* (September 19, 1873): 4.

136. Samuel Johnson, *A Dictionary of the English Language* (London, 1755), s.v. "professional." Robert DeMaria, Jr., recently analyzed some 1,300 entries in Johnson's *Dictionary,* but not "profession" or its permutations. *Johnson's DICTIONARY and the Language of Learning* (Chapel Hill, NC, 1986).

they "have in great measure corrupted our language and taste." The reason for this opinion was that Richardson's novels were said to employ "minute flippancies of expression, colloquial phrases, new-coined words, and involved periods" often derived from the idiom of the day.[137] In the preface to *Clarissa*, Richardson acknowledged that "his Language ... is not always to be found in the Works of some of the most celebrated modern Writers'; and scholars have maintained that he "invented a new species of writing" by employing "the normal language of his time."[138] Whether idiomatic, novel, or both, his use of language was highly self-conscious, and so it is fitting that *Clarissa* provides the fulcrum for the shift in meaning of "professional."

In his various writings Richardson generally employed the term "profession" and its permutations in the sense of "vow," and he repeated this sense in 1755 when he compiled a book of quotations from his own writings. Indeed, it was under the category "Church, Clergy" that Richardson included the quotation: *"Professional* as well as *national* reflexions are to be avoided."[139] This quotation book is, in fact, the source of Johnson's quotation of Richardson, notwithstanding Johnson's and the *OED*'s references to *Clarissa*.[140] The significance of the quotation book is that it reaffirms the ambiguity of the original text, which reads: "I must needs say, that the clergy should practise what they preach.... For my part, I don't

---

137. Quotations are from James Boswell, *Boswell's Life of Johnson* (1791), ed. George B. Hill and L. F. Powell, 6 vols. (Oxford, 1934–50), vol. 4, p. 4; A Lover of Virtue, *Critical Remarks on Sir Charles Grandison, Clarissa and Pamela* (1754; Los Angeles, 1950), p. 3; Edward Mangin, ed., *The Works of Samuel Richardson with a Sketch of his Life and Writings* (London, 1811), vol. 1, p. xxiii.

138. Samuel Richardson, *Clarissa or, The History of a Young Lady*, 8 vols. (London: 1748), vol. 1, p. iv; Irwin Gopnik, *A Theory of Style and Richardson's CLARISSA* (Paris, 1970), p. 42; Terry Eagleton, *The Rape of Clarissa: Writing, Sexuality and Class Struggle in Samuel Richardson* (Oxford, 1982), p. 40. See Wilhelm Uhrstrom, *Studies on the Language of Samuel Richardson* (Upsala, 1907), p. 3. As a result Richardson is vastly influential and much studied, but even those who have examined related topics have not addressed his importance for "professional." See Cynthia G. Wolff, *Samuel Richardson and the Eighteenth-Century Puritan Character* (Hamden, CT, 1972); Richard G. Hannaford, *Samuel Richardson: An Annotated Bibliography of Critical Studies* (New York, 1980).

139. Samuel Richardson, *A Collection of the Moral and Instructive Sentiments*, p. 100. For other examples of "profess-," see Richardson, "Hints of Prefaces for *Clarissa*" (n.d.), in *Clarissa: Preface, Hints of Prefaces, and Postscript*, introduction by R. F. Brissenden (Los Angeles, 1964), p. 1; Richardson, *Clarissa*, vol. 1, p. iv; Richardson, *A Collection of the Moral and Instructive Sentiments*, pp. 91, 67.

140. This fact is evident because Richardson misquoted and mis-cited himself, and Samuel Johnson and the *OED* used the misquotations and mis-citations. The errors are not surprising because *Clarissa* appeared first as seven volumes published in three installments, then, after a partial reprinting, in an edition of 1751 consisting of eight volumes published in twelve books. A fourth edition of seven volumes published in eight books also appeared in the 1750s. Abridged editions appear in the United States in 1795, 1798 and 1800. "Bibliographical Note," pp. ix–x, in *Clarissa or, The History of a Young Lady*, by Samuel Richardson, 8 vols. (1751; Oxford, 1930); R. F. Brissenden, "Introduction," p. i, in *Clarissa: Preface, Hints of Prefaces, and Postscript*, by Samuel Richardson (Los Angeles, 1964).

love *professional* any more than *national* reflections."[141] By categorizing the quotation under "Church, Clergy," Richardson seems to stress the ambiguity between "religious" and "occupational," which comports with the transition being made at the time between the general and particular calling.

Samuel Johnson, however, and later the *OED*, obliterated the ambiguity and transition by citing Richardson's quotation solely for support of the occupational sense of "professional." This interpretation was made authoritative by the facts that Johnson's dictionary was the first to include the term and that it next appeared, along with Johnson's exact definition, in John Walker's *A Critical Pronouncing Dictionary* (1791), which was reprinted 100 times by 1904.[142] The interpretation then fit perfectly with twentieth-century concern for professionalization and professionalism, and this twentieth-century neglect of the religious sense of "professional" has corresponded with inattention to the adjective "professed" that had denoted "occupational" until surrendering that usage to "professional."

Although the word "professed" often implies deception to recent scholars of the professions, it usually conveyed sincere belief and commitment to seventeenth- and eighteenth-century "professors." In addition, this past participle became the natural adjective to describe those who "professed" a certain vocation. In the 1600s Francis Bacon referred to "professed lawyers" and "professed soldiers," and Samuel Langley complained that "Men are grown professed politicians."[143] In the 1700s the term appeared in treatises by or about various kinds of "professors": a "professed cook," "professed author," or "professed housekeeper." Other adjectives, such as "professionary" and "professionist" occasionally were employed as well, but "professed" appeared most commonly in this vocational sense.[144] Into the nineteenth century "professed" continued to be used in the same fashion. Contemporaneous with the first appearance of the word "professional" in *American Bibliography* in 1811 is a tract by a "professed botanist." In 1828 the famous *Yale*

---

141. Richardson, *Clarissa* (1748), vol. 5, p. 19; (1751), vol. 5, p. 81.

142. John Walker, *A Critical Pronouncing Dictionary* (1791; Menston, UK, 1968), s.v. "professional." On seventeenth-century dictionaries, see the discussion in Note 14 of Chapter 2. In the eighteenth century, "professional" did not appear in J. K. [John Kersey], *A New English Dictionary* (1702; Menston, UK, 1969); Nathan Bailey *Dictionarium Britannicum: Or a more Compleat Universal Etymological English Dictionary than any Extant* (1730; Menston, UK, 1969); James Buchanan, *Linguae Britannicae Vera Pronunciatio* (1757; Menston, UK, 1967); Thomas Spence, *The Grand Repository of the English Language* (1775; Menston, UK, 1969). See De Witt T. Starnes and Gertrude E. Noyes, *The English Dictionary from Cawdrey to Johnson, 1604–1755* (Chapel Hill, NC, 1946), p. 146.

143. Francis Bacon, *Maxims of the Law* (1597), in *The Works*, ed. James Spedding et al. (Boston, 1861), vol. 14, p. 183; Bacon, "The Essayes or Counsels, Civill and Morall" (1625), in *The Works*, vol. 12, p. 183; Langley, *The Persecuted Minister, In defence of the Ministerie*, p. 159.

144. Ann Cook, *Professed cookery: Containing Boiling, Roasting …*, 2d edn (London, 1755); [B. Clermont], *The Professed Cook, or the modern art of cookery*, 2d edn (London, 1769), 10th edn (London, 1812); Charlotte Mason, *The Lady's Assistant … now First Published … from a Professed Housekeeper* (London, 1773); *A Key to the Drama, or Memoirs, Intrigues and Atchievements* [sic] *… By a Gentleman no Professed Author but a lover of History and of the Theatre* (London, 1768).

Report referred to a "professed chemist" having "superior knowledge in his profession."[145] In the 1830s civil engineers and railroad companies debated the merits of hiring a technically educated "professed Engineer." In 1845 the pastor of First Baptist Church in Philadelphia spoke of "the ministers of religion" as "the professed friends of Christ," and the future president of Brown University called them "the professed moral and religious teachers of the community" in 1853.[146] As late as the 1860s a "professed launderer" published *The LAUNDRY manual; or, Washing Made Easy* and an essay appeared on "training professed teachers."[147]

By that time, however, such references were anomalous, and the adjective "professional" was conventional. In the Eighteenth-Century Short Title Catalog "professional" appears only once in the 1760s and 1770s, while "professed" is found several times in the sense of "occupational." But in the 1780s usage of "professional" in reference to ministers, lawyers, and doctors increased, as seen in the *State Gazette of Georgia* and the *Pennsylvania Packet.* Meanwhile Alexander Hamilton recorded that the British spy Major John André requested "to be indulged with a professional death," meaning that he wished to die as a soldier by a firing squad rather than by hanging as a spy.[148] In 1799 Samuel Knox, longtime principal of an academy in Maryland, argued that teachers should be paid relative to "their professional industry and exertion." In 1809 Englishman Richard Edgeworth devoted his *Essays on Professional Education* to divinity, law, medicine, and the military; and soon thereafter Jacob Bigelow, MD directed *A Poem on Professional Life* to doctors, lawyers, and divines. In the early 1830s the Western Literary Institute and College of Professional Teachers was founded in Cincinnati, although a foreign visitor to the United States distinguished "professional men" from teachers, merchants, and mechanics in 1837.[149]

In this fashion, between the 1750s and the 1850s the usage of "professed" and "professional" reversed. The former became anomalous, the latter commonplace,

---

145. Jacob Bigelow, *A Poem on Professional Life, delivered by Appointment of the Society of Phi Beta Kappa* (Boston, 1811); William Steward, Jr., *The Healing Art, or Art of Healing disclosed by a professed botanist* (Ballston Spa, NY, 1812); *Reports on the Course of Instruction in Yale College,* p. 32.

146. Quotations are from Calhoun, *The American Civil Engineer,* p. 137; Barnas Sears, *An Educated Ministry* (New York, 1853), p. 16; George B. Ide, *The Ministry Demanded by the Present Crisis* (Philadelphia, 1845), pp. 37, 41.

147. "A professed launderer," *The LAUNDRY manual; or, Washing Made Easy* (New York, 1863); [anon.], "A True College for Women," *London Quarterly Review* (April 1869), reprinted in *The Liberal Education of Women,* ed. James Orton (New York, 1873), pp. 144, 149.

148. *State Gazette of Georgia* (November 27, 1783): 1; *Pennsylvania Packet* (February 21, 1787): 1; Alexander Hamilton, "Letter to Colonel John Laurens [October 11, 1780]," *The Papers of Alexander Hamilton,* ed. Harold C. Syrett, vol. 2 (New York, 1961), p. 468.

149. Samuel Knox, "An Essay on the Best System of Liberal Education, Adapted to the Genius of the Government of the United States" (1799), reprinted in *Essays on Education in the Early Republic,* ed. Frederick Rudolph (Cambridge, MA, 1965), pp. 279–80, 291–2, 315–6, 362–3; Richard L. Edgeworth, *Essays on Professional Education* (London, 1809); Bigelow, *A Poem on Professional Life;* Francis J. Grund, *The Americans in their Moral, Social, and Political Relations* (London, 1837), vol. 1, p. 214.

as an adjective referring to occupations. Even the clergy no longer employed "professional" in the sense of "religious." In words that would have been a self-contradiction a century earlier, Rev. Robert T. Middleditch of the New Jersey Baptist Association noted in 1856 that a minister's "personal religion may suffer in the routine of professional duty." A decade later the National Council of Congregational Churches called for developing a "professional ministry" to stem the decline in clerical status, tenure, and authority. As if in response, Henry Ward Beecher warned divinity students in 1871 not to "wrap yourselves in professional mystery."[150]

In one respect this transition in the usage of "professional" is simply an extension of the earlier developments in the rhetoric of "profession." The adjective "professional" was taken from its theological context, in which it meant "avowed" or "religious," and applied to particular callings or employments, dignifying them with higher status. This background helps to account for otherwise perplexing usages in the early 1800s, such as "a professional gentleman."[151] In addition to that aspect, however, the role of lawyers transformed the meaning of "professional" into a singular moment in the rhetoric of "profession." That transformation occurred in three ways and constituted the fourth moment in the rhetoric of "profession."

Lawyers, first of all, appear to have been the "professors" who most prominently adopted the new usage of "professional" as it gained popularity in the United States between about 1780 and 1830. To be sure, such a generalization is difficult to prove. By the year 1800 there were 178 weekly newspapers in the United States and 56 others that appeared more frequently, with an estimated circulation of 200,000. By 1829 some 1,000 newspapers were publishing with a total circulation of at least 1 million.[152] Given the expanse of this small segment of the rhetoric of a culture, one can scarcely claim certainty for what is, finally, an impressionistic judgment. Even so, I have the impression that jurists, whose "profession" was rising to preeminence by any measure, were most inclined to describe themselves and to be described as "professional" in the late eighteenth and early nineteenth century. Other occupations then emulated the practice of "professional" lawyers.

Whereas it is uncommon to find instances of "professional" in other kinds of publications and writings in the 1780s and 1790s, courts, legislatures, or individuals referring to lawyers – from the *[Boston] Independent Chronicle* to the Georgia legislature, from Noah Webster to the very first term of the United States Supreme Court – frequently mention lawyers' "professional character" or "professional

150. Robert T. Middleditch, "Prayer For Ministers," *Minutes of the East New Jersey Baptist Association* (June 3, 1856), p. 26; Calhoun, *Professional Lives in America,* p. 174; Henry Ward Beecher, *Yale Lectures on Preaching* (New York, 1872), p. 88.

151. "A Professional Gentleman," *Trial of [John] Davison, convicted ... of Felony and Shoplifting* (Taunton, UK, [1809]); "A Professional Gentleman," *The London Minstrel; being a collection of ... English, Irish and Scotch songs* (London, 1820, 1825); "A professional Gentleman," *Plan for Establishing a Safe and Economical Currency* (Edinburgh, 1821); "A professional Gentleman," *Considerations on the Present State of the Country in Respect to Income and Taxation* (Edinburgh, 1822).

152. Stewart, "Jeffersonian Journalism: Newspaper Propaganda and the Development of the Democratic-Republican Party, 1789–1801," ch. 1; Aronson, *Status and Kinship in the Higher Civil Service,* p. 20.

business."[153] In the first decade of the nineteenth century, when not a single instance of "professional" appears in the some 20,000 titles of *American Bibliography*, writings by or about lawyers, including case reports, were studded with references to the "professional man" in law. Between 1810 and 1825, when the first seven legal periodicals in the United States were founded and abuzz with "professional" issues, merely three different titles among the 56,000 in *American Bibliography* include the term "professional."[154] Lawyers thus appear to have sponsored the transition of "professional" from a religious to an occupational sense.

The second aspect of the fourth moment in the rhetoric of profession was that these newly "professional" lawyers began to invoke the religious ethic of selfless service. This invocation was part of a general tendency by jurists to don the still respected mantle of theology. In his 1829 inauguration as professor of law at Harvard, Joseph Story urged lawyers to judge themselves as if "standing in the temple and in the presence of the law ... What sacrifice [could be] more pure than, in such a cause? What martyrdom more worthy to be canonized in our hearts?" Speaking at Wesleyan University in 1835, the Honorable E. Jackson, Jr., extolled "the source and the safeguard of our dearest rights – I mean the science of law ... whose 'seat ... is the bosom of God and its voice the harmony of the world.'" Subsequently Timothy Walker lectured at Cincinnati College that "the province of a lawyer is to vindicate rights and redress wrongs; and it is a high and holy function," and Daniel Lord in New York equated "the extra-professional influence of the pulpit and the bar."[155]

Interwoven in these religious metaphors and comparisons was a call for selfless service on the part of the bar. Opening his law lectures at the University of Maryland in 1823, David Hoffman opined that a lawyer "labours not for those alone

---

153. Honestus [Benjamin Austin], *Observations on the Pernicious Practice of the Law* (1819), passim; Horatio Marbury and William H. Crawford, *Digest of the Laws of the State of Georgia from 1755 to 1800* (Savannah, GA, 1802), p. 41, passim; "Supreme Court of the United States ... Rules," 2 Dallas (2 US) 390 (1790); Rollins, *The Long Journey of Noah Webster*, p. 20; David Ramsay, *History of the American Revolution*, 2 vols. (1793; New York, 1968), vol. 1, p. 134.

154. *American Bibliography, 1801–1825.* Bigelow, *Poem on Professional Life* (1811); John Trenor, *On the Professional Education of Dentists* (New York, 1812); [United States' Congressional] Committee of Ways and Means, "Report ... on the professional income of lawyers, solicitors, and counsellors" (Washington, DC, 1814). The seven periodicals are *American Law Journal* (Philadelphia, 1808–1817); *Carolina Law Repository* (Raleigh, NC, 1813–6); *New York Judicial Repository* (New York, 1818–9); *Journal of Jurisprudence* (Philadelphia, 1821); *Annual Law Register of the United States (Griffith)* (Burlington, VT, 1821–2); *Journal of the Law School* (Needham, VA, 1822); *United States Law Journal* (New Haven, New York, 1822–6). Frederick C. Hicks, *Materials and Methods of Legal Research* (Rochester, NY, 1923), pp. 165–72.

155. Joseph Story, *Discourse Pronounced upon the Inauguration of the Author, as Dane Professor of Law in Harvard University* (1829), in *Legal Mind in America*, pp. 180, 182; E. Jackson, Jr., *An Address Delivered to The Peithologian Society of Wesleyan University* (New York, 1835), p. 10; Timothy Walker, *Introductory Lecture on the Dignity of the Law as a Profession, Delivered at the Cincinnati College* (1838), in *Legal Mind in America*, p. 251; Daniel Lord, *On the Extra-Professional Influence of the Pulpit and the Bar* (New York, 1851).

who can afford the *honorarium,* but the widow, the fatherless, and the oppressed are ever in his mind." "What is morally wrong, cannot be professionally right," he concluded in a noted essay of 1836. In the 1840s the *Pennsylvania Law Journal* approved those who "regard the profession of the law, not as a mere money-getting business, nor the remuneration of their 'labours'."[156] Lecturing to the law department at the University of Pennsylvania in 1854, George Sharswood stated: "There is, perhaps, no profession, after that of the sacred ministry, in which a high-toned morality is more imperatively necessary than that of the law." Unwilling to concede higher moral aspirations even to the clergy, a future Chief Justice of the Wisconsin Supreme Court reclaimed the highest ground for lawyers in a speech at the University of Wisconsin:

> If our profession be, as I believe, the most honorable, it is also the most ardu-
> ous.... There it stands, the profession of the law; subrogated on earth, for
> the angels who administer God's law in heaven.... This is the true ambition of
> the lawyer. To obey God in the service of society ... to minister to His justice,
> by the nearest approach to it, under the municipal law.[157]

Such allusions and comparisons to religion certainly had antecedents in the colonial period, but this invocation of selfless service was novel. Indeed, the invocation commenced during a brief interlude near the turn of the century when the common law prohibition on English barristers suing to collect their fees was observed in American courts. Scholars from Harold Laski to Paul Starr have maintained that this prohibition whereby English law regarded barristers "to be above material motives ... never successfully crossed the Atlantic."[158] And it is true that, in a series of cases beginning in the 1820s in the Carolinas and Tennessee, jurists permitted lawyers to sue in order to collect their fees.[159] However, in 1796 the US Supreme Court had objected to this prospect, declaring, "We do not think this ... ought to be allowed. The general practice of the United States is in opposition to it, and ... is entitled to the respect of the Court, till it is changed, or

---

156. David Hoffman, *A Lecture, Introductory to a Course of Lectures, Now Delivered in the University of Maryland* (1823), in *Legal Mind in America,* pp. 86–7; Hoffman, *A Course of Legal Study, Addressed to Students and the Profession Generally,* 2d edn (Baltimore, MD, 1836), vol. 2, p. 765; "Physicians' and Counsels' Fees," 2 *Pennsylvania Law Journal* (1843–4): 128.

157. H. George Sharswood, *A Compend of Lectures on the Aims and Duties of the Profession of the Law* (Philadelphia, 1854), p. 2; Edward G. Ryan, "Address to the Graduating Law Students of the University of Wisconsin" (1873), reprinted in *Notre Dame Lawyer,* 19 (1943): 118–21.

158. Paul Starr, *The Social Transformation of American Medicine* (New York, 1982), pp. 61–2. Harold J. Laski, "The Decline of the Professions," *Harper's Magazine* (1935): 676–85. Starr cites *Judah* v. *M'namee,* 3 Blackford 269 (Indiana 1833) on this point. But the court there refers only to physicians, not to lawyers.

159. *Duncan* v. *Breithaupt,* 1 McCord 149 (South Carolina 1821); *Leach* v. *Strange,* 3 Hawks 601 (North Carolina 1825); *Newnan* v. *Washington,* 1 Martin & Yerger 79, 80–1 (Tennessee 1827); *Stevens* v. *Adams,* 23 Wendell 56 (New York 1840); *Adams* v. *Stevens,* 26 Wendell 451, 455 (New York 1841). See Baker, *An Introduction to English Legal History,* ch. 10.

modified, by statute." Subsequently, while citing the English prohibition against barristers" suing to collect fees, the Supreme Court of Pennsylvania held in 1819 that lawyers "cannot sue for their fees" in order "to recover for professional services" beyond amounts provided in the fee statutes. A South Carolina court later noted that the prohibition had applied there as well.[160] This temporary endorsement of the prohibition demonstrates the significance of the "professional" rhetoric of selfless service, which jurists were adopting contemporaneously.

The third aspect of this transformation of the term "professional" is that jurists, even while adopting the religious sense of "service," added their own characteristic nuance to "professional service." Beside the continuing theological conception of "service" as selfless charity, a contractual notion of "service" as the feeable use or benefit to a client gradually appeared. In 1821 the Constitutional Court of South Carolina held: "In suits requiring great professional labor ... an attorney may rightfully and legally charge ... a sum proportioned to the value of the services." Citing this case a decade later, the South Carolina Court of Appeals decided, in regard to "professional services," that "an attorney is intitled to recover for his services in managing a suit, as much as they were worth."[161] Meanwhile the Supreme Court of North Carolina in 1825 and the Supreme Court of Pennsylvania in 1830 ruled on suits by attorneys seeking to recover "compensation for professional services." The same contractual denotation appeared in the 1835 opinion of the Chief Justice of the Supreme Court of Pennsylvania that "it is hard to imagine a principle of policy that would forbid compensation for services in a profession."[162] The principle of being a "servant unto all" was in this way supplemented by the idea that "professional services" were entitled to "a fair compensation" in the words of the Chancellor of New York.[163] The financial implications of these decisions and their connection to larger economic changes will be considered below. What is important to see here is the rhetorical development that "professional service" had acquired a new meaning quite apart from selfless charity. It now signified as well the contractual and feeable use or benefit provided to a client by "professional exertion," "professional labour," or "professional business."[164] In the words of a widely reprinted article that commented on these cases in 1882, "the [attorney-client] relation is contractual in its nature."[165]

160. *Arcambel* v. *Wiseman,* 3 Dallas (3 US) 306, 306 (1796); *Mooney* v. *Lloyd,* 5 Sergeant & Rawle 412, 412, 413, 416 (Pennsylvania 1819); *Clendinen* v. *Black,* 2 Bailey 488, 489 (South Carolina 1831). The Pennsylvania Supreme Court neglected an earlier decision in the Allegheny County court of common pleas in which Hugh H. Brackenridge sued successfully to recover additional compensation beyond what the fee tables provided. *Brackenridge* v. *McFarlane,* Addison 49 (Pennsylvania 1793).
161. *Duncan* v. *Breithaupt,* 1 McCord 149, 149 (South Carolina 1821); *Clendinen* v. *Black,* 2 Bailey 488, 489 (South Carolina 1831).
162. *Gray* v. *Brackenridge,* 2 Penrose & Watts 75, 80 (Pennsylvania 1830); *Leach* v. *Strange,* 3 Hawks 601, 602 (North Carolina 1825); *Foster* v. *Jack,* 4 Watts 334, 337 (Pennsylvania 1835).
163. *Adams* v. *Stevens,* 26 Wendell 451, 463, 455 (New York 1841).
164. *Newnan* v. *Washington,* 1 Martin & Yerger 79, 81 (Tennessee 1827); *Duncan* v. *Breihaupt,* 1 McCord 149, 151–2 (South Carolina 1821); [John Livingston, ed.], *United States Monthly Law Magazine Advertiser and Examiner,* 3 (1851): 30–2.
165. "Lawyer and Client – Right of Action for Fees," *Virginia Law Journal,* 5 (1882): 612.

The fourth moment in the rhetoric of profession thus comprised three aspects. Jurists had first sponsored the transition of "professional" from a religious to an occupational sense by adopting this usage for the preeminent profession. In addition, they accommodated their own language to the religious nuance in the rhetoric of "profession" by invoking the notion of selfless service, thereby ensuring its transmission to subsequent "professions." Finally, they informed that same rhetoric, especially the new term "professional," with their own character, resulting in a profound ambiguity. Henceforth, "professional service" would convey the idea of contractual and feeable use or benefit to a client, as well as selfless charity. This rhetorical development was accompanied, indeed sustained, by a remarkable increase in the juridical, political, social, and economic influence of lawyers.

Institutional, Political, and Social: "the most formidable & influential ordir of any"

The colonial governments and judiciary had generally not enlisted the services of "professional" lawyers. But the perception of need changed dramatically in the 1770s when, although many remained loyal to Britain, attorneys dominated the leadership of the Revolution.[166] "Gentlemen of that profession had acquired the confidence of the inhabitants by their exertion in the common cause," which "had been planned and carried into effect more by lawyers than by any other order of men," wrote David Ramsay in 1789. "Professionally taught the rights of the people, they were among the foremost to decry every attack made on their liberties." In this way, lawyers not only contributed personally, but were "professionally taught" to lead at a time when "in America THE LAW IS KING," in the words of Thomas Paine, and when "every class of people should *know* and *love* the laws," according to Noah Webster.[167] The legal profession thus furnished the architects of polity, whose authority encroached upon several domains by professing law and politics. As a self-taught farmer chided in 1798: "The Lawyers have ... become the most formidable & influential ordir of any in the Government, & though they are

Reprinted in *Central Law Journal [St. Louis]*, 13 (1882): 43; *Pittsburgh Legal Journal*, 29 (1882): 15; *Irish Law Times*, 15 (1882): 455.

166. *Who was Who during the American Revolution* (Indianapolis, IN, 1976); Nolan, "The Effect of the Revolution on the Bar: The Maryland Experience," pp. 969–90; Charles H. Van Tyne, "Lawyers and the American Revolution," *Law Times*, 163 (1927): 523–5; Erwin C. Surrency, "The Lawyer and the Revolution," *AJLH*, 8 (1964): 135; Charles R. McKirdy, "A Bar Divided: The Lawyers of Massachusetts and the American Revolution," *AJLH*, 16 (1972): 205–14; Milton M. Klein, "New York Lawyers and the Coming of the American Revolution," *New York History*, 55 (1974): 383–407.

167. Ramsay, *History of the American Revolution* (1793), vol. 1, p. 134; Thomas Paine, *Common Sense Addressed to Inhabitants of America, A New Edition* (1776), reprinted in *Thomas Paine Common Sense and Other Political Writings*, ed. Nelson F. Adkins (New York, 1953), p. 32; Noah Webster, "On the Education of Youth in America," in *A Collection of Essays and Fugitive Writings. On Moral, Historical, Political and Literary Subjects* (Boston, 1790), p. 30.

nither Juditial nor Executive officers, but a kind of Mule ordir, ingendered by & many times overawing both."[168]

Lawyers' "overawing" of the judiciary was certainly not inevitable in the young nation where citizens feared the despotism of an appointed, tenured judiciary. The early constitutions of some states, such as Rhode Island and Pennsylvania, required judges to be elected, and this requirement was adopted by certain new states, such as Mississippi in 1821. Nevertheless, demands arose soon after the Revolution, as in Virginia, Maryland, and North Carolina, to replace the untrained JPs, who served in the local courts where government most directly influenced people's lives. By the end of Jefferson's presidency in 1808, an independent, appointed, tenured judiciary sat in the federal and most state courts, and their ranks were dominated by trained lawyers. In Massachusetts, for example, where only two of the eleven justices on the highest court from 1760 to 1774 were lawyers, 24 of the 26 who sat in the half-century after independence were members of the bar. Election of judges was not widely instituted until the 1850s. Only in 1846 did another state, New York, follow Mississippi's example, and when Justice Frederick Grimké of the Ohio State Supreme Court proposed the election of judges in 1848, the proposal was regarded as radical by members of the bench and bar.[169]

Meanwhile the judicial power to determine law increased dramatically. Before 1800 American leaders generally regarded the judiciary as the weakest of the three branches of government, but over the first quarter of the nineteenth century, Chief Justice John Marshall "invincibly expanded the power of the [US] Supreme Court and indirectly the prestige of the whole judiciary." At the same time, courts of common law adopted three mechanisms to restrict the authority of juries: according "special" cases to the discretion of a judge, awarding new trials for jury verdicts "contrary to the weight of the evidence," and distinguishing between questions of fact and law and reserving the latter for judges.[170] Although some frontier states, such as Missouri, attempted to hold the bench and bar "strictly accountable to the popular will," recent research has demonstrated that backcountry courts, like those

168. William Manning, *The Key of Libberty* (1798), ed. Samuel E. Morison in *WMQ*, 3d ser., 13 (1956): 230.

169. Risjord, *Chesapeake Politics, 1781–1800*, p. 182; Roeber, *Faithful Magistrates and Republican Lawyers ... 1680–1810*, chs. 5–6; Everett C. Goodwin, *The Magistracy Rediscovered: Connecticut, 1636–1818* (Ann Arbor, MI, 1981), pp. 76ff.; Ellis, *The Jeffersonian Crisis: Courts and Politics in the Young Republic*, chs. 9–15; Robert M. Ireland, *The County Courts in Antebellum Kentucky* (Lexington, KY, 1972), passim; Gawalt, *The Promise of Power: The Emergence of the Legal Profession in Massachusetts, 1760–1840*, ch. 2; Nelson, *Americanization of the Common Law ... 1760–1830*, p. 70; Cover, *Justice Accused: Antislavery and the Judicial Process*, pp. 145–7; Bloomfield, *American Lawyers in a Changing Society, 1776–1876*, pp. 260–2.

170. Quotations are from Schlesinger, *The Age of Jackson*, p. 15; Horwitz, *The Transformation of American Law, 1780–1860*, pp. 141–3. See Nelson, *Americanization of the Common Law ... 1760–1830*, pp. 18–35, 165–74; Jerold S. Auerbach, *Justice Without Law?* (New York, 1983), pp. 48–9. Even a sharp critic of Horwitz acknowledges the "that the development of contract law considerably reduced the sovereignty of the jury, whose discretionary power came to be restricted." Simpson, "The Horwitz Thesis and the History of Contracts," p. 600.

in Kentucky, adhered to formal legal procedures far more than has traditionally been understood.[171] As a result, the more eminent members of the bar, who in the first quarter of the nineteenth century tended to enter politics, began in the second quarter to seek appointments to the bench. All these factors suggest that "in the first half of the nineteenth century ... despite some ambivalence, judges as a group were consistently held in the highest esteem in American society."[172]

Part of the reason that lawyers came to dominate the judiciary was the increasingly technical nature of jurisprudence. In matters of private law, concerning disputes between individuals, the English common law was adopted in the states and territories either by explicit constitutional or statutory provision or by unbroken custom. This fact would have provided professional mystery enough. But the common law was made more mysterious by its state-by-state adoption only to the extent that it was not repugnant to statutes or the new constitutions. "Hence, he who shall travel through the different States will soon discover, that the whole of the common law of England has been no where introduced," stated US Supreme Court Justice Samuel Chase in 1798, "there is, in short, a great and essential diversity, in the subjects to which the common law is applied, as well as in the extent of its application."[173]

This confusing diversity was somewhat ameliorated by the introduction of written case reports and digests of statutes in the early decades of the Republic. The first case reporter appeared in Connecticut in 1789, followed by Pennsylvania in 1790, Virginia in 1795, the US Supreme Court in 1798, Kentucky in 1803, and New York in 1804. Even so, the common law was "no *written* or *printed* thing," but the abstracted rules from decisions in past cases.[174] The appearance of this legal literature therefore increased the technical sophistication of jurists' expertise, without conceding accessibility to the laity. The rapid development of private law also contributed to lawyers' professional mystery. In contract law, for example, Morton Horwitz has identified a shift between 1780 and 1820 from the colonial "objective theory of value" based upon "just price" and fair exchange to a "subjective theory

171. William F. English, *The Pioneer Lawyer and Jurist in Missouri* (Columbia, MO, 1947), pp. 12–3, 19–20; Mary K. B. Tachau, *Federal Courts in the Early Republic: Kentucky, 1789–1816* (Princeton, NJ, 1978), pp. 14–5. Cf. Ellis, *The Jeffersonian Crisis: Courts and Politics in the Young Republic*, chs. 9, 10; George Dangerfield, *The Awakening of American Nationalism, 1815–1828* (New York, 1965), p. 102.

172. Linford, "The Mormons, the Law, and the Territory of Utah," pp. 230–2; Stephen Botein, "'What shall we Meet Afterwards in Heaven?': Judgeship as a Symbol for Modern Lawyers," in *Professions and Professional Ideologies in America*, ed. Gerald L. Geison (Chapel Hill, NC, 1983), pp. 49–54.

173. *United States* v. *Worrall*, 2 Dallas (2 US) 384, 394 (1798). Louisiana was the chief exception to the adoption of common law. On the adoption of equity, see Stanley N. Katz, "The Politics of Law in Colonial America: Controversies over Chancery Courts and Equity Law in the Eighteenth Century," in *Colonial America*, ed. Katz, 2d edn (Boston, 1976), pp. 401–22.

174. William J. Cobbett, *A Year's Residence in the United States of America, Part II* (London, 1819), p. 397; Ellis, *The Jeffersonian Crisis: Courts and Politics in the Young Republic*, pp. 118–9; Charles M. Cook, *The American Codification Movement: A Study of Antebellum Legal Reform* (Westport, CT, 1981), ch. 1.

of contract" reflected in the rule "caveat emptor" which was compatible with the emerging freemarket economy. Subsequently, Horwitz argues, a formalistic theory of contract was introduced in order to meet "the need for a uniform and consistent set of essentially impersonal commercial rules" in the even larger commercial markets of the mid-nineteenth century. Horwitz's interpretation has been challenged, but no one denies that the jurisprudence of private law became increasingly protean and technical between 1776 and 1870.[175]

Yet another source of professional mystery was that most closely associated with revolutionary excitement: the creation of a new polity. The individual states generally went through two rounds of constitution-making. The first came in the 1770s, when, fearing a tyrannical executive, states invested abundant power in legislatures. But these legislatures quickly became overbearing and arbitrary, and another wave of constitution-making ensued in the 1780s. Attempts were made to balance legislative and executive authority, and much of the theoretical groundwork was laid for the federal Constitution.[176] The resulting legal-political conceptions established in that Constitution were novel, a fact that has often gone unappreciated.

Daniel Boorstin, for example, stated that "the Revolution ... did not produce in America a single important treatise on political theory," by which he meant that "the United States was being born in an atmosphere of legal rather than philosophical debate." One might expect Boorstin to have studied the legal developments, but both he and more recent historians "honor the Revolution by treating it as though it had no impact on the history of American law," according to Stanley Katz. In response, Katz insightfully suggests that "the truly novel idea of American constitutionalism" took place at the "legal-constitutional" stratum between the level of technical law and "the higher plane of political theory."[177] Indeed, the originality of certain American legal-political conceptions is remarkable.

In 1760 the English idea of "constitution" meant simply the existing arrangement of governmental institutions and their rationale. By definition, a part of the English constitution, such as the king, could not violate the constitution. By 1790 in the United States "Constitution" meant several new and different things.[178] It was,

175. Horwitz, *The Transformation of American Law, 1780–1860*, pp. 180–2, 196–201. See Gilmore, *The Death of Contract*, ch. 1; Nelson, *Americanization of the Common Law ... 1760–1830*, pp. 163–4; Simpson, "The Horwitz Thesis and the History of Contracts," pp. 533ff.; Peter Gabel and Jay M. Feinman, "Contract Law as Ideology," pp. 172–84, in *The Politics of Law: A Progressive Critique*, ed. David Kairys (New York, 1982).

176. Allan Nevins, *The American States during and after the Revolution, 1775–1789* (New York, 1924); Wood, *The Creation of the American Republic, 1776–1787*, ch. 8.

177. Boorstin, *The Genius of American Politics*, pp. 66, 88; Katz, "The Legal and Religious Context of Natural Rights Theory," pp. 38, 40, 42; Cf. Daniel J. Boorstin, *The Americans: The Colonial Experience* (New York, 1958), pp. 191–205; Ellis, *The Jeffersonian Crisis: Courts and Politics in the Young Republic*, pp. 269–70; Botein, "Income and Ideology: Harvard-Trained Clergymen in Eighteenth-Century New England," p. 14.

178. Here and below, I draw from Bailyn, *The Ideological Origins of the American Revolution*, ch. 5; Wood, *The Creation of the American Republic, 1776–1787*, pts. 2, 5; Charles F. Mullett, *Fundamental Law and the American Revolution, 1760–1776* (New York, 1933); Edward S. Corwin, *The "Higher Law" Background of American Constitutional Law* (Ithaca, NY, 1955); Leonard W. Levy, ed., *Essays on the Making of the Constitution*, 2d edn (New

first of all, a written document. Royal and proprietary charters had long been written down, of course. But "the great emotional and philosophical capital that the Revolutionary generation invested in ... written constitutional arrangements" arose from the fact that the document described higher law. This idea that a constitution set forth higher or fundamental law validating the existing arrangements of government was another innovation. Such higher or fundamental law, US Supreme Court Justice William Johnson stated, "will impose laws even on the deity" and is, therefore, "permanent," the Court noted in *Cohens* v. *Virginia* (1821).[179]

Permanent, that is, unless the "people" change their mind. The idea that the Constitution originated in what Madison called the "fountain of authority, the people" – in other words, that sovereignty was invested in the "people" – was also an invention, apparently devised in order to circumvent the eighteenth-century prohibition on dividing power among different entities and thereby creating the political solecism of *imperio in imperium*. Instead, ultimate power was attributed to one nebulous source, the people.[180] With that theoretical issue resolved, authority was then innovatively apportioned among three separate branches of government. To be sure, the idea of "mixed government" was a commonplace in English political theory, and Montesquieu had written about "separation of powers" while the early state constitutions had envisioned counterbalancing authority among the executive, legislative, and judicial branches. But in these cases, each entity of government carried an indistinct portion of power and shared overlapping functions. The idea of according power to functionally defined branches, all-powerful within their functional spheres, was novel. So novel, in fact, that it was realized only gradually between intimations in *The Federalist*, the US Supreme Court's early references in *Ogden* v. *Blackledge* (1804), and subsequent judicial decisions, such as *Merrill* v. *Sherburne* (1818).[181]

These legal-political innovations, among others, made the Constitution and the polity it described unique. They also provided a special role for the judiciary as guardians of the constituted polity. That role was "the uniquely American institution of judicial review,"[182] which was constructed gradually in the early national

---

York, 1987). An argument for seventeenth-century antecedents of many of these innovations can be found in Thomas Grey, "Origins of the Unwritten Constitution: Fundamental Law in American Revolutionary Thought," *Stanford Law Review*, 30 (1978): 843–93

179. Quotations are from: George Dargo, "Parties and the Transformation of the Constitutional Idea in Revolutionary Pennsylvania," in *Party and Political Opposition in Revolutionary America*, ed. Patricia U. Bonomi (Tarrytown, NY, 1980), p. 100; *Fletcher* v. *Peck*, 6 Cranch (10 US) 87, 143 (1810); *Cohens* v. *Virginia*, 6 Wheaton (19 US) 264, 380–1 (1821). See John M. Murrin, "A Roof without Walls: The Dilemma of American National Identity," in *Beyond Confederation*, ed. Richard Beeman et al. (Chapel Hill, NC, 1987), pp. 346–8.

180. [James Madison], *Federalist No. 51*, in *The Federalist, A Commentary on the Constitution of the United States* (1788; reprint, New York, 1964). See Wood, *The Creation of the American Republic, 1776–1787*, ch. 9; Edmund S. Morgan, *Inventing the People: The Rise of Popular Sovereignty in England and America* (New York, 1988).

181. [Madison], *Federalist Nos. 37, 51*; [Hamilton], *Federalist No. 78*; *Ogden* v. *Blackledge*, 2 Cranch (6 US) 272, 276 (1804); *Merrill* v. *Sherburne*, 1 New Hampshire 199, 212–6 (1818).

182. Dargo, "Parties and the Transformation of the Constitutional Idea in Revolutionary

period. *Marbury* v. *Madison* (1803) was the first instance in which the US Supreme Court refused to give effect to a federal statute, and the President and Congress meanwhile felt themselves no less obliged to evaluate the constitutionality of their actions. Nevertheless, the role of examining the written Constitution, of discerning the higher law attributed to the people's will, and, finally, of adjudicating the boundaries between the functionally separate branches of government was more and more assumed by the federal and state courts. In this fashion, "the question, whether an act repugnant to the constitution, can become the law of the land," in Chief Justice John Marshall's words, became increasingly a judicial question. And an English case of 1610 was recalled anachronistically in the early nineteenth centuries to provide a precedent for the new doctrine of judicial review.[183]

Judicial review elevated the traditionally weakest branch of government to the final arbiter not only within government, but also within the overarching innovation of the new polity: the federal system itself. As with other legal-political inventions, the meaning and significance of federalism appeared slowly. Through 1800 "the United States was seen as a community of states," and only gradually, stimulated by the resolution of territorial controversies between the states, did a new notion of polity arise: the idea of diminutive states within a sovereign union, the idea of a polity of polities. It was assigned to the courts, especially the federal courts, to adjudicate disputes between states and between a state and the federal government.[184] In this way, too, courts expanded their purview at the same time that professional lawyers were coming to dominate the judiciary. On both accounts, the authority of attorneys encroached upon judicial institutions.

Pennsylvania," p. 99. William E. Nelson, "Changing Conceptions of Judicial Review: The Evolution of Constitutional Theory in the States, 1790–1860," *University of Pennsylvania Law Review*, 120 (1972): 1166–85; Ellis, *The Jeffersonian Crisis: Courts and Politics in the Young Republic*, ch. 4; Wood, *The Creation of the American Republic, 1776–1787*, ch. 10; Sylvia Snowiss, *Judicial Review and the Law of the Constitution* (New Haven, CT, 1990); Shannon C. Stimson, *The American Revolution in the Laws: Anglo-American Jurisprudence before John Marshall* (Princeton, NJ, 1990).

183. *Marbury* v. *Madison*, 1 Cranch (5 US) 137, 176 (1803). Decided by Chief Justice Edward Coke, *Dr. Bonham's Case*, 8 Coke Reports 107 (London 1610), was cited only a few times in the seventeenth century and then neglected. American jurists in the early nineteenth century interpreted the case to announce a doctrine of judicial review requiring that judges compare statutes to a higher or fundamental law. Coke's authority and *Dr. Bonham's Case* were thus invoked to justify and authorize an American innovation. (Samuel E. Thorne, "Dr. Bonham's Case," *Law Quarterly Review*, no. 216 (1938): 543–52. Cf. Grey, "Origins of the Unwritten Constitution: Fundamental Law in American Revolutionary Thought," pp. 851–4.) A profound irony in *Dr. Bonham's Case* has gone unmentioned by legal scholars. Coke's decision had the effect of undermining the guild of doctors, because he held that the Royal College of Physicians could not identify or fine unlicensed or incompetent practitioners since a party "cannot be a judge in his own case." But, in making this decision, Coke voided a legislative statute. The decision thus made common law jurists the judges of the limits of their own authority. In one stroke the guild of physicians was undercut by the sword that defended the legal profession.

184. Peter S. Onuf, *The Origins of the Federal Republic: Jurisdictional Controversies in the United States, 1775–1787* (Philadelphia, 1983), pp. 20, 46, 168, 171; Tachau, *Federal Courts in the Early Republic: Kentucky, 1789–1816*, p. 29.

In this developing polity of polities, lawyers' authority likewise encroached upon political institutions. Attorneys succeeded in the rough and tumble of political life not only because they were "professionally taught the rights of the people," but also because they had "the kind of individualism and often the combativeness, sometimes shaped in litigation, that made a political career seem not too wounding and also attractive in its potential for gaining clients."[185] Granted, the early "politicians" – those who attended to the polity – had envisioned a gentlemanly sort of politics. Thus, lawyers established themselves in Virginia between 1774 and 1790 by wedding the traditional "Country" ideology to the revolutionary movement and portraying themselves as Republican gentlemen. Meanwhile statesmen everywhere viewed partisanship as evidence of a lack of Republican virtue and complained about the "party spirit" and political parties that first appeared in the 1770s and 1780s. In 1794 George Washington denounced parties as "self-created bodies ... forming themselves under the shade of Night in a conclave," and Judge William Wyche of New York proclaimed, "Party is a monster who devours the common good, whose destructive jaws are dangerous to the felicity of nations."[186] By the late 1790s, however, the term "party" had virtually lost its pejorative connotations, and some 35 popular "Democrat" or "Republican" societies had been formed throughout the colonies. These were followed in the late 1790s by a new wave of political associations that produced the first party system.[187]

Lawyers dominated the political institutions, unlike in the colonial period. In 1663 the Massachusetts legislature had prohibited any "usual and common attorney" from sitting as a representative, and in 1729 the General Assembly of Rhode Island forbade lawyers from becoming deputies. In Virginia merely 6 percent of the members of the House of Burgesses between 1720 and 1776 were lawyers, while in Massachusetts the fraction of representatives who were lawyers did not exceed 9 percent between 1760 and 1770.[188] Such proportions changed

185. Quotations are from: Ramsey, *History of the American Revolution* (1793), vol. 1, p. 134; David Riesman, personal correspondence (January 7, 1987).

186. George Washington, "Letter to Burges Ball" (September 25, 1794), in *The Writings of George Washington*, ed. John C. Fitzpatrick (Washington, DC, 1931–49), vol. 33, p. 506; William Wyche, *Party Spirit: An Oration* (New York, 1794), p. 16; Roeber, *Faithful Magistrates and Republican Lawyers ... 1680–1810*, ch. 5.

187. Risjord, *Chesapeake Politics, 1781–1800*, pp. 407, 414, 431; Cunningham, *The Jeffersonian Republicans: The Formation of Party Organization, 1789–1801*, p. 168; Eugene P. Link, *Democratic-Republican Societies, 1790–1800* (New York, 1942), pp. 13–5. The literature on political partisanship and parties through 1860 is enormous and growing. Here and below, I draw upon Richard Hofstadter, *The Idea of a Party System: The Rise of Legitimate Opposition in the United States, 1780–1840* (Berkeley, CA, 1969); Arthur M. Schlesinger, Jr., ed., *History of US Political Parties*, vol. 1: *1789–1860, From Factions to Parties* (New York, 1973); Lance Banning, *The Jeffersonian Persuasion: Evolution of a Party Ideology* (Ithaca, NY, 1978); Patricia U. Bonomi, ed., *Party and Political Opposition in Revolutionary America* (Tarrytown, NY, 1980); John F. Hoadley, *Origins of American Political Parties, 1789–1803* (Lexington, KY, 1986).

188. *Records of Massachusetts Bay*, vol. 4, pt. 2, p. 87; *Records of the Colony of Rhode Island and Providence Plantations in New England*, 10 vols. (1856; New York, 1968), vol. 4, p. 430; Roeber, *Faithful Magistrates and Republican Lawyers ... 1680–1810*, p. 145.

markedly after 1776, when 25 of 56 signers of the Declaration of Independence were trained in law, as were 31 of the 55 delegates to the subsequent Constitutional Convention in Philadelphia. In 1789 law was the chief occupation of 55 percent of United States senators, and by 1845 that fraction had risen to 86 percent. Meanwhile a lawyer occupied the presidency in all but two years between 1797 and 1865, and those lawyer presidents appointed attorneys to staff the government. Between 1789 and 1861, out of 167 appointments to cabinet and high diplomatic posts, 77 percent went to lawyers, 11 percent went to businessmen, and 6 percent went to farmers or large land owners. Among lesser but still elite positions in the civil service, lawyers constituted 68 percent under President Adams (1797–1801), 62 percent under Jefferson (1801–9), and 83 percent under Jackson (1829–37).[189]

At the state level, lawyers dominated political offices not only in older, well established areas, such as New England, but also in frontier states. "The frontier lawyer, in fact, was almost compelled to become a politician," according to Jack Northrup. Indiana, for example, held a constitutional convention in 1816, and seven of the first eight governors, eleven of the thirteen lieutenant governors, and seven of the eight secretaries of state were lawyers. Between 1816 and 1852 all but one presiding officer in both the Indiana House of Representatives and state Senate were lawyers, and 75 out of 95 terms of Indiana Congressmen were filled by lawyers. In Wisconsin attorneys similarly dominated political and judicial offices both before and after 1848, when the territory joined the union. Meanwhile, in certain regions where anti-lawyer animus was fervent, such as Cumberland County, North Carolina, attorneys played a lesser role in politics.[190]

The Cumberland County situation demonstrates not only the regional discontinuities, but also the changing status of politicians over time. The first American party system lasted from Thomas Jefferson's election to the presidency in 1800 to the death of the Federalist Party in about 1815. After the "Era of Good Feelings" under President James Monroe (1817–25), the second party system emerged with the election of Andrew Jackson in 1828. This resurgence of what John Nevin in 1840 called "the Vile Spirit of Party" was commonly criticized as another blow to Republican virtue, following what some had hoped was the temporary anomaly of the first party system.[191] But the party system was resilient, and partisan politics

189. Surrency, "The Lawyer and the Revolution," p. 134; Chroust, *The Rise of the Legal Profession in America,* vol. 2, pp. 4–5; Donald R. Matthews, "United States Senators and the Class Structure," *Public Opinion Quarterly,* 18 (1954): 13; Philip H. Burch, Jr., *Elites in American History* (New York, 1981), vol. 1, pp. 244–5; Aronson, *Status and Kinship in the Higher Civil Service,* vol. 1, pp. 86–7. Between 1797 and 1865 the only non-lawyer presidents were Generals William Henry Harrison (1841) and Zachary Taylor (1849–50).

190. Jack Northrup, "The Education of a Western Lawyer," *AJLH,* 12 (1968): 305. Gawalt, *The Promise of Power: The Emergence of the Legal Profession in Massachusetts, 1760–1840,* chs. 2, 3; Chroust, *The Rise of the Legal Profession in America,* vol. 2, p. 127; Howard Feiginbaum, "The Lawyers in Wisconsin, 1836–1860: A Profile," *Wisconsin Magazine of History,* 55 (1971): 100–6; Watson, *Jacksonian Politics and Community Conflict,* p. 302; Joy B. and Robert R. Gilsdorf, "Elites and Electorates: Some Plain Truths for Historians of Colonial America," in *Saints and Revolutionaries,* ed. David D. Hall et al. (New York, 1984), pp. 231–5.

191. Theodore Appel, *The Life and Work of John Williamson Nevin* (Philadelphia, 1889), pp. 116–25. Richard P. McCormick, *The Second American Party System: Party Formation in*

soon were dominated by lawyers with lesser status. Highly pedigreed members of the bar began to be attracted instead by the "science" of the law and to eschew politics for the now prestigious judiciary, as happened to Joseph Story, one of the most distinguished antebellum jurists.[192] Consequently, whatever their individual status in the profession, lawyers as a group gained judicial and political authority in the late eighteenth and early nineteenth centuries. The new Professor of Law at the College of William and Mary was well justified in observing in his inaugural lecture of 1834, "The history of our country is full of proof that the bar is the road to eminence ... [F]ew ... have attained to this eminence in public life, without having been first distinguished in the profession."[193]

Beyond the legal and political authority gained in formal institutions, lawyers accrued a great deal of informal social authority due to "the substitution of political for clerical leadership and of politics for religion as the most challenging area of human thought and endeavor."[194] Indeed, the United States could not match Europe in art, literature, or other cultural pursuits, but its jurisprudence was equal to the European, observed Richard Rush, who served as US Attorney General and Secretary of State in the 1810s. Even contemporary English jurists, such as Samuel Warren, conceded the high technical quality of "AMERICAN LAW ... entitling it to the respect of English lawyers."[195] As a result, when American literature flowered in the second quarter of the century, the polity and the law were prominent in the minds of leading authors, editors, and journalists. This prominence was also manifested in rural communities, such as Edgefield, South Carolina, where "lawyers were important in the spreading of ideas. They rode circuit with judges and traveled from one small district seat to another, as well as to the state capital." The itinerations of the bar thus contributed to lawyers' intellectual sovereignty over settled clergy, while the itinerant preachers were generally less educated and respected than the circuit-riding jurists.[196]

---

the Jacksonian Era (Chapel Hill, NC, 1966); Kohl, *The Politics of Individualism: Parties and the American Character in the Jacksonian Era,* passim.

192. Bloomfield, *American Lawyers in a Changing Society, 1776–1876,* pp. 148–51; Stephen Botein, "'What shall we Meet Afterwards in Heaven?': Judgeship as a Symbol for Modern Lawyers," pp. 49–54; R. Kent Newmyer, *Supreme Court Justice Joseph Story: Statesman of the Old Republic* (Chapel Hill, NC, 1985), p. 38.

193. Nathaniel Beverly Tucker, "A Lecture on the Study of the Law; Being an Introduction to a Course of Lectures on that Subject in the College of William and Mary," *Southern Literary Messenger,* 1 (1834–5): 145–6.

194. Morgan, "The American Revolution Considered as an Intellectual Movement," p. 11. Bloomfield considers this view to be an exaggeration of Perry Miller, but abundant opinion supports the point. Cf. Bloomfield, *American Lawyers in a Changing Society, 1776–1876,* p. 151; Brooke Hindle, *The Pursuit of Science in Revolutionary America, 1735–1789* (Chapel Hill, NC, 1956), pp. 248–77, 382–5; Gawalt, *The Promise of Power: The Emergence of the Legal Profession in Massachusetts, 1760–1840,* p. 118; Humphrey, *From King's College to Columbia, 1746–1800,* p. 225.

195. Richard Rush, *American Jurisprudence* (1815), in *Legal Mind in America,* pp. 43–52; Samuel Warren, *A Popular and Practical Introduction to Law Studies and to Every Department of the Legal Profession,* 2 vols., 3d edn (London, 1870), p. xiii.

196. Orville V. Burton, *In my Father's House are Many Mansions: Family and Community in Edgefield, South Carolina* (Chapel Hill, NC, 1985), p. 21. See Patterson, *Authority, Autonomy, and Representation in American Literature, 1776–1865.*

Attorneys' encroachment upon the intellectual leadership, and thus social authority, of ministers appeared also in the learned societies that were springing up. In the newly founded American Academy of Arts and Sciences jurists achieved a distinction in 1780 that would have been unthinkable 50 years earlier: they outnumbered the clergy and every other occupational group among the 62 founding members. This intellectual stature grew as time passed. Through 1860 the Maine Historical Society, for example, counted among its 238 members 140 lawyers, 56 ministers, 16 physicians, and 26 others. No less did lawyers play a role in natural science. They were second only to businessmen and college faculty among participants in local committees of the American Association for the Advancement of Science from 1848 to 1860. Meanwhile the foremost interpreter of Baconianism, the standard epistemology of antebellum science in America, "was not a scientist but a Maryland attorney, Samuel Tyler," who "was highly acclaimed by his contemporaries as the greatest philosopher [in] America." And the first American *Treatise on Sociology* (1854) was written by a lawyer from Mississippi, Henry Hughes.[197]

While these intellectual accomplishments elevated the social authority of lawyers, their influence in social affairs was also extended by reason of their formal authority in legal and political institutions. The idea of social deviance and crime, for example, shifted from offenses against a moral code, based on religion or honor, to offenses against property and person. Needless to say, the shift was not uniform. The religious mediation of disputes in the North dissolved quickly and rather completely, while the "honorable" resolution of disputes by fighting in the South eroded slowly. In particular, a "prototypical, industrial, urbanizing state," such as Massachusetts, changed more rapidly than "the most aristocratic rural slave state," South Carolina. Nevertheless, the definition of crime was gradually transformed, and during the first third of the nineteenth century American criminal law emerged as a cognizable, if still disorganized, field from the antecedent motley of common law, Constitutional provisions, and state statutes. Police forces, prisons, parole, and probation also emerged during the first two-thirds of the century. In these ways both the definition of crime and the institutions for addressing it were transformed by the systematic and regulatory character reflected in the rule of law.[198] Hence, "it

197. George H. Daniels, *American Science in the Age of Jackson* (New York, 1968), p. 69. Leslie W. Dunlap, *American Historical Societies, 1790–1860* (Madison, WI, 1944), p. 27; Walter M. Whitehill, "Early Learned Societies in Boston and Vicinity," p. 159, and Sally G. Kohlstedt, "Savants and Professionals: The American Association for the Advancement of Science, 1848–1860," p. 312, in *The Pursuit of Knowledge in the Early American Republic,* ed. Alexandra Oleson and Sanborn C. Brown (Baltimore, MD, 1976); Arthur J. Vidich and Stanford M. Lyman, *American Sociology: Worldly Rejections of Religion and their Directions* (New Haven, CT, 1985), pp. 4–5.

198. Quotation is from Hindus, *Prison and Plantation: Crime, Justice, and Authority in Massachusetts and South Carolina, 1767–1878,* pp. 183–4. William E. Nelson, "Emerging Notions of Modern Criminal Law in the Revolutionary Era: An Historical Perspective," *New York University Law Review,* 42 (1967): 450–532; Edward L. Ayers, *Vengeance and Justice: Crime and Punishment in the Nineteenth-Century American South* (New York, 1984); Dwight F. Henderson, *Congress, Courts, and Criminals: The Development of Federal Criminal Law, 1801–1829* (Westport, CT, 1985); Bertram Wyatt-Brown, *Yankee Saints and Southern Sinners* (Baton Rouge, LA, 1985); William H. Pease and Jane H. Pease, *The Web of Progress:*

was clear to laymen as it was to lawyers that the nature of American institutions, whether economic, social, or political, was largely to be determined by judges." On this point, apologist, consensus, and critical revisionist historians concur: "common law judges came to play a central role in directing the course of social change."[199]

Apart from the direct control by judges, the jurisprudential influence is demonstrated by the social treatment of the sick and indigent. In colonial times, the ill, the poor, and the orphan were provided for personally on the basis of reciprocal obligations in a close-knit community. In the first half of the nineteenth century these problematic individuals were institutionalized in asylums. "The well-ordered asylum would exemplify the proper principles of social organization," writes David Rothman, "and thus ensure the safety of the republic and promote its glory."[200] Those proper principles were precisely the substantively neutral and procedurally uniform rule of law that was reflected in functional, institutional organization. Institutions such as prisons, asylums, hospitals, and orphanages arose when the response to social problems was shaped by the architectonical rule of law.

The response to social abnormality was thus to create smaller polities of abnormality within the polity of normal citizens, and this response supports Perry Miller's view that jurists assumed from the clergy the role of protecting the morality of the nation. That view is further supported by the religious historiography arising from the late nineteenth-century social gospel movement, which portrays the antebellum decades as a glacial period in the social activism of the church. To be sure, clerical abolitionists tried to influence social issues through internal reform of individuals, but the clergy retreated when abolitionism challenged the public order.[201] A similar but more subtle retreat occurred in the field of education.

In the first half of the nineteenth century the rationale that education serves religious ends persevered in the religiously controlled voluntary associations devoted to the advancement of education. In the American Education Society, for

---

Private Values and Public Styles in Boston and Charleston, 1828–1843 (New York, 1985). On "Southern Distinctiveness" and the Chesapeake region, see Allan Kulikoff, *Tobacco and Slaves: The Development of Southern Cultures in the Chesapeake, 1680–1800* (Chapel Hill, NC, 1986); Timothy H. Breen, *Tobacco Culture: The Mentality of the Great Tidewater Planters on the Eve of the Revolution* (Princeton, NJ, 1985); Frederick F. Siegel, *The Roots of Southern Distinctiveness: Tobacco and Society in Danville, Virginia, 1780–1865* (Chapel Hill, NC, 1987).

199. Mark DeWolfe Howe, "The Creative Period in the Law of Massachusetts," *Proceedings of the Massachusetts Historical Society,* 69 (1947–50): 237; Horwitz, *The Transformation of American Law, 1780–1860,* p. 1. Horwitz quotes Howe and cites Roscoe Pound and Daniel Boorstin.

200. David J. Rothman, *The Discovery of the Asylum: Social Order and Disorder in the New Republic* (New York, 1971), p. xix. Cf. Gerald N. Grob, "Rediscovering Asylums: The Unhistorical History of the Mental Hospital," pp. 135–48, in *The Therapeutic Revolution,* ed. Morris J. Vogel and Charles E. Rosenberg (Philadelphia, 1979).

201. Miller, *The Life of the Mind in America: From the Revolution to the Civil War,* pp. 186–206; Gordon A. Riegler, *Socialization of the New England Clergy 1800 to 1860* (Greenfield, OH, 1945), p. 1; Scott, *From Office to Profession: The New England Ministry, 1750–1850,* chs. 5, 6.

example, "the education of ministers and revitalization of religion were the primary concerns ... not education per se." The use of revivalistic methods to spread the educational gospel, as well as the development of evangelical "Sunday schools," demonstrate the instrumentality of education to religion over this period. Hence, teaching continued to be regarded as a "lesser ministry" by clergy and educators.[202]

In the larger social arena, however, the instrumentality of education to religious ends was eclipsed by the conviction that shaping good citizens and the polity was the primary purpose of education. This political rationale was first announced in late eighteenth-century colleges and in repeated proposals to create a national university, was then endorsed for the common schools in the form of "Republican ideology," and finally suffused public discussion as "a republican style of educational thought" in the early national period.[203] In fact, members of Congress and delegates to the state constitutional conventions "seemed to regard the common school as the *sine qua non* of republicanism, in effect a fourth branch of government." Similarly, educational periodicals before the Civil War expressed "an unbounded faith in education as the means of transforming society and an oft-expressed belief that general diffusion of knowledge is the foundation of liberty and republican institutions."[204] Textbooks and curriculum for the schools and colleges likewise reflected that belief.[205]

Two other significant ways in which the polity eclipsed religion as the goal for education are often overlooked. First, legislation leading to the disestablishment of state churches sometimes funneled the ecclesiastical monies into education. For example, the general assessments bill proposed for Virginia in 1784 maintained that all religious taxes not designated under the check-off system for a particular denomination would be spent on schools. Similarly, Vermont in 1805 granted the colonial glebes of the Church of England to the towns for the support of schools, a

202. Natalie N. Naylor, "'Holding High the Standard': The Influence of the American Education Society in Ante-Bellum Education," *HEQ*, 24 (1984): 479. David Tyack, "The Kingdom of God and the Common School: Protestant Ministers and the Educational Awakening in the West," *Harvard Educational Review*, 36 (1966): 447–69; Paul H. Mattingly, *The Classless Profession: American Schoolmen in the Nineteenth Century* (New York, 1975), chs. 3, 4; Anne M. Boylan, *Sunday School: The Formation of an American Institution, 1790–1880* (New Haven, CT, 1988).

203. Lawrence Cremin, *American Education: The National Experience, 1783–1876* (New York, 1979), pp. 124–5; Edgar B. Wesley, *Proposed: The University of the United States* (Minneapolis, MN, 1936); Donald O. Schneider, "Education in Colonial American Colleges, 1750–1770, and the Occupations and Political Offices of their Alumni" (PhD diss., George Peabody College for Teachers, 1965), pp. 19–23; Carl F. Kaestle, *Pillars of the Republic: Common Schools and American Society, 1780–1860* (New York, 1983), p. 198, ch. 5.

204. David Tyack, Thomas James, and Aaron Benavot, *Law and the Shaping of Public Education, 1785–1954* (Madison, WI, 1987), p. 14, ch. 2; Sheldon E. Davis, *Educational Periodicals in the Nineteenth Century* (Washington, DC, 1919), p. 18, ch. 2.

205. Michael V. Belok, *Forming the American Minds: Early School-books and their Compilers (1783–1837)* (Agra, India, 1973), ch. 2; Michael V. Belok, "The Instructed Citizen: Civic Education in the United States during the Nineteenth Century," *Paedagogica Historica*, 18 (1978): 257–74; Robson, *Educating Republicans: the College in the Era of the American Revolution*, chs. 3, 5, 6.

grant that was upheld by the US Supreme Court. Meanwhile, in the Northwest Ordinance of 1789, Congress declared, "Religion, morality, and knowledge, being necessary to good government and the happiness of mankind, schools ... shall forever be encouraged."[206] In each case, religion was not only displaced by the polity as the goal of education, but funding for religion was reallocated to education.

A second highly symbolic aspect of this displacement was the matter of academic degrees. In a political age, the Doctor of Laws was introduced as the honorary degree that would distinguish men of accomplishment. Princeton awarded the first LLD in 1769, followed by Yale in 1773 and Harvard in 1776. Not to be outdone, the College of William and Mary awarded the first earned bachelor of laws degree in 1793.[207] By that time Isaac Royall had bequested to Harvard College an endowment for a chair either in law or medicine. The bequest became available in 1815, at which point four attorneys constituted a majority of the seven Fellows of the Harvard Corporation, and the Fellows decided to designate the bequest for a Royall Professorship of Law.[208]

This direct exercise of social authority in the field of education became typical as lawyers gradually usurped clerical leadership in the first half of the nineteenth century. In 1707 Cotton Mather had not succeeded in blocking the election of attorney John Leverett to the Harvard presidency. But Mather's point was generally conceded "that, to make a lawyer ... a praesident for a College of Divines, will be a very preposterous thing, a thing without precedent." And every other college president of every colonial college was drawn from the clergy.[209] Immediately in 1777, however, a group of representatives in the Connecticut legislature sought to oust the ministers from the Yale Corporation and to appoint its members like those of the judiciary. In 1787 attorney William S. Johnson was elected president of Columbia College, and the 1805 plan for the University of Virginia required the chancellor to be "learned in the law." In 1829 the lawyer-dominated Harvard Corporation named one of its own Fellows, attorney Josiah Quincy, to the presidency. Quincy served until 1845 and was followed by Edward Everett, who, though an ordained minister, was a politician and diplomat, having served as a Congressman, Governor of Massachusetts, and ambassador to Great Britain.[210] Mean-

---

206. "A Bill establishing a Provision for Teachers of the Christian Religion," reprinted as a Supplemental Appendix to the dissenting opinion of Justice Rutledge in *Everson* v. *Board of Education*, 330 US 1, 72–4 (1947); *Town of Pawlet* v. *Clark*, 9 Cranch (13 US) 292 (1815); 1 *US Statutes*, 50 (1789).

207. *Princetonians*, vol. 2, p. xxvi; George W. Pierson, *A Yale Book of Numbers: Historical Statistics of the College and University, 1701–1976* (New Haven, CT, 1983), pp. 18–9; Harvard University, *Quinquennial Catalogue of the Officers and Graduates, 1636–1925* (Cambridge, MA, 1925), pp. 28–32; Walter C. Eells, *Baccalaureate Degrees Conferred by American Colleges in the 17th and 18th Centuries* (Washington, DC, 1958), p. 26.

208. Sutherland, *The Law at Harvard ... 1817–1967*, pp. 38–45.

209. Mather is quoted in Samuel E. Morison, *Harvard College in the Seventeenth Century* (Cambridge, MA, 1936), pt. 2, p. 552. George P. Schmidt, *The Old Time College President* (New York, 1930), p. 184.

210. John S. Whitehead, *The Separation of College and State: Columbia, Dartmouth, Harvard, and Yale, 1776–1876* (New Haven, CT, 1973), p. 39; *Yale Graduates*, vol. 1,

while ministers generally "insisted on preserving for themselves the role of advisors and overseers as members of the school committee in local communities."[211] Even so, by the 1840s and 1850s the fourteen "chief reformers" of the "common school crusade" included nine lawyers and merely four clergymen – a dramatic shift from the 1700s or even the early 1800s.[212]

Beyond their authority evident in social institutions such as education, lawyers by virtue of their profession also exercised considerable personal influence over people whom they met individually. In their formal role as adjudicators, jurists' personal influence increased as the law of familial and domestic relations developed. Divorce, for example, shifted from requiring a legislative act to being a judicial matter resolved in the courts, and two key issues for women during this period were the legality of divorce and the property rights of married women.[213] Marriage was relieved of the requirement for ecclesiastical or state formalization or confirmation. Under the contractual architectonic of the liberal polity, marriage "like any other civil contract ... depended for its validity solely on a meeting of minds, on the free consent of the parties," as demonstrated in a landmark New York case of 1809.[214]

This formal role of adjudicator in personal matters translated into a great deal of

---

p. 763; Roeber, *Faithful Magistrates and Republican Lawyers ... 1680–1810*, p. 238; Samuel E. Morison, *Three Centuries of Harvard, 1636–1936* (Cambridge, MA, 1936), pp. 1–272. The shift from clerical to legal control of the seven-member Harvard corporation is shown by these decade-by-decade totals of corporation members from each professional category:

Year	1800	1810	1820	1830	1840	1850
Theology	4	3	3	1	1	1
Law	2	4	4	4	4	4

Source: Ronald Story, *The Forging of an Aristocracy: Harvard and the Boston Upper Class, 1800–1870* (Middletown, CT, 1980), pp. 34, 38, 42, 44, 47, 208–9.

211. Mattingly, *The Classless Profession: American Schoolmen in the Nineteenth Century*, p. 22, chs. 1, 2, 4.

212. David Tyack, *Turning Points in American Educational History* (New York, 1967), p. 125. Tyack and Elisabeth Hansot repeat the list in *Managers of Virtue: Public School Leadership in America, 1820–1980* (New York, 1982), p. 45, while invoking the authority, without citation, of Ellwood P. Cubberley and Lawrence Cremin. Meanwhile, Cremin offered a slightly different list with somewhat different occupations. *American Education: The National Experience, 1783–1876*, p. 175.

213. Michael Grossberg, *Governing the Hearth: Law and the Family in Nineteenth-Century America* (Chapel Hill, 1985), pp. 289ff.; Norma Basch, *In the Eyes of the Law: Women, Marriage and Property in Nineteenth-Century New York* (1984); Bloomfield, *American Lawyers in a Changing Society, 1776–1876*, ch. 4; Jamil S. Zainaldin, "The Emergence of a Modern American Family Law: Child Custody, Adoption and the Courts, 1796–1851," *Northwestern University Law Review*, 73 (1979): 1038–89; Lawrence M. Friedman, "Rights of Passage: Divorce Law in Historical Perspective," *Oregon Law Review*, 63 (1984): 650–3.

214. Bloomfield, *American Lawyers in a Changing Society, 1776–1876*, p. 106; *Fenton v. Reed*, 4 Johnson 54 (New York 1809).

informal personal influence over individuals, whom lawyers counseled in the privacy of their offices. In his *Introductory Lecture on the Dignity of the Law as a Profession, Delivered at the Cincinnati College*, Timothy Walker described how an attorney's consultation with a client assumed the nature of a colonial minister counseling his parishioners:

> Men come to him in their hours of trouble.... The guilty and the innocent, the upright and the dishonest, the wronging and the wronged, the knave and the dupe, alike consult him, and with the same unreserved confidence.... It is not given to man to see the human heart completely unveiled before him. But the lawyer perhaps comes more nearly to this, than any other, for there is no aspect in which the character does not present itself, in his secret consultations.[215]

In providing legal counsel, lawyers thus gained entry into the personal lives of the laity. As Judge Peter Thatcher observed in 1831: "What place is so barren, what village so small, in which is not found its lawyer, as well as its pastor? We mingle with the people in all their concerns, at home and abroad, in public and private, in the field and on the exchange. The influence of the profession is not confined to the administration of justice; it is felt in all the concerns of life and government."[216] And prominent among those "concerns of life and government" was money.

Economic: "an honorable and an expensive science"

In the decades after 1783, the young American nation was preoccupied with laying down what Stuart Bruchey calls "'structural overhead capital' – adopting the Constitution of 1787 and putting it into effect, organizing the federal government and incipient political parties, spelling out 'the rules of the game'." Public capital was predominantly invested in building these institutions and the necessary material accouterments, including the nation's capital, army, navy, and various judicial and governmental buildings. By the election of 1800, these expenses and the national debt led to frequent protests, such as Thomas Cooper's *Political Arithmetic* (1798). Nevertheless, the public structures were a source of pride and began to serve many of the functions that churches had in the colonial era. According to Herbert Johnson and Robert Andrist, "the courthouse was the scene of most local entertainment, including concerts, theatrical performances, and various exhibitions. More often, though, it was court trials and political debate that drew crowds into the building."[217] As these structures were erected, the lawyers and politicians inside naturally began to correspond and publish about the law. Before 1815 scarcely 30 books had been published about American jurisprudence, and few of these

215. Walker, *Introductory Lecture on the Dignity of the Law as a Profession*, p. 251.
216. Quoted in Newmyer, *Supreme Court Justice Joseph Story*, pp. 263–4.
217. Bruchey, "Law and Economic Change in the Early American Republic," pp. 88–9; Herbert A. Johnson and Ralph K. Andrist, *Historic Courthouses of New York State* (New York, 1977), p. 14.

addressed substantive law. By 1820, the amount spent on publishing legal treatises and court reporters had surpassed that devoted to either theology or medicine, and in subsequent decades the margin widened, according to the estimate of one major publisher of the time.[218]

These expenditures in the public sphere were indicative of the close relationship between law and commerce that originated in the commercial development of the eighteenth and early nineteenth century. This "business revolution" involved new political mechanisms addressing national economic issues, as well as new financial instruments needed to conduct more complex transactions involving longer terms, more parties and agents, and fluctuating value based upon the free market.[219] The complexity of business transactions was further heightened by the increasing size, density, and diversity of the population. The number of people in the United States, which approached 4 million in 1790, increased eightfold by 1860. Over the same period, the fraction of the population living in cities went from 6 percent to almost 20 percent, and immigration increased dramatically, reaching its highest historical level in relation to the existing population during the second quarter of the nineteenth century. Transportation also developed, as the 23 miles of railroad track in 1830 grew to nearly 31,000 miles in 1860. The size and complexity of the country and its economy were growing with the love of money, and in 1859 the word "millionaire" was for the first time included in a school speller "as a useful term for the young American."[220]

Commensurately, "political economy" had become a prominent field of inquiry, stimulated in the 1780s by the appearance of Adam Smith's *An Inquiry into the Nature and Causes of the Wealth of Nations* (1776). "Political economy" primarily denoted public policy designed to promote national wealth in a free market economy, but the term was also used interchangeably with "moral philosophy" and "political science" and therefore signified a broad area of inquiry that was further stimulated by the first American edition of Jean-Baptiste Say's *Treatise on Political*

218. Cook, *The American Codification Movement: A Study of Antebellum Legal Reform*, p. 9; Cremin, *American Education: The National Experience, 1783–1876*, p. 301.

219. Virginia D. Harrington, *The New York Merchant on the Eve of the Revolution* (New York, 1935), chs. 2–7; Samuel P. Huntington, *Political Order in Changing Societies* (New Haven, CT, 1968), pp. 33ff.; Thomas C. Cochran, "The Business Revolution," *AHR*, 79 (1974): 1449–66; Diane Lindstrom, *Economic Development in the Philadelphia Region, 1810–1850* (New York, 1978); Howard B. Rock, *Artisans of the New Republic: The Tradesmen of New York City in the Age of Jefferson* (New York, 1979), ch. 9; Pease and Pease, *The Web of Progress: Private Values and Public Styles in Boston and Charleston, 1828–1843*, passim; Joyce Appleby, *Capitalism and the New Social Order: The Republican Vision of the 1790s* (New York, 1984).

220. Elson, *Guardians of Tradition: American Schoolbooks of the Nineteenth Century*, p. 255. *Historical Statistics*, series A6–8, 57–72, Q321–8; Thomas Bender, *Toward an Urban Vision: Ideas and Institutions in Nineteenth Century America* (Lexington, KY, 1975); George R. Taylor, *The Transportation Revolution, 1815–1860* (New York, 1951); John F. Stover, "Canals and Turnpikes: America's Early-Nineteenth-Century Transportation Network," pp. 60–98, in *An Emerging Independent American Economy, 1815–1875*, ed. Joseph R. Frese and Jacob Judd (Tarrytown, NY, 1980); Howard P. Chudacoff, *The Evolution of American Urban Society* (Englewood Cliffs, NJ, 1975), ch. 2.

Economy in 1821. This ambiguity only contributed to the importance of "political economy, the new queen of the sciences," and by 1876 Francis Wayland's summative textbook, *The Elements of Political Economy* (1837), had been through 23 editions.[221]

The concern for political economy reflected America's general preoccupation with the relationship between polity and wealth, and this preoccupation was manifested particularly in links between law and commerce. Historian J. W. Hurst made the seminal analysis in this regard, demonstrating that law sponsored "the release of energy" in early nineteenth-century society and fostered commercial development. Lawrence Friedman then did much to explain this sponsorship, while Morton Horwitz has critically analyzed the relationship between law and commerce. Looking at private law – property, contracts, and torts – Horwitz emphasizes that the personal and collective interests of lawyers and merchants were served by "a major transformation of substantive legal rules governing commercial disputes," and he portrays this transformation as a willful bargain between merchants and attorneys.[222] Horwitz's intimation that lawyers and judges shaped private law *in order* to serve their personal and corporate interests is speculative. But his evidence for the jurisprudential sponsorship of entrepreneurial commerce is solid, whatever the conscious or unconscious motives of merchants and jurists.

One example of this sponsorship was the Constitutional doctrine of vested rights that arose in the late 1700s and persevered until the mid-nineteenth century. This doctrine held "that the legislature cannot ... except for reasons of public policy, enact laws impairing vested rights" which "are rights vested in specific individuals." The doctrine pertained especially to property, as the US Supreme Court made clear in *Calder* v. *Bull* (1798). It was then interpreted in *Fletcher* v. *Peck* (1810) to ensure the reliability of contractual obligations, and in *Dartmouth College* (1819) the court disallowed a state's revocation of a corporate charter, thus ensuring the vested rights of corporations and the legal reliability of their contractual obligations.[223]

221. Charles F. Mullett, "No Intellectual Voluptuary But a Sagacious Dictionary: George Cornewall Lewis, 1806–1863," in Lewis, *Remarks on the Use and Abuse of some Political Terms*, p. 21; Francis Wayland, *The Elements of Political Economy* (New York, 1837). See Henry C. Carey, *The Principles of Social Science* (Philadelphia, 1859), vol. 2, p. 409; Nelson, *Liberty and Property: Political Economy and Policymaking in the New Nation, 1789–1812*, passim; Drew R. McCoy, *The Elusive Republic: Political Economy in Jeffersonian America* (Chapel Hill, NC, 1980).

222. Horwitz, *The Transformation of American Law, 1780–1860*, pp. 154, 253, ch. 3; James W. Hurst, *Law and the Conditions of Freedom in the Nineteenth-Century United States* (Madison, WI, 1956), pp. 10–25; Lawrence M. Friedman, *A History of American Law*, 2d edn (New York, 1985). Horwitz's key argument is that private law jurisprudence shifted from promoting monopoly until the 1830s to attacking monopoly after the 1830s. Anti-competitive, pro-monopoly jurisprudence was necessary in the first third of the nineteenth century in order to encourage initial investment in large projects. In subsequent decades a pro-competitive, anti-monopolistic jurisprudence was necessary in order to encourage new investors to enter markets dominated by monopolies. Thus, jurists, early and late, had the same view in mind: to encourage economic development.

223. Edward S. Corwin, "The Basic Doctrine of American Constitutional Law," *Michigan Law Review*, 12 (1914): 271–3; *Calder* v. *Bull*, 3 Dallas (3 US) 386, 388 (1798). *Fletcher* v.

Dartmouth College (1819) demonstrates another jurisprudential innovation that sponsored commerce: the invention of the private corporation endowed with the vested rights of individuals. In English law, corporations – what Blackstone called "bodies politic" – were a mixed category having some legal attributes of the state and some of an individual citizen. In addition, English law made no distinction between corporations of private individuals seeking to advance their own ends, and corporations of public entities, such as cities, towns, or colonies. The state could intrude at any time and change the terms of the charter because all corporations were regarded as instruments of the state.[224]

American courts became uncertain about state authority to intrude in this fashion, and this uncertainty led to questions about the nature of corporations: were they like private individuals with inviolable vested rights, or were they like public towns, whose charters and rights could be modified? In 1815 Justice Story introduced a distinction between public corporations, which could be regulated by the state, and private corporations, whose charters, once granted, could not be altered. *Dartmouth College* (1819) then enshrined this distinction between public and private corporations,[225] and the American conception of corporations subsequently moved further away from the English view of these "bodies politic" serving state purposes, to a vision of corporations as private associations serving their own ends. With the shield of vested rights erected, private corporations began to proliferate. Only eight of the 310 corporations chartered by American states through 1800 had been dedicated to producing goods for sale. By 1830, 600 corporations in New England alone were devoted to this end. In this fashion, "the chartered corporation ... began its rise to dominance, first in banking, then in insurance and inland transportation, soon in manufacturing."[226]

In these technical but highly significant ways, jurists constructed a polity conducive to investment and commercial development. Whether by design or circumstance, they consequently allied themselves with merchants, the wealthiest vocational group in society. The alliance between merchants and lawyers was relatively new, because merchants in mid-eighteenth-century commercial centers had tended to favor commercial arbitration due to "its speed and low cost." Only gradually and unevenly in the second half of the eighteenth century did the complexity of commercial transactions begin to justify to merchants the need for the rule of law in resolving disputes. By the 1770s, in commercial centers such as New York, "the merchants with the lawyers and landholders formed an aristocracy

---

Peck, 6 Cranch (10 US) 87, 135 (1810); *Dartmouth College* v. *Woodward,* 4 Wheaton (17 US) 518 (1819).

224. William Blackstone, *Commentaries on the Laws of England* (Oxford, 1765), vol. 1, ch. 18.

225. *Terrett* v. *Taylor,* 9 Cranch (13 US) 43, 51–2 (1815); *Dartmouth College* v. *Woodward,* 4 Wheaton (17 US) 518 (1819).

226. Schlesinger, *The Age of Jackson,* p. 9; Oscar Handlin and Mary F. Handlin, "Origins of the American Business Corporation," *Journal of Economic History,* 5 (1945): 1–23; Nelson, *Americanization of the Common Law ... 1760–1830,* chs. 2, 3, 4; Hendrik Hartog, "Because all the World was not New York City: Governance, Property Rights, and the State in the Changing Definition of a Corporation, 1730–1860," *Buffalo Law Review,* 28 (1979): 91–109; Newmyer, *Supreme Court Justice Joseph Story,* p. 128.

which was able to control elections both in the city and in the country."²²⁷ Similarly in North Carolina in the 1780s there arose what Norman Risjord labels the "Lawyers' Party," an alliance of attorneys and merchants opposing the larger, rural "Farmers' Party." Small wonder that Hector de Crèvecoeur noted in the same decade that "Lawyer or merchant are the fairest titles our towns afford."²²⁸

The alliance between merchants and lawyers led attorneys to begin working on retainer for merchant houses and corporations and, eventually, to serve in that capacity full time. From 1810 to 1840 almost 20 percent of college-trained lawyers in Maine and Massachusetts left general court practice to apply their legal skills in banks, railroads, and industries. Notwithstanding "southern distinctiveness," these trends also appeared in southern communities such as Nashville, where after about 1820 leading lawyers earned the bulk of their income through business retainers and left debt collection to lesser attorneys. Louisiana society was similarly dominated by an alliance of lawyers, merchants, and planters. Touring the United States in the mid-1830s, Michael Chevalier noted this alliance, and by the following decade the same path to a handsome legal practice existed even on the frontier. After moving from Kentucky to Texas and joining the bar in the 1840s, William Ballinger made a fortune by contacting businessmen in eastern commercial centers and arranging to represent their accounts in Texas for a commission.²²⁹

Though allied in this way, lawyers, whose economic status is discussed below, did not earn as much as merchants, who dominated the wealthiest segment of the population, as indicated on Table 3.1. This high financial status enjoyed by merchants, bankers, and businessmen elevated their self-esteem and prompted them to denigrate those in the professions, as reported by Englishman Isaac Fidler, who visited the United States in 1833. There was some defensiveness in this denigration, however, because wealth did not necessarily imply the highest social status. "There are few who would not prefer a very moderate independence, with a *genteel* position, to wealth, with the drawback of a vulgar occupation," John Lalor noted in 1839, "The liberal professions gratify this love of gentility.... The briefless barrister, the unemployed physician, the humblest starving curate ... is still, according to common notions, undeniably in the position of a gentleman." Hence, Byerly Thomson observed in 1857, "a business secures an earlier means of access to

227. Quotations are from Auerbach, *Justice Without Law?*, p. 32; Harrington, *The New York Merchant on the Eve of the Revolution*, p. 37. E. B. O'Callaghan, ed., *Documents Relative to the Colonial History of the State of New York* (Albany, NY, 1859), vol. 7, p. 795; Main, *The Social Structure of Revolutionary America*, p. 155.
228. Risjord, *Chesapeake Politics, 1781–1800*, pp. 88–95; J. Hector St. John de Crèvecoeur, *Letters from an American Farmer* (1782; London: 1783), ed. Albert E. Stone (New York, 1981), letter 3.
229. Shugg, *Origins of Class Struggle in Louisiana*, pp. 28, 133, 138, 141; Chevalier, *Society, Manners and Politics in the United States*, p. 282; Gawalt, "Sources of Anti-Lawyer Sentiment in Massachusetts, 1740–1840," p. 287; Gawalt, *The Promise of Power: The Emergence of the Legal Profession in Massachusetts, 1760–1840*, chs. 2, 3; Newmyer, *Supreme Court Justice Joseph Story*, p. 39; Horwitz, *The Transformation of American Law, 1780–1860*, ch. 5; Calhoun, *Professional Lives in America*, pp. 83–5; Bloomfield, *American Lawyers in a Changing Society, 1776–1876*, ch. 8.

Table 3.1   Occupational groups among wealthiest citizens in antebellum America

	New York 1828 (%)	Boston 1830 (%)	Brooklyn 1841 (%)	New York 1845 (%)	Philadelphia 1845–6 (%)	Boston 1850 (%)
Merchants[1]	81	72	59	76	63	71
Attorneys	7	11	5	9	5	10
Widows	3	7	7	3	3	7
Builders[2]	4	2	8	4	5	3
Physicians	1	3	2	3	5	3
Distillers	–	2	3	1	1	1
Publishers[3]	–	–	1	2	2	1
Misc.	4	3	15[4]	2	16[5]	4
Total	100	100	100	100	100	100

[1] Includes bankers
[2] Includes manufacturers
[3] Includes booksellers
[4] Includes 5 percent farmers
[5] Includes 13 percent "gentlemen"
Sources: Adapted from Edward Pessen, *Riches, Class and Power Before the Civil War* (Lexington, MA, 1973), pp. 47–8, 303; Pessen, "The Business Elite of Antebellum New York City: Diversity, Continuity, Standing," in *An Emerging Independent American Economy, 1815–1875*, ed. Joseph R. Frese and Jacob Judd (Tarrytown, NY, 1980), pp. 164–5. The criteria of "wealthy" varied in the lists used by Pessen.

competence, and wealth; and ... a profession presents a readier road to position in society, and to honour."[230]

At the other end of the financial spectrum, workers did not fare well during the economic fluctuations of the War of 1812 and the Panics of 1819, 1837, and 1857. In the early national period between 1790 and 1830, workers' real wages increased slightly more than 60 percent, much of it in the 1790s. From 1830 to 1860 real wages increased only about 12 percent. Because the economy grew at a much higher rate, scholars are agreed that economic and social stratification increased between 1800 and 1860. The formerly artisan workforce split into two classes: entrepreneurs who supplied the capital and workers who toiled for wages. This stratification occurred at different rates in different industries, and by mid-century was quite uneven. Nevertheless, the hard times of the late 1830s and early 1840s

230. Isaac Fidler, *Observations on Professions, Literature, Manners and Emigration in the United States and Canada* (New York, 1833), p. 20; John Lalor, "The Social Position of Educators," in *The Educator. Prize Essays on the Means and Expediency of Elevating the Profession of the Educator in Society* (London, 1839), pp. 77–8; Thomson, *The Choice of a Profession*, p. 11.

sharpened class divisions and produced what Robert Wiebe has called "a society in halves." In 1860 only about 60 percent of free adult males had a personal estate valued at more than $100, and only 40 percent of free adult males owned real estate. In annual income at this time, unskilled workers earned between $200 and $400; domestic servants who constituted about 6 percent of the workforce earned from $300 to $500; skilled artisans, mechanics, and craftsmen, from $400 to $800; the "middle class," comprising perhaps a fifth of the workforce, from $800 to $5,000; and the "rich," comprising less than 1 percent, more than $5,000. Overall, the average income for non-farm employees in 1860 was $363.[231]

Among the professors of the liberal professions, the clergy continued their long decline in economic status that had begun early in the eighteenth century. In 1837 Edward Hazen described the situation well:

> The salary received by ministers of the gospel, in the United States, is exceedingly various in the different denominations, and in the same denomination from different congregations. In some instances, they receive nothing for their services; in others a liberal compensation.... [B]ut ... taking the ability of its members into account, there is no employment less productive of wealth.[232]

Many of the ministers who enjoyed "a liberal compensation" belonged to the Protestant Episcopal Church, or reconstituted Anglican church, which generally provided salaries of $500 to $1,000 in an average parish and $1,000 to $5,000 in large parishes. Presbyterians also did well, particularly in southern cities, where "the average wealth of the town preachers far exceeded the average of free white adult males in 1860." Similarly, in New England Unitarian ministers, the liberal descendants of the Congregationalists, generally received between $700 and $2,000.[233] Most clergy, however, belonged to the income level of skilled artisans.

An important reason for ministers' lower income, in addition to factors noted earlier, was the explosion of the Baptist and Methodist denominations, whose

231. Wiebe, *The Opening of American Society*, ch. 16; *Historical Statistics*, series D715–21, 735; Edgar W. Martin, *The Standard of Living in 1860* (Chicago, 1942), ch. 13, pp. 393–4, app. B; Donald T. Adams, "Wage Rates in the Early National Period: 1785–1830," *Journal of Economic History*, 28 (1968): 404–26; Pessen, *Riches, Class and Power before the Civil War*, ch. 3; Edward Pessen, "Builders of the Young Republic," in *A History of the American Worker*, ed. Richard B. Morris (Princeton, NJ, 1983), pp. 43–78; Paul G. Faler, *Mechanics and Manufacturers in the Early Industrial Revolution: Lynn Massachusetts, 1780–1860* (Albany, NY, 1981), ch. 5; W. J. Rorabaugh, *The Craft Apprentice: From Franklin to the Machine Age in America* (New York, 1986), chs. 1, 3, 5–7; Lee Soltow, *Men and Wealth in the United States, 1850–1870* (New Haven, CT, 1975), p. 174, ch. 4; Daniel E. Sutherland, *Americans and their Servants: Domestic Service in the United States from 1800 to 1920* (Baton Rouge, LA, 1981), pp. 45, 104; Bruce Laurie, *Artisans into Workers: Labor in Nineteenth-Century America* (New York, 1989), pp. 56–61.

232. Hazen, *The Panorama of Professions and Trades*, p. 123.

233. Quotation is from Holifield, *Gentleman Theologians ... in Southern Culture, 1795–1860*, p. 32. Hanley, *The American Revolution and Religion, Maryland, 1770–1800*, pp. 227–8; William W. Manross, *The Episcopal Church in the United States, 1800–1840* (New York, 1938), pp. 98–9; Charles Brooks, *A Statement of Facts from Each Religious Denomination in New England Respecting Ministers' Salaries* (Boston, 1854), pp. 5–7.

clergy were often poorly educated and paid. A recent study of one antebellum community in South Carolina found, for example, that preachers were spread evenly across the top three-quarters of the population in wealth, with only a few in the bottom quarter. The wealthy ministers in the top two quarters were generally Episcopalians, whereas those in the bottom two quarters were largely Baptists or Methodists. These evangelical denominations, which grew especially in the South between 1787 and 1825, tended to regard clerical poverty as evidence of religious commitment.[234] Nevertheless, many Baptist and Methodist clergymen believed they had entirely too much evidence.

Looking back to the beginning of the century, a prominent Virginia clergyman later wrote, "among all the Baptist ministers of Virginia, not one received an adequate or even stinted support." In 1826 Joseph Warne reported that 154 of 156 Baptist clergy in part of North Carolina could not support themselves by their ministry. In the 1830s William C. Buck, a leader of the Kentucky Baptists, stated that although his was the largest denomination in Kentucky – more numerous than all other sects put together – there was not a single minister with a full-time salary.[235] An 1845 survey of Baptist ministers in New Jersey concluded that "the average amount of salary paid to each minister does not exceed $350 annually; neither is that all received." Things were little better even in New England, where an 1854 survey of some 1,500 clergy, conducted by the Society for the Relief of Aged and Destitute Clergymen, found that non-Unitarians generally earned between $350 and $650.[236]

Rev. T. C. Teasdale accurately summed up the situation in 1846, estimating that "the average compensation of ministers, of all denominations, in the United States, does not exceed three or four hundred dollars per annum." This compensation meant that "Americans ... have cheaper preachers than can be found in any part of Europe," and ministers complained loudly, but to no avail.[237] The clergy were

234. Burton, *In my Father's House are Many Mansions: Family and Community in Edgefield, South Carolina*, pp. 57–8, 69, 351; John B. Boles, *The Great Revival, 1787–1825: Origins of the Southern Evangelical Mind* (Lexington, KY, 1972), p. 170.

235. Jeremiah B. Jeter, *The Recollections of a Long Life* (Richmond, VA, 1891), p. 311; Joseph A. Warne, *The Duty of Supporting the Christian Minstry, Stated and Enforced* (Newbern, NC, 1826), p. 11; Spencer, *A History of Kentucky Baptists*, vol. 1, pp. 496, 660, 937–8, 959; Randall A. Corkern, "A Study of the Education, Morals, Salary and Controversial Movements of the Frontier Baptist Preacher in Kentucky from its Settlement until 1830" (ThD thesis, Southern Baptist Theological Seminary, 1960), pp. 134–96.

236. John M. Carpenter, *The Duty of the Churches to Recognize and Appreciate their Pastors ... delivered before the New Jersey [Baptist] Association* (Philadelphia, 1845), p. 15; Brooks, *A Statement of Facts from Each Religious Denomination in New England Respecting Ministers' Salaries*, pp. 5–7. Most clerical salaries reported in *Yale Graduates* for the period between 1800 and 1850 are below $500.

237. T. C. Teasdale, "Sermon on Ministerial Education," in *Minutes of the Fourteenth Anniversary of the Monogahela Baptist Association* (Pittsburgh, 1846), p. 23; Grund, *The Americans in their Moral, Social, and Political Relations*, vol. 1, pp. 291–2. See James Walker, "Difficulties in Parishes," *Christian Examiner*, 9 (1830): 18; [anon.], "The Value of the Minister's Work, an Argument for His Support," *[Richmond] Baptist Preacher*, 6 (June 1847): 97–100; C. Goodwin, "Trials and Tribulations of the Christian Pastor," in *Minutes of the New Jersey Baptist Association* (1851): 17–20; Amzi Benedict, "Ministerial Support," *American National Preacher*, 29 (1855): 129–40.

increasingly drawn from the families of farmers and artisans both because their sons saw it as the next step up in social status and because "wealthy Christians are not, as a class, disposed to educate their sons for the ministry. They commonly prefer to see them engaged in some more lucrative profession or pursuit."[238]

Physicians were in no better economic position, being "bitterly divided and financially insecure in the nineteenth century."[239] Between 1790 and 1860 the number of physicians rose about eleven times, from some 5,000 to perhaps 55,000, whereas the population rose only eight times from about 4 million to some 32 million. Overcrowding therefore increased, and by 1860 "the number of physicians per person was the highest in known American history." In addition, "trained physicians crowded into urban areas, which increased competition for patients and lowered earnings."[240] Moreover, as the Committee on Medical Education of the American Medical Association noted in 1851, "the profession is not only crowded, but a large portion of it is made up of ignorant and unworthy men."[241] The profession's ignorance of effective therapies before the Civil War was thus compounded by the lack of education and social graces on the part of many physicians.

The result was that "the income of doctors varied more than did that of ministers but apparently averaged about the same." Hence, Edward Pessen found that there were perhaps a third as many wealthy doctors as lawyers, and more wealthy doctors than wealthy clergymen. Nevertheless, most doctors stood "at the lower end of the middle class" earning about $400–800 in the second quarter of the nineteenth century.[242] It is telling that one medical historian has argued that early-nineteenth-century physicians enjoyed high status in Rochester, New York, which, at the time, was the nation's largest city founded after the Revolution.

238. Teasdale, "Sermon on Ministerial Education," p. 23; Julian Sturtevant, "The Education of Indigent Young Men for the Ministry," *American Biblical Repository,* 10 (1843): 465–8; Scott, *From Office to Profession: The New England Ministry, 1750–1850,* ch. 4; David F. Allmendinger, Jr., *Paupers and Scholars: The Transformation of Student Life in 19th Century New England* (New York, 1975), ch. 1. Fewer young men with fortunes went into ministry, and fewer ministers amassed a comfortable estate, as demonstrated by the estates of ministers who graduated from Yale reported in Table 2.2. If one arranges the estates by graduation date, the value of the estate declines over time. All ten of those who graduated in 1712 or earlier left estates valued over £1,000, while only four of the thirteen who graduated after 1712 did so. Similarly, 35 percent of the future ministers in the Harvard classes of 1715–39 came from prosperous backgrounds, whereas 18 percent in the classes 1740–64 did so. Botein, "Income and Ideology: Harvard-Trained Clergymen in Eighteenth-Century New England," pp. 404–5.

239. Starr, *The Social Transformation of American Medicine,* pp. ix, 30–232.

240. Colin B. Burke, *American Collegiate Populations: A Test of the Traditional View* (New York, 1982), p. 186; William G. Rothstein, *American Medical Schools and the Practice of Medicine* (New York, 1987), p. 41. The increase was initially due to the number of individuals who were drawn into medicine by being drafted as surgeons during the Revolution or the War of 1812. See, for example, *Yale Graduates,* vol. 3, p. 540; Seebert J. Goldowsky, *Yankee Surgeon: The Life and Times of Usher Parson, 1788–1868* (Boston, 1988).

241. Worthington Hooker et al., "Report of the Committee on Medical Education," *Transactions of the American Medical Association,* 4 (1851): 417.

242. Quotations are from Main, *The Social Structure of Revolutionary America,* p. 99; Starr, *The Social Transformation of American Medicine,* pp. 63, 84. See Pessen, *Riches, Class and Power before the Civil War,* ch. 4; Martin, *The Standard of Living in 1860,* ch. 8.

However, even the better educated of these high-status physicians "found it necessary to have additional means of support beside the practice of their profession."
And from this high point early in the nineteenth century "the financial situation of
the profession deteriorated." By 1860 merely one-third of Rochester physicians
owned real property, which qualified them to vote. Thus, two-thirds of Rochester
physicians probably owned less wealth than the average voter. And the estates of
the enfranchised physicians had an average value of $1,500, which was almost
exactly the average value of all voters' estates. This was the situation in a city
where physicians supposedly had high status.[243]

If ministers and physicians generally earned less than lawyers, teachers were at a
lower rank still. In 1842 the President of Brown University summarized the situation for the upper echelon of educators:

> [T]he instructors of Colleges in this country, are remunerated, at a lower rate
> than almost any other professional men. I know but very few who ... might not
> earn a larger compensation in any other profession.... [P]rofessorships in New
> England Colleges vary from six hundred to twelve hundred dollars per annum.
> And I ask, what inducements could such an income offer to a lawyer, physician,
> or a cle[r]gyman?[244]

These figures fit closely with recent estimates about college professors' income in
other parts of the country during the first half of the nineteenth century. To be
sure, there were exceptions. At Harvard the average faculty salary in 1825 was
$1,400; in 1845, $1,950; and in 1865, $2,550. Joseph Story, the professor of law,
earned $4,000, the highest of any professor. As a result, three-fifths of the Harvard
professors appointed before 1830 and three-fourths of those appointed after 1830
left estates in the top 2 percent of the Massachusetts population. At the University
of Virginia in the 1820s each professor was provided a rent-free residence, a fixed
salary, and the fees paid by the students enrolled in his subject. In total, professors'
annual income reached $2,500. South Carolina College offered similar inducements,
and Columbia University paid professors between $2,000 and $3,000 through the
1840s and about $4,000 in the 1850s. At the same time, professors in the most
successful proprietary professional schools associated with colleges might approach
this income.[245]

243. Edward C. Atwater, "The Medical Profession in a New Society, Rochester, New
York (1811–60)," *Bulletin of the History of Medicine,* 47 (1973): 223, 227–9.
244. Francis Wayland, *Thoughts on the Present Collegiate System in the United States*
(Boston, 1842), pp. 136–7.
245. Pierson, *A Yale Book of Numbers: Historical Statistics ... 1701–1976,* pp. 538–9,
599–600; Story, *The Forging of an Aristocracy: Harvard and the Boston Upper Class, 1800–
1870,* pp. 81–2; Whitehead, *The Separation of College and State ... 1776–1876,* p. 101; Sister
M. St. Mel Kennedy, "The Changing Academic Characteristics of the Nineteenth-Century
American College Teacher," *Paedagogica Historica,* 5 (1965): 366; Burke, *American Collegiate
Populations,* p. 233; Dumas Malone, *Jefferson and His Time: The Sage of Monticello* (Boston,
1981), p. 398; Franek Rozwadowski, "From Recitation Room to Research Seminar: Political
Economy at Columbia University," in *Breaking the Academic Mould: Economists and
American Higher Learning in the Nineteenth Century,* ed. William J. Barber (Middletown, CT,
1988), p. 172; Freidel, *Francis Lieber,* pp. 239–40; Rothstein, *American Medical Schools,*
p. 62; Johnson, *Schooled Lawyers,* p. 13.

However, in the hundreds of little liberal arts colleges springing up across the country faculty members were fortunate to make $500 annually. Even at the well established colleges in New England, such as Williams or Bowdoin, professors earned about $700 through 1840. The administrative leaders of these colleges did slightly better with some negotiating. When Professor Stephen Olin of Franklin College in Athens, Georgia, was named president of Randolph-Macon College in 1832, he exaggerated his salary in order to induce Randolph-Macon to raise their offer to $1,500 plus housing. A similar offer was accepted in 1849 by the new vice-president at Centenary College in Louisiana, and Brown University meanwhile responded to its president's complaint quoted above by offering faculty a fixed salary of $1,200 or $500 plus fees of students enrolled in their courses.[246]

The income of those teaching in the schools was lower still. "The salaries of teachers ... in most of the States are mere pittances, when compared with the remuneration of professional men, or clerks in the counting rooms of respectable merchants," observed English visitor Francis Grund. Even worse was the judgment in 1829 of Samuel Hall, the founder of the first normal school in the United States: "The monthly wages of the teachers of district schools are frequently one third less than the amount paid to experienced clerks and journeymen mechanics in the same vicinity." In 1837 the American Institute of Instruction noted that "the wages of a teacher are below those given in the humblest of the mechanic arts," and John Kingsbury stated in 1848 that "no intellectual labor is so poorly paid."[247]

Typically a male teacher might earn $400 to $600, while principals, who supervised small staffs of teachers in the urban schools that were founded by the 1850s, earned as much as $1,000. These generalized estimates must, however, be adjusted in light of what Francis Grund in 1837 called the "sordid practice introduced throughout the United States" that women who taught were generally paid two-fifths to three-fifths of the salary paid to men. Over the course of the nineteenth century, the precollegiate teaching force changed from being almost exclusively male in 1800 to about 70 percent female by 1900. A key shift occurred from 1830 to 1860, when common schools were organized into districts under state departments of education. The push for expansion and centralization was accompanied by a desire for economy, which resulted in the hiring of more women, who, without any options for professional work, taught for less money. Thus, the Massachusetts teaching force went from 56 percent female in 1834 to 78 percent female in 1860. In the South this feminization of the teaching force did not reduce women teachers' salaries as much as in the North due to the southern labor shortage. Nevertheless, the income of schoolmistresses everywhere, such as those sent by the

246. Barber, "Political Economy from the Top Down: Brown University," pp. 84–5; Holifield, *Gentleman Theologians ... in Southern Culture, 1795–1860*, p. 136; Frederick Rudolph, *The American College and University, A History* (New York, 1962), p. 193; James E. Scanlon, *Randolph-Macon College: A Southern History, 1825–1967* (Charlottesville, VA, 1983), pp. 53–4.

247. Grund, *The Americans in their Moral, Social, and Political Relations*, vol. 1, p. 214; Samuel R. Hall, *Lectures on School-Keeping* (1829), ed. Arthur D. Wright and George E. Gardner (Hanover, NH, 1929), p. 29; American Institute of Instruction, *Memorial of the Directors* (Boston, 1837), p. 5; John Kingsbury, *Lecture on Failures in Teaching delivered before the American Institute of Education* (Boston, 1848), p. 5.

National Popular Board of Education in the 1840s and 1850s to Iowa, Wisconsin, Ohio, Missouri, Illinois, Indiana, and Kentucky, generally hovered at about $150 with room or board, or $300 without.[248]

While ministers, physicians, and educators saw their relative income from "professional service" declining or, at best, holding even between 1750 and 1860, lawyers' personal wealth rose dramatically. True, attorneys' income varied greatly from the railroad lawyer to the debt-collecting pettifogger, and young lawyers faced a "starving time" at the outset of their careers. It has also been said that judicial salaries were so low that lawyers refused to sit on the bench, and that attorneys acquired wealth only through earnings outside of their legal practice. In fact, it has even been suggested "that most lawyers had no greater direct compensation in fees or salary" than did ministers or college faculty members.[249] However, lawyers attained positions where they could earn outside income, as in corporations and merchant houses, precisely because of their legal and political expertise. Thus, the far more common misperception among scholars is to inflate lawyer's financial status, suggesting that lawyers were "earning as a group ten times as much as doctors and ministers and as much as the very wealthiest merchants and planters."[250]

On balance, it may simply be asserted that attorneys did much better financially than other professions and not as well as merchants. The 1789 Judiciary Act provided salaries of $1,000 or more for federal district judges, $3,500 for justices of the US Supreme Court, and $1,500 for the Attorney General. In 1801 federal district and circuit judges were given a salary of between $1,500 and $2,000. Some legalistic states, such as Massachusetts, soon matched or exceeded those salaries, whereas a justice on the Ohio Supreme Court was not paid $1,500 until 1837.[251]

248. Grund, *The Americans in their Moral, Social, and Political Relations,* vol. 1, p. 222n. Estimates are drawn from Kaestle, *Pillars of the Republic: Common Schools and American Society, 1780–1860,* pp. 123–5; Polly Welts Kaufman, *Women Teachers on the Frontier* (New Haven, CT, 1984), pp. 32, 148, 160, 174, 178, 204; Frederick M. Binder, *The Age of the Common School, 1830–1865* (New York, 1975), p. 78; Kathryn Kish Sklar, *Catharine Beecher: A Study in American Domesticity* (New Haven, CT, 1973), p. 312; Richard M. Bernard and Maris A. Vinovskis, "The Female School Teacher in Ante-bellum Massachusetts," *Journal of Social History,* 10 (1977): 332–45; Amelia Akehurst Lines, *To Raise Myself a Little: The Diaries and Letters of Jennie, a Georgia Teacher, 1851–1886,* ed. Thomas Dyer (Athens, GA, 1984), pp. 11, 17, 25, 103, 134, 145, 170; Mattingly, *The Classless Profession: American Schoolmen in the Nineteenth Century,* pp. 104–5, 147, 213.

249. Gawalt, *The Promise of Power: The Emergence of the Legal Profession in Massachusetts, 1760–1840,* pp. 127, 102. Fannie M. Farmer, "The Bar Examination and Beginning Years of Legal Practice in North Carolina, 1820–1860," *North Carolina Historical Review,* 29 (1952): 159–70; Edward Pessen, *Most Uncommon Jacksonians: Radical Leaders of the Early Labor Movements* (Albany, NY, 1967), pp. 52, 58; Chroust, *The Rise of the Legal Profession in America,* vol. 2, p. 46; Story, *The Forging of an Aristocracy: Harvard and the Boston Upper Class, 1800–1870,* pp. 83–4.

250. Klein, "New York Lawyers and the Coming of the American Revolution," pp. 388–9. See James K. Martin, *Men in Rebellion* (New Brunswick, NJ, 1973), pp. 66–9; Main, *The Social Structure of Revolutionary America,* p. 101.

251. 1 *US Statutes,* 72 (1789); 2 *US Statutes,* 89 (1801); 2 *US Statutes,* 121 (1801); Ellis, *The Jeffersonian Crisis: Courts and Politics in the Young Republic,* pp. 216–7; Bloomfield, *American Lawyers in a Changing Society, 1776–1876,* p. 248.

Meanwhile successful lawyers earned at least as much as leading judges in corresponding regions of the country. Indeed, a retainer of $1,000 per month for successful entrepreneurial attorneys such as John Taylor in Virginia, Waightstill Avery in North Carolina, Benjamin C. Yancey in South Carolina, or Daniel Webster in Boston, "would have been but a moderate allowance," as the Constitutional Court of South Carolina noted in 1821. Certainly, frontier lawyers received less. Those in Alabama, Mississippi, Louisiana, or Tennessee, after five or six lean years, would "lay up money, ranging from $250 to 500, according to merit and good fortune, *per annum.*"[252] Nevertheless, throughout the country in the first half of the nineteenth century, a greater fraction of wealthy citizens occupied themselves in the law than in any other professional occupation, as demonstrated in Table 3.1. Hence, New York attorney Theodore Sedgwick correctly responded to the inquiry *How Shall the Lawyer be Paid* by characterizing the law as "a toilsome, an honorable and an expensive science." Likewise, John Livingston was generally accurate in his estimate that across the United States lawyers earned on average about $1,500 in 1850, an estimate that he reduced to $1,000 after the Panic of 1857.[253]

Economic: "seting the Cat to watch the Creem pot"

The relative wealth of attorneys between the Revolution and the Civil War is, therefore, easily demonstrated. In fact, the point is well known, unlike the high financial status of the colonial clergy. What has not been appreciated about antebellum lawyers is how their rise in wealth occurred despite fee statutes restricting attorneys' income from legal practice. Indeed, the way in which lawyers were able to circumvent the statutes that regulated their fees is no less significant than their rise in income. This circumvention demonstrates in a very specific and material way the increased authority acquired by lawyers as a result of their professional mastery of the architectonic of culture.

In the decades leading up to the Revolution, it was generally known that lawyers

252. Baldwin, *The Flush Times of Alabama and Mississippi, A Series of Sketches,* p. 48; *Duncan* v. *Breithaupt,* 1 McCord 149, 150 (South Carolina 1821); M. E. Bradford, "A Virginia Cato: John Taylor of Caroline and the Agrarian Republic," in *Arator, Being a Series of Agricultural Essays, Practical and Political: In Sixty-Four Numbers* (1818), by John Taylor (Indianapolis, IN, 1977), pp. 12–3; Clement Eaton, "A Mirror of the Southern Colonial Lawyer: The Fee Books of Patrick Henry, Thomas Jefferson and Waightstill Avery," *WMQ,* 3d ser., 8 (1951): 520–34; Sutherland, *The Law at Harvard … 1817–1967,* pp. 43–4; Martin, *The Standard of Living in 1860,* pp. 393–4; Gawalt, *The Promise of Power: The Emergence of the Legal Profession in Massachusetts, 1760–1840,* pp. 110–5.

253. Theodore Sedgwick, Jr., *How Shall the Lawyer Be Paid, or some Remarks upon Two Acts recently Passed on the Subject of the Cost of Legal Proceedings* (New York, 1840), pp. 10–1; [John Livingston, ed.], *The United States Monthly Law Magazine,* 4 (1851): iv; Livingston, *Livingston's United States Law Register and Official Directory for 1860: Being a Handbook Useful to Every Lawyer and Business Man, as well as to all Executive, Judicial, Legislative, and County Officers* (New York, 1860), p. ix.

were chipping away at the authority of the fee statutes. They sometimes charged for services not listed in the statutes or accepted gratuitous payments exceeding the fee limits.[254] Nevertheless, states continued to enact fee statutes after the Revolution, the last ones being passed by New York in 1840 and Pennsylvania in 1868.[255] It is important to see that these statutes had explicitly prohibited lawyers from charging more than the stated sums for handling a given case. The 1710 New York ordinance, in force for almost 60 years, declared that any lawyer who "shall any time hereafter exact, demand or ask any greater or other fee ... shall be liable to ... such ... Fines and Penalties as the Utmost Rigour of the Law can Inflict." The Pennsylvania statutes of 1723 and 1752 required each attorney to display a table of the statutory fees "where it shall be constantly exposed to view and inspection of all persons." The 1742 Virginia law declared that lawyers "shall not exact, take, or receive, directly or indirectly, any greater or other fees or rewards, for the following services, than what are herein particularly mentioned and expressed."[256] The 1770 North Carolina act prohibited a lawyer from "exacting, taking, receiving, or demanding any greater Fee, or other Reward, for any of the above services," and the South Carolina acts in the 1790s stated simply: "the attornies fees ... shall not exceed the present fees ... in all cases whatsoever." In 1795 Massachusetts proscribed "any greater fee or fees for any of the services aforesaid than are by this Act allowed," and Vermont did likewise in 1802 and 1839.[257] All these declarations were buttressed by laws against champerty (promising to pay one's attorney a share of the proceeds won in a case) and against maintenance (interfering in a law suit by aiding one party in suing another).[258]

254. Erwin C. Surrency, "The Pernicious Practice of Law – A Comment," *AJLH*, 13 (1969): 242; Honestus, *Observations on the Pernicious Practice of the Law*, passim; John Adams, *Legal Papers*, ed. with an introduction by L. Kinvin Wroth and Hiller B. Zobel (Cambridge, MA, 1965), vol. 1, pp. lxix–lxxi. Virginia statutes of 1757 and 1761 provided that lawyers could receive more than the fee statutes but prohibited them from suing to enforce contracts for the additional amount. Statutes of 1765 and 1778 justified raising the fees by the fact that lawyers were charging and receiving more than the statutes allowed. (*Statutes of Virginia*, vol. 7, pp. 124–5, 400–1; vol. 8, pp. 184–5; vol. 9, pp. 528–9.) In the following, I draw upon Ruth E. Peters, "Statutory Regulation of Lawyers' Fees in Massachusetts, New York, Pennsylvania, South Carolina, Tennessee and Virginia from the Mid-Seventeenth Century to the Mid-Nineteenth Century" (Third-year JD paper, Harvard Law School, 1975).

255. *New York Laws* (Albany, NY, 1840): 386; *Laws of Pennsylvania* (Harrisburg, PA, 1868), p. 1, ss. 9. Chroust identifies many of the statutes passed between 1776 and 1840. *The Rise of the Legal Profession in America*, vol. 2, ch. 5.

256. Paul M. Hamlin and Charles E. Baker, eds., *Supreme Court of Judicature of the Province of New York, 1691–1704*, 3 vols. (New York, 1959), vol. 1, pp. 265, 272–4; *Statutes of Pennsylvania*, vol. 3, p. 379 (1722–3), vol. 5, p. 177 (1751–2); *Statutes of Virginia*, vol. 5, p. 182.

257. *State Records of North Carolina*, vol. 23, pp. 788–9; *Statutes of South Carolina*, vol. 5, pp. 154–5 (1791), 265 (1792); vol. 6, p. 265 (1798); *Session Laws of Massachusetts* (Boston, 1795): 41; *Laws of the State of Vermont ... 1802* (Bennington, VT, 1808), pp. 401–4; *Revised Statutes of the State of Vermont ... 1839* (Burlington, VT, 1840), pp. 471–2.

258. See *Thurston* v. *Percival*, 1 Pickering 415 (Massachusetts 1823); Baker, "The English Legal Profession, 1450–1550," pp. 16–41.

Despite these numerous and longstanding declarations, lawyers and judges in a series of cases beginning in Pennsylvania in 1819 maintained that the fee statutes never could have meant their explicit historical meaning. "It cannot seriously be thought that the general assembly intended the tax fee ... as the sole reward of professional exertion," the Supreme Court of Tennessee stated in 1827.[259] Such an intention "was not and has not been the understanding of the practice of the profession, of the courts, or of the people," maintained a jurist on the New York Court of Errors in 1841. To be sure, added a fellow jurist in the same case, the fees for sheriffs, clerks, and other court officers were also listed in the same statutes, and regarding *those* fees, "it cannot be doubted that the policy and intent of the legislature are in accordance with the most obvious and primary interpretation of the statute." However, "the most obvious and primary interpretation" did not apply to attorneys. "Higher compensation for counsel services" was allowable, he maintained, "as it falls within a fair and reasonable use of the words, though not the first and most obvious." He concluded: "my only doubt or difficulty in this case has been the fear of giving such a general construction to the statute, as would legalize extortionate bargains" by clerks, sheriffs, and others "whose fees are fixed in the same chapter."[260] Consequently, not only were attorneys allowed to receive more than the fees provided in the statutes, but "clerks, sheriffs, and the like" were regarded as bound by "the most obvious and primary interpretation" of the same statutes, which attorneys could evade!

It is difficult to escape the conclusion here that these jurists were influenced by professional allegiance and that their decisions ironically confirm one of the first principles of the rule of law set forth by the US Supreme Court in 1798: "a law that makes a man a judge in his own cause" is "contrary to the great principles of the social compact." In the very same year the point was also expressed by a self-taught farmer, who warned that putting lawyers in charge of "the Juditial power ... appears to me like seting the Cat to watch the Creem pot."[261] Even so, the naked self-interest of this profession sitting in judgement of its own fee statutes was clothed in legitimacy, and this fact demonstrates with exceptional clarity how the "professional exertion" in legal and political domains translated into economic and social authority. Moreover, the texture of that legitimacy, as exhibited in the reasoning of the courts, demonstrates perfectly how the cultural architectonic justified and shaped jurists' authority in all these domains.

One way of circumventing "the most obvious and primary interpretation" of the fee statutes was to distinguish between remuneration for legal "counsel," or advice, which was held to be subject to private arrangement, and fees for legal process and actual litigation, which were held to be subject to the statutes.[262] Many fee tables,

259. *Newnan* v. *Washington*, 1 Martin & Yerger 79, 82 (Tennessee 1827). See *Mooney* v. *Lloyd*, 5 Sergeant & Rawle 412 (Pennsylvania 1819). Jurists even acknowledged subsequently that the fee statutes had been intended to limit the total compensation of lawyers. "Compensation of Lawyers," *Albany Law Journal*, 10 (1874): 193–4; "Lawyers' Fees," *Albany Law Journal*, 13 (1877): 379–80.

260. *Adams* v. *Stevens*, 26 Wendell 451, 457–8, 461, 464, 466 (New York 1841).

261. *Calder* v. *Bull*, 3 Dallas (3 US) 386, 388 (1798); Manning, *The Key of Libberty*, p. 227.

262. *Adams* v. *Stevens*, 26 Wendell 451, 457–8 (New York 1841).

however, included fees both for counsel and for process. In these instances, and others as well, courts adopted another approach of distinguishing between "party to party" obligations (the amount that the losing party had to pay the winning party's attorney, which was said to be the object of the fee statutes) and "client to lawyer" obligations, which could be privately negotiated. This distinction was made in nearly identical language by the Supreme Court of Pennsylvania in 1835 and the Special Court of Appeals in Virginia in 1855. The fee statutes had to be understood in this way, held the New York Supreme Court of Judicature in 1840, "Otherwise the provisions, when taken in their full extent, would seem to be absurd."[263]

The patent absurdity of the "full extent" and "first and most obvious" reading of the fee statutes – that lawyers' total compensation should be limited by statute to slightly more than that of sheriffs, clerks, and other court officers – led jurists to a third and predominant approach of circumventing the statutes, an approach that directly reflected the liberal architectonic of culture. Attorneys argued and judges agreed that lawyers should be paid *in quantum meruit:* how much the service was worth, which is to say, what the free market would bear. In fact, jurists were even willing to demean the legal profession by doffing the mantle of professional dignity, in order to claim for themselves the freedom of the marketplace that was intrinsic to the architectonic and was supposedly enjoyed by any common laborer.

"The handicraftsman ... can look with confidence to the law for a full indemnity for his services; and the law mechanic ... may with equal confidence and right look to the same principle for his indemnity," held the Constitutional Court of South Carolina in 1821 and the North Carolina Supreme Court in 1825 on behalf of lawyers' right to contract and sue for remuneration beyond the fee statutes.[264] Dismissing the English tradition that "the profession of the law is of an honorable character, and services rendered by its professors gratuitous," the Tennessee Supreme Court held in 1827, "he who works at the bar and he who works at the plane – the physician, the farrier, the carpenter, and the smith, should all possess an equality of rights and be paid what they reasonably deserve to have, according to the value of their respective services.... We have here no separate *orders in society* – none of those *exclusive privileges*, which distinguish the lawyer in England ... and which constitutes him a sort of *noble* in the land." Indeed, maintained the Chief Justice of the Supreme Court of Pennsylvania in 1835, no principle "would forbid compensation for services in a profession which is now as purely a calling as any mechanical art."[265]

263. *Major's* v. *Gibson*, 1 Patton & Heath 48, 58 (Virginia 1855); *Foster* v. *Jack*, 4 Watts 334, 339 (Pennsylvania 1835); *Stevens* v. *Adams*, 23 Wendell 56, 60 (New York 1840). See *Duncan* v. *Breithaupt*, 1 McCord 149 (South Carolina 1821); *Clendinen* v. *Black*, 2 Bailey 488 (South Carolina 1831); *Adams* v. *Stevens*, 26 Wendell 451, 458 (New York 1841). The 1855 Virginia court was evenly divided and thus allowed to stand a lower court decision upholding the right of lawyers to sue to recover compensation under a contract providing an amount exceeding that prescribed by the fee statutes.

264. *Duncan* v. *Breithaupt*, 1 McCord 149, 151–2 (South Carolina 1821); *Leach* v. *Strange*, 3 Hawks 601 (North Carolina 1825).

265. *Newnan* v. *Washington*, 1 Martin & Yerger 79, 80–1 (Tennessee 1827); *Foster* v. *Jack*, 4 Watts 334, 337 (Pennsylvania 1835).

Likewise, the Chancellor of the New York Court of Errors in 1841 denied that lawyer's work "is so much more honorable than the business of other members of the community as to prevent him from recovering a fair compensation for his services on that account."[266] "[I]n our 'Bank Note World' ... in an age when the greatest poets or novelists are willing to confess that they toil 'for gain, not glory,' it is ridiculous to attempt to perpetuate a monstrous legal fiction, by which the hard working lawyers of our day, toiling in their offices, are to be regarded [like] ... the patrician jurisconsults of ancient Rome," agreed a fellow member of the New York Court of Errors.[267] Hence, the New York General Assembly in 1848 repealed the statutory prescription of lawyers" fees, as had been recommended by the Commissioners on Practice and Pleading, who argued that such prescription violated "the first principles of political economy," namely the principle of the free market in which "a professional person" should be free to sell services and enter into contracts.[268]

In this fashion, lawyers were able to attack restrictions on their financial standing by invoking "the first principles of political economy" in a "Bank Note World," namely the freedom of the marketplace. Moreover, this invocation implicitly denied both poles of the dialectic of service derived from the theological profession. On the one hand, lawyers endorsed self-interested pursuit of material gain rather than selfless service; on the other hand, they eschewed the higher dignity purchased by that selflessness and equated the "law mechanic" with "the handicraftsman." Of course, the ethic of selfless service and its associated dignity were invoked by attorneys in other contexts, and remained constituent in the idea of "profession." In fact, some jurists, such as a member of the Virginia Court of Appeals in 1855, specifically noted that the freemarket rationale ought not to undermine the dignity of the learned professions because the market would check "the abuse of professional confidence or professional influence."[269] But in a new age with different values and ideas, new arguments had to be employed, and lawyers came to profit both personally and corporately by professing the cultural architectonic. By invoking that new worldview in their judicial capacity, lawyers were able to free themselves from strictures on their income, even as clergy, unable to cope with the liberal ideas and values, had seen their economic position erode in the mid-eighteenth century.

Comparative: "the most elevated in the land"

These various kinds of authority – intellectual, juridical, political, social, economic – conferred upon law the highest status among the "learned professions" in the first half of the nineteenth century. "If I were asked where I place the

266. *Adams* v. *Stevens*, 26 Wendell 451, 455 (New York 1841).
267. *Adams* v. *Stevens*, 26 Wendell 451, 466 (New York 1841).
268. Field, Graham, Loomis, *First Report of the New York Commissioners on Practice and Pleading,* p. 207; *New York Laws* (Albany, NY, 1848), p. 544.
269. *Major's* v. *Gibson*, 1 Patton & Heath 48, 84 (Virginia 1855).

American aristocracy," wrote Alexis de Tocqueville, "I should reply without hesitation that it is not among the rich who are united by no common tie, but that it occupies the judicial bench and bar." These words have been quoted and cited so often that it has become fashionable to dispute them. Yet, countless observers across the country testified to the same point. Writing about lawyers in South Carolina, Crèvecoeur stated that "nothing can exceed their wealth, their power, and their influence." In 1834 Nathaniel Beverly Tucker affirmed, "The history of our country is full of proof that the bar is the road to eminence." Similarly, in his inaugural lecture at Cincinnati College in 1837, Timothy Walker exuded, "I would hold up the legal profession as an end in itself.... He who stands at the head of this profession, is on a level with the most elevated in the land."[270] So, too, modern studies of Massachusetts, Connecticut, New York, Virginia, and South Carolina indicate that by 1800 "law had become America's leading profession."[271]

Law consequently became the most desirable career, the path chosen by those seeking to elevate themselves. Martin Van Buren personified what the popular literature described. Van Buren's only schooling was at the village academy, yet by age 30 he was earning $10,000 per year in legal practice, and this success led directly to political opportunity and, ultimately, the White House. Although Van Buren often spoke of himself as ascending from "rags to riches," the mobility of a legal career was enjoyed most often by middle-class boys moving into the upper ranks of society.[272] In Philadelphia, for example, the percentage of lawyers who came from middle-class backgrounds rose from 16 percent at the beginning of the nineteenth century to 44 percent in 1860. This trend contrasted with that of the ministry. Whether in New England, the South, or the western frontier, the clergy increasingly drew its recruits from lower class boys seeking to move into middle-class respectability.[273]

270. Alexis de Tocqueville, *Democracy in America*, ed. Phillips Bradley (1834; New York, 1945), vol. 1, p. 288; Crèvecoeur, *Letters from an American Farmer*, letter 9; Tucker, "A Lecture on the Study of the Law," pp. 145–6; Walker, *Introductory Lecture on the Dignity of Law as a Profession*, p. 253.

271. Nelson, *Americanization of the Common Law ... 1760–1830*, p. 2; Roeber, *Faithful Magistrates and Republican Lawyers ... 1680–1810*, p. 228; Surrency, "The Lawyer and the Revolution," p. 126; Goodwin, *The Magistracy Rediscovered: Connecticut, 1636–1818*, p. 76; Harrington, *The New York Merchant on the Eve of the Revolution*, p. 15; Hoyt P. Canady, Jr., "Gentlemen of the Bar: Lawyers in Colonial South Carolina" (PhD diss., University of Tennessee, 1979), passim.

272. Donald B. Cole, *Martin Van Buren and the American Political System* (Princeton, NJ, 1984), pp. 14, 22. See Bloomfield, *American Lawyers in a Changing Society, 1776–1876*, ch. 5; Murrin, "The Legal Transformation: The Bench and Bar of Eighteenth-Century Massachusetts," pp. 550–1; Canady, "Gentlemen of the Bar: Lawyers in Colonial South Carolina," ch. 8; Alan M. Smith, "Virginia Lawyers, 1680–1776, The Birth of an American Profession" (PhD diss., Johns Hopkins University, 1967), chs. 3, 4.

273. Gary B. Nash, "The Philadelphia Bench and Bar, 1800–1861," *Comparative Studies in Society and History*, 7 (1965): 216. This trend had begun in mid-eighteenth-century New England, where the social ranking of the 60 boys admitted to the Harvard class of 1765 placed those who later spent their career in law at ranks 15, 17, 20, 25, 29, 35, 36; and those who eventually worked as ministers at 18, 24, 41–4, 48–9, 53–5, 59–60. *Harvard Graduates*, vol. 16, pp. 118–295; Allmendinger, *Paupers and Scholars*, ch. 1.

The rising preference of college graduates to set aside *"Miss Theology"* for the charms of "Miss Law, a grave and comely young lady, a little pitted with the small pox," had begun as early as the second quarter of the eighteenth century.[274] This trend then became pronounced between 1750 and 1776, when the fraction of graduates entering a career in the ministry dropped by about 30 percent, the fraction bound for the law rose by about 55 percent, and the fraction headed for medicine remained constant at about one-seventh of the graduates.[275] For the century after the Revolution, various studies indicate that, despite brief resurgences by theology during revivalist periods, particularly at rural denominational colleges, the fraction of college graduates entering theology continued to slide in the first half of the nineteenth century, eventually being surpassed by the fraction in law, which grew commensurately larger.

In 1851 the Committee on Medical Education of the AMA studied the vocational choices of the graduates of Amherst, Brown, Dartmouth, Hamilton, Harvard, Princeton, Union, and Yale from 1800 to about 1850 and reported that 8 percent chose medicine, while 26 percent chose divinity and the same percentage law. In 1882 another investigator reported to the AMA that, among the alumni of 58 colleges who graduated between 1825 and 1882, 21 percent entered theology, 20 percent law, and 9 percent medicine. The investigator suggested that law was relatively underrepresented in this report.[276] In contrast to these averages across the entire time period, a 1908 study of selected Yale classes between 1797 and 1866 lends a sense of the changes within the time period, as indicated on Table 3.2. These trends at Yale are significant not only due to the prominence of the College, but also because it was regarded as a religiously "safe" institution compared to Harvard. Looking at selected Harvard classes between 1798 and 1860, a recent scholar found an even sharper decline in theology revealed in Table 3.3.

The new propensity to choose law over theology that was evident at Harvard appeared as well in other institutions that were not founded by a religious denomination. For example, graduates at the University of Vermont, chartered by the state in 1791, overwhelmingly went into law, as evident in Table 3.4.

These figures from Vermont also indicate the resurgence of graduates' choosing the ministry during the revivalist period of the 1820s and 1830s This trend was even more pronounced at small, rural, denominational colleges, such as the Maine Literary and Theological Institution, which was founded by the Baptists in 1820 and eventually became Colby College. There the overall trend of graduates going

274. Hugh Henry Brackenridge, *The United States Magazine: A Repository of History, Politics, and Literature* (Philadelphia, 1779), pp. 312–3. See *Harvard Graduates*, vol. 9, pp. 67, 591; vol. 15, pp. 393–4; *Yale Graduates*, vol. 1, pp. 207–11, 216, 247–51, 267, 278, 354–7, 442, 453–4, 565–6, 638–9, 658, 709, 762–5, vol. 2, p. 118. Whereas only two of the thirteen lawyers in the Harvard classes from 1700 to 1727 prepared first for careers in theology, eight of the eleven lawyers in the classes from 1731 to 1735 did so. *Harvard Graduates*, vol. 5, 6, 7, 8; Murrin, "The Legal Transformation: The Bench and Bar of Eighteenth-Century Massachusetts," p. 551n.

275. Figures are computed from Table A2.5 in Appendix 2.

276. Hooker et al., "Report of the Committee on Medical Education," p. 421; Charles McIntyre, "The Percentage of College-Bred Men in the Medical Profession," *The Medical Record*, 22 (December 16, 1882): 681.

Table 3.2   Vocational choices of Yale graduates from selected classes,* 1797–1866

	1797–1833 (%)	1834–49 (%)	1850–66 (%)
Theology	29	25	18
Law	26	33	32
Medicine	13	9	9
Education	9	9	9
Commerce/Manufacturing	7	10	17
Other/Unknown	16	14	15
Total	100	100	100

* The records of some classes were unusable.
Source: Data from Ronald M. Byrnes, "A Statistical Study of the Yale Graduates, 1797–1866," *Yale Review*, 17 (1908): 316–38.

Table 3.3   Vocational choices of Harvard graduates from selected classes, 1798–1860

	1798–1830 (%)	1835–60 (%)
Theology	24	9
Law	33	33
Medicine	13	15
Commerce	17	24
Other	13	19
Total	100	100

Source: Adapted from Story, *The Forging of an Aristocracy: Harvard and the Boston Upper Class, 1800–1870*, p. 95.

Table 3.4   Vocational choices of University of Vermont graduates in all classes, 1804–1860

	1804–20 (%)	1821–40 (%)	1841–60 (%)
Theology	16	21	16
Law	54	44	44
Medicine	6	4	6
Education	6	14	10
Other/Unknown	18	17	24
Total	100	100	100

Source: [J. E. Goodrich], *General Catalogue of the University of Vermont and State Agricultural College, 1791–1900* (Burlington, VT, 1901).

into law was temporarily stemmed by a countervailing movement into the ministry during the revivalist period. Law then recovered as the field of occupational choice by the 1850s.[277]

In sum, these various analyses confirm Bailey Burritt's conclusion based upon his study of the vocational choices of graduates of 28 colleges that granted bachelor's degrees before 1860: "From 1642 to 1780 the ministry was clearly the dominant profession. Though surpassed by law between 1780 and 1820, it again led between 1820 and 1840.... Law, accordingly, was in the ascendancy during the early part of the nineteenth century, and once more between 1840 and 1885."[278] This conclusion is further confirmed by a complementary trend in the American students who went to German universities after studying in American colleges. Following 1850, the number and proportion of American students registering to study theology at these universities declined, while the number registering for law increased sharply.[279]

These trends naturally affected the fraction of educated talent within each of the learned professions and thus, to some degree, their social status. In general,

277. The fractions of graduates from Colby College were:

	1822–30 (%)	1831–40 (%)	1841–50 (%)	1851–60 (%)
Theology	32	39	31	20
Law	35	23	23	29

Colby College, *General Catalogue of Officers, Graduates and Former Students of Colby College, Centennial Edition, 1820–1920* (Waterville, ME, 1920).

278. Bailey B. Burritt, *Professional Distribution of College and University Graduates* (Washington, DC, 1912), p. 76. Those 28 institutions were Harvard, Yale, Pennsylvania, Columbia, Brown, Dartmouth, Oberlin, Michigan, Wisconsin, Union, Princeton, Vermont, Middlebury, New York University, Bowdoin, Beloit, Syracuse, Haverford, Northwestern, Rochester, Miami, Hanover, DePauw, Bucknell, Dickinson, Jefferson, Washington, and Colgate. Additional tables of New England colleges are available in Gawalt, *The Promise of Power: The Emergence of the Legal Profession in Massachusetts 1760–1840*, pp. 141–3. Colin Burke's often cited analysis of student careers in the first half of the nineteenth century is not helpful. He rarely identifies the colleges or the sources on which he relied. Nor does he explain the size or nature of the samples of "alumni and former students" from which he derived his percentages of careers. Moreover, because Burke "allowed up to four occupations for each student" by counting "multiple, concurrent, or sequential occupations," different individuals are apparently counted different numbers of times. His deceptively precise figures therefore report the vocations that some students who spent some period of time at some colleges pursued for some period of time. Consequently, one cannot make inferences about vocational choices from Burke's data. *American Collegiate Populations*, pp. 154, 183, 265–6, ch. 4.

279. Carl Diehl, *Americans and German Scholarship, 1770–1870* (New Haven, CT, 1978), pp. 56–7, 155. Diehl reported these registrations by American students in faculties of German universities:

medicine had the lowest number and percentage of college graduates, with law challenging theology, which nevertheless retained its supremacy. For example, at Harvard in the six decades before 1879, 74 percent of the theology students, 56 percent of those in law, and 35 percent in medicine had earned bachelor degrees. At Yale 81 percent of the theology students from 1867 to 1880, 32 percent of the law students from 1843 to 1880, and 24 percent of the medical students from 1825 to 1880 had earned bachelor degrees. Nationwide in the year 1879, the fractions of professional school students holding a bachelor's degree in science or arts were 31 percent in theology, 25 percent in law, and 8 percent in medicine, according to the professional schools reporting to the US Commissioner of Education.[280]

Apart from college degrees, the generalization about educational levels also holds with respect to professional training. Among the some 3,500 physicians who practiced during the Revolution, it was estimated that only about 400 had any formal education. In 1835 in Ohio, only about one-fifth of physicians had degrees from medical schools, while in five New England counties between 1790 and 1840, only one-fifth to one-third of physicians were medical school graduates. A decade later, less than one-fifth out of 201 physicians in eastern Tennessee had graduated from a medical school, and merely another fifth claimed to have taken a course of medical lectures.[281] Consequently, the Committee on Medical Education of the AMA complained that "the general standard of education and attainment is much lower in the medical than it is in the other professions ... of law and theology."[282] In 1882 Charles McIntyre reported to the AMA that, among those responding to a survey among New Jersey and Pennsylvania medical societies, merely 20 percent had been to college and only 13 percent held college degrees. "Can you escape the conclusion that classing the *medical business* among the learned *professions* is altogether a mistake?" asked McIntyre.[283]

Meanwhile ministers comforted themselves with being "the best instructed"

	Theology	Law	Medicine	Philosophy	Unknown
1810–49	26	5	9	50	0
1850–59	8	12	5	54	3
1860–69	8	10	17	54	6

280. McIntyre, "The Percentage of College-Bred Men in the Medical Profession," p. 682.

281. Starr, *The Social Transformation of American Medicine,* pp. 63–4; Richard H. Shryock, *Medicine and Society in America, 1660–1860* (New York, 1960), p. 9; Shryock, *Medical Licensing in America, 1650–1965* (Baltimore, MD, 1967), pp. 31–2; Frederick C. Waite, "The Professional Education of Pioneer Ohio Physicians," *Ohio State Archaeological and Historical Quarterly,* 48 (1939): 190.

282. Hooker et al., "Report of the Committee on Medical Education," pp. 409, 412. See Daniel Drake, *Practical Essays on Medical Education and the Medical Profession in the United States* (Cincinnati, OH, 1832).

283. McIntyre, "The Percentage of College-Bred Men in the Medical Profession," pp. 681–2.

among the professions,[284] although they acknowledged profound discontinuities in this regard. For example, a study of fully half of the Episcopal clergy between 1800 and 1840 found that 77 percent were known to have attended college. In contrast, only 8 percent of the southern delegates to the Methodist General Conference in 1844 were college graduates, and the Southern Aid Society reported in 1853 that merely "one fifth of the preachers are regularly educated for their business."[285] It was indeed the evangelical denominations – the Methodists and Baptists – that feared that learning would intellectualize the "religion of the heart" and that "*Learning makes young ministers proud.*"[286] Pleas for education in these denominations were therefore aimed, at best, at a meager standard: "the ministry should not fall below the average standard of intelligence of the community they instruct."[287]

The concern for educational standards was manifested in the founding of many professional schools for the liberal professions between 1780 and 1830. Samuel Haber has insightfully labeled this phenomenon "America's first wave of professionalization," and this phrase has become a standard *topos* in modern sociology and historiography of the professions.[288] This process commenced with the establishment of professorships at colleges, such as in divinity at Harvard in 1722, in medicine at Philadelphia in 1765, and in law at the College of William and Mary in 1779. These professorships were not always intended to offer professional training, but they gradually led, at least indirectly, to establishing proprietary professional schools at colleges. Thus, a medical school was founded at the College of Philadelphia in 1765 and one at King's College in 1767. The University of Maryland chartered a law school in 1812, and Harvard opened the first law school formally associated with a college in 1817. In the interim the first professional

284. Theodore Parker, "Thoughts on Labor," p. 73; Henry N. Day, "The Training of the Preacher," *American Biblical Repository*, 8 (1842): 71ff.

285. Holifield, *The Gentleman Theologians ... in Southern Culture, 1795–1860*, pp. 24–5; Manross, *The Episcopal Church in the United States, 1800–1840*, ch. 2. Congregationalists and Presbyterians also maintained high educational standards, as did the New England clergy as a whole. Sloan, *The Scottish Enlightenment and the American College Ideal*, pp. 38–42, appendix; Scott, *From Office to Profession: The New England Ministry, 1750–1850*, pp. 124–5.

286. John Stanford, *The Utility of Learning to a Young Minister Considered* (New York, 1814), p. 16; Robert C. Monk, "Early American Methodist Ministerial Education," pp. 63–80, in *The Divine Drama in History and Liturgy*, ed. John E. Booty (Allison, PA, 1984).

287. William R. Williams, *The Doctrine of Scripture concerning the Holy Ghost, in its Relations to Minsterial Education* (New York, 1844), p. 41. Even so, the aversion to learning among the Baptists and Methodists should not be overemphasized. See William Fristoe, *A Concise History of the Ketocton Baptist Association* (Stanton, VA, 1808), pp. 32–8; David Benedict, *A General History of the Baptist Denomination in America and Other Parts of the World* (New York, 1855), p. 938; John L. Burrows, "The Need of the Age for an Educated Ministry," *Baptist Memorial and Monthly Chronicle*, 13 (1854): 289–91, 321–4, 353–6; 14 (1855): 2–4, 33–7.

288. Samuel Haber, "The Professions and Higher Education in America: A Historical View," in *Higher Education and the Labor Market*, ed. Margaret S. Gordon (New York, 1974), p. 240. Burke offers a list of medical, law, theological, and normal schools founded from 1800 to 1860. *American Collegiate Populations*, pp. 319–40.

school that expected its students to have earned a bachelor's degree was founded independently in 1808 – Andover Seminary in Massachusetts. Dozens of these professional schools were established at colleges by 1830, and they struggled for survival.[289] Meanwhile apprenticeship was the more accessible and popular route by which one trained for the liberal professions, and many lawyers and physicians earned fees from apprentices who wanted to be inducted into the mysteries of a profession.

This flowering of professional education, which accompanied the introduction of licensing requirements to practice medicine and law, was followed by a decline in educational standards. By 1840 nearly every state had repealed statutes excluding or disadvantaging "irregular" medical practitioners. By 1860 merely one-quarter of the states and territories required professional study to practice law, whereas in 1800 three-quarters had.[290] Scholars have offered different explanations for this decline. Regarding medicine, some have traditionally said that doctors had little functional expertise, so increased educational requirements were pointless until medical science was developed.[291] Others have dismissed this functionalist view as "the usual explanation" and proposed that the necessary social and economic infrastructure was not in place to support the medical profession.[292] Somewhat ancillary to this second view, another conventional explanation, emphasized particularly by those who study law, attributes the decline in educational and licensing standards to "a widespread and powerful egalatarian impulse" in the Jacksonian era.[293]

289. Taylor and Parsons, *Professional Education in the United States*, pp. 154, 350; Rothstein, *American Medical Schools*, p. 31; Redlich, *The Common Law and the Case Method in American University Law Schools*, p. 7n.
290. Joseph F. Kett, *The Formation of the American Medical Profession: The Role of Institutions, 1780–1860* (New Haven, CT, 1968), p. 13; Ronald L. Numbers, "The Fall and Rise of the American Medical Profession," in *The Professions in American History*, ed. Nathan O. Hatch (Notre Dame, IN, 1988), p. 52; James W. Hurst, *The Growth of American Law: The Law Makers* (Boston, 1950), pp. 250, 280. By 1860, only one southern state (North Carolina), one western state (Ohio), and seven others, out of 39 jurisdictions, required some period of study for admission to practice law.
291. Richard H. Shryock, *The Development of Modern Medicine: An Interpretation of the Social and Scientific Factors Involved* (Philadelphia, 1936), ch. 14; Henry B. Shafer, *The American Medical Profession, 1783–1850* (New York, 1937); Daniels, *American Science in the Age of Jackson*, ch. 7; William G. Rothstein, *American Physicians in the Nineteenth Century: From Sects to Science* (Baltimore, MD, 1972); Rothstein, *American Medical Schools*, p. 39, ch. 2; Charles E. Rosenberg, *The Care of Strangers: The Rise of America's Hospital System* (New York, 1987), ch. 3.
292. Starr, *The Social Transformation of American Medicine*, pp. 94–5, passim. Ironically, Peter D. Hall overemphasizes the strength and accomplishment of early medical education at colleges because he wishes to undermine the claim that late-nineteenth-century medicine gained legitimacy due to the rise of therapeutic expertise. "The Social Foundations of Professional Credibility: Linking the Medical Profession to Higher Education in Connecticut and Massachusetts, 1700–1830," in *The Authority of Experts*, ed. Thomas L. Haskell (Bloomington, IN, 1984), pp. 107–41.
293. Haber, "The Professions and Higher Education in America: A Historical View,"

It may be doubted, however, whether all this attention devoted to "America's first wave of professionalization" followed by "The Fall" over the next three decades really says very much about the meaning of "profession" in America. Centuries before they were known as "the professions," clergy, lawyers, physicians, and teachers had been educated in graduate *scholae* at universities. When these fields subsequently became normative for a "profession," not a single professional school existed in the colonies, and occupational responsibilities were conventionally learned via apprenticeship. Almost a century passed before the movement arose to found professional schools. Moreover, some scholars have astutely observed that the rise and fall of professional education and licensing in the first half of the nineteenth century had little effect on the actual status and authority of the professions.[294] They continued on the same trajectories: theology declining, law ascending, and medicine and education muddling along.

Consequently, if the emergence of "the true professional ideal" or "professionalization" refers to what were known as "professions," that emergence seems little influenced by this particular episode of professional education. The four professions were highly educated centuries before they became normative for "professions," and they became normative well before professional education arose in America. Thus, the early nineteenth-century episode of professional education cannot be considered "America's first wave of professionalization," unless one applies the anachronistic standard of subsequent "professionalization." Antebellum jurists were, however, convinced that they were fully "professional," and this belief was justified, as is shown by a concluding comparison with the fields of theology, medicine, and education.

In the early 1800s, the clergy still spoke boldly of *The Comparative Advantages of the Ministerial Profession* and noted with pride that Rev. William Ellery Channing had contemplated both the law and medicine at the end of the eighteenth century, and that Charles Grandison Finney in the 1820s and Horace Bushnell in the 1830s left the law for preaching. Nevertheless, the clergy were very much aware that "within a few years past, scores of individuals have left the ministry for other professions"; that "the present low salaries paid to the clergy ... prevent many young men of talent and character from entering the sacred profession'; and that, even worse, the ministry was declining "more rapidly than the numbers indicate."[295] A central reason for this last fact was the increasing proportion of

---

p. 246; Pound, *The Lawyer from Antiquity to Modern Times,* pp. 223f.; Sutherland, *The Law at Harvard ... 1817–1967,* ch. 5; Chroust, *The Rise of the Legal Profession in America,* vol. 2, pp. 166–7; Reed, *Training for the Public Profession of the Law,* pp. 82–93; Stevens, *Law School ... from the 1850s to the 1980s,* pp. 7–8.

294. Bloomfield, *American Lawyers in a Changing Society, 1776–1876,* ch. 5; Johnson, *Schooled Lawyers,* p. 26. See Calhoun, *Professional Lives in America,* ch. 3.

295. Quotations are, respectively, from Nathaniel Colver, *A Call of God to the Christian Ministry, Definite and Imperative* (Boston, 1847), p. 18; Brooks, *A Statement of Facts from Each Religious Denomination,* p. 24; Francis Wayland, *The Apostolic Ministry: A Discourse Delivered ... before the New York Baptist Union for Ministerial Education* (Rochester, NY, 1853), p. 78; Aaron Bancroft, *The Comparative Advantages of the Ministerial Profession* (Portsmouth, NH, 1808).

evangelical denominations, the Methodists and Baptists, which included almost 70 percent of the Protestants in the United States by 1855. These enthusiastic denominations and the religious revivals that spread to other groups exacerbated the erosion of clerical learning, income, and authority that had begun in the Great Awakening nearly a century earlier. Consequently, the ministry, in spite of the continuing influence of religion, was slowly being reduced to a "business," the pastor to a "religious tradesman."[296]

Lamenting the clergy's lack of influence over public affairs, such as the slavery question in Nebraska, Rev. Charles M. Bowers complained that unlike the clergy "in by-gone days," ministers and their sermons were now "slapped at as so many mere mosquitoes." Hoping to gain a measure of influence, some clergy adopted their rhetoric to politics and law in a way that would have been inconceivable a century earlier. Sermons proclaimed the *"Sacred Right of Free Speech"* or sought "to direct [parishioners] in casting their votes in a political canvass." In 1855 one Tennessee Baptist minister went so far as to preach: "In the dawning of our liberty we have a counterpart of Christianity.... Our Nazareth [is] the Quaker colony of Pennsylvania ... Philadelphia, our Bethlehem; Carpenter's Hall, our manger; Parliament, our Caesar Augustus; George III, our Herod; Valley Forge, our Gethsemane; Yorktown, our Calvary, and the Constitution, our promised Comforter."[297]

Other ministers, however, resisted the professional and architectonical eclipse as long as possible: "When the Son of God ... appeared in our world, he chose to sustain the character, not of a *prince, a legislator, a conqueror,* but of a *poor, itinerant preacher,*" observed Rev. John Ryland. True, "a minister of the Gospel ... is not indeed called to manage the intricate affairs of state," conceded Rev. Thomas Baldwin of Boston, "but subjects of infinitely greater moment call for his fidelity." Meanwhile, as if regretting the painful demise of a longtime competitor, members of the bench and bar spoke respectfully and no longer begrudgingly of the clergy and theology. In fact they began to employ theological and ecclesiastical metaphors, particularly in regard to the selfless service of a profession. After all, "the Christian religion is the common law of the land," stated Joseph Story.[298]

Physicians, meanwhile, were held in virtual contempt by jurists, for "midway through the nineteenth century American medicine lay in a shambles," notwithstanding the presence of well educated doctors at certain private, urban hospitals.[299]

296. US Bureau of the Census, *Census of Religious Bodies* (Washington, DC, 1919), p. 24; John Close, *A Discourse on the Qualifications and Business of a Gospel Minister* (Waterford, NY, 1807); [Richard Steele], *The Religious Tradesman* (Charlestown, MA, 1804).

297. Charles M. Bowers, *Discourse on the Nebraska Bill* (Clinton, NY, 1854), p. 2; Middleditch, "Prayer for Pastors," pp. 24–5; Scott, *From Office to Profession: The New England Ministry, 1750–1850,* p. 139; Bitting, *Liberty and Literature, or Moral, Political and Intellectual Freedom,* p. 6.

298. John Ryland, Jr., "Paul's Charge to the Corinthians respecting ... the Conduct of the Churches toward their Pastors," in *Two Discourses* (London, 1787), p. 37; Thomas Baldwin, *The Christian Ministry, A Sermon* (Boston, 1814), p. 16. Story is quoted in Alvah S. Hobart, *American Opportunities for Ministers, A Minister's Meditation in Troas* (n.p., 1919), p. 5.

299. Numbers, "The Fall and Rise of the American Medical Profession," p. 51; Starr, *The Social Transformation of American Medicine,* pp. 30–59; Rosenberg, *The Care of Strangers: The Rise of America's Hospital System,* ch. 2.

Jurists would have found it unthinkable that, say, a doctor of the life sciences who never earned a law degree could be named dean of the nation's leading law school. A leader of the Philadelphia bar expressed the common view:

> And what shall we say of doctors of medicine? ... "Theirs is the least learned of the professions, in this country at least. They have not half the general culture of the lawyers, nor a quarter of that of the ministers." ... We have more physicians in proportion to our population than any other country in the world, and every year increases the evil.[300]

This view confirms not only that medicine was the profession chosen least by college graduates, but also that the best students chose it proportionately less. Based on a survey of college graduates from 1800 to 1850, the Committee on Medical Education of the AMA reported "that of those who have received honours in our colleges, the proportion that has entered the medical profession is smaller than that which has entered it from the whole body of graduates." As a result, "in all of our American colleges medicine has ever been, and is now, the most despised of all the professions which liberally-educated men are expected to enter," observed George Shrady in 1869. College faculty, said Shrady, commonly advise undergraduates: "Don't study medicine; anybody can be a doctor. Study law or theology." In fact, when loyalty oaths were introduced after the Civil War to keep former Confederates out of important offices, Missouri's extreme version was directed also to the professions, and the state ignored doctors, while including clergymen, lawyers, and schoolteachers.[301]

Schoolteaching began to be called a "profession" more frequently and prominently early in the nineteenth century through the efforts of schoolmen such as Samuel R. Hall and William A. Alcott.[302] Following the practice of jurists, schoolmen applied the adjective "professional" to teaching during the 1830s, a decade when *The Common School Advocate and Journal of Education* of Illinois solicited essays on the topic: "Teaching Made a Profession." In the 1830s and 1840s lyceums and teachers' institutes, which were invented to give periodic instruction to schoolmasters, flourished in New England, New York, Pennsylvania, and the upper Midwest. Attention and resources then commenced to shift to founding normal schools, and by 1860 twelve had been established.[303]

---

300. George G. Mercer, *The American Scholar in Professional Life* (Philadelphia, 1889), pp. 26, 29.

301. Hooker et al., "Report of the Committee on Medical Education," p. 422; George F. Shrady, "American vs. European Medical Science," *The Medical Record*, 4 (May 15, 1869): 133. The Missouri oath was struck down by the United States Supreme Court in *Cummings v. Missouri*, 4 Wallace (71 US) 277 (1867).

302. Mattingly, *The Classless Profession: American Schoolmen in the Nineteenth Century*, pp. 9–23. Samuel R. Hall tended not to employ the word "profession," but was conscious of avoiding "schoolkeeping" in preference for such terms as *"science of teaching." Lectures on School-Keeping*, pp. iv, v, 13.

303. *The Common School Advocate and Journal of Education*, 1 (1837): 3. "Professional Education of Teachers," *American Annals of Education*, 3 (October 1833): 455–7; Samuel N. Sweet, *Teachers' Institutes, Temporary Normal Schools; their Origin and Progress* (Utica, NY,

Meanwhile women were entering teaching, which they began to view as their profession since man "closes against her all the avenues to wealth and distinction ... theology, medicine, or law," as stated the *Declaration of Sentiments* of the first American women's rights conference held in 1848. The most influential spokeswoman for this inchoate movement was perhaps Catharine Beecher, who commenced writing on *"the profession* of a *woman"* as early as 1829 and continued through an important address delivered in major eastern cities during 1845 and 1846. *"The educating of children* ... is the true and noble profession of a woman," stated Beecher, "like law, medicine, and theology, [it] opens the way to competence, influence, and honor."[304] Nevertheless, women were excluded from membership in major professional teaching movements, such as the American Institute of Instruction and the National Teachers' Association, until after the Civil War.

Though proud enough to exclude women, these movements had modest influence before the 1860s. The popular judgment remained that "persons too lazy to work, and unfit for other profitable employments, were usually engaged as pedagogues," as the leading Baptist clergyman in Virginia, Jeremiah B. Jeter, observed. Certain handbooks, such as *The Teacher* by Principal Jacob Abbott, insisted on calling the vocation a "business," "work," or "employment," rather than "profession." In the 1830s Anglican clergyman Isaac Fidler toured the United States looking for a position as a schoolmaster, and was repulsed by the low status, authority, and remuneration of American teachers. His countryman Francis Grund agreed: "The profession of teacher is embraced by large numbers of men ... only as a temporary means of subsistence.... Many of the most eminent lawyers, ministers, and physicians ... consider ... the employment of an instructor as a sort of relief from the most pressing necessities; but not as *an end* to be proposed by a man who aspires at honourable distinction. This creed, once established in the minds of professional men, has communicated itself to all ranks of society."[305] Such views

---

1848); Allen O. Hansen, *Early Educational Leadership in the Ohio Valley: A Study of Educational Reconstruction through the Western Literary Institute and College of Professional Teachers, 1829–1841* (Bloomington, IL, 1923); Jonathan Messerli, *Horace Mann: A Biography* (New York, 1972), pp. 298–369; Mattingly, *The Classless Profession: American Schoolmen in the Nineteenth Century,* chs. 4, 6, table 15.

304. *Declaration of Sentiments* (drafted and signed on July 16–20, 1848; reprinted Seneca Falls, NY, 1986); Catharine E. Beecher, *Suggestions Respecting Improvement in Education, Presented to the Trustees of the Hartford Female Seminary* (Hartford, CT, 1829), p. 7; Beecher, *The Evils Suffered by American Women and American Children: The Causes and the Remedy* (New York, 1847), pp. 18–20. Joan N. Burstyn, "Catharine Beecher and the Education of American Women," *New England Quarterly,* 47 (1974): 386–403; Sklar, *Catharine Beecher,* pp. 180–2.

305. Jeter, *The Recollections of a Long Life,* p. 4; Jacob Abbott, *The Teacher: or Moral Influences Employed in the Instruction and Government of the Young; Intended Chiefly to Assist Young Teachers in Organizing and Conducting their Schools* (Boston, 1833), passim; Fidler, *Observations on Professions, Literature, Manners and Emigration in the United States and Canada,* chs. 3, 4; Grund, *The Americans in their Moral, Social, and Political Relations,* vol. 1, pp. 215–6.

confirm a recent scholar's estimate that the efforts to make teaching a profession influenced only "the top 10 to 20 percent of the teachers of the antebellum period."[306]

Nor did educators strengthen their "private calling" in the colleges, which were neither intellectually vibrant nor financially strong before the Civil War.[307] A study of the majority of the some 210 individuals who worked as college teachers between 1750 and 1800 found that less than 35 percent could be identified primarily with that vocation. The primary occupation for most of the other 65 percent was another liberal profession. The situation did not change appreciably in the first half of the nineteenth century. Studies of Bowdoin, Brown, Dartmouth, Harvard, Yale, and the University of Michigan have shown that only "during the decade immediately following the Civil War" did professors begin to feel a commitment to the dignity of the academic vocation above that to a particular college or other vocation.[308]

These findings are perfectly reflected in the decision of one young South Carolinian who had failed in managing his father's plantation in 1858. "I have for nearly 27 years dreamt of doing a great many things," he wrote, "I have accomplished nothing.... I had failed in everything. I was the living, walking realization of utter incompetency, patent to every eye." With this in mind, the ne'er-do-well "went to Harvard, where he prepared to become a college professor."[309] Small wonder, then, that professors with more self-esteem left the college faculties to join the leading profession, especially when the revolutionary polity became the focus of excitement. David Howell, the first professor of the College of Rhode Island, resigned his position in 1779 to take up the practice of law. Two years later, Rev. Abraham Baldwin declined the Professorship of Divinity at Yale to join the bar. And in 1783 the first Professor of Mathematics and Natural

---

306. Kaestle, *Pillars of the Republic: Common Schools and American Society, 1780–1860*, p. 131, ch. 6.

307. My own view on the historiographical controversy surrounding this point is set forth in *Orators and Philosophers: A History of the Idea of Liberal Education* (New York, 1986), app. 1; and "Writing the History of Universities: A New Approach?", *Minerva*, 23 (1986): 375–89.

308. Quotation is from Martin J. Finkelstein, who, contrary to his announced intent and conclusion, demonstrates that "the modern academic career had come of age" only after the Civil War. ("From Tutor to Specialized Scholar: Academic Specialization in Eighteenth and Nineteenth Century America," *History of Higher Education Annual*, 3 (1983): 113.) William D. Carrell, "American College Professors, 1750–1800," *HEQ*, 8 (1968): 301; Kennedy, "The Changing Academic Characteristics of the Nineteenth-Century American College Teacher," pp. 351–99; Robert A. McCaughey, "The Transformation of American Academic Life: Harvard University, 1821–1892," *Perspectives in American History*, 8 (1974): 239–332; Alan Creutz, "From College Teacher to University Scholar: The Evolution and Professionalization of Academics at the University of Michigan, 1841–1900" (PhD diss., University of Michigan, 1981), ch. 6; Marilyn Tobias, *Old Dartmouth on Trial: The Trans-formation of the Academic Community in Nineteenth-Century America* (New York, 1982).

309. Quoted in Burton, *In my Father's House are Many Mansions: Family and Community in Edgefield, South Carolina*, p. 109.

Philosophy at Princeton resigned in order to devote himself to law and public affairs.[310]

Rhetorical: "Lawyers are inclined to ... association"

We have seen that politics, jurisprudence, and attorneys eclipsed religion, theology, and the clergy in the second half of the eighteenth century, with lawyers rising to juridical, political, social, and economic preeminence among the "professions." In the course of these developments, the term "professional" was transmuted from its original sense of "avowed" or "religious" into its customary modern meaning of "vocational." This fourth moment in the rhetoric of "professions," I have proposed, was largely sponsored by jurists, who adopted the term "professional," rather than "professed," while embracing the dignity and service ethic of the theological profession. Moreover, this relationship between rhetoric and the lawyers' vocation was reflexive. Not only did the inherited meaning of "profession" influence how lawyers talked about their own vocation, but the nature of the legal vocation also informed the subsequent understanding of "profession" and "professional." This legal influence appeared first in the development that "professional service" commenced to signify contractual and feeable use or benefit to a client, in addition to the theological service ethic implying selflessness. A second way in which law informed how people thought and talked about "profession" was the defining and emphasizing of the professional polity, or professional association, as a characteristic of a "profession."

The rise of professional associations has been the subject of a number of speculative interpretations. Following Émile Durkheim, some scholars have linked the phenomenon to ancient and medieval guilds, but this tenuous link has justifiably been questioned in recent time.[311] In contrast to Durkheim, others find professional association beginning in the late nineteenth century as part of the rise of bureaucracy, the middle class, and the "search for order" in an industrializing society. One corollary to this view attributes the origins of professional association to the 1847 founding of the American Medical Association, an attribution that suits the predominant influence assigned to the medical profession by the same scholars.[312] Another corollary emphasizes the Jacksonian complaints about the arcane and unwritten nature of legal science, especially case law, which prompted antebellum demands to codify the law. By this corollary "the advent of 'Jacksonian democracy' probably dealt the death blow to any organization of the legal profession," and it is

---

310. *Princetonians*, vol. 1, pp. 562–6, 643–6; *Yale Graduates*, vol. 3, p. 432.

311. Émile Durkheim, *Professional Ethics and Civic Morals*, tr. Cornelia Brookfield (London, 1957), ch. 2. Cf. Michael Schudson, "Public, Private and Professional Lives: The Correspondence of David Dudley Field and Samuel Bowles," *AJLH*, 21 (1977): 207.

312. Morris Fishbein, *A History of the American Medical Association, 1847 to 1947* (Philadelphia, 1947); Harold L. Wilensky, "The Professionalization of Everyone?", *American*

true that the Jacksonian period witnessed the reversal of efforts to strengthen the bar and restrict admission to the practice of law. Subsequently, according to this view, the demands to codify the law were answered by jurists' writing of scientific legal treatises. As a result "the bar-association movement" commenced with the reformation of Harvard Law School and the founding of the ABA in the 1870s. The rise of legal science thus accompanied "the bar-association movement" after the Civil War.[313]

It may be wondered, however, whether the founding date of professional organizations is an artificially discrete criterion for identifying the concern for professional association. By any other measure, antebellum physicians, whose "orientation ... in short, was *competitive* rather than *corporate*," cannot be said to have led the movement for professional association. Though founded in 1847, the AMA adopted its federal structure only in 1901 and borrowed that structure, in fact, from other professional associations.[314] Moreover, if one attends to founding dates, then teachers might be regarded as the creators of modern professional guilds in America. Established in 1794, the Society of Associated Teachers of New York, for example, has been called "the first professional organization" in the United States, and state teachers' organizations with professional journals were founded in Illinois, New York, Rhode Island, and Massachusetts in the 1840s.[315] This record of association founding is earlier and more enduring than that of other professional fields. On the other hand, the ABA, founded in 1878, was essentially a social club for elite lawyers summering in Saratoga Springs until they were aroused by the Progressive demand for recall of judges and reversal of judicial decisions. Only in

Journal of Sociology, 70 (1964): 141; Robert H. Wiebe, *The Search for Order, 1877–1920* (New York, 1967), pp. 111–63; Burton J. Bledstein, *The Culture of Professionalism: The Middle Class and the Development of Higher Education in America* (New York, 1976), pp. 318–31; Magali Sarfatti Larson, *The Rise of Professionalism: A Sociological Analysis* (Berkeley, CA, 1977), pp. 5, 246; Michael J. Powell, *From Patrician to Professional Elite: The Transformation of the New York City Bar Association* (New York, 1988).

313. Quotations are from Chroust, *The Rise of the Legal Profession in America,* vol. 2, p. 156; Friedman, *A History of American Law,* pp. 648–9. See Reed, *Training for the Public Profession of the Law,* pp. 82–93; Roscoe Pound, *The Formative Era of American Law* (Boston, 1938), p. 154; Schlesinger, *The Age of Jackson,* ch. 25; Miller, *The Life of the Mind in America: From the Revolution to the Civil War,* pp. 239–65; Cook, *The American Codification Movement: A Study of Antebellum Legal Reform,* p. 204; Charles R. McKirdy, "Massachusetts Lawyers on the Eve of the American Revolution: The State of the Profession," pp. 318–28, and Daniel R. Coquillette, "Justinian in Braintree: John Adams, Civilian Learning, and Legal Elitism, 1758–1775," in *Law in Colonial Massachusetts, 1630–1800* (Boston, 1984), pp. 359–82.

314. Starr, *The Social Transformation of American Medicine,* pp. 88–92, 111; Kett, *The Formation of the American Medical Profession ... 1780–1860,* passim; Calhoun, *Professional Lives in America,* ch. 2; Johnson, *Schooled Lawyers,* p. 2, ch. 2.

315. Alfred F. Young, *The Democratic Republicans of New York: The Origins, 1763–1797* (Chapel Hill, NC, 1967), pp. 406–7; Davis, *Educational Periodicals in the Nineteenth Century,* p. 37.

the second decade of the twentieth century did the ABA discuss comprehensive, rather than exclusive, membership, and only then did local, state, and national bar associations undertake to expand their membership.[316] Consequently, it could be argued that bar organizations began in the second quarter of the twentieth century, not the 1870s.

The founding dates of organizations can therefore be manipulated in different ways. If, instead, one looks beneath the formal shell of organization, it may be the case that Charles Warren was quite perceptive when he announced at the *end* of his history of the American bar: "it is fitting that the *last* fact to be recorded should be the foundation of the American Bar Association, in 1878."[317] From this perspective, the flock of bar organizations that appeared after the Civil War – twelve in the 1870s and nineteen in the 1880s – is the culmination, not the beginning, of a concern for association.

Lawyers' professional devotion to the polity led them by nature to associate. "[T]hey naturally constitute *a body*," wrote Tocqueville, "the analogy of their studies and the uniformity of their methods connect their minds as a common interest might unite their endeavors."[318] Comparing "Lawyers and Doctors," one jurist noted:

> Lawyers are inclined to congregation – association; and if they are not positively clannish or cliquish, are frequently brought together in the practice of their profession, and learn to seek counsel.... [T]he lawyer's habit of association of effort and thought, his disinclination to isolation, his consequent ability to see both sides of a question, his more liberal and tolerant notions of things render him a companion for lawyers as well as for others.... The legal profession is thus always a brotherhood, and in this respect a direct contrast from the medical profession.[319]

In the antebellum era, members of the bench and bar "maintained professional discipline through the 'convivial' life of the judicial circuit."[320] Relative to physicians and clergy, lawyers were regarded, even after the Jacksonian challenge, as having successfully barricaded their profession through formal and informal association, as noted by delegates to the state constitution conventions of Michigan in 1850 and Indiana in 1851.[321] Indeed, recent scholars have argued that, in certain states, "rather than the collapse of the legal profession, the Jacksonian years marked the emergence of the modern legal profession.... Brought together in part by group consciousness or a sense of common interest and by societal hostility,

---

316. Hurst, *The Growth of American Law: The Law Makers*, pp. 286–92; Whitney N. Seymour, "The First Century of the American Bar Association," *American Bar Association Journal*, 64 (1978): 1038–42; Philip J. Wickser, "Bar Associations," *Cornell Law Quarterly*, 15 (1930): 390–419.

317. Warren, *A History of the American Bar*, p. 562. Emphasis added.

318. Tocqueville, *Democracy in America*, vol. 1, pp. 283–4.

319. Lawyers and Doctors," *Albany Law Journal*, p. 36.

320. Johnson, *Schooled Lawyers*, p. xiii, ch. 2; Calhoun, *Professional Lives in America*, ch. 3; Bloomfield, *American Lawyers in a Changing Society, 1776–1876*, p. 139.

321. Stevens, *Law School ... from the 1850s to the 1980s*, p. 18; Chroust, *The Rise of the Legal Profession in America*, vol. 2, p. 165.

lawyers unintentionally formed a prototype for professionalization through group voluntarism."[322]

My contention here is not, as some studies would suggest, that attorneys were racing toward an alluring hypostasis of "professionalization." The claim is that the pervading concern for polity resulted in the founding of "voluntary associations" and "societies" in all aspects of American culture, including the professions. This phenomenon informed the conception of "profession" in a special way because, on the one hand, the chief "politicians" – what Samuel Goodrich in his popular text-book called the "political architects" – were also the preeminent "profession."[323] On the other hand, the very notion of voluntary association, which captivated Americans in the first half of the nineteenth century, was simply the liberal jurisprudence applied to social organizations: individuals freely choosing to make small social contracts among themselves.

The enthusiasm for voluntary association had to overcome the perception of the 1790s that "a voluntary association or coalition" of the diverse American colonies was "difficult to be supposed."[324] In addition, there was the fear through the 1790s that political parties or "self-created societies" were divisive. But with the estab-lishment of the federal system – a polity of polities – Americans proceeded to politize the world. By 1795 many individuals, such as a writer in the *New York Journal*, were proudly discussing many "a little self-created society to which I belong." By 1812 Lyman Beecher was preaching that "local voluntary associations" are the best instruments to effect "A Reformation of Morals Practicable and Indispensable."[325] By 1820 thousands of voluntary associations had been formed, and in 1830 William Ellery Channing observed:

> In truth, one of the most remarkable circumstances or features of our age, is ... that every thing is done now by societies. Men have learned what wonders can be accomplished in certain cases by union, and seem to think that union is competent to every thing.... Would men spread one set of opinions, or crush another? They make a society. Would they improve the penal code, or relieve poor debtors? They make societies. Would they encourage agriculture, or manufacturers, or science? They make societies.[326]

In the second quarter of the century, the national Lyceum movement led to the founding of innumerable "*town lyceums*," which the early leader of the movement,

---

322. Gawalt, *The Promise of Power: The Emergence of the Legal Profession in Massachusetts, 1760–1840*, pp. 4–5, 13; Hurst, *The Growth of American Law: The Law Makers*, pp. 285–9; Stevens, *Law School ... from the 1850s to the 1980s*, p. 8.

323. Goodrich, *The Young American: or Book of Government and Law*, p. 1. See Jack C. Ross, *An Assembly of Good Fellows: Voluntary Associations in History* (Westport, CT, 1976), pp. 283–95; James L. Adams, *Voluntary Associations: Socio-cultural Analyses and Theological Interpretation*, ed. J. Ronald Engel (Chicago, 1986).

324. Andrew Burnaby, *Travels through the Middle Settlements in North America in the Years 1759 and 1760*, 3d edn (London, 1798), p. 152.

325. *[Greenleaf's] New York Journal and Patriotic Register* (February 24, 1795): 1; Lyman Beecher, "A Reformation of Morals Practicable and Indispensable," in *Sermons, Delivered on Various Occasions* (Boston, 1852), p. 95. Young, *The Democratic Republicans of New York: The Origins, 1763–1797*, ch. 18.

326. William E. Channing, *The Works*, 11th edn, 6 vols. (Boston, 1849), vol. 1, p. 282.

Josiah Holbrook, defined as "a voluntary association of individuals." At the national level more than 55 scientific societies were similarly established by 1855.[327] Meanwhile reformatories, orphanages, asylums, and prisons were created as polities of abnormality. Social problems, it appeared, could be solved by politizing them. No less in business and employment was the desire for association manifest. Corporations – what Blackstone had called "bodies politic" – emerged as the new and primary vehicle of private enterprise, and laborers and journeymen meanwhile formed fraternal organizations and "mutual aid societies," many of which gradually merged into "trades' unions." These unions were largely defeated or kept in check by industrialists before the Civil War. But the defeat was not for lack of workers' appreciation for the importance of association and its role in the free market. Mark Twain addressed a public attitude as broad and sweeping as the Mississippi in his tale of how a riverboat pilots' "benevolent association" became "the compactest monopoly in the world."[328]

Tocqueville was correct, then, in stating that "as soon as several of the inhabitants of the United States have taken up an opinion or a feeling which they wish to promote in the world, they look out for mutual assistance; and as soon as they have found one another out, they combine." Hence, "voluntary associations ... have been denominated the peculiar glory of the present age," observed Francis Wayland. In fact, "the idea expressed by the magic word, ASSOCIATION" is the "greatest need" of human beings and "the great and really fundamental law" of social science, theorized Henry Carey in 1859.[329]

By that time lawyers were the indisputably preeminent profession, just as they were the architects of polity. The importance of association in all spheres of life, especially in the "professions," was henceforth unquestioned, and all that remained was the working out of the principle after the Civil War. The conception of a professional polity had been established in the antebellum era, and physicians and clergy, like teachers, felt the imprint of the political architectonic and endorsed the new conception. In 1851 the Committee on Medical Education of the AMA proposed that the problems of the medical profession "have no better cure, or

327. [Josiah Holbrook], *American Lyceum, or Society for the Improvement of Schools and Diffusion of Useful Knowledge* (Boston, 1829), pp. 1–2; [Holbrook], *The Lyceums* (Boston, 1829), pp. 2–3; Leah G. Stambler, "The Lyceum Movement in American Education, 1826–1845," *Paedagogica Historica,* 21 (1981): 157–85; Ralph S. Bates, *Scientific Societies in the United States,* 3d edn (Cambridge, MA, 1965), ch. 2; A. Hunter Dupree, "The National Pattern of American Learned Societies, 1769–1863," pp. 21–32, and Joseph Ewan, "The Growth of Learned and Scientific Societies in the Southeastern United States to 1860," pp. 208–18, in *The Pursuit of Knowledge in the Early American Republic,* ed. Alexandra Oleson and Sanborn C. Brown (Baltimore, MD, 1976).

328. Mark Twain, *Life on the Mississippi* (1875), 2d edn (1883; New York, 1961), p. 109, ch. 15. Walter E. Hugins, *Jacksonian Democracy and the Working Class: A Study of the New York Workingmen's Movement, 1829–1837* (Stanford, 1960); Calhoun, *The American Civil Engineer,* ch. 8; Rorabaugh, *The Craft Apprentice: From Franklin to the Machine Age in America,* pp. 87ff.; Rock, *Artisans of the New Republic,* chs. 5, 10.

329. Tocqueville, *Democracy in America,* vol. 2, p. 117; Francis Wayland, *The Limitations of Human Responsibility,* 2d edn (New York, 1838), p. 96; Carey, *The Principles of Social Science,* vol. 1, pp. vi, 41–2; vol. 3, pp. 409–10.

rather preventive, than is to be found in what may be termed scientific socialism." For "the chief means of removing abuses ... is *the influence that can be exerted through the organizations of the profession*.... The voluntary principle imparts great power to associated action. These organizations are, therefore, to do a peculiarly important work for the profession in this country."[330] Similarly, "by the 1850s, in institutional terms, the clergy had become ... a coherent, self-conscious body, organized and defined by a set of institutions which were outside lay or public control," as studies have shown for New England clergy, evangelical Baptists, Methodists in North Carolina, and Presbyterians generally.[331]

Like the new meanings of "professional" and "service," the importance of professional association derived from the example and influence of attorneys through their mastery of the cultural architectonic. How could it be otherwise when observer after observer concurred with Charles Daubeny's judgment of 1837: "It is too true that Americans ... interest themselves but little in anything but politics.... Science and literature seem almost unknown, schools are very rare, and it is said, extremely bad."[332] Quite soon, however, this situation would be reversed. The association of "professors of law" on the bench and at the bar would be eclipsed by "professors of law" in the university.

---

330. Hooker et al., "Report of the Committee on Medical Education," pp. 427, 425–6.

331. Scott, *From Office to Profession: The New England Ministry, 1750–1850*, pp. 154–5, chs. 4, 8, 9; Benedict, *A General History of the Baptist Denomination*, p. 841; John B. Weaver, "Charles F. Deems: The Ministry as Profession in Nineteenth-Century America," *Methodist History*, 21 (1983): 156–68; Miller, *The Revolutionary College: American Presbyterian Higher Education, 1707–1837*, pp. 222–33, 246. On the "ministerial associations," which "were intended primarily for the devotional life of the clergy," compare Charles E. Hambrick-Stowe, *The Practice of Piety: Puritan Devotional Disciplines in Seventeenth-Century New England* (Chapel Hill, NC, 1982), p. 142; Harlan, *The Clergy and the Great Awakening in New England*, ch. 6; [Cotton Mather], *RATIO DISCIPLINAE FRATRUM NOV-ANGLORUM: A Faithful Account of the Discipline Professed and Practised in the Churches of New-England* (1726; New York, 1972), p. 181; with Perry Miller, *The New England Mind: From Colony to Province* (Cambridge, MA, 1953), pp. 257–68; Cotton Mather, *Magnalia Christi Americana; or The Ecclesiastical History of New-England* (1702; Hartford, CT, 1855), vol. 2, p. 655; Youngs, *God's Messengers: Religious Leadership in Colonial New England*, pp. 69–78; Wilson, *The Benevolent Deity*, p. 54; Bonomi, *Under the Cope of Heaven*, pp. 40, 61–6.

332. Charles Daubeny, *Journal of a Tour through the United States, and in Canada, made during the Years, 1837–38* (Oxford, 1843), pp. 148, 216–7. Daubeny was specifically addressing New Orleans.

4

1860s–1910s

SCIENCE AND EDUCATION: "PROFESSOR" BECOMES "PROFESSIONAL"

Let us make our education brave and preventive. Politics is an afterwork, a poor patching. We are always a little late.... We shall one day learn to supersede politics by education.... We must begin higher up, namely in Education.

Ralph Waldo Emerson, "Culture" (1860)

Within 100 years the profession of teaching has grown from about one-twentieth to one-fourth of the [college] graduates.... Since 1880 the line for teaching has crossed that of the ministry, and since 1890 that of law. Thus at the close of the century it is the dominant profession.

Bailey B. Burritt, Professional Distribution of College and University Graduates
(1912)

Education has, thus, become the chief problem of the world, its one holy cause.... Never so much as now is education *the* one and chief hope of the world.

G. Stanley Hall, Life and Confessions of a Psychologist *(1923)*

We have seen that changes in the way people thought and spoke about "profession" corresponded to changes in the nature of cultural ideals, in the dominant forms of knowledge associated with those cultural ideals, and in the status of the preeminent vocation that upheld the ideal, possessed the knowledge, and exercised authority in various domains of society. These cultural ideals, forms of knowledge, and pre-eminent vocations informed the meaning of "profession." In the predominantly religious culture through the mid-eighteenth century, "profession" acquired several theological denotations: a secular vocation invested with special dignity, the group of people who practice that vocation, and the dialectical ethic of selfless service associated with that practice. In the political culture of the late eighteenth and early nineteenth century, the meaning of "profession" was informed by certain jurisprudential characteristics: the organization of the vocation into a polity, or guild, and the contractual sense of "professional service." Interwoven in these developments were four moments in the rhetoric of profession: four specific changes in the usage of the term and its derivatives.

First was the extension of "profession" from referring to a religious vow to signifying the group of people, especially the clergy, who made the vow. Second was the shift in reference from the clergy to dignified, non-religious occupations. Third was the introduction of the terms "learned profession" and "liberal profession." These denoted the dignified occupations of theology, law, medicine, and education, four fields that originally became associated in the medieval university. Fourth was the replacement of the adjective "professed" by "professional" to denote "occupational" or "vocational."

Between the 1860s and the 1910s another transformation occurred in the "professions." This change involved a shift in status both within the echelon of that small group of vocations known as "learned" or "liberal" professions, as well as for the echelon as a whole. Law declined to the position that it has held for most of American history and to which it seems especially well suited – the second-best profession. Whether due to the seeming amoralism of the advocacy system, described above, or the fact that lawyers must lose half of their cases, as Karl Llewellyn remarked, or to the long tradition of Anglo-American animus toward lawyers, which Max Weber noted, the legal profession seems to attract an extraordinary amount of criticism, particularly when exposed as the foremost profession.[1] Attorneys fare much better when counseling in the shadow of another preeminent profession, which then attracts the bulk of egalitarian criticism directed against elites. As the status of law declined, so did that of the entire echelon of liberal and learned professions, while the educational profession ascended dramatically within that echelon. For men or for women, within their respective spheres, education became the preeminent profession, and this ascendance was accompanied by a fifth moment in the rhetoric of "profession."

These propositions contradict the views of many scholars who have asserted that the final third of the nineteenth century was the formative period of professions, particularly law. It is said that professions were invented or developed by the middle class during the industrialization and urbanization of this period. But this claim relies upon the presumptive definition that a "profession" is a middle-class job in an urban, industrial society. These scholars therefore tell us more about the history of such jobs than about the historical echelon of what were conventionally called "professions." Indeed, it is nearer the truth to consider this period the *decline* of professions inasmuch as the authority of this vocational group eroded

---

1. Karl N. Llewelyn, *The Bramble Bush: On our Law and its Study* (1930; 2d edn, New York, 1951), p. 171; Max Weber, *Economy and Society: An Outline of Interpretive Sociology*, ed. Guenther Roth and Claus Wittich, tr. Ephraim Fischoff et al. (New York, 1968), vol. 2, p. 891.

during the last half of the nineteenth century. The decline, in fact, helps to explain why education for a brief period could emerge as the preeminent profession at all: the ascendance of education was made more dramatic by the fact that other professions declined. All these developments inevitably influenced the usage of "profession" and produced a sixth rhetorical moment at the beginning of the twentieth century.

Intellectual: "Man, the molecule of society"

In the United States during the second half of the nineteenth century, the cultural ideal, the fundamental source of cultural inspiration and legitimacy, shifted from "polity" to "science." Such a broad generalization, needless to say, is subject to many qualifications and rejoinders. Even so, there is convincing evidence that devotion to politics declined and was redirected to "science" and to the locus of the definition, production, and transmission of science – the educational institutions.

The Civil War – whether arising from slavery or class struggle, whether resulting in a "New South" or the same economic and social structure[2] – literally destroyed the polity for a time and exposed the nation's deep political divisions. In this respect the 1860s "changed the politics of a people," as Mark Twain and Charles Warner observed. Not only did the Civil War destroy on the battlefield the idealized American polity, but the war also impressed upon many citizens a personal sense of vulnerability and destruction.[3] Political idealism was further weakened by the nation's expansionism in the second half of the nineteenth century, culminating in the war with Spain. True, some regarded expansion as the consummation of the polity. Yet by 1898 "talk of American uniqueness, of the nation as a lonely polity whose goal was the isolated preservation of an inspired design, diminished," as Paul Nagel has remarked.[4]

Apart from fighting on battlefields at home and abroad, other factors contributed to the loss of political idealism. Political corruption had become a prominent issue in the 1850s, and by the following decade the public longed for "the days when to be a politician was to be a man of ability," according to the *Hartford Courant.* The Congressional scandals of the 1870s, especially Crédit Mobilier, further tarnished

2. Cf. William A. Dunning, *Reconstruction, Political and Economic, 1865–1877* (New York, 1907); Mark V. Tushnet, *The American Law of Slavery, 1810–1860: Considerations of Humanity and Interest* (Princeton, NJ, 1981); Richard H. Sewell, *A House Divided: Sectionalism and Civil War, 1848–1865* (Baltimore, MD, 1988); Stephen V. Ash, *Middle Tennessee Society Transformed, 1860–1870: War and Peace in the Upper South* (Baton Rouge, LA, 1988); Robert C. Kenzer, *Kinship and Neighborhood in a Southern Community: Orange County, North Carolina, 1849–1881* (Knoxville, TN, 1988).

3. Mark Twain and Charles D. Warner, *The Gilded Age: A Tale of To-day* (New York, 1915), p. 336; Randall C. Jimerson, *The Private Civil War: Popular Thought during the Sectional Conflict* (Baton Rouge, LA, 1988).

4. Paul C. Nagel, *This Sacred Trust: American Nationality, 1798–1898* (Oxford, 1971), p. 325; Irwin Unger and Debi Unger, *The Vulnerable Years: The United States, 1896–1917* (New York, 1978), ch. 2.

the image of politics, and the General Secretary of the American Social Science Association observed in 1876, "we have come into one of those seasons of political and social collapse when the worst and most ignoble aspects of human nature offer themselves shamelessly to view." As urbanization proceeded, municipal politics were thought to be no improvement upon the national variety. Indeed, political corruption was "the shame of the cities" according to Lincoln Steffens's famous series of articles published in 1904.[5]

The judiciary also lost prestige and legitimacy after the Civil War. By the turn of the century courts attracted widespread criticism from populists, labor leaders, small businessmen, legislators, and even respected members of the bar.[6] The most intense criticism arose in response to a series of late-nineteenth-century Constitutional cases wherein the US Supreme Court extended freedom of contract in order to strike down progressive labor legislation. Historians have debated the reasons for these decisions, but what is not disputed is that the judiciary, led by the Supreme Court, was perceived as siding with wealthy industrialists against labor in the incipient class conflict arising from the industrialization and immigration during the second half of the nineteenth century.[7] This perception prompted efforts, beginning at mid-century and intensifying by the late nineteenth century, to end the appointing and life tenure of judges in favor of periodic public elections. Every new state entering the union between 1846 and 1912 adopted the popular election of judges, and by 1914 only seven states did not elect their judiciary. By that point, however, reformers had begun to reverse themselves and call for the appointment of judges because judicial elections had become totally politicized.

In this fashion even the judiciary was seen to be compromised by discredited political mechanisms, and the disillusionment with electoral process spread to nearly all levels and offices. After the contested presidential election between

5. Quotations are from Robert V. Bruce, *The Launching of American Science, 1846–1876* (New York, 1987), p. 329; F. B. Sanborn, "The Work of Social Science, Past and Present," *Journal of Social Science Containing the Transactions of the American Association*, 8 (1876): 24; Jon C. Teaford, *The Unheralded Triumph: City Government in America, 1870–1900* (Baltimore, MD, 1984), p. 1; Mark W. Summers, *The Plundering Generation: Corruption and the Crisis of the Union, 1849–1861* (New York, 1987). Lincoln Steffens articles were collected in *The Shame of the Cities* (New York, 1904).

6. Stephen Botein, "'What shall we Meet Afterwards in Heaven?': Judgeship as a Symbol for Modern American Lawyers," in *Professions and Professional Ideologies in America*, ed. Gerald L. Geison (Chapel Hill, NC, 1983), p. 55; Charles E. Merriam, *American Political Ideas: Studies in the Development of American Political Thought, 1865–1917* (1920; New York, 1969), p. 147; Joseph F. Wall, "*Lochner v. New York*: A Study in the Modernization of Constitutional Law," in *American Industrialization, Economic Expansion, and the Law*, ed. Joseph R. Frese and Jacob Judd (New York, 1981), pp. 113–41.

7. Cf. Edward S. Corwin, *The Twilight of the Supreme Court: A History of our Constitutional Theory* (New Haven, CT, 1934), ch. 1; Benjamin Twiss, *Lawyers and the Constitution: How Laissez-Faire Came to the Supreme Court* (Princeton, NJ, 1942); Charles W. McCurdy, "The *Knight* Sugar Decision of 1895 and the Modernization of American Corporation Law, 1869–1903," *Business History Review*, 53 (1979): 304–12; James C. Foster, *The Ideology of Apolitical Politics: The Elite Lawyers' Response to the Legitimation Crisis in American Capitalism, 1870–1920* (New York, 1986).

William McKinley and William Jennings Bryan in 1896, voter participation began to decline, and this symptom of "the decline of popular politics" extended to local, as well as national, elections.[8] Consequently, polity eroded as a cultural ideal and primary source of inspiration and legitimation over the second half of the nineteenth century, and science ascended in its place.

Although scholars have traditionally maintained that American interest and accomplishment in science appeared only after the Civil War, important scientific work has recently been credited to individuals and institutions from the antebellum and Jeffersonian periods, if not earlier.[9] Whether a historian concludes that "American Science Comes of Age … 1850–1930" or that "American Science Comes of Age, 1780–1820," has often depended on the definition of science employed and the branch of science being studied. Historians have been preoccupied with physics and biology and neglected other fields, such as geology or chemistry, which included the largest number of scientists in the United States before World War I.[10] These definitional problems mean that the dispute over the coming-of-age of American science probably cannot be resolved. Yet, given that the greatest scientific endeavors before the Civil War were government-sponsored surveys and that the membership of the American Association for the Advancement of Science before 1860 "was a heterogeneous mix of practicing scientists, interested participants, and onlookers," it is reasonable to endorse the conclusion of Robert Bruce that "American scientists … launched their momentous enterprise … in the years from 1846 to 1876."[11]

8. Botein, "… Judgeship as a Symbol for Modern American Lawyers," p. 57; Kermit L. Hall, "Constitutional Machinery and Judicial Professionalism: The Careers of Midwestern State Appellate Court Judges, 1861–1899," in *The New High Priests: Lawyers in Post-Civil War America,* ed. Gerard W. Gawalt (Westport, CT, 1984), p. 29; Michael E. McGerr, *The Decline of Popular Politics: The American North, 1865–1928* (New York, 1986), ch. 7; Kermit L. Hall, *The Magic Mirror: Law in American History* (New York, 1989), p. 196.

9. For the traditional view, see Alexis de Tocqueville, *Democracy in America,* ed. Phillips Bradley (1834; New York, 1945), vol. 2, p. 36; Richard H. Shryock, "American Indifference to Basic Science during the Nineteenth Century," *Archives Internationales d'histoire de science,* 28 (1948): 50–65; I. Bernard Cohen, "Science in America: The Nineteenth Century," in *Paths of American Thought,* ed. Arthur M. Schlesinger, Jr., and Morton White (Boston, 1963), pp. 167–89. For the revised view, see George H. Daniels, *American Science in the Age of Jackson* (New York, 1968); Stanley M. Guralnick, *Science and the Ante-Bellum American College* (Philadelphia, 1975); John C. Greene, *American Science in the Age of Jefferson* (Ames, IA, 1984).

10. Mott T. Greene, "History of Geology," p. 97, and John W. Servos, "History of Chemistry," p. 132, in *Historical Writing on American Sciences,* ed. Sally Gregory Kohlstedt and Margaret W. Rossiter (Baltimore, MD, 1985). Cf. Charles E. Rosenberg, *No Other Gods: On Science and American Social Thought* (Baltimore, MD, 1976), ch. 6. See Hamilton Cravens, "American Science Comes of Age: An Institutional Perspective, 1850–1930," *American Studies,* 17 (1976): 49–70; John C. Greene, "American Science Comes of Age, 1780–1820," *Journal of American History,* 55 (1968): 22–41.

11. Quotations are from Nathan Reingold, "American Indifference to Basic Research: A Reappraisal," in *Nineteenth-Century American Science,* ed. George H. Daniels (Evanston, IL, 1972), pp. 38–62; Sally G. Kohlstedt, "Savants and Professionals: The American Association for the Advancement of Science, 1848–1860," in *The Pursuit of Knowledge in the Early*

By the 1870s, then, science was underway while the ship of state was headed for dry dock. In 1876 the noted astronomer Simon Newcomb called upon Americans to establish their greatness by pursuing science. By 1884 scientific bureaus in the national government had expanded to the point that a federal commission was formed to consider whether a Department of Science should be established. In 1898 W. J. McGee announced, "America has become a nation of science." It is telling that McGee's announcement appeared in a popular magazine. In the decade after 1866, *Harper's Monthly, Atlantic, New York Times, New York Tribune,* and *Chicago Inter-Ocean* introduced regular series on science topics. In 1872 *Popular Science Monthly* began publication, and over the last three decades of the nineteenth century prominent scientists assumed leadership in publicizing science.[12] What has often been called a "religion of science" consequently gained adherence both among intellectuals and in the popular mind. "[A]nalogies and arguments of science or drawn from science became ... an increasingly plausible idiom in which to formulate – and in that sense control emotionally – almost every aspect of an inexorably modernizing world," writes Charles Rosenberg. Commensurately, "the man of science" appeared in the second half of the nineteenth century as "a special breed" having great cultural authority.[13]

On the other hand, it has been argued that "the prophets of profit and progress – Rockefeller, Carnegie, Vanderbilt, Morgan, Gould, et al. – became the cultural heroes for their time." These "robber barons" spawned a great increase in national wealth, accompanying the industrialization, bureaucratization, incorporation, urban-ization, and immigration that occurred between the Civil War and World War I.[14] In the celebrated interpretations of Samuel Hays and Robert Wiebe, these developments are regarded as hallmarks of the era, linked by the desire to systematize and order society for the sake of efficiency. Americans are thus said to have reoriented themselves from identification with geographic communities to identification with their occupations. "The Job" in "The Office" became "An

---

American Republic, ed. Alexandra Oleson and Sanborn C. Brown (Baltimore, MD, 1976), p. 299; Bruce, *The Launching of American Science,* p. 3. See A. Hunter Dupree, *Science in the Federal Government: A History of Policies and Activities* (Cambridge, MA, 1957), ch. 5.

12. Simon Newcomb, "Exact Science in America," *North American Review,* 119 (1874): 286–308; W. J. McGee, "Fifty Years of American Science," *Atlantic Monthly,* 82 (1898): 320; John C. Burnham, *How Superstition Won and Science Lost: Popularizing Science and Health in the United States* (New Brunswick, NJ, 1987), p. 162, ch. 4; Matthew D. Whalen and Mary F. Tobin, "Periodicals and the Popularization of Science in America, 1860–1910," *Journal of American Culture,* 3 (1980): 195–203; Dupree, *Science in the Federal Government,* ch. 11; Bruce, *The Launching of American Science, 1846–1876,* pp. 354–5.

13. Quotations are from Rosenberg, *No Other Gods: On Science and American Social Thought,* p. 7; Burnham, *How Superstition Won and Science Lost,* pp. 29–31, 151–2, 163–7. See Donald H. Meyer, "Paul Carus and the Religion of Science," *American Quarterly,* 14 (1962): 597–607; Donald Fleming, *John William Draper and the Religion of Science* (Philadelphia, 1950).

14. David G. Pugh, *Sons of Liberty: The Masculine Mind in Nineteenth-Century America* (Westport, CT, 1983), p. xix; Matthew Josephson, *The Robber Barons: The Great American Capitalists, 1861–1901* (New York, 1934).

American Novel," as Sinclair Lewis described.[15] Following Hays and Wiebe, others have pronounced that "an industrializing society is a professionalizing society," that "professionalism" is "a cultural process by which the middle class in America matured and defined itself," and that "the modern professions came into being" in the "industrializing society of late-nineteenth-century America."[16]

Such pronouncements, which treat industrial and economic changes as formative and foremost in the development of "profession," presuppose that the term means a middle-class occupation. But this is a premise that no one – even Burton Bledstein, who has discussed the use of "words" in "the culture of professionalism" – has demonstrated from the rhetorical evidence of the time. In fact the premise is an assumption drawn from the twentieth century. Industrialization, corporate capitalism, and the new middle class were not equated with "professionalism" or "professionality," words that began to appear in the mid-1800s.[17] To be sure, the broad economic and industrial changes were intricately related to the professions. But this relationship derived from the fact that both these changes and the meaning of "profession" were fundamentally influenced by the new "religion of science."

The nature of this architectonical influence was dynamic and multiform because "science" itself changed over time. In the antebellum period this popular term usually denoted Baconianism, meaning the gathering, description, and taxonomic classification of data. Because Baconianism was subsequently eclipsed, it is often forgotten that this inductive method itself had several different interpretations. Induction might be considered a process of inquiry and discovery, as William Whewell seemed to hold. Or, though primarily a method of discovery, induction might also be considered a form of verification, as John Herschel suggested. Indeed, for John Stuart Mill induction was the only way to verify scientific theories, which, he felt, must rely on causal and, therefore, empirical arguments.[18]

Herschel and Whewell emphasized the testing of consequences deduced from hypotheses as a process of verification, laying important groundwork for the

15. Sinclair Lewis, *The Job: An American Novel* (New York, 1917); Samuel P. Hays, *The Response to Industrialism: 1885–1914* (Chicago, 1957); Robert H. Wiebe, *The Search for Order, 1877–1920* (New York, 1967).

16. William J. Goode, "Encroachment, Charlatanism, and the Emerging Profession: Psychology, Sociology, and Medicine," *American Sociological Review*, 25 (1960): 902; Burton J. Bledstein, *The Culture of Professionalism: The Middle Class and the Development of Higher Education in America* (New York, 1976), p. ix; Penina Migdal Glazer and Miriam Slater, *Unequal Colleagues: The Entrance of Women into the Professions, 1890–1940* (New Brunswick, NJ, 1987), pp. 2–3. See Wiebe, *The Search for Order, 1877–1920*, ch. 5.

17. *OED*, s.v. "professionalism"; Bledstein, *The Culture of Professionalism*, pp. 65–79.

18. William Whewell, *Novum Organum Renovatum* (London, 1858), p. 59; Whewell, *The Philosophy of the Inductive Sciences*, 2 vols. (London, 1840); John F. W. Herschel, *A Preliminary Discourse on the Study of Natural Philosophy* (1830; New York, 1966), pp. 186–230; John S. Mill, *A System of Logic: Ratiocinative and Inductive* (London, 1843), vol. 2. See Daniels, *American Science in the Age of Jackson*, chs. 3, 7; Theodore D. Bozeman, *Protestants in an Age of Science: The Baconian Ideal and Antebellum Religious Thought* (Chapel Hill, NC, 1977), ch. 1; Herbert Hovenkamp, *Science and Religion in America, 1800–1860* (Philadelphia, 1978).

hypothetico-deductive method. This method and the "religion of science" thus gained ascendance in the second half of the nineteenth century, particularly after the publication of Charles Darwin's *Origin of Species* (1859).[19] The hypothetico-deductive method was initially accompanied by a positivist desire for and faith in certitude, just as Baconian induction had been. But this positivism broke down in the face of the slowly realized impermanence of even scientific findings.[20] Consequently, by the turn of the century the hypothetico-deductive method was transmuted into the "experimental method," as the methodological emphasis shifted from *verifying* hypotheses to *falsifying* them.

Though tentative, the new findings of natural and physical sciences acquired more and more credibility, and intellectual authority gradually shifted toward these new fields and away from the metaphysical and moral sciences. Deductions from those older sciences, including "the *architectonic* science of theology," had previously been employed to explain the natural world, as Henry Tappan observed in his inaugural address at the University of Michigan in 1851. But the moral and social sciences now began to look for confirmation from the natural and physical sciences and to draw from them germinal concepts. Early social scientists thus wrote freely about "Man the molecule of society" and "the identity of physical and social laws."[21] Part of the reason for this shift in authority was that the increasing complexity of society overwhelmed the capacity of mid-century social and political leaders to understand and explain events.[22] These leaders therefore joined with college faculty members holding generalist appointments in moral philosophy and

19. Ironically, Darwin suggested that he had adhered to traditional Baconian induction, rather than the hypothetico-deductive method. Recent scholars have concluded, however, that Darwin used the latter method and relied upon Whewell and Herschel in doing so. Michael T. Ghiselin, *The Triumph of the Darwinian Method* (Berkeley, CA, 1969), p. 67; Hamilton Cravens, *The Triumph of Evolution: American Scientists and the Heredity-Environment Controversy, 1900–1941* (Philadelphia, 1978). ch. 1; Peter J. Bowler, *Evolution: The History of an Idea* (Berkeley, CA, 1984), p. 202.

20. Paul S. Buck, ed., *Social Sciences at Harvard, 1860–1920: From Inculcation to the Open Mind* (Cambridge, MA, 1965), p. 15; Mary O. Furner, *Advocacy and Objectivity: A Crisis in the Professionalization of American Social Science, 1865–1905* (Lexington, KY, 1975), p. 289; Burnham, *How Superstition Won and Science Lost*, p. 167.

21. Henry P. Tappan, *University Education* (New York, 1851), p. 31; Henry C. Carey, *The Principles of Social Science* (Philadelphia, 1858–9), vol. 1, pp. vi, 41, vol. 3, pp. 466–7. In the late twentieth century, the interpretation of the relationship between natural and social sciences has reversed again, as the universality and objectivity of natural science have come under attack. Historians now suggest that social conditions shaped natural science. See Bowler, *Evolution: The History of an Idea*, ch. 6; Robert M. Young, *Darwin's Metaphor: Nature's Place in Victorian Culture* (Cambridge, UK, 1985).

22. See Furner, *Advocacy and Objectivity ... American Social Science, 1865–1905;* Cravens, "American Science Comes of Age: An Institutional Perspective, 1850–1930," pp. 49–70; Thomas L. Haskell, *The Emergence of Professional Social Science: The American Social Science Association and the Nineteenth-Century Crisis of Authority* (Urbana, IL, 1977), chs. 2, 10; Dorothy Ross, "The Development of the Social Sciences," in *The Organization of Knowledge in Modern America, 1860–1920*, ed. Alexandra Oleson and John Voss (Baltimore, MD, 1979), pp. 107–38.

political economy in order to form organizations devoted to scientific, social study, chiefly the American Social Science Association, founded in 1865.

Within a few decades this association and similar associations of generalists were undermined by the inability of generalists to keep pace with the increasingly specialized areas of knowledge, by the inability of social and political leaders to keep up with full-time scholars, and by the discrediting of utility and advocacy as motives or rationales for scientific study. By the 1910s psychology, economics, history, political science, and sociology had all broken away from "political economy" and "moral philosophy" to become independent disciplines. Meanwhile Baconianism and historicism had largely been repudiated as "scientific" methods, and this repudiation led to an even closer bond between the new social sciences and the natural sciences. Indeed, recent commentators, from Friedrich Hayek to Dorothy Ross, have noted the early twentieth-century "scientism ... the belief that the objective methods of the natural sciences should be used in the study of human affairs; and that such methods are the only fruitful ones in the pursuit of knowledge."[23] This scientism appeared as well in fields that eventually became known as the "humanities." Philosophy hatched out psychology, while the modern languages found their scientists in German-trained philologists who "wanted to teach modern languages on a scientific model" and organized the Modern Language Association in 1883 to do so.[24] Hence, the humanities also drew upon scientific methods and concepts, as did the learned professions.

Among the professions, medicine got science last. This ironical tardiness was due to the fact that jurists and theologians were the intellectual and cultural leaders before the Civil War. Hence, they were poised, indeed challenged, to square their own field with the new science. Physicians – no medical term analogous to "theologian" and "jurist" even existed – scrambled along, lugging their sectarianism with them. Antebellum scientists thus distinguished medicine from "dearly beloved science," as did Asa Gray, who left medicine after earning an MD in 1831 to became a prominent botanist.[25] The distinction continued through the 1880s, when leading physicians still maintained that "there is no likelihood that medicine will take its rank among the exact sciences" because "the final test of a science is the possibility of *predicting* the phenomena belonging to its domain," and "the physician can never know beforehand the precise effect which a drug will produce in a given case."[26] Even at medical schools in the early 1900s "the quality of clinical instruc-

23. Ross, "The Development of the Social Sciences," p. 131; F. A. Hayek, *The Counter-Revolution of Science: Studies in the Abuse of Reason* (Glencoe, IL, 1952), ch. 1.

24. Bruce Kuklick, *The Rise of American Philosophy: Cambridge, Massachusetts, 1860–1930* (New Haven, CT, 1977), p. 461; Michael Warner, "Professionalization and the Rewards of Literature: 1875–1900," *Criticism*, 27 (1985): 2–3; Gerald Graff, *Professing Literature: An Institutional History* (Chicago, 1987), pp. 55–118.

25. A. Hunter Dupree, *Asa Gray: American Botanist, Friend of Darwin* (1959; Baltimore, MD, 1988), pp. 46–9; Daniels, *American Science in the Age of Jackson*, p. 32, chs. 2–7; William G. Rothstein, *American Medical Schools and the Practice of Medicine* (New York, 1987), p. 52.

26. George G. Mercer, *The American Scholar in Professional Life* (Philadelphia, 1889), pp. 29–30.

tion ... lagged considerably behind that of the basic science teaching." And the great majority of clinicians expressed ambivalence about the scientific medicine appearing in physiology, bacteriology, and biochemistry. Due to this ambivalence, physicians were widely disparaged by scientists.[27]

In contrast, religion and science had enjoyed a fairly harmonious relationship in the antebellum period. This harmony was owed to their mutual reliance upon Baconian natural theology, which "was not a case of theologians misusing science for their own ends, but of scientists trying to attach some of the aura of the theologian to their own profession."[28] The harmony soon dissipated, however, as the relationship reversed between these intellectual fields. By the early 1880s this reversal and consequent loss of harmony were observed by many individuals. Sociologist Lester Ward expressed the changes in this way: "the territory once belonging to the gods, which has been contested and reclaimed by science, embraces the entire fields of astronomy, physics, chemistry, and geology. That of biology has now fairly passed out of theological supremacy, while those of moral and social phenomena are at present time the battle-ground between science and religion."[29]

This traditional view that religion and science warred against each other in the late nineteenth century is now regarded by up-to-date scholars as "historically bankrupt." After all, it is said, one cannot credit the statements of "protagonists" of the time, such as Lester Ward. Nor can one credit the "Whiggish and conflict-oriented historical canon" established by John W. Draper's *History of the Conflict between Religion and Science* (1874) and Andrew Dixon White's *A History of the Warfare of Science with Theology* (1896). Finally, it is said, "there never was a pervasive and genuinely divisive discontinuity between scientific and religious

27. Quotation is from Kenneth M. Ludmerer, *Learning to Heal: The Development of American Medical Education* (New York, 1985), p. 165; Russell C. Maulitz," 'Physician versus Bacteriologist': The Ideology of Science in Clinical Medicine," p. 93, and Gerald L. Geison, "Divided we Stand: Physiologists and Clinicians in the American Context," pp. 67–90, in *The Therapeutic Revolution*, ed. Morris J. Vogel and Charles E. Rosenberg (Philadelphia, 1979); Leila Zenderland, "The Debate over Diagnosis: Henry Herbert Goddard and the Medical Acceptance of Intelligence Testing," in *Psychological Testing and American Society, 1890–1930*, ed. Michael M. Sokal (New Brunswick, NJ, 1987), pp. 46–62; Robert E. Kohler, *From Medical Chemistry to Biochemistry: The Making of a Biomedical Discipline* (Cambridge, UK, 1982).

28. Daniels, *American Science in the Age of Jackson*, p. 53; Bozeman, *Protestants in an Age of Science*; Hovenkamp, *Science and Religion in America, 1800–1860*; Bruce Kuklick, *Churchmen and Philosophers: From Jonathan Edwards to John Dewey* (New Haven, CT, 1985), pt. 2; Ronald L. Numbers, "Science and Religion," in *Historical Writing on American Science*, ed. Sally Gregory Kohlstedt and Margaret W. Rossiter (Baltimore, MD, 1985), pp. 68–70. Cf. Bruce, *The Launching of American Science, 1846–1876*, pp. 121ff.; James Turner, *Without God, Without Creed: The Origins of Unbelief in America* (Baltimore, MD, 1985), pp. 160–1.

29. Frank Lester Ward, *Dynamic Sociology, or Applied Social Science* (New York, 1883), vol. 2, p. 269. See Charles W. Eliot, "On the Education of Ministers" (1882), in Educational Reform (New York, 1898), pp. 69–71; Andrew Dixon White, *What Profession shall I Choose, and How shall I Fit myself for it?* (Ithaca, NY, 1884), p. 50.

imperatives in the minds of most educated Americans."[30] Taken together, these statements mean that there is no way to disprove the up-to-date view. One cannot believe the contemporary testimony or historiography about the conflict, and the educated, and presumably the uneducated, simply did not see a conflict either.

Such revisionist scholarship testifies to the complexity of the relationship between religion and science. Different interpretations are reasonable depending on whether one defines the issue as dogmatism versus skepticism, metaphysics versus naturalism, belief versus unbelief, theology versus philosophy, traditionalism versus modernism, stasis versus evolution.[31] Yet, however the relationship is interpreted, it seems capricious to sweep away the testimony of Ward, Draper, White, and a host of others about their own time. Certainly, theology could and did accommodate virtually any scientific finding, as well as the various definitions of the scientific method. But when science started to ascend in the hierarchy of belief, theologians were bound to resist, even as they were "beginning to see that the divine methods are scientific and that if we are to be effective 'laborers together with God,' our methods must be scientific," as one Baptist minister remarked.[32]

The divinely scientific method was no less protean than the naturally scientific. It led first and foremost to philological and historical scholarship, indeed, to "a historical emphasis to all study."[33] For Catholics this emphasis was reflected in an "Americanist Era" in diocesan seminaries from 1884 to 1910. For Protestants the historicism was complemented, on the one hand, by a "natural" style of pastoral care, including the assimilation of empirical psychology.[34] On the other hand, it was

---

30. Quotations are from Numbers, "Science and Religion," p. 80; Rosenberg, *No Other Gods: On Science and American Social Thought*, p. 3. John W. Draper, *History of the Conflict between Religion and Science* (New York, 1874); Andrew Dixon White, *A History of the Warfare of Science with Theology in Christendom*, 2 vols. (New York, 1896).

31. See, respectively, James R. Moore, *The Post-Darwinian Controversies: A Study of the Protestant Struggle to Come to Terms with Darwin in Great Britain and America, 1870–1900* (New York, 1979); J. David Hoeveler, Jr., *James McCosh and the Scottish Intellectual Tradition: From Glasgow to Princeton* (Princeton, NJ, 1981); Turner, *Without God, Without Creed*, chs. 4, 5, 6; Louise L. Stevenson, *Scholarly Means to Evangelical Ends: The New Haven Scholars and the Transformation of Higher Learning in America, 1830–1890* (New Haven, CT, 1986); Kuklick, *Churchmen and Philosophers: From Jonathan Edwards to John Dewey*, pt. 3; Charles D. Cashdollar, *The Transformation of Theology, 1830–1890: Positivism and Protestant Thought in Britain and America* (Princeton, NJ, 1989); Jon H. Roberts, *Darwinism and the Divine in America: Protestant Intellectuals and Organic Evolution, 1859–1900* (Madison, WI, 1988).

32. Josiah Strong, *Religious Movements for Social Betterment* (New York, 1900), p. 17; "The Place of Science in Ministerial Education," *Baptist Review & Expositor*, 3 (1906): 588–96.

33. Levering Reynolds, Jr., "The Later Years (1880–1953)," in *The Harvard Divinity School: Its Place in Harvard University and American Culture*, ed. George H. Williams (Boston, 1954), p. 170; Kuklick, *Churchmen and Philosophers*, chs. 12, 13, 14; Jurgen Herbst, *The German Historical School in American Scholarship: A Study in the Transfer of Culture* (Ithaca, NY, 1965), ch. 4; Turner, *Without God, Without Creed*, pp. 146, 185.

34. Joseph M. White, *The Diocesan Seminary in the United States: A History from the 1780s to the Present* (Notre Dame, IN, 1988), pp. 165–264; E. Brooks Holifield, *A History of*

enthusiastically amplified with "Christian sociology" by the 1900s. Theologians, including Graham Taylor of Chicago Theological Seminary and Alfred Anthony of Cobb Divinity School, therefore assessed "The Sociological Function of the Ministry" and "The Preacher and the Study of Sociology." Meanwhile social scientists, such as Richard Ely, proposed "that half of theological students' time be devoted to social science and that divinity schools be the chief intellectual centers for sociology."[35]

Just as "natural theology" had testified to the authority of antebellum religion over science, so antebellum jurists confidently claimed to have a "science" that was "the perfection of reason," in the words of seventeenth-century English jurist Sir Edward Coke. Coke was frequently quoted in the young United States, and, mindful of his authority, American jurists treated Constitutional law as formal, scientific, and devoid of discretion.[36] Jurists may have adopted a "subjective" viewpoint in early-nineteenth-century private law, as Morton Horwitz suggests. But the Cokean objective of "a *science* of jurisprudence" was espoused in the treatises of leading jurists, including Joseph Story at Harvard, James Kent at Columbia, David Hoffman at Maryland, Daniel Mayes at Transylvania, Bellamy Storer at Louisville, and Christian Roselius at Tulane.[37] This antebellum legal science, though influenced by Baconianism, was largely rationalistic and axiomatic, and proudly so. Antebellum jurists called law "a *moral* science" and clearly distinguished between

---

Pastoral Care: from Salvation to Self-Realization (Nashville, TN, 1983), pp. 164–5, ch. 5. Thus, in 1895 G. Stanley Hall undertook his study, *Jesus, the Christ, in the Light of Psychology* (New York, 1917).

35. Charles H. Hopkins, *The Rise of the Social Gospel in American Protestantism, 1865–1915* (New Haven, CT, 1940), p. 108; Alfred W. Anthony, *A Post-seminarial Curriculum or the Minister's Self-Culture* (Boston, [1900]), p. 20; "The Sociological Function of the Ministry," *Baptist Review & Expositor*, 5 (1908): 213–27; "The Preacher and the Study of Sociology," *Baptist Review & Expositor*, 7 (1910): 49–56; Robert S. Michaelson, "The Protestant Ministry in America: 1850 to the Present," in *The Ministry in Historical Perspectives*, ed. H. Richard Niebuhr and Daniel D. Williams (New York, 1956), p. 261; John F. McClymer, *War and Welfare: Social Engineering in America, 1890–1925* (Westport, CT, 1980), p. 20. Marty argues that mainline Protestants sold out to fashionable ideas of sociology, science, and education, and found themselves dated almost immediately. Conversely Vidich and Lyman rely heavily on metaphor to argue that sociology rose "out of Protestant theology" and was infused with "a mission ... of establishing the Kingdom of God on Earth." Martin E. Marty *The Irony of it all: 1893–1919* (Chicago, 1986); Arthur J. Vidich and Stanford M. Lyman, *American Sociology: Worldly Rejections of Religion and their Directions* (New Haven, CT, 1985), p. xi.

36. Sir Edward Coke, *Institutes of the Laws of England* (London, 1628), pt. 1, p. 232b.

37. Morton J. Horwitz, *The Transformation of American Law, 1780–1860* (Cambridge, MA, 1977), pp. 196–9, 256, chs. 7, 8. Daniel Mayes, *An Address to the Students of Law in Transylvania University* (Lexington, KY, 1834), pp. 1–2; Bellamy Storer, *The Legal Profession* (Cincinnati, OH, 1856), p. 8; Christian Roselius, "Introductory Lecture" (1854), in *The Gladsome Light of Jurisprudence*, ed. Michael H. Hoeflich (Westport, CT, 1988), p. 224. The testimony of David Hoffman, James Kent, and Joseph Story is reprinted in *Legal Mind in America*, pp. 68–75, 87, 95, 182–7. See Perry Miller, *The Life of the Mind in America: From the Revolution to the Civil War* (Cambridge, MA, 1965), pp. 156–85.

"physical and moral law."[38] Then, in the final third of the nineteenth century, the rising authority of empirical science undermined this rationalistic and axiomatic "moral science," and jurisprudence encountered "a crisis of legitimacy." After all, said Dean C. C. Langdell of Harvard Law School, "If law be not a science, a university will consult its own dignity in declining to teach it."[39]

It was, in fact, Langdell who introduced the most successful legitimating analogy between jurisprudence and the new natural science when he introduced the case method of teaching in 1871 with these words:

> Law considered as a science, consists of certain principles or doctrines.... Each of these doctrines has arrived at its present state by slow degrees; in other words, it is a growth, extending ... through centuries ... [T]he shortest and best, if not the only way of mastering the doctrine effectually is by studying the cases in which it is embodied ... Moreover, the number of fundamental legal doctrines is much less than is commonly supposed.... It seemed to me, therefore, to be possible to take ... a branch of the law ... and ... to select, classify, and arrange all the cases which had contributed in any important degree to the growth, development, or establishment of any of its essential doctrines.[40]

Here the characteristics attributed at the time to Darwinian biology are readily apparent: historicism, empiricism, certitude, and induction of a taxonomy of a few laws. Langdell later elaborated the analogy by noting "that law is a science, ... the library is the proper workshop of professors and students alike ... [just as] the laboratories of the university are to the chemists and physicists, the museum of natural history to the zoologists, the botanical garden to the botanists."[41] Such analogies were significant because there was "a very real connection between this prevailing vogue of the physical and applied sciences and the fact that Langdell's innovation in legal education was also introduced comparatively quickly," according to the 1914 Carnegie Foundation study of the case method.[42]

---

38. Daniel Mayes, *An Address to the Students of Law*, p. 1; Christian Roselius, "Introductory Lecture," p. 224. Maxwell Bloomfield, *American Lawyers in a Changing Society, 1776–1876* (Cambridge, MA, 1976), p. 163; Stephen Botein, "Professional History Reconsidered," *AJLH*, 21 (1977): 67.

39. Christopher C. Langdell, "Harvard Celebration Speeches," *Law Quarterly Review*, 3 (1887): 124. Thomas C. Grey, "Langdell's Orthodoxy," *University of Pittsburgh Law Review*, 45 (1983): 1–53; Foster, *The Ideology of Apolitical Politics ... 1870–1920*, passim.

40. Christopher C. Langdell, *A Selection of Cases on the Law of Contracts* (Boston, 1871), "Preface."

41. Langdell, "Harvard Celebration Speeches," p. 124. Langdell scarcely said another thing about the case method. Albert J. Harno, *Legal Education in the United States* (San Francisco, CA, 1953), p. 56.

42. Josef Redlich, *The Common Law and the Case Method in American University Law Schools* (New York, 1914), p. 16. Robert W. Gordon dismisses the "notion" that the modeling of jurisprudence on natural and physical science was an effort to legitimate jurisprudence in the late nineteenth century. His dismissal relies on the fact that antebellum jurists had already referred to law as a "science." But this well known fact ignores the points that the meaning of "science" changed and gained tremendous cultural authority in the second half of the nineteenth century. It also ignores the testimony from Langdell, Redlich,

Even as the case method triumphed, however, the Darwinian model of legal science was overthrown. The method of teaching from cases remained, while the leading edge of jurisprudence moved three steps further on. The first development ran parallel to the transmutation of the hypothetico-deductive method into the experimental method: Langdell's desire for positive, legal rules was undercut by skepticism. "Certainty generally is illusion, and repose is not the destiny of man," admonished Oliver Wendell Holmes, Jr., in 1897. And, again, in 1905 from the US Supreme Court: "General propositions do not decide concrete cases."[43] This skepticism about the verity and applicability of legal principles led, secondly, to a pragmatic view that social policy and societal results must guide jurists in decisions. Roscoe Pound was the exemplary figure here: "[T]his scientific character of law is a means – a means toward the end of law, which is the administration of justice. Law is not scientific for the sake of science.... it must be judged by the results it achieves.... We have to ... attain a pragmatic, a sociological legal science."[44]

Pound's "sociological legal science" referred to jurists treating social policy and societal results as the standard for deciding cases, and this reference demonstrates the ambiguity of the new disciplines and their terminology in the 1900s. What might today be called "sociological jurisprudence" – the informing of jurisprudence by social science – was the third development of legal science. Having replaced formal legal principles with social policy and societal results as the standard by which cases should be decided, jurists turned to social science to calculate those results. Louis Brandeis was the exemplar in this regard. In a famous case of 1908, attorney Brandeis submitted to the US Supreme Court a 113-page brief that consisted of three pages of legal opinion supplemented by a mass of psychological, medical, economic, and sociological data and analysis.[45] This empiricism would quickly pose tremendous problems, not only for jurisprudence, but for all social, political, and ethical theory of the time. It would lead to the skeptical view that all events and entities were interdependent and in flux, as Edward Purcell has shown. Nevertheless, for the moment, "the slogan 'law is a science' became 'law is a social science'."[46] In this sense, the scientism of Langdell persisted through the 1910s.

Science thus gained authority over other domains of intellectual life in the second half of the nineteenth century. To be sure, the term "science" had long

---

and Pound, among many others. Gordon also omits any reference to natural or physical sciences when identifying "three distinct versions of the ideology of legal science." "Legal Thought and Legal Practice in the Age of American Enterprise," in *Professions and Professional Ideologies in America*, ed. Gerald L. Geison (Chapel Hill, NC, 1983), pp. 97, 81–94.

43. Oliver W. Holmes, Jr., "The Path of the Law," *Harvard Law Review*, 10 (1897): 466; J. Holmes dissenting in *Lochner v. New York*, 198 US 45, 76 (1905). Grey, "Langdell's Orthodoxy," pp. 1–53.

44. Roscoe Pound, "Mechanical Jurisprudence," *Columbia Law Review*, 8 (1908): 605–10; Pound, "The Need of a Sociological Jurisprudence," *The Green Bag*, 19 (1907): 607–15.

45. Louis D. Brandeis and Josephine Goldmark, *Women in Industry ... Brief for the State of Oregon* (New York, 1908); *Muller v. Oregon*, 208 US 412 (1908).

46. Grant Gilmore, *The Ages of American Law* (New Haven, CT, 1977), p. 87; Edward A. Purcell, Jr., *The Crisis of Democratic Theory: Scientific Naturalism and the Problem of Value* (Lexington, KY, 1973), chs. 9, 10, 11.

conveyed legitimacy and dignity. In the high Middle Ages *scientia* had carried greater weight than *disciplina* or *ars*, though all three terms were interchangeable in many instances; and from the seventeenth century "science" had been growing in intellectual authority due to new findings about the natural and physical world. But it was only in the second quarter of the nineteenth century that the primary usage of the English word narrowed to natural and physical sciences.[47] From that point "the *architectonic* science" had rapidly shifted, as Henry Tappan observed at mid-century. Indeed, the very term "architectonic science" became outmoded, ironically signifying the utter domination of the new architectonic. Whereas "serving sciences" had previously retained their distinct identity while nevertheless being modeled upon the "master science," now the word "science" came to mean, first and foremost, natural science. Other terms, such as "legal science" or "theological science," gradually began to look and sound improper. No previous architectonic had so completely mastered epistemology as to nearly obliterate alternative understandings of "science." The usage of "architectonic" thus disappeared when the master science became the only science.

Institutional: *Science and Education*

Education became the institutional locus for the cultural ideal of science. That this should be so might, in retrospect, appear to be inevitable, just as churches were the institutional locus of religion. Yet we have seen that the polity was not always confided to the care of lawyers, and this fact should alert us to examine other possibilities. The military, for example, might have become the institutional locus of science. As late as the 1860s future Nobel-prize winner Albert Michelson studied at the Naval Academy because he believed that no other college offered adequate instruction in physics. However, science in the military services subsequently declined, as A. H. Dupree has shown.[48] Another possibility was the federal government. In the late 1860s more scientists resided in Washington, DC, than in any other part of the country due to the presence of the Department of Agriculture, the Army Engineers, and the Geological, Coastal, and Geodetic Surveys. But appropriations did not increase significantly, and the 1884 campaign to create a federal Department of Science foundered. Consequently, the prospect of the government becoming the locus for science soon dissipated.[49] Yet another possi-

47. John T. Merz, *A History of European Thought in the Nineteenth Century* (London, 1904), vol. 1, p. 89n. Cf. *OED*, s.v. "science," "scientist'; Daniels, *American Science in the Age of Jackson*, p. 38; Bruce, *The Launching of American Science, 1846–1876*, p. 80.

48. Alex Roland, "Science and War," in *Historical Writing on American Science*, ed. Sally G. Kohlstedt and Margaret W. Rossiter (Baltimore, MD, 1985), p. 260; Dupree, *Science in the Federal Government*, ch. 9.

49. Dupree, *Science in the Federal Government*, pp. 151–6, 215–31, 294–5; J. Kirkpatrick Flack, *Desideratum in Washington: The Intellectual Community in the Capital City, 1870–1900* (Cambridge, MA, 1975); Gary S. Dunbar, "Credentialism and Careerism in American Geography, 1890–1915," in *The Origins of Academic Geography in the United States*, ed. Brian W. Blouet (Hamden, CT, 1981), p. 71.

bility was the growing industrial corporations, but here, too, the formation of in-house laboratories straggled behind the achievements of scientists. Even when American physicists and chemists achieved preeminence in the twentieth century, businessmen and industrialists were slow to hire them or to draw upon their findings. Corporate leaders likewise neglected the social sciences. For example, Frederick W. Taylor's methods of improving the efficiency of labor and capital were ignored by the managers of most of America's largest companies until about 1920.[50]

Finally, it should be noted that engineering might have become the institutional, or professional, locus of science, but did not.[51] Elite engineers, who traditionally rose up through the shop culture of "mechanics," had long aspired for professional status. But these aspirations had been hindered, in part, by bickering among the engineering specialities over their relative importance.[52] This internal conflict was overshadowed in the late nineteenth century, when graduates of newly founded engineering schools desired to ascend, by way of their learning, into the ranks of the learned professions. These young upstarts quickly came into conflict with the established shop-culture elite, but this conflict also became moot. Most engineering

50. Louis Galambos, "The American Economy and the Reorganization of the Sources of Knowledge," pp. 271–2, and Daniel J. Kevles, "The Physics, Mathematics, and Chemistry Communities: A Comparative Analysis," pp. 139–45, in *The Organization of Knowledge in Modern America, 1860–1920,* ed. Alexandra Oleson and John Voss (Baltimore, MD, 1979); Servos, "History of Chemistry," p. 132; George Wise, "A New Role for Professional Scientists in Industry: Industrial Research at General Electric, 1900–1916," *Technology and Culture,* 21 (1980): 408–29; Wise, "Ionists in Industry: Physical Chemistry at General Electric, 1900–1915," *Isis,* 74 (1983): 7–21. Some scholars have maintained that industry did draw upon the findings of the natural and social scientists. See Monte A. Calvert, *The Mechanical Engineer in America, 1830–1910* (Baltimore, MD, 1967), p. 235; Samuel Haber, *Efficiency and Uplift: Scientific Management in the Progressive Era, 1890–1920* (Chicago, 1964).

51. Engineering and technology have long been understood as developing and applying ideas that are discovered by scientists. Even revisionist historians, such as David F. Noble, have viewed engineering and technology as "the wedding of science to the useful arts." In contrast, some historians, such as George Wise, have begun calling this "the oversimplified model ... [of] an assembly line," and are now "treating science and technology as separate spheres of knowledge, both man-made." Hence, the thrust of recent scholarship is toward distinguishing science from engineering even more than did the traditional or revisionist views. Noble, *America by Design: Science, Technology, and the Rise of Corporate Capitalism* (New York, 1977), ch. 1; Wise, "Science and Technology," in *Historical Writing on American Science,* ed. Sally G. Kohlstedt and Margaret W. Rossiter (Baltimore, MD, 1985), pp. 229, 244. See Melvin Kranzberg, "The Disunity of Science-Technology," *American Scientist,* 56 (1968): 21–34; Edwin T. Layton, Jr., "Mirror Image Twins: The Communities of Science and Technology in 19th Century America," in *Nineteenth-Century American Science,* ed. George H. Daniels (Evanston, IL, 1972), pp. 210–30.

52. Calvert, *The Mechanical Engineer in America, 1830–1910,* chs. 6, 11; Bruce, *The Launching of American Science, 1846–1876,* pp. 150–65, 341; Bruce Sinclair, "Episodes in the History of the American Engineering Profession," in *The Professions in American History,* ed. Nathan O. Hatch (Notre Dame, IN, 1988), pp. 127–44.

schools had not yet attained college-level work in the 1910s, when the learned professions were moving toward a norm of graduate-level training. The lower educational standards in engineering naturally encouraged those in the learned professions to believe that "the discipline of the modern engineer ... is less complex and exacting," as Abraham Flexner maintained.[53] Consequently, engineering did not become the locus of science. Only in 1916 were engineers invited for the first time to serve on national scientific advisory boards and thereby recognized as part of the established scientific community or as a learned profession, according to the 1918 Carnegie Foundation report on engineering education.[54]

Hence, engineering, industry, the federal government, or the military might have become the institutional locus of science, but education assumed the role with an ease that seemed as natural as evolution. As early as 1850 members of the new American Association for the Advancement of Science founded the American Association for the Advancement of Education, dedicated to reforming higher education. The annual meetings of the two organizations were scheduled concurrently so members could attend both, and in 1857 the latter was subsumed by the National Teachers Association, which broadened the reform agenda to include secondary and elementary education. Meanwhile the leading institutions of antebellum science and intellectual life – gentlemanly associations of urban clergy, lawyers, and physicians – were migrating into colleges and aborning universities. In New York City, for example, the *Times* noted this migration in 1859, and by the mid-1890s the "popular, participatory scientific movement in New York City ... had been taken over by academic scientists – most of them members of the Columbia University faculty."[55]

Whereas in 1846 educators constituted less than half of the leading scientists listed in the *Dictionary of American Biography*, they formed a majority by 1876, and the proportion of educators rose dramatically thereafter. In the final quarter of the nineteenth century 81 percent of the physicists, chemists, and mathematicians in the United States were employed in education, merely 13 percent in government, and 6 percent in some other field. Between about 1890 and 1915 the percentage in

53. Abraham Flexner, *Medical Education in the United States and Canada* (New York, 1910), pp. 23–4; Edwin T. Layton, Jr., *The Revolt of the Engineers: Social Responsibility and the American Engineering Profession* (Baltimore, MD, 1986), p. 4; Calvert, *The Mechanical Engineer in America, 1830–1910*, chs. 7, 8.

54. Charles R. Mann, *A Study of Engineering Education* (New York, 1918), pp. 107, ch. 16. David Noble, who wishes to demonstrate the dominance of technology, engineering, and their links to corporate capitalism, tends to locate "the emergence of the professional engineers" earlier in time, and does not acknowledge that many engineers and observers did not consider engineering a profession. He also states that in 1900 there were 45,000 engineers, inferring that "excepting teachers, it was already the largest professional occupation in America." But census data indicate that in 1900 there were some 77,000 engineers in the country, as compared to 108,000 lawyers and judges, 114,000 clergymen, and 131,000 physicians and surgeons. *America by Design*, pp. 38–9; *Historical Statistics*, series D233–682.

55. Quotations are from "College Progress," *New York Times* (August 16, 1859): 4; Douglas Sloan, "Science in New York City, 1867–1907," *Isis*, 17 (1980): 36. Sally G. Kohlstedt, *The Formation of the American Scientific Community: The American Association for the Advancement of Science, 1848–60* (Urbana, IL, 1976), p. 136.

education reached 84 percent, while the fraction in government dropped to 10 percent.[56] In 1910 J. McKeen Cattell published a famous analysis of the one thousand "best" scientists in the United States. He concluded, "Nearly three-quarters of our scientific men earn their livings by teaching, and a large proportion of the others have done so." In striking contrast to the antebellum membership of learned societies, Cattell's list included "no lawyer or man of business." With this in mind, Cattell began editing "*Science and Education.* A series of volumes for the promotion of scientific research and educational progress."[57]

Within the field of education, it was the university that "gained ascendancy over other institutional forms for the discovery and diffusion of knowledge," as Edward Shils has remarked.[58] The number of associated "scientific schools" and "scientific departments," which had first appeared in the 1850s, grew sharply in the 1870s along with the new land-grant universities, which were dubbed "Our National Schools of Science." University libraries shifted their purpose from accumulation to use for research; the undergraduate major was established as a kind of apprenticeship to specialized research; and, when the US Bureau of Education introduced "an academic quality rating" of colleges in 1911, the scale was "based on only *one* criterion – the success of their graduates in well-regarded graduate schools."[59] Flushed with the apparent fulfillment of their commitment to science and reflecting the clerical lineage from which many were descended, the scientific researchers and university leaders shared the enthusiasm later recalled by G. Stanley Hall:

> We felt that we belonged to the larger university ... eternal in the world of science and learning ... [and] that research is nothing less than a religion....

56. Bruce, *The Launching of American Science, 1846–1876,* p. 136; Kevles, "The Physics, Mathematics, and Chemistry Communities," pp. 167–8.

57. J. McKeen Cattell, *American Men of Science: A Biographical Dictionary,* 2d edn (New York, 1910), pp. 583–4; Cattell, "*Science and Education*" (New York, 1913).

58. Edward Shils, "The Order of Learning in the United States: The Ascendancy of the University," in *The Organization of Knowledge in Modern America, 1860–1920,* ed. Alexandra Oleson and John Voss (Baltimore, MD, 1979), p. 19; Charles D. Walcott, "Relations of the National Government to Higher Education and Research," *Science,* n.s., 13 (1901): 1004–11; Sally Gregory Kohlstedt, "Institutional History," *Historical Writing on American Science,* ed. Kohlstedt and Margaret W. Rossiter (Baltimore, MD, 1985), p. 30.

59. Bruce, *The Launching of American Science, 1846–1876,* pp. 327–30; "Our National Schools of Science," *North American Review,* 105 (1867): 495–520; John Y. Cole, "Storehouses and Workshops: American Libraries and the Uses of Knowledge," in *The Organization of Knowledge in Modern America, 1860–1920,* ed. Alexandra Oleson and John Voss (Baltimore, MD, 1979), pp. 364–85; David S. Webster, "Bureau of Education's Suppressed Ratings of Colleges, 1911–1912," *HEQ,* 24 (1984): 509. This does not mean that all institutions embraced the research ideal or that no other purposes and rationales existed in higher education. But research gradually became preeminent among the rationales and goals cited by university leaders. The classic treatment in this regard is Laurence R. Veysey, *The Emergence of the American University* (Chicago, 1965). See Hugh Hawkins, "University Identity: the Teaching and Research Functions," in *The Organization of Knowledge in Modern America, 1860–1920,* ed. Alexandra Oleson and John Voss (Baltimore, MD, 1979), pp. 285–312; Charles C. Bishop, "Teaching at Johns Hopkins: The First Generation," *HEQ,* 27 (1987): 499–515.

[E]ducation has, thus, become the chief problem of the world, its one holy cause.... Never so much as now is education *the* one and chief hope of the world."[60]

In this fashion the university assumed leadership of the crusade for science. But it is important to recognize that the leadership extended throughout a host of educational institutions accompanying the university. This extended leadership reflects the fact that the entire field of education during this period was far less structured and differentiated than has commonly been portrayed. Scholars depicting education as rigidly and hierarchically bureaucratized before 1900 have focused upon urban school systems, and it is true that New York city had commenced, even before 1850,[61] building "the one best system" of schools that began to emerge 50 years later in Philadelphia, Chicago, St. Louis, and San Francisco. However, these initial efforts encountered stiff resistance even at the turn of the century in those major cities. In smaller cities, the "system" was small or nonexistent. San Diego, for example, had but one high school at the end of the nineteenth century, and Seattle had not yet begun to plan a system of schools.[62] As late as 1920, 58 percent of the nation's schoolchildren were living in rural areas, where a "locally controlled, nonbureaucratic mode of education" dominated "without regard to region."[63] As a result, most schools were in a "muddle over what distinguished an administrator from a teacher."[64]

Meanwhile much of "higher" education was lower. In 1898 the US Commissioner of Education noted "the large number of weak, so-called colleges and universities," which "do not furnish as good an education as may be obtained in good secondary schools." Likewise the vast majority of schools for the learned professions, except divinity, operated at the level of secondary schools or lower. Schools for vocations aspiring to the status of the learned professions were often at the elementary level. On the other hand, elite high schools were sometimes

60. G. Stanley Hall, *Life and Confessions of a Psychologist* (New York, 1923), pp. 338, 521–3.

61. On the antebellum "consolidation of schools into a single articulated, hierarchical system," see Carl F. Kaestle, *The Evolution of an Urban School System: New York City, 1750–1850* (Cambridge, MA, 1973), p. viii; Kaestle, *Pillars of the Republic: Common Schools and American Society, 1780–1860* (New York, 1983), p. 221; Lawrence Cremin, *American Education: The National Experience, 1783–1876* (New York, 1980), pp. x, 124–5.

62. David B. Tyack, *The One Best System: A History of American Urban Education* (Cambridge, MA, 1979), pp. 147–67; Jesse B. Sears and Adin D. Henderson, *Cubberley of Stanford and His Contribution to American Education* (Stanford, CA, 1957), ch. 4; Bryce E. Nelson, *Good Schools: The Seattle Public School System, 1901–1930* (Seattle, WA, 1988), pp. 3–22; David Tyack, Thomas James, and Aaron Benavot, *Law and the Shaping of American Public Education, 1785–1954* (Madison, WI, 1987), p. 19.

63. William A. Link, *A Hard Country and a Lonely Place: Schooling, Society, and Reform in Rural Virginia, 1870–1920* (Chapel Hill, NC, 1986), pp. ix, 5. *Historical Statistics*, series A199–209; Wayne E. Fuller, *The Old Country School: The Story of Rural Education in the Middle West* (Chicago, 1982), ch. 5.

64. David F. Labaree, "Career Ladders and the Early Public High-School Teacher: A Study of Inequality and Opportunity," in *American Teachers*, ed. Donald Warren (New York, 1989), p. 177.

empowered by the state to grant bachelor degrees, as in the case of Central High School in Philadelphia. And governmental efforts to systematize educational institutions proceeded slowly. The federal Office of Education had no authority in this regard, and state efforts were small, as shown by the fact that in 1890 half of the state departments of education comprised merely the superintendent and, at most, one assistant.[65]

Quite correct, then, was the description in the *United States Exhibit Prepared for the Paris Exposition 1900:*

> Spontaneity is the keynote of education in the United States. Its varied form, its uneven progress, its lack of symmetry, its practical effectiveness, are all due to the fact that ... local preference and individual initiative have been ruling forces....
> As a result, there is, in the European sense, no American system of education.[66]

That "no American system of education" existed was further demonstrated by the fact that educational leaders actively involved themselves in all aspects of the field. The involvement of Harvard President Charles Eliot is perhaps best known. But the effort was also made by President Henry Tappan at Michigan, where the university faculty was statutorily charged to visit the schools in the state. In Minnesota, University president William Folwell led the drive to organize public schools, and in Tennessee Charles Dabney became president of the University in 1887 and championed the Southern Education Board founded in 1901. Meanwhile Brown University President Barnas Sears became General Agent of the Peabody Education Fund in Virginia, and Columbia President N. M. Butler was a leader of the National Council of Education, College Entrance Examination Board, and *Educational Review.*[67]

This intensive involvement across the spectrum of education was not limited to university presidents. "From 1850 to the end of the century, in stark contrast to the twentieth-century collegiate professoriate, many ... professors not only thought of themselves as professional schoolmen but participated with teachers at all levels to determine a comprehensible expertise for the work of education as a whole."[68] Eminent science professors, such as Asa Gray, Louis Agassiz, N. S. Shaler, and H. N. Martin, offered courses and institutes for schoolteachers on how to teach their disciplines. At Johns Hopkins philologist Basil Gildersleeve organized a "pedagogical seminary," and in Wisconsin Frederick Jackson Turner traveled widely as a school inspector and offered his university course on the teaching of history in high

---

65. Quotations are from *USCommEd* (1896–7), p. 1647; David Tyack, "Pilgrims Progress: Towards a Social History of the School Superintendency, 1860–1960," 16 *HEQ* (1976): 257. Henry L. Taylor and James R. Parsons, Jr., ed., *Professional Education in the United States* (Albany, NY, 1899), pp. 3–49; David F. Labaree, *The Making of an American High School: The Credentials Market and the Central High School of Philadelphia, 1838–1939* (New Haven, CT, 1988), pp. 109–10.

66. Nicholas M. Butler, ed., *Education in the United States* (Albany, NY, 1900), p. vii.

67. Tappan, *University Education*, p. 68; Charles W. Dabney, *Universal Education in the South* (Chapel Hill, NC, 1936), vol. 1; Mary D. Vaughan, comp., *Historical Catalogue of Brown University, 1764–1904* (Providence, RI, 1905), p. 145.

68. Paul Mattingly, "Academia and Professional School Careers, 1840–1900," *Teachers College Record*, 83 (1981): 221–2.

schools. Even among the Harvard faculty "professors in all fields ... spoke at teachers' gatherings, and published articles on curriculum and methods."[69]

Consequently, I am proposing that, in order to understand professions during the late nineteenth and early twentieth centuries, it is necessary to recognize the cultural ideal of science and its locus in the domain of education. And in order to understand the domain of education, it is vital to see that the institutional and occupational boundaries within that domain were crossed relatively easily and often during this period. To be sure, there existed severe gender discrimination, and its implications for professional status will be discussed below. But occupational movement was common for men, who constituted about 80 percent of those working in higher education, 85 percent of public school administrators, and about 30 percent of public schoolteachers in the year 1900. These male educators moved back and forth across a wide range of positions in universities, colleges, schools, and educational offices that subsequently became separated by rigid boundaries of custom and administrative regulation.[70]

William Payne, who had been a teacher, principal, and superintendent, was named the first professor of pedagogy at the University of Michigan in 1879 and then Chancellor of the University of Nashville. His successor at Michigan, Elmer Brown, subsequently became professor of education at the University of California and chancellor of New York University. In 1887 Burke Hinsdale became the next professor of pedagogy at Michigan after serving as a teacher, college president, and the superintendent of schools in Cleveland. In that superintendency, Hinsdale succeeded Andrew Draper, who became president of the University of Illinois and then the first Commissioner of Education for the state of New York in 1904. Meanwhile Henry Judson became a schoolteacher for 15 years, then a professor at the University of Minnesota and president of the University of Chicago. E. C. Elliott went from schoolteaching to graduate study at Teachers College, and then to a professorship at the University of Wisconsin, the presidency of the University of Montana, and the presidency of Purdue University. Born in 1862, Philander Claxton taught school and then pedagogy at a normal school in North Carolina, becoming head of the department of education at the University of Tennessee, US Commissioner of Education, and provost of the University of Alabama. Martin Brumbaugh served as a teacher, principal, and county superintendent of schools before being appointed president of Juniata College and then Superintendent of Schools in Philadelphia. Edwin Alderman became a schoolteacher and school superintendent, then professor of education at the University of North Carolina, and successively president of that university in 1896, Tulane University in 1900,

69. Arthur G. Powell, *The Uncertain Profession: Harvard and the Search for Educational Authority* (Cambridge, MA, 1980), p. 17. Bishop, "Teaching at Johns Hopkins: The First Generation," pp. 507–10; Dupree, *Asa Gray*, p. 345.

70. *Historical Statistics*, series D233–682, H520–30, H689–99; Tyack, "Pilgrims Progress ... the School Superintendency, 1860–1960," p. 261; David Tyack and Elisabeth Hansot, *Managers of Virtue: Public School Leadership in America, 1820–1980* (New York, 1982), pp. 129–44. Cf. Geraldine Jonçich Clifford and James W. Guthrie, *Ed School: A Brief for Professional Education* (Chicago, 1988), p. 142; Labaree, "Career Ladders and the Early Public High-School Teacher: A Study of Inequality and Opportunity," pp. 159f.

and the University of Virginia in 1904. Born in 1875, Rufus Kleinsmid served as professor of education at DePauw University from 1905 until 1914, when he became president of the University of Arizona and then president of the University of Southern California. Also born in 1875, Henry Suzzalo studied at San Jose Normal School and Stanford, before working as a principal and earning a doctorate at Teachers College. He then became a professor of education, president of the University of Washington and president of the Carnegie Foundation for the Advancement of Teaching.[71]

This occupational mobility within education is evident in the careers of the presidents of leading midwestern state universities during this period. In her study of eleven such universities from 1867 to 1911, Joland Mohr found that nearly two-thirds of the presidents had served as superintendents of schools, normal school principals, or schoolteachers before becoming university presidents. Due to this personal background, these presidents, as well as those of the wealthy private institutions who were drawn from the social elite, maintained their active involvement across the spectrum of education.[72]

Thus, the institutional and occupational boundaries in late nineteenth- and early twentieth-century education were crossed far more often and easily than subsequently in the field of education or contemporaneously in other learned professions. Schoolteachers became university professors who became school superintendents who became college or university presidents, and vice versa. At the same time impermeable institutional, vocational, and sectarian boundaries existed within the other learned professions. It was inconceivable for itinerant Baptist preachers to ascend to leading Episcopal pulpits, for sectarian physicians to pass easily and credibly among the "regulars," or for rural debt-collectors or urban ambulance-chasers to rise to the US Supreme Court or the "Great Bar" on Wall Street. Conversely, eminent attorneys, physicians, or clergy often dismissed – or disowned – these lesser members of their profession, who actually constituted the majority of the membership. In contrast, 77 college and university presidents, state school

71. Vaughan, *Historical Catalogue of Brown University, 1764–1904*, p. 299; Allen S. Whitney, *History of the Professional Training of Teachers at the University of Michigan for The First Half-Century 1879 to 1929* (Ann Arbor, MI, 1931), pp. 37–59; Simon F. Kropp, "Hiram Hadley and the Founding of New Mexico State University," *Arizona and the West*, 9 (1967): 21–40; Raymond Callahan, *Education and the Cult of Efficiency: A Study of the Social Forces that have Shaped the Public Schools* (Chicago, 1962), pp. 111–3; Clinton B. Allison, "Early Professors of Education: Three Case Studies," in *The Professors of Teaching: An Inquiry*, ed. Richard Wisniewski and Edward R. DuCharme (Albany, NY, 1989), pp. 35–40; Donald T. Williams, "Henry Suzzallo and the University of a Thousand Years," *History of Higher Education Annual*, 5 (1985): 57–82; Barry M. Franklin, *Building the American Community: The School Curriculum and the Search for Social Control* (Philadelphia, 1986), pp. 35. See also entries in the *Biographical Dictionary of American Educators*.

72. Joland E. Mohr, "Higher Education and the Development of Professionalism in Post-Civil War America: A Content Analysis of Inaugural Addresses given by Selected Land-Grant College and University Presidents, 1867–1911" (PhD diss., University of Minnesota, 1984), pp. 198–251. See Thomas J. Cullen and Kathryn Sutton Cullen, comps., *The Obituaries of University of Washington Presidents, 1861–1958* (Seattle, WA, 1989); Bledstein, *The Culture of Professionalism*, app. 1.

superintendents, and other prominent citizens published a formal statement as early as 1874, affirming that schoolteaching "has become a regular occupation. Teachers mingle freely in the best social circles and enjoy the respect of the community."[73] However roseate this view, it was unthinkable for leading members of the bench and bar to express analogous sentiments about debt-collecting lawyers, or for eminent "regular" physicians to commend the Homeopaths or Eclectics.

Notwithstanding the permeability of institutional and occupational boundaries within the educational profession, a clearly delineated, lower-status majority did exist, constituting about 65 percent of educators in the year 1900. This majority comprised the women in the field.[74] In effect a gender boundary in education substituted for the impermeable sectarian, institutional, and occupational boundaries in the other learned professions. Within the educational crusade addressing "the chief problem of the world, its one holy cause," male educators moved easily among the various offices and institutions as need and opportunity arose. But women could not. Hence, these two points distinguished education from the other learned professions at the time: occupational mobility among offices and ranks and a gender distinction that effectively circumscribed the majority of the profession. The impermeable boundary within education was defined not by sect, institution or vocational role, as in theology, medicine, and law, but by gender.[75]

This argument can be roughly schematized as in Figure 4.1. The pyramids represent the status hierarchy of occupations and institutions in each profession. Within each pyramid, the line signifies a virtually impermeable boundary; within each sector, there was relative mobility occupationally and institutionally.

The mobility of male educators enhanced the intimate relationship between science and education, particularly the diffusion of science from the universities into all educational institutions. Secondary schools, even elementary schools, became imbued with the missionizing scientific spirit.[76] Commensurately, this broad-based educational sponsorship of the cultural ideal of science made it inevitable that "education *the* one and chief hope of the world" would be scientized along with theology, law, and medicine. As in those three fields, discussion about a "science of education" commenced in the antebellum era and grew louder after the Civil War.

73. Duane D. Doty and William T. Harris, *A Statement of the Theory of Education in the United States of America as Approved by Many Leading Educators* (Washington, DC, 1874), p. 19.

74. *Historical Statistics*, series D233–682, H520–30, H689–99.

75. I am indebted to my colleague Lynn D. Gordon for helping me to think about the issue of gender.

76. William T. Harris, *How to Teach Natural Science in Public Schools* (New York, 1871; 2d edn, 1895); E. L. Youmans et al., "Science Teaching in the Public Schools," *Popular Science Monthly*, 23 (1883): 207–14; Orra E. Underhill, *The Origins and Development of Elementary-School Science* (Chicago, 1941), chs. 1–3; Hanor A. Webb, "How General Science Began," *School Science and Mathematics*, 59 (1959): 421–30; Sidney Rosen, "The Rise of High-School Chemistry in America (to 1920)," *Journal of Chemical Education*, 33 (1956): 627–33; Rosen, "The Origins of High School General Biology," *School Science and Mathematics*, 59 (1959): 473–89; Geraldine Jonçich [Clifford], "Scientists and the Schools of the Nineteenth Century: The Case of American Physicists," *American Quarterly*, 18 (1966): 667–85.

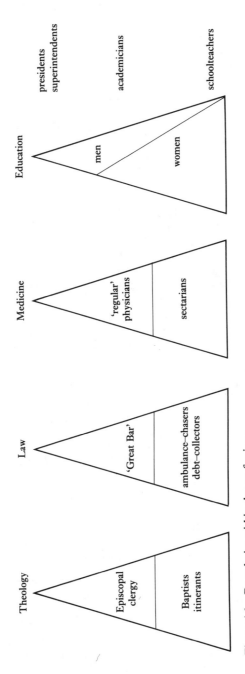

Figure 4.1 Boundaries within the professions

From the State Superintendent in Pennsylvania in 1865 to the nation's first full-time Professor of the Science and Art of Teaching in 1879, to Nicholas Murray Butler writing in *Science* in 1885, to Edward Thorndike in the 1900s, educators declaimed on "the science of education," "the scientific study of education," and "the mission of science in education."[77] This development deserves some attention because the relationship between science and education was formative for professions during this period and because recent scholars have often interpreted this relationship mindful more of subsequent experience than the context of the time.

The educational science came with a German pedigree. The precise nature of German influence upon American education in the second half of the nineteenth century has been much debated. But there is no doubt that the attribution of American practices to Germany, accurate or not, helped to legitimate those practices. "It is natural for us to look to Germany for significant educational movements," wrote a Stanford University professor in *Science* in 1909. Nor is it doubted that German universities advanced the study of *Pädagogik*, beginning in 1776 when Immanuel Kant offered the first lectures on the topic. By 1875 some 50 courses of lectures for teachers in the higher schools were offered in German universities, and Americans studying in Europe observed this practice, while those who remained at home consulted German texts.[78] With this in mind, educational leaders, such as the president of the University of Michigan, affirmed that "pedagogy should be an established course in the American university, as it is in the German," and some institutions, such as Wellesley College, hired a German professor to offer its first course in teaching. Meanwhile American educators published numerous studies comparing their practices, institutions, ideas, and salaries to the German.[79]

77. Samuel P. Bates, "Liberal Education," *American Journal of Education*, 15 (1865): 176; William H. Payne, *Contributions to the Science of Education* (New York, 1886); Nicholas Murray Butler, "The Science of Teaching," *Science*, 6 (1885): 529–30; Edward L. Thorndike, *Education: A First Book* (New York, 1914), p. 8; James R. Robarts, "The Quest for a Science of Education in the Nineteenth Century," *HEQ*, 8 (1968): 431–46; Paul H. Mattingly, *The Classless Profession: American Schoolmen in the Nineteenth Century* (New York, 1975), pp. 84–97.

78. Guido H. Marx, "Some Trends in Higher Education" *Science*, 29 (1909): 759; Heinrich G. Brzoska, *Die Notwendigkeit pädagogischer Seminare auf der Universität und ihre zweckmässige Einrichtung* (1835) newly ed. Wilhelm Rein (Leipzig, 1887); Friedrich A. W. Diesterweg, *Pädagogik; in systematischer Anordnung und zu Einführung in das Studium der wissenschaftlich Pädagogik* (1850), rev. H. Scherer (Giessen, 1890); Whitney, *History of the Professional Training of Teachers at the University of Michigan*, pp. 2–4; Jurgen Herbst, *And Sadly Teach: Teacher Education and Professionalization in American Culture* (Chicago, 1989), ch. 2. Clifford and Guthrie dismiss the influence of "a few German universities which had pioneered chairs in education." *Ed School*, p. 123.

79. James B. Angell, "Relations of the University to Public Education," *NEA* (1887): 147; Barbara Beatty, " 'The Kind of Knowledge of Most Worth to Young Women': Post-Secondary Vocational Training for Teaching and Motherhood at the Wheelock School, 1888–1914," *History of Higher Education Annual*, 6 (1986): 32. See Fred W. Atkinson, "The Professional Preparation of Secondary School Teachers in the United States" (Ph.D. diss.,

The "science of education" naturally entailed research and publication. The National Teachers Association had begun publishing proceedings and documents in 1858, and the US Commissioner of Education began issuing annual statistical reports in 1868. By 1900 nearly 300 periodicals were substantially devoted to education, and a *Bibliography of Education* had appeared. Bureaus of educational research then sprouted up, and *A Bibliography of Bibliographies ... of Educational Research* appeared soon after World War I.[80]

Notwithstanding this bulk and enthusiasm, the educational science encountered an increasing amount of skepticism as time passed. Indeed, scholars of education from Evelyn Clement in 1937 to Clifford and Guthrie in 1988 have maintained that nineteenth- and early twentieth-century academicians adopted an "adverse posture" toward the science and departments of education.[81] This conventional judgment, however, overlooks several important kinds of discontinuity in the assessment of educational science during this period.

One sort of discontinuity was definitional because "science of education" had various meanings between the 1860s and 1910s. These varieties may be enumerated in different ways, but at least four major types of educational science are easily identified. Reflecting the German pedigree of the field, there was, first, a tendency to define *Pädagogik* as an introspective "science of mind." This approach was particularly attractive to what Hamilton Cravens calls "philosopher-psychologists" who opposed Herbert Spencer's materialism, but it quickly gave way, second, to empirical educational science.[82] This second approach treated education as the professional field surmounted upon empirical or experimental psychology. Educational science thus became linked to the experimental New Psychology, which grew phenomenally between 1900 and 1920. Proponents, such as E. L. Thorndike, enthusiastically declared, "through the knowledge of the science of human

University of Leipzig, 1893); John F. Brown, *The Training of Teachers for Secondary Schools in Germany and the United States* (New York, 1911); Edward L. Thorndike et al., *The Financial Status of the Professor in America and in Germany* (New York, 1908); William H. Carpenter, "The Financial Status of the Professor in America and Germany," *Educational Review*, 36 (1908): 325–41.

80. Butler, ed., *Education in the United States*, p. viii; Will S. Monroe, *Bibliography of Education* (New York, 1897); Walter S. Monroe et al., *Ten Years of Educational Research, 1918–27* (Urbana, IL, 1928), p. 32; Walter S. Monroe et al., *A Bibliography of Bibliographies ... of Educational Research* (Urbana, IL, 1928).

81. Clifford and Guthrie, *Ed School*, p. 123; Evelyn A. Clement, "The Antagonism against the Departments of Education," *School and Society*, 49 (1937): 659–62. My analysis in this chapter differs from the helpful work of Clifford and Guthrie, who regard the period 1900–1940 as "formative" for the educational profession and who rely almost exclusively on Magali Sarfatti Larson and Burton Bledstein for their understanding of professionalism. *Ed School*, pp. 47–166. In his good book, Jurgen Herbst also follows Larson and Bledstein and expresses dismay that "professionalization takes command" in education. *And Sadly Teach: Teacher Education and Professionalization in American Culture*, p. 102, passim.

82. Arthur G. Powell, "The Education of Educators at Harvard, 1891–1912," in *Social Sciences at Harvard, 1860–1920*, ed. Paul S. Buck (Cambridge, MA, 1965), pp. 229–31, 252–3; Powell, *The Uncertain Profession*, pp. 41–3; Cravens, *The Triumph of Evolution ... 1900–1941*, pp. 69–70, 196–201.

nature ... the average graduate of Teachers College in 1950, ought to be able to give better advice to a high-school boy ... than Solomon, Socrates, and Benjamin Franklin all together could give."[83]

Partly in reaction to the popularity of this empirical, psychological variety, a third kind of "science of education" arose contemporaneously. Writing in 1896 on "The Demands of Sociology upon Pedagogy," Albion Small criticized "the naively mediaeval psychology" and argued for emphasizing the social conditions in which personality is formulated. This third kind of educational science, then, was "sociological," although this term was highly ambiguous. It meant the study of social policy to many, while to others, such as Émile Durkheim in France, it meant a distinct and precise methodology serving as the basis of a science of education.[84] Finally, between about 1905 and 1915 a fourth kind of educational science attempted to apply Frederick Taylor's principles of "scientific management" to the administration of burgeoning school systems. The "scientific" aspect of this science lay chiefly in statistics, which legitimated it in the eyes of Harvard President A. L. Lowell, for one. Whatever the legitimacy of this applied, quantitative, administrative science, it attracted funding for research, and this strengthened its position as well.[85]

By the 1910s observers explicitly recognized these successive approaches to the scientific study of education.[86] Indeed, it appears that these changes in the meaning of educational science roughly correspond to notable shifts in terminology.[87] Be that as it may, what cannot be denied is that "science of education" was defined in

83. Edward L. Thorndike, "The University and Vocational Guidance" (1913), in *Readings in Vocational Guidance*, ed. Meyer Bloomfield (Boston, 1915), p. 100. See, too, Thorndike, "The Contribution of Psychology to Education," *Journal of Educational Psychology*, 1 (1910): 6–7; Herman H. Horne, *The Psychological Principles of Education: A Study in the Science of Education* (New York, 1911), p. 21; W. L. Gooding, "Psychology and Pedagogy," *School Review*, 3 (1895): 559–61; Reuben P. Halleck, "Introduction," *Report of the Committee of Seventeen on the Preparation of High-School Teachers*, in *NEA* (1917): 523–35.

84. Albion W. Small, "The Demands of Sociology upon Pedagogy," *NEA* (1896): 174–5; Émile Durkheim, *Moral Education, A Study in the Theory and Application of the Sociology of Education* (1925), tr. Everett K. Wilson and Herman Schnurer (New York, 1961), ch. 1.

85. Powell, *The Uncertain Profession*, p. 85, ch. 4; Tyack and Hansot, *Managers of Virtue: Public School Leadership in America, 1820–1980*, pp. 152–60. The classic analysis is Callahan, *Education and the Cult of Efficiency* (1962).

86. Henry Suzzallo, "Editor's Introduction," in Arthur C. Perry, Jr., *The Status of the Teacher* (Boston, 1912), p. viii; Frank T. Carlton, *Economic Influences upon Educational Progress in the United States, 1820–1850* (1908; New York, 1965), pp. 2–3; Franklin Bobbitt, *The Curriculum* (Boston, 1918), p. 41.

87. Discussion about "science of education" before 1870 was often linked to proposals for professorial chairs in "didactics." This happened, for example, at Brown, Harvard, and Iowa. The shift to philosophical psychology reflected influence from Germany, where *Pädagogik* or "pedagogy" had been coined in the late eighteenth century, and the expressions "science of pedagogy" and "science of teaching" then became prominent in the 1870s, 1880s, and 1890s. For example, the nation's first full-time chair in education, at the University of Michigan, and first graduate school of education, at New York University, were designated in "teach-

different ways, and an "adverse posture" toward one sometimes implied advocacy toward another. This definitional discontinuity in the assessment of educational science was accompanied by another, temporal discontinuity.

Until the 1900s academicians in other fields were not particularly critical of educationists. Testimony to this fact comes from Allen S. Whitney and Walter S. Monroe, two prominent education professors who lived through the period and wrote on the topic. A committee of the American Academy of Arts and Sciences likewise testified that the period through 1905 comprised "the years of cooperation" between the professors of education and those of other disciplines.[88] To be sure, critical assessments could be heard about the study of education, but such criticism was encountered by most new disciplines of the time. This comparative point has not been appreciated by a number of recent scholars. Bernard Bailyn has intimated, while Arthur Powell and Theodore Sizer have stated explicitly, that education "in the 1880s and early 1890s ... hardly existed at all in the sense of other academic subjects."[89] But this view profoundly misrepresents the state of "other academic subjects" in the late nineteenth-century, ranging from biology to English, especially those that would become the social sciences.[90]

---

ing" and "pedagogy" respectively. Then, in the 1890s the terms "didactics" and "pedagogy" were sloughed away, and "education" predominated. By 1908, when William H. Burnham observed, "The word pedagogy itself is in disrepute," many departments of "pedagogy" had been renamed or superseded by departments of "education," as happened at the University of Tennessee at the turn of the century. Burnham, "The History of Education," in *The History of Education as a Professional Subject*, ed. William H. Burnham and Henry Suzzallo (New York, 1908), p. 4. Thomas Hill, "Remarks on the Study of Didactics in Colleges," *American Journal of Education*, 5 (1865): 177–9; Timothy F. O'Leary, *An Inquiry into the General Purposes, Functions, and Organization of Selected University Schools of Education* (Washington, DC, 1941), p. 240; Edmund J. James, *Chairs of Pedagogics in our Universities: A Discussion of the Science and Art of Education as University Disciplines* (Philadelphia, 1887); Charles K. Adams, "The Teaching of Pedagogy in Colleges and Universities," *Addresses and Proceedings of the New England Association of Colleges and Preparatory Schools* (1888): 16–29; Butler, "The Science of Teaching," pp. 529–30; Whitney, *History of the Professional Training of Teachers at the University of Michigan*, pp. 2–3; Albert E. Winship, *Is there a Science of Pedagogy?* (Boston, 1892); Payne, *Contributions to Education as a Science*; Allison, "Early Professors of Education: Three Case Studies," pp. 29–34.

88. Often, the neighboring normal schools offered the stiffest resistance to the establishment of chairs and departments of pedagogy at colleges and universities. Whitney, *History of the Professional Training of Teachers at the University of Michigan*, pp. 28–40, 88–91, 113–4; Walter S. Monroe, *Teaching-Learning Theory and Teacher Education, 1890–1950* (Urbana, IL, 1952), p. 209, chs. 6, 7, 9–12; Howard M. Jones, Francis Keppel, Robert Ulich [Committee on the Teaching Profession of the American Academy of Arts and Sciences], "On the Conflict between the 'Liberal Arts' and the 'Schools of Education'," *ACLS Newsletter*, 5 (1954): 17–9; Willard S. Elsbree, *The American Teacher: Evolution of a Profession in a Democracy* (New York, 1939), ch. 23.

89. Theodore R. Sizer and Arthur G. Powell, "Changing Conceptions of the Professor of Education," in *To be a Phoenix: The Education Professoriate*, ed. J. S. Counelis (Bloomington, IN, 1969), p. 62; Bernard Bailyn, "Education as a Discipline: Some Historical Notes," in *The Discipline of Education*, ed. John Walton and J. L. Kuethe (Madison, WI, 1963), pp. 125–7.

90. Charles W. Eliot, "Liberty in Education" (1885), in *Educational Reform* (New York,

Psychology was relatively well established among the young social sciences. Yet the first professorship in the United States appeared only in 1887, fifteen years after that in pedagogy, and historians have shown that psychologists" "desire for scientific stature was ... largely frustrated in the years before 1917.... They were unable to reach agreement among themselves as to the definitions of their field and its phenomena, or with regard to proper methods of investigation."[91] Meanwhile political science and anthropology were fledgling disciplines. Of the some 400 colleges and universities in the country in 1890, merely ten claimed to teach "political science," and none anthropology, while 114 colleges and universities offered courses in pedagogy, and 31 had established professorial chairs in the subject. By 1903 only five colleges and universities had established professorships in anthropology, while 135 had chairs of pedagogy or heads of education departments, and 230 offered courses in pedagogy. By the start of the World War less than one-tenth of the some 600 colleges and universities taught anthropology, about one-quarter taught "political science," and almost half offered courses in pedagogy.[92]

Scarcely more than a tenth of those 600 institutions offered courses in "sociology," which also had severe problems of legitimation. "Neither in 1892 nor in 1901 had sociology justified itself as a body of doctrine, as a point of view, or as a method of research," noted a prominent sociologist in *American Journal of Sociology* in 1916. Indeed, the study of education was in many institutions through this period explicitly more legitimate than sociology. Émile Durkheim was the world's leading scientific sociologist, and his first faculty appointment, in 1887 at Bordeaux, was to teach pedagogy. "[T]his was the cover under which sociology was first officially introduced into a French university," notes Stephen Lukes, "Indeed it was only as a special favour that [Durkheim] was allowed to add the word 'Sociology' to 'Pedagogy' in the Faculty List." In 1902 Durkheim assumed the chair in "Science of Education" at the Sorbonne, and not until 1913 was he permitted to add the word 'sociology' to this title.[93] Since Durkheim was at the forefront of the

1898), pp. 138–40; Louis F. Snow, *The College Curriculum in the United States* (New York, 1907), p. 180; Dorothy Ross, "American Social Science and the Idea of Progress," in *The Authority of Experts*, ed. Thomas L. Haskell (Bloomington, IN, 1984), pp. 157–8. On the "unimpressive" results of social science, see Richard J. Bernstein, *The Restructuring of Social and Political Theory* (New York, 1976), p. 32; Jeffrey T. Bergner, *The Origin of Formalism in Social Science* (Chicago, 1981), p. ix, passim.

91. Quotations are from Thomas M. Camfield, "The Professionalization of American Psychologists, 1870–1917," *Journal of the History of the Behavioral Sciences*, 9 (1973): 73; Burnham, *How Superstition Won and Science Lost*, p. 91; Sheldon M. Stern, "William James and the New Psychology," in *Social Sciences at Harvard, 1860–1920*, ed. Paul S. Buck (Cambridge, MA, 1965), pp. 205, 219–22; Cravens, *The Triumph of Evolution ... 1900–1941*, pp. 56–86, 196–201.

92. *USCommEd* (1904), pp. 1169–71, 1688; Carter Alexander, "Aims of Departments of Education in Colleges and Universities," in *Work in Education in Colleges and Universities* (Chicago, IL, 1915), pp. 3–6; Elsbree, *The American Teacher*, pp. 320–31; Cravens, *The Triumph of Evolution ... 1900–1941*, pp. 89–120; Daniel T. Rodgers, *Contested Truths: Keywords in American Politics since Independence* (New York, 1987), p. 156.

93. Albion W. Small, "Fifty Years of Sociology in the United States (1865–1915)," *American Journal of Sociology*, 21 (1916): 802; Steven Lukes, *Émile Durkheim: His Life and*

field, it is scarcely surprising that in the United States in 1916 Albion Small affirmed that "the designation 'sociology' is a mischievously ambiguous middle term."[94]

Consequently skepticism could be heard about the study of education before 1910. But this was scarcely anomalous. The fact that pedagogy might be attacked by some for not being scientific and by others for trying to be too scientific reflected a pattern of discussion concerning many humanistic, social, and professional studies of the time. Moreover, educational science in the United States, as well as Germany and France, seemed to be validated by enrollments and funding exceeding those of other new disciplines.

By about 1910, however, the view of education began to turn from this conventional skepticism to a deep antipathy that was expressed even in the popular press. In his dissertation on "The Opposition to Schools of Education by Professors of the Liberal Arts," Eugene Auerbach found relatively little vituperation before 1910. But in subsequent years "Hard Words About Pedagogy" began to appear: philosopher Charles Gayley charged educationists with "fallacies of ignorance and personal conceit"; Warner Fite complained in the *Nation* of "soft pedagogics"; a writer in *The Unpopular Review* wished to "shut the mouths and vacate the chairs of the professors of pedagogy"; Alfred Stearns in *Atlantic Monthly* lamented "all the latest educational nostrums that have been foisted upon us"; and classicist Louis Ford maintained that the requirements of educationists were like "asphyxiating gas." Meanwhile the director of the School of Education at the University of Chicago examined the "attacks on departments of education."[95] The recent view that an "adverse posture" toward "science of education" predominated in nineteenth- and twentieth-century higher education therefore has to be qualified in light of this temporal discontinuity. The nature and amount of criticism of pedagogy changed markedly in the first decade of the twentieth century.

In addition to definitional and temporal differences, geographical and gender differences introduced discontinuity in the assessment of pedagogy. Opposition to the "science of education" existed primarily in eastern colleges and universities, particularly the private elite institutions, as C. C. Rounds noted already in 1881. Because these institutions, particularly Harvard, have dominated the historiography of higher education, judgments about the status of pedagogy have tended to be

---

Work, A Historical and Critical Study (Stanford, CA, 1985), pp. 109, 364–6. See Frank L. Tolman, "The Study of Sociology in Institutions of Learning in the United States," *American Journal of Sociology*, 7 (1902): 797–838; *ibid*, 8 (1902–3): 85–121, 251–72, 531–58.

94. Small, "Fifty Years of Sociology in the United States (1865–1915)," p. 830.

95. [anon.], "Hard Words About Pedagogy," *Dial*, 51 (1911): 239–41; Charles M. Gayley, *Idols of Education* (New York, 1910), p. 137; Warner Fite, "Pedagogy and the Teacher," *Nation*, 93 (1911): 207–9; "If I were a College President," *Unpopular Review*, 5 (1916): 64–5; Alfred E. Stearns, "Some Fallacies in the Modern Educational Scheme," *Atlantic Monthly*, 118 (1916): 650; Louis E. Ford, "Classics and the Asphyxiating Gas of the Educational Requirements," *School and Society*, 5 (1917): 336. C. H. Judd, "Editorial Notes," *Elementary School Journal*, 12 (1911): 138–40; Eugene C. Auerbach, "The Opposition to Schools of Education by Professors of the Liberal Arts: A Historical Analysis" (PhD diss., University of Southern California, 1957), chs. 1–3.

made from their perspective.[96] Apart from this group, however, the story is rather different. University departments and schools of education in Iowa, Michigan, Wisconsin, Indiana, Illinois, Ohio, and Washington experienced relatively little antipathy through the first decade of the twentieth century. For example, in her unpublished autobiography, political scientist Theresa McMahon spoke respectfully of "professors of education" at the universities of Wisconsin and Washington early in the twentieth century. In contrast, the faculty of the college of business, McMahon wrote, "brought into the university a destructive force as far as the intellectual caliber of the teaching force was concerned," and "were treated by the rest of the faculty with a sort of mild contempt."[97]

That McMahon was a woman at public western universities is telling because the geographic discontinuity in views of educational science generally corresponded with views on the education of women. Mid-western and far western universities were the first to admit women: Iowa in 1855, Wisconsin in 1867, Kansas, Indiana, and Minnesota in 1869, Michigan, Missouri and California in 1870. These universities also led the movement to establish chairs and departments of pedagogy, in which women predominantly enrolled. Conversely, opposition to the study of education usually accompanied resistance to the enrollment of women, and both kinds of opposition generally obtained in elite eastern institutions. At Columbia University, for example, the University Council responded to an 1892 proposal to incorporate Teachers College by adjudging: "there is no such subject as Education and moreover it would bring into the University women who are not wanted." Meanwhile the perception that normal schools, which enrolled mostly women, were inferior to colleges, which enrolled mostly men, was offered as a reason to deny admission to either women or pedagogy.[98] Whether such opposition was directed more to women or to educational science is difficult to determine; and whether western openness arose from principle, politics, or desire for enrollment is likewise obscure. What is clear is that geography and gender together introduced more discontinuity in attitudes toward educational science.

Finally, beyond the definitional, temporal, geographical, and gender-related discontinuities in the supposedly universal "adverse posture" toward educational science, there was a good deal of ambivalence within institutions, especially within

96. C. C. Rounds, "Lines of Advance," *NEA* (1881): 15; J. Stephen Hazlett, "Education Professors; The Centennial of an Identity Crisis," in *The Professors of Teaching: An Inquiry,* ed. Richard Wisniewski and Edward R. DuCharme (Albany, NY, 1989), pp. 21–2.

97. Theresa McMahon, "My Story" (1958), in *Lone Voyagers: Academic Women in Coeducational Institutions, 1870–1937,* ed. Geraldine Jonçich Clifford (New York, 1989), pp. 255, 261–2, 270, 276–7; Angell, "Relations of the University to Public Education," p. 147; Leigh G. Hubbell, *The Development of University Departments of Education in Six States of the Middle West* (Washington, DC, 1924); Auerbach, "The Opposition to Schools of Education by Professors of the Liberal Arts," chs. 1–3.

98. Quoted in James E. Russell, *Founding Teachers College: Reminiscences of the Dean Emeritus* (New York, 1937), pp. 26, 64ff.; Lawrence A. Cremin, David A. Shannon, and Mary E. Townsend, *A History of Teachers College, Columbia University* (New York, 1954), pp. 19–31, 70ff; William McAndrew, "The Present Status of the Professions – Public-School Teaching," *World's Work,* 5 (1902): 3192; Auerbach, "The Opposition to Schools of Education by Professors of the Liberal Arts," pp. 41–3.

elite universities where the "adverse posture" was most pronounced. The pattern of ambivalence, which has generally gone unnoticed, was that the reforming president befriended, if not championed, pedagogy, while the faculty in competing disciplines were skeptical, and the rest of the faculty indifferent. At Johns Hopkins, for example, President D. C. Gilman announced in his 1876 inaugural address that "philosophy, principles, and methods" of education would be a formal part of the curriculum. At Columbia three successive presidents from 1864 through the first World War advocated the study of education and supported the founding of Teachers College and its incorporation as a graduate faculty into the university, despite opposition from the faculty. Similarly, Presidents J. B. Angell at Michigan, C. K. Adams and J. G. Schurman at Cornell, D. S. Jordan at Stanford, W. R. Harper at Chicago, and A. T. Hadley at Yale promoted and protected their department of education.[99]

The efforts of these presidents were part of their promotion and protection of a broad range of humanistic, social, and professional studies that were emerging at elite research universities through the early twentieth century. This fact is exemplified by the situation at Harvard, where the view of educational studies was not uniformly hostile, or even hostile at all, at least through the 1900s. There was a good deal of skepticism, combined with some optimism, all of which amounted to institutional ambivalence and contradiction.[100] This situation typified the status of

99. Quotation is from Bishop, "Teaching at Johns Hopkins: The First Generation," p. 511; Cremin, Shannon, and Townsend, *A History of Teachers College*, pt. 1; Russell, *Founding Teachers College*, chs. 2–3; Whitney, *History of the Professional Training of Teachers at the University of Michigan*, pp. 88–91, 113–4; Adams, "The Teaching of Pedagogy in Colleges and Universities," pp. 16–29; Jacob G. Schurman, "Teaching – a Trade or a Profession?", *Forum*, 21 (1896): 171–85; Sears and Henderson, *Cubberley of Stanford*, pp. 61–103; Thomas W. Goodspeed, *A History of the University of Chicago: The First Quarter-Century* (Chicago, 1916), p. 207; John S. Brubacher et al., *The Department of Education at Yale University, 1891–1958* (New Haven, CT, 1960), ch. 1.

100. While the nondescript President Thomas Hill in 1865 had recommended "*the establishment of a Normal School in a University*," President Charles W. Eliot, the innovator in professional education, rejected a proposal to establish professional training of teachers at Harvard. In 1890, however, he reversed himself and persuaded the Harvard faculty to establish a committee to plan such a course. To chair this committee, Eliot appointed Josiah Royce who denied the possibility of a "science of education." To teach the non-scientific "history and art of teaching," Eliot in 1891 appointed Paul Hanus, whose only degree was in science. William James was assigned to teach the scientific side of pedagogy, and he promptly declared that he knew nothing about pedagogy. Meanwhile, Eliot publicly denied that the Harvard faculty had any interest in pedagogy, although Hanus reported that Harvard opposition to the study of education was virtually extinct. In 1901 Hanus was promoted and tenured, a decision that Eliot regarded as signifying Harvard's commitment to the study of education and that John Dewey noted with mischievous delight. By World War I, antipathy toward the study of education at Harvard had grown enormously along with the Division of Education. Hill, "Remarks on The Study of Didactics in Colleges," p. 179; Josiah Royce, "Is there a Science of Education?", *Educational Review*, 1 (1891): 132; John Dewey, "Education as a University Study," *Columbia University Quarterly*, 9 (1907): 284; Hugh Hawkins, *Between Harvard and America: The Educational Leadership of Charles W. Eliot* (New York, 1972), pp. 254–6; Powell, *The Uncertain Profession*, p. 41, chs. 2–4.

many humanistic, social, and professional disciplines. Until about 1910 the "science of education" was at the very least holding its own, even within elite universities.

In sum, we have seen that the cultural ideal of science was manifested in the widespread acclaim for and fascination with natural and physical sciences and their architectonical influence over other domains of knowledge. Concurrently, the institutional locus of science was established in education, whose institutional and occupational boundaries were crossed relatively easily and often by men, and this fact enhanced the diffusion of science through schools and colleges as well as universities. Meanwhile the educational sponsorship of science prompted enthusiastic efforts to develop a "science of education." Due to all these developments, it became increasingly difficult to discuss science apart from educational institutions, and education basked in the reflected cultural authority of science. This development magnified the estimable status that learning had long conveyed, and resulted in a brief era of intense excitement about education.

Commencing in the 1860s with the appearance of the Morrill Act, the US Bureau of Education, the National Education Association, and a host of other agencies and institutions, this brief educational era lasted the duration of the Peabody Fund in the South (1867–1914) and the administrations of C. W. Eliot at Harvard (1869–1909), J. B. Angell at Michigan (1871–1909), and a legion of other leading educational reformers at all levels. This era peaked between about 1890 and 1905, a time that the dean of the nation's leading college of education later called "the richest of our lives." It was a period that members of the American Academy of Arts and Sciences later described as "the years of cooperation" between educationists and other professors, a period when education "was under the guidance of a group of men who spoke with authority because they were considered leaders both in education and in the cultural life of the nation."[101] Americans had developed an "educational consciousness," affirmed the President of the Carnegie Foundation for the Advancement of Teaching in 1910. It was "a stage in civilization in which the people conceive of education as a natural and necessary activity of the State itself."[102] Between the 1860s and the 1910s it thus became possible to regard "education as the last and highest form of evolution" and "*the* one and chief hope of the world."[103]

"history written by historians for historians"

Such testimony declaring the importance of education is well known to historians; the interesting point is that it is not believed. The growth of science and education

---

101. Russell, *Founding Teachers College*, p. 51; Jones, Keppel, Ulich, "On the Conflict between the 'Liberal Arts' and the 'Schools of Education'," p. 17.

102. Henry S. Pritchett, "The Spirit of the State Universities," *Atlantic Monthly*, 105 (1910): 741–4.

103. Thomas Davidson, *A History of Education* (New York, 1900), p. v; Hall, *Life and Confessions of a Psychologist*, p. 521.

and their intimate relationship are not doubted, but the educational enthusiasm, particularly expressed by educationists near the turn of the century, is scarcely credited. In fact, the dominant view in historiography is that educators at all levels constituted a demeaned and relatively undesirable profession. This paradox of an exalted view of education cobbled to a degraded view of the educational profession is partly explained by the neglect of comparative standards – both temporal and professional – for what is inherently a relative judgment. Scholars' assessments of professional status are often derived from studying one profession over a relatively brief time period. But in order to assess professional status, the observer must have a sense of change over time and of the experience of other professions.[104] Historians often cite praise or criticism of one profession in order to demonstrate its status without recognizing that similar praise of criticism was being expressed about other fields.

Without such comparative standards derived from studying the full context, scholars examining one vocation in one period have tended to impose their *a priori* views upon the past. This imposition has particularly influenced recent historiography regarding the educational profession, which has been shaped by the increasing concern in the 1970s and 1980s about school reform and historical injustices suffered by women. The problem here, needless to say, is not the validity of these concerns, but the assumption that those issues presented themselves at the beginning of the century much as they do at the end. Beyond these concerns, which will be addressed below, another kind of presentism has recently skewed the historical understanding of professions in the late nineteenth and early twentieth century and, particularly, the educational profession. This kind appears in the broad revisionist movement occurring in historiography since the late 1950s.

In regard to education, the *locus classicus* of this movement is an essay published by Bernard Bailyn in 1960. In this essay and another from 1963, Bailyn seemingly devastated the historiography written by turn-of-the-century educationists and proceeded to offer a new historical approach. As a result he has been routinely and enthusiastically cited by way of dismissing the old historiography. Ironically, however, the indictments made against this older work can also be turned against the revisionist scholarship, a fact that calls into question the greater validity attributed to the newer work.

Bailyn charged, first, that the educationists' historiography was moralistic and teleological, while, by implication, professional historiography was free of these presumptions.[105] Yet it has been shown that in the two decades after the founding of the American Historical Association (AHA) in 1884 Darwinian historicism dominated the viewpoint of most historians, and those in the vanguard were

---

104. Richard Hofstadter, *The Age of Reform from Bryan to F.D.R.* (New York, 1955), p. 153; Joseph Greenblum and Leonard I. Pearlin, "Vertical Mobility and Prejudice: A Socio-psychological Analysis," in *Class, Status, and Power,* ed. Reinhard Bendix and Seymour M. Lipset (Glencoe, IL, 1953), pp. 480–91.

105. Bernard Bailyn, *Education in the Forming of American Society: Needs and Opportunities for Study* (1960; New York, 1972), p. 9; Bailyn, "Education as a Discipline: Some Historical Notes," p. 132.

only beginning to enshrine the "objectivity" of "scientific history."[106] Hence, professional historians of the time were addressing history very much "in the fashion of contemporary educationists," as Wilson Smith noted in a careful response to Bailyn.[107] In addition, Bailyn proposed that turn-of-the-century educationists "directed their attention almost exclusively to the ... formal institutions of instruction" and neglected the social context and varied forms of all the institutions that transfer culture. The irony here is that a "sociological" viewpoint had emerged as a dominant perspective among educationists by the 1900s. Meanwhile the leaders of the AHA concluded that this emphasis on the social context of education undermined their historicism, which they sought to defend in order to preserve their own influence over history curricula in the public schools. Contrary to Bailyn's view, then, the educationists were in "advance" of the historians in relating education to social context, as Ray Hiner has demonstrated. In fact, it was the educationists who sounded the earliest and loudest warning that "the school cannot be understood in isolation. It has no meaning outside of its social setting. It is social life which has created the school," as Henry Suzzallo observed from Teachers College in 1908.[108]

This attention to social context also controverts Bailyn's further charge that early educationists wrote their history "in almost total isolation" from the leading historians of the day. This indictment was, first of all, no great criticism in itself, given the context of historiography at the time. Moreover, it was not true. The leaders of the AHA and National Education Association (NEA) shared a Darwinian historicism through 1900, and collaborated closely on planning the history curriculum for the secondary and elementary schools. Albert Bushnell Hart, one of Bailyn's forerunners in the Harvard history department, was a key figure in this collaboration, serving as a leading member of the AHA and the NEA Committee of Ten. Meanwhile another active member of the AHA, who was a history professor

---

106. Peter Novick, *That Noble Dream: The "Objectivity Question" and the American Historical Profession* (Chicago, 1988), pt. 1; Carol F. Baird, "Albert Bushnell Hart: The Rise of the Professional Historian," in *Social Sciences at Harvard, 1860–1920,* ed. Paul S. Buck (Cambridge, MA, 1965), pp. 135–6; John Higham, *History: Professional Scholarship in America* (Baltimore, MD, 1965), pp. 1–103; George H. Callcott, *History in the United States, 1800–1860* (Baltimore, MD, 1970), p. 225; N. Ray Hiner, "Professions in Process: Changing Relations between Historians and Educators, 1896–1911," *HEQ,* 12 (1972): 34.

107. Wilson Smith, "Comments," in *The Discipline of Education,* ed. John Walton and J. L. Kuethe (Madison, WI, 1963), p. 141; Lawrence A. Cremin, *The Wonderful World of Ellwood Patterson Cubberley: An Essay on the Historiography of American Education* (New York, 1965), p. 33, ch. 3.

108. Bailyn, *Education in the Forming of American Society,* p. 9; Henry Suzzallo, "The Professional Use of the History of Education," in *The History of Education as a Professional Subject,* ed. W. H. Burnham and Suzzallo (New York, 1908), p. 55; Hiner, "Professions in Process: Changing Relations between Historians and Educators, 1896–1911," pp. 34–56. See Burnham, "The History of Education," p. 21; Ernest C. Moore, "The History of Education," *School Review,* 11 (1903): 356; Arthur O. Norton, "The Scope and Aims of the History of Education," *Educational Review,* 27 (1904): 443–55. Bailyn cites some of these individuals but dismisses their insight because they did not complete the task. "Education as a Discipline: Some Historical Notes," p. 129n.

at Hiram College, became the second occupant of the nation's first full-time chair in pedagogy at the University of Michigan in 1887.[109] Leading educationists were scarcely isolated from professional historians of the day.

Finally, Bailyn maintained that the historiography of the educationists was self-centered and self-aggrandizing. "Its purpose was to dignify a newly self-conscious profession, education.... [T]he history written by the educational missionaries of the turn of the century derived directly from their professional interests."[110] We shall return to this point below, but it should be noted here that, just as Bailyn overlooked the shared perspective of historians and educationists and their collaboration in planning the history curricula for the schools, so he neglected the fact that this collaboration "manifested the professional ideology and interests of the leadership of the history profession," as well as of educationists.[111]

Overall, it is fair to say that Bailyn's assessment of the educationists' historiography was cursory. Ignoring the turn-of-the-century context, he held up as typical two textbooks intended for college sophomores and another textbook for school administrators,[112] and compared them to the standards of professional historiography from a half century later. In so doing, he neglected the educationists' acknowledgement that the books were flawed and the testimony of contemporary scholars that these textbooks were the best thing available on the topic.[113]

Invoking Bailyn's authority and example, a line of revisionist social historiography nevertheless appeared and grew increasingly moralistic, teleological, and self-aggrandizing. In this way, the methodological revision that Bailyn envisioned was combined with an ideological revisionism, as demonstrated in the works of Michael Katz. The distinction between methodological and ideological revisionism was, needless to say, not sharp and clean. Many scholars, such as Katz, seemed to believe that the latter necessarily accompanied the former, and the distinction was further muddled by cannonades against "revisionism."[114] Meanwhile the work of

109. Bailyn, *Education in the Forming of American Society*, p. 9; Baird, "Albert Bushnell Hart: The Rise of the Professional Historian," p. 142; Powell, *The Uncertain Profession*, p. 59; Whitney, *History of the Professional Training of Teachers at the University of Michigan*, pp. 37–59.

110. Bailyn, *Education in the Forming of American Society*, pp. 7, 9.

111. Hiner, "Professions in Process: Changing Relations between Historians and Educators, 1896–1911," p. 39.

112. Paul Monroe, *Textbook in the History of Education* (New York, 1906); Davidson, *A History of Education*; Ellwood P. Cubberley, *Public Education in the United States* (Boston, 1919).

113. Burnham, "History of Education," pp. 1–27; Suzzallo, "The Professional Use of the History of Education," pp. 29–57; Moore, "The History of Education," p. 356; Norton, "Scope and Aims of the History of Education," pp. 443–55; Gayley, *Idols of Education*, p. 136; "Hard Words About Pedagogy," p. 239; Sears and Henderson, *Cubberley of Stanford*, pp. 93–7, 108, 121–2; Cremin, *The Wonderful World of Ellwood Patterson Cubberley*, pp. 1–5; Jones, Keppel, and Ulich, "On the Conflict between the 'Liberal Arts' and the 'Schools of Education'," p. 37.

114. See Michael B. Katz, *The Irony of Early School Reform: Educational Innovation in Mid-Nineteenth Century Massachusetts* (Cambridge, MA, 1968); Diane Ravitch, *The Revisionists Revised: A Critique of the Radical Attack on the Schools* (New York, 1978).

some historians, such as Lawrence Cremin, demonstrated the possibility of writing sophisticated historiography without casting the turn-of-the-century educationists as historiographical villains, as they were for Bailyn, or historical villains, as they were for Katz. These broad contours of the historiography of education since 1960 are well known, and it scarcely needs to be said that "great good resulted" from this revisionism, as Bailyn conceded to the educationists.[115] But the question remains: why were revisionist historians so quick to invoke Bailyn and dismiss the educationists' historiography and, concomitantly, the educationists' views about their own profession and time?

We have noted some of the educationists' optimistic testimony about themselves and their work, and David Tyack has observed "the powerful optimism so many superintendents displayed in the face of immense challenges in the early twentieth century." Indeed, the most snobbish meritocrats of science at the turn of the century conceded the promise, even the accomplishment, of the scientific professors of education. In 1906 and again in 1910 J. McKeen Cattell drew up a famous list of the 4,000 foremost American scientists with stars indicating the top 1,000. The eligible fields from which individuals were drawn included "education, economics or other subjects not commonly included under the exact and natural sciences."[116] At the same time Abraham Flexner, who unflinchingly noted the inferiority of engineers and consigned the majority of medical schools to oblivion, nevertheless observed,

> The professors of secondary education in the state universities are the evangelists of this genuine [educational renaissance]. Young, intelligent, well trained, these sturdy leaders ceaselessly traverse the length and breadth of their respective states, stimulating, suggesting, guiding, organizing. It is an inspiring spectacle.[117]

Cattell and Flexner cannot be dismissed as self-aggrandizing educationists. Moreover, it is significant that educationists' confidence and pride constituted a new attitude, for earlier pedagogues had freely lamented their low status. The change in attitude must be explained, and a change in status is the most straightforward explanation. One must therefore ask why Bailyn and those who followed him doubted the educationists' testimony about their own time. The answer seems to be twofold.

First is the context of educational studies in the 1950s and 1960s. After the so-called "pioneer period" in educational research through the 1910s, the field did

115. Bailyn, "Education as a Discipline: Some Historical Notes," p. 129. See *Education and History,* a special issue of the *Harvard Educational Review,* 46 (1976): 293–508; John H. Best, ed., *Historical Inquiry in Education: A Research Agenda* (Washington, DC, 1983); "New Business in the History of Education," *Educational Studies,* 18 (1987): 34–52.

116. Tyack, "Pilgrims Progress: Towards a Social History of the School Superintendency, 1860–1960," p. 262; J. McKeen Cattell, *American Men of Science: A Biographical Dictionary* (New York, 1906), preface; Cattell, *American Men of Science* (1910).

117. Flexner, *Medical Education in the United States,* p. 40. Paul Shorey even associated Flexner with the educationists in his attack upon them in "The Assault on Humanism (II)," *The Atlantic Monthly,* 120 (1917): 98. By 1930, Flexner saw little merit in education schools, and recent scholars have projected his later view on to the past. *Universities: American, English, German* (New York, 1930), pp. 96–110.

not fulfill the expectations of the first generation of educationists. The second and third generations, notwithstanding their roseate pronouncements, made little creative contribution to scholarship and pointed to healthy enrollments as evidence of the quality of their work. This situation was vilified by Arthur Bestor in 1953, and the following year a committee of the American Academy of Arts and Sciences observed that conflict between liberal arts faculties and schools of education had reached "a degree of vehemence." In 1957 the launching of Sputnik sparked criticism of the schools and educational studies, and in 1958 Yale University closed its department of education. The following year Bailyn presented his initial essay at a conference of historians, and it is scarcely surprising that he found the enthusiasm of turn-of-the-century educationists "strange as it may now seem."[118] Consequently the state of educational studies in the 1950s prompted one kind of presentist doubting that anyone could have taken the educationists seriously at the turn of the century.

Second, the professional context of historians also influenced their assessment of educationists' historiography. Bailyn was calling for professional historians to rescue the historiography of education so that it "will no longer suffer from neglect and ill-founded conclusions."[119] He argued that only a professional historian could write the history of education, because "[t]he guidelines for the historian probing these problems of American education lie outside the area of education itself; the story ... will not be grasped by one who approaches it with the special problems of education exclusively, or even primarily, in mind." He then moved quickly to the conclusion that "the study of education for the historian is not a science and ... not a discipline."[120]

This reasoning indicates the nature of historians' professional context, and provides the link between educational historiography and the historiography of other professions. To see this link, one must underscore the four points of Bailyn's argument: (i) educationists cannot tell their own history; (ii) one reason is because the history told by educationists is self-serving and not to be trusted; (iii) another reason is that educationists lack the requisite expertise, which concerns the social context at large rather than the internal developments of education; (iv) in fact, these internal developments – the educationists' expertise – exist only due to their artificial isolation from the social context and explain very little at all. While applauding his reasoning, subsequent historians of education rarely recognized that "what Bailyn has said about the limitations of educational history written by

118. Monroe et al., "Ten Years of Educational Research, 1918–27," ch. 2; Jones, Keppel, Ulich, "On the Conflict between the 'Liberal Arts' and the 'Schools of Education'," pp. 17–38; Bailyn, "Education as a Discipline: Some Historical Notes," p. 126; Arthur Bestor, *Educational Wastelands: The Retreat from Learning in our Public Schools* (Urbana, IL, 1953); Brubacher et al., *The Department of Education at Yale University, 1891–1958*, ch. 4; Auerbach, "The Opposition to Schools of Education by Professors of the Liberal Arts"; Elsie A. Hug *Seventy-five Years in Education: The Role of the School of Education, New York University, 1890–1965* (New York, 1965), ch. 7.

119. Lester J. Cappon, "Foreword," in Bailyn, *Education in the Forming of American Society*, p. x.

120. Bailyn, "Education as a Discipline: Some Historical Notes," pp. 138–9.

schoolmen applies equally well to the bulk of the historical literature in a field like medicine or law" and other professional fields.[121]

From the turn of the century historians trained in history departments had been applying the slightly disparaging term "church historian" to scholars trained and teaching in divinity schools about the history of Christianity. The point of the distinction was that "church historians" made certain doctrinal assumptions and neglected the influence of social forces upon the ecclesiastical institutions. Meanwhile Benjamin Twiss in 1942 had emphasized the pejorative term "lawyers' history," and in 1958 Christopher Hill called on historians "to take legal history out of the hands of lawyers, as religious history has been taken away from the theologians, and to relate them both to social development."[122] Professional historians thus began to dismiss lawyers' history as, at worst, undisguised apologetics, and, at best, "genetic legal history" meaning "that the history of the law is treated as a biologically closed system whose development is governed by a genetic code rather than by the interactive influence of environment."[123]

These developments in theology and law were precisely analogous to Bailyn's approach to education, and medicine was soon abducted by the historians as well. The revisionist medical historiography attacked the traditional view that improved therapeutic expertise, derived from nineteenth-century natural sciences, elevated the authority and status of physicians in the early twentieth century. Various strategies were adopted in this attack, such as discounting medical science as a conspiratorially conceived "ideological weapon," or arguing that medical science, though somewhat therapeutic, was also dysfunctional; or maintaining that social and political factors, especially public-health policy, outweighed the importance of therapeutic advances in elevating physicians' authority and status.[124] By 1980 these strategies prompted complaints that the revisionist social history had reduced physicians to "no more than a bit of flotsam on a great economic or social current."[125]

121. William R. Johnson, "Professions in Process: Doctors and Teachers in American Culture," *HEQ*, 15 (1975): 185.

122. Higham, *History: Professional Scholarship in America*, p. 17; Twiss, *Lawyers and the Constitution*, pp. 54, 104, 147, 150, 223–4; Christopher Hill, *Puritanism and Revolution: The English Revolution of the Seventeenth Century* (London, 1958), p. 28.

123. Peter C. Hoffer, "Disorder and Deference: The Paradoxes of Criminal Justice in the Colonial Tidewater," in *Ambivalent Legacy: A Legal History of the South*, ed. D. J. Bodenhamer and J. W. Ely, Jr. (Jackson, MS, 1984), p. 199n. See Jamil S. Zainaldin, "The Emergence of a Modern Family Law: Child Custody, Adoption and the Courts, 1796–1851," *Northwestern University Law Review*, 73 (1979): 1038–9.

124. See, respectively, E. Richard Brown, *Rockefeller Medicine Men: Medicine and Capitalism in America* (Berkeley, CA, 1979), p. 10; Stanley J. Reiser, *Medicine and the Reign of Technology* (Cambridge, UK, 1978); Barbara Gutmann Rosenkrantz, "Cart before Horse: Theory, Practice, and Professional Image in American Public Health, 1870–1920," *Journal of the History of Medicine and Allied Sciences*, 29 (1974): 55–73; John H. Warner, "Science in Medicine," in *Historical Writing on American Science*, ed. Sally Gregory Kohlstedt and Margaret W. Rossiter (Baltimore, MD, 1985), pp. 48–52.

125. Lloyd G. Stevenson, "A Second Opinion," *Bulletin of the History of Medicine*, 54 (1980): 135. See "History versus the Historians," *Journal of the History of Medicine and Allied Sciences*, 33 (1978): 127–8; "Medical History without Medicine," *Journal of the*

From medicine it was only a step to the history of science where a longstanding "internalist" view was attributed to scientists writing their own history. This view was rejected by "externalists" whose "focus is not on the scientific discipline, but on sets of scientific communities" due to "the conviction that the history of American science is interesting and important only if it is viewed as an especially significant factor in the history of American national development."[126] The externalists explicitly preferred "the professional history of science, a discipline that may be defined as history written by historians for historians." This preference was owed to the fact that scientists' expertise and standards employed in writing history are "well below what a professional historian would deem adequate."[127] Furthermore, such professional historians maintained, ironically enough, that the historiography written by professional scientists was untrustworthy inasmuch as the professionals tended to demean the efforts of amateur scientists, who represented "a potential challenge to the hegemony of the professionals."[128]

Revisionist historians likewise proposed that social sciences were "the product of an egoistic quest for status and power, threatening the old establishment elites, the last generation of amateurs." Whereas the traditional historiography of social science focused upon the substance of the disciplines and their shift from morality to objectivity, "a more accurate and revealing point of view ... interprets the

History of Medicine and Allied Sciences, 35 (1980): 5–7. Revisionist analysis of the Flexner report (1910) is indicative of the interpretive shift and its contradictions. Once regarded as the keystone to uplifting the medical profession by enshrining functional medical science in medical education, the Flexner report is now treated as uninfluential. Sociologist Starr discredits the "Flexner Myth" by way of emphasizing the role of social forces on the medical profession; medical academician Ludmerer also dismisses the Flexner report by way of crediting medical academicians. Rosenberg likewise deemphasizes the report but then, like Ludmerer, eviscerates this view to the point of conceding great influence to the report after all. On the other hand, Markowitz and Rosner emphasize the report as a vehicle "to establish modern professional elitism in medicine." Paul Starr, *The Social Transformation of American Medicine* (New York, 1982), pp. 118–26, 230; Ludmerer, *Learning to Heal*, pp. 4, 166ff., 191ff., 236ff; Charles E. Rosenberg, *The Care of Strangers: The Rise of America's Hospital System* (New York, 1987), pp. 192–211, 292; Gerald E. Markowitz and David K. Rosner, "Doctors in Crisis: A Study of the Use of Medical Education Reform to Establish Modern Professional Elitism in Medicine," *American Quarterly*, 25 (1973): 83–107.

126. George H. Daniels, ed., *Nineteenth-Century American Science: A Reappraisal* (Evanston, IL, 1972), p. ix; Edward Lurie, "The History of Science in America: Development and New Directions," in ibid., pp. 3–21. Reingold regards the internalist/externalist distinction as a simple dichotomy that has now been superseded, but some externalists believe that villainous internalism has not yet been vanquished. Cf. Nathan Reingold, ed., *The Sciences in the American Context: New Perspectives* (Washington, DC, 1979), pp. 2–3; Margaret W. Rossiter and Sally Gregory Kohlstedt, "Introduction," in *Historical Writing on American Science*, ed. Kohlstedt and Rossiter (Baltimore, MD, 1985), p. 9.

127. Greene, "History of Geology," pp. 97–8, 100. See, too, Jane Maienschein, "History of Biology," in *Historical Writing on American Science*, ed. Sally Gregory Kohlstedt and Margaret W. Rossiter (Baltimore, MD, 1985), p. 150.

128. Marc Rothenberg, "Organization and Control: Professionals and Amateurs in American Astronomy, 1899–1918," *Social Studies of Science*, 11 (1981): 305.

various definitions of social science as different strategies adopted at different times to enhance the social scientists' influence outside the academy." Neither psychologists, sociologists, economists, nor anthropologists escaped the revisionist skewer.[129]

Overall, then, professional historians began to revise the history of professional fields and disciplines in the 1950s, 1960s, and 1970s, and adopted a relatively uniform framework for this historiography. That framework involved four basic points: (i) professionals cannot tell their own history; (ii) one reason is that the history told by professionals is self-serving and cannot be trusted; (iii) another reason is that professionals lack the requisite expertise, which concerns the social and economic context rather than the internal developments of the professional field; (iv) in fact these internal developments – the professionals' expertise – exist only due to their artificial isolation from social context and explain very little at all. In this way historians substituted their expertise for other professionals' expertise, while claiming that professional expertise was unimportant, at best, and artificial, at worst. By this claim and the associated charge that professionals were serving their interests, historians deflected attention from their own effort to "take" the historiography of the professions "out of the hands" of competing professionals, in the words of Christopher Hill.

Needless to say, much good has come from the new dispensation in historiography of the professions. But the fact remains that the revisionist "history written by historians for historians" may be interpreted as no less a project of professional legitimation than is lawyers' history or, for that matter, lawyers' law. The evaluation of turn-of-the-century educationists' historiography must therefore be understood in the context of this new dispensation. That is to say, the revisionist historians may be no less susceptible to the motives that Bailyn attributed to the "early evangelists of professionalism in American education."[130] Confident of their superior expertise and ability, as well as their pure motives, the new historians of the 1960s, 1970s, and 1980s dismissed the turn-of-the-century educationists for imposing their anachronistic assumptions on the history of American education, and not allowing the past to speak for itself. The historians have likewise dismissed what the educationists were saying about their own time.

If, however, we suspend the presentist assumption about educational studies and the presumption that social historians' expertise trumps other professionals' expertise, it becomes possible to consider the question: why were educationists, unlike in the past, congratulating themselves in the 1900s? How was it possible, as never before, for educationists to assert:

129. Quotations are from A. W. Coats, "The Educational Revolution and the Professionalization of American Economics," in *Breaking the Academic Mould: Economists and American Higher Learning in the Nineteenth Century*, ed. William J. Barber (Middletown, CT, 1988), p. 354; Robert L. Church, "Economists as Experts: The Rise of an Academic Profession in America, 1870–1917," in *The University in Society*, ed. Lawrence Stone (Princeton, NJ, 1974), p. 571. See Cravens, *The Triumph of Evolution … 1900–1941*, pp. 61–2, 91, 121, 191–223; Thomas Bender, "The Erosion of Public Culture: Cities, Discourses, and Professional Disciplines," in *The Authority of Experts*, ed. Thomas L. Haskell (Bloomington, IN, 1984), p. 100; George W. Stocking, Jr., "On the Limits of 'Presentism' and 'Historicism' in the Historiography of the Behavioral Sciences," in *Race, Culture and Evolution: Essays in the History of Anthropology* (Chicago, 1982).

130. Bailyn, "Education as a Discipline: Some Historical Notes," p. 125.

From many points of view, the educator's profession ... is seen to be the noblest of professions, and that which ought to call for the highest devotion and enthusiasm.[131]

The answer usually advanced since Bailyn's treatise of 1960 is that the educationists were bad historians. Yet this explanation cannot explain the change in pedagogues' self-esteem, among other things. Mindful, then, that professionals are never so blind as when they are defending their profession against interlopers – for at that moment virtue, expertise, and interest coincide – let us examine the institutional, political, social, and economic authority of educators following the Civil War.

Institutional, Political, and Social: "All the great questions of today ... are educational questions"

It is often said, notwithstanding the excitement about education during this era, that educators' authority within their institutions was small. Schoolteachers were tightly leashed by new educational administrators, and both administrators and teachers were subservient to publicly elected school boards. Meanwhile professorial laments about "The Administrative Peril in Education" were already standard fare by 1913, when J. McKeen Cattell published a 400-page compendium of such complaints. Cattell himself opined, "The first step of a really great university president would be to refuse to accept a larger salary than is paid to the professors. The second step would be to make himself responsible to the faculty instead of holding each professor responsible to him." On the other hand, many presidents of colleges and universities felt the rein of lay boards of trustees who maintained final authority over finances, buildings, personnel, and curriculum.[132] Consequently, there exists abundant testimony that educators at all levels were denied authority over educational institutions through at least the opening decade of the twentieth century. Such testimony, however, is burdened with inconsistencies, as well as normative assumptions about the degree of authority any given group of educators deserves. If the situation in the 1910s is compared to that of 50 years earlier, rather than an *a priori* norm, it becomes clear that the autonomy and authority of educators increased extraordinarily over this period.

Presidents and deans gained considerably in these regards, as A. F. West observed in 1906. As a result, college and university administration became for the first time a subject of study. In 1900, the president of Western Reserve University published the first book on the subject, and the president of Harvard in 1908 addressed "university administration" in a series of lectures dedicated "to stimulate scientific research of the highest type."[133] Meanwhile the autonomy and authority

131. Davidson, *A History of Education*, pp. v–vi.
132. J. McKeen Cattell, ed., *University Control* (New York, 1913), p. 44; Joseph Jastrow, "The Administrative Peril in Education," in ibid., pp. 315–48; Walter P. Metzger, "College Professors and Big Business Men: A Study of American Ideologies, 1880–1915" (PhD diss., University of Iowa, 1950), ch. 4.
133. Andrew F. West, "The Changing Conception of 'The Faculty' in American Universities," in *Short Papers on American Liberal Education* (New York, 1907), pp. 35–42;

of the faculty also rose dramatically, notwithstanding the complaints of Cattell, Veblen, and others that the faculty deserved more.

Before the Civil War it was common for trustees, even at leading colleges, to exercise "entire control over the discipline, the choice of text-books, and the whole place of education," as Ronald Story has observed. The faculty, meanwhile, were charged with the thankless task of disciplining students.[134] After the war, as the ideal of scientific research took hold, the faculty at universities inevitably gained substantial control over the curriculum and pedagogy, while sloughing off responsibility for student discipline. Commensurately, they acquired greater security of tenure and greater freedom to express themselves publicly. Antebellum professors had been virtually prohibited from expressing controversial or unorthodox views, whereas academic freedom and security of tenure had become the expressed norm at leading universities by 1915. The same point holds with respect to faculty appointments, about which professors had scarcely been consulted in the past. Although lay trustees still initiated appointments in many sectarian and state institutions in the South and West, a 1910 survey "indicated that departments in major universities had gained a close-to-discretionary power over junior appointments and that presidents had largely made it their custom not to act on senior appointments without the concurrence of affected departments."[135]

In addition, the assertion that increases in administrators' authority came at the expense of the faculty overlooks the fact that bureaucratization of colleges and universities served the interests of the faculty. It did so by providing professors with departmental sanctuaries away from colleagues who disagreed with them, as Robert Wiebe and Laurence Veysey have described.[136] The accusation also neglects the fact that presidents and deans after the mid-nineteenth century were in-

---

Charles F. Thwing, *College Administration* (New York, 1900), ch. 1; Charles W. Eliot, *University Administration* (Boston, 1908), title page. See Earl J. McGrath, *Evolution of Administrative Offices in Institutions of Higher Education in the United States, 1860–1933* (PhD diss., University of Chicago, 1936); Veysey, *The Emergence of the American University,* pp. 302–17, 346–56.

134. Ronald Story, *The Forging of an Aristocracy: Harvard and the Boston Upper Class, 1800–1870* (Middletown, CT, 1980), p. 73; Kathryn McDaniel Moore, "The War with the Tutors: Student–Faculty Conflict at Harvard and Yale, 1745–1771," *HEQ,* 18 (1978): 115–27; Steven J. Novak, *The Rights of Youth: American Colleges and Student Revolt, 1798–1815* (Cambridge, MA, 1977); Jennings L. Wagoner, Jr., "Honor and Dishonor at Mr. Jefferson's University: the Antebellum Years," *HEQ,* 26 (1986): 155–79; Martin J. Finkelstein, *The American Academic Profession: A Synthesis of Social Scientific Inquiry since World War II* (Columbus, OH, 1984), pp. 19–20.

135. Walter P. Metzger, "The Academic Profession in the United States," in *The Academic Professor,* ed. Burton R. Clark (Berkeley, CA, 1987), p. 186; Arthur T. Hadley, "Academic Freedom in Theory and in Practice," *Atlantic Monthly,* 91 (1903): 152–60; Charles W. Eliot, *Academic Freedom: An Address* (Ithaca, NY, 1907); Nicholas Murray Butler, "Academic Freedom," *Educational Review,* 47 (1914): 291–4; Metzger, "Academic Tenure in America: A Historical Essay," in *Faculty Tenure* (San Francisco, CA, 1973), pp. 123–48.

136. Veysey, *The Emergence of the American University,* pp. 311–23; Wiebe, *The Search for Order, 1877–1920,* p. 121.

creasingly drawn from the faculty. Indeed, the shift toward choosing institutional leaders from the professoriate is remarkable. At Harvard, only one of the permanent rectors or presidents prior to 1849 came directly from an academic position; between 1850 and 1920 every one did. At Princeton, only one of the permanent presidents before 1854 was not called from a pulpit; from 1854 through World War I, every one came from an academic position. At Brown, only one of the permanent presidents before 1855 was called from academe; between 1855 and 1929 all but one came from an academic background. At Yale, all of the permanent rectors and presidents before 1817 were called from positions outside of education; between 1817 and 1921 all were called from the faculty.[137]

Overall, it may be said that presidents and deans gained considerable institutional authority in higher education, while faculty did as well, though not to the extent of the new administrators. Certain faculty members begrudged presidents and deans their greater gains. But those administrative leaders were drawn increasingly from faculty ranks rather than from outside education, and their leadership of the institutions served the interests of the teachers and researchers by creating departmental sanctuaries for them. These points, which attest to the rising autonomy and authority of educators within colleges and universities, apply to educators in the schools as well.

No one disputes the appearance of the "scientific" school superintendency, which Raymond Callahan described and attributed to the 1910s. Other scholars have dated it from the 1880s, and already in 1898 the president of Western Reserve University observed about this "New Profession":

It is indeed a blessed fortune when a good superintendent is supported by a school board that is so wise as to know it knows little, and therefore commits all educational questions to him.... Boston, Worcester, Springfield, Brooklyn, Philadelphia, Cleveland, Chicago, Minneapolis, St. Paul, St. Louis, Kansas City, Denver and other towns bear testimony.[138]

The authority of superintendents and other educational administrators was thus apparent by the turn of the century. This rise in authority, however, is commonly portrayed as occurring at the expense of teachers, particularly in light of the feminization of the teaching force. And it is true that superintendents exerted

137. Samuel E. Morison, *Three Centuries of Harvard, 1636–1936* (Cambridge, MA, 1936); George W. Pierson, *Yale College: An Educational History, 1871–1921* (New Haven, CT, 1952), pp. 695–705; Pierson, *A Yale Book of Numbers: Historical Statistics of the College and University, 1701–1976* (New Haven, CT, 1983), pp. 343–7, 428–31; Thomas J. Wertenbaker, *Princeton, 1746–1896* (Princeton, NJ, 1946); Vaughan, comp., *Historical Catalogue of Brown University, 1764–1904*; Louise Bauer and William T. Hastings, comps., *The Historical Catalogue of Brown University, 1764–1934* (Providence, RI, 1936).

138. Charles F. Thwing, "A New Profession," *Educational Review*, 15 (1898): 28, 30. Cf. Callahan, *Education and the Cult of Efficiency*, pp. 216–9; Mattingly, *The Classless Profession: American Schoolmen in the Nineteenth Century*, pp. 179–83; Tyack, "Pilgrims Progress ... the School Superintendency, 1860–1960," pp. 257–300; Teaford, *The Unheralded Triumph: City Government in America, 1870–1900*, pp. 161–2; Tyack and Hansot, *Managers of Virtue: Public School Leadership ... 1820–1980*, chs. 9–11.

substantial control over the hiring and activities of teachers. But this fact does not mean that late-nineteenth-century teachers *lost* autonomy or authority relative to antebellum pedagogues, who answered to local school boards of laymen with whom they often "boarded round." Nor is it the case that rural teachers in the late nineteenth century, who still answered directly to local school boards, had more authority than teachers in urban school systems, where superintendents reigned.[139] The superintendents acquired their institutional authority at the expense of lay persons, rather than teachers.

Moreover, as with college and university presidents, there was a remarkable shift toward school leaders rising up through the ranks rather than being drawn from the other learned professions. For example, the schoolmen belonging to the American Institute of Instruction generally came from outside of the schools between 1830 and 1860, whereas most schoolmen between 1860 and 1890 rose up through teaching.[140] This fact that authority over educational institutions came to be vested in career educators comports with teachers' increased autonomy derived from rising standards of certification.

The situation in Colorado typified this development. Colorado's first licensing exam for teachers was established in 1861, and decade by decade the exam was made more difficult while educational qualifications were introduced and raised, a process that culminated in the opening of the first state normal school in 1890. By 1906 the State Superintendent of Public Instruction, Katherine Craig, reported

---

139. Harold W. Foght, *The Rural Teacher and His Work* (New York, 1919); Link, *A Hard Country and a Lonely Place: Schooling ... in Rural Virginia, 1870–1920*, pp. 61–4; Fuller, *The Old Country School ... in the Middle West*, chs. 9–10; Polly Welts Kaufman, *Women Teachers on the Frontier* (New Haven, CT, 1984). See these essays from the Country School Legacy Project of the National Endowment for the Humanities (Silt, CO, 1982): Robert J. Barthell, "Wyoming's Country Schools. Comprehensive Report"; Scott B. Birkinshaw, "The Legacy of Utah's Country Schools, 1847–1896"; Herbert Blakely, "Southeastern South Dakota's Country Schools"; Philip Brown, "Northeastern South Dakota's Country Schools"; James Dertien, "Eastern Nebraska's Country Schools"; Joanne L. Dodds and Edwin Dodds, "Country School Legacy Report for Southern Colorado"; Ernest Grundy, "Central Nebraska's Country Schools"; Andrew Gulliford et al., "Work and Leisure in Country Schools in Wyoming"; Caroline Hatton, "Western South Dakota's Country Schools"; Warren A. Henke, "North Dakota's Country Teachers: Their Roles, Rules, and Restrictions"; Sara E. Judge, "Eastern and Central Kansas Country Schools"; Sandra Scofield, "The Country School Legacy in Western Nebraska."

140. Mattingly, *The Classless Profession: American Schoolmen in the Nineteenth Century*, ch. 7. Mattingly attributes high status to antebellum schoolmen because high-status *outsiders* contributed to and led the profession. Then, because teachers, who were from lower status backgrounds, assumed leadership after 1860, Mattingly infers that schoolmen's status declined from 1830–60 to 1860–90. But this development signifies an increase in the autonomy and authority of the educational profession, not a decline in status, because antebellum schoolmen brought their status to education and did not derive it from education. In contrast to Mattingly's reasoning, Thomas Haskell, for example, considers "a change in the locus of social authority from the older genteel elites to the new academic professionals" to be a rise in the autonomy and authority of the latter, not a decline in the status of the professoriate. Mattingly, pp. 136, 154; Haskell, *The Emergence of Professional Social Science*, pp. 24–7, 211–2, 234–56.

that "higher scholarship and higher professional qualifications seem to be the watchword of the hour," and the following year the state university founded a school of education. This process, coupled with efforts to establish security of tenure for teachers, resulted in confiding to career educators the hiring of teachers and offering those teachers, once hired, a measure of security from local politics.[141] Schoolteachers thus gained greater autonomy by virtue of increased certification requirements and security of tenure, while they indirectly acquired substantial institutional authority because external school boards ceded much of their authority to career educators who had risen up through the schools, as had Katherine Craig.

In these ways educators, considered as a group, saw their authority and autonomy increase within their institutions, and this increase ramified into political, social, and economic life during the Progressive Period extending from about 1890 through 1920. Naturally, different interpretations can be made of this development in line with the various interpretations of Progressivism. Some scholars, such as Harold Faulkner, have considered Progressivism to be a popular and heroic movement sponsored by labor, immigrants, and other outsiders who struggled against social injustice and exclusion. With respect to education, this heroic view has been contradicted by those, such as Michael Katz, who contend that the laboring classes did not support Progressive high schools, and this contention has, in turn, been challenged on both methodological and ideological grounds.[142] Another interpretation has applauded elite college-educated reformers who called themselves "Progressives" and instituted public policy derived from the social sciences and administered through apolitical bureaucracies, as in the Seattle school system in the early 1900s.[143]

In yet another interpretation, Richard Hofstadter has characterized those elite Progressives as anxious about their loss of influence relative to uneducated bosses of machine politics, on the one hand, and to big business, on the other. Hence, the reformers emphasized scientific expertise in order to preserve their "social control."[144]

---

141. Katherine L. Craig, *Report of the State Superintendent of Public Instruction of the State of Colorado for the Years, 1905–1906* (Denver, CO, 1906), p. 3; Samuel N. Willett, "A History of the Certification of Teachers in Colorado, 1861–1945" (MS thesis, Colorado College, 1946), chs. 2–3. See Elsbree, *The American Teacher*, ch. 24.

142. Cf. Harold U. Faulkner, *The Quest for Social Justice, 1898–1914* (New York, 1931); Katz, *The Irony of Early School Reform*; Katz, *Class, Bureaucracy and Schools: The Illusion of Educational Change in America*, expanded edn (New York, 1974); Maris A. Vinovskis, *The Origins of Public High Schools: A Reexamination of the Beverly High School Controversy* (Madison, WI, 1985); Paul E. Peterson, *The Politics of School Reform, 1870–1940* (Chicago, 1985).

143. See Joseph M. Rice, *The Public-School System of the United States* (New York, 1893); Nelson, *Good Schools: The Seattle Public School System, 1901–1930*, ch. 3.

144. Hofstadter, *Age of Reform*, pp. 148–64. "Social control" initially denoted benign reform, when introduced by sociologist Edward A. Ross, who published *Social Control* (1901), based upon a series of articles in *American Journal of Sociology*. The interpretive ambiguity as to whether "urban service professionals" were motivated by a desire for justice or for control is expressed in Don S. Kirschner, *The Paradox of Professionalism: Reform and Public Service in Urban America, 1900–1940* (Westport, CT, 1986); Barry M. Franklin, *Building the American Community: The School Curriculum and the Search for Social Control* (Philadelphia, 1986).

In regard to education, Hofstadter's interpretation has implied a critical assessment of the "administrative progressives" who built large school systems near the turn of the century.[145] Still another interpretation has come from historians, such as Gabriel Kolko, who maintain that Progressivism was a reform movement, perhaps initially heroic, but soon co-opted by financiers and industrial capitalists. These wealthy men sought to consolidate their economic dominance by encouraging government regulation that would control the market and education and placate the underclass under the guise of advancing the public interest.[146]

Other interpretations also exist, contributing to what has been called the "historiographic Babel" regarding Progressivism.[147] Babel or not, at least one common theme has consistently appeared in this historiography: "the Progressive mind was ultimately an educator's mind." Progressivism was a broad movement with many branches, but it was rooted in a concern for education.[148] True, Progressivism involved political, economic, and social reforms. But into each of these fields education encroached, and educators gained authority just as clergy and lawyers had done in earlier eras.

With respect to the polity, Ralph Waldo Emerson was prescient in 1860, writing that: "Politics is an afterwork, a poor patching. We are always a little late…. We shall one day learn to supersede politics by education." President Rutherford B. Hayes repeated the point in his 1880 State of the Union address: "political reconstruction" must give way to "educational reconstruction" as the vehicle to "peace, virtue, and social order." Educational missionaries, such as Amory Mayo, then endorsed the president's speech: "new education" was called for; it was time for the "soldier to give way to the schoolmaster in the complete reconstruction of national affairs."[149] When the regents of the University of Kansas came to Johns Hopkins University in 1889 to recruit a department chairman for the social sciences, their hosts proposed that the new department be named either "History and Politics" or "History and Political Science." Neither would do, said the regents, because Kansans "had politics enough in the state already." However naive, this new, pejorative sense of "politics" and "political" could not be denied.[150] Politicians thus tried to sanitize their campaigns by making them "educational." Meanwhile efforts were made to keep politics out of science and education at all costs, lest efforts for improvement be "defeated … through the efforts of politicians

145. Tyack, *The One Best System: A History of American Urban Education,* p. 127.

146. Gabriel Kolko, *The Triumph of Conservatism: A Reinterpretation of American History, 1900–1916* (New York, 1963); James Weinstein, *The Corporate Ideal in the Liberal State, 1900–1918* (Boston, 1968).

147. Unger and Unger, *The Vulnerable Years: The United States, 1896–1917,* p. 101.

148. Lawrence A. Cremin, *The Transformation of the School: Progressivism in American Education, 1876–1957* (New York, 1961), p. 89.

149. Ralph Waldo Emerson, "Culture," pp. 135–6, in *Conduct of Life* (1860), vol. 6 of *Emerson's Complete Works* (Boston, 1884); Dan T. Carter and Amy Friedlander, eds., *Southern Women in the Recent Educational Movement in the South* (Baton Rouge, LA, 1978), pp. xi–xii; Amory D. Mayo, "The President's Speech," *Education,* 1 (1880): 84; Mayo, "The New Education and Colonel Parker," *Journal of Education,* 18 (1883): 84–7.

150. Small, "Fifty Years of Sociology in the United States (1865–1915)," p. 760.

and others in favor of low standards," as noted the United States' exhibit on "Professional Education" prepared for the Paris Exposition of 1900.[151]

The polity could not be ignored, of course, and ways were found to turn it to educational ends. Beginning in Massachusetts in 1852 and concluding with Mississippi in 1918, compulsory education laws were enacted in every state. At the federal level, the National Department of Education was created in 1867, then converted to a Bureau within the Department of the Interior in 1869. In the 1870s proposals to establish a national university were repeatedly made in the National Education Association and by President Hayes. In the 1880s several bills to establish a national university were filed in Congress, then 15 more in the 1890s, and another nine by 1910, at which point interest waned. Meanwhile the seven state Constitutions approved by Congress between 1881 and 1900 included on average more than twice as many provisions regarding education as did the eight new state Constitutions written between 1841 and 1860.[152] Political authority was also invested in individual professors. This happened not so much through their election to public office, although it is no coincidence that the three Presidents serving from 1901 to 1921 have been identified as the most "learned presidents" since the early 1800s.[153] Rather, professors generally acquired political authority by virtue of the rising status of the expert in all fields.

Social scientists through the 1880s were highly prescriptive and moral in their investigations. Toward the end of the nineteenth century they began to portray themselves as objective and impartial experts, influencing public policy by supplying expertise. A shift from advocacy to impartiality thus accompanied the increasing specialization and complexity of science, and these two developments resulted in transferring authority from clergy, attorneys, physicians, and other elites to academicians who founded specialized associations of study. In the words of Lester Ward, "if government could be in the hands of social scientists, instead of social empiricists, it might be elevated to the rank of an applied science."[154] This influence was manifested in the "sociological jurisprudence" of Roscoe Pound. It likewise appeared even in havens of machine politics, such as Chicago, and reached

151. Henry L. Taylor and James R. Parsons, Jr., *Professional Education in the United States* (Albany, NY, 1899), p. 23n.; McGerr, *The American North, 1865–1928: The Decline of Popular Politics*, ch. 4.

152. Donald R. Warren, *To Enforce Education: A History of the Founding Years of the United States Office of Education* (Detroit, MI, 1974); Edgar B. Wesley, *NEA: the First Hundred Years: The Building of the Teaching Profession* (New York, 1957), ch. 18; Tyack, James, and Benavot, *Law and the Shaping of Public Education, 1785–1954*, pp. 55–9.

153. Theodore Roosevelt, William Howard Taft, Woodrow Wilson. David H. Burton, *The Learned Presidency: Theodore Roosevelt, William Howard Taft, Woodrow Wilson* (Cranbury, NJ, 1988), p. 12.

154. Ward, *Dynamic Sociology*, vol. 2, p. 249. Church, "Economists as Experts: The Rise of an Academic Profession in America, 1870–1917," p. 577; Furner, *Advocacy and Objectivity ... American Social Science, 1865–1905*; Haskell, *The Emergence of Professional Social Science*, chs. 2, 10; Alan Creutz, "From College Teacher to University Scholar: The Evolution and Professionalization of Academics at the University of Michigan, 1841–1900" (PhD diss., University of Michigan, 1981), ch. 6.

new heights in Wisconsin, where *World's Work* identified "A University That Runs a State."[155]

In addition to the political authority that their expertise conveyed, educators acquired a great deal of social authority in a variety of ways. For one, educators gained new social authority, because, as Willard Waller observed in his classic work, "the teacher has a special position as a paid agent of cultural diffusion." In this sense, "all the great questions of today, the problems of social reform, of philanthropy and politics, and even ... the problems of hygiene and psychiatry, are educational questions," affirmed William Burnham of Clark University in 1908.[156] Educational institutions therefore assumed a role similar to that of the colonial meetinghouse. Rural schoolhouses became "the social and religious center of the neighborhood," as in Clay County, Nebraska, in 1873. Similarly, "in Colorado towns ... the most precious institution [is] the public school," observed the state Superintendent of Public Instruction in 1881.[157] In major cities such as New York this prominent role meant that the schools began to require "grand public buildings which would be permanent and prominent." To be sure, in New York as in other cities, a broad array of institutions – museums, parks, churches, art institutes, settlement houses – also served "as agencies of education," as Douglas Sloan has demonstrated. But at the center of the array stood the formal institutions of education. The school, the college, or the university became the "cathedral of culture" in its particular locale over the second half of the nineteenth century.[158]

Commensurately, the number and variety of formal institutions of education increased sharply between the Civil War and World War I. Counting the myriads of short-lived institutions is difficult to do, but overall enrollment figures lend a sense of the growth. Between 1860 and 1910 the United States population increased about threefold, from 31.5 million to 92.4 million. Meanwhile the total enrollment in schools, colleges, and universities jumped about six times to almost 20 million.

155. Vidich and Lyman, *American Sociology*, p. 161; Steven J. Diner, *A City and its Universities: Public Policy in Chicago, 1892–1919* (Chapel Hill, NC, 1980), passim.

156. Willard Waller, *The Sociology of Teaching* (New York, 1933), p. 40; Burnham, "History of Education," p. 21.

157. [US Bureau of Education], *The Rural Teacher of Nebraska* (Washington, DC, 1919), p. 33; [Joseph C. Shattuck], *Second Biennial Report of the Superintendent of Public Instruction of the State of Colorado* (Denver, CO, 1881), p. 56. See these essays from the Country School Legacy Project of the National Endowment for the Humanities (Silt, CO, 1982): Barthell, "Wyoming's Country Schools"; Birkinshaw, "The Legacy of Utah's Country Schools, 1847–1896"; Blakely, "Southeastern South Dakota's Country Schools"; Brown, "Northeastern South Dakota's Country Schools"; Dertien, "Eastern Nebraska's Country Schools"; Dodds and Dodds, "Country School Legacy Report for Southern Colorado"; Grundy, "Central Nebraska's Country Schools"; Gulliford et al., "Work and Leisure in Country Schools in Wyoming"; Hatton, "Western South Dakota's Country Schools"; Judge, "Eastern and Central Kansas Country Schools"; Scofield, "The Country School Legacy in Western Nebraska."

158. Quotations are from Kaestle, *The Evolution of an Urban School System: New York City, 1750–1850*, p. 177; Sloan, "Science in New York City, 1867–1907," p. 35; William W. Cutler, III, "Cathedral of Culture: The Schoolhouse in American Educational Thought and Practice since 1820," *HEQ*, 29 (1989): 1–33.

This relative and absolute increase indicates that "by 1900 America had the best-educated population in the world."[159] The increase in enrollment, which contributed to the social authority of educators, was due not only to the proliferation of existing models of educational institutions, but also to their growing variety.

The land-grant colleges, for example, were established by the Morrill Act of 1862, and by 1870, 37 states had accepted the federal grants and agreed to found colleges teaching "agriculture and the mechanic arts."[160] Kindergartens were founded in the 1870s and 1880s with an enthusiasm that outstripped even Germany, where they had originated. Public kindergartens were established in San Francisco in 1878, Cincinnati in 1879, Chicago in 1880, Philadelphia in 1881, and Boston in 1883, "and by 1914 most major cities had public kindergarten systems." At the same time, secondary schools received special emphasis as Americans attempted to build what Princeton President James McCosh described as the missing stairway between the primary floor and higher floor of the American house of education.[161] One such attempt was the private boarding school movement, which took hold from about 1880 to 1910. While these schools were marble staircases, the conventional stairway became the public high schools, which appeared in great numbers in the 1870s, 1880s, and early 1890s. Then the junior high school and the junior college appeared between 1900 and 1920.[162]

Accompanying these new institutions was the widespread introduction of educational requirements for vocational licenses, certificates, and credentials, which provided another dimension of social authority. To be sure, diplomas and degrees had long elevated a graduate's social status quite apart from their utility in meeting vocational requirements. Hence, a college degree had increasingly become an expectation among the "best men" of society, and the fraction of "American leaders" who attended college rose from about one-third to more than one-half over the second half of the nineteenth century.[163] But quite apart from this elevation of status, diplomas and degrees now began to assume a new dimension of social

159. Susan B. Carter, "Occupational Segregation, Teachers' Wages, and American Economic Growth", *Journal of Economic History*, 46 (1986): 374. In 1910 there were about 19,371,000 school students and 598,000 higher education students, constituting about 21.6 percent of the population. *Historical Statistics*, series A6–8, H412–32, H700–715; Colin B. Burke, "The Expansion of American Higher Education, in *The Transformation of Higher Learning, 1860–1930*, ed. Konrad H. Jarausch (Chicago, 1983), p. 111.

160. 12 *US Statutes* 503 (1862); Henry S. Brunner, *Land-Grant Colleges and Universities, 1862–1962* (Washington, DC, 1962); Mohr, "Higher Education and the Development of Professionalism ... 1867–1911," ch. 2.

161. Ann Taylor Allen, "'Let Us Live with our Children': Kindergarten Movements in Germany and the United States, 1840–1914," *HEQ*, 28 (1988): 46; William Hooper, *A Lecture on the Imperfections of our Primary Schools Delivered before the North Carolina Institute of Education* (Newbern, NC, 1832); James McCosh, "Upper Schools," *NEA* (1873): 23.

162. Edward N. Saveth, "Education of an Elite," *HEQ*, 28 (1988): 367–86; Edward A. Krug, *The Shaping of the American High School* (Madison, WI, 1969); Leonard V. Koos, *The Junior-College Movement* (Boston, 1924), pp. 1–2.

163. "American leaders" being defined as individuals in the *Dictionary of American Biography*. George W. Pierson, *The Education of American Leaders: Comparative Contributions of US Colleges and Universities* (New York, 1969), pp. 2–5.

authority because the road to good employment – particularly the learned professions – was being rerouted through educational institutions.

The call for vocational education was expressed in a torrent of literature describing "the financial return of education to the individual" and to industrial society in general. By the 1880s the demand for vocational education led to the diploma mill scandals, in which one of the most notorious entrepreneurs admitted to selling some 60,000 fake diplomas. These scandals only stimulated further demand, and *The Money Value of Education* (1916) included a bibliography of 126 essays published between 1900 and 1916 on the topic.[164] This movement toward vocational guidance and education has been much debated along the lines of Progressive historiography described above. Whatever the normative assessment, it is clear that from California to New York the movement gained popularity, fueled by the demand for scientific efficiency in industry. "Between 1906, when Massachusetts proposed the first statewide system of vocational schools, and 1917, when Congress passed the Smith-Hughes Act mandating federal aid for vocational education, almost every group in the nation ... demanded that the schools be refashioned along vocational lines."[165]

The public demand was manifested in occupational and professional licensing laws. After the Jacksonian retrenchment, licensing had lain dormant until it was revived in the 1880s, a revival typified by the experience in West Virginia. There professional education went from being viewed as a *helpful* source of acculturation and expertise, to being viewed as *sufficient*, when professional schools gained the "diploma privilege" whereby graduation from an accredited school legally entitled the graduate to practice the profession in the state. Then, near the turn of the century, professional education became viewed as *necessary* in order for a citizen to be licensed to practice in the state. This development was evident in the US Supreme Court's first ruling on the constitutionality of a state law licensing professions, wherein the Court in 1889 upheld a West Virginia statute licensing physicians. With this precedent established, from "1890 to 1910, occupational licensing first achieved a firm foothold in the statute-books of most American states," according to Lawrence Friedman.[166]

164. A. Caswell Ellis, *The Money Value of Education* (Washington, DC, 1917); Doty and Harris, *A Statement of the Theory of Education in the United States of America as Approved by Many Leading Educators*, p. 12; Martin Kaufman, *Homeopathy in America: The Rise and Fall of a Medical Heresy* (Baltimore, MD, 1971), p. 142.

165. Harvey A. Kantor, *Learning to Earn: School, Work, and Vocational Reform in California, 1880–1930* (Madison, WI, 1988), p. 17. Cf. W. Carson Ryan, Jr., *Vocational Guidance and the Public Schools* (Washington, DC, 1919); Meyer Bloomfield, ed., *Readings in Vocational Guidance* (Boston, 1915); Cremin, *The Transformation of the School ... 1876–1957*, ch. 2; Katz, *Class, Bureaucracy and Schools*, ch. 3; Walter Feinberg and Henry Rosemont, Jr., eds., *Work, Technology and Education: Dissenting Essays in the Intellectual Foundations of American Education* (Urbana, IL, 1975); Samuel Bowles and Herbert Gintis, *Schooling in Capitalist America: Educational Reform and the Contradictions of Economic Life* (New York, 1976), ch. 7; Paul C. Violas, *The Training of the Urban Working Class: A History of Twentieth Century Urban Education* (Chicago, 1978).

166. Lawrence M. Friedman, "Freedom of Contract and Occupational Licensing, 1890–1910: A Legal and Social Study," *California Law Review*, 53 (1965): 489. *Dent* v. *West Virginia*, 129 US 114 (1889); Frances P. DeLancy, *The Licensing of Professions in West Virginia* (Chicago, 1938), p. 56, chart 9.

The kinds and number of vocational degrees, vocational schools, and vocational students expanded commensurately, and at the turn of the century the US Bureau of Education introduced a separate chapter on "Professional Education" into its annual reports. Meanwhile Henry Taylor and James Parsons prepared a massive report on "Professional Education" for the United States' exhibit at the Paris Exposition of 1900. This report highlighted the traditional learned professions, which continued to dominate analysis of "professions" even after the appearance of the nation's first business school at the University of Pennsylvania in 1881, the first forestry school at Cornell in 1898, and the first journalism school at Missouri in 1908. The pattern in theological, legal, and medical education was strikingly similar: reforming presidents of universities edged out part-time practitioners and appointed full-time academicians to professional school faculties. These academicians then redefined professional expertise and training along the lines of "scientific" specialities, while professional degrees became successively helpful, sufficient, and necessary elements for professional licensing. In this fashion, education encroached on the other professions, turning professional questions into "educational questions" – to paraphrase Abraham Flexner and Henry Pritchett.[167] In fact, when the new word "professionalization" was introduced at the turn of the century, it was defined in the educational terms of the distribution and acquisition of knowledge:

> the process by which we may perhaps be allowed to call by the clumsy name of professionalisation, and which in every walk of life makes for the distribution and enforces the necessity of knowledge.[168]

In medicine there were some 50 professional schools offering degrees in 1850. That number doubled by 1880, tripled by 1900, and reached a peak of 162 in 1906, when medical schools began merging and closing. Commensurate with the numerical growth, there was a gradual shift in governance from proprietary to non-profit, in pedagogy from lecture and apprenticeship to laboratory and clinic, and in purpose from practical to scientific. Whereas medical specialization at the beginning of the nineteenth century was seen as "a style of quackery," the new medical science had established specialists as the most prestigious medical professionals by the beginning of the twentieth century. Meanwhile the medical school course was lengthened to a norm of four years by 1900, and entrance requirements for medical school rose to a norm of a high school diploma by 1910, when Abraham Flexner aspired to establish a standard of two years of college work.[169]

167. Taylor and Parsons, *Professional Education in the United States.* Abraham Flexner and Henry Pritchett, the president of the Carnegie Foundation, justified their authority to speak on medical education by maintaining that "the question is not a medical question, but an educational question." Steven C. Wheatley, *The Politics of Philanthropy: Abraham Flexner and Medical Education* (Madison, WI, 1988), p. 52; Ludmerer, *Learning to Heal,* pp. 170–1. Notwithstanding this encroachment, I regard as speculative Bledstein's view that "the American university came into existence to serve and promote professional authority in society," that is, to serve "the ego-satisfying pretensions of professionalism." *The Culture of Professionalism,* pp. x, 289.

168. "Modern Bowling," *Saturday Review* (August 24, 1901): 233.

169. Quotation is from Rosenberg, *The Care of Strangers,* p. 169. Ludmerer, *Learning to Heal,* chs. 2–5; Flexner, *Medical Education,* pp. 47–8; Rothstein, *American Medical Schools,*

In law merely 25 percent of the states or territories had any education requirement for admission to the bar in 1860. By 1890 the fraction had grown to
47 percent and then to 73 percent by 1917. Commensurately, the number of law
students grew from about 1,500 in 1860 to almost 23,000 by 1916; the number of
law schools rose from 21 to 140 over the same period. These increases were
particularly marked in the 1890s, when the diploma privilege in law became widespread. Meanwhile the average law course was lengthened from one year to three
years, and admission standards were introduced. By 1900 three states – Connecticut, New York, and Illinois – required at least three years of high school work
for admission to law school, and two schools – Harvard and Yale – required at least
two years of college work for admission.[170] These increases appropriately coincided
with the introduction of the new scientific jurisprudence and case method.

In theology the number of divinity students and schools increased, though not as
fast as those in the other learned professions. Between 1870 and 1900 the number
of students rose two-and-half times to about 8,000, compared to a fourfold increase
to over 25,000 in medicine and an eightfold increase to over 12,500 in law. The
number of divinity schools almost doubled, rising from 80 to 154 over the same
period. This relatively smaller increase indicated less interest in the ministry as a
career, rather than less interest in education on the part of the clergy, for the
importance of a learned ministry, indeed a "scientific ministry," was vociferously
emphasized.[171]

While medical, legal, and theological education expanded greatly, the growth in
teacher education was phenomenal. Quite apart from the expansion of graduate
study required for college and university teaching, the growth in training for
schoolteachers surpassed every other form of professional or vocational education.
The nineteen normal schools on the eve of the Civil War grew to 139 by 1876 and
then 242 by 1892, while the US Commissioner of Education reported that normal
schools and education departments and courses "are being so rapidly established ...
that it is hard to keep up with the increase or even to tell where it is occurring." By
the turn of the century there existed some 362 public and private normal schools,
and 929 public and private high schools and academies that were offering courses
in professional training for teachers. At that point the value of the property and
endowment of normal schools was about thirteen times that of law schools, twice
that of medical schools (including hospitals), and almost nine-tenths that of divinity

pp. 142–3. Here and below, I draw from Alfred Z. Reed, *Training for the Public Profession of
the Law* (New York, 1921), pp. 91–2, 442–3.

170. William R. Johnson, *Schooled Lawyers, A Study in the Clash of Professional Cultures*
(Chapel Hill, NC, 1981), pp. 55–6, 120–53; Taylor and Parsons, *Professional Education in the
United States*, pp. 9, 11; Robert Stevens, *Law School: Legal Education in America from the
1850s to the 1980s* (Chapel Hill, NC, 1983), p. 36; chs. 4–7; Jerold S. Auerbach, *Unequal
Justice: Lawyers and Social Change in Modern America* (New York, 1976), ch. 3.

171. Milton G. Evans, "The Purpose and Meaning of an Educated Ministry," *Baptist
Review & Expositor*, 1 (1904): 5–17; Archibald T. Robertson, "Preaching and Scholarship
[Inaugural Address, Southern Baptist Theological Seminary]" (Louisville, KY, 1890); David
S. Hill, *The Problems and Education of the Protestant Ministry* (PhD diss., Clark University,
1908).

schools.[172] Most of these normal schools, like most medical and law schools, were on the level of high schools and duplicated much of the secondary curriculum, although a few in New York and Massachusetts approached college-level work and hoped to offer the new degrees of Bachelor, Master, and Doctor of Pedagogy.[173] Those new degrees were conferred by many of the universities that established chairs, departments and, finally, schools of education in the late nineteenth century: Iowa, Michigan, Utah, Minnesota, Wisconsin, Indiana, Illinois, Northwestern, North Carolina, Johns Hopkins, Cornell, Clark, Stanford, California, Texas, Nebraska, Missouri, Chicago, Ohio State, Harvard, Columbia, and New York University.[174]

By 1906, when John Dewey declared that education had attained "standing as a university subject," educators had gained institutional autonomy and authority vastly exceeding that prior to the Civil War. In addition, the rise of scientific expertise had conveyed to those in colleges and universities greater say in public affairs. Meanwhile the road to a great many occupations, including the learned professions, had been rerouted through formal institutions of education. Educators acquired enormous social authority by encroaching upon those other fields, and the need for credentials and accreditation was creating a "pedagocracy," one observer noted in 1911.[175] Commensurate with this increased institutional, political, and social authority, educators and their institutions began to receive a larger share of the financial resources of society.

Economic: "It Pays the State to Educate"

Between the 1860s and 1910s the nation's wealth grew enormously but discontinuously, as the overheated economy alternately boomed and busted. The Panic of 1857 yielded to a war-time boom that crashed with the Panic of 1873. Then followed the "Gilded Age" boom of the 1880s, the Panic of 1893, a recovery begin-

---

172. *USCommEd* (1888–9), vol. 2, p. 956; Winship, *Is there a Science of Pedagogy?*, p. 15; Burke A. Hinsdale, "The Training of Teachers," in *Monographs on Education in the United States*, ed. Nicholas M. Butler (Albany, NY, 1900), pp. 359–408; Taylor and Parsons, *Professional Education in the United States*, pp. 19–20; Mattingly, *The Classless Profession: American Schoolmen in the Nineteenth Century*, table 15.

173. Atkinson, "The Professional Preparation of Secondary School Teachers," ch. 2; Elsbree, *The American Teacher*, ch. 23; Mattingly, *The Classless Profession: American Schoolmen in the Nineteenth Century*, pp. 143–51; Monroe, *Teaching-Learning Theory ... 1890–1950*, chs. 6, 7, 9–12.

174. Burke A. Hinsdale, *Pedagogical Chairs in Colleges and Universities* (Syracuse, NY, 1889); Hubbell, *The Development of University Departments of Education*; Auerbach, "The Opposition to Schools of Education by Professors of the Liberal Arts," chs. 3, 4; O'Leary, *An Inquiry into ... Selected University Schools of Education*, p. 240; Clifford and Guthrie, *Ed School*, ch. 2.

175. Dewey, "Education as a University Study," p. 284; "Hard Words About Pedagogy," pp. 240–1.

ning in 1897, and the Panic of 1907. Due, in part, to these recessions, prices deflated by 52 percent between the end of the Civil War and the start of World War I. $100 in 1914 would have been worth $152 in 1866, $105 in 1875, $92 in 1885, $84 in 1895, $88 in 1905. Between 1905 and 1914 there was inflation of about 12 percent.[176]

Amid these volatile conditions, the level of public and private expenditure upon science and education rose phenomenally. Relative to other professional fields, in fact, this rise was unparalleled both in absolute terms and, especially, when compared to expenditures before the Civil War. The half-million dollar gift of 1835 that endowed the Smithsonian Institution was the greatest single benefaction toward "the increase and diffusion of knowledge" in America to that point. Even this gift lay fallow for a decade because Congress could not agree on how to use it, and, despite the delay, the endowment in 1846 still exceeded that of every college and university in the country.[177] Given this background, the AAAS in 1853 voted against even trying to raise an endowment, and in 1863 Congress created the National Academy of Science but repeatedly declined to fund it.[178]

By that point, however, conditions were beginning to change. Between 1850 and 1870 aggregate expenditures on education rose "roughly 400 percent in constant dollar values ... as contrasted with a 170 percent increase in the total population."[179] Subsequently "total expenditures for education in the United States ... increased from about $75,000,000 a year in 1870 to $240,000,000 in 1900 and to nearly a billion in 1916," according to a study for the Carnegie Foundation in 1918. Recent economic historians have confirmed this trend. Albert Fishlow found that public and private expenditures on education in the United States approximately tripled from 1870 to 1900, and Theodore Schultz reported that they tripled again by 1916. That this ninefold increase between 1870 and 1916 represented a relatively greater fraction of social resources may be seen by comparing it to budgeted expenditures for the federal government over the same period. The aggregate expenditures on education represented about 31 percent of those of the federal government in 1870, 56 percent in 1900, and 137 percent in 1915.[180]

These figures do not even include students' foregone earnings that scholars have computed in order to arrive at "total" educational expenditures.[181] Nor do they include most of the land "set apart by Congress for the endowment of public

176. *Historical Statistics,* series D722–7, D735–8.

177. Dupree, *Science in the Federal Government,* p. 284, ch. 4; Bruce, *The Launching of American Science, 1846–1876,* ch. 14. Only the Harvard endowment approached that of the Smithsonian.

178. Bruce, *The Launching of American Science, 1846–1876,* p. 259, 305; Rexmond C. Cochrane, *The National Academy of Sciences: The First Hundred Years, 1863–1963* (Washington, DC, 1978), pp. 80–97.

179. Cremin, *American Education: The National Experience, 1783–1876,* pp. 179–80.

180. Mann, *A Study of Engineering Education,* p. 17; Albert Fishlow, "Levels of Nineteenth-Century American Investment in Education," *Journal of Economic History,* 26 (1966): 420–3; Theodore W. Schultz, "Capital Formation by Education," *Journal of Political Economy,* 68 (1960): 578–80; *Historical Statistics,* series Y335–8.

181. Schultz, "Capital Formation by Education," pp. 571–83; Fishlow, "Levels of Nineteenth-Century American Investment in Education," pp. 418–36.

education [which] amounts to 86,138,473 acres.... This is an area larger than that of the six New England states, New York, New Jersey, Maryland and Delaware added together. It is ... as great as the kingdom of Prussia, about seven-tenths as great as France, and considerably greater than the combined areas of Great Britain, including the Channel Islands, and the Kingdom of Holland," as N. M. Butler observed in 1900.[182] By that time, education had also become the largest category of expenditures made by state and local governments. In 1902, out of expenditures of $1,013 million, state and local governments spent 25 percent on "education" with the next highest categories being "highways" at 17 percent and "administration" at 14 percent. In 1913, out of expenditures of $2,064 million, state and local governments spent 28 percent on "education," compared to the next highest categories of "highways" at 20 percent and "administration" at 10 percent.[183]

These figures confirm the judgment of Tyack, James, and Benavot that "in the nineteenth century, state school systems represented ... a more universal and costly public service than any other.... While many other public services in the United States were meager, and often privatized, education became the largest part of the public sector in a period marked by distrust of government."[184] These expenditures were rationalized by the "World Wide Law" announced in 1899 by the president of the University of Tennessee: "It Pays the State to Educate." The South straggled in this regard, as Amory Mayo noted in 1892. Nevertheless, it was generally conceded that "the wealth and the wealth-producing power of any people depend on the quantity and quality of education."[185]

Spurred by Andrew Carnegie's widely reprinted article "The Gospel of Wealth" (1889), private contributions to education also poured in, particularly to higher education, where science was rooted. Over 1 million dollars to each of their name-sake institutions came from Cornelius Vanderbilt, Paul Tulane, Jonas Clark, John Creighton, Asa Chandler (to Emory), Seth Low (to Columbia), and John Green (to Princeton). Over 2 million came from Ezra Cornell, Benjamin and James Duke, Henry Sage (to Cornell), and Jay Gould (to New York University). Over 3 million from Anthony Drexel, George Peabody, Johns Hopkins, and Robert Brookings (to Washington University in St. Louis). About 8 million from William Rice; over ten million, after the dust had settled, from Leland and Jane Stanford, and at least 27 million from John D. Rockefeller to the University of Chicago. Meanwhile less fortunate places not in receipt of these enormous gifts, such as Harvard, fared satisfactorily. The Harvard endowment tripled between 1869 and 1878, then tripled again by 1898, and exceeded $22 million by 1909.[186] By that point private

182. Butler, *Education in the United States*, pp. vii–viii.

183. *Historical Statistics*, series Y682–709.

184. Tyack, James, and Benavot, *Law and the Shaping of Public Education, 1785–1954*, pp. 45, 54.

185. Quotations are from Charles W. Dabney, "A World Wide Law," in *University of Tennessee Index* (1899): series 2, no. 10; Amory D. Mayo, *Southern Women in the Recent Educational Movement of the South* (1892), ed. Dan T. Carter and Amy Friedlander (Baton Rouge, LA, 1978), p. 136; Ellis, *The Money Value of Education*, p. 3.

186. Robert H. Bremner, *American Philanthropy* (Chicago, 1960), p. 105; Merle E. Curti and Roderick Nash, *Philanthropy in the Shaping of American Higher Education* (New Brunswick, NJ, 1965), chs. 6, 7, 9, 12; Daniel A. Wren, "American Business Philanthropy and Higher Education in the Nineteenth Century," *Business History Review*, 57 (1983): 321–46.

Table 4.1   Educational expenditure in the United States and Europe, 1900

	Expenditure per student (1900 dollars)	Students per capita	Expenditure per capita (1900 dollars)
United States	16.78	0.23	3.86
United Kingdom	16.40	0.18	2.95
Germany	13.57	0.20	2.71
France	12.79	0.15	1.92

Source: Adapted from Fishlow, "Levels of Nineteenth-century American Investment in Education," pp. 432–4.

benefactors were donating almost $26 million annually to higher education, compared to about $6 million in the 1870s.[187] Even the social scientists who expressed reservations about accepting "tainted money" from industrialists succumbed to the temptations of this munificence and agreed to "serve power," according to Silva and Slaughter. As a result, the value of the property, including endowment, of institutions of higher education grew by 110 percent in the 1880s, 158 percent in the 1890s, and 75 percent in the 1900s.[188]

It is therefore evident that schools, colleges, and universities received unprecedented resources from private sources as well as the federal, state, and local governments. Not only did these expenditures surpass those in other professional fields, such as religion, health, government, or military, but also the United States' educational expenditures per capita, exceeded that of other major western powers by the turn of the century, as indicated on Table 4.1.

Thus – relative to the past, relative to other professional fields, and relative to other countries – the aggregate expenditure by Americans on education over this period was phenomenal. In this broad sense the economic status of formal institutions of education rose tremendously. With respect to individual members of the learned professions, however, the question remains as to whether and how the ninefold increase in aggregate spending between 1870 and 1916 translated into elevated financial status for educators.

The assessment of personal economic status begins by observing that, between 1860 and 1914, the average annual earnings of all full-time employees grew merely 65 percent, as indicated on Table 4.2. The earnings naturally varied by vocation. In 1900, for example, farm laborers earned on average $247 in current dollars, factory

187. *USCommEd* (1875), pp. lxxxii–lxxxiii; *USCommEd* (1902), vol. 2, pp. 1354; Mann, *A Study of Engineering Education*, p. 17; Henry A. Rowland, "A Plea for Pure Science" *Science*, 2 (1883): 247.

188. The figures are $83 million in 1880, $174 million in 1890, $449 million in 1900, and $785 million in 1910. Rowland, "A Plea for Pure Science," p. 247; *Historical Statistics*, series H739–50; Edward T. Silva and Sheila A. Slaughter, *Serving Power: The Making of the Social Science Expert, 1860–1920* (Westport, CT, 1984), ch. 10.

Table 4.2   Average annual earnings of all full-time employees, 1860–1914

	Money earnings (current dollars)	Real earnings (1914 dollars)	Cumulative change in real earnings from 1860
1860	303*	381	–
1870	439*	351	–8%
1880	336*	344	–10%
1890	438	479	+26%
1900	438	520	+36%
1910	574	606	+59%
1914	627	627	+65%

* Estimated from figures for non-farm employees reported in *Historical Statistics*, series D735–8; Edgar W. Martin, *The Standard of Living in 1860* (Chicago, 1942), pp. 399n., 415.

Source: Historical Statistics, series D722–7, D735–8, D779–93.

workers and coal miners $435, highly skilled workers $800–1,000, and clerical workers $1,011. Notwithstanding this variety, most of the working population occupied a fairly narrow range of income; at least 92 percent of all American families had earnings under $1,300 in 1900. The top 2 percent of the population, meanwhile, controlled some 60 percent of the country's wealth, which was generally derived from large manufacturing, commercial, or financial enterprises.[189]

As more of the nation's wealth became concentrated in these enterprises, academicians sought to study them and to forge links with potential benefactors, while businessmen sought new dignity and status commensurate with their economic power. As a result, collegiate business schools began to appear, the first ones being founded at the universities of Pennsylvania, California, and Chicago by 1900. This development was accompanied by the rise of "scientific management," and together these events stimulated efforts to identify business as a "profession." In fact, business historians have maintained that "by the time the Harvard Graduate School of Business Administration was organized in 1908, business education had attained a complete professional status."[190] Such statements do not, however, reflect

189. *Historical Statistics*, series D739–64, D779–93; Stanley Lebergott, *The American Economy: Income, Wealth and Want* (Princeton, NJ, 1976), p. 321; Merriam, *American Political Ideas … 1865–1917*, p. 13; James R. Green, *The World of the Worker: Labor in Twentieth-Century America* (New York, 1980), ch. 1; Bruce Laurie, *Artisans into Workers: Labor in Nineteenth-Century America* (New York, 1989), pp. 127–9.

190. Irving G. Wylie, *The Self-Made Man in America: The Myth of Rags to Riches* (New Brunswick, NJ, 1954), p. 113. See Haber, *Efficiency and Uplift: Scientific Management in the Progressive Era, 1890–1920*. Alfred D. Chandler, Jr., talks repeatedly about business management becoming a "profession" in the late nineteenth century, but does not quote anyone using this language. *The Visible Hand: The Managerial Revolution in American Business* (Cambridge, MA, 1977), pp. 8, 130–3, 143, 281–2, 456, 464–8.

contemporary opinion. Rather than affirming business to be a profession, observers tended to express the qualified hope that "business should be, and to some extent already is, one of the professions," as Justice Louis Brandeis stated in 1912. It was this prospective sense "that business is becoming a profession" that characterized discussion on the topic through the 1950s.[191]

This is not to say that business had lower status than the "learned professions," but rather that two countervailing factors were involved in assessing their relationship. On the one hand, members of the professions, as well as most businessmen, expressed the traditional view that amassing wealth did not merit the high dignity of a profession. In the words of Edward Everett Hale:

> the men of liberal culture, of the liberal arts and professions ... all deal with infinite values, not to be weighed, counted, or measured.... [T]he essential principle which lifts the liberal professions to their place above all other callings, is that they deal with infinite values.... Justice, Beauty, Truth, Life.[192]

This opinion in the United States was buttressed by the English view that a liberally educated person deigns not to enter business. On the other hand, members of the professions were forced to concede the importance of material wealth because "solid pudding is better than empty praise," in the words of one attorney in 1872. Added another in 1874:

> There is a great deal too much of this sentimental nonsense in regard to the members of the learned professions. A physician must not advertise; a clergyman must not care for the amount of his salary; a lawyer must not have pecuniary interest in the result of his client's cause.[193]

Between these two factors of dignity and wealth, the balance point increasingly tipped toward the latter, as it became clear that "in Gilded Age America the ability to achieve professional status offered no guarantee of prosperity or even security."[194] While tycoons, industrialists, and business managers grew ever more wealthy and

191. Louis D. Brandeis, *Business – A Profession* (Boston, 1914), p. 1; James H. S. Bossard and J. Frederic Dewhurst, *University Education for Business: A Study of Existing Needs and Practices* (Philadelphia, 1931), p. 12. See A. M. Carr-Saunders and P. A. Wilson, *The Professions* (Oxford, 1933), pp. 491–4; C. Wright Mills, *White Collar: The American Middle Classes* (New York, 1951), p. 138; Howard R. Bowen, "Business Management: A Profession?", *Annals of the American Academy of Political and Social Science*, 297 (1955): 112–7; Bernard Barber, "Is American Business Becoming Professionalized?", in *Sociological Theory, Values and Sociocultural Change*, ed. Edward A. Tiryakian (London, 1963), pp. 121–46.

192. Edward E. Hale, "Noblesse Oblige" (1871), in *What Career? Ten Papers on the Choice of a Vocation and the Use of Time* (Boston, 1878), pp. 55, 65, 71. See Hofstadter, *Age of Reform*, pp. 148–9; James B. Gilbert, *Work without Salvation: America's Intellectuals and Industrial Alienation, 1880–1910* (Baltimore, MD, 1977), pp. vii–ix. For the debate among university dons at Cambridge University, see Sheldon Rothblatt, *The Revolution of the Dons: Cambridge and Society in Victorian England* (New York, 1968), pp. 248–73.

193. "Lawyers' Incomes," *Albany Law Journal*, 6 (1872): 249; "Compensation of Lawyers," *Albany Law Journal*, 10 (1874): 193–4.

194. Cindy Sondik Aron, *Ladies and Gentlemen of the Civil Service: Middle-Class Workers in Victorian America* (New York, 1987), p. 28.

powerful, members of the professions were forced to concede the rising status of "the industrial aristocracy." As a result they often fell to self-pity while exaggerating their late nineteenth-century decline in social status relative to "the captain of industry." Or they trumpeted the traditional norm that professional dignity offset wealth, given a reasonable degree of material security.[195] Whatever the response, the professions watched their prestige and appeal decline relative to business and industry, where fortunes could be amassed.[196]

Fortunes could not easily be made in the professions, even in the practice of law. The average salary of attorneys from the 1870s through about 1910 was between $2,000 and $3,000. True, a clutch of Wall Street lawyers near the turn of the century received yearly fees totaling between $50,000 and $100,000, but even these sums did not compare to the fortunes of industrial barons. Already by the 1870s "the status of the lawyers had ... eroded in relation to the rich, who had grown vastly richer with the advent of financial capitalism."[197] With this in mind, attorneys, though well off compared to the average income of full-time employees, grumbled. Writing to the *Central Law Journal* of St. Louis, one Cincinnati attorney observed: "Lawyers as a class are proverbially poor.... Lawyers as a rule are underpaid for their work.... And as for our judges, it is a source of universal complaint that they are the most poorly paid of any judges in the world."[198]

195. Merriam, *American Political Ideas ... 1865–1917*, p. 2. See Winship, *Is there a Science of Pedagogy?*, p. 12; Flexner, *Medical Education*, p. 45; Hofstadter, *The Age of Reform*, pp. 148–64.

196. In a study of the career choices of college graduates at 37 colleges and universities across the country, Burritt concluded that "commercial pursuits" had experienced a "phenomenal rise" in the last half of the nineteenth century. At the end of the nineteenth century, commerce was the choice of about 20 percent of the baccalaureates of these institutions, and theology, law and medicine combined, about 27 percent. Soon commerce passed those three fields, according to a study of more than 24,000 graduates of six New England colleges between 1904 and 1926. Bailey B. Burritt, *Professional Distribution of College and University Graduates* (Washington, DC, 1912), p. 78; McGruder E. Sadler, "A Comparative Personnel Study of Ministerial, Medical, and Law Students" (PhD diss., Yale University, 1929), ch. 1.

197. John A. Matzko, " 'The Best Men of the Bar': The Founding of the American Bar Association," in *The New High Priests: Lawyers in Post-Civil War America* (Westport, CT, 1984), ed. Gerard W. Gawalt (Westport, CT, 1984), pp. 78–9. In addition to sources cited below, my estimates are drawn from: "Compensation of Lawyers," *Albany Law Journal*, 10 (1874): 193–4; "Lawyers' Fees," *Albany Law Journal*, 13 (1877): 379–80; "Breadgetting of the Legal Profession," *Albany Law Journal*, 20 (1880): 306; Henry Strong, "Waiting for Clients," *Chicago Legal News*, 11 (1881): 300–1; "Lawyer and Client – Right of Action for Fees," *Central Law Journal [Des Moines]*, reprinted in *Virginia Law Journal*, 5 (1882): 610; "Lawyers' Fees," *Washington Law Reporter*, 14 (1886): 376; T. A. McNeal, "Compensation of Lawyers," *Kansas State Bar Association Reports*, 2 (1889): 28; "Lawyers' Fees," *American Law Review [St. Louis]*, 26 (1892): 107–10; Charles N. Gregory, "Wage of Law Teachers," *ABA Reports* (1897): 511–22; "Compensation of Attorneys," *Oklahoma Law Journal*, 3 (1905): 348–52; Gerard W. Gawalt, "The Impact of Industrialization on the Legal Profession in Massachusetts, 1870–1900," in *The New High Priests: Lawyers in Post-Civil War America*, ed. Gawalt (Westport, CT, 1984), p. 99.

198. W. H. W., "Lawyers' Fees," *Central Law Journal* (St. Louis) 11 (1880): 219–20.

If lawyers sensed they were losing ground to businessmen, notwithstanding new openings for railroad and corporate attorneys, much more was this the case for physicians. Doctors received "little economic reward" for their efforts and generally belonged to "the lower end of the middle class," earning between $700–1,500 at the turn of the century.[199] In the cities medicine was highly competitive, and most physicians had few regular patients. In small towns and rural areas doctors had a more stable and regular patronage, but earned even less while working longer hours. As late as 1914 in a rural state like Wisconsin three-fifths of the state's approximately 2,800 physicians earned less than $1,500 annually. The fundamental problem was that "the medical profession is very full – indeed, in its lower ranks, overcrowded," as noted A. D. White in 1884 and Abraham Flexner in his famous report of 1910. Under these circumstances it is scarcely surprising that only a tiny fraction of the investment in higher education before 1910 was directed toward medical schools.[200]

The clergy, whose relationship to mammon was most problematic, experienced the greatest relative decline of income among the learned professions. The average salary of most full-time Protestant ministers on the eve of the Civil War was about $500. Given this figure as a baseline, Table 4.3 compares clerical earnings with the average annual earnings of all full-time employees over time.

The figures in Table 4.3 are based upon reports from Congregational and Methodist ministers, and therefore provide a high estimate of clerical income. Other studies drawing upon a broader sampling of denominations confirm the pattern that, on the eve of World War I, Protestant clergy still earned somewhat more than the average income of all full-time employees, although they had lost considerable ground relative to that average. By 1920 clerical income fell almost to that average – $1,428 compared to $1,407, respectively. As to maximum income, it should be noted that less than 1 percent of all clergy in the late nineteenth or early twentieth century earned over $3,000.[201] With this in mind, clergy – from the Rector of Episcopal Grace Church in New York City to Baptist W. C. Bitting in Missouri – concluded, regretfully, that ministers earned less than lawyers, physicians, or professors and about as much as schoolteachers, but, hopefully, that their traditional status offset their lesser wealth among the professions.[202]

199. George Rosen, *The Structure of American Medical Practice, 1875–1941,* ed. Charles E. Rosenberg (Philadelphia, 1983), p. 35; Starr, *The Social Transformation of American Medicine,* pp. 84–5, 142. Rosen cites higher estimates that do not count the bottom third, at least, of physicians (p. 35).

200. White, *What Profession shall I Choose?,* p. 44; Flexner, *Medical Education,* p. 17; Ludmerer, *Learning to Heal,* chs. 7, 10; Rothstein, *American Medical Schools,* pp. 67, 110–1, 162–3; Ronald L. Numbers, "The Fall and Rise of the American Medical Profession," in *The Professions in American History,* ed. Nathan O. Hatch (Notre Dame, IN, 1988), p. 62.

201. Figures in current dollars. *Historical Statistics,* p. 152, series D735–8. See Mark A. May and Frank K. Shuttleworth, *The Education of American Ministers* (New York, 1934), vol. 4, p. 51; Ferenc M. Szasz, *The Protestant Clergy in the Great Plains and Mountain West, 1865–1915* (Albuquerque, NM, 1988), p. 67; Mary E. Moxcey, *Some Qualities Associated with Success in the Christian Ministry* (New York, 1922), p. 70; Robert L. Webb, *The Ministry as a Life Work* (New York, 1922), p. 11.

202. Charles L. Slattery, *The Ministry* (New York, 1921), ch. 8; W. C. Bitting, *Shall the*

Table 4.3   Average annual earnings of all full-time employees compared to
Protestant ministers' salaries, 1860–1914

	Money earnings (current dollars)		Real earnings (1914 dollars)		Cumulative increase in real earnings since 1860	
	All	Clergy	All	Clergy	All	Clergy
1860	303*	500	381	629	–	–
1890	438	794	479	868	26%	38%
1900	438	731	520	867	36%	38%
1910	574	802	606	847	59%	35%
1914	627	938	627	938	65%	49%

*Estimated from the figures for non-farm employees reported in *Historical Statistics*, series D735–8; Martin, *Standard of Living in 1860*, pp. 399n., 415.
Source: *Historical Statistics*, series D722–7, D735–8, D779–93.

The clergy's assessment of schoolteachers' earnings is high compared to the conventional view "that the salary American teachers receive is very close to the bare living wage," in the words of Lotus Coffmann from 1911. Various individuals from the president of the University of Chicago, to an education professor of Hampton Institute, to the editor of the *Journal of Education*, concurred at the time – and subsequent historians have agreed – that "at no time in the half century after 1870 did teachers receive more than minimal compensation."[203] Similar testimony was also heard about college and university faculty. "[P]rofessors ... are thus placed in ... humiliating contrast with men of nearly every occupation above unskilled labor," wrote An American Professor in the *Educational Review*, quoting the *Nation* and citing a number university presidents. Studies of professorial income by W. R. Harper, Guido Marx, E. L. Thorndike, and J. M. Cattell came to

Old Preacher Suffer? (New York, 1910), pp. 4–5. See George W. Samson, *An Appeal to the Churches of Maryland ... to Educate and Support Men for the Ministry* (Baltimore, MD, 1870); "The Pastor's Economy," *Seminary Magazine*, 1 (October 1888): 153–5; "The Preacher's Pay," *Seminary Magazine*, 8 (May 1895): 451–3; "Pastoral Support," *Southwestern Journal of Theology*, 1 (July 1917): 31–47; Henry H. Tweedy, Harlan P. Breach, and Judson J. Smith, *Christian Work as a Vocation* (New York, 1922). p. 34.
203. Lotus D. Coffman, *The Social Composition of the Teaching Population* (New York, 1911), p. 83; William Graebner, "Retirement in Education: The Economic and Social Functions of the Teachers' Pension," *HEQ*, 18 (1978): 397. See William R. Harper, *The Trend in Higher Education in America* (Chicago, 1905), p. 187; Charles B. Dyke, *The Economic Aspect of Teachers' Salaries* (New York, 1899), pp. 7, 15, 51; Arthur C. Perry, Jr., *The Status of the Teacher* (Boston, 1912), p. 12; Willard S. Elsbree, *Teachers' Salaries* (New York, 1931), pp. 5–6; Theodore R. Sizer, *Secondary Schools at the Turn of the Century* (New Haven, CT, 1964), p. 42; Michael W. Sedlak and Steven Schlossman, *Who will Teach? Historical Perspectives on the Changing Appeal of Teaching as a Profession* (Santa Monica, CA, 1986), ch. 2.

the same conclusion.[204] Relying on these studies, recent historians have likewise testified to the "genteel poverty" of late-nineteenth and early twentieth-century professors.[205]

Such testimony about educators' relatively low financial status is problematic in several respects, however. For one thing, scholars from E. L. Thorndike to Howard Bowen have noted the "definitional and statistical problems" encountered in evaluating the compensation of faculty at all levels.[206] For another, such testimony was usually leavened with a strong sense of optimism. "[T]he future of the American teacher looks brighter than it ever has before," observed the president of the Carnegie Foundation for the Advancement of Teaching, the US Commissioner of Education, and the editor of the *Journal of Education* in the 1900s.[207]

An important reason for this optimism lies in another issue that is often overlooked by those asserting educators' low financial status: the deflation between the Civil War and World War I. Contemporary educators arguing for salary increases often proposed that "a period of great increase in the cost of living" followed the 1880s,[208] and recent scholars have suggested that educators' salaries "did not rise significantly" in constant dollars after 1867, and have even conveyed the impression of "falling salaries" against a background of "the rising cost of living" from the 1880s onward.[209] The cost-of-living estimates from the time have been shown to be inflated, however, for there existed about 52 percent deflation in consumer prices

204. An American Professor, "The Status of the American Professor," *Educational Review*, 16 (1898): 422. Harper, "The Pay of College Professors," *The Forum*, 16 (1893): 96–109; Guido H. Marx, "The Problem of the Assistant Professor," *Journal of Proceedings and Addresses of the Association of American Universities Journal*, 11 (1910): 29; Flexner, *Medical Education*, p. 45; Cattell, *American Men of Science* (1910), pp. 578–9; Thorndike et al., *The Financial Status of the Professor*, pp. 22–5.

205. Margaret W. Rossiter, *Women Scientists in America: Struggles and Strategies to 1940* (Baltimore, MD, 1982), pp. 197, 369n. See Cravens, *The Triumph of Evolution ... 1900–1941*, p. 206; Helen Lefkowitz Horowitz, *Alma Mater: Design and Experience in the Women's Colleges from their Beginnings to the 1930s* (Boston, 1984), p. 185; Rothstein, *American Medical Schools*, p. 106.

206. Howard R. Bowen, "Faculty salaries: Past and Future," *Educational Record*, 49 (1968): 11; Thorndike, *The Financial Status of the Professor*, pp. 22–3.

207. Henry S. Pritchett, in Thorndike, *The Financial Status of the Professor*, p. viii. See Perry, *The Status of the Teacher*, pp. 59–60; William T. Harris, "The Future of Teachers' Salaries," *Independent*, 69 (1905): 255–8.

208. Marx, "Some Trends in Higher Education," p. 775; Wayne J. Urban, *Why Teachers Organized* (Detroit, MI, 1982), pp. 115–6.

209. Barbara Miller Solomon, *In the Company of Educated Women: A History of Women and Higher Education in America* (New Haven, CT, 1985), p. 225; Frank Stricker, "American Professors in the Progressive Era: Incomes, Aspirations, and Professionalism," *Journal of Interdisciplinary History*, 19 (1988): 240, 247. See Sedlak and Schlossman, *Who will Teach?*, p. 5. Some scholars have noted the deflationary conditions, which increased the value in teachers' salaries over the last half of the nineteenth century. Elsbree, *The American Teacher*, pp. 432–3; Sizer, *Secondary Schools at the Turn of the Century*, p. 42; Graebner, "Retirement in Education: The Economic and Social Functions of the Teachers' Pension," p. 397.

between the Civil War and World War I. In fact, the international depression from 1873 to 1896 involved "the most drastic deflation in the memory of man," according to David Landes and Alan Trachtenberg.[210] Consequently, unless one were to argue that educators' actual money earnings declined by half – a proposition that no one suggests – then their real earnings must have risen significantly in constant dollars.[211]

Finally, it must be noted that complaints about educators' compensation generally do not pertain to administrators. On the eve of the Civil War the salaries for male high school principals in large cities ranged from $1,500–3,000, while male grammar school principals earned $700–2,000, and female grammar school principals earned $400–1,000. These amounts increased as school systems appeared and expanded in subsequent decades. Meanwhile the school superintendency was accorded a salary commensurate with the best paid minister or physician in the locale: $2,000–3,000 in small communities, $5,000–6,000 in middle-sized cities, and about $10,000 in major cities.[212] In rural states, such as Colorado, district Superintendents were paid $3,000–5,000 and principals $1,000, while in Vermont the state superintendent of schools was paid more than the governor. By the turn of the century, it was said that merely 5 percent of the university professors in the country "may hope to receive a salary equal to that of the superintendent of schools of such cities as Athens, Ohio, and Fort Wayne, Indiana."[213]

In colleges and universities presidents were paid at about the same level as school superintendents in their locale. At the close of the Civil War presidents of leading eastern colleges earned about $3,000, which was the amount paid to presidents of mid-western state universities in the 1870s and 1880s.[214] In 1893 the

210. Alan Trachtenberg, *The Incorporation of America: Culture and Society in the Gilded Age* (New York, 1982), p. 39. *Historical Statistics*, series D722–27, D735–8; Stricker, "American Professors in the Progressive Era," p. 248n.

211. There were occasional cutbacks as when the forerunner of the University of Illinois cut professors' salaries by 10 percent in 1873. But such cuts were, as in this case, temporary. Winton U. Solberg, *The University of Illinois, 1867–1894; An Intellectual and Cultural History* (Urbana, IL, 1968), pp. 125, 257.

212. Thwing, "A New Profession," pp. 31–2; Dyke, *The Economic Aspect of Teachers' Salaries*, ch. 2; Edward L. Thorndike, *The Teaching Staff of Secondary Schools in the United States: Amount of Education, Length of Service, Salaries* (Washington, DC, 1909); Ellwood P. Cubberley, *Public School Administration: A Statement of the Fundamental Principles Underlying the Organization and Administration of Public Education* (Boston, 1916), pp. 130–2; Elsbree, *The American Teacher*, pp. 272–9.

213. Thorndike, *The Financial Status of the Professor*, p. 24. Ira M. DeLong and Fred Dick, eds., *1896–97 Educational Directory for the State of Colorado* ([Denver, CO, 1897]), pp. 3–7; William S. Learned, William C. Bagley, et al., *The Professional Preparation of Teachers for American Public Schools ... in the State of Missouri* (New York, 1920), p. 9n.

214. John S. Whitehead, *The Separation of College and State: Columbia, Dartmouth, Harvard, and Yale, 1776–1876* (New Haven, CT, 1973), p. 220; Earle D. Ross, *A History of the Iowa State College of Agriculture and Mechanic Arts* (Ames, IA, 1942), pp. 78–9; Solberg, *The University of Illinois, 1867–1894*, pp. 99, 103–4, 125, 257, 333; Allan Nevins, *The State Universities and Democracy* (Urbana, IL, 1962), p. 50; Merle Curti and Vernon Carstensen, eds., *The University of Wisconsin: A History, 1848–1925* (Madison, WI, 1949), vol. 1, pp. 593–4n.

Table 4.4   Average annual earnings of all full-time employees compared to the salaries of public school teachers, 1870–1914

	Money earnings (current dollars)		Real earnings (1914 dollars)		Cumulative change in real earnings since 1870	
	All	P.S. Teachers	All	P.S. Teachers	All	P.S. Teachers
1870	439*	189	351	151	–	–
1880	336*	195	344	199	–2%	+32%
1890	438	252	479	275	+36%	+82%
1900	438	325	520	386	+48%	+156%
1910	574	485	606	512	+73%	+239%
1914	627	525	627	525	+79%	+248%

* Estimated from the figures for non-farm employees reported in *Historical Statistics*, series D735–8.
Source: *Historical Statistics*, series D722–27, D735–8, D779–793, H520–30.

president of the University of Chicago surveyed 124 "representative" colleges and universities and found that the average salary of presidents was just over $3,000, with about one-sixth of presidents receiving housing in addition. By the turn of the century presidents of major universities earned about $10,000, and college presidents about $5,000. These figures put the income of presidents, as well as superintendents, in about the top 2 percent of American families.[215]

Since educational administrators were well compensated relative both to the general population and to the other learned professions, the question of the low financial status of educators narrows to that of schoolteachers and professors. For the former group, a general comparison to the average annual earnings of all full-time employees is presented in Table 4.4.[216]

Table 4.4 demonstrates the remarkable relative gain in the real income of public school teachers between the Civil War and World War I, particularly between 1890 and 1910. This relative gain – more than three times the average gain of all employees – is confirmed by other studies. For example, Paul Douglas found that, among thirteen groups of workers, teachers' income had the biggest gain in purchasing power between 1900 and 1926. Since the purchasing power of teachers' incomes began to stagnate after about 1915 due to the rise of inflation, Douglas's

215. Harper, "The Pay of College Professors," p. 97; Andrew F. West, "American Colleges," in *Education in the United States*, ed. Nicholas M. Butler (Albany, NY, 1900), p. 237; Veysey, *The Emergence of the American University*, pp. 263, 391n.; Viva Boothe, *Salaries and the Cost of Living in Twenty-Seven State Universities and Colleges, 1913–1932* (Columbus, OH, 1932), p. 29.

216. The contemporary bibliography on this topic is enormous. See Charles A. Nelson, "Bibliography of Teachers' Salaries and Pensions," *Educational Review*, 33 (1907): 24–35, including over 350 items; and Thorndike, *The Teaching Staff of Secondary Schools*, pp. 51–7, including another 80 sources published between 1905 and 1909.

finding means that the remarkable increase in teachers' real income occurred between 1900 and the early 1910s. This increase helps to explain why great optimism was expressed at the same time that the average income of all teachers in 1913 ($512) was still below that of factory workers ($578), and merely half that of salaried employees ($1,066).[217]

Notwithstanding such optimism, scholars have long maintained "that teachers" salaries were lamentably low in 1913."[218] This assertion requires that one make a number of assumptions about the "definitional and statistical problems" concerning that income. These problems include the variation in income by geographic area, by locale in urban or rural areas, by level of school, and by race. A black, elementary teacher in a rural southern school was paid perhaps a third of the salary of a white, northern, urban high school teacher.[219] Such contextual, structural, and prejudicial factors obtained also in the other professions, however. What particularly complicates the assessment of teachers' income is a number of additional problems.

First, there is the evaluation of perquisites accorded to teachers. Room and board had traditionally been provided, and, although this arrangement was generally unsatisfactory to teachers and gradually eliminated, it continued to supplement the compensation in many rural school districts. Tenure for schoolteachers was championed by educational spokesmen, such as Charles Eliot, and was introduced in most urban school systems by the turn of the century. States began enacting laws establishing tenure for teachers: the District of Columbia in 1906, New Jersey and Wisconsin in 1909, Oregon in 1913, Massachusetts in 1914, Maryland in 1916, and New York and Illinois in 1917. Furthermore, inasmuch as "long tenures logically involve pensions or annuities," in the words of Eliot, retirement benefits were provided for many teachers. Some 65 cities established pensions for teachers between 1905 and 1914, and by 1916 a retirement system for public schoolteachers had been established in 33 states.[220]

Beyond the value of these perquisites, which did not accrue to workers in most other fields, the length of the school year was not equivalent to the work year of other employees. In 1870 the average school year was about 132 days, and in 1916 about 159. Teachers' income at the time was therefore generally based on seven

217. Paul H. Douglas, *Real Wages in the United States, 1890–1926* (New York, 1930), p. 395–7; Walter C. Eells, *Teacher's Salaries and the Cost of Living* (Stanford, CA, 1933), ch. 4; E. S. Evenden, *Teachers' Salaries and Salary Schedules in the United States, 1918–19* (Washington, DC, 1919), p. 117; Elsbree, *The American Teacher*, p. 433, ch. 29; Willford I. King, *The National Income and its Purchasing Power* (New York, 1930), p. 87; Perry, *The Status of the Teacher*, pp. 59–60.

218. Eells, *Teacher's Salaries and the Cost of Living*, p. 71.

219. Mayo, *Southern Women in the Recent Educational Movement of the South*, p. 263; Dyke, *The Economic Aspect of Teachers' Salaries*, ch. 2; Thorndike, *The Teaching Staff of Secondary Schools*, pp. 39–52; Elsbree, *The American Teacher*, p. 273.

220. Charles W. Eliot, "Teachers' Tenure of Office," in *Educational Reform: Essays and Addresses* (New York, 1898), pp. 52–3; Elsbree, *The American Teacher*, p. 477, ch. 30; Graebner, "Retirement in Education: The Economic and Social Functions of the Teachers' Pension," p. 401; Teaford, *The Unheralded Triumph: City Government in America, 1870–1900*, p. 159.

months of teaching.[221] In view of this factor and the perquisites, it is possible to argue that teachers' income should be as much as *doubled* when compared to the average income of all full-time employees. But even this adjustment does not reach the fundamental difficulty in such comparisons, which are the basis for the judgment that teachers were poorly paid in the late nineteenth and early twentieth centuries. The fundamental issue in evaluating schoolteachers' income is gender.

The feminization of the teaching force began in the Northeast and mid-West in the second quarter of the nineteenth century, and occurred in the South in the decades following the Civil War. By the turn of the century, more than two-thirds of teachers were women, and in 1908 the US Commissioner of Education reported that 78 percent of teachers were women, a fraction that rose to 86 percent by 1920.[222] It is equally well known that these women were paid less than men. The differential between men and women, like the absolute amount of compensation, varied according to the geographic area, the locale in urban or rural areas, and the level of teaching. But in general it may be said that women were paid one-third to one-half the salaries of men until the 1860s. Subsequently the fraction rose to between two-thirds and four-fifths in the 1900s, according to studies of the time.[223]

It has been suggested that feminization was a cause of teachers' low compensation in the sense that the increased supply of teachers arising from the education of women meant that well qualified, low-paid women could be substituted for higher-paid men. Other scholars suggest that low compensation was a cause of feminization, since men left teaching when salaries did not keep up with other

221. *Historical Statistics*, series H520–30; William T. Harris, "Elementary Education," in *Education in the United States*, ed. Nicholas M. Butler (Albany, NY, 1900), p. 103; Dyke, *The Economic Aspect of Teachers' Salaries*, pp. 18–28.

222. Mayo, *Southern Women in the Recent Educational Movement in the South*, p. 178; *USCommEd* (1908), vol. 2, p. 396; Myra H. Strober and Audrey G. Lanford, "The Feminization of Public School Teaching: Cross-Sectional Analysis, 1850–1880," *Signs*, 11 (1986): 212–35; Robert C. Morris, *Reading, 'Riting, and Reconstruction: The Education of Freedmen in the South, 1861–1870* (Chicago, 1976), chs. 2, 4; John G. Richardson and Brenda Wooden Hatcher, "The Feminization of Public School Teaching, 1870–1920," *Work and Occupations*, 10 (1983): 81–99; Geraldine Jonçich Clifford, "Man/Women/Teacher: Gender, Family, and Career in American Educational History," in *American Teachers: Histories of a Profession at Work*, ed. Donald Warren (New York, 1989), p. 294.

223. Dyke, *The Economic Aspect of Teachers' Salaries*, pp. 31–41; *USCommEd* (1896–97), vol. 2, p. 1537; National Education Association, *Report of the Committee on Salaries, Tenure, and Pensions* (Winona, MN, 1905), pp. 190–205; Ernest C. Moore, *Fifty Years of American Education ... from 1867 to 1917* (Boston, 1917), p. 61; Elsbree, *The American Teacher*, ch. 21; Sedlak and Schlossman, *Who will Teach?*, ch. 2. Studying 5,000 teachers chosen from communities representative of the teaching staff of the country, Thorndike concluded that the average salary for male public high school teachers was about $700, the median, about $900; the average for women, about $550; the median, about $650. (*The Teaching Staff of Secondary Schools*, pp. 13–4.) In another prominent study, Coffman examined teachers in 17 states, concluding that "the typical American male public-school teacher" earned $489; "the typical American female teacher" $485. (*The Social Composition of the Teaching Population*, pp. 79–81.) Coffman's lower estimates may be explained by a moderate bias toward rural teachers. Cf. John L. Rury, "Who Became Teachers? The Social Characteristics of Teachers in American History," in *American Teachers*, ed. Donald Warren (New York, 1989), p. 31.

options.[224] It has also been argued that the disparity in average income persisted, despite the gradual elimination of differential salary schedules for men and women, because women were relegated to teaching in "lower" levels of schooling and denied administrative responsibilities that supplemented teaching salaries.[225]

Whatever the nature and direction of these causal relationships, the inference that teachers' salaries were low is drawn from comparisons to other workers' income. But such comparisons reveal differences among vocations only if the groups of workers are alike in other respects. In these comparisons the variable of vocation is confounded by the variable of gender, because the predominantly female population of teachers is being compared to the predominantly male population of other workers. The confounding is demonstrated by the contradictory recommendations made to improve the inferred low status of teachers' salaries. On the one hand, early-twentieth-century scholars who made this inference, such as Lotus Coffman, recommended that teachers should be men who should be paid as much as, or more than, other men. "How great is the need for many more 'regular fellows' to follow the calling," agreed Riverda Jordan, "[teaching] is a real 'MAN'S JOB'."[226] On the other hand, recent scholars, who have cited the same comparative studies, conclude that women teachers should have been paid as much as other male workers.[227] Consequently, although the two groups of scholars talk about teaching being poorly paid, they both would change the situation by addressing the gender variable in ironically different ways: either barring women from teaching, or welcoming them and paying them as much as men.

In contrast, Susan Carter has avoided confounding vocation and gender and recently made some of the most informative analyses of women's salaries. She maintains that "although much has been made of the fact that wages of women teachers were low, it is also true that, when compared with other employment opportunities open to women, teaching was a *good job*."[228] The point was made as

224. Cf. Carter, "Occupational Segregation, Teachers' Wages, and American Economic Growth," pp. 373–83; Kathleen C. Berkeley, "'The Ladies Want to Bring about Reform in the Public Schools': Public Education and Women's Rights in the Post-Civil War South," *HEQ*, 24 (1984): 45–58.

225. Thorndike, *The Teaching Staff of Secondary Schools*, pp. 20–1; Coffman, *The Social Composition of the Teaching Population*, p. 83; John L. Rury, "Gender, Salaries, and Career: American Teachers, 1900–1910," *Issues in Education*, 4 (1986): 215–35; Myra H. Strober and David B. Tyack, "Why do Women Teach and Men Manage? A Report on Research on Schools," *Signs*, 5 (1980): 494–503.

226. Riverda H. Jordan, *Education as a Life Work: An Introduction into Education* (New York, 1930), pp. 5, 28; Coffman, *The Social Composition of the Teaching Population*, ch. 11; Elsbree, *The American Teacher*, p. 433.

227. Sedlak and Schlossman, *Who will Teach?*, ch. 2; Clifford, "Man/Women/Teacher: Gender, Family, and Career in American Educational History," p. 298; David Tyack and Elisabeth Hansot, "Silence and Policy Talk: Historical Puzzles About Gender and Education," *Educational Researcher*, 17 (April 1988): 33–41.

228. Susan B. Carter and Mark Prus, "The Labor Market and the American High School Girl, 1890–1928," *Journal of Economic History*, 42 (1982): 166; Carter, "Academic Women Revisited: An Empirical Study of Changing Patterns in Women's Employment as College and University Faculty, 1890–1963," *Journal of Social History*, 14 (1981): 690; Carter, "Incentives and Rewards to Teaching," in *American Teachers: Histories of a Profession at Work*, ed. Donald Warren (New York, 1989), p. 49.

well in writings of the time, when $4–6 per week was a good wage for a female factory worker. "When the girl got $10.00, $12.00 and $15.00 a week it became a rather respectable job," according to University of Washington professor Theresa McMahon, who worked on behalf of a minimum wage law in the 1900s. Meanwhile in other feminized professions, such as social work, "salaries, on the whole, compared unfavorably with those of schoolteachers." Overall, "education surpassed by far any other field employing women," according to Barbara Miller Solomon.[229]

If schoolteaching was the most remunerative vocational option for the great majority of those who were teachers – notwithstanding the injustice of the fact – then it may also be worthwhile to reconsider the abundant historical and historiographical testimony that college and university teachers were poorly paid. There exists important testimony contradicting the often cited view "that the least rewarded of all the professions is that of the teacher in our higher educational institutions," as Andrew Carnegie wrote in 1905. Indeed, Carnegie's "shock" at discovering in the 1890s "that college teachers were paid less than many of his office clerks" is often recounted as part of the lore of professors' "genteel poverty."[230] But it is telling that this specific comparison breaks down when examined closely. Many office clerks were, in fact, well paid. The average annual salary of male clerks in the federal civil service was $1,200, a figure in about the top 10 percent of the income of American families. Furthermore, the average faculty salary in the 1890s was some 75 percent higher than the average clerical salary of about 900 dollars.[231] Other such comparisons also become problematic when examined closely.[232] Consequently, scholars from Claude Bowman to Richard Shryock have labeled as "exaggeration" the view that professors were poorly paid, and Howard Bowen has recently observed "that the pre-World War I era was a golden age for the academic profession."[233]

229. McMahon, "My Story" (1958), pp. 257–61; Roy Lubove, *The Professional Altruist: The Emergence of Social Work as a Career, 1880–1930* (Cambridge, MA, 1965), p. 133; Solomon, *In the Company of Educated Women*, pp. 127–8. See J. M. Bancroft, "Occupations and Professions for College Bred Women," *Education*, 5 (1885): 486–95; Margaret MacKintosh, "Women as Professional Teachers," *Education*, 7 (1887): 556–8; Roberta Frankfort, *Collegiate Women: Domesticity and Career in Turn-of-the-Century America* (New York, 1977), p. 102.

230. Quoted from Carnegie's "Letter of Gift to the Trustees" establishing the Carnegie Foundation for the Advancement of Teaching in 1905, in Rainard R. Robbins, *College Plans for Retirement Income* (New York, 1940), pp. 24–5; Andrew Carnegie, *Autobiography* (Boston, 1920), p. 268.

231. Aron, *Ladies and Gentlemen of the Civil Service ... in Victorian America*, p. 21; *Historical Statistics*, series D739–64, 779–93.

232. Ronald L. Numbers states that in 1914 the average income of the top 40 percent of Wisconsin's physicians was "$1,488 ... more than twice what professors earned." But University of Wisconsin faculty salaries approached $2,000 in the 1880s and $3,000 in the 1890s. Numbers, "The Fall and Rise of the American Medical Profession," p. 62; Nevins, *The State Universities and Democracy*, p. 50; Curti and Carstensen, *The University of Wisconsin*, vol. 1, pp. 593, 594n.; Cattell, *American Men of Science* (1910), p. 579. Numbers's view is astutely contradicted in Solomon, *In the Company of Educated Women*, p. 225; Stricker, "American Professors in the Progressive Era, p. 236.

233. Claude C. Bowman, "The College Professor in America: An Analysis of Articles

Many studies of academic salaries were conducted in the late nineteenth and early twentieth centuries. In 1893 University of Chicago President W. R. Harper surveyed 124 "representative" colleges and universities and concluded that $1,470 was "a very fair approximation of the actual average pay" of professors across the country. A widely cited study of twenty leading universities in 1910 concluded that their professors at age 37 earned on average $1,800. One scholar estimated that the average faculty salary in 1912–13 was $1,550, while another study of faculty salaries at 27 state colleges and universities from 23 different states concluded that in 1913–14 the median salary of full professors was $2,530, associate professors $1,862, and assistant professors $1,567.[234] Perhaps the most careful study was published in 1908 by the Carnegie Foundation for the Advancement of Teaching. Out of the some 700 colleges and universities in the United States and Canada, the 102 "financially strongest" reported that "the average salary of a full professor ... is somewhere near $2,500." Among the 471 colleges and universities actually sampled, the "median for all full professors" in the lower half was "somewhat higher than $1,299."[235]

When these data are evaluated in light of the fact that at least 92 percent of American families had an income below $1,300 in the 1900s, the inference follows that about three-quarters of the full-professors at colleges and universities probably had earnings of more than $1,300, that is, in the top 8 percent of family income in the country.[236] Regarding the entire professoriate, we know that the great majority of faculty at the poorer colleges and universities earned less than $1,300 because only half of the full professors earned that amount. We also know that the great majority of faculty at wealthier institutions earned over $1,300 because most assistant professors at the leading institutions earned well over $1,300. Because the wealthier colleges and universities had many more faculty members than the poorer institutions, we may infer that perhaps half of the entire professoriate had a salary

---

Published in the General Magazines, 1890–1938" (PhD diss., University of Pennsylvania, 1938), pp. 63–8; Richard H. Shryock, "The Academic Profession in the United States," *Bulletin of the American Association of University Professors*, 38 (1952): 52; Bowen, "Faculty salaries: Past and Future," p. 10. This view is confirmed by a close study of "faculty status and pay in four [Pennsylvania] colleges ... between 1860 and 1910" in W. Bruce Leslie, "When Professors had Servants: Prestige, Pay, and Professionalization, 1860–1917," *History of Higher Education Annual*, 10 (1990): 19–30. Stricker contends that "in the late 1890s ... dissatisfaction with salaries intensified, erupting in dozens of articles." But among his 64 sources attesting to this point, merely three are from the 1890s, and 51 are dated after 1905. "American Professors in the Progressive Era," p. 234.

234. Harper, "The Pay of College Professors," p. 99; Marx, "The Problem of the Assistant Professor," pp. 25–9; Bowen, "Faculty salaries: Past and Future," p. 10; Boothe, *Salaries and the Cost of Living in Twenty-Seven State Universities and Colleges, 1913–1932*, p. 12.

235. Thorndike, *The Financial Status of the Professor*, pp. vi, 21, 32; Stricker, "American Professors in the Progressive Era," p. 238.

236. This inference follows by reasoning that more than half of the full professors in the poorer half of institutions (one-quarter of all full professors) and almost all of the professors in the wealthier half of institutions (two quarters of all full professors) earned more than $1,299, and by assuming that the "more than" in the former case will approximately balance off the "almost" in the latter.

above $1,300, and the average faculty salary was doubtlessly higher.[237] By this reasoning, we reach the conclusion that at the beginning of the twentieth century most professors and the great majority of all full professors had a salary in about the highest tenth of the incomes of American families. And nearly all professors attained that status in the course of their career.

This income was augmented by a number of perquisites. Leading institutions began granting unlimited tenure in the late nineteenth century, and in 1905 the Carnegie Foundation for the Advancement of Teaching was founded in order to establish a pension system for professors in "accepted" private colleges and universities. The purposes and administration of the system were much debated, but the project nevertheless established the expectation of some pension perquisite for faculty. Meanwhile sabbaticals were introduced by three institutions in the 1880s, another six in the 1890s, and a host of others after 1900.[238] Finally, there was the "independence of the work [which] has quite as much to do as the salary, with attracting men of high type," observed a law professor at the University of Wisconsin. "[T]here is a freedom about it that is inexpressibly fascinating. The professor is his own master," agreed James Hart, a professor of modern languages.[239]

In sum, it is evident that professors' economic status was relatively high from the 1870s through at least 1910. Apart from considerable perquisites, they earned four or five times the income of unskilled laborers and two or three times the average income of all full-time employees. They generally earned more than clergy or physicians, and stood in better straits than many lawyers. Even as their real earnings began to erode after 1910, the average faculty salary was about two-and-a-half times the average earnings of manufacturing employees.[240] Standing financially in at least the top tenth of all American families, professors occupied a position comparable to ministers in the colonial era and to attorneys between the Revolution and Civil War, whose incomes, however, had greater variation. In view of this financial status, the question to be addressed is not the one that has occupied most scholars of the time and since, namely, why were professors paid so poorly? Rather, the

237. Marx, "The Problem of the Assistant Professor," pp. 25–9; Cattell, *American Men of Science* (1910), p. 578. Recall Harper's survey, which found the average faculty salary in all ranks at 124 "representative" institutions to be $1,470. "The Pay of College Professors" (1893).

238. Walter C. Eells and Ernest Hollins, *Sabbatical Leaves in American Higher Education* (Washington, DC, 1962), p. 10. See J. McKeen Cattell, *Carnegie Pensions Together with Extracts from Letters from Two Hundred and Fourteen College and University Professors* (New York, 1919); Ellen Condliffe Lagemann, *Private Power for the Public Good: A History of the Carnegie Foundation for the Advancement of Teaching* (Middletown, Conn, 1983), ch. 3.

239. Gregory, "Wage of Law Teachers," p. 520; James Morgan Hart (1874), quoted in *The Origins of Literary Studies in America: A Documentary Anthology*, ed. Gerald Graff and Michael Warner (New York, 1989), p. 22.

240. Bowman, *The College Professor in America*, pp. 39–63; Beardsley Ruml and Sidney G. Tickton, *Teaching Salaries Then and Now: A 50-Year Comparison with Other Occupations and Industries* (New York, 1955), pp. 32–3; Veysey, *The Emergence of the American University*, p. 390; Solomon, *In the Company of Educated Women*, pp. 65, 225; Carter, "Academic Women Revisited … 1890–1963," p. 698.

question is why did professors think they were paid so poorly when they were relatively well off? To be sure, the clergy and bar were not wholly satisfied with their financial status during their heyday. But why were professorial laments about finances louder and more numerous than those of other leading professions in earlier times?

Half of the answer lies paradoxically in the greater aspirations of faculty. Precisely because they had more, they envisioned more. Endowed with greater intellectual, institutional, political, and social authority than they had ever known, professors naturally aspired to see that manifested in higher economic status, not only through public investment, but also through elevated personal status. Professors therefore developed "new expectations" and made what they considered a justified "demand for privileged treatment." This demand for "a 'professorial' standard of living" arose commensurately with their higher status and increased authority in general and seemed only commensurate with the public investment that had been made in education.[241] The other half of the answer lies in the fact that during this period the United States spawned "a culture in which everything hinges on money," as Robert and Helen Lynd later maintained. At the very time that professors were coming into their own and beginning to earn a "good living," as the clergy and bar had done before them, the standard of what constituted a "good living" rose dramatically. "An American Professor" complained in 1898, "There is no reason for reserving for the professor the exercise of the virtues of self-denial and endurance, when everyone else is striving for all the comfort and luxury attainable."[242]

This striving in late-nineteenth-century and early-twentieth-century America resulted in a widening gap between the rich and poor. A greater fraction of wealth became concentrated in the hands of a smaller percentage of the population. As a result, professors did not *feel* well off, even though they stood financially in at least the highest tenth of family income. The chasm that separated professors from the wealthy was so much greater than professors' distance from the average worker that they felt their economic status was not commensurate with their talent or the presumed importance and dignity of their profession. "There is practically no class of college professors whose pay is on a level with the pay of men in positions of first or second rank and responsibility in the industrial community," observed W. R. Harper. Consequently, professors demanded more, not so much, they said, because they wanted more, but because they deserved to be elevated by virtue of their talent and importance. "The value of genius to the world is of course inestimable. A great man of science may contribute more than even the most successful promoter – a Rockefeller, a Carnegie, or a Morgan – gets," argued James Cattell.[243]

241. Stricker, "American Professors in the Progressive Era," pp. 234, 249. Stricker is one of the few to recognize that professorial laments about low economic status arose more from "new expectations" than from low economic status.

242. Robert S. Lynd and Helen Merrell Lynd, *Middletown: A Study in Modern American Culture* (New York, 1929), pp. 206–7; An American Professor, "Status of the American Professor," p. 422.

243. Harper, "The Pay of College Professors," pp. 103–4; Cattell, ed., *University Control,* pp. 45–6. Green, *The World of the Worker: Labor in Twentieth-Century America,* ch. 1; Laurie, *Artisans into Workers: Labor in Nineteenth-Century America,* pp. 127–9.

And how much money did professors feel was commensurate with their dignity and worth? Estimates of the hypothetical are understandably difficult to find, although ratios of the shortfall against industrialists and financiers are not uncommon, as E. L. Thorndike noted:

> In other callings great ability brings a proportionate reward; the best man may expect from twenty to forty times the reward of the average man.... But in teaching and scholarship the best man cannot ... expect much more than from two to four times the financial reward of the average man.[244]

In 1893, the president of the University of Chicago proposed that a professor "deserves, at the lowest, an increase of about fifty percent in his pay, over the present rates.... The payment of such salaries would be only a matter of simple justice." At the turn of the century, after a decade of deflation, this proposal was cited by others and described as "indeed a conservative estimate." Meanwhile a University of Wisconsin professor proposed that "$5,500 would represent an income which would enable the professor to marry and move in any circle of society which he desires."[245]

This "conservative estimate" of "simple justice" and the standard "to move and marry in any circle of society" meant, in effect, that professors envisioned jumping from the top 8 percent of family income in the United States to about the top 3 or 4 percent. Doubtlessly, the fact that presidents and superintendents occupied that position made professors' claim appear all the more just and righteous. Relative to this desirable " 'professorial' standard of living," they felt themselves living in genteel poverty and lamented their shortfall. But compared to the great majority of fellow citizens and most members of other professions, professors were well off, just as most schoolteachers found their work to be the most remunerative vocational option open to them.

Considered in the context of the time, educators were well paid, notwithstanding historical and historiographical testimony to the contrary. That very testimony, in fact, demonstrates educators' increased expectations, which were stimulated by their enormously improved financial status relative to other learned professions. Those increased expectations throughout the field were accompanied by a new sense of corporate identity and career commitment. We now turn to examine these new attitudes and their expression in the fifth moment of the rhetoric of profession.

Rhetorical: "a truly liberal Profession of Teaching"

In the first half of the nineteenth century, a few American scientists and professors began to endorse "the vocation of scholar" advanced by German academics such as F. A. Wolff. Whether these Americans understood or appropriated the German

---

244. Thorndike, *The Financial Status of the Professor*, p. 25.

245. Harper, "The Pay of College Professors," p. 109; An American Professor, "Status of the American Professor," pp. 419–20, 427; Gregory, "Wage of Law Teachers," p. 519.

conception is much debated.[246] But it is clear that the American profession of scholarship meant attending to academic, rather than student, discipline. Over the second half of the nineteenth century the "men of science," expressing "this pietistic commitment to science as a vocation,"[247] became increasingly prominent in universities, as we have seen.

This prominence of scientists and science accompanied the emergence of specialized disciplines. The scientific pursuit of knowledge required specialization, which became the "distinctive characteristic of nineteenth-century knowledge [that] impelled its creators and custodians to turn their particular competences into professions."[248] Whether adopting an internalist or externalist perspective, historians are agreed that chemists, physicists, biologists, astronomers, and botanists developed a corporate identity and a career commitment to studying and teaching their specialty between about 1880 and 1914.[249] At the same time psychology, anthropology, economics, sociology, and political science "became professions and disciplines."[250] Likewise, in the fields that became the humanities, "the

246. Carl Diehl, *Americans and German Scholarship, 1770–1870* (New Haven, CT, 1978), pp. 42, 149, ch. 2; Kohlstedt, *The Formation of the American Scientific Community*, pp. 138–53; Nathan Reingold, "Definitions and Speculations: The Professionalization of Science in America in the Nineteenth Century," in *The Pursuit of Knowledge in the Early Republic*, ed. Alexandra Oleson and Sanborn C. Brown (Baltimore, MD, 1976), pp. 33–69.

247. Rosenberg, *No Other Gods: On Science and American Social Thought*, pp. 138, 3, 15. David A. Hollinger, "Inquiry and Uplift: Late Nineteenth-Century American Academics and the Moral Efficacy of Scientific Practice," in *The Authority of Experts*, ed. Thomas L. Haskell (Bloomington, IN, 1984), p. 144; Bruce, *The Launching of American Science, 1846–1876*, p. 4; Daniels, *American Science in the Age Jackson*, p. 35, ch. 2.

248. John Higham, "The Matrix of Specialization," in *The Organization of Knowledge in Modern America, 1860–1920*, ed. Alexandra Oleson and John Voss (Baltimore, MD, 1979), pp. 3–4. Sister M. St. Mel Kennedy, "The Changing Academic Characteristics of the Nineteenth-Century American College Teacher," *Paedagogica Historica*, 5 (1965): 399; Buck, ed., *Social Sciences at Harvard, 1860–1920*, p. 8; Geraldine Jonçich Clifford, ed., *Lone Voyagers: Academic Women in Coeducational Institutions, 1870–1937* (New York, 1989), p. 25; Novick, *That Noble Dream: The "Objectivity Question" and the American Historical Profession*, p. 52.

249. Edward H. Beardsley, *The Rise of the American Chemistry Profession, 1850–1900* (Gainseville, FL, 1964); Kevles, "The Physics, Mathematics, and Chemistry Communities," pp. 139–72; Rachel Volberg, "Constraints and Commitments in the Development of American Biology, 1880–1920" (PhD diss., University of California, 1983); Eugene Cittadino, "Ecology and the Professionalization of Botany in America, 1890–1905," *Studies in the History of Biology*, 4 (1980): 171–98; Rothenberg, "Organization and Control: Professionals and Amateurs in American Astronomy, 1899–1918," pp. 305–25.

250. Hamilton Cravens, "History of the Social Sciences," in *Historical Writing on American Science*, ed. Sally Gregory Kohlstedt and Margaret W. Rossiter (Baltimore, MD, 1985), p. 202. In addition to cited sources by Dorothy Ross, Hamilton Cravens, Thomas Haskell, and Mary Furner, I draw from Coats, "The Educational Revolution and the Professionalization of American Economics," pp. 340–75; Camfield, "The Professionalization of American Psychologists, 1870–1917," p. 67; George J. Stigler, *The Economist as Preacher and Other Essays* (Chicago, 1988), p. 77.

university ... paid the salaries of nearly all" of the 50 or so individuals who contributed most to scholarship. Hence, there occurred "the triumph of professionalism" in philosophy, literature, and history over this same period.[251]

In line with the model of professional polity imparted to the meaning of "profession" by attorneys, these scholarly specialties formed voluntary associations. The American Philological Association, founded in 1869, was followed by at least 79 learned societies in the 1870s and some 121 in the 1880s. By the 1910s associations of associations began to appear, such as the American Council of Learned Societies, and in 1915 the American Association of University Professors was formed. To be sure, these associations exercised little authority over the formal institutions of education. But the associations did become the source of national standards by which the scholarship and status of "professor" were evaluated. In this sense the faculty became more autonomous, however circumscribed their direct institutional authority may have been, and professors began to shift their loyalty and attention from their college or university to these associations of colleagues, who trained and evaluated them.[252]

The drive to establish and strengthen a profession appeared no less among those in the schools. Expressing the aspirations of schoolmen at the end of the Civil War, the Superintendent of Public Instruction in Pennsylvania proposed in 1865: "It remains for the last half of the nineteenth century to read well a science of Education, and to train a truly liberal Profession of Teaching."[253] Subsequently "the interesting query 'Is teaching a profession?'" began to appear repeatedly in educational journals, and the speakers at the annual conventions of the National Education Association (NEA) in the 1880s and 1890s devoted great effort to "proving that teaching was a profession."[254]

---

251. Quotations are from Laurence R. Veysey, "The Plural Organized Worlds of the Humanities," in *The Organization of Knowledge in Modern America, 1860–1920,* ed. Alexandra Oleson and John Voss (Baltimore, MD, 1979), p. 92; Kuklick, *The Rise of American Philosophy ... 1860–1930,* p. 565; Graff, *Professing Literature,* chs. 3, 4; Baird, "Albert Bushnell Hart: The Rise of the Professional Historian," pp. 129–74; David D. Van Tassel, "From Learned Society to Professional Organization: The American Historical Association, 1884–1900," *AHR,* 89 (1984): 929–56. Cf. Novick, *The Noble Dream: The "Objectivity Question" and the American Historical Profession,* p. 48, ch. 2.

252. Higham, *History: Professional Scholarship in America,* p. 8; Kennedy, "The Changing Academic Characteristics of the Nineteenth-Century American College Teacher," pp. 351–99; Marilyn Tobias, *Old Dartmouth on Trial: The Transformation of the Academic Community in Nineteenth-Century America* (New York, 1982), apps. 2–9; Martin J. Finkelstein, "From Tutor to Specialized Scholar: Academic Specialization in Eighteenth and Nineteenth Century America," *History of Higher Education Annual,* 3 (1983): 99–121; W. Bruce Leslie, "Between Piety and Expertise: Professionalization of College Faculty in the 'Age of the University'," *Pennsylvania History,* 46 (1979): 245–65; Glazer and Slater, *Unequal Colleagues: The Entrance of Women into the Professions, 1890–1940,* ch. 2; Creutz, "From College Teacher to University Scholar ... at the University of Michigan, 1841–1900," ch. 6; Robert A. McCaughey, "The Transformation of American Academic Life: Harvard University, 1821–1892," *Perspectives in American History,* 8 (1974): 243ff.

253. Bates, "Liberal Education," p. 176.

254. Sheldon E. Davis, *Educational Periodicals in the Nineteenth Century* (Washington, DC, 1919), p. 69; Wesley, *NEA: the First Hundred Years:,* p. 50.

The story of the NEA demonstrates both the professional aspirations of educators in the schools, as well as the conflicts that resulted from those aspirations. The NEA was founded in 1870 as the successor to the National Teachers Association, which had been organized in 1857. In 1880 the NEA established an elite inner circle of some 60 members who were called the National Council of Education and represented the "old guard" of schoolmen who had traditionally come from the social elite and professions outside of education. Tension inevitably developed between this Council and the new generation of educators who rose up through the schools to leadership positions. The latter group finally wrested control of the NEA away from the "old guard" in the 1900s, an event that accompanied the contemporary shift toward denigrating educationists. Meanwhile within the new generation there developed a conflict between teachers and the administrators of the new and growing school systems, a conflict that was deepened and made more complex by the increasing gender differentiation between these two groups. Partly in order to advance teachers' interests against those of the old guard and the administrators, state and local teachers associations began to appear over the last half of the nineteenth century, and by 1900 more than 50 had been founded. The most militant of these was the Chicago Teachers' Federation, which championed the formation of the American Federation of Teachers (AFT) in 1916. The prospect of competition from the AFT pushed the NEA to disengage from the old guard and devote itself to the new generation of school leaders.[255]

In all these ways, between the Civil War and World War I professors, administrators, and schoolteachers became more and more concerned with corporate identity, career commitment, and the idea of being a "profession." Historians conventionally regard these groups as separate vocations, distinguishing them according to the formal institutional boundaries that eventually appeared within the field of education. This approach contrasts sharply with historians' commitment over the past three decades to vitiate the external boundaries between formal educational institutions and other social institutions that transfer culture, such as churches, newspapers, and families. That is to say, historians, looking internally *within* the field of education, have tended to emphasize formal institutional divisions, discussing educators in colleges and universities apart from those in schooling and, within the latter, teachers apart from administrators. But looking *outside* at the context of education, historians have minimized or even dismissed formal institutional boundaries and treated "education" as a broad cultural process occurring across many social institutions.

It is noteworthy that these two approaches to historiography seem to be inconsistent: proposing distinct subdivisions within a field that is itself indistinct. The apparent inconsistency becomes even more noteworthy in view of the fact that the two approaches can be reconciled on the grounds that they both aggrandize academicians. The first proposition elevates academicians above schoolteachers.

255. Wesley, *NEA: the First Hundred Years*, p. 334; Richard Whittemore, "Nicholas Murray Butley and the Teaching Profession," *HEQ*, 1 (1961): 35; Urban, *Why Teachers Organized*, chs. 5, 6; David J. Hogan, *Class and Reform: School and Society in Chicago, 1880–1930* (Philadelphia, 1985), pp. 195, 222; Graebner, "Retirement in Education: The Economic and Social Functions of the Teachers' Pension," p. 397.

The second proposition elevates academicians above other professions in line with the earlier discussion about professional historiography. Whatever the degree of academicians' self-aggrandizement, an alternative to the two approaches to historiography is proposed in this chapter. On the one hand, education should be distinguished as a separate social endeavor among others. On the other hand, within the field of education boundaries between institutions and vocations should not be emphasized, because they were crossed relatively easily. In this early period of massive unsystematic growth in education, schoolteachers became university faculty members who became school superintendents who became college and university presidents. The impermeable boundary within the educational profession was defined not by sect, institution or vocational role as in theology, law, and medicine, but by gender. Male educators moved relatively easily; women could not. Given this, my proposal is that a proper understanding of the so-called "professionalization" of professors, administrators, and teachers in the late nineteenth and early twentieth centuries involves reversing the now conventional historiographical approach. The external boundaries *between* education and other social institutions, rather than the institutional and occupational boundaries *within* education, should be emphasized.

This proposal is supported by the contemporaneous rhetoric of "profession." The external boundaries between educational institutions and other social institutions are demonstrated by the fifth moment in the rhetoric of "profession": the narrowing and elevating of the usage of "professor" and the introduction of the noun "professional" to fill the lacuna left by the narrowed usage of "professor." The reference of "professors" to practitioners of non-academic vocations was sloughed away over this period, and the adjective "professional" began to serve as a noun in the place of "professor." This fifth moment in the rhetoric of "profession" was owed to the fact that education became the preeminent profession over the final third of the nineteenth century and imparted its own character to the meaning and usage of "profession."

In early American culture "professor" most prominently denoted a religious believer, and this usage gradually declined in the first half of the nineteenth century, as indicated by a review of entries in the dictionaries published in the United States before 1861.[256] In religious literature, such as the 1849 compendium *The Clergy of America,* the term "professors of religion" continued to appear in regard to believers. But by the 1870s and 1880s this usage, even in religious writings, became occasional and then quite rare, as the academic sense of "professor" held sway. The transition can be seen notably in the writings of prominent clergymen, such as Theodore Parker and Barnas Sears. This shift from religious usage to academic usage was exemplified in a commemorative biography of a deceased faculty member of Dartmouth College in 1861. The biographer observed on one page that the deceased had been a faithful "professor of religion" as an undergraduate and, on the next page, that he became a learned "Professor of Divinity" some years after graduation.[257] In subsequent decades, most educators repeated this process – vocationally and rhetorically.

Meanwhile "professor" carried forward another prominent denotation from early American culture: one who practices any art, craft, or mystery. Apart from "medi-

256. See Appendix 3.
257. Joseph Belcher, *The Clergy of America, Anecdotes Illustrative of the Character of*

cal professors" or "professors of law," colonial Englishmen could hire a "professor of predictions by stargazing," "professors of the drama," "eminent and dexterous professors of slight of hand'; and "professors of painting, sculpture, & architecture," as well as professors of any of the conventional arts and crafts. In addition, stories were told of "the most remarkable professors of villainy" and "professors in the black arts."[258] Such usage continued through the first half of the nineteenth century, when the terms "professors of science," "professors of education," and "professors of teaching" referred to *practitioners*, rather than *teachers*, of these fields.[259]

When "professional" appeared early in the nineteenth century this term was employed only as an adjective: "Relating to a calling or profession; done by a professor." "Professor" thus served as the standard nominative form, and was often interchanged with "professional man."[260] According to the *OED*, the first use of

---

Ministers of Religion in the United States (Philadelphia, 1849); Clement Long, *Serving God with the Mind: A Discourse Commemorative of Rev. Roswell Shurtleff* (Concord, NH, 1861), pp. 28–31. Cf. Theodore Parker, "The American Scholar," in *Works: The American Scholar*, ed. Samuel A. Eliot (Boston, 1907), p. 25; Barnas Sears, *An Educated Ministry* (New York, 1853), p. 16; John Dowling, *Humility as an Element of Ministerial Character* (New York, 1877), p. 1; Jeremiah B. Jeter, *The Recollections of a Long Life* (Richmond, VA, 1891), p. 171.

258. The word "teacher" was often added to "professor" when teaching as well as practice was intended. *Merry Andrew, Or, an almanack after a new fashion ... By Merry Andrew, professor of predictions by star-gazing* (Edinburgh, 1702); *The State of Surgery: but more particularly, the disadvantages its professors lie under considered* (London, 1752); Gentleman of the Middle Temple, *Seasonable Thoughts offered to ... all those who are, or intend to be, professors of the law* (London, 1758); *Theatrical disquisitions ... with an impartial examen of the profession and professors of the drama ... By a Lady* (London, 1763); Henri Decremps, *The conjurer unmasked; being a clear and full explanation of all the surprizing performances exhibited ... by the most eminent and dexterous professors of slight of hand* (London, 1785); James Caulfield, *Blackguardiana: or, a dictionary of rogues, bawds, pimps, whores, pickpockets, shoplifters ... the most remarkable professors of villainy* ([London, 1793?]); Laurent F. Boutmy, *To the nobility and gentry: Mr. Boutmy from Brussells, Professor of mussic [sic] and teacher in the harpsichord* ([London, 1795?]); *An entire range of performances? The public having been for a long series of years entertained at a prodigious expence with the unrivall'd deceptions of ... professors in the black arts* ([London, 1795?]); Gustavus Katterfelto, *Dr. Katterfelto, MD Professor and Teacher of natural experimental philosophy* ([Newcastle, UK, 1795]); Anthony Pasquin, *An authentic history of the professors of painting, sculpture, & architecture, who have practised in Ireland* ([London, 1796]).

259. H. Byerly Thomson, *The Choice of a Profession* (London, 1857), pp. 1–2, 7; John A. Heraud, "Expediency and Means of Elevating the Profession of the Educator in the Public Estimation," pp. 142–58, and Edward Higginson, "On the Expediency and the Means of Elevating the Profession of the Educator in Public Estimation," pp. 276, 304, in *The Educator. Prize Essays on the Means and Expediency of Elevating the Profession of the Educator in Society* (London, 1839).

260. Joseph E. Worcester, *Universal and Critical Dictionary of the English Language* (Boston, 1846), s.v. "professional"; *The MAGIC Oracle; or, The black art made easy ... by a professional wizard* (Boston, 18–); *The MAGIC Oracle; or, The black art made easy ... by a professor of magic* (Boston, [1867]); *Newnan* v. *Washington*, 1 Martin & Yerger 79, 80–1 (Tennessee 1827); Thomas S. Grimké, *An Oration on ... Reducing the Whole Body of the Law to the Simplicity of a Code* (1827), in *Legal Mind in America*, pp. 148–58.

"professional" as a noun appeared in a letter of Jane Austen from 1811, but, as with all such shifts in rhetorical usage, the change occurred gradually, not discretely. "Professionalist" appeared as early as 1786, though the *OED* cites the earliest instance from 1825, and this form gained initial acceptance.[261] Indeed, the noun "professional" does not even appear in American dictionaries published before 1861, and writers who employed the word as a noun alternated this new usage with the traditional "professor."[262] Over time, however, the noun "professional" became conventional while "professor" was reserved for educators. In his influential *Critical Pronouncing Dictionary* (1791) John Walker had defined "professor" as "one who publickly practices or teaches an art," and when Lyman Cobb abridged Walker's dictionary in 1828, he eliminated the word "practices."[263]

This fifth rhetorical moment therefore involved narrowing the traditional term for one who practiced any craft or vocation – "professor" – to the field of education, which was rapidly ascending in status and dignity. It meant restricting and elevating the usage of the term "professor" and substituting "professional" in its place. This transformation – from the religious and general vocational usage of "professor" to a restricted educational usage, accompanied by a shift to the nominative usage of "professional" – was remarkably complete. So complete, in fact, that by the end of the nineteenth century this transformation had been forgotten, and university "professors" began to complain that non-academics were trying to steal their name and gain some of their prestige. In 1904 the President of Iowa State College warned that loose standards in granting academic and honorary degrees had made "professors ... as thick as colonels in Kentucky."[264] Subsequently authorities such as the *OED*, I. B. Cohen, and Burton Bledstein suggested that in nineteenth-century America the "grandiose title" of "professor" was expanded from its narrow, prestigious, academic meaning to a wider, popular, non-academic meaning.[265] In fact, the historical process was the reverse.

This new way in which people talked and thought about "professors" evidences the boundary between formal educational institutions and other social institutions. The term that had conventionally referred to a member of any profession became restricted to the field of education, and this restriction demonstrates both the preeminence of the field and its discrete character. Meanwhile the fact that institutional and occupational boundaries within the field were crossed relatively easily and often was also expressed through this fifth moment in the rhetoric of "profession." Although the usage of "professor" was narrowed to education, it was

261. *OED*, s.v. "professional," "professionalist." See Honestus [Benjamin Austin], *Observations on the Pernicious Practice of the Law* (1786, 1819), p. 14, reprinted in *AJLH*, 13 (1969); Joseph E. Worcester, *Dictionary of the English Language* (Boston, 1860), s.v. "professionalist."

262. See Appendix 3; J. S. Douglas, *Homeopathy. A Lecture* (Hamilton, NY, 1845), pp. 3–4.

263. John Walker, *A Critical Pronouncing Dictionary* (1791; Menston, UK, 1968), s.v. "professor"; Lyman Cobb, *Cobb's Abridgement of J. Walker's Critical Pronouncing Dictionary* (New York, 1828), s.v. "professor."

264. Albert B. Storms, *The Outlook* (Ames, IA, 1904), p. 6.

265. *OED*, s.v. "professor"; I. Bernard Cohen, *Science and American Society in the First Century of the Republic* (Columbus, OH, 1961), p. 21; Bledstein, *The Culture of Professionalism*, pp. 21, 281.

not yet restricted *within* education. The term "professor" was widely applied to teachers and administrators in schools, as well as colleges and universities. From 1858 in the *Southern School of Georgia* or the rules for the New Braunfels Academy in Texas, to the 1860s in rural Colorado, to physicist Henry Rowland in 1883, to the 1890s in Philadelphia, to the 1910s in the famous Flexner Report or small towns throughout the country, teachers and administrators in high school, and sometimes in grammar schools, were called "professors."[266] This usage of "professor" testifies to the fact that boundaries within education were crossed far more easily and often than would subsequently be the case. The usage also demonstrates the coordinate gender boundary within education because, while "professor" was applied to teachers and administrators in both schools and higher education, it was generally restricted to men. In schools where male teachers were called "professor" female teachers were still often called "Miss."[267]

Between the Civil War and World War I, educators therefore became more and more concerned with corporate identity and career commitment and with the idea of being a profession. This concern was manifested through a fifth development in the rhetoric of profession: the usage of "professor" was narrowed to its application to educational institutions, an application that was nevertheless much broader than the usage of "professor" would become. Commensurately, the adjective "professional" became employed as a noun, serving in the role that "professor" formerly had. On the one hand, this relative narrowing of the meaning of "professor" evidences the formal distinction between education and other social institutions of the time. On the other hand, the breadth of the meaning of "professor" within education demonstrates that the institutional and occupational boundaries were crossed relatively easily and often by men. This vocation – whose external boundaries were fortified by association and expressed in rhetoric and whose internal boundaries were permeable for male "professors" – meanwhile became the most attractive profession for men or women, within their respective spheres.

Comparative: "the very highest vocation"

Believing that education during this period "was a poorly paid profession," scholars have often asserted that "one can safely surmise that fewer people of quality were

266. Editor, *Southern School of Georgia*, 1 (1858): 185; "Rules for the Regulation of the Professors and Teachers of the New Braunfels [Texas] Academy" (1858), in *The Age of the Academies*, ed. Theodore R. Sizer (New York, 1964), pp. 181–7; Rowland, "A Plea for Pure Science" p. 245; H. M. Barrett et al., *Colorado: Short Studies of its Past and Present* (Boulder, CO, 1927), p. 123; Labaree, *The Making of an American High School*, p. 4; Ludmerer, *Learning to Heal*, p. 125; Flexner, *Medical Education*, p. 32; Cubberley, *Public School Administration*, p. 267; Waller, *The Sociology of Teaching*, pp. 49ff., 387; Lynd and Lynd, *Middletown*, p. 209; William W. Brickman, "Tax Exemption Privileges for Professors of Brown University," *HEQ*, 6 (1966): 72. This usage appeared "chiefly" in the United States, according to *OED*, s.v. "professor."

267. I am grateful to Geraldine Jonçich Clifford for pointing out to me this gender restriction. (Personal correspondence, November 1990.)

willing to enter it."[268] We have seen that the premise of this longstanding view is untrue, and even those who have gone beyond surmising to examine evidence on the point have tended to rely on unsupported conjecture from the period.[269] What is required to make a more informed judgment about the relative appeal of the learned professions is an assessment of the career choices of individuals at the time.

Among those who suffered great discrimination in all the learned professions, the most advantaged predominantly chose to work in education. This was the case for what W. E. B. Du Bois and others called the "Talented Tenth" of African-Americans, referring to the college-educated. In 1910 there were some 3,200 living black college graduates, and a study by DuBois and A. G. Dill found that 54 percent were teachers, 20 percent ministers, 7 percent physicians, 4 percent lawyers, 4 percent students, and 11 percent in other occupations.[270] Meanwhile educated women, who had the most freedom to choose vocations among the limited choices open to women, also elected to work in education. The other "female professions" of social work, librarianship, and nursing were beginning to emerge at this time. But neither these, nor writing, the other prominent alternative, remotely challenged women's preference for teaching before World War I.[271] At eighteen leading co-educational colleges and universities the fraction of female graduates entering teaching rose as follows: 39 percent in the classes 1881–5, 45 percent 1886–90, 55 percent 1891–5, and 55 percent 1896–1900.[272] Even at elite women's colleges the pattern did not vary. Graduates of Smith College, Bryn Mawr, and Wellesley during the 1880s and 1890s predominantly entered teaching. A study of 3,500 graduates of such institutions from 1869 to 1898 found that 72 percent had taught. In the year 1900, 70 percent of the 61,000 women studying in coeducational institutions in the United States were reported to be in teacher training courses.

268. Sizer, *Secondary Schools at the Turn of the Century*, p. 42; Thorndike et al., *The Financial Status of the Professor*, p. 25.

269. Veysey cites opinions from the 1900s that graduate students in the arts and sciences were not as good as students entering business, law, or medicine, and Veysey's authority has been invoked by others. But these views ignore the more abundant and severe complaints about the quality of law and medical students. Veysey, *The Emergence of the American University*, pp. 178–9; Hawkins, "University Identity: the Teaching and Research Functions," p. 296; Ludmerer, *Learning to Heal*, p. 92. Cf. Taylor and Parsons, *Professional Education in the United States*, pp. 3–49; Flexner, *Medical Education*, p. 45; Cattell, *American Men of Science* (1910), appendix.

270. W. E. B. Du Bois and Augustus G. Dill, *The College-Bred Negro American* (Atlanta, GA, 1910), pp. 45–7, 65; Louis R. Harlan, *Booker T. Washington* (New York, 1983), vol. 2, p. 85, chs. 2–4; Linda M. Perkins, "The History of Blacks in Teaching: Growth and Decline within the Profession," in *American Teachers*, ed. Donald Warren (New York, 1989), p. 345.

271. Carter and Prus, "The Labor Market and the American High School Girl, 1890–1928," p. 166; Carter, "Academic Women Revisited ... 1890–1963," p. 690; Frankfort, *Collegiate Women*, pp. 91ff.; Solomon, *In the Company of Educated Women*, pp. 36, 124–7; Lubove, *The Professional Altruist: The Emergence of Social Work as a Career, 1880–1930*, p. 132; Frances B. Cogan, *All-American Girl: The Ideal of Real Womanhood in Mid-Nineteenth-Century America* (Athens, GA, 1989), pp. 250–1.

272. Percentages calculated by Stephen Appel from Burritt, *Professional Distribution of College and University Graduates*, pp. 94–141.

Another study of over 16,000 female college graduates in 1915 found that 84 percent of those who worked were teachers.[273]

This vocational preference of blacks and women can be discounted in view of the discrimination that circumscribed their choices. Yet, white men also predominantly chose careers in education. Among all male students in higher education, the percentage enrolled in normal schools and teachers colleges rose to become a plurality by 1900: 6 percent in 1860, 12 percent in 1870, 23 percent in 1880, 19 percent in 1890, 27 percent in 1900. The significance of this trend may, likewise, be discounted on the grounds that many of these men were not of the socially advantaged and their career choices were restricted. However, the group in normal schools and teachers colleges was matched by a plurality of male graduates from liberal arts colleges and universities who also chose a career in education.[274]

Even at leading colleges and universities, the proportion of male graduates entering education surpassed the proportions entering other learned professions. A study of 37 leading colleges and universities from across the country found that the fraction of male graduates working in education increased in this way: 13 percent for the classes 1871–80, 16 percent 1881–90, 20 percent 1891–1900.[275] Since these 37 institutions were flagship state universities and well established private colleges and universities, the findings are particularly significant because they indicate the career choices made by relatively elite and educated men. Even the leading students at the most elite institutions exhibited the same preference. Among Phi Beta Kappa graduates of Yale, for example, the greatest fraction were attracted to law between 1780 and 1819 and to medicine during the 1950s. In between those two periods, from 1880 to 1919, the greatest fraction were attracted to education and science. Among Harvard graduates who received their degrees *summa cum laude* between 1895 and 1908, 56 percent entered the graduate school of arts and sciences to prepare for careers in teaching and research, while merely 19 percent entered any of the Harvard professional schools, a striking contrast to the late twentieth-century experience, for example.[276]

Consequently, whether one looks at groups whose career choices were unjustly restricted according to race or gender; at white male college graduates, who could choose relatively freely; at the men who attended leading colleges and universities; or even at those who succeeded at the most elite institutions in the country, the evidence indicates that education was the leading vocational choice for each group in the late nineteenth and early twentieth century. It follows, then, that education

273. Sarah H. Gordon, "Smith College Students: The First Ten Classes, 1879–1888," *HEQ,* 15 (1975): 163; Frankfort, *Collegiate Women,* pp. 56, 60; Roberta Wein, "Women's Colleges and Domesticity, 1875–1918," *HEQ,* 14 (1974): 37–45; Solomon, *In the Company of Educated Women,* p. 127; Clifford, *Lone Voyagers: Academic Women … 1870–1937,* p. 16.

274. Burke, "The Expansion of American Higher Education," p. 112; Colin B. Burke, *American Collegiate Populations: A Test of the Traditional View* (New York, 1982), p. 222.

275. Percentages calculated by Stephen Appel from Burritt, *Professional Distribution of College and University Graduates,* pp. 94–141. Cf., note 278 below and ch. 3, note 278.

276. Charles H. Haskins, "The Graduate School of Arts and Sciences, 1872–1929," in *The Development of Harvard University … 1869–1929,* ed. Samuel E. Morison (Cambridge, MA, 1930), p. 451n.; Albert B. Crawford, *Phi Beta Kappa Men of Yale, 1780–1959* (New Haven, CT, 1968), pp. 30–42. For medicine, the period was 1950–9.

was the leading vocational choice among all students in higher education. Indeed, the enrollment in higher education rose sevenfold from 1870 to 1910, and "the curricula that brought about most of the growth in enrollment ... was education itself.... [T]he training of teachers and professors accounts for most of the increase in attendance."[277] As Bailey Burritt concluded in 1912:

> Within 100 years the profession of teaching has grown from about one-twentieth to one-fourth of the [college] graduates.... Since 1880 the line for teaching has crossed that of the ministry, and since 1890 that of law. Thus at the close of the century it is the dominant profession.[278]

The relative educational level of the learned professions reflected these trends. Through the end of the nineteenth century, the theological institutions maintained their academic edge over other professional schools. In 1899 43 percent of the divinity schools in the country required four years of college work for admission, compared to only one medical school and no law schools. Nevertheless, there were signs that the standards of divinity schools were fast eroding. The specialized study of philosophy eclipsed theology at universities, and divinity schools' practice of subsidizing their students' tuition was said "to have drawn inferior men to the church."[279] Meanwhile a leading member of the Philadelphia bar observed:

277. Burke, *American College Populations*, p. 222. *Historical Statistics*, series H700–15; Auerbach, "The Opposition to Schools of Education by Professors of the Liberal Arts," p. 62; Merle L. Borrowman, "About Professors of Education," in *The Professor of Education: An Assessment of Conditions*, ed. Aryes Bagley (Minneapolis, MN, 1975), p. 58. Burke calculated that, of all the students enrolled in higher education, the fraction in normal schools and teachers colleges grew as follows: 16 percent in 1870, 35 percent in 1880, 29 percent in 1890, 30 percent in 1900, 37 percent in 1910. In addition, Burke estimated that about 30 percent of college undergraduates were enrolled in teacher training courses. *American Collegiate Populations*, p. 216; Burke, "The Expansion of American Higher Education," pp. 112–5.

278. Burritt, *Professional Distribution of College and University Graduates*, p. 77. The following table presents the composite percentages calculated by Burritt for the career choices of male and female graduates of the 37 leading colleges and universities that he studied.

Vocation	1871–5	1876–80	1881–5	1886–90	1891–5	1896–1900
Education	13	16	19	19	24	27
Law	28	24	22	20	19	16
Theology	17	14	12	12	10	6
Medicine	9	9	9	8	9	7
Commerce	16	20	22	21	18	19

Source: Adapted from Burritt, p. 144.

279. Quotation is from Cattell, *American Men of Science* (1910), p. 577. Taylor and Parsons, *Professional Education in the United States*, pp. 10, 19–21; Marx, "Some Trends in Higher Education" p. 785; Kuklick, *The Rise of American Philosophy ... 1860–1930*, pp. 191–2.

that ... the relative learning of the ministry is not what it was formerly, that the average preacher is not a scholar, and that we frequently find to-day what was seldom, if ever, found in olden time: the shallow man in the pulpit and the scholar in the pew.[280]

Even so, ministers were generally better educated than lawyers or physicians, as this Philadelphia attorney conceded. Only a quarter of lawyers admitted to the bar in 1870 were law school graduates, and in 1885 only one law school in the country had a course of study longer than two years. As late as 1910 only two-thirds of those admitted to the bar were law school graduates, and only about one-tenth of the law students were college graduates. Due to more stringent licensing requirements, a greater proportion of doctors went to professional school, but the fraction of college graduates among medical students was even smaller than the one-tenth of law students.[281] In 1910 only about 8 percent of those admitted to the bar were college graduates, and the fraction of physicians who were college graduates was no higher. A contemporaneous study confirmed that more divinity students were college graduates than law students or medical students but that, among "the four learned professions," professors "have here shown a greater educational investment than for any of the other professions."[282]

These facts demonstrate that clergy, as well as professors, were better educated than lawyers or physicians. They also demonstrate the anachronism of the often made assumption that legal and medical education conventionally occurred at the graduate or even collegiate level. This anachronism has contributed to the long-standing deprecation of normal schools and teachers colleges during this period. Granted, if comparing normal schools to professional schools at the universities that were leading the late nineteenth-century reform in professional education, one could justifiably assert that "the teachers stand below the other professions.... The Normal Schools at present occupy the same position as the old Medical Schools."[283]

280. Mercer, *The American Scholar in Professional Life,* pp. 6–7.

281. Charles McIntyre, "The Percentage of College-Bred Men in the Medical Profession," *The Medical Record,* 22 (December 16, 1882): 682; "Report of the Committee on Legal Education," *Reports and Transactions of the ABA,* 14 (1891): app. B; Richard G. Boone, *Education in the United States: Its History from the Earliest Settlement* (New York, 1890), pp. 211–20; Auerbach, *Unequal Justice: Lawyers and Social Change in Modern America,* p. 94; Reed, *Training for the Public Profession of the Law,* pp. 50ff., 90–3; Taylor and Parsons, *Professional Education in the United States,* p. 13; Gert N. Brieger, "'Fit to Study Medicine': Notes for a History of Pre-Medical Education in America," *Bulletin of the History of Medicine,* 57 (1983): 1–21. By 1895 three-quarters of the students at Harvard Law School had degrees. From there the fraction dropped to between one-third and one-half at California, Columbia, Northwestern, and Yale. Next came Michigan with about one-sixth degree-holders, and so on down. Stevens, *Law School ... from the 1850s to the 1980s,* pp. 44–5; Mercer, *The American Scholar in Professional Life,* p. 20.

282. Edwin G. Dexter, "Training for the Learned Professions," *Educational Review,* 25 (1903): 37; Jerold S. Auerbach, "Enmity and Amity: Law Teachers and Practitioners, 1900–1922," *Perspectives in American History,* 5 (1971): 574; Reed, *Training for the Public Profession of the Law,* pp. 50ff., 90–3; Bledstein, *The Culture of Professionalism,* p. 278.

283. Albert B. Hart, "The Teacher as a Professional Expert," *School Review,* 1 (1893): 7. See Russell, *Founding Teachers College,* p. 30; Elsbree, *The American Teacher,* ch. 23;

However, within the broad context of professional education, it was true that "many of our American law, medical and theological schools require a standard of admission, no higher" than normal schools, as F. W. Atkinson observed in his 1893 dissertation for the University of Leipzig. When the School of Pedagogy at the University of the City of New York (later New York University) was founded in 1890 its admission standard constituted "a larger requirement than is demanded by any school of law or medicine in New York."[284]

Consequently the education of schoolteachers was relatively higher than has often been portrayed. In 1910, when no more than 8 percent of those admitted to practice law or medicine were college graduates, the average length of education for male and female secondary school teachers in the country was two years beyond high school. Thus, when the Denver city schools were requiring in 1905 that all high school teachers hold the AB, it would have been an unreasonable standard for Denver lawyers or physicians.[285] Similarly, in Missouri, the normal schools compared quite well to law and medical schools. Through at least 1910, the "regular" medical schools were found to have "abysmally low educational standards," and the law schools were little better. The normal schools, meanwhile, were elevated from the secondary level to "early college work," and a study of 299 normal school students who registered at the state university between 1912 and 1915 found that 63 per cent earned better grades than the other university students.[286]

If, therefore, education was the profession of choice and if professors at all levels were relatively well educated, it comes as no surprise that this vocation was accorded high status at the turn of the century. To be sure, distinguished scholars from Richard Shryock to I. B. Cohen to Martin Trow have asserted quite the opposite.[287] But before the Civil War no college professor or president called his profession

---

Monroe, *Teaching-Learning Theory ... 1890–1950*, chs. 6, 7, 9–12; Hug, *Seventy-five Years in Education ... the School of Education, New York University, 1890–1965*, p. 14.

284. Atkinson, "The Professional Preparation of Secondary School Teachers in the United States," p. 33; Winship, *Is there a Science of Pedagogy?*, p. iv. Hug maintains that the school quickly had to compromise this standard. *Seventy-five Years in Education ... the School of Education, New York University, 1890–1965*, p. 13.

285. Aaron Grove, ed., "The Denver Examinations," *Colorado School Journal*, 20 (1905): 235; Thorndike, *The Teaching Staff of Secondary Schools*, pp. 14–5, 19. Cf. Coffman, *The Social Composition of the Teaching Population*, pp. 79–81.

286. Harold W. Eickhoff, "The Organization and Regulation of Medicine in Missouri, 1883–1901" (PhD diss., University of Missouri, 1964), ch. 1; Learned, Bagley, et al., *The Professional Preparation of Teachers for American Public Schools ... in the State of Missouri*, pp. 34–41, 360; Flexner, *Medical Education*, pp. 251–8; Reed, *Training for the Public Profession of the Law*, pp. 446–7, app. 1.

287. Shryock, "The Academic Profession in the United States," pp. 32–70; Cohen, "Science in America: the Nineteenth Century," p. 183; Martin Trow, "American Higher Education: Past, Present and Future," *Educational Researcher*, 17 (April 1988): 18–9. This proposition is linked to scholars' increased expectations described earlier and, more generally, to intellectuals' sense of themselves "as members of a beleaguered minority." Christopher Lasch, *The New Radicalism in America [1889–1963]: The Intellectual as a Social Type* (New York, 1965), p. x, passim.

"the very highest vocation," "the highest occupation of mankind," or "the only recognized aristocracy in America."[288] To emphasize university professors' complaints at the turn of the century, as does Shryock, for example, is to miss the really dramatic shift: in the final third of the nineteenth century it became possible for professors to conceive of their profession as "the very highest vocation" and to begrudge slights to their dignity and authority according to a presumed standard of what the highest vocation deserved. Late nineteenth-century educators may not have achieved the singular preeminence that colonial ministers or Republican lawyers did in earlier periods, a fact owed largely to the decline of the learned professions relative to business in the late nineteenth century. Yet, precisely because of that decline, the educational profession, whose status increased by any measure, made even greater gains relative to the other learned professions.

When the first prestige scale of occupations was published in 1925 it reported that professors ranked ahead of physicians, clergy, and lawyers, and second only to businessmen, among "forty-five occupations" that respondents arranged "in the order of their social standing." In the 1930s an opinion poll of "representative citizens" of small towns and cities found that professors were ranked second only to physicians "in the *order of your admiration*" for 25 occupations.[289] The professor had thus become an estimable figure for the first time in America, as Edward Everett Hale observed in 1899. The professor stood first rank in "the only recognized aristocracy in America," maintained the president of the Carnegie Foundation for the Advancement of Teaching in 1908.[290]

As president of the Carnegie Foundation, Henry Pritchett was obliged to extoll the professorial role. But he had served as president of the Massachusetts Institute of Technology and, like many of his executive colleagues, considered presidents to be "the best men," as the phrase went.[291] Professors might claim for themselves "the very highest vocation of man," and note that nine college and university presidents left their offices to join the first faculty of the University of Chicago.[292] But presidents nevertheless displayed "increasing self-consciousness" that their office was a special vocation, as revealed in the inaugural addresses of presidents at land-grant universities between 1867 and 1911. Apart from such public oratory, a

288. Hall, *Life and Confessions of a Psychologist,* p. 338; Rowland, "A Plea for Pure Science," pp. 243–4; Henry S. Pritchett, in Thorndike et al., *The Financial Status of the Professor,* p. ix.

289. George S. Counts, "The Social Status of Occupations: A Problem in Vocational Guidance," *School Review,* 33 (1925): 16–27; George W. Hartmann, "The Prestige of Occupations: A Comparison of Educational Occupations with Others," *Personnel Journal,* 13 (1934–5): 144–52; Logan Wilson, *The Academic Man: A Study in the Sociology of a Profession* (New York, 1942), p. 16; Theodore Caplow, *The Sociology of Work* (Minneapolis, MN, 1954), p. 32.

290. Edward E. Hale, *James Russell Lowell and His Friends* (New York, 1899), ch. 9; Henry S. Pritchett, in Thorndike et al., *The Financial Status of the Professor,* p. ix. See Leslie, "When Professors had Servants ... 1860–1917," pp. 19–30.

291. Bernard Crick, *The American Science of Politics: Its Origins and Conditions* (Berkeley, CA, 1959), p. 32; Bledstein, *The Culture of Professionalism,* p. 131, chs. 4, 5.

292. Hall, *Life and Confessions of a Psychologist,* p. 338; Goodspeed, *A History of the University of Chicago,* ch. 7.

professional, even a "scientific," literature on the topic began to appear with the publication of *College Administration* (1900) and *University Administration* (1908).[293]

Like the presidents, the new school administrators also felt their status rising. This feeling grew commensurately with the size of their institutions, their authority, and the legitimacy of the "science of education." When schoolman E. P. Cubberley became Superintendent of Schools in San Diego in 1896, many citizens felt the position called for a businessman, rather than a professional educator. When Cubberly left in 1898 the School Board was convinced that it needed a professional, rather than a businessman, as superintendent. In that same year C. F. Thwing, who was not a superintendent, described this "New Profession" in words that Cubberley repeated almost verbatim in 1916:

> School supervision represents a new profession.... In pecuniary, social, professional, and personal rewards it ranks with the other learned professions, while the call for city school superintendents of the right type is today greater than the call for lawyers, doctors, or ministers.[294]

This opinion was validated by the experience of school administrators across the country from St. Louis in the 1870s and 1880s to Seattle in the 1900s.[295]

Regarding schoolteachers, 77 college and university presidents, state school superintendents, and other prominent citizens publicly affirmed as early as 1874 that "teaching, particularly in cities, has become a regular occupation. Teachers mingle freely in the best social circles and enjoy the respect of the community." This statement may be interpreted as a roseate apology, but recent scholarship has confirmed that by the 1890s the urban schools had generally been freed from political patronage, and "most teachers in city school systems regarded teaching as a profession."[296] As implied by these statements, there has long existed a historical and historiographical tendency to view rural schools as professional wastelands. But here, too, recent research has demonstrated the estimable leadership role played by teachers in rural communities, and it is important in this regard to note that the rural teaching force was largely feminized. Though earning lower salaries, rural female teachers enjoyed far more autonomy than in urban areas; they could control

293. Mohr, "Higher Education and the Development of Professionalism ... 1867–1911," pp. 261ff.; Thwing, *College Administration* (1900); Eliot, *University Administration* (1908).

294. Cubberley, *Public School Administration*, p. 130; Thwing, "A New Profession," p. 33.

295. Sears and Henderson, *Cubberley of Stanford*, pp. 34, 51–2; Elinor M. Gersman, "Progressive Reform of the St. Louis School Board, 1897," *HEQ*, 10 (1970): 3–4; Nelson, *Good Schools: The Seattle Public School System, 1901–1930*, ch. 1. This validation was the germ of later difficulties because schoolmen's rising status and authority soon made them "arrogant and overconfident of their ability to prescribe solutions for all educational problems." (Fuller, *The Old Country School ... in the Middle West*, p. 105; Auerbach, "The Opposition to Schools of Education by Professors of the Liberal Arts, p. 87.) Callahan astutely noted that the status and authority conferred upon superintendents was balanced by "the vulnerability of the schools and schoolmen; and the great strength of the business community." *Education and the Cult of Efficiency*, p. 179, ch. 8.

296. Doty and Harris, *A Statement ... Approved by Many Leading Educators*, p. 19; Teaford, *The Unheralded Triumph: City Government in America, 1870–1900*, p. 157.

their money, own property, travel on their own, and fill roles of municipal leadership.[297]

Well established by the 1890s, these professional developments among urban and rural teachers were then extended, for better or worse, by Progressivism. "For in progressivism teachers soon found that they had an ideology that dignified in the noblest terms their own quest for status, while in professionalism progressives had the key to their demand for scientifically trained pedagogues."[298] Compared to these developments for schoolteachers – as well as professors and educational administrators of all types – the professionals in the other learned professions generally felt discouraged.

Medicine, through at least 1900, was "a beleaguered profession," "a profession in disarray," or, at best, "an emerging profession."[299] Even physician historians, such as George Rosen, freely acknowledge that "in 1875 ... the condition of medicine appeared to be one of utter confusion and anarchy.... [T]here was no clear improvement in the situation of the profession until the turn of the century." Contemporary observers testified that among "the recognized 'learned professions' " none "meets with less real consideration than the medical."[300] Hence, "merely a handful of students entering medical school had college preparation ... and those who did have college degrees tended to be academically inferior, since the better students generally chose careers in teaching, law, or the clergy."[301]

Meanwhile academic physicians wrested leadership of medicine away from practicing clinicians. Full-time professors of medicine first appeared in the 1870s, and they "were driven by a single overriding purpose: to make academic medicine a secure career in America."[302] Their rationale for this seemingly self-interested goal

297. Bernard Wishy, *The Child and the Republic: the Dawn of Modern American Child Nurture* (Philadelphia, 1968), pp. 146–51; Kaufman, *Women Teachers on the Frontier*, passim. Barthell, "Wyoming's Country Schools"; Birkinshaw, "The Legacy of Utah's Country Schools, 1847–1896"; Blakely, "Southeastern South Dakota's Country Schools"; Brown, "Northeastern South Dakota's Country Schools"; Dertien, "Eastern Nebraska's Country Schools"; Dodds and Dodds, "Country School Legacy Report for Southern Colorado"; Grundy, "Central Nebraska's Country Schools"; Gulliford et al., "Work and Leisure in Country Schools in Wyoming"; Hatton, "Western South Dakota's Country Schools"; Judge, "Eastern and Central Kansas Country Schools"; Scofield, "The Country School Legacy in Western Nebraska." Cf. Henke, "North Dakota's Country Teachers: Their Roles, Rules, and Restrictions"; Jessie L. Embry, "Schoolmarms of Utah: 'Separate and Unequal' " (Silt, CO, 1982).

298. Cremin, *The Transformation of the School ... 1876–1957*, p. 175.

299. Starr, *The Social Transformation of American Medicine*, p. 198; Ludmerer, *Learning to Heal*, pp. 24–8; Leo J. O'Hara, "An Emerging Profession: Philadelphia Medicine 1860–1900" (PhD diss., University of Pennsylvania, 1976).

300. Rosen, *The Structure of American Medical Practice, 1875–1941*, pp. 15–6; Hart, "The Teacher as a Professional Expert," p. 5.

301. Ludmerer, *Learning to Heal*, pp. 12–3.

302. Ludmerer, *Learning to Heal*, pp. 6, 101, 125–6. Scholars have sometimes attributed high status to faculty members in earlier medical schools, but such faculty members achieved high status because they were leading clinicians before they taught. See Starr, *The Social Transformation of American Medicine*, pp. 122, 462 (n. 104); Rothstein, *American Medical Schools*, pp. 61–7, 98, 106.

was to reform medical education by informing it with medical science. Competition and conflict inevitably developed between the academic physicians and the clinicians, particularly as state licensing laws established requirements for medical education and then increased those requirements. Just as inevitably in an educational era, the full-time professors, who had acquired control over leading medical schools, gained the upper hand. In his 1869 inaugural address Harvard President Eliot had proposed that professional students be examined by practicing members of the professions in order to provide an "effective examination of the teacher." In 1898, however, he explicitly renounced this proposal of having professionals examine the work of professional school faculty. By that point, the lines of intellectual and professional authority ran in the opposite direction.[303] When the Flexner report was published in 1910 the public was already accustomed to prefer "the reassuring authority embodied in a 'professor'" over that of a practicing clinician.[304]

If medicine was struggling upward, led by full-time professors, theology was stumbling ever lower. In fact "the clergy were probably the most conspicuous losers from the status revolution" prompted by industrial capitalism. "The secular and materialistic spirit of the age is a powerful cause in diverting young men from entering the ministry," observed the General Secretary of the World's Student Christian Federation in 1911.[305] In response, Victorian "princes of the pulpit," such as Henry Ward Beecher and Lyman Abbott, attempted to preserve clerical status, it is said, by allying themselves with business interests and rationalizing industrial capitalism through "the American cult of self-help." This alliance then prompted a reaction in the Social Gospel movement of the 1890s, which anticipated the work of liberal clergy in the Progressive movement.[306] Yet neither pulpit princes, Social Gospel, nor liberal clergy could halt the slide of ministers' status.

Church leaders observed "in nearly all denominations and theological seminaries a serious decline in the number of candidates for the ministry." In 1905 the president of the University of Chicago noted that "the number of students preparing for the ministry ... has decreased considerably within the last decade.... It is undoubtedly true that the other professions are relatively more attractive in these modern times."[307] The Secretary of the Northern Baptist Education Society explained: "The first and most obvious reason is found in the economic situation.... The minister ... is required to spend in training for his work just as many years as the lawyer or physician or professor, but ... he finds himself discounted." Another

303. Eliot, *Educational Reform: Essays and Addresses* (New York, 1898), pp. viii, 9. Ludmerer, *Learning to Heal*, pp. 123–8, 235–40; Rothstein, *American Medical Schools*, ch. 5.

304. Rosenberg, *The Care of Strangers*, p. 174, chs. 7, 8.

305. Hofstadter, *Age of Reform*, p. 150; John R. Mott, *The Future Leadership of the Church* (New York, 1911), p. 57.

306. Wylie, *The Self-Made Man in America*, ch. 4; Holifield, *A History of Pastoral Care in America*, p. 168; Richard Hofstadter, *Social Darwinism in American Thought*, rev. edn (Boston, 1955), ch. 6; Robert T. Handy, *A Christian America: Protestant Hopes and Historical Realities* (New York, 1971), pp. 95–183.

307. James H. Snowden, *The Attractions of the Ministry* (Philadelphia, 1921), p. 114; Harper, *The Trend in Higher Education in America*, pp. 197–8.

reason for the decline was that "the ministry no longer seemed intellectually respectable.... Educated men and women ... groped toward new professions."[308] By the 1920s it was reported that those bound for the ministry generally scored lower on intelligence tests than those planning to enter other professions, and research in the scientific psychology found that "inferiority attitudes and introversion may be regarded as a condition which predisposes an individual toward the religious life."[309]

The significance of this decline in intellectual standards was magnified by the rising importance of education, and resulted in the disappearance of the clergy from prominent and influential positions in colleges and universities. According to one survey of private institutions, the fraction of trustees who were clergy fell from 39 percent in 1869 to 7 percent in 1930. Similarly, the fraction of college presidents who were clergy shrank dramatically from the antebellum figure of 90 percent.[310] No less significant than these declines was the disappearance of clergy from college and university faculties.

In the first half of the nineteenth century ministers dominated college faculties, which generally provided little outlet for intellectual inquiry or innovation. Clergy inclined in these directions either remained in their pulpits, as did eleven of the original seventeen clerical leaders of New England Transcendentalism, or took up public lecturing, which afforded a living by the 1840s. Ralph Waldo Emerson was the exemplar. Having left the ministry, he saw little prospect for his vision of "Man Thinking" in the colleges of the time, and embarked on the lecture circuit with great success, leading others to follow.[311] By 1876 transcendentalist clergyman Octavius Frothingham complained that "preaching is giving place to lecturing; the pulpit has been taken down; science alone is permitted to speak with authority." Even as Frothingham wrote, however, the vocational half-way house of public lecturing had "virtually disappeared."[312] In its place arose the university, which

308. Webb, *The Ministry as a Life Work*, pp. 9, 12–3; Robert M. Crunden, *Ministers of Reform: The Progressives' Achievement in American Civilization, 1889–1920* (New York, 1982), p. ix.

309. K. Sward, "Temperament and Religious Experience," *Journal of Social Psychology*, 2 (1931): 374; Mark A. May, *The Education of American Ministers*, vol. 2: *The Profession of the Ministry* (New York, 1934), ch. 14; Sadler, "A Comparative Personnel Study of Ministerial, Medical, and Law Students," passim.

310. Earl J. McGrath, "The Control of Higher Education in America," *Educational Record*, 17 (1936): 259–72; George P. Schmidt, *The Old-Time College President* (New York, 1930), p. 185; Richard Hofstadter and C. Dewitt Hardy, *The Development and Scope of Higher Education in the United States* (New York, 1953), pp. 33–6.

311. William R. Hutchison, *The Transcendentalist Ministers: Church Reform in the New England Renaissance* (New Haven, CT, 1959), p. viii; Donald M. Scott, "The Profession that Vanished: Public Lecturing in Mid-Nineteenth-Century America," in *Professions and Professional Ideologies in America*, ed. Gerald L. Geison (Chapel Hill, NC, 1983), pp. 12–28; Henry N. Smith, "Emerson's Problem of Vocation," *New England Quarterly*, 12 (1939): 52–67.

312. Octavius B. Frothingham, *Transcendentalism in New England: A History* (New York, 1876), p. 320; Scott, "The Profession that Vanished: Public Lecturing in Mid-Nineteenth-Century America," pp. 26–7.

attracted many young men who would have – or had – entered the ministry in the past. Departments of philosophy and the new social sciences attracted many such individuals.[313] Commensurate with this shift in career choice, there emerged "the idea of the university as a paradise of learning ... from the earlier idea of the whole Church as a provisional paradise." Even faculties suspicious of modernism and committed to "evangelical ends," as at Yale, embraced the new "scholarly vocation" in lieu of the ministerial vocation in the church.[314]

That the clergy were eclipsed in this way is well known, but that law reached "its lowest ebb" after the Civil War[315] is much disputed. In fact the predominant view in recent scholarship is that "the country's first truly professional bar" did not appear "until the end of the nineteenth century," a time that supposedly became "the most critical period of this process of professionalization ... when law replaced religion as the controlling element in American society."[316] Three primary reasons are offered to support the predominant view. First is the multiplication of bar associations between 1880 and the 1910s. Second is the appearance both of corporate lawyers, who "became the new professional men of the new century," and of the large law firm, which became "the symbol of the new profession." Third is the rise of legal science and legal education, which are believed to have formed "a symbiotic relationship" with bar associations and corporate lawyers.[317]

313. Turner, *Without God, Without Creed,* pp. 121–2; Kuklick, *Churchmen and Philosophers,* pp. 117–9, 196; Wilson Smith, *Professors and Public Ethics: Studies of Northern Moral Philosophers before the Civil War* (Ithaca, NY, 1956), pp. 5–6; Vidich and Lyman, *American Sociology,* pp. 34, 282; Kennedy, "The Changing Academic Characteristics of the Nineteenth-Century American College Teacher," p. 360.

314. George H. Williams, "The Theological Idea of the University: The Paradise Theme and Related Motifs in the History of Higher Education," in *Wilderness and Paradise in Christian Thought* (New York, 1962), p. viii; Stevenson, *Scholarly Means to Evangelical Ends ... 1830–1890,* pp. 11, 30–49. Arthur J. Engel has described the contemporaneous shift from the role of the Oxford University don, who viewed his Fellowship primarily as a step on the career ladder of the Church, to professors who were viewed their academic position as a separate profession preferable to the Church. *From Clergyman to Don: The Rise of the Academic Profession in Nineteenth-Century Oxford* (New York, 1983).

315. Taylor and Parsons, *Professional Education in the United States,* p. 8; W. Raymond Blackard, "The Demoralization of the Legal Profession in Nineteenth Century America," *Tennessee Law Review,* 16 (1940): 323; John S. Bradway, *The Bar and Public Relations: An Introduction to the Public Relations Field of the Bar* (Indianapolis, IN, 1934), p. 48.

316. John W. Johnson, *American Legal Culture, 1908–1940* (Westport, CT, 1981), p. 3; Richard L. Abel, *American Lawyers* (New York, 1989), p. 40; Gerard W. Gawalt, ed., *The New High Priests: Lawyers in Post-Civil War America* (Westport, CT, 1984), p. vii. Hall, *The Magic Mirror: Law in American History,* ch. 11.

317. Quotations are from Auerbach, *Unequal Justice: Lawyers and Social Change in Modern America,* p. 23; Wayne K. Hobson, "Symbol of the New Profession: Emergence of the Large Law Firm, 1870–1915," in *The New High Priests: Lawyers in Post-Civil War America,* ed. Gerard W. Gawalt (Westport, CT, 1984), pp. 3–28; Gordon, "Legal Thought and Legal Practice in the Age of American Enterprise," p. 72. See also Lawrence M. Friedman, *A History of American Law,* 2d edn (New York, 1985) chs. 11, 12; Matzko, " 'The Best Men of the Bar': The Founding of the American Bar Association," pp. 76–7; Roscoe

In regard to the first reason, it may be said that, although many state bar associations were founded between 1880 and the 1910s, the movement toward voluntary association originated in the antebellum period, as demonstrated earlier. Moreover, even in the late nineteenth century, many of the new state bar associations were ineffective "false starts," as in Virginia and Mississippi. Indeed, the membership of most of these bar associations was exclusive and small. The American Bar Association was founded in 1878, which is often regarded as a signal date in the predominant view. But in 1900 only about 1 percent of lawyers in the country belonged to the ABA, and in 1910 only 3 percent. These facts demonstrate Maxwell Bloomfield's warning not to "overemphasize the role of formal organization as the appropriate yardstick by which to measure the strength of professionalism within the bar."[318]

In regard to the rise of corporate lawyers in large law firms, it should be noted that this development resulted in the "cleavage of the American Bar into two bars, the Great Bar and the bar in general."[319] The corporate Great Bar may have been the object of envy, but it was also thought to be "captured" by business interests, leading to "the erosion of the independent professional and the autonomous profession." Hence, "many lawyers were convinced that their profession had declined in its intellectual standards and in its moral and social position."[320] As Thomas Grey has observed: "It is hardly possible to read a speech given at a bar association meeting during that period without finding either lamentation for the lost independence of the American lawyer, newly in servitude to business, or defensive bluster against charges that the profession had been commercialized and degraded."[321] Jerold Auerbach has suggested that such speeches and bluster have been misinterpreted inasmuch as "corporate lawyers repudiated the notion of professional decline" and attributed the commercialization of the bar to Jewish and Catholic immigrant lawyers, who, in their view, were dragging the profession down. Whatever the degree of demeaning commercialization and captivity owed to corporate lawyers, the fundamental point to see is that the Great Bar was, in fact,

---

Pound, *The Lawyer from Antiquity to Modern Times* (St. Paul, MN, 1953); Foster, *The Ideology of Apolitical Politics,* ch. 4; Stevens, *Law School ... from the 1850s to the 1980s,* p. 21, passim.

318. Bloomfield, *American Lawyers in a Changing Society, 1776–1876,* p. 137; Reed, *Training for the Public Profession of the Law,* p. 216; W. Hamilton Bryson and E. Lee Shepard, "The Virginia Bar, 1870–1900," pp. 171–85, and Michael de L. Landon, "Another False Start: Mississippi's Second State Bar Association, 1886–1892," pp. 187–200, in *The New High Priests: Lawyers in Post-Civil War America,* ed. Gerard W. Gawalt (Westport, CT, 1984).

319. Edward S. Corwin, "Foreword," p. x, in Twiss, *Lawyers and the Constitution.*

320. Gawalt, "The Impact of Industrialization on the Legal Profession in Massachusetts, 1870–1900," p. 110; Hofstadter, *The Age of Reform,* p. 158.

321. Grey, "Langdell's Orthodoxy," p. 37. Joseph Katz, "The Legal Profession, 1890–1915: The Lawyer's Role in Society: A Study of Attitudes" (MA thesis, Columbia University, 1954), pp. 6–7, 18–21; Robert W. Gordon, "'The Ideal and the Actual in the Law': Fantasies and Practices of New York City Lawyers, 1870–1910," in *The New High Priests: Lawyers in Post-Civil War America,* ed. Gerard W. Gawalt (Westport, CT, 1984), pp. 61–2; Foster, *The Ideology of Apolitical Politics,* p. 137.

a tiny bar. In 1898 it constituted less than one-half of 1 percent of the nation's lawyers and little more than 1 percent in 1915.[322] The conception of powerful, prestigious, and wealthy attorneys in the late nineteenth century is actually derived from the experience of a minute fraction of the legal profession.

Finally, in regard to the rise of legal science and legal education, it may be said – to paraphrase Abraham Flexner and Henry S. Pritchett – that legal education was a matter more of education than of law.[323] In 1870 C. C. Langdell, "a shy, retiring scholar" rather than a practicing attorney, was appointed dean of Harvard Law School.[324] At that point, "the teaching of law *as a career* was a thing unknown in this country," observed Langdell, who then appointed the nation's first law professor who was a graduating law student who had never practiced law, J. B. Ames. By 1894 Langdell observed that

> Of the eight professors ... now in the [Law] School ... all of them deliberately chose the teaching of law as a career in preference to the practice of it. Many of the recent graduates of the School are also now actively engaged in teaching law in other institutions.... The School may, therefore, fairly claim ... that it has succeeded in inspiring its students with enthusiasm for the cultivation of law as a science and for a professorial life.[325]

Added Professor Ames in 1901: "In the thirty-five years since the Civil War ... this remarkable growth of law schools ... means, first of all, the opening of a new career ... the career of the law professor." Ames estimated that "about one-fourth of the law professors of this country give themselves wholly to the duties of their professorships" and that the proportion would grow to three-quarters "in the next generation."[326]

In 1892 the ABA formed a Section of Legal Education, and in 1900 the Association of American Law Schools (AALS) was founded by the elite law schools, which sought to advance their model of full-time study both for students and faculty. Inevitably competition and conflict developed, just as it had in medicine, among elite law professors, elite attorneys, country lawyers, urban immigrant lawyers, and night law schools. Different interpretations of the competition and conflict are possible, but the end result was that elite professors and elite attorneys

322. Auerbach, *Unequal Justice: Lawyers and Social Change in Modern America*, pp. 36–7, ch. 2; Hobson, "Symbol of the New Profession: Emergence of the Large Law Firm, 1870–1915," p. 6.

323. Flexner and Pritchett deflected questions about their authority to speak on medical education by maintaining that "the question is not a medical question, but an educational question." Wheatley, *The Politics of Philanthropy*, p. 52; Ludmerer, *Learning to Heal*, pp. 170–1.

324. Robert T. Swaine, *The Cravath Firm and its Predecessors, 1819–1947* (New York, 1946), vol. 1, pp. 143–4; Charles W. Eliot, "Langdell and the Law School," *Harvard Law Review*, 33 (1920): 518.

325. Christopher C. Langdell, "The Harvard Law School, 1869–1894," *Harvard Graduates Magazine*, 2 (1894): 497–8.

326. James B. Ames, "The Vocation of the Law Professor" [1901], in *Lectures on Legal History and Miscellaneous Legal Essays* (Cambridge, MA, 1913), pp. 360–2; Gregory, "Wage of Law Teachers," pp. 513–5.

overcame their differences, joined hands, and established the AALS model as the professional norm. This result demonstrated "the undoubtedly increasing influence that American university professors of law exert upon ... the legal profession in America, and the ... development of the entire legal system."[327]

This conclusion from a 1914 report to the Carnegie Foundation for the Advancement of Teaching indicates that the rise of legal science, education, and professors attests more to the status of "the teaching of law *as a career*," in the words of Langdell, than to the status of the bench and bar. Other contemporary observers agreed that law professors' influence was already "comparable in degree" to that of judges, and was "likely to increase in the future more rapidly than that of judges."[328] Indeed, the ABA later commissioned an extensive Survey of the Legal Profession, which reported that the some 1,000 law professors in the nation had contributed more to elevating the legal profession than the more than 7,000 judges. This was partly because most of the judiciary were selected by "political considerations" as much as "judicial fitness," but primarily because lawyers increasingly drew their legitimacy from law degrees due to the transformation in legal science, education, and professors. In fact, lawyers were forced to define themselves in terms of their education as the number of "lawyer jobs" increased in society.[329]

In fine, there is good reason to discount the three reasons conventionally cited to support the predominant view that in the late nineteenth century attorneys first became "professionalized" and attained high status among professions. The rise of bar associations was not particular to this period; the emergence of corporate lawyers in large firms possibly detracted from professional dignity and status and,

---

327. Redlich, *The Common Law and the Case Method*, p. 5. See Hofstadter, *The Age of Reform*, pp. 157–8; Auerbach, "Enmity and Amity: Law Teachers and Practitioners, 1900–1922," pp. 551–601; Johnson, *Schooled Lawyers*, p. 105, chs. 5–7; Johnson, *American Legal Culture, 1908–1940*, p. 6; Gawalt, "The Impact of Industrialization on the Legal Profession in Massachusetts, 1870–1900," p. 110; Reed, *Training for the Public Profession of the Law*, chs. 22, 31; Stevens, *Law School ... from the 1850s to the 1980s*, ch. 6. Just as he dismisses the scientific and academic influence upon jurists and jurisprudence, so Gordon maintains that "lines of specialization between the practitioner and the academic had not yet hardened" before 1920. "Legal Thought and Legal Practice in the Age of American Enterprise," pp. 99–100.

328. Joseph H. Beale, *A Treatise on the Conflict of Laws or, Private International Law* (Cambridge, MA, 1916), vol. 1, p. 150; Ames, "The Vocation of the Law Professor," p. 369; G. Edward White, *Tort Law in America: An Intellectual History* (New York, 1980), p. xii.

329. Albert P. Blaustein and Charles O. Porter, *The American Lawyer: A Summary of the Survey of the Legal Profession* (Chicago, 1954), chs. 5, 6. Noting that lawyers left the courtroom and law office for non-legal settings and functions, scholars have tended to view the new kinds of "lawyer jobs" as evidence of the rising influence of lawyers. See Hall, *The Magic Mirror: Law in American History*, p. 212; Gordon, " 'The Ideal and the Actual in the Law' ... New York City Lawyers, 1870–1910," p. 61; Friedman, *A History of American Law*, pp. 633–4. However, the development indicates even more the influence of legal education, inasmuch as, once lawyers left the courtroom and the subject matter of the law, what defined them as a "lawyer" was that they had been to law school. The expansion of lawyers' jobs to non-legal functions meant that legal education, not the legal function or the law, became the defining characteristic of the lawyer.

in any case, was confined to a tiny fraction of the bar. Finally, the ascendance of legal science and education attests more to the encroachment of science and education upon law than to the rising status of the bench and bar.

While the Great Bar practiced on Wall Street in the late nineteenth century, immigrant lawyers in eastern cities hustled to make ends meet. In southern states, such as Mississippi, "the great majority of ... lawyers were still concerned only with the everyday problems of petty crimes, family estates, and small-scale farming and retailing that they encountered in their rural small-town practices." In "most Western states," testified a professor at the University of Iowa, the bar was "an unorganized body of very fluctuating membership, without fixed professional traditions, made up of newcomers from all parts of the Union, many of them without experience and almost all without legal training." In the Rocky Mountain states and territories of Nevada, Wyoming, Idaho, Arizona, Colorado, New Mexico, and Utah, "law was a nominal occupation.... many lawyers were also miners, ranchers, merchants, and the like." In California, apart from the fortunate few who represented railroads or manufacturers, most legal practice until the turn of the century consisted of collecting debts and validating land titles drawn up hastily by speculators or swindlers.[330] Meanwhile lawyers retreated from influential governmental and political positions, as the president of the ABA lamented in 1894. The fraction of US Senators whose chief occupation was law, which had risen from 54 percent in 1789 to 86 percent in 1845, declined to 60 percent by 1895. Similarly, the percentage of appointees to major cabinet and diplomatic posts who were lawyers declined from 78 percent between 1789 and 1861 to 42 percent between 1861 and 1923. Also declining was the fraction of graduates of 37 leading state universities and private colleges who chose law for a career: 26 percent in the classes 1871–80, 21 percent 1881–90, 17 percent 1891–1900.[331]

By the 1900s and 1910s observations about "The Passing of the Legal Profession" were common.[332] When recent scholars claim that "legal periodical

330. Quotations are from Landon, "Another False Start: Mississippi's Second State Bar Association, 1886–1892," p. 198; W. G. Hammond, "Legal Education and the Study of Jurisprudence in the West and North-West," *Journal of Social Science*, 8 (1876): 166; Gordon M. Bakken, *Rocky Mountain Constitution Making, 1850–1912* (Westport, CT, 1987), p. 18. Bakken, "Industrialization and the Nineteenth-Century California Bar," pp. 125–70, in *The New High Priests: Lawyers in Post-Civil War America,* ed. Gerard W. Gawalt (Westport, CT, 1984); Auerbach, *Unequal Justice: Lawyers and Social Change in Modern America,* ch. 2.

331. Merriam, *American Political Ideas ... 1865–1917,* p. 147n.; Donald R. Matthews, "United States Senators and the Class Structure," *Public Opinion Quarterly,* 18 (1954): 13; Philip H. Burch, Jr., *Elites in American History* (New York, 1981), vols. 1, 2; Burritt, *Professional Distribution of College and University Graduates,* p. 143.

332. Robert T. Platt, "The Decadence of Law as a Profession and its Growth as a Business," *Yale Law Journal,* 12 (1903): 441–5; Harry D. Nims, "The Present Status of the Professions – The Law," *World's Work,* 5 (1903): 3085; John R. Dos Passos, *The American Lawyer as he was – as he is – as he can be* (New York, 1907); George W. Bristol, "The Passing of the Legal Profession," *Yale Law Journal,* 22 (1913): 590–613; Julius H. Cohen, *The Law: Business or Profession?* (New York, 1916); T. J. O'Donnell, "Has the Lawyer Lost Caste?", *Chicago Legal News,* 49 (1917): 310; W. R. Vance, "Is the Legal Profession Losing its Influence in the Community?", *Central Law Journal,* 91 (1920): 77–8.

articles from the end of the century resound with praises of the legal profession," they are likely to be referring to articles about legal education.[333] And this kind of praise – to recur to Flexner and Pritchett – was a matter more of education than of law, inasmuch as "the vocation of the law professor" was for those "who devote the whole of their time to the university."[334]

Rhetorical: the "ideal of expert service"

During the late nineteenth and early twentieth centuries, education became the preeminent profession for women, within their sphere, or for men, who constituted about 80 percent of those working in higher education, 85 percent of public school administrators and 30 percent of public schoolteachers in the year 1900.[335] This "very highest vocation" acquired intellectual, institutional, political, social, and economic authority and status that made it, for this brief period, the most attractive among the liberal professions. In advancing and articulating their "profession," educators of all types inevitably appropriated the characteristics of a "profession" that had been bequeathed by the antecedent theological and legal exemplars.

In calling their work a "profession," these individuals meant an especially dignified vocation to which they professed deep commitment. These theological characteristics were complemented by a professed ethic of selfless service in two respects. On the one hand, teachers at all levels professed an ethic of serving others. "[T]eaching, like virtue, is its own reward," wrote Arthur Perry from Boston in 1912, calling on the teacher to offer "his most devoted service" and "best serve the pupils before him." Indeed, "the teaching service ... fulfills the foremost requirement of a profession," affirmed educationists from the president of the New York State Teachers College to John Almack and Albert Lang in California.[336] For male administrators, the professional ethic of serving others was often construed as "public service" or "social service." For women, the ethic was generally interpreted in terms of self-sacrificing domesticity. Meanwhile the commitment to selfless service, particularly in liberal arts colleges, was amplified by the historical and continuing association of ministers with teachers.[337]

---

333. Stevens, *Law School ... from the 1850s to the 1980s*, p. 101. Stevens cites five articles to prove his point, and all five concern legal education and admission requirements to the bar.

334. Ames, "The Vocation of the Law Professor," p. 361.

335. *Historical Statistics*, series D233–682, H520–30, H689–99.

336. Perry, *The Status of the Teacher*, p. 54; A. R. Brubacher, *Teaching: Profession and Practice* (New York, 1927), p. 22; John C. Almack and Albert R. Lang, *Problems of the Teaching Profession* (Boston, 1925), pp. 16, 59.

337. See Doty and Harris, *A Statement ... Approved by Many Leading Educators*, p. 19; Noah Porter, *The American College and the American Public* (New Haven, CT, 1870), chs. 2, 11, 15; Matthew J. Walsh, *Teaching as a Profession: Its Ethical Standards* (New York, 1926); Francis B. Pearson, *The Teacher* (New York 1921), ch. 2. While language about the professional ethic of service was doubtlessly employed in order to induce women and working class men into teaching and to rationalize their salaries, the ethic was not invented to

On the other hand, many faculty members in universities and to a lesser extent in colleges professed an ethic of serving science and pursuing truth. Scientists "linked belief in natural order with a lifestyle emphasizing service and self-denial as well as the courageous pursuit of reality," in the words of William Burnham. Thus, "science, like religion, offered an ideal of selflessness, of truth, of the possibility of spiritual dedication ... [to] the cause of abstract research ... a cause transcending mere personal ambition," according to Charles Rosenberg. That scientists disavowed material reward for the sake of "higher things" and that this disavowal involved hard work cannot be doubted. But it is difficult to see how the idea of selflessness or "secular altruism" arises from research or science *per se*, as recent scholars have maintained.[338] Researchers at the time became notorious for their "personal ambition" and for identifying themselves with their findings, inasmuch as "the pursuit of fame or reputation is usually far more selfish" than the pursuit of wealth.[339] Hence, it is nearer the truth to say that this selflessness associated with the vocation of scientists came not from science, but from the professional ethic of service that originated in the theological profession.

In addition to these theological denotations, those working in education adopted certain legal characteristics that historically informed the meaning of "profession." They formed voluntary associations in order to pursue and protect their professional interests, though they were no more successful than lawyers, physicians, or clergy during this period in establishing guilds competent to these ends. They also professed a contractual notion of professional service through their demands for increased compensation as "a matter of simple justice," to quote the president of the University of Chicago.[340] These legal characteristics of "profession," how-

---

achieve these ends. Rather, it was a theological characteristic of the meaning of "profession" that shaped how people thought and spoke about professional service after theology declined. Cf. Mattingly, *The Classless Profession: American Schoolmen in the Nineteenth Century*, pp. xvi, xx; Cogan, *All-American Girl ... in Mid-Nineteenth-Century America*, pp. 238ff.; Solomon, *In the Company of Educated Women*, p. 124; Frankfort, *Collegiate Women*, p. 41; Glazer and Slater, *Unequal Colleagues: The Entrance of Women into the Professions, 1890–1940*, p. 145; Hogan, *Class and Reform: School and Society in Chicago, 1880–1930*, p. 221.

338. Quotations are from Burnham, *How Superstition Won and Science Lost*, pp. 7–8; Rosenberg, *No Other Gods: On Science and American Social Thought*, pp. 3, 15, 138–9; James Reed, "Robert M. Yerkes and the Mental Testing Movement," in *Psychological Testing and American Society, 1890–1930*, ed. Michael M. Sokal (New Brunswick, NJ, 1987), p. 78. See Veysey, *The Emergence of the American University*, pp. 138–9, 150–1; Hollinger, "Inquiry and Uplift: Late Nineteenth-Century American Academics and the Moral Efficacy of Scientific Practice," pp. 143, 152.

339. Cattell, *American Men of Science* (1910), p. 578. This is not say that "the idealistic disinterestedness of ... the 'scholarly' American professor" was a disguise for "the ego-satisfying pretensions of professionalism." Bledstein, *The Culture of Professionalism*, pp. 288–9, 334; Diner, *A City and its Universities ... Chicago, 1892–1919*, pp. 5–6. The service ethic is explained not by the altruism of science or the egoism of professions, but rather as a constituent of the inherited rhetoric of "profession," shaping how people thought and spoke about a dignified vocation.

340. Harper, "The Pay of College Professors," p. 109. Dismissing the tradition of selflessness, Silva and Slaughter argue that "the service component of the expert" should be under-

ever, were less pronounced than the theological, due, in part, to the historical links between ecclesiastical and educational institutions.

While the semantic inheritance of the term shaped the "profession" of education in these ways, the relationship was reflexive. The particular character of the new preeminent profession influenced the meaning and usage of the term "profession." One aspect of this influence was the fifth moment in the rhetoric of profession: the appearance of the noun "professional" to replace the conventional usage of "professor," which became reserved for the preeminent profession. Henceforth only educators, not practitioners, could legitimately call themselves "professors." In addition, a sixth moment in the rhetoric of profession occurred as educators informed the meaning of "profession" with a substantive characteristic of their vocation – learning. This semantic development was revealed by two changes in usage. First, the term "liberal profession" was sloughed away, and then, ironically enough, "learned" disappeared from "learned profession."

We have seen that the terms "liberal professions" and "learned professions" were introduced early in the eighteenth century and subsequently became conventional. They routinely referred to theology, law, medicine, and education, four fields that originally became associated in the medieval university. As an abbreviated form of the two longer terms, the word "professions" acquired the same denotation, and the distinct nature of the "professional class" and the identity of its few members were matters of general consensus in the course of the eighteenth and nineteenth centuries. Thus, when the American Social Science Association was founded in 1865 it was divided into the four departments of education, public health, jurisprudence, and social economy, which reflected the social functions of the four professions.[341] Fifty years later, US Census bulletins observed the same convention: "Professional occupations ... especially what are often styled the learned professions are clearly distinguished.... Numerically, teachers constitute the most important professional class, exceeding the total number of lawyers, clergymen, and doctors." Meanwhile a University of Illinois professor sought to eliminate confusion on the point:

> These four then – the minister, the doctor, the lawyer, and the college professor – comprise the learned professions.... It must not be inferred that there are no other professions, which might with propriety lay claim to the title learned.... but ... the line must be drawn somewhere, and we have drawn it here, with ... the four leading professions.[342]

Such testimony, even while affirming longstanding usage, demonstrated that the convention was weakening over the final third of the nineteenth century. To be sure, there had always existed variation in usage, stemming from the fact that

---

stood as reciprocal and contractual. *Serving Power: The ... Social Science Expert, 1860–1920,* pp. 4, 9. Cf. Loren Baritz, *The Servants of Power: A History of the Use of Social Science in American Industry* (Middletown, CT, 1960).

341. Sanborn, "The Work of Social Science," pp. 26–7; Ross, "The Development of the Social Sciences," p. 110.

342. Dexter, "Training for the Learned Professions," p. 28; [Walter F. Willcox], *Census Statistics of Teachers, Bulletin 23 of the U.S. Bureau of the Census* (Washington, DC, 1905), p. 7.

"professions" originally denoted vocations in general. But this variation intensified as many employments sought to join the "professional class." In 1869 President William Folwell of the University of Minnesota anticipated that the category of "professions" would be gradually expanded as a function of "the rise and progress of professional education": from the learned professions to the commercial occupations, to the industrial and laboring classes. Subsequently engineers, funeral directors, baseball players, detectives, journalists, plumbers, and a host of others claimed that their vocation "is no longer merely a trade.... It is clothed with the responsibility of the learned professions and the dignity of the sciences."[343]

This self-conscious claim nevertheless acknowledged the continuing norm that the "learned professions" were, in fact, the "professions." They might be called the "intellectual professions," the "great professions," or even "professional profession[s]."[344] Whatever the adjective, the existence of a special "professional class" was evident. At the same time, the adjectival variation demonstrates the first aspect of the sixth moment in the rhetoric of "profession": the term "liberal professions," long the synonym for "learned professions," slipped out of customary usage over the second half of the nineteenth century. The link between "liberal education" and "learned professions" was still cited and explained, as did John Raymond in 1870, Charles Eliot in 1884, and Justin Morrill in 1888. But the term "liberal professions" was scarcely heard by the turn of the century.[345] The premium on *learning* in an educational age appears to have edged the synonym out of customary usage.

If the popularity of learning outmoded the usage of "liberal professions," the same thing happened, ironically enough, to "learned professions" shortly thereafter. This was the second aspect of the sixth moment in the rhetoric of profession: the usage of "learned professions" became infrequent near the turn of the century, leaving the word "professions" to denote an ever broadening class of vocations. In a culture where education and science were the chief source of legitimacy, "the status of the layman was now defined in relation to congregations of the learned rather than congregations of the saints."[346] This truth was literal as well as metaphorical. In 1904 Rev. O. J. Sturgis addressed *The Relation of an Educated Laity to*

343. William W. Folwell, "Inaugural Address, 1869," in *University Addresses* (Minneapolis, MN, 1909), p. 14, passim; Bledstein, *The Culture of Professionalism*, p. 35. Frank L. Mott, *A History of American Magazines, 1865–1885* (Cambridge, MA, 1938), pp. 17–8.

344. John H. Raymond, "The Demand of the Age for a Liberal Education for Women," in *The Liberal Education of Women*, ed. James Orton (New York, 1873), p. 32; W. H. H. Russell, "Professional Ethics," *Chicago Legal News*, 18 (September 12, 1886): 6; Winship, *Is there a Science of Pedagogy?*, p. 10; Henry S. Pritchett, "Introduction," in Abraham Flexner, *Medical Education*, p. xiv.

345. Raymond, "The Demand of the Age for the Liberal Education of Women," pp. 27–57; Charles W. Eliot, "What is a Liberal Education," *Century Magazine*, 28 (1884) 203–12; Justin S. Morrill, *State Aid to the Land-Grant Colleges* (Burlington, VT, 1888), p. 6. On contemporary shifts in the "liberal professions" in England see Rothblatt, *The Revolution of the Dons*, pp. 86–93, 248–73.

346. Neil Harris, "The Lamp of Learning: Popular Lights and Shadows," in *The Organization of Knowledge in Modern America, 1860–1920*, ed. Alexandra Oleson and John Voss (Baltimore, MD, 1979), p. 430.

an Educated Ministry, and in 1916, a University of Chicago sociologist proclaimed that Americans had become "a learned public."[347] For such a public, "learned professions" was redundant, because a "profession" had to be learned. As occupations sought to join the professional class, the term "learned professions" bulged more and more until it finally burst and fell into disuse. In 1900 Melville Dewey listed six vocations among "the learned professions"; in 1911 John Mott counted thirteen "and many others." Subsequently, the "exclusion acts," limiting immigration into the United States, contained exemptions for immigrants "belonging to any recognized learned profession."[348] Meanwhile individuals began referring to "the learned professions" in quotation marks or to the "so-called learned professions" or the "traditional 'learned' professions," references demonstrating that the term was becoming antiquated. By 1927 observers were recalling the time when "we used to speak of the learned professions."[349]

In this fashion the terms that had appeared at the beginning of the eighteenth century and signified the dignity attaching to a small group of vocations – "liberal professions" and "learned professions" – fell out of customary usage near the beginning of the twentieth century. In the early 1700s the terms denoted the few, special vocations that were dignified by learning, which was afforded by liberality. In the early 1900s the disappearance of the two terms coincided with and confirmed the preeminence of the educational profession. In an educational era "liberal" was overshadowed by "learned," and then "learned" itself became redundant in regard to professions. As the University of Missouri president noted in his 1908 inaugural, "We must add ... schools which will take care of the new professions as they appear," and by 1918 the number of degrees granted yearly in professional fields surpassed for the first time the total of those granted in the liberal arts.[350]

These changes in usage constituted the sixth moment in the rhetoric of profession, and signified how educators were informing the meaning of profession with a substantive characteristic of their vocation. That substantive characteristic was learning, which, in regard to "professions," came to mean functional expertise. This functional expertise denoted two conceptions. On the one hand, "expertise"

347. O. J. Sturgis, *The Relation of an Educated Laity to an Educated Ministry* (Philadelphia, 1904); Small, "Fifty Years of Sociology in the United States (1865–1915)," p. 769.

348. Melville Dewey, "Preface," in Taylor and Parsons, *Professional Education in the United States*, pp. 3–4; Mott, *The Future Leadership of the Church*, p. 62; 39 *US Statutes* 875 (1917); 41 *US Statutes* 981 (1921).

349. *USCommEd* (1899–1900), vol. 1, p. 620; W. E. Wickenden and Adelaide Dick, "Professional Organizations and Professional Schools," *Journal of Engineering Education*, n.s., 15 (1924): 226; Brubacher, *Teaching Profession and Practice*, p. 3. Denying that the Sherman Anti-Trust Act (1890) excluded the "learned professions" from its purview, the US Supreme Court later noted pointedly, "The language ... of the Sherman Act, of course, contains no exception." 26 *US Statutes* 209 (1890); *Goldfarb* v. *Virginia State Bar* 421 US 773, 787 (1975).

350. Albert R. Hill, "Inaugural Address," in *Exercises at the Inauguration of Albert Ross Hill, LLD, as President of the University* (Columbia, MO, 1909), p. 89; Auerbach, "The Opposition to Schools of Education by Professors of the Liberal Arts," p. 62.

was now expected to emulate the architectonic of natural science as closely as possible – empirical, quantitative, and experimentally verifiable. On the other hand, "functional" implied that the knowledge or science was instrumental to some desirable end. Identifying such an end might have become problematic, but the professional ethic of service was at hand to provide a common reference point for functionality, even though interpretations of "professional service" might differ. In this way, a difficult and contentious debate about ends was avoided, while the notion of functional expertise helped to integrate the ideas of service and science that were central to the educational profession but potentially difficult to reconcile.[351] This notion and its reconciling capacity appeared in the dual themes of research and reform, or scholarship and service, that were exemplified in the social sciences.

The individuals who founded the American Social Science Association in 1865 devoted their work to serving and improving society. In the 1880s there appeared a new generation of social scientists, committed primarily to "objectivity" and "science," as befitted the contemporary rise of scientific expertise in the profession and culture at large. Within the Association, conflict developed between the proponents of service and the advocates of science, resulting in the formation of a number of new, more specialized professional associations. The conflict also resulted in melding together the commitments to service and science in the role of the social scientist who would prescribe or recommend policy based on scientific expertise.[352]

In addition to social science, many other fields began to proclaim and discuss the "ideal of expert service," "expert knowledge," and "the professional expert." These topics appeared, for example, in the literature on teachers and engineers and in the inaugural addresses of university presidents.[353] But most demonstrative of

351. Many scholars have discussed the tension between utility and research as rationales and purposes advanced for education in the late nineteenth and early twentieth centuries. See Veysey, *The Emergence of the American University,* pp. 57–179. However pronounced this tension was in some respects, functionality and scientific expertise reached an accommodation in the domain of "professions."

352. Herbert Spencer contributed to this process with the American editions of *The Principles of Sociology* (New York, 1896), in which he discussed "Professional Institutions" by tracing the origins of professions among primitive peoples and analyzing the application of specialized, functional skills to human problems: vol. 2, pt. 7, pp. 179–324. The process has been most fully explicated in Furner, *Advocacy and Objectivity … American Social Science, 1865–1905;* Haskell, *The Emergence of Professional Social Science.* Other scholars noting or adumbrating the point include: David B. Potts, "Social Ethics at Harvard, 1881–1931, A Study in Academic Activism," in *Social Sciences at Harvard, 1860–1910,* ed. Paul S. Buck (Cambridge, MA, 1965), p. 91; Church, "Economists as Experts: The Rise of an Academic Profession in America, 1870–1917," pp. 571–4; Ross, "The Development of the Social Sciences," pp. 113–21; Ellsworth R. Fuhrman, *The Sociology of Knowledge in America, 1883–1915* (Charlottesville, VA, 1980), ch. 1. Cf. Buck, *Social Sciences at Harvard, 1860–1920,* p. 10; David M. Grossman, "Professors and Public Service, 1885–1925: A Chapter in the Professionalization of the Social Sciences" (PhD diss., Washington University, St. Louis, 1973); Shils, "The Order of Learning in the United States," p. 32.

353. Henry Suzzalo, "The Reorganization of the Teaching Profession," *NEA* (1913): 362–3. George H. Palmer, *The Ideal Teacher* (Boston, 1910), p. iv; Hart, "The Teacher as

the import of functional expertise for the meaning of "profession" was a series of Constitutional cases concerning occupational licensing. In the 1880s states began enacting laws requiring that more and more occupations be licensed, and then raising the educational requirements for those licenses. The US Constitution offered a number of possible grounds for challenging these licensing laws,[354] and in a series of cases posing such challenges, the US Supreme Court evaluated state licensing statutes according to an implied standard of whether a given occupation had functional expertise.

The Court held, in effect, that a state was entitled to license an occupation – to use police power to abridge certain obligations, rights, and privileges of citizens – insofar as the occupation's expertise was difficult and its function related to the public good. These two criteria are evident in the first ruling made by the Court on state licensing laws, *Dent* v. *West Virginia* (1889). The Court upheld both the licensing of physicians and the specific licensing requirement of either passing an examination or graduating from a reputable medical college, because "few professions require more careful preparation ... than that of medicine," which demands "knowledge of ... the human body in all its complicated parts," and because the requirement has an "appropriate" and "reasonable" relationship to the "general welfare." A decade later in *Hawker* v. *New York* (1898) the Court upheld another licensing statute for physicians and made explicit that, in licensing professions, "character is as important a qualification as knowledge" because the nature of the functional service is as important as the difficulty of the expertise.[355]

With the standard established in *Dent* and *Hawker*, the Supreme Court in a series of decisions over the next 30 years maintained the doctrine that the state's authority to license occupations depended upon the difficulty of the expertise and the nature of the function that the occupation performed.[356] State courts invoked

---

a Professional Expert," pp. 4–14; Layton, *The Revolt of the Engineers*, pp. 53–4; Calvert, *The Mechanical Engineer in America, 1830–1910*, p. 160; Mohr, "Higher Education and the Development of Professionalism ... 1867–1911," p. 323.

354. The statutes could be alleged to infringe the antecedent contractual obligations of citizens or the privileges or liberties of citizens, to deprive professionals of a vested property right to practice, or to deprive the nonlicensed citizens of equal protection of the law because other individuals, being licensed, would be allowed to practice. *US Constitution*, Art. 1 sect. 10, art. 2 sect. 2, amendments 6, 14.

355. *Dent* v. *West Virginia*, 129 US 114, 122–3 (1889); *Hawker* v. *New York*, 170 US 189, 194 (1898). Friedman maintains that "no consistent ideological pattern emerges from the case law" concerning occupational licensing during the emergent period between 1890 through 1910. But he assumes that "occupational associations take as their goal the task of defining an area of exclusive economic jurisdiction and protecting that area against economic competition." "Freedom of Contract and Occupational Licensing, 1890–1910," pp. 504, 526. My view is that interpreting the cases as relying on a standard of functional expertise is both plausible and more compelling than Friedman's interpretation of anomic professional self-interest.

356. See *Reetz* v. *Michigan*, 188 US 505, 506 (1902); *Collins* v. *Texas*, 223 US 288, 296 (1911); *Crane* v. *Johnson*, 242 US 339 (1916); *McNaughton* v. *Johnson*, 242 US 344 (1916); *Douglas* v. *Noble*, 261 US 165, 169 (1922); *Graves* v. *Minnesota*, 272 US 425, 427 (1926); *Roschen* v. *Ward*, 279 US 337 (1929).

the doctrine when overturning licensing statutes that did not meet the standard, such as "An Act to Insure the Better Education of Practitioners of Horse-shoeing, and to Regulate the Practice of Horse-shoers in the State of Illinois." In 1901 an Illinois court voided this law on the grounds that horse-shoers' skill was not sufficiently difficult to require advanced education and their service not sufficiently instrumental to "the public health or comfort, or to the safety or welfare of society." After all, said the court, "if this act is valid, then the legislature of the state can regulate almost any employment of the citizen by the requirement of previous study, and previous examination."[357] In contrast, courts held "that there is a marked distinction between the business of plumbers and that of horseshoers" in regard to both the requisite level of skill and the functional relationship to "the health, welfare, and comfort" of the public. Thus, minimal licensing requirements for the training of plumbers were normally sustained.[358]

At the peak of "the educational ideal,"[359] medicine thus appeared prominently and favorably in the leading Constitutional cases on occupational licensing. Like Cinderella, medicine had long been the last of the liberal and learned professions that anyone expected to achieve preeminence. Given doctors' attendance on unmentionable bodily functions and given their longstanding disagreements about therapies, which, in any case, were ineffective, it had long seemed incredible that physicians could become the preeminent "professionals." But a new leading profession was appropriate for a new word in a new century. "Professionals" had become those who professed dialectically selfless and contractual service, membership in a strong association, and functional expertise modeled on the architectonic of natural science. Once medical schools were reformed in light of the educational standard of functional science, medicine would fit remarkably well into this idea of "profession," whose characteristics derived from the vocations of theology, law, and education in American culture.

357. *Bessette* v. *People*, 193 Illinois 334, 344, 346 (1901); *In re Aubry*, 36 Washington 308, 316 (1904).

358. *Singer* v. *Maryland*, 72 Maryland 464 (1890).

359. James P. Munroe, *The Educational Ideal, An Outline of its Growth in Modern Times* (Boston, 1896).

5

CONCLUSION

———

I have, alas, studied philosophy,
Jurisprudence and medicine, too,
And, worst of all, theology
With keen endeavor, through and through.

Goethe, Faust[1]

The experience of each new age requires a new confession.

Ralph Waldo Emerson

We have seen that in the fifteenth, sixteenth, and seventeenth centuries the mean-ing of "profession" was extended from reference to a religious vow to denoting the act of joining and belonging, then to signifying the group of those who made the vow. Under the influence of Protestantism that meaning was further extended from denoting the "regular" monastic clergy to signifying the "secular" clergy and the laity. These semantic developments assumed special significance in the religious culture of colonial America, where they constituted the first moment in the rhetoric of "profession," which would eventually lead to "the true professional ideal" in the United States.

In that religious culture, theology and the clergy became preeminent in intellec-tual, political, social, and economic life. The Calvinist cast of the theological archi-tectonic and the preeminent status of the clergy led to emphasizing and dignifying all vocations as the fulfillment of a Christian's spiritual calling. That dignification,

———

1. Johann Wolfgang von Goethe, *Faust* (1808), tr. Walter Kaufmann (Garden City, NY, 1961), pt. 1, ll. 354–7.

in turn, elevated the vocational sense of the term "profession," and this sense became paramount by the end of the eighteenth century while the reference to religious vows declined. These developments constituted the second moment in the rhetoric of "profession." Meanwhile, as the vocational sense of "profession" gained dignity, it also narrowed, and these trends were expressed by two new terms. "Liberal professions" and "learned professions" appeared early in the eighteenth century in reference to the preeminent occupation of theology and to the fields with which theology had been associated since the thirteenth century: law, medicine, and learning. This was the third moment in the rhetoric of "profession."

Interwoven in these three rhetorical changes was an additional nuance derived from the nature of the preeminent profession. The clergy informed the meaning of "profession" with an ethic of selfless service. This ethic, being a central tenet of Christian theology, was shaped by the dialectical character of the theological architectonic. Selfless service implied that the servant would gain in status through the act of selflessness. The preeminence of the colonial clergy thus resulted in the special weight and dignity of "profession" in its religious sense being extended to vocations. The fact that "profession" came to refer to a group of people; the fact that it began to denote the work, or "particular calling," which those people did; the fact that "profession" began to signify the most dignified kind of work; and the fact that a dialectical ethic of selfless service came to be associated with a "profession" – these developments are explained by the preeminence of theology as an architectonic and an occupation in the colonial period.

In the second half of the eighteenth century religion, theology, and ministers were eclipsed by the cultural ideal of building a polity, the architectonic of liberal jurisprudence and politics, and the profession of law. In the course of this intellectual, institutional, social, and economic shift, the term "professional" was transmuted from its original sense of "avowed" or "religious" into its customary modern meaning of "vocational." This fourth moment in the rhetoric of "professions" was largely sponsored by lawyers who employed the adjective "professional," rather than the conventional "professed." They did, however, adopt the dignity and service ethic of the theological profession, and in this fashion, the inherited meaning of "profession" informed the way in which lawyers talked and thought about their vocation. At the same time the legal vocation reflexively informed the understanding of "profession" and "professional." This legal influence appeared first in the development that "professional service" commenced to signify contractual and feeable use or benefit to a client, in addition to the theological service ethic implying selflessness. Another way in which law informed how people thought and talked about "profession" was the defining and emphasizing of the professional polity, or professional association, as a characteristic of a "profession."

Between the 1860s and 1910s another shift occurred as "science" became the architectonic and the fundament of cultural legitimacy. Indeed, the very term "architectonic science" became outmoded, ironically signifying the utter domination of the new master science. Whereas "serving sciences" had previously retained their distinct identity, while nevertheless modeling themselves upon the architectonic, now the word "science" came to be identified with natural, experimental science, and other meanings were forgotten or ignored. Commensurately, the field of education emerged for a brief period as the most attractive among the "learned professions." This emergence was owed, in part, to the fact that a gender boundary in education substituted for the impermeable sectarian, institutional, and occupational boundaries in the other professions, resulting in relative mobility for male educators and restrictions upon women in the field. As a result, education became the most attractive profession for men or women, within their respective spheres.

Accompanying this development was a fifth moment in the rhetoric of "profession." The noun "professional" was introduced to replace "professor," which became reserved for the preeminent profession; henceforth, only educators could legitimately call themselves "professors." A sixth moment subsequently occurred as these professors informed the meaning of "profession" with a substantive characteristic of their vocation: learning. This semantic development was revealed by two changes in usage. First, the term "liberal professions" became outmoded and disappeared. Then, ironically enough, "learned" became redundant and was sloughed away from "learned professions." "Professions" alone began to refer to the expanding group of vocations that were acquiring the patina of learning, as manifested in the phenomenal growth of professional education. And this "learning" in professional education, being shaped by the architectonic, implied functional expertise modeled upon the natural sciences.

Through this process, schematized in Figure 5.1, the ground was prepared, by the beginning of the twentieth century, for the idealization of "profession." The term denoted a dignified vocation practiced by "professionals" who professed selfless and contractual service, membership in a strong association, and functional expertise modeled on the natural sciences. This conception then became hypostatized as professionals announced "The True Professional Ideal" and advocated "a nearer approach to the ideal" and "idealizing an occupation."[2]

"the queen of the professions, medicine"

"The true professional ideal" fit twentieth-century medicine remarkably well, and it rapidly became the preeminent profession in what has been called the "the health century."[3] In 1925 the first public opinion survey of vocational status indicated that doctors had passed lawyers and ministers, though not professors, in public esteem. Within a decade, another survey of "representative citizens" of small towns and cities reported that physicians ranked first "in the *order of your admiration*" for 25 occupations, and this preeminent status of medicine was confirmed in surveys of 1947 and 1963, by which point scholars were discussing "the queen of the

2. John F. Dillon, "The True Professional Ideal," *Reports and Transactions of the ABA* (1894): 409; James C. Carter, Jr., "The Ideal and the Actual in the Law," *Reports and Transactions of the ABA* (1890): 3; Albert E. Winship, *Is there a Science of Pedagogy?* (Boston, 1892), pp. 8, 10, 12.

3. See Edward Shorter, *The Health Century* (New York, 1987); Susan Sontag, *Illness as Metaphor* (New York, 1978).

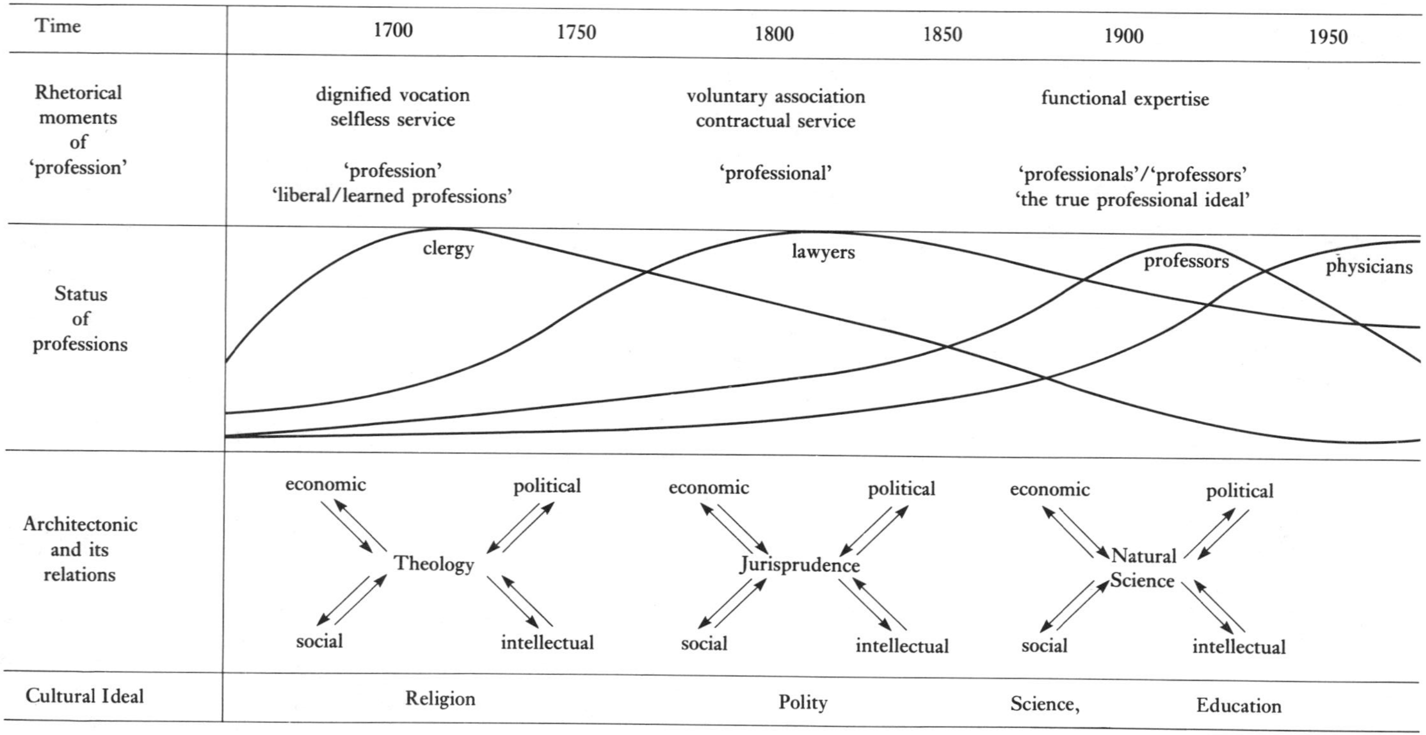

Time	1700	1750	1800	1850	1900	1950
Rhetorical moments of 'profession'	dignified vocation selfless service 'profession' 'liberal/learned professions'		voluntary association contractual service 'professional'		functional expertise 'professionals'/'professors' 'the true professional ideal'	
Status of professions	clergy		lawyers		professors	physicians
Architectonic and its relations	economic — Theology — political / social — Theology — intellectual		economic — Jurisprudence — political / social — Jurisprudence — intellectual		economic — Natural Science — political / social — Natural Science — intellectual	
Cultural Ideal	Religion		Polity		Science,	Education

Figure 5.1   The emergence of "the true professional ideal" in America

professions, medicine."[4] As with preeminent professions in the past, the average personal income and public expenditures in the field rose dramatically, rivaling that of any other profession.[5] The factors contributing to medicine's rise to be the "sovereign profession" in the twentieth century have often been described and will not be repeated here.[6] What must be noted in light of the foregoing analysis is medicine's relationship to other longstanding professions.

The sovereignty of medicine appeared unmistakably in its relations with education. Medical schools became more closely associated with their teaching hospitals than their universities,[7] and the contrast here to legal education is telling. Law schools had essentially been subsumed by universities. Geographically, they were usually located on campus; organizationally and financially, they answered to the central administration; and professionally, the leading law faculties tried to model themselves and their practices as much as possible upon conventional professorial norms. In contrast, medical schools were generally built near their teaching hospitals, often distant from the campus of the university on the other side of a river, thoroughfare, city, or state. This geographical separation both symbolized and contributed to the relative independence, organizationally and financially, that was ceded to the medical complex, which was often administered by a semi-autonomous vice-president or even a separate president. In addition, the social authority of clinical medicine obviated the professorial norms that law faculties had embraced. The striving for tenure and the preference for academic above clinical expertise did not become normative in medical centers, where an average clinician could earn social status and income exceeding professors in the rest of the university. All these factors demonstrate how medicine successfully resisted or transmuted the educational norms that reshaped law schools.

Like education, religion genuflected before the new sovereign profession. The "cure of souls," derived from the medieval *cura animarum* and Socratic *iatros tes psychēs*, was transformed, as it was transliterated, into the "psychiatrist."[8] This

4. Everett C. Hughes, "Professions" (1963), reprinted in *The Professions in America*, ed. Kenneth S. Lynn (Boston, 1967), p. 1; George S. Counts, "The Social Status of Occupations: A Problem in Vocational Guidance," *School Review*, 33 (1925): 16–27; George W. Hartmann, "The Prestige of Occupations: A Comparison of Educational Occupations with Others," *Personnel Journal*, 13 (1934): 144–52; Frances K. Zemans and Victor G. Rosenblum, *The Making of a Public Profession* (Chicago, 1981), p. 3.

5. *Historical Statistics*, series D739–64, D913–26; Milton H. Friedman and Simon Kuznets, *Income from Independent Professional Practice* (New York, 1945), pp. 390–3; William G. Rothstein, *American Medical Schools and the Practice of Medicine* (New York, 1987), pp. 151, 162–3.

6. See Richard H. Shryock, *Medicine in America: Historical Essays* (Baltimore, MD, 1966), pp. 149–76; Paul Starr, *The Social Transformation of American Medicine* (New York, 1982); Charles E. Rosenberg, *The Care of Strangers: the Rise of America's Hospital System* (New York, 1987); William G. Rothstein, *American Medical Schools and the Practice of Medicine* (New York, 1987), pp. 119–79.

7. Kenneth M. Ludmerer, *Learning to Heal: The Development of American Medical Education* (New York, 1985), chs. 10–2.

8. John T. McNeill, *A History of the Cure of Souls* (London, 1952), pp. vii–viii, 20, ch. 2; Plato, *Apology* 29d, 30b; Werner Jaeger, *Paideia: The Ideals of Greek Culture*, tr. Gilbert

transformation was prepared by the discrediting of irregular and sectarian medicine, which had often invoked religious and spiritual ideas. In response, ministers began associating religion with the new "medical science" and dissociating themselves from the legal profession, as did Rev. Leonidas Crawford in the Abingdon Religious Education Texts.[9]

This desire of professions to associate with medicine in "the health century" and, commensurately, to dissociate from fallen sovereign professions of the past was no less pronounced in law. Through the end of the nineteenth century jurists usually referred to theology with respect, often invoking religious metaphors while appealing to the "eternal and indestructible sense of justice and right, written by God on the living tablets of the human heart, and revealed in his Holy Word."[10] By the 1910s this practice had reversed, as leading jurists dissociated theology from jurisprudence and employed religious metaphors disparagingly.[11] This reversal accompanied the attack on formalist jurisprudence and the rise of skepticism in legal realism during the 1920s and 1930s, by which point jurists were freely condemning "all true believers in the orthodox legal theory" and "dogmas of legal theology" and arguing that "we must blaspheme the legal oracles."[12]

While dissociating themselves from the fallen sovereign profession of theology, leading jurists reversed their view of the relationship between law and medicine. In the second half of the nineteenth century they had tended to dissociate law from medicine due to its lower intellectual and social status among the professions.[13] But as medicine rose to become the "sovereign profession" jurists began to invoke me-

---

Highet (New York, 1943), vol. 2, pp. 38–43; Kaspar Naegale, "Clergymen, Teachers, and Psychiatrists: A Study in Roles and Socialization," *Canadian Journal of Economics and Political Science*, 22 (1956): 46–62; Andrew Abbott, *The System of Professions: An Essay on the Division of Expert Labor* (Chicago, 1988), pp. 308–10.

9. Leonidas W. Crawford, *Vocations within the Church* (Cincinnati, OH, 1920), pp. 49–53; Robert C. Fuller, *Alternative Medicine and American Religious Life* (New York, 1989).

10. George Sharswood, *An Essay on Professional Ethics*, 5th edn (1884; Philadelphia, 1907), pp. 10–1. See Perry Miller, *The Life of the Mind in America: From the Revolution to the Civil War* (New York, 1965), pp. 186–206; John F. Dillon, "Address of the President," *Reports and Transactions of the ABA* (1892): 200–3; Committee on a Code of Professional Ethics, *Reports and Transactions of the ABA*, 29 (1906): 600–2; Stephen Botein, "Professional History Reconsidered," *AJLH*, 21 (1977): 67; Grant Gilmore, *The Ages of American Law* (New Haven, CT, 1977), ch. 3; Elizabeth Mensch, "The History of Mainstream Legal Thought," in *The Politics of Law: A Progressive Critique*, ed. David Kairys (New York, 1982), p. 19.

11. See Oliver W. Holmes, Jr., *The Common Law* (Boston, 1881), p. 234; Roscoe Pound, "Liberty of Contract," *Yale Law Journal*, 18 (1909): 461; Leon Green, *Rationale of Proximate Cause* (Kansas City, Missouri, 1927), pp. 74–7, 135–6; Henry Edgerton, "Legal Cause," *University of Pennsylvania Law Review*, 72 (1924): 211.

12. Felix S. Cohen, "Transcendental Nonsense and the Functional Approach," *Columbia Law Review*, 35 (1935): 820–3; Karl N. Llewelyn, *The Bramble Bush: On our Law and its Study* (1930; 2d edn, New York, 1951), p. 148.

13. "Lawyers and Doctors," *Albany Law Journal*, 7 (1873): 35; George G. Mercer, *The American Scholar in Professional Life* (Philadelphia, 1889), pp. 29–30; W. W. Davies, "The Lawyer and Physician: A Contrast," *American Law Review*, 48 (1914): 874.

dical metaphors, as did Frank Goodnow in 1905: "Constitutional law deals with the anatomy of government; administrative law and administration have to do with the functions, the physiology of government, so to speak." In the same year, the Supreme Court in a famous decision referred to "doctors, lawyers, scientists, all professional men," demonstrating the emerging tendency of jurists to define doctors and lawyers as the archetypal professionals.[14]

In 1916 a life scientist who never earned a law degree was named dean of the nation's leading law school at Harvard University and served in that post for twenty years. Meanwhile, being "greatly impressed" by the 1910 Flexner report and its influence on medical education, the ABA in 1913 wrote to the Carnegie Foundation for the Advancement of Teaching, saying that it was "most anxious to have a similar investigation made" into legal education. The resulting Carnegie study, published in 1921, made clear that physicians had become paragons for lawyers,[15] and eminent jurists, such as Felix Frankfurter, began calling for "research in crime, as there is research in medicine and research in the natural sciences."[16] This call was echoed so loudly and so often that by the 1940s what was repugnant a half century earlier had become normative: jurists referred predominantly to "lawyers and physicians" when discussing professions, as did Roscoe Pound in his history of the legal profession commissioned by the ABA.[17]

This novel association of law with medicine was meanwhile adopted by scholars studying the professions, who began to describe medicine and law as the "classic" or "major" professions "*par excellence.*"[18] At the same time jurists attempted to justify the association in some principled way beyond the fact that the two

14. Frank J. Goodnow, *The Principles of the Administrative Law of the United States* (New York, 1905), p. 3; *Lochner* v. *New York* 198 US 45, 60 (1905).

15. Quoted from Michael Schudson, "The Flexner Report and the Reed Report: Notes on the History of Professional Education in the United States," *Social Science Quarterly*, 55 (1974): 351; Alfred Z. Reed, *Training for the Public Profession of the Law* (New York, 1921), pp. 3, 41–3.

16. Felix Frankfurter, *The Public and its Government* (New Haven, CT, 1930), p. 156; Henry M. Hart and Albert M. Sacks, *The Legal Process*, tent. edn (Cambridge, MA, 1958), pp. 1–6.

17. Roscoe Pound, *The Lawyer from Antiquity to Modern Times* (St. Paul, MN, 1953), pp. 7–10; Roscoe Pound, "The Profession in the Society of Today," *New England Journal of Medicine*, 241 (1949): 351–7.

18. Harold J. Laski, "The Decline of the Professions," *Harper's Magazine* (1935): 676; Nathan Glazer, "The Schools of the Minor Professions," *Minerva*, 12 (1974): 346–8; Magali Sarfatti Larson, *The Rise of Professionalism: A Sociological Analysis* (Berkeley, CA, 1977), ch. 1; Michael J. Powell, "Developments in the Regulation of Lawyers: Competing Segments and Market, Client and Government Controls," *Social Forces*, 64 (1985): 281. See Dietrich Rueschemeyer, "Doctors and Lawyers: A Comment on the Theory of the Professions," *Canadian Review of Sociology and Anthropology*, 1 (1964): 17; Wilbert E. Moore and Gerald W. Rosenblum, *The Professions: Roles and Rules* (New York, 1970); William R. Johnson, *Schooled lawyers: A Study in the Clash of Professional Cultures* (New York, 1978), ch. 2; William F. May, *Notes on the Ethics of Doctors and Lawyers* (Bloomington, IN, 1977); Robert Dingwall and Philip Lewis, *The Sociology of the Professions: Lawyers, Doctors and Others* (London, 1983).

professions had relatively greater social and economic status. Leading efforts to posit a "special" principled symmetry between doctors and lawyers were not convincing, however.[19] Jurists' century-long movement toward dissociating theology from jurisprudence and associating lawyers with doctors can best be explained, therefore, by jurists' interest in aligning themselves with the "sovereign profession."

In its relations with other traditional professions of education, theology, and law, twentieth-century medicine thus established its sovereignty, and its remarkable success in this regard helped to establish "the true professional ideal" as the model for all vocations. The number of "professional persons"[20] and fields called "professions" increased commensurately with the status of medicine. Through a kind of mitosis, "professions, formerly complete units, have been divided, re-divided, and divided again. Each new fractional part of the unit profession has become as extensive ... as the profession whence it originated."[21] However, even as this mitotic process was leading some to anticipate "The Professionalization of Everyone,"[22] medicine was becoming the target of widespread criticism, and its fortunes began to decline in the 1970s. The number of malpractice suits and third-party payments increased, and the profession became "proletarianized," with more physicians entering large health companies than private practice. The number of medical school applicants meanwhile declined, and the number of medical schools increased, leading to a drop, some said, in the quality of medical graduates. In

19. Charles Fried, "The Lawyer as Friend: The Moral Foundations of the Lawyer–Client Relation," *Yale Law Journal*, 85 (1976): 1072. See Bruce A. Kimball, "The Inclination of Modern Jurists to Associate Lawyers with Doctors: Plato's Response in *Gorgias* 464–5," *Journal of Medical Humanities and Bioethics*, 9 (1987): 17–31. For examples of the continuing association by jurists, see Richard Wasserstrom, "Lawyers as Professionals: Some Moral Issues," *Human Rights*, 5 (Fall 1975): 1, 5; Charles Frankel, "Review, Code of Professional Responsibility," *University of Chicago Law Review*, 43 (1976): 875; Zemans and Rosenblum, *The Making of a Public Profession*, p. 3; Julie Taylor, "Appendix," in Andrew L. Kaufman, *Problems in Professional Responsibility*, 2d edn (Boston, 1984), p. 837; Roger C. Cramton, "Professional Education in Medicine and Law: Structural Differences, Common Fallacies, Possible Opportunities," *Cleveland State Law Review*, 34 (1986): 349–62.

20. Cf. Theodore Caplow, *The Sociology of Work* (Minneapolis, MN, 1954), appendix, table G; Friedman and Kuznets, *Income from Independent Professional Practice*, p. 3; C. Wright Mills, *White Collar: The American Middle Classes* (New York, 1951), p. 113; John W. Wright, *The American Almanac of Jobs and Salaries* (New York, 1982), p. 1; Laurence Veysey, "Higher Education as a Profession: Changes and Discontinuities," in *The Professions in American History*, ed. Nathan O. Hatch (Notre Dame, IN, 1988), p. 15.

21. Robert J. Leonard, "Trends in Professional Education," *Teachers College Record*, 26 (1924): 180. Regarding the increasing number of "professions" cf. Henry L. Taylor and James R. Parsons, Jr., *Professional Education in the United States* (Albany, NY, 1900), p. 4; Abraham Flexner, "Is Social Work a Profession?", *School and Society*, 1 (1915): 911; A. M. Carr-Saunders and P. A. Wilson, *The Professions* (Oxford, 1933), p. 507, table 3; US Bureau of the Census, *US Summary of Detailed Characteristics* (Washington, DC, 1950), p. 261, table 124; Lloyd E. Blauch, *Education for the Professions* (Washington, DC, 1955); Geoffrey Millerson, *The Qualifying Associations: A Study in Professionalization* (London, 1964).

22. Harold L. Wilensky, "The Professionalization of Everyone?", *American Journal of Sociology*, 70 (1964): 137–58.

Conclusion 309

addition the proportion of female medical students increased, and this incipient feminization of the profession was also interpreted as a sign of the declining status of physicians.[23] Hence, the popular and academic press from San Francisco to Boston began asking "What's Ailing Doctors?"[24] Meanwhile professionalization became unfashionable among the cognoscenti, prompting studies of the prospect of "The Deprofessionalization of Everyone."[25]

In sum, the phenomenal rise of medicine as a sovereign profession contributed to establishing "the true professional ideal" as the model for vocations in American culture, and the decline of medicine was likewise accompanied by the decline of that ideal. Contemporaneously, twentieth-century scholarship about the professions underwent corresponding shifts that were shaped, on the one hand, by the inherited rhetoric of professions with its theological, legal, and educational characteristics and, on the other hand, by scholars' preoccupation with the status of their own profession. This preoccupation has been so consuming, in fact, that scholars have neglected the inherited rhetoric, and thus failed to see how that inheritance shaped the history of "professions," as well as their understanding of their own vocation. We turn now to examine that scholarship.

"a truly tremendous literature"

In the course of the twentieth century hundreds, if not thousands, of articles and books appeared on the topic of the professions, and already in 1970 a bibliography listed 56 pages of sources "selected" from "a truly tremendous literature" on the professions.[26] While the literature mounted, various scholars tried unsuccessfully to

23. Ronald L. Numbers, "The Fall and Rise of the American Medical Profession," in *The Professions in American History*, ed. Nathan O. Hatch (Notre Dame, IN, 1988), p. 67; John McKinlay, "Toward the Proletarianization of Physicians," in *Professionals as Workers: Mental Labor in Advanced Capitalism*, ed. Charles Derber (Boston, 1982), pp. 37–62; *Minority Students in Medical Education: Facts and Figures, II* (Washington, DC, 1985), pp. 4, 8; Bernadine Healy, "Innovators for the 21st Century: Will we Face a Crisis in Biomedical-Research Brainpower?", *New England Journal of Medicine*, 319 (1988): 1058–64; Janet Bickel, "Women in Medical Education: A Status Report," *New England Journal of Medicine*, 319 (1988): 1579.

24. John C. Burnham, "American Medicine's Golden Age: What Happened to it?", *Science*, 215 (1982): 1474–9; Robert Pear, "Doctors Fear they're Losing Status," *San Francisco Chronicle* (December 31, 1987): 16A; Richard A. Knox, "What's Ailing Doctors? Examining the National Malaise," *Boston Globe Magazine* (March 18, 1990): 16–9.

25. M. R. Huag, "The Deprofessionalization of Everyone," *Sociological Focus*, 9 (1975): 197–213; N. A. Touren, "Deprofessionalization and its Sources," *Sociology of Work and Occupations*, 2 (1975): 323–37; Laurence Veysey, "Who's a Professional? Who cares?", *Reviews in American History*, 3 (1975): 419–23; Robert A. Rothman, "Deprofessionalization: The Case of Law in America," *Work and Occupations*, 11 (1984): 183–206; Martin Oppenheimer, "The Proletarianization of the Professional," *Sociological Review Monograph*, 20 (1973): 213–27; Magali Sarfatti Larson, "Proletarianization and Educated Labor," *Theory and Society*, 9 (1980): 131–75; McKinlay, "Toward the Proletarianization of Physicians," pp. 37–62.

26. Moore and Rosenblum, *The Professions*, pp. 245–91.

systematize these writings and arrive at a definition of a profession,[27] an effort that
has periodically been declared both fruitless and wrongheaded.[28] Yet, even those
who announced in one decade that "there are no definitive criteria" of a profession
could be found in the following decade seeking such criteria.[29] Thus, it became
difficult to generalize about this contradictory mass of writings beyond Eliot
Freidson's recent assessment "that scholarship concerned with the professions is in
an intellectual shambles."[30]

Nevertheless, a distinction may be made between those who have written about
their own profession and those who have studied others' professions. Although
some individuals in the former group have recently become critical of professions,[31]
generally this group has been sympathetic toward their topic.[32] Among the latter
group, a temporal distinction may be discerned. Before the 1950s, most scholars
and outside observers praised professionals and encouraged their commitment to
professionalism or "professional patriotism," as it was termed by the president of
the Carnegie Foundation for the Advancement of Teaching.[33] This Whiggish
outlook could be heard from "Thorstein Veblen's ... dream of a professionally

27. See Ernest Greenwood, "Attributes of a Profession," *Social Work*, 2 (1957): 45–55;
Morris L. Cogan, "Toward a Definition of Profession," *Harvard Educational Review*, 23
(1953): 33–50; Cogan, "The Problem of Defining a Profession," *Annals of the American
Academy of Political and Social Science*, 297 (1955): 105–11; Howard S. Becker, "The Nature
of a Profession," in *Education for the Professions*, ed. Nelson B. Henry (Chicago, 1962), pp.
29–34; Millerson, *The Qualifying Associations: A Study in Professionalization*, table 1-1.
28. Friedman and Kuznets, *Income from Independent Professional Practice*, p. 7; Robert W.
Habenstein, "Critique of 'Profession' as a Sociological Category," *Sociological Quarterly*, 4
(1963): 291–300; Moore and Rosenblum, *The Professions*, ch. 1; J. A. Roth, "Professionalism:
the Sociologist's Decoy," *Sociology of Work and Occupations*, 1 (1974): 6–23; Eliot Freidson,
Professional Powers: A Study of the Institutionalization of Formal Knowledge (Chicago, 1986),
pp. 31–2, chs. 2–3.
29. Cf. G. Lester Anderson, "Professional Education: Present Status and Continuing
Problems," in *Education for the Professions*, ed. Nelson B. Henry (Chicago, 1962), p. 4;
Anderson, *Trends in Education for the Professions* (Washington, DC, 1974).
30. Eliot Freidson, "Are Professions Necessary?", in *The Authority of Experts: Studies in
History and Theory*, ed. Thomas L. Haskell (Bloomington, IN, 1984), p. 5.
31. The Critical Legal Studies movement exemplifies this phenomenon. See Duncan
Kennedy, *Legal Education and the Reproduction of Hierarchy: A Polemic against the System*
(Cambridge, MA, 1983); Roberto M. Unger, *The Critical Legal Studies Movement*
(Cambridge, MA, 1986).
32. Law school dean Paul Carrington has responded to the Critical Legal Scholars: "For
those university law teachers able to keep the faith of the secular religion, let there be no
shame in the romantic innocence with which they approach the ultimate issue of their
profession." "Of Law and the River," *Journal of Legal Education*, 34 (1984): 222. See
Thomas L. Shaffer, *Faith and the Professions* (Provo, UT, 1987).
33. Henry S. Pritchett, "Introduction," in Abraham Flexner, *Medical Education in the
United States and Canada* (New York, 1910), p. xiii. This is not to deny that there had long
existed opprobrium toward professions, as expressed in George Bernard Shaw's famous line:
"All professions are conspiracies against the laity." *The Doctor's Dilemma* (1906), Act 1, in
Bernard Shaw's Complete Plays with Prefaces (New York, 1962), vol. 1, p. 110.

run society" and Abraham Flexner's contention that "what matters most is professional spirit," to the first Minnesota Occupational Scale of 1931, which ranked "professional" at the top of the seven groups of occupations.[34] In 1935 Harold Laski observed that "it is impossible to draw up an indictment against a profession," and in 1954 the chancellor of New York University affirmed that "prosperity and ... happiness can both be attributed – insofar as we attain them – to the professions: To their growth, to their ever-increasing assumption of responsibility in providing for the needs and wants of the people."[35]

By the 1950s, however, scholars and outside observers began to voice criticism of professionals and professions even as their numbers grew. In a frequently cited article of 1953 Morris Cogan noted that a minor, but vocal chorus of criticism could be heard, and Myron Lieberman echoed that point in a popular textbook from 1956.[36] Typical during this transitional period was the attitude of Milton Friedman and Simon Kuznets in 1945 and Howard Becker in 1962, each of whom noted the possibility of an unflattering interpretation of professions, but wished to avoid being "accused of cynicism or muckraking" and doubted "that the symbol of the profession is used simply as a device by which the self-interest of the work group can be furthered."[37] Analysts became less deferential as time passed, and by 1972 it was not uncommonly claimed that "virtually every one of the major professions is deeply troubled, and most are in the process of renewal, reconstruction, reform and, occasionally, revolution." Subsequently the vehemence and amount of criticism of the professions has increased.[38]

Contemporaneous with this normative shift in the general assessment of professions, there occurred a theoretical shift as well. The favorable attitude toward the professions that predominated through the 1950s was accompanied by a functionalist analysis. It was said that specialized "scientific" knowledge that serves a social function – and is usually produced in a university – constitutes the foundation of a profession.[39] The functionalist view was heard from many scholars in

34. Quotations are respectively from Kenneth S. Lynn, ed., *The Professions in America* (Boston, 1967), p. ix; Flexner, "Is Social Work a Profession?", pp. 903–4; Florence L. Goodenough and John E. Anderson, *Experimental Child Study* (New York, 1931).

35. Laski, "The Decline of the Professions," p. 676; Henry T. Heald, *The Responsibility of the Professions to Future Society* (New York, 1954), pp. 1–2.

36. Cogan, "Toward a Definition of Profession," pp. 41–2; Myron Lieberman, *Education as a Profession* (Englewood Cliffs, NJ, 1956), pp. 16–7.

37. Becker, "The Nature of a Profession," pp. 39–40; Friedman and Kuznets, *Income from Independent Professional Practice*, p. 137. Everett C. Hughes was one of the leaders to question scholars' enthusiasm for the professions. "Professions," p. 4.

38. Ronald Gross and Paul Osterman, *The New Professionals* (New York, 1972), p. 9. See Jacques Barzun, "The Professions under Siege," *Harper's*, 257 (October 1978): 61–8; Nathan Glazer, "The Attack on the Professions," *Commentary*, 66 (November 1978): 34–41; Gerald L. Geison, ed., *Professions and Professional Ideologies in America* (Chapel Hill, NC, 1983), pp. 3–7; Walter P. Metzger, "A Spectre is Haunting American Scholars: The Spectre of 'Professionism'," *Educational Researcher* (August–September 1987): 10–9.

39. Although widespread usage requires that "functionalism" be employed here, the term is problematic. On the one hand, its usage among scholars is not consistent. For example, it has been applied to various instrumental relationships regarding professions, as when

the early twentieth century, including Herbert Spencer, Thorstein Veblen, Alfred North Whitehead, and R. H. Tawney.[40] In 1933 A. M. Carr-Saunders and P. A. Wilson enshrined this analysis in a classic work that was soon hailed as "undoubtedly the best general study in the field."[41] Carr-Saunders and Wilson wrote,

> At the present day many professions are based upon sciences; and nothing, short of the onset of a glacial age in the history of human mental activity, could now check the onward march of these sciences. The scientific professions are obviously borne along by the progress of the knowledge upon which they are based.... Therefore it is reasonable to anticipate that the progressiveness shown by the scientific professions will in [the] future be characteristic of all.[42]

Notwithstanding the contribution of Carr-Saunders and Wilson, the individual most responsible for articulating the functionalist analysis was Talcott Parsons. In 1939 he published an important essay, which, after several reprintings and revisions, led to his canonical article in the *International Encyclopedia of Social Sciences* in 1968, by which time the functionalist view was on the wane. Parsons took for granted that "cognitive rationality" was invested in "the intellectual disciplines – the humanities, and the sciences natural and social." These disciplines were institutionalized in "the university–academy complex" that provided the basis, first and foremost, for "the profession of learning itself " and, secondarily, for "the 'applied' branch of the professions ... its historic focuses ... represented by the two fields of law and medicine." Not only did this mean that "professionalization" was "a process which in one aspect is almost synonymous with that of rationalization," but it also suggested that professions were relatively high-minded and disinterested.[43]

---

professional knowledge or codes of ethics have been said to serve the function of disguising the self-interest of a profession and thus propping up its legitimacy. Cohen, "Transcendental Nonsense and the Functional Approach," p. 809; Deborah Rhode, "Why the ABA Bothers: A Functional Perspective on Professional Codes," *Texas Law Review*, 59 (1981): 689–721. On the other hand, individual scholars discussing functionalism often fail to define clearly the instrumentality under consideration or to maintain consistently the identity of the means and ends.

40. Herbert Spencer traced the origins of "professions" among primitive peoples emphasizing the functional application of specialized skills to various problems. *The Principles of Sociology* (New York, 1896), vol. 2, pt. 7, pp. 179–324. Thorstein Veblen, *The Higher Learning in America* (New York, 1918), ch. 7; Alfred N. Whitehead, *Adventures in Ideas* (New York, 1933), pp. 72–3; R. H. Tawney, *The Acquisitive Society* (New York, 1920), chs. 6–7.

41. Frances P. DeLancy, *The Licensing of Professions in West Virginia* (Chicago, 1938), p. v. Even today, the work is regarded as "still the standard general history of the professions in England." Wilfrid R. Prest, ed., *The Professions in Early Modern England* (London, 1987), p. 1.

42. Carr-Saunders and Wilson, *The Professions*, p. 496. See pp. 284, 295–7, 307, 365, 491, 499.

43. Talcott Parsons, "Professions," *International Encyclopedia of the Social Sciences*, vol. 12 (1968), pp. 536–7, 544; Parsons, "The Professions and Social Structure," *Social Forces*, 17 (1939): 457–67, reprinted in *Essays in Sociological Theory, Pure and Applied* (Glencoe, IL, 1948), pp. 185–99, 2d edn (New York, 1954), pp. 34–49.

The Parsonian view continued to be expressed,[44] but by the late 1950s a number of scholars who endorsed the legitimating capacity of professional expertise began to emphasize contextual and structural factors in analyzing how professionals gained authority over a social function.[45] As the normative attitude toward the professions shifted more and more in the 1960s and Parsons' benign judgment was replaced by cynicism and disfavor, the analysis of "structural" factors came to the fore.

In these refulgent days of post-structuralism and deconstruction, "structural" is a term no less problematic than "functional." Indeed, although "functionalism" is sometimes employed in ways meaning precisely the opposite of Parsons' model,[46] there is, at least, agreement on applying the term to his approach.[47] In contrast, the anti-Parsonian, or post-Parsonian, view has been called "a radically sociological view," a "power analysis," a "dominance model," and "the alternative 'capitalist' model."[48] It might also be called a constructivist view. Yet, "underlying structural

---

44. Edward Shils, "The Profession of Science," *Advancement of Science*, 24 (1968): 469–80; Joseph Ben-David, "The Profession of Science and its Powers," *Minerva*, 10 (1972): 362–83; Daniel Bell, *The Coming of PostIndustrial Society* (New York, 1976), p. 374.

45. William J. Goode, "Community within a Community, The Professions," *American Sociological Review*, 22 (1957): 194–200; Goode, "Encroachment, Charlatanism, and the Emerging Profession: Psychology, Sociology, and Medicine," *American Sociological Review*, 25 (1960): 902–14; Robert K. Merton, "The Functions of the Professional Association," *American Journal of Nursing*, 58 (1958): 504; Robert K. Merton, *Some Thoughts on the Professions in America*, Brown University Papers 37 (Providence, RI, 1960). Contemporaneously, an almost unnoticed new trend in structural organization of professions was inaugurated, and may have indirectly contributed to this shift in analysis. In 1961, fifteen states enacted legislation allowing professionals for the first time to form corporations and associations taxable as corporations. Commerce Clearing House, *New Professional Corporation Laws Explained* (Washington, DC, 1962), p. 5.

46. See Cohen, "Transcendental Nonsense and the Functional Approach," p. 809; Rhode, "Why the ABA Bothers: A Functional Perspective on Professional Codes," pp. 689–721.

47. Meanwhile, Parsons' view is sometimes called a "structural functionalist theory." This usage is accurate in the sense that "structural functionalism" is applied to theories relying on Durkheim's notion that structural "divisions of labor" exist by virtue of their social function. But the usage obscures what has become the more conventional distinction between functionalist and structuralist views of the professions because Durkheim, as French and German scholars have traditionally done, applied the word *profession* to all vocational groups, without the sense of special dignity that the word carried in England and America. Émile Durkheim, *The Division of Labor in Society* (1893), tr. W. D. Halls with an introduction by Lewis A. Coser (New York, 1984), p. xxxv; Joyce Appleby, "Value and Society," in *Colonial British America*, ed. Jack P. Greene and J. R. Pole (Baltimore, MD, 1984), pp. 292–5; Caplow, *The Sociology of Work*, ch. 1; Philip R. C. Elliott, *The Sociology of the Professions* (New York, 1972), pp. 6–13; Gerald L. Geison, ed., *Professions and the French State, 1700–1900* (Philadelphia, 1984), pp. 2–3, 10–1; Richard L. Abel, *American Lawyers* (New York, 1989), pp. 34–9.

48. Quotations are respectively from: Becker, "The Nature of a Profession," pp. 32; Starr, *The Social Transformation of American Medicine*, pp. 143–4; Rothman, "Deprofessionalization: The Case of Law in America," p. 185; Geison, ed., *Professions and Professional Ideologies in America*, pp. 7–8; Abbott, *The System of Professions*, pp. 5–6.

processes," "structural effects," and "structural necessities" are most generally
associated with this analysis,[49] so the term "structuralist" will be employed here to
refer to this general category, which was nevertheless informed by intellectual
developments termed "post-structural."[50]

Whereas the functionalist analysis explains "professions" in terms of the validity
and utility of expertise, the structuralist analysis emphasizes the organizational
structure of professional associations and the socio-economic structures that sustain
the associations. It challenges professions' claims to possess objective expertise and
tends to regard professions as self-conscious monopolies seeking to maximize their
income and prestige. By this view, "professionalization is thus an attempt to trans-
late one order of scarce resources – special knowledge and skills – into another –
social and economic rewards." The key point is that the scarcity of such "special
knowledge and skills" is usually regarded as structural and artificial due to "the
gnawing suspicion that [professional] self-regulation generally manifests itself in
anticompetitive restrictions."[51] For example, a recent historical study of "the social
dynamics of professionalism" is said to find that a medical speciality "developed
deliberately and consciously as the best way to enhance the careers, social status,
and income of doctors.... The suggestion that specialization has been caused in
part by the tremendous increase in scientific knowledge is given very little attention."[52] The structuralist thus questions the integrity and objectivity of scientific
expertise, the cornerstone of the functionalist view. Professionals are said to barri-
cade their expertise, while making it artificially abstruse and arcane, so that they
can "mystify" and exclude the laity.[53] This challenge to functional expertise and,

49. Larson, *The Rise of Professionalism*, p. 208; Starr, *The Social Transformation of
American Medicine*, pp. 65–7, 143, 231; Abbott, *The System of Professions*, p. 319. See, too,
Steven J. Diner, *A City and its Universities ... Chicago, 1892–1919* (Chapel Hill, NC, 1980),
p. 5; Paul Mattingly, "Academia and Professional School Careers, 1840–1900," *Teachers
College Record*, 83 (1981): 219. Although the anthropological school of "structuralism" and
the Marxist sense of "structures" are to be clearly distinguished, the claim that transcultural
social structures exist and help to explain human experience is common to both and
contributes to this general approach to studying professions.

50. Such informing appears in Stanley Fish's discussion of the interpretation of legal texts.
Is there a Text in this Class? (Cambridge, MA, 1980), chs. 13–6; Fish, "Working on the
Chain Gang: Interpretation in Law and Literature?', *Texas Law Review*, 60 (1982): 551–67;
Fish, "Wrong Again." *Texas Law Review*, 62 (1983): 299–316.

51. Quotations are respectively from Larson, *The Rise of Professionalism*, p. xvii, chs. 1, 9;
Ira Horowitz, "The Economic Foundations of Self-Regulation in the Professions," in
Regulating the Professions, ed. Roger D. Blair and Stephen Rubin (Lexington, MA, 1980),
p. 4. See Terence J. Johnson, *Professions and Power* (London, 1972), pp. 41–61; Barbara
Melosh, *The Physician's Hand: Work, Culture and Conflict and American Nursing* (Philadel-
phia, 1982); Wade L. Robison, Michael S. Pritchard, and Joseph Ellin, eds., *Profits and
Professions: Essays in Business and Professional Ethics* (Clifton, NJ, 1983).

52. John P. Hubbell, Jr., "[Review of] *American Pediatrics: The Social Dynamics of
Professionalism, 1880–1980* by Sydney A. Halpern ... 1988," *New England Journal of Medi-
cine*, 320 (1989): 1358. See Penina Migdal Glazer and Miriam Slater, *Unequal Colleagues: The
Entrance of Women into the Professions, 1890–1940* (New York, 1987), p. 16.

53. See, for example, Jethro K. Liebermann, *The Tyranny of the Experts: How Professionals are Closing the Open Society* (New York, 1970); Gerald E. Markowitz and David

thus, to the legitimacy of professional authority is intimately linked with charges that the ethic of selfless service was invented to deflect criticism of professionals' power and prestige by disguising their self-interest.

The tendency of pre-1950s functionalism to credit the professional service ethic was inaugurated by Louis Brandeis and Abraham Flexner and echoed by most social scientists in subsequent decades,[54] with the notable exception of Talcott Parsons.[55] Meanwhile professionals credited the service ethic as well, observing that "the labor union exercises its monopoly for the sole purpose of gaining an economic advantage for its membership.... The monopoly on professional service rests on higher ground.... It is unthinkable that a professional secret should be used for personal gain."[56] Even acerbic critics of their own profession, such as Roscoe Pound, became apologists in this regard. In 1933 the State Supreme Court of Washington gave legal standing to the professional service ethic by upholding an exemption of "professions" from an excise tax upon "business activities" on the grounds that

A profession is not a money getting business. It has no element of commercialism in it. True, the professional man seeks to live by what he earns, but his main

Karl Rosner, "Doctors in Crisis: A Study of the Use of Medical Education Reform to Establish Modern Professional Elitism in Medicine," *American Quarterly*, 25 (1973): 83–107; Ivan Illich et al., *Disabling Professions* (Salem, NH, 1977); Douglas Klegon, "The Sociology of Professions: An Emerging Perspective," *Sociology of Work and Occupations*, 5 (1978): 259–83.

54. Flexner, "Is Social Work a Profession?", pp. 901–11; Louis D. Brandeis, *Business – A Profession* (Boston, 1914), p. 2. See Clyde L. King, ed., "Ethics of the Professions and of Business," *Annals of the American Academy of Political and Social Science*, 306 (1922): 1–300; T. H. Marshall, "The Recent History of Professionalism in Relation to Social Structure and Policy," *Canadian Journal of Economics and Political Science*, 5 (1939): 327.

55. Parsons maintained that professional ethics was merely expected behavior that persisted only due to its functionality in helping the professional to perform the service for the patient or client. ("The Professions and Social Structure," pp. 457–67.) In contrast, Durkheim and Tawney feared the unbridled and amoral free market of liberal capitalism, and thus were delighted to find associations that explicitly claimed and did seem to be elevated above the market. Thomas L. Haskell, "Professionalism *versus* Capitalism: R. H. Tawney, Émile Durkheim, and C. S. Peirce on the Disinterestedness of Professional Communities," pp. 180–225, in *The Authority of Experts*, ed. Haskell (Bloomington, IN, 1984).

56. A. R. Brubacher, *Teaching Profession and Practice* (New York, 1927), pp. 11, 15. In an ironic reversal the early twentieth-century literature about schoolteaching extolled the service ethic, not as a way for a high-status profession to deflect criticism of its power and prestige, but as way for this low-status group to gain some status by way of the dialectic of selflessness. The argument ran: high-status professions emphasize service; teaching emphasizes service; thus, teaching is a high-status profession. See Arthur C. Perry, Jr., *The Status of the Teacher* (Boston, 1912), ch. 3; Francis B. Pearson, *The Teacher* (New York 1921), chs. 8, 10; John C. Almack and Albert R. Lang, *Problems of the Teaching Profession* (Boston, 1925), ch. 4; Matthew J. Walsh, *Teaching as a Profession: Its Ethical Standards* (New York, 1926), chs. 1–3; Riverda H. Jordan, *Education as a Life Work: An Introduction into Education* (New York, 1930), p. 22; National Education Association, "The Yardstick of a Profession," *Institute on Professional and Public Relations* (Washington, DC, 1948), p. 8; Albert J. Huggett and T. M. Stinnett, *Professional Problems of Teachers* (New York, 1956), p. 20.

purpose and desire is to be of service to those who seek his aid and to the community of which he is a necessary part.[57]

In this fashion, professional service was credited by the functionalist analysis just as it credited professional expertise. The service ethic is still recited faithfully today,[58] "but reactions to it range from mild skepticism to curt dismissal. Some modern writers regard it a harmless myth.... Others share [the] hostile conviction that professionals are wolves in sheep's clothing, monopolists who live by the rule of caveat emptor, but lack the integrity to admit it."[59] The prevailing structuralist skepticism, which emphasizes desires for money and prestige, has thus put in doubt all testimony on behalf of professional service, though it should be noted that the service ethic is a good deal more complex than either its traditional proponents or its recent critics have commonly understood. Not only is there the historical ambiguity between contractual and selfless service, but the latter can mean benefiting the individual client or the society at large, or upholding some abstract virtue underlying the profession, such as health, justice, or truth. These different kinds of selfless service are not necessarily compatible, and proponents and critics generally have not analyzed their complex relationship with much rigor.[60]

Overall, twentieth-century scholarship about the professions reveals two marked shifts, both beginning in the 1950s and culminating in the 1970s and 1980s: a normative shift from approbation to criticism and a theoretical shift from functionalist to structuralist analyses of professions. Needless to say, these simple sketches of functionalism and structuralism do not do justice to the subtleties of scholars' individual analyses.[61] But it is important to gain a sense of the large

57. *State Ex Rel. Stiner* v. *Yelle* 174 Washington 402, 411 (1933); Pound, *The Lawyer from Antiquity to Modern Times*, p. 5.

58. Anton-Hermann Chroust, *The Rise of the Legal Profession in America* (Norman, OK, 1965), vol. 1, p. xi; Zemans and Rosenblum, *The Making of a Public Profession*, p. 126 (n. 8); *Goldfarb* v. *Virginia State Bar* 421 US 773, 786; Warren Burger quoted in Steven Brill, "Headnotes: Uncle Warren," *American Lawyer*, 5 (October 1984): 9.

59. Haskell, "Professionalism *versus* Capitalism," p. 181.

60. Another important ambiguity is whether the individual or the association or both are expected to serve. Similar to Durkheim and Tawney, Parsons argued that individual professionals rationally seek to pursue their own interests, but that the collectivity of a profession tends to encourage altruistic behavior. ("The Professions and Social Structure," 458–64.) After World War II certain professionals repeated the view that individuals are probably self-interested, but that the group, by virtue of association, tends inevitably toward altruism and service. (Huggett and Stinnett, *Professional Problems of Teachers*, p. 24; Lieberman, *Education as a Profession*, pp. 4–5.) Yet the failure to explain exactly why or how the collectivity should encourage altruistic behavior is underscored by the fact that other observers, such as Reinhold Niehbuhr, proposed just the opposite: that individuals can be expected to act morally while groups tend to protect their self-interest. *Moral Man and Immoral Society* (New York, 1932).

61. Paul Starr, for example, has explicitly tried to balance the two analyses, although he clearly favors the structuralist. This effort at balance might be more compelling, had Starr emphasized the functionalist approach regarding the initial rise of the medical profession through the early twentieth century, and the structuralist analysis regarding the subsequent consolidation of physicians' authority. *The Social Transformation of American Medicine*.

picture. The conceptual difference between functionalism and structuralism turns on whether expertise or organizational and social structure is regarded as the taproot of professional authority and status. But this conceptual difference is not the only way to explain the theoretical and normative shifts. Both may be attributed to a third shift: the change in social status of the professoriate in the course of the twentieth century.

"the profession of learning itself"

Studies of the social status of occupations before World War II indicate that professors were highly regarded. Public opinion surveys in the 1920s found that professors were ranked second only to bankers among "forty-five occupations" that respondents arranged "in the order of their social standing." In the 1930s an opinion poll of "representative citizens" of small towns and cities found that professors were ranked second only to physicians.[62] Nevertheless, the general decline of optimism that followed the first World War had already given professors, and intellectuals in general, a sense of becoming "members of a beleaguered minority."[63] This sense became more pronounced after 1945, the point that some have identified as the beginning of the "decline" of American professors as "a cultural elite."[64] By 1951 C. Wright Mills observed:

> The increase in enrollment and the consequent mass-production methods of instruction have made the position of college professor less distinctive than it once was.... The type of man who is recruited for college teaching and shaped for this end by graduate school training is very likely to have a strong plebeian strain.... The Arts and Sciences graduate schools, as the president of Harvard has indicated, do not receive "their fair share of the best brains and well-developed, forceful personalities". Law and medical schools have done much better.[65]

62. Counts, "The Social Status of Occupations," pp. 16–27; Hartmann, "The Prestige of Occupations: A Comparison of Educational Occupations with Others," pp. 144–52; Logan Wilson, *The Academic Man: A Study in the Sociology of a Profession* (New York, 1942), p. 16; Robert W. Hodge, Paul M. Siegel, and Peter H. Rossi, "Occupational Prestige in the United States, 1925–63," *American Journal of Sociology*, 70 (1964): 291–6.

63. Christopher Lasch, *The New Radicalism in America [1889–1963]: The Intellectual as a Social Type* (New York, 1965), p. x. Laurence Veysey, "The Plural Organized Worlds of the Humanities," in *The Organization of Knowledge in Modern America, 1860–1920*, ed. Alexandra Oleson and John Voss (Baltimore, MD, 1979), p. 91; Paul Fussell, *The Great War and Modern Memory* (New York, 1975); David M. Kennedy, *Over Here: The First World War and American Society* (New York, 1980), p. vii.

64. Joseph Gusfield, "American Professors: The Decline of a Cultural Elite," *School Review*, 83 (1975): 595–616; Paul F. Lazarsfeld and Wagner Thielens, Jr., *The Academic Mind: Social Scientists in a Time of Crisis* (Glencoe, IL, 1958).

65. Mills, *White Collar*, pp. 129–30. See, too, H. M. Wriston, "Fire Bell in the Night," *Bulletin of the American Association of University Professors*, 35 (1949): 441; Richard H. Shryock, "The Academic Profession in the United States," *Bulletin of the American Association of University Professors*, 38 (1952): 32–70.

The boom in higher education between about 1955 and 1970 brought some renewal in the prosperity and esteem of professors. Their income, which, from a high point in 1913, had decreased in value relative to that of the average worker, increased enormously in this period.[66] However, "public disenchantment with higher education developed during the late 1960s and early 1970s," and this disenchantment subsequently continued "to sap the professional pride and confidence of the academic teaching corps."[67] In addition, salary increases fell far behind inflation, a fact that may account for recent scholars' readiness to attend to their forerunner's complaints about income during the 1890s and 1900s, just as the disenchantment of the 1970s and 1980s may explain recent scholars' readiness to credit their forerunners' complaints about being unappreciated.

The status of the academic profession thus changed markedly and concurrently with the normative and theoretical shifts in scholarship analyzing professions. In fact these changes were not only concurrent but may be profoundly related. On the one hand, the functionalist analysis that predominated before World War II was a patronizing view of the non-academic professions. Veblen, Tawney, Carr-Saunders, Wilson, Whitehead, and other professors were generally agreed, in Parsons words, that "cognitive rationality" was expressed most fully in "the profession of learning itself" and, secondarily, in "the 'applied' branches of the professions" including law and medicine, the chief competitors to professors.[68] This view was tantamount to parents commending their children for their fine upbringing: the praise returned to the praiser, while patronizing the one praised. What is not sufficiently appreciated by many critics today who regard functionalism as naive praise of professions is that the functionalist scholars were praising themselves.

On the other hand, what is equally unappreciated is the extent to which the recent decades of critical scholarship of the professions can be understood as sour grapes hidden in the dense foliage of an "alternative 'capitalist,'" "radically sociological," "power" analysis. As MDs and JDs more and more outstripped PhDs in social and economic status and authority after World War II, the scholarly attitude toward professions shifted, and an analytic frame was found to legitimate that attitude. At least, this is a plausible explanation for why the theoretical shift

---

66. Beardsley Ruml and Sidney G. Tickton, *Teaching Salaries Then and Now: A 50-Year Comparison with Other Occupations and Industries* (New York, 1955), pp. 32–9; Viva Boothe, *Salaries and the Cost of Living in Twenty-Seven State Universities and Colleges, 1913–1932* (Columbus, OH, 1932), pp. 6–7, 65; [Ford Foundation], *The Pay of Professors* (New York, 1962), p. 1; Howard R. Bowen, "Faculty salaries: Past and Future," *Educational Record*, 49 (1968): 17; Frank Stricker, "American Professors in the Progressive Era: Incomes, Aspirations, and Professionalism," *Journal of Interdisciplinary History*, 19 (1988): 256.

67. Logan Wilson, *American Academics: Then and Now* (New York, 1979), pp. 8–9; Howard R. Bowen and Jack H. Schuster, *American Professors: A National Resource Imperiled* (New York, 1986), pp. 4–5; Metzger, "A Spectre is Haunting American Scholars: The Spectre of 'Professionism'," p. 17. Christopher Jencks and David Riesman, *The Academic Revolution* (Garden City, NJ, 1968), ch. 5; Walter P. Metzger, "The Academic Profession in Hard Times," *Daedalus*, 104 (Winter 1975): 25–44; Martin J. Finkelstein, *The American Academic Profession: A Synthesis of Social Scientific Inquiry since World War II* (Columbus, OH, 1984), passim.

68. Parsons, "Professions," pp. 536–7.

corresponds both with the normative shift and with professors' decline in social and economic status in the decades after 1945. To be sure, this correspondence does not prove that the change in status caused the other two shifts. But it does offer a plausible explanation, just as functionalism and structuralism plausibly explain professionalization.[69]

The fact, then, may be that the recent "critical" scholarship of the professions is no less teleological and self-aggrandizing than Parsonian functionalism is said to be. For example, the dean among recent scholars of the professions, Eliot Freidson, has dismissed the capacity of other professions to analyze themselves and the functionalist analysis which they usually employ, that analysis being "both logically and substantively in contrast with the principle generally employed by sociologists."[70] Hence, in his award-winning book on the medical profession Freidson wrote:

> I assume that the analytical variables of social organization are more useful discriminants than those of norms, attitudes, or ethics and that, in fact, the former has a closer relationship to behavior than the latter.... Medicine, then, in this sociological usage, is an organized consulting occupation which may serve as the discoverer, carrier, and practitioner of certain kinds of knowledge, but which is not a body of knowledge as such.[71]

In contrast to the functionalist thesis that cognitive rationality naturally and necessarily legitimates authority over a social function, Freidson states: "Obviously, an occupation does not 'naturally' come by so unusual a condition as professional autonomy.... A profession attains and maintains its position by virtue of the protection and patronage of some elite segment of society ... Its position is thus secured by the political and economic influence of the elite which sponsors it." By this formulation, the fundamental question of professionalism becomes the structural relations of "political and economic power" – "the capacity to control and regulate." But it is no less true than for Parsons that "the profession of learning itself" is the only group that can understand and explain these relations.[72]

69. Metzger says the causes of "antiprofessionalism" arising in the 1950s are unclear, but suggests that "professional expansion" in recent time may be a contributing factor because "it became virtually impossible to aim a critical arrow at any social institution or public policy without piercing professional flesh." "A Spectre is Haunting American Scholars: The Spectre of 'Professionism'," p. 17.

70. Eliot Freidson, ed., *The Professions and their Prospects* (Beverly Hills, CA, 1971), p. 8.

71. Eliot Freidson, *Profession of Medicine: A Study of the Sociology of Applied Knowledge* (New York, 1970), pp. 4–5. Hence, his "basic thesis ... that the actual substance of the knowledge that is ultimately involved in influencing human activities is different from the formal knowledge that is asserted by academics and authorities" does not seem to apply to the formal knowledge of sociology. *Professional Powers*, p. xi; "Professions and the Occupational Principle," in *The Professions and their Prospects*, ed. Eliot Freidson (London, 1971), pp. 24–5.

72. Freidson, *Profession of Medicine*, pp. 72–3, 82; Freidson, "Are Professions Necessary?", p. 10; Parsons, "Professions," pp. 536–7. The self-interest underlying the two schools of analysis is demonstrated also by the irony that the functionalism of Kenneth Ludmerer and the structuralism of Paul Starr lead them each to dismiss the "mythical" influence of the Flexner report in elevating the medical profession. In each case, the "Flexner myth"

This "profession of learning" that Parsons and Freidson enshrined as the oracle
of professions was their own discipline of sociology, and other scholars have taken
offense at what they regarded as the imperiousness of sociology: "the discipline that
has sometimes aspired to be crowned the modern queen of the sciences."[73] Indeed,
a distinguished historian of professions in the early modern period has expressed
herself stridently on this point:

> If the sociologist is happy to find structures and neglect meaning, the historian
> finds such an exercise most unrewarding.... Sociology is a simple science.
> Historians know only too well the complexity of human society.[74]

Surely this response is extreme, not only because the social and behavioral sciences
have contributed greatly to historical analysis, but also because historians of the
professions have pursued their own imperial designs, as we have seen. Recent
sociology of the professions "neglects meaning" no more than the rest of the
twentieth-century scholarship on the professions, and this neglect of meaning is
better understood as presentism, for it is presentism that conditions the great bulk
of that scholarship, whether early or late, approving or critical, functionalist or
structuralist. This presentism is revealed by certain continuities in the twentieth-
century scholarship of the professions that underlie the theoretical and normative
shifts discussed above.

One presentist continuity is the assumption that medicine is the universal arche-
type of a profession. From the Flexner report of 1910 to the prize-winning works of
Eliot Freidson and Paul Starr, scholars have focused upon medicine, "the queen of
the professions," "the prototypical" and "paradigmatic" case. Indeed, the assumption is often baldly stated: "I assume that if anything "is" a profession, it is
contemporary medicine." Accordingly, if something can be proven with respect to
medicine, then it is deemed to characterize "professionalization," because "the rise
of medicine" is interchangeable with "the rise of professions."[75]

---

challenges the expertise of the professional academics represented by the author: medical
scientists for Ludmerer, sociologists for Starr. Ludmerer, *Learning to Heal: The Development
of American Medical Education*, pp. 4, 166ff., 191ff., 236ff.; Starr, *The Social Transformation
of American Medicine*, pp. 118–26, 230.

73. Sidney E. Mead, "Christendom, Enlightenment, and the Revolution," in *Religion and
the American Revolution*, ed. Jerald C. Brauer (Philadelphia, 1976), p. 39. See Hubbell,
"[Review of] *American Pediatrics: The Social Dynamics of Professionalism, 1880–1980* by
Sydney A. Halpern," p. 1358.

74. Rosemary O'Day, "The Anatomy of a Profession: the Clergy of the Church of
England," in *the Professions in Early Modern England*, ed. Wilfrid Prest (London, 1987),
pp. 26, 59.

75. Quotations are respectively from Hughes, "Professions," p. 1; William J. Goode,
"Theoretical Limits of Professionalization," in *The Semi-Professions and their Organization*,
ed. Amitai Etzioni (New York, 1969), pp. 294–5; Freidson, *Profession of Medicine*, p. 4;
Starr, *The Social Transformation of American Medicine*, pp. 17, 28–9, 39–40, 79, 453. See
Bernard Barber, "Some Problems in the Sociology of the Professions" (1965), reprinted in
The Professions in America, ed. Kenneth S. Lynn (Boston, 1967), p. 31; Larson, *The Rise of
Professionalism*, ch. 3. The lone qualification is the explicit or implicit exaltation of the
academic profession.

A related continuity is the assumption that modern science is the architectonic. Here again, little explanation is required with respect to the pre-1950s functionalism, which enshrined "cognitive rationality." However, this continuity seems decidedly contradicted by the last three decades of structuralist scholarship, much of which invokes theorists of deconstruction, post-structuralism, constructivism and hermeneutics in order to challenge the privileged epistemological status of modern science. Ironically, however, the constructivist sword used to eviscerate the functionalist belief in ahistorical, transcultural, and objective expertise is somehow transformed into a scientistic shield to fend off claims for the ethical character of professions. Freidson, for example, having challenged the view "that there are objective rather than historical and social criteria by which differential salience and superior knowledge and skill are determined," elsewhere discounts the ethical ideal of professional service as a chimerical notion that cannot be confirmed "by reliable information," "empirical evidence," or "*objectively determinable attributes.*" Similarly, Larson rebuts claims on behalf of objective professional expertise, but then dismisses the "ideal of service" as an artifact of a nebulous "traditional moral law" that has no empirical basis other than to deflect criticism of professional monopolies.[76]

In this way, notwithstanding the constructivist arguments that are applied to "scientific" professions, the structuralist analysis remains very much what Parsons or Veblen would have understood as "scientific" when it comes time to rebut claims for professional service or to explain the context and structure of professions. The explanation is not, for example, substantively rational, as in Constitutional law, or dialectical, as in Pauline theology, or interpretative, as in both fields. Whether in the strident terms of Larson or the more evenhanded approach of Hughes, Freidson or Starr, the structuralist analysis exhibits a preference for the empirical, causal, formally rational, and quantitative.

Another presentist continuity is the proposition that professions were invented or first appeared in modern industrial, bureaucratic society. This point is so firmly established that it is held to be "the orthodox interpretation" of the history of professions.[77] As a result, "their history before the development of industrial

76. Eliot Freidson, "Professions and the Occupational Principle," pp. 24–5, 31; Freidson, *Profession of Medicine*, pp. 80–3; Larson, *The Rise of Professionalism*, pp. 222–3; Larson, "The Production of Expertise and the Constitution of Expert Power," in *The Authority of Experts*, ed. Thomas L. Haskell (Bloomington, IN, 1984), pp. 28–80.

77. Daniel Duman, "The English Bar in the Georgian Era," in *Lawyers in Early Modern Europe and America*, ed. Wilfrid R. Prest (New York, 1981), p. 95; Duman, *The English and Colonial Bars in the Nineteenth Century* (London, 1983), pp. 200–1. Marshall, "The Recent History of Professionalism in Relation to Social Structure and Policy," p. 325; Elliott, *The Sociology of the Professions*, pp. 14, 32; William J. Reader, *Professional Men: The Rise of the Professional Classes in Nineteenth-Century England* (New York, 1966), pp. 2, 11; Burton J. Bledstein, *The Culture of Professionalism: The Middle Class and the Development of Higher Education in America* (New York, 1976), p. 20; Nathan Reingold, "Definitions and Speculations: The Professionalization of Science in America in the Nineteenth Century," in *The Pursuit of Knowledge in the Early Republic*, ed. Alexandra Oleson and Sanborn C. Brown (Baltimore, MD, 1976), p. 37; Brian Greenberg, *Worker and Community, Response to Industrialization in a Nineteenth-Century American City, Albany, New York, 1850–1884*

capitalism tends to be ignored," because "an industrializing society is a professionalizing society," and the professions were "brought into being to serve the needs of
an industrial society."[78] This view was axiomatic for the functionalist analysis since
"cognitive rationality" was associated with the advance of science and the concomitant technological advancements. For the structuralist analysis, the chronology
stems from Karl Polanyi's thesis that the rise of the free market and industrial capitalism engendered a "countermovement" among the intellectual bourgeoisie, who
protected themselves from the savage free-for-all of the marketplace by forming
associations, such as professional guilds.[79] Polanyi's thesis has been extended and
applied in different ways, but the fundamental continuity in all such interpretations
is the close link posited between professionalization and the emergence of the
middle class in industrial and bureaucratic culture of the nineteenth century.

Still another presentist continuity is the neglect of theology as an important
profession, or even as a profession at all. While Abraham Flexner and Beatrice and
Sydney Webb omitted theology from their lists of professions with little comment,
the explicit rationale of Carr-Saunders and Wilson for this neglect is revealing.
These social scientists dismissed the clergy and the military with the ironical
reasoning that the former was no longer socially important and the latter ought no
longer be socially important. They further avowed that law and medicine were "the
two medieval professions which demanded the most specialized training" and that
from the early 1700s, when theology "had divested itself of duties relating to the
ordinary business of life, its position on the list [of professions] was anomalous."[80]
This omission of theology was subsequently endorsed by many others studying the
professions, and the omission fits perfectly the twentieth-century tendency to identify law and medicine as "the older professions," which were "historically considered as 'the professions'."[81]

(Albany, NY, 1985), p. 4; Prest, *The Professions in Early Modern England*, p. 4; Maxwell H.
Bloomfield, "Law: The Development of a Profession," in *The Professions in American
History*, ed. Nathan O. Hatch (Notre Dame, IN, 1988), p. 33.

78. Quotations are respectively from: C. W. Brooks, *Pettifoggers and Vipers of the
Commonwealth: The "Lower Branch" of the Legal Profession in Early Modern England*
(Cambridge, UK, 1986), p. 263; Goode, "Encroachment, Charlatanism, and the Emerging
Profession," p. 902; Reader, *Professional Men ... in Nineteenth-Century England*, p. 2. Even
those who attempt to revise this chronology push back the origins of professions merely to
the early nineteenth century or mid-eighteenth century. Duman, "The English Bar in the
Georgian Era," p. 104; Samuel Haber, "The Professions and Higher Education in America:
A Historical View," in *Higher Education and the Labor Market*, ed. Margaret S. Gordon
(New York, 1974). p. 238.

79. Karl Polanyi, *The Great Transformation* (New York, 1944).

80. Carr-Saunders and Wilson, *The Professions*, pp. 3, 294, 309; Flexner, "Is Social Work
a Profession?", pp. 901–11; Sidney and Beatrice Webb, "Special Supplement on Professional
Associations," *New Statesman*, 9 (April 21–8, 1917): 4.

81. Quotations are respectively from Freidson, "Are Professions Necessary?", p. 3;
DeLancy, *The Licensing of Professions in West Virginia*, p. 15; Mills, *White Collar*, p. x;
Hughes, "Professions," p. 7; Larson, *The Rise of Professionalism*, p. xiii, 216, but cf. p. 236;
Taylor, "Appendix," p. 837; Powell, "Developments in the Regulation of Lawyers," p. 281.
Donald W. Light astutely notes, "Most accounts of the professions do not include the minis-

Not only do these judgments rely on incorrect beliefs about past centuries, but they also misunderstand occupations in the current epoch. At the turn of the century, the academic standards of divinity schools were, on average, much higher than those of law or medical schools, while the value of the endowments and property of divinity schools was more than twice the total value of the endowments and property of law and medical schools combined. The higher academic standards and greater wealth of divinity schools persisted for some time. As late as 1916, after medical education had begun its reforms, the value of the endowment and property of theological schools was about 63 million dollars; that of medical schools, including associated hospitals, about 54 million dollars; and all other professional schools combined, about 16 million dollars.[82] This was the same year when Abraham Flexner, for example, was omitting theology from his list of professions, a fact that suits perfectly his assumption that natural science is the architectonic and his neglect of the word "profession."

This neglect of the rhetoric of profession is the final continuity underlying the twentieth-century scholarship of the professions. Notwithstanding their different normative or theoretical viewpoints, scholars have persistently failed to examine carefully, or even to ask, what the word "profession" and its cognates meant in the past. This point was discussed in the introduction, and subsequent chapters have offered an alternative view. I have tried to explain how that meaning changed reflexively and episodically over time as the nature of what was actually called a "profession" changed. By the beginning of the twentieth century, the term denoted a dignified vocation with three fundamental characteristics. These three characteristics then came to constitute the basic topics of discussion in the twentieth-century debate about the meaning and nature of professions, notwithstanding the normative and theoretical shifts described above. One topic concerns the body of functional knowledge, or expertise, associated with a profession and involves issues of epistemology, utility, and education. A second topic concerns the profession's organization into an association and involves such issues as autonomy, exclusion, licensing, and certification. The third fundamental topic is the ethic of professional service.

Needless to say, these three basic topics – expertise, association, service – have often been subdivided by scholars into lists of six, eight, ten, or more characteristics. But such characteristics are often redundant or may easily be aggregated on grounds of parsimony.[83] Meanwhile a good deal of testimony affirms that "there

---

try; for scholars find it easiest to leave its difficulties behind. It was a profession in decline, and were one to account for that one would have to revise most of the theories of the professions, which rely so heavily on the medical profession and the themes of monopoly and dominance that ... cannot explain decline." Donald W. Light, "The Development of Professional Schools in America," in *The Transformation of Higher Learning, 1860–1930*, ed. Konrad H. Jarausch (Chicago, 1983), p. 346.

82. Taylor and Parsons, *Professional Education in the United States*, pp. 10–1, 19–21; *USCommEd* (1916), vol. 2, p. 353.

83. See, for example, Flexner, "Is Social Work a Profession?", pp. 902–4; Rothman, "Deprofessionalization: The Case of Law in America," pp. 183–4. See, too, Jan Goldstein, "Foucault among the Sociologists: The 'Disciplines' and the History of the Professions," *History and Theory* (1984): 174–5; National Education Association, "The Yardstick of a

are three ideas involved in a profession: organization, learning ... and a spirit of public service." Such testimony comes from Pritchett, Brandeis, and the Webbs in the 1910s, and Taeusch, DeLancy, Pound, Carr-Saunders, and Wilson in the 1920s and 1930s.[84] More recently Tyler, Cogan, and Blauch in the 1950s, Chroust and Barber in the 1960s, Goode and Elliott in the 1970s, and Starr, Berman, Rich, and Hatch in the 1980s have said that "three important aspects" – the "collegial, cognitive, and moral," that is, "autonomy, service and knowledge" – are characteristics of the "ideal" of a profession.[85]

To be sure, there is great disagreement over the nature and legitimacy of the expertise, association, and service ethic. But that disagreement attests all the more to the fundamental character of these topics in the debate about professions in twentieth-century America. The three topics have arisen not out of some natural law or necessity based either in "cognitive rationality" or in the "social structure" of industrial society, but rather out of the untoward experience of vocations called "professions," experience that has then informed the meaning of the term. The hypostatization of the tripartite "true professional ideal" at the turn of the century established the "groove," to use Whitehead's term,[86] within which discussion and analysis of professions has largely remained in the course of the twentieth century.

The failure of scholars to recognize these points stems directly from the

---

Profession," p. 8; Lieberman, *Education as a Profession*, pp. 1–6; Huggett and Stinnett, *Professional Problems of Teachers*, p. 9; Edgar H. Schein and Diane W. Kommers, *Professional Education: Some New Directions* (New York, 1972), pp. 8–9; Moore and Rosenblum, *The Professions*, ch. 1; Millerson, *The Qualifying Associations*, table 1-1.

84. Quotation is from Pound, *The Lawyer from Antiquity to Modern Times*, pp. 5–8. See Pritchett, "Introduction," p. xiii; Brandeis, *Business – A Profession*, p. 2; Sidney and Beatrice Webb, "Special Supplement on Professional Associations," p. 4; W. E. Wickenden and Adelaide Dick, "Professional Organization and Professional Schools," *Journal of Engineering Education*, n.s., 15 (1929): 225; Carl F. Taeusch, *Professional and Business Ethics* (New York, 1926), pp. 13–5; Carr-Saunders and Wilson, *The Professions*, pp. 284–7, 307, 421, 491; Roscoe Pound, "Modern Organization and an Old Profession," *ABA Journal*, 22 (1936): 768; Delancy, *The Licensing of Professions in West Virginia*, pp. 14–5.

85. Quotations are from Elliott, *The Sociology of the Professions*, p. 94; Starr, *The Social Transformation of American Medicine*, p. 15; Goode, "The Theoretical Limits of Professionalization," pp. 290–1. See Ralph W. Tyler, Jr., "Distinctive Attributes of Education for the Professions," *Social Work Journal*, 23 (1952): 52–62, 94; Cogan, "Toward a Definition of Profession," pp. 39–49; Blauch, *Education for the Professions*, p. 3; Samuel P. Huntington, *The Soldier and the State* (Cambridge, MA, 1957), pp. 8–10; Chroust, *The Rise of the Legal Profession in America*, vol. 1, p. xii; Timothy K. Nenninger, *Leavenworth Schools and the Old Army: Education, Professionalism, and the Officer Corps of the United States Army, 1881–1918* (Westport, CT, 1978), p. 5; Harold J. Berman, *Law and Revolution: The Formation of the Western Legal Tradition* (Cambridge, MA, 1983), p. 159; John M. Rich, *Professional Ethics in Education* (Springfield, IL, 1984), pp. 155ff.; Nathan O. Hatch, ed., *The Professions in American History* (Notre Dame, IN, 1988), pp. 1–2. Barber lists "four essential attributes" of a profession: these three plus a "system of rewards." "Some Problems in the Sociology of Professions," p. 18.

86. Alfred N. Whitehead, *Science in the Modern World* (1925; New York, 1963), pp. 78, 275–6.

presentism of modern scholarship about professions. Twentieth-century scholars have been telling the story of past professions in terms of the present experience of their own profession. The presentism of analysis has derived from professors' preoccupation with the status and nature of the professoriate, which entered the twentieth century preeminent and gradually declined. That this analysis could have been avoided for the sake of a fuller, more disinterested account is, perhaps, gratuitous or speculative. But what is certain is that listening seriously and in detail to the rhetoric – the professions – of the past, may assist in opening ourselves to the self-understanding of that past and, in turn, to the present.

APPENDIX 1

____

In the following tables figures indicate annual salaries unless otherwise stated. Towns have generally been identified by their current state rather than their original colony. Sources in parentheses indicate volume and pages in *Harvard Graduates, Yale Graduates,* or *Princetonians* as indicated by institution and date of graduation. Note that in many cases these works do not specify the currency of the salary.

Table A1.1   Sample of salaries of colonial college graduates who became Anglican clergy or missionaries of the Society for the Propagation of the Gospel

1697	Bishop of London provided £100 annuity for Samuel Myles, assistant minister for Anglican church in Boston (3: 289).
1698	William Vesey (HC 1693) was Rector of Trinity Church in New York, 1698–1746 at £60 (4: 175–9).
1723	Timothy Cutler (HC 1701) inducted into Christ Church, Boston, at about £150 in colonial currency from the church and £60 sterling from SPG (5: 45–66); John Usher (HC 1719) became SPG missionary to Bristol, RI, at salary of £60 sterling from SPG and £15 sterling from the congregation (6: 345–7).
1731	Samuel Seabury (HC 1724) declined call from North Yarmouth, ME, at £120 and settlement of £200, and went as SPG missionary to New London at £50 sterling supplemented by contribution of £40 in colonial currency (7: 433–6).
1735	John Sergeant (YC 1729) sent as SPG missionary to western Massachusetts at £150 (1: 396).
1736–late 1740s	Jonathan Arnold (YC 1723) itinerated as SPG missionary through New England, New York, and New Jersey on £30 (1: 274–6).

1737	Henry Barclay (YC 1734) appointed SPG missionary to northern New York at £50 (1: 504); Christopher Bridge (HC 1733) went to Anglican pulpit in Jamaica on £150 plus £50 in lieu of glebe (9: 282).
1744	Isaac Browne (YC 1729) sent as SPG missionary to Newark, NJ, on £50 (1: 381).
1738–48	Daniel Dwight (YC 1721) sent by SPG to parish outside of Charleston, SC, at £50 (1: 247).
late 1740s	Hezekiah Watkins (YC 1737) served as SPG missionary along the Hudson River at £30, and Richard Mansfield (YC 1741) did so in western Connecticut at £20 (1: 594, 687).
1750s	Thomas Chandler (YC 1745), missionary in New Jersey, paid £50 by SPG plus allowance from the British Government of £200 (2: 24–5); William Sturgeon (YC 1745) assistant minister of Christ Church, Philadelphia, earned £30 from SPG, and £50 in 1756; becoming rector in 1762, he earned high salary of £200, including £50 from SPG (2: 61–2); John Ogilvie (YC 1745) served as SPG missionary to Mohawk Indians in New York on £50, and in 1764 named assistant minister to Trinity Church of New York at £200 (2: 174–5).
1760	Marmaduke Browne (HC 1752) installed at Newport, RI, at £100 sterling plus stipend from SPG (13: 202); Jacob Bailey (HC 1755) named SPG missionary in Maine at £50 (13: 526).
1760s	Samuel Fayerweather (HC 1743) paid £50 as SPG missionary in North Kingston, RI (11: 226); Bela Hubbard (YC 1758) appointed SPG missionary to New Haven at £60 (2: 538); and Ebenezer Moseley (YC 1763) ordained SPG missionary for area of New York along the Susquehanna at £100 (3: 40); Samuel Auchmuty (HC 1741) installed as Rector of Trinity Church in New York in 1764 at £250, one of the best livings in the colonies (11: 117–18).
1770s	Luke Babcock (YC 1755) received £30 as SPG missionary in Westchester County, plus allowance and glebe from local church (2: 363); Robert Blackwell (PC 1768) in 1772 began tour as SPG missionary in New Jersey at £50 salary (1: 633).

Table A1.2   Sample of salaries and settlements of colonial college graduates who became ministers in New England and the Middle Colonies

1651	Samuel Phillips (HC 1650) settled in Rowley, MA, at £50–90, depending on cost of living (1: 221–7).
1658	Joseph Rowlandson (HC 1652) settled in Lancaster, MA, at £55 (1: 317).
1659	Hampton, NH, settled Seaborn Cotton (HC 1651) at £60, which rose to £80 in 1667 (1: 286–9).
1660	John Russell (HC 1645) settled in Hadley, MA, at £80 (1: 110–16).
1661	Gershom Bulkeley (HC 1655) contracted to preach as the unordained minister at New London, CT, for £80 (1: 389–96); John Emerson (HC 1656) began ministry in Gloucester, MA, at £60 (1: 485–6).
1663	Samuel Whiting (HC 1653) settled in Billerica, MA, at £70 (1: 363–4); Northampton, MA, voted to settle Joseph Eliot (HC 1658) at £60 plus initial payment of £80 and to build him a house (1: 530–2).
1665	John Woodbridge (HC 1664) paid £60 during his ministry in Connecticut, 1665–78 (2: 156–7).
1666	Simon Bradstreet (HC 1660) called to New London, CT, at £80, which rose to £100 by his ordination in 1670 (2: 55–6).
1668	Nehemiah Hobart (HC 1667) ordained in Newton, MA, at £65, which rose to £80 in 1703 (2: 235).
1669	John Cotton (1657) settled in Plymouth at £90 (1: 496–501).
1670	Northampton, MA, voted to provide Solomon Stoddard (HC 1662) £100 yearly (2: 111–16).
1671	Hope Atherton (HC 1665) settled in Hatfield, MA, at £60 (2: 193–5).
1672	Samuel Willard (HC 1659), in his first year at the church of Groton, MA, in 1663, paid £40, which rose to £80 by 1672 (2: 13–15).
1673	William Adams (HC 1671) settled in Dedham, MA, at £60 (2: 383).
1674	Moses Fiske (HC 1662) settled in Braintree at £80 (2: 123–5).
1675	John Richardson (HC 1666) settled in Newbury, MA, at £100 (2: 210–11).
1678	Abraham Pierson (HC 1668) assumed full-time ministry in Newark, NJ, at £80 (2: 253–5); Thomas Clark (HC 1670) called to Chelmsford, MA, for £80 (2: 320–1).
1679	Nathaniel Chauncy (HC 1661) served churches in Connecticut and Massachusetts during his career and received £60 in 1679 (2: 74–87); Josiah Flynt (HC 1664) received £100 from Dorchester, £60 of it in money (2: 150–3); Gershom Hobart (HC 1667) began ministry at Groton, MA, that lasted until 1707 at £50–100, depending on how much was to be paid in money and different kinds of "country pay" (2: 229–33); Samuel

	Angier (HC 1673) paid £70 during his ministry in Rehoboth, MA, 1679–93, and in Watertown, 1697–1718 (2: 422–6).
1680	Southampton, Long Island, called Joseph Taylor (HC 1669) for £100 (2: 288–91); Thomas Shepard (HC 1676) ordained in Charlestown, MA, at £100 (2: 484).
1681	Samuel Mather (HC 1671) called by Windsor, CT, at £100 (2: 365–6); Joseph Capen (HC 1677) called to Topsfield, MA, at £70 in country pay or £20 in silver and £45 in country pay (2: 519–20); Thomas Cheever (HC 1677) ordained in Malden, MA, at £50 (2: 502); Thomas Mighill (HC 1663) served as assistant minister in Scituate, MA, at £60 (2: 145); Jeremiah Shepard (HC 1669) ordained in Lynne, MA, at £80 (2: 271–2).
1682	Zechariah Symmes (HC 1657) received £60 in country pay at Bradford, MA (1: 492); Nathaniel Gookin (HC 1675) ordained in Cambridge, MA, at £100 (2: 475–7); John Danforth (HC 1677) ordained in Dorchester at £100 (2: 508).
1683	Hempstead, Long Island, settled Jeremiah Hobart (HC 1650) at £70 (1: 214–5); Percival Green (HC 1680) received £50 for preaching in Wells, ME (3: 208–9); James Bayley (HC 1654) settled in Killingworth, CT, where his salary was reported at £70 (2: 294–5); John Wise (HC 1673) ordained at Ipswich, MA, at £60 (2: 429); Nicholas Noyes (HC 1667) called to Salem, MA, at £80 (2: 240).
1684	New London, CT, offered Edward Oakes (HC 1679) £100 (3: 171–2); Grindall Rawson (HC 1678) ordained in Mendon, MA, at £15 sterling and £40 in country pay (3: 161–2).
1685	Hartford, CT, ordained Timothy Woodbridge (HC 1675) at £100 (2: 465).
1686	Edward Taylor (HC 1671), minister of Westfield, MA, earned £50 in 1678, which rose to £80 in 1686, and continued at that rate to the end of the century (2: 406–7).
1687	Elizabeth, NJ, paid John Harriman (HC 1667) £60, 1687–1705 (2: 216–21).
1688	Joseph Gerrish (HC 1669) received £60 from Wenham, MA (2: 301); Middletown, CT, ordained Noadiah Russell (HC 1681) at £100 (3: 216–19).
1689	Wells, ME, paid Richard Martyn (HC 1680) £50 (3: 179).
1691	Jeremiah Cushing (HC 1676) ordained in Scituate, MA, at £60 (2: 499).
1692	John Prudden (HC 1668) became minister in Newark, NJ, at £50 (2: 259–62); Samuel Carter (HC 1660) called to Groton, MA, at £60 (2: 65–7).
1693	Stamford, CT, voted John Davenport (HC 1661) £70 until the senior minister died, at which point he would receive £100 (3: 370); Joseph Belcher (HC 1690) ordained in Dedham, MA, at £60 (4: 28–9); Nathaniel Clap (HC 1690) refused offer of £60 to settle in Suffield, CT (4: 36); Timothy Stevens (HC 1687) settled in Glastonbury, CT, at £70 (3: 386–7).
1694	Kittery, ME, paid John Newmarch (HC 1690) £40 in money

and £15 in board (4: 72); Michael Wigglesworth (HC 1651), minister of Malden, MA, paid £55 (1: 276–7).

1695   Woodbridge, NJ, paid Samuel Shepard (HC 1685) £50 (3: 342); Thomas Ruggles (HC 1690) ordained in Roxbury, MA, at £80 (4: 76); Charles Chauncy (HC 1686) ordained at Stratford, CT, £70 (3: 365–6); John Pike (HC 1675), minister in Dover, NH, received £65 (2: 450).

1696   Wallingford, CT, paid Samuel Street (HC 1664) £50 in 1673, which rose to £100 by 1696 (2: 160–2); Rowland Cotton (HC 1685) received £80 from Sandwich, MA (3: 323–4).

1697   Dudley Woodbridge (HC 1694) settled at Simsbury, CT, at £60, including £20 in silver (4: 215); Stephen Buckingham (HC 1693) ordained in Norwalk, CT, at £80 (4: 158); Edward Payson (HC 1677) received £100 from Rowley, MA (2: 515); James Pierpont (HC 1681) minister of New Haven, CT, at £120 (3: 225); Joseph Baxter (HC 1693) settled in Medfield, MA, at £60 (4: 146–7).

1698   Dorchester, MA, established a minimum of £85 to be gathered by free contribution for John Danforth (HC 1677) (2: 508–9); John Cotton (HC 1681) voted £70 by Yarmouth, MA (3: 212–15); Simon Bradstreet (HC 1693) ordained in Charlestown, MA, at £98 (4: 156); Salmon Treat (HC 1694) settled in Preston, CT, at £46 in money (4: 207–9); Joseph Green (HC 1695) ordained in Salem, MA, at £60 in money (4: 230); Benjamin Ruggles (HC 1693) ordained in Suffield, CT, at £80 (4: 172).

1699   Ephraim Little (HC 1695) ordained in Plymouth, MA, at £60, which rose to £70 in 1706 and to £80 in 1711 (4: 248–9).

1700   Newark, NJ, settled Jabez Wakeman (HC 1697) at £60 in 1700, which rose immediately to £80 and yearly thereafter due to marriage, birth of children, and inflation (4: 391–2); Rehoboth, MA, paid Thomas Greenwood (HC 1690) £70 (4: 61); John Hale (HC 1657) received £74 yearly for the last quarter of the seventeenth century from Beverly (1: 509–18); Jabez Fox (HC 1665) settled in Woburn at £50 (2: 196–7); Timothy Edwards (HC 1691) paid £100 during the first quarter of eighteenth century by Windsor Farms, MA (4: 94–7).

1701   Jedediah Andrews (HC 1695) ordained as the first Presbyterian minister of Philadelphia at £105 (4: 219–24); John Swift (HC 1697) ordained in Framingham, MA, at £60 (4: 388–90); Thomas Blowers (HC 1695) settled in Beverly, MA, at £80, which rose to £140 by 1729 (4: 225–8); Samuel Emery (HC 1691) settled in Wells, ME, at £45 (4: 99).

1703   John Fox (HC 1698) succeeded his father as minister of Woburn, MA, at £80 (4: 404–5); Benjamin Rolfe (HC 1684) voted £70 by Haverhill, MA (3: 312); Jabez Fitch settled in Ipswich, MA, at £130 (4: 202); John White (HC 1998) settled in Gloucester, MA, at £70 which rose to £560 by his death in 1760 (4: 421–3).

1704   Robert Breck (HC 1700) ordained at Marlborough, MA, at £70

(4: 515–17); Ephraim Woodbridge (HC 1701) ordained in Groton, CT, at £80 (5: 130); Nathaniel Eells (HC 1699) preached in Scituate in 1703 for £65, and ordained there in 1704; his salary rose to £200 as the currency fluctuated in value (4: 468–70); Stephen Hosmer (HC 1699) ordained in East Haddam, CT, at £80 (4: 478–9); Josiah Torrey (HC 1698) settled in Tisbury, Martha's Vineyard, at £20, plus settlement of one-sixteenth of the town's land (4: 419).

1705   Samuel Whitman (HC 1696) accepted call from Farmington, CT, at £90, which rose to £100 in his second year (4: 315–16); John Southmayd (HC 1697) ordained in Waterbury, CT, at £60–70 (4: 379–81).

1706   Exeter, NH, ordained John Odlin (HC 1702) at £70 plus £200 settlement and 200 acres (5: 168); Moses Hale (HC 1699) settled in Byfield, MA, at £65 (4: 476–8); Israel Loring (HC 1701) ordained in Sudbury at £70 (5: 76); Jacob Heminway (YC 1704) agreed to settle in East Haven, CT, at £50 (1: 24).

1707   Berwick, ME, ordained Jeremiah Wise (HC 1700) at £80 (4: 550–1); John Hart (HC 1704) ordained in Guilford, CT, at £90 (5: 252–4); the General Court of Massachusetts settled Samuel Hunt (HC 1700) in Dartmouth at £60, raised to £100 in 1722 (4: 527–9), and settled Joseph Marsh (HC 1705) in Tiverton (now in Connecticut) at £50 (5: 281) because the two towns refused to pay a minister; Jacob Heminway (YC 1704) accepted the offer of East Haven, CT, for £50 (1: 24).

1708   Falmouth, MA, ordained Joseph Metcalf (HC 1703) at £40 (5: 220–2); Samson Stoddard (HC 1701) ordained in Chelmsford, MA, at £70 (5: 120); Malden, MA, offered Joseph Parsons (HC 1695) £60 (4: 366–7); Thomas Symmes (HC 1698) in 1708 became Assistant Minister to his father in Bradford, MA, at £60 (4: 413); Daniel Greenleaf (HC 1699) settled in Yarmouth at £80 (4: 473–6).

1709   New London, CT, settled Eliphalet Adams (HC 1694) at £90 (4: 191); George Curwin (HC 1701) accepted offer from Reading, MA, at £80, and moved to Salem in 1714 at £90 (5: 37–43); Joseph Marsh (HC 1705) ordained in Braintree at £70 (5: 282); David Parsons (HC 1705) ordained in Malden, MA, at £60 (5: 283–6).

1710   Hampton, NH, ordained Nathaniel Gookin (HC 1703) at £70, £10 of it in money (5: 206–7); Azariah Mather (YC 1705) ordained in Windsor, CT, at £80 in country pay for two years, £100 for the next two, and £120 subsequently (1: 33); Ebenezer Devotion (HC 1707) ordained in Suffield, CT, at £80, to be raised to £100 after five years (5: 329–30); Timothy Cutler (HC 1701) settled in Stratford, CT, at £80 (5: 45–66); Jonathan Marsh (HC 1705) ordained minister of Windsor, CT, at £100 (5: 279); Samuel Treat (HC 1769) received £70 in silver from Eastham, MA (2: 307); Eleazer Williams (HC 1708) settled in Mansfield, CT, at £40 plus large settlement (5: 472).

1711	Nicholas Sever (HC 1701) ordained in Dover, NH, at £80 (5: 91); John Avery (HC 1706) ordained in Truro, MA, at £60 (5: 302–3); John Williams (HC 1683) received £60 from Deerfield, MA, (3: 257); Joshua Gardner (HC 1707) ordained in Haverhill, MA, at £70 (5: 331–3); Thomas Barnard (HC 1679) elected salary from Andover, MA, of £42 in money, rather than £60 in corn (3: 174–6); John Woodward (HC 1693) asked Norwich, CT, for increase in his £70 salary (4: 186–7).
1712	New Castle, NH, ordained William Shurtleff (HC 1707) at £65 while single and £80 if he married (5: 396–9); Jonathan Russell (YC 1708) settled in Barnstable, MA, at £80 (1: 78); Daniel Lewes (HC 1707) settled in 1712 in Pembroke, RI, at £80, which gradually rose to £150 by his death in 1742 (5: 335–6); John Whiting (HC 1700) ordained in Concord, MA, at about £100, which gradually rose to £190 before his death in 1752 (4: 532–4); Theophilus Cotton (HC 1701) settled in Hampton Falls, NH, at £60 (5: 34–7); Phineas Fiske (YC 1704) settled as associate pastor in Haddam, CT, at salary to reach £70 (1: 21).
1713	Daniel Baker (HC 1706) ordained in Reading, MA, at £70 upon the death of the senior minister (5: 307–9); Benjamin Prescott (HC 1708) ordained in Salem, MA, at £80 in Old Tenor (5: 485–6); Aaron Porter (HC 1708) ordained as first minister of Medford, MA, at £55, to be raised £2 per year until it reached £70 (5: 441); Hadley, MA, changed the salary of its minister, Isaac Chauncy (HC 1693), from £80 in provisions to £60 in province bills (4: 160); Joseph Stevens (HC 1703) settled in Charlestown, MA, at £80, which rose to £150 by 1721 when he died (5: 240–3).
1714	Bristol, RI, raised the salary of John Sparhawk (HC 1689) from £80 to £100 (3: 421–2); John Cotton (HC 1710) ordained in Newton, MA, at £80, to be raised to £100 when he acquired a family (5: 517–21); John Tufts (HC 1708) ordained in Newbury, MA, at £80 upon the death of the senior ministers (5: 457–60); Samuel Wigglesworth (HC 1707) ordained in Ipswich, MA, at £60 (5: 406–8); Pomfret, CT, ordained its first minister, Ebenezer Williams (HC 1708), at £60 to be raised to £70 (5: 499); Samuel Wiswall (HC 1701) ordained in Egartown, MA, at £50 (5: 128); Joseph Avery (HC 1706) ordained in Norton, MA, at £50 (5: 305–6); Glastonbury, CT, raised the salary of Timothy Stevens (HC 1687) to £100 (3: 386–7).
1715	Newington, NH, ordained Joseph Adams (HC 1710) at £80–90 (5: 503); David Deming (HC 1700) ordained in Medway, MA, at £60 (4: 518–19); John Emerson (HC 1689) settled in Portsmouth, NH, at £100 (3: 419–20); Caleb Trowbridge (HC 1710) ordained in Groton, MA, at £80 (5: 545); John Chipman (HC 1711) ordained in Beverly, MA, at £60, which rose to £600 by 1770 (5: 563–7).
1716	New Haven, CT, ordained Joseph Noyes (YC 1709) at £120 (1: 85); Ames Cheever (HC 1707) ordained in Manchester, MA, at

£70 (5: 326–7); Samuel Cooke (YC 1705) ordained in Stratfield, CT, at £100 (1: 29); Samuel Tompson (HC 1710) ordained in Gloucester, MA, at £60 (5: 544); Joseph Dorr (HC 1711) ordained in Mendon, MA, at £75 annually (5: 575–8).

1717   Dover, NH, ordained Jonathan Cushing (HC 1712) at £90 (5: 634–5); Peter Clark (HC 1712) settled in Danvers, MA, at £90 (5: 616–21); Benjamin Shattuck (HC 1709) settled in Littleton, MA, at £55, to be raised gradually to £70 by 1730 (5: 493–4); Daniel Brewer (HC 1687), minister of Springfield, MA, voted £85 (3: 384); Thomas Cheney (HC 1711) ordained in Brookfield, MA, at £52, to be raised gradually to limit of £70 (5: 561–2); Thomas Foxcroft (HC 1714) settled as one of the two ministers of First Church of Boston, at more than £160 (6: 47–54).

1718   James Allin (HC 1710) settled in Brookline, MA, at £80, which was augmented each year by grant of between £40 and £80 (5: 506–9); James Hale (HC 1703) ordained in Ashford, CT, at £60 (5: 217–8); Thomas Prince (HC 1707) ordained co-minister of Old South Church at about £80 (5: 341–61); John Gardner (HC 1715) ordained in Stow, MA, at £70 (6: 88–9); James Wetmore (YC 1714) ordained minister of North Haven at £80 in country pay plus settlement of £150 in money or grain (1: 133–4).

1719   Stratham, NH, paid Henry Rust (HC 1707) £80 (5: 371–4); John Brown (HC 1714) ordained in Haverhill, MA, at £100 (6: 38–9); Joseph Lord (HC 1691) settled in Chatam, MA, at £80 (4: 104); Benjamin Webb (HC 1715) ordained in Eastham, MA, at £90 (6: 112); Nathanial Prentice (HC 1715) accepted call from Dunstable, MA, at £80, after the offer had been declined by Jonathan Pierpont (HC 1714) and Enoch Coffin (HC 1715), due, in part, to the threat of Indian attack (6: 42, 69, 104–6); Ebenezer Pierpont (HC 1715) rejected offer of £90 to settle in Springfield, MA (6: 101).

1720   Great Valley, DE, in the Presbytery of Philadelphia called David Evans (YC 1713) for £25 (1: 111–12); Arundel, ME, paid John Eveleth (HC 1689) £50 to preach (3: 424–7); William Cooper (HC 1712), minister in Cambridge, MA, voted £169 upon his marriage (5: 624–6); Nathaniel Sparhawk (HC 1715) settled in Lynnfield, MA, at £65 (6: 106–8); Jonathan Townsend (HC 1716) ordained in Needham at £80 (6: 150–2); Nathaniel Cotton (HC 1717) settled in Bristol, Rhode Island, at £100 (6: 168); Thomas Parker (HC 1718) ordained in Chelmsford, MA, at £80 (6: 266); Joseph Stacey (HC 1719) ordained in Kingston, MA, at £80, which rose to £145 by his death in 1741 (6: 343–4); David Parsons (HC 1705) declined offer of £60 from Leicester, MA, and agreed to £75 (5: 283–6; *Yale Graduates* 1: 56).

1721   John Rogers (HC 1711) ordained in Kittery, ME, at £100 (5: 581–3); David Turner (HC 1718) settled in Rehoboth, MA, at £70 (6: 287); Joseph Emerson (HC 1717) called to Malden, MA, at £100 (6: 171).

1722   Matthew Short (HC 1707) settled in Easton, MA, at £40 (5: 395); William Welsteed (HC 1716) rejected offer from Waltham, MA, for £84, and Benjamin Fessenden (HC 1718) accepted for £90 (6: 155, 243–4).

1723   Joshua Gee (HC 1717) settled in Boston at more than £150 (6: 177); Job Cushing (HC 1714) ordained in Shrewsbury, MA, at £100 (6: 45); Woodstock, CT, raised the salary of Josiah Dwight (HC 1687) from £60 to £75 (3: 396); James Bayley (HC 1719) ordained in Weymouth at £76 (6: 293–4); Timothy Collins (YC 1718) ordained at salary of £57, which rose to £80 by 1727, £90 in 1729, £100 in 1735, and £170 in 1740 (1: 183).

1724   Isaac Stiles (YC 1722) ordained at North Haven, CT, at £70, to be raised to £120 gradually (1: 265); Nathaniel Leonard (HC 1719) ordained in Plymouth, MA, at £110 (6: 324–6); Ebenezer Parkman (HC 1721) ordained in Westborough, MA, at £80 (6: 512–13).

1725   Richard Jaques (HC 1720) ordained in Gloucester at salary of £100, which was cut to £44 when the currency deflated (6: 387–8); Benjamin Wadsworth (HC 1690) earned about £169 from First Church of Boston (4: 85–6); Peter Reynolds (HC1720) ordained in Enfield, CT, at £100 (6: 398).

1726   Nehemiah Bull (YC 1723) settled in Westfield, MA, at £100, which rose to £240 by the time of his death in 1740 (1: 280); John Lowell (HC 1721) ordained in Newburyport, CT, at £130 (6: 497); John Hancock (HC 1719) ordained in Braintree, MA, at £110 (6: 317); Joseph Parsons (HC 1720) ordained in Bradford, MA, at £110 (6: 393); Thomas Clap (HC 1722) settled in Norwich, CT at £100 plus settlement of £300 (7: 28).

1727   Amos Throop (HC 1721) ordained in Woodstock, CT, at £100 (6: 573); Nathaniel Rogers (HC 1721) ordained in Ipswich, MA, at £130; (6: 556–7); Thomas Smith (HC 1720) ordained in what is now Portland, ME, at £70 plus his board (6: 402); Joseph Whipple (HC1720) ordained in Hampton Falls, NH, at £120 (6: 415); Jonathan Mills (HC 1723) received £75 from Bellingham, MA (7: 240); Moses Hale (HC 1722) turned down offer of £100 plus £200 settlement from Barrington, MA (7: 77); John Wadsworth (HC 1723) rejected call from Barrington, RI, for £100 plus £100 settlement, and in 1729 rejected one from Canterbury, CT, of £100 plus £150 settlement (7: 266); Samuel Dunbar (HC 1723) ordained in Stoughton at £100 plus £200 settlement (7: 167); Habijah Weld ordained in Attleborough, MA, at £100 plus settlement of £200 (7: 269).

1728   William Tompson (HC 1718) ordained in Scarborough, ME, at £100 (6: 284–5); Charles Chauncy (HC 1721) received £225 from First Church of Boston upon his marriage (6: 440–1); Benjamin Bass (HC 1715) ordained in Hanover, MA, at £130 (6:

73); Theophilus Pickering (HC 1719) settled in Ipswich at paper equivalent of 300 ounces of silver, which varied from £120 to £232 in subsequent decades (6: 331); Samuel Jennison (HC 1720) accepted call to Canterbury, CT, at £100 (6: 389).

1729   Barnabas Taylor (HC 1721) ordained in Bristol, RI, at £240 (6: 568); Edward Jackson (HC 1719) ordained in Woburn, MA, at £120 (6: 321); Joseph Champney (HC 1721) accepted call to Beverly, MA, at £140 and settlement of £200 (6: 438); John Wadsworth (HC 1723) accepted the offer of Canterbury, CT, at £110 (7: 266); Christopher Sargeant (HC 1725) ordained in Kittery, ME, at £80 plus settlement of £100 (7: 567); Ezra Whitmarsh (HC 1723) rejected call from Barrington, RI, at £90 plus settlement of £120 (7: 280–1); Samuel Seabury (HC 1724) declined offer of £120 plus settlement of £200 from North Yarmouth, ME (7: 433–4); and Marston Cabot (HC 1724) rejected offer from Killingly, CT, of £80 plus settlement of £200; the church raised the settlement to £300 and he accepted (7: 320–1).

1730   Arundel, ME, ordained Thomas Prentice (HC 1726) at £130 plus £200 settlement (8: 82).

1731   New Castle, NH, raised the salary of William Shurtleff (HC 1707) to £100 (5: 396–9); Stephen Sewall (HC 1721) offered salary of £160 by Marlborough, MA (6: 561–3); Daniel Rogers, II (HC 1725) rejected offer of £100 plus settlement of £200 from Littleton, MA, which finally made acceptable offer of £140 plus £300 settlement (7: 561); Joseph Belcher (HC 1723) ordained in Easton, MA, at £100 plus settlement of £200 (7: 145).

1732   Daniel Wadsworth (YC 1726) ordained at Hartford at £130 (1: 340).

1733   Abraham Todd (YC 1727) ordained in Greenwich, CT at £100 (1: 361); Benjamin Kent (HC 1727) offered £180 plus settlement of £400 by Marlborough, MA (8: 221); James Chandler (HC 1728) ordained in Rowley, MA, at £110 plus settlement of £300 (8: 376).

1734   William Smith (HC 1725) ordained in Weymouth at £160 plus £300 settlement (7: 589); Seth Payne (YC 1726) ordained in Stafford, CT, at £100 (1: 334).

1736   Eleazar Wheelock (YC 1733) ordained in Lebanon, CT, at £140 (1: 493); James Bridgham (HC 1726) rejected offer from Brimfield, MA, at £120 plus £300 settlement until the salary was raised to £140 (8: 7–8); North Yarmouth, ME, ordained Nicholas Loring (HC 1731) at £150 plus settlement of £250 (9: 180); John Hovey (HC 1725) turned down offer from Woodstock, CT, of £150 plus settlement of £400, and in 1740 he accepted call from Arundel, ME, at £180 (7: 538–9).

1737   Lancaster, MA, raised the salary of John Prentice (HC 1700) to £210 (4: 529–31).

1738	William Seward (YC 1734) ordained in Killingworth, CT, at £140 (1: 512); Jacob Bacon (HC 1731) ordained in Upper Ashulet, NH, at £130 plus settlement of £150 (9: 18–19); Aaron Whittemore (HC 1734) settled in Pembroke, NH, for £120 plus settlement of £300 (9: 461).
1739	Samuel Veazie (HC 1736) ordained in Duxbury, MA at £150 and settlement of £400 (10: 85); Marlborough, MA offered Aaron Smith (HC 1735) £240 Old Tenor or £80 New Tenor plus settlement of £400 Old Tenor (9: 575); Mark Leavenworth (YC 1737) settled in Waterbury, CT, at £150 (1: 581).
1740	Abner Bayley (HC 1736) ordained in Salem, NH, at £150 (10: 11–13); Stephen White (YC 1736) settled in Windham, CT, at £100 salary and £300 settlement (1: 568); Daniel Bliss (HC 1731) ordained at Concord, MA, at £200 plus settlement of £500 (9: 131).
1741	Bristol, RI, ordained John Burt (HC 1736) at £250 (10: 29); Killingworth CT, voted £210 for Jared Eliot (YC 1706; 1: 52–6) (HC 1703; 5: 191–5); Joshua Tufts (HC 1736) ordained in Litchfield, NH, at £150 plus settlement of £300 (10: 82); Ebenezer Bridge (HC 1736) ordained in Chelmsford, MA, at £200 plus settlement of £500, and in 1749 Bridge rejected offer of £500 from the town (10: 18).
1742	Solomon Townsend (HC 1735) ordained over Barrington, RI, at £90 (9: 586); John Woodbridge (YC 1726) installed in Hadley, MA, £150 (1: 345).
1743	The General Assembly of Connecticut ordered East Hartford to pay Samuel Woodbridge (HC 1701) salary of £150 Old Tenor (5: 131–4); Moses Morrill (HC 1737) ordained in Biddeford, ME, at £200 (10: 209); John Bass (HC 1736) ordained in Ashford, CT, at £200 plus settlement of £400 (10: 115); Richard Salter (HC 1739) declined call from Mansfield, CT, at £200 plus settlement of £400 (10: 404).
1744	John Rogers (HC 1739) ordained in Gloucester, MA at £250 plus settlement of £400 (10: 401); Nathaniel Stone (HC 1690) received £200 Old Tenor from Harwich, MA, in 1744 (4: 80); Isaac Chalker (YC 1728) installed in Glastonbury, CT, at £300 (1: 369–70).
1747	Setauket, Long Island, paid George Phillips (HC 1686) £40 (3: 361); Eastham, MA, offered Isaiah Dunster (HC 1741) £350 and settlement of £600 (11: 27) John Brown (HC 1741) ordained in Cohasset, MA, at £350 in goods (11: 13); Aaron Cleveland (HC 1735) settled in Malden, MA, at £350 and settlement of £300 (9: 495).
1748	Timothy Harrington (HC 1737) ordained in Lancaster, MA, at £480 and settlement of £1,000 (10: 189); Jacob Bacon (HC 1731), minister of Upper Ashulet, NH, refused offer of £300 plus settlement of £500 to move to Union, CT, and in 1749 accepted call from Plymouth, MA at £500 (9: 18–19); Cotton

Brown (HC 1743) rejected offer of £480 plus settlement of £2,000 from Lancaster, MA, and accepted offer of £1,000 plus settlement of £600 from Brookline, MA (11: 182); Berwick, ME, voted to raise the salary of Jeremiah Wise (HC 1700) to £500 Old Tenor (4: 552); Farmington, CT, paid William Burnham (HC 1702) £350 (5: 137–40); Peter Thacher (HC 1737) declined call from Attleboro, MA, at £600 and then accepted £400 (10: 247).

1749
Fairfield, CT, paid £340 to Nathaniel Hunn (YC 1731), who was ordained in 1733 at £100 (1: 429); Chatam, MA, offered Stephen Emery (HC 1730) £170 and £800 settlement (8: 709).

1750
Oliver Peabody (HC 1721) offered £300 in paper to serve the English parish in the Indian reservation of Natick, MA (6: 533); Stephen Chase (HC 1728) accepted call to Newcastle, NH, at £50 hard money (8: 384); Moses Parsons (HC 1736) settled in Byfield, MA, at £100 hard money (10: 53–4); Joseph Swain settled in Wenham, MA, at about £65 and settlement of £133 specie (11: 475).

1751
Ebenezer Booge (YC 1748) ordained in Farmington, CT, at £50 or £165 Old Tenor (2: 148).

1752
Brunswick, ME ordained John Miller (HC 1752) at about £65 and £133 settlement in specie (13: 272); Eliakim Willis (HC 1735) accepted offer of about £53 hard money to settle in Malden, MA (9: 607).

1753
David Ripley (YC 1749) ordained at Pomfret, CT, at £600 Old Tenor (2: 217); Elisha Eaton (HC 1729) installed in North Yarmouth, ME, at £460 currency or £60 lawful money (8: 571); Joseph Palmer (HC 1747) settled in Norton, MA, at about £65 and £133 settlement in specie (12: 197–8); Edward Billing (HC 1731), preacher in Dutchess County, New York, called to Deerfield, MA, at £200 and settlement of £600 Old Tenor (9: 26).

1754
Thomas Smith (HC 1725) paid £625 by Yarmouth, MA (7: 587); Joseph Roberts (HC 1741) ordained in Leicester, MA, at about £65 and £133 settlement in specie (11: 66).

1756
Marston Cabot (HC 1724) paid £600 by Killingly, CT, upon his death (7: 321); Robert Cutler (HC 1741) accepted call from Epping, NH, at £350 Old Tenor (11: 23); Jason Haven (HC 1754) ordained in Dedham for £500 and settlement of £1,000 (13: 447); Sandown, NH, offered Josiah Cotton (HC 1722) £1,000 and £500 settlement (7: 55).

1757
Abraham Keteltas (YC 1752) ordained in Elizabethtown, NJ, at £130 (2: 289); Mather Byles (HC 1751) ordained in New London, CT, at £100 plus settlement of £240 New Tenor (13: 7).

1758
Jonathan Eames (HC 1752) turned down offer of £1,000 NH currency and accepted £1,600 NH currency from Newton, NH (13: 227); Stephen Farrar (HC 1755) accepted call to New Ipswich, NH, at £40 sterling (13: 587).

1759	Caleb Barnum (PC 1757) settled in Wrentham, MA, at about £65 and £133 settlement in specie (1: 172).
1760	Nathan Williams (YC 1755) ordained in Tolland, CT, at £80 (2: 395); Chandler Robbins (YC 1756) ordained in Plymouth, MA, at £100 (2: 424); Robie Morrill (HC 1755) accepted call to Boscawen, NH, at £700 Old Tenor to be raised to £1,000 (13: 629).
1761	Israel Cheever (HC 1749) installed in Liverpool, Nova Scotia, at £80 (12: 364).
1762	Ebenezer Kellogg (YC 1757) ordained in Vernon, CT, at £70 (2: 477); Peter Thacher Smith (HC 1753) settled in Windham, ME, at £80 and £83 settlement (13: 356); Samuel Foxcroft (HC 1754) settled in New Gloucester, ME, for £80 and £100 settlement (13: 411).
1763	John Huntington (PC 1759) called to Salem, MA, at £100 plus £200 settlement (1: 270).
1764	Samuel Deane ordained in Portland, ME, at £100 and £133 settlement (14: 592).
1765	Seth Dean (YC 1738) ordained in Rindge, NH, at £40 (1: 600); Avery Hall ordained in Rochester, NH, at £80 (2: 587); Benajah Phelps (YC 1761) ordained in Cornwallis, Nova Scotia, at £80 (2: 713); Basking Ridge, NJ, paid Samuel Kennedy (PC 1754) £110 (1: 101); Robert Cooper (PC 1763) ordained by the Presbytery of Carlisle over church in Cumberland County, PA, at £110 (1: 421).
1766	Jesse Ives (YC 1758) called to Norwich, CT at £95 (2: 542).
1767	Rockaway, NJ, paid James Tuttle (PC 1764) £60 for half-time position (1: 473).
1768	Ebenezer Martin (YC 1756) ordained in Westford, CT, at £60 (2: 420–1); Thomas Cary (HC 1761) ordained in Newburyport, MA, at £845 Old Tenor (15: 29).
1769	William Woodhull (PC 1764) settled in Morris County, NJ, at £40 (1: 475–6).

Table A1.3   Sample of salaries and settlements of colonial college graduates who became schoolmasters in New England and the Middle Colonies

1661–2	John Barsham (HC 1658) received £26 from Hampton, NH (1: 539–40).
1664–87	Caleb Watson (HC 1661) taught in Hadley, MA, and Hartford, CT, for promised salary of £60 that was rarely paid in full (2: 95–7).
1670–99	Daniel Epes (HC 1669) – "the most Eminent SchoolMaster in *New-England*" – taught in Salem intermittently with £60 guaranteed by the town, if student fees fell short (2: 265–6); from 1685 to 1695 Samuel Cobbet (HC 1663) earning salary of £12 plus a house lot (2: 136–7); Edward Mills (HC 1685), who taught school near Boston until 1732, was paid £30 in 1687, £10 in money and £20 in grain (3: 337–8).
1705	Josiah Cotton (HC 1698) accepted job to teach at Plymouth for salary of £40 in 1705 (4: 398–401).
1708	Upon the death of Ezekiel Cheever, Nathaniel Williams (HC 1693), who was paid £80 as assistant schoolmaster, named schoolmaster at the Boston Latin School at £100 (4: 184).
1712	John Emerson (HC 1675) died after teaching for most of his adult life just north of Boston, where the towns guaranteed to supplement student fees up to £50–60 (2: 472–4); Samuel Burr (HC 1697) taught school in eastern Massachusetts for salary ranging up to £40 (4: 341–2).
1714	Benjamin Tompson (HC 1662) died after teaching for his career in Braintree, MA, where he was paid up to £30 per year plus the use of one-and-a-half acre house lot (2: 103–9).
1715	Samuel Cooke (YC 1705) completed eight years as Rector of the grammar school in New Haven at £60 (1: 29).
1718	John Woodbridge (HC 1710) schoolmaster in Newbury, MA, had his salary raised to £40 from £25 in 1713 (5: 555–6).
1717–28	Henry Wise (HC 1717) kept school near Boston for £55 from 1717 to 1727 (6: 219); Amos Throop (HC 1721) taught during 1724–8 in Bristol, RI, at £50 until becoming minister there (6: 573); Benjamin Fessenden (HC 1718) kept school at Watertown from 1718 to 1722 at salary of £44 (6: 243); John Hancock (HC 1719) taught at Lexington and Woburn, MA, for £40–50 (6: 316); James Bayley (HC 1719) taught school in Andover, MA, after graduation for £44 (6: 293); Ebenezer Roby (HC 1719) taught at Weymouth, MA, after graduation at £42 (6: 336); Robert Ward (HC 1719) taught Charlestown, MA, after graduation for £60 (6: 351); in 1720 Ames Angier (HC 1701), lifetime schoolmaster in Boston, voted salary of £100 to become schoolmaster of the new South Grammar School (5: 27–9); Daniel Dwight (YC 1721) taught Hopkins grammar school in Connecticut at £40 (1: 246).

1729	Thomas Norton (HC 1725) began career teaching at Ipswich, MA, at £55 (7: 548); Ezra Whitmarsh (HC 1723) rejected pastoral call from Barrington, RI, at £90 and £120 supplement and became schoolteacher and occasional preacher in Plymouth at salary of £100 during 1730s (7: 280–1).
1731	Zechariah Hicks (HC 1724) earned £100 as assistant schoolmaster in Boston (7: 358).
1732	John Janvrin (HC 1728) paid £65 in Kittery, ME (8: 436).
1733	Nathaniel Harrington (HC 1729) earned £55 in Watertown, MA (8: 429).
1734	John Lovell named headmaster of South Grammar School in Boston at £150 plus use of house and garden; his salary rose to £600 at peak of inflation and dropped to £120 when hard money was restored (8: 442–3).
1728–38	John Wight (HC1721) taught at Bristol, RI, for £50 (6: 585).
1728–31	David Stearns (HC 1728) paid £45 to keep Watertown, MA school (8: 496).
1738	Ezra Whitmarsh (HC 1723) schoolteacher and occasional preacher in Plymouth at £100 (7: 280–1).
1739	Richard Caner (YC 1736) became SPG schoolmaster in Fairfield, CT, at £10 sterling (1: 557).
1740	Daniel Dodge (HC 1700) died after career as schoolmaster in eastern Massachusetts at £30–40 (4: 519–20); Benjamin Choat (HC 1703) became schoolmaster in Kingston, NH, at £36, after preaching for several years without obtaining settlement (5: 184–5).
1741	John Moore (YC 1741) became SPG schoolmaster in Long Island at £15 sterling (1: 689).
1742	Samuel White (HC 1740) taught in Boston at £90, raised to £130 by 1745 (10: 539).
1744–9	Shadrach Hathaway (YC 1738) taught 1745–9 in Bristol County, MA, for £75 Old Tenor (1: 601); Stephen Longfellow (HC 1742) schoolmaster in Falmouth, ME, for £200 and tuition from private school that he kept on the side (11: 155).
1747	Elihu Lyman (YC 1745) at Oyster Bay, Long Island, received £6 per quarter plus board and a horse for school of 30 or more students (2: 50).
1748	Thomas Frink (HC 1722) earned £200 teaching in Rutland, MA (7: 73).
1749	John Noyes (HC 1733) taught in Rowley, MA, for £200 Old Tenor plus board (9: 313).
1750s	Peleg Wiswall (HC 1702), schoolmaster in Boston for over 40 years saw his salary grow to several hundred pounds Old Tenor by late 1740s, and then cut to £60 after the currency stabilized with the return to hard currency (5: 177–9); in Newport, RI, Jeremiah Leaming (YC 1745) kept SPG school at £20 sterling (2: 39–40); Samuel Payson (HC 1716) schoolmaster of Rowley, MA, from 1722 to 1757 earned between £30 and £80 (6: 148–

9); Seth Sweetser (HC 1722) in 1724 became schoolmaster at Charlestown, MA, at £75 with salary rising to £500 Old Tenor by 1752 (7: 125); Abraham Bradley (YC 1723) taught school in Guildford, CT intermittently during 1723–50 at £40 (1: 277); in 1750s Nathaniel Gardner (HC 1739) taught in Boston at salary of £50–60 (10:367–8).

1760s   John Fowle (HC 1747) taught Woburn at £40 (12: 158); Ephraim Langdon (HC 1752) taught in Boston at £60 (13: 243); John Nutting (HC 1712), career schoolmaster of Salem, MA, earned about £70, after the currency stabilized (5: 641–4).

1762   Ephraim Avery (YC 1761) employed as SPG schoolmaster in Second River, NJ, at £10 sterling (2: 685).

1770   John Avery (YC 1761) SPG schoolmaster in Rye, Long Island, at £10 sterling (2: 687); Jacob Coggin (HC 1763) began long career as schoolmaster in Woburn, MA, at £40 salary (15:374).

1771   Samuel Hunt (HC 1765) accepted offer in Boston for £100 (16: 178).

1773   Isaac Alexander (PC 1772) taught near Charlotte, NC, at £80 (2: 177); Philip V. Fithian (PC 1772) became tutor in home of Robert Carter III in Virginia at £35 per year plus room, board, horse, and servant (2: 218).

APPENDIX 2

Although some scholars have recently evaluated the vocational choices of college graduates in American history during the early national and antebellum periods,[1] the classification of the vocations of those who earned bachelor's degrees at the colonial colleges has not been adequately addressed. There is, in fact, no accurate, comprehensive enumeration of vocational choices of the colonial college graduates. Drawing upon the best biographical and historical catalogues available for each colonial college, I attempt here to provide such a categorization and enumeration for the colleges, individually and collectively.[2] Because this undertaking forces one to make problematic choices in light of the available information and the social context of the time, it is worthwhile to explain in some detail the method of categorization and its rationale, a discussion that has usually been made insufficiently or omitted entirely in enumerations of vocational choices.

The best strategy for assessing the vocational choices of those who graduated before the Revolution has long been that adopted by Lawrence Cremin in his magisterial history of American colonial education. This approach involves supplementing the "classic analysis"[3] of Bailey Burritt with the later and more reliable data supplied by Samuel E. Morison on seventeenth-century Harvard and

1. See, for example, Colin B. Burke, *American Collegiate Populations: A Test of the Traditional View* (New York, 1982), ch. 4; Gerard W. Gawalt, *The Promise of Power: The Emergence of the Legal Profession in Massachusetts, 1760–1840* (Westport, CT, 1979), ch. 4.

2. The College of William and Mary is not included in the numerical tables due to the paucity and uncertainty of information described in Table A2.14, where I have listed the persons believed to have attended the College for at least three years prior to 1777.

3. Lawrence A. Cremin, *American Education: The Colonial Experience, 1607–1783* (New York, 1970), p. 666. See Mark A. May, *The Education of American Ministers,* vol. 2: *The Profession of the Ministry* (New York, 1934), p. 24; Paul H. Mattingly, *The Classless Profession: American Schoolmen in the Nineteenth Century* (New York, 1975), p. 218 (n. 10); Stephen Botein, "Income and Ideology: Harvard-Trained Clergymen in Eighteenth-Century New England," *Eighteenth-Century Studies,* 13 (1980): 404n.

by Donald O. Schneider on the third quarter of the eighteenth-century.[4] There are, however, several problems both with this approach and with the sources themselves.

Burritt's study on the colonial colleges is flawed. It has been criticized by Colin Burke for its "focus upon a single major occupation, a very modern notion" and for using less than "ninety-nine different occupational categories."[5] These two points are not the most serious flaws, however, or even flaws at all. It may well be Burke who is being anachronistic in suggesting that a "focus upon a single major vocation" is "a very modern notion." In fact Burke's own approach of categorizing each individual into as many as "four different occupations" creates as many problems as it solves. This approach devalues the choices of individuals who remained in their occupations by counting disproportionately the decisions of individuals who wandered from occupation to occupation. Burke also criticized Burritt for using only a handful of occupational categories, but here again, it may be both anachronistic and overly discrete to employ the 99 categories that Burke proposes. If such categories as "Principals & Superintendents," "Professors," "College Presidents," "State-Local Government," "National Government," and "Diplomatic Service" are not artificially discrete for the antebellum period, they are certainly so for the colonial period.[6]

It is true that Burritt's criteria for classifying individuals into vocations and his application of those criteria are suspect, about which more will be said below. But the more serious deficiencies concern his sources. Burritt gave only a vague description of his sources, so it is impossible to determine his accuracy. Moreover, he appears to have missed some sources that are still important today, such as the *University of Pennsylvania Biographical Catalogue* (1894),[7] and there are better sources now available, including the later volumes of *Harvard Graduates*, Thomas's work on Columbia, Pierson's collection of historical statistics on Yale, and the recent volumes on Princeton, which Burritt identified as a particular problem.[8]

4. Bailey B. Burritt, *Professional Distribution of College and University Graduates* (Washington, DC, 1912); Samuel E. Morison, *Harvard College in the Seventeenth Century* (Cambridge, MA, 1936), pt. 2, pp. 556–65; Donald O. Schneider, "Education in Colonial American Colleges, 1750–1770, and the Occupations and Political Offices of their Alumni" (PhD diss., George Peabody College for Teachers, 1965).

5. Burke, *American Collegiate Populations*, p. 139. Burritt employed the classifications of ministry, law, medicine, education, commercial pursuits, public service, engineering, agriculture, literature and journalism, and unclassified (p. 11).

6. Burke, *American Collegiate Populations*, p. 139, table 4.3. According to this approach, Achilles Mansfield, who graduated from Yale in 1770 and spent his entire career ministering to the established church in Killingworth, Connecticut, until his death in 1814, would be counted once as a minister, whereas Asa Spaulding, who graduated from Yale in 1752, served as a minister and chaplain in Connecticut and New Hampshire until about 1763, then became an innkeeper, while doing some surveying on the side, and eventually went into law, would be listed in four different categories. *Yale Graduates*, vol. 3, p. 389; vol. 2, pp. 296–7.

7. Burritt, *Professional Distribution*, pp. 9–10, 29; [Persifor Frazier et al.], *University of Pennsylvania Biographical Catalogue of the Matriculates of the College ... of Philadelphia ... 1749–1857* (New York, 1894).

8. Burritt, *Professional Distribution*, p. 10; Milton H. Thomas, *Columbia University, Officers and Alumni, 1754–1857* (New York, 1936); George W. Pierson, *A Yale Book of*

Schneider's dissertation is more recent and reliable than Burritt, but has the drawbacks that it is not readily accessible to many scholars, has been superseded by later sources, and has a relatively narrow focus. Schneider looks only at the years from 1750 to 1770 and only at the colleges of Harvard, William and Mary, Yale, and New Jersey. He also treats the various vocations as though they were equally attractive and does not consider how relative attractiveness influenced vocational choice. For example, he regards the positions of schoolmaster or college tutor, which many graduates pursued for a few years after graduation, as an option comparable to other fields, rather than a preparatory stage, and thus considers the move from teaching to ministry as a career change rather than a normal progression in a ministerial career.[9]

Morison's figures on seventeenth-century Harvard are also more recent and reliable than Burritt's, but Morison was more concerned with depicting the fortunes of all the "Sons of Harvard" than with providing information about choices among vocations.[10] He therefore counted in his figures all those who attended Harvard, whether or not they graduated. As a result, one problem with using Morison to supplement Burritt and Schneider is that Morison's figures include non-graduates and the others' do not. A second problem is that examining college graduates, rather than all individuals who ever attended college, provides better information about preferences among vocations, and this issue will be discussed below.

Other scholars have attempted partial enumerations of the career choices made by graduates of the colonial colleges. In a recently published list of the "Professional Choices of Harvard Graduates: 1642–1760," Charles R. McKirdy does not explain how he categorizes individuals in careers, so one can only speculate about what his numbers actually mean. Moreover, he looks only at the fields of law, medicine, and theology and, as a result, appears to inflate these categories.[11] The recently published biographical volumes of Princeton graduates also include among

Numbers: Historical Statistics of the College and University, 1701–1976 (New Haven, CT, 1983); *Princetonians.*

9. Schneider, "Education in Colonial American Colleges," ch. 5, pp. 194–200.

10. Morison, *Harvard College,* pt. 2, pp. 556–65.

11. Charles R. McKirdy, "Massachusetts Lawyers on the Eve of the American Revolution: The State of the Profession," in *Law in Colonial Massachusetts, 1630–1800* (Boston, 1984), app. 2, p. 316n. For example, McKirdy counts seven clergymen in the Harvard class of 1749, whereas I count five. Of the only two possible additional candidates, one is Abijah Thurston who had begun to preach in his hometown but died within a year of graduation. Since many graduates commenced to study divinity and to preach and never entered the ministry, I have counted Thurston in the indeterminate category of "Died Young." The other possibility is Edward Wigglesworth, who was promoted from college tutor to Hollis Professor of Divinity at Harvard, in which capacity he served from 1765 to 1791. Even though Wigglesworth taught divinity, he was never ordained and never settled in a church, and I have placed him in the category of "College Educator." *Harvard Graduates,* vol. 12, pp. 488–9, 507–17. Most of these points apply also to: Paul M. Hamlin, *Legal Education in Colonial New York* (New York, 1939), app. 1: "Students of King's College, 1758–1784, who became Lawyers, Doctors, Ministers."

the appendices a categorization of the graduates by their "professional occupations," but these tables must be consulted with caution. They do not distinguish between graduates, non-graduates, and certain honorary graduates who did not attend Princeton at all but were later granted honorary degrees and, as was the custom of the colonial colleges, entered on the rolls of the class that they would have joined had they attended. Incorporating these individuals not only leads to duplication of the graduates of other colleges, but also presents a misleading picture of the vocations pursued by those who actually studied at and graduated from Princeton. In addition, the reader is not told how the sorting into occupations was made, and thus does not know the meaning of the various categories really mean, such as "School Masters," given that many other "professionals" had taught school and that some of the listed school masters left teaching or died young and would doubtlessly have entered other vocations. Nor does one know why Nathaniel Niles, who graduated in 1766, studied law and medicine, taught school, was licensed to preach in 1769, served churches in Vermont while practicing law and medicine, and was eventually elevated to the Vermont Supreme Court and other public offices, is not categorized at all or where he would be if he were.[12]

The problematic nature of the categorization provided in an otherwise excellent biographical dictionary of college graduates extends also to Dexter's *Yale Graduates*. Dexter provided summaries of the "professional callings" of Yale graduates in a few sentences at the end of his volumes, and historians have relied on these statements to derive numerical categorizations.[13] But Dexter's figures are somewhat inaccurate,[14] and his categorization, which historians have tended to take at face value, is equivocal and unclear.[15]

Mindful of these past studies and their difficulties, I have included in this categorization only those individuals who earned a bachelor's degree[16] from a

12. Jane E. Weber, "Appendix," in *Princetonians*, vol. 1, pp. 585–7, 670–3; vol. 2, pp. 546–7; vol. 3, pp. 463–4.

13. Gawalt, *The Promise of Power*, ch. 4, p. 141; Everett C. Goodwin, *The Magistracy Rediscovered Connecticut, 1636–1818* (Ann Arbor, MI, 1981), p. 67. Like McKirdy, these authors do not explain their criteria for classification or how they dealt with the numerous ambiguous cases.

14. There were, for example, 482 graduates from Yale in the classes from 1702 to 1744, not 483, because David Parsons, listed in the class of 1705, actually received his BA from Harvard. Similarly, William Phelps should not be counted as a BA graduate in the Yale class of 1776 because he apparently did not receive the degree. *Yale Graduates*, vol. 1, p. 36; vol. 3, p. 630. On the difficulties of counting the class of 1705 at both Yale and Harvard, see *Harvard Graduates*, vol. 5, pp. 261–301.

15. A typical statement of graduates' "professional callings" by Dexter reads: "about one-half entered the ministry.... Not more than 33 of these graduates are known to have devoted themselves exclusively to the legal profession.... But 30 of the whole number are known to have become physicians." *Yale Graduates*, vol. 1, p. 773.

16. This enumeration includes the 28 graduates who earned bachelor of medicine or physic degrees from the College of Philadelphia between 1768 and 1776 and the twelve such graduates who earned MB degrees from King's College between 1769 and 1776. (Some of these graduates earned a BA before the MB and are counted only once and under the earlier BA class.) Because the BA degree was the more demanding and prestigious degree, these

colonial college. Those who attended but did not graduate or who received honorary or *ad eundem* ("courtesy") degrees are excluded. One reason for this exclusion is that the graduates constitute a more discrete and clearly defined population. They were distinguished by their common experience and lengthy socialization at college and by their degree, which served as a professional credential in certain contexts and conferred a great deal of status in general.

Although this approach provides greater precision of definition, it is sometimes difficult even to identify those who earned a bachelor's degree. *Harvard Graduates* is particularly obscure on this point because graduates, non-graduates, and honorary graduates are listed together. This arrangement has misled even scholars who have read the seventeen volumes carefully, let alone those who have succumbed to the understandable temptation to skim the 11,000-odd pages.[17] Even Clifford K. Shipton, the author of the later volumes of *Harvard Graduates*, neglected to note, for instance, that two individuals who were later placed in the class of 1770 – John Porter, who received an *ed eundem* MA in 1777, and Thomas Kittredge, who received an honorary MD in 1811 – did not graduate with a BA from Harvard. And regarding the class of 1762, Shipton stated that 51 students were admitted, then listed 52 admittees.[18] In addition, Shipton was somewhat tendentious in his introductory descriptions of graduates, emphasizing public offices, professional vocations, however temporary, and academic appointments, particularly those having to do with Harvard or the Massachusetts Historical Society. Consequently a cursory reading of the volumes will give a misleading impression of the career of some graduates.

A second reason for focusing upon college graduates is the greater accuracy of the records concerning this group. Although even these records are in many instances suspect or lacking, the identity of many of the students who attended but did not graduate from the colonial colleges is unknown, as Morison observed about seventeenth-century Harvard.[19] Notwithstanding the greater accuracy of the records of graduates, it is important to note the tradeoff between abundance and

---

medical degrees might be eliminated. But the standards of the BA course were not at all consistent over time and among institutions, so it seems reasonable to include all college graduates. See Frederic C. Waite, "Medical Degrees Conferred in the American Colonies and in the United States in the Eighteenth Century," *Annals of Medical History*, 9 (1937): 314–20; David C. Humphrey, *From King's College to Columbia, 1746–1800* (New York, 1976), chs. 13, 14. The first bachelor of laws degree appears to have been granted in 1793 by the College of William and Mary.

17. For example, McKirdy, appears to count William Crawford and George Sparhawk incorrectly as graduates, as does Schneider for Peter R. Livingston, and Walter C. Eells for either John Hart or John Russell and for either Benjamin Viall and Thomas West. McKirdy, "Massachusetts Lawyers," p. 335; Schneider, "Education in Colonial American Colleges," p. 202; Walter C. Eells, *Baccalaureate Degrees Conferred by American Colleges in the 17th and 18th Centuries* (Washington, DC, 1958), pp. 34–5; *Harvard Graduates*, vol. 5, pp. 252–8; vol. 8, pp. 793–4; vol. 13, pp. 561–3; vol. 14, pp. 125, 184, 242, 314.

18. *Harvard Graduates*, vol. 17, pp. 332–3, 402, 423; vol. 15, pp. 148–9.

19. Morison, *Harvard College*, pt. 2, p. 557. See Table A2.14 on the College of William and Mary, Table A2.13 on Queen's College, and *Harvard Graduates*, vol. 5, pp. 261–301, on the Harvard class of 1705.

accuracy of information in the college catalogues. The earlier catalogues tend to include significant vocational and biographical information about the alumni. The later catalogues, which subsume the earlier ones, tend to be more accurate, for they include corrections of earlier editions, but also excise more and more of the vocational and biographical information due to the increasing number of alumni. These two tendencies are exemplified in the catalogues of Columbia University.[20]

For the information provided in the tables below, I have compared the several catalogues listed. Where information has been changed or omitted by reason of earlier error, I have obviously relied on the information in the later catalogue. However, where a later catalogue omits all vocational information, I have used the information provided in the earlier catalogues, particularly those cited by later editors as the more accurate of the earlier catalogues. For example, the 1905 catalogue of Brown University, which Gawalt employed in his analysis, should be evaluated in light of the catalogues of 1914 and 1934, which make some emendations in the earlier edition.[21]

A third reason for focusing upon college graduates is that an analysis of this group offers more information about colonists" intrinsic preferences among vocations. Because college graduates were privileged by reason of holding a degree, they were freer to make choices among occupations. Their choices thus reflect more accurately the colonists' intrinsic preferences than would those of a general sample of the population. This greater accuracy is complemented by the consistency in the ratio of college graduates to the total population. In a dated but still useful study, Eells found that there existed in America from 1642 to 1800 a "remarkable uniformity of the ratio of college graduates to the total population ... varying only from 8 to 14 per 10,000 population. Most of the time it hovered close to the average ratio of the entire period of 11.5 per 10,000 population."[22] To this third reason it might be objected that a college degree was not the normal prerequisite for a career in law or medicine in the colonial period, and so the focus upon college graduates skews the data away from those fields. But this point merely goes to say that neither law nor medicine were the vocation preferred by the most advantaged of the population for much of the colonial period. And the objection neglects the fact that a college degree was deemed a prerequisite by the leaders of the legal and medical fields; and it was considered desirable, if one had the opportunity and means, by the practitioners at large.

20. Cf. *Catalogue of the Governors, Trustees, and Officers and of the Alumni and other Graduates of Columbia College ... from 1754 to 1882* (New York, 1882), p. 5; *Catalogue of the Officers and Graduates of Columbia University from the Foundation of King's College in 1754* (New York, 1906), p. 5; *Catalogue of the Officers and Graduates of Columbia University from the Foundation of King's College in 1754* (New York, 1912), p. 5; Thomas, *Columbia University*, p. xi.

21. Gawalt, *The Promise of Power*, p. 142; Mary D. Vaughan, comp., *Historical Catalogue of Brown University, 1764–1904* (Providence, RI, 1905); [Louise P. Bates, ed.], *Historical Catalogue of Brown University, 1764–1914* (Providence, RI, 1914); Louise Bauer and William T. Hastings, comps., *The Historical Catalogue of Brown University, 1764–1934* (Providence, RI, 1936).

22. Eells, *Baccalaureate Degrees*, p. 37.

While addressing only those who earned a bachelor's degree from a colonial college, I have followed the practice of most scholars in classifying each graduate into a single major field. As discussed above, the notion of classifying one individual into several vocations as that individual changed vocations gives undue weight to those who made such changes. On the other hand, the approach of classifying "secondary careers," which is adopted by Richard Warch,[23] does not really avoid the problem of deciding on one primary career and introduces an additional level of ambiguity. Since many college graduates farmed, taught, or practiced "physick" in some fashion at some point, it is ambiguous as to when a graduate should be considered to have a "secondary career" in these fields and others not. Another drawback to classifying "secondary careers," is that, although *Harvard Graduates*, *Yale Graduates*, and *Princetonians* have in many instances enough information to make multiple or secondary classifications, in many other cases the graduates of these and the other colonial colleges are known only well enough to estimate, at best, their primary vocation. Thus, it would be inconsistent to estimate secondary or multiple vocations for some better known individuals, and not for all other graduates.

Consequently, the colonial college graduates are each classified into no more than one vocation on the following numerical tables, and the classifications are made according to four criteria. The first criterion is evidence of training and, especially, an apprenticeship or a second degree completed in a particular field. In the absence of other evidence or data about a graduate's occupation, I have counted such an apprenticeship or study as determinative. Thus, Samuel Bellingham (HC 1642), who reportedly earned a doctorate in medicine at Leyden, and Henry Saltonstall (HC 1642), who supposedly did likewise at Padua, are classified as physicians in the absence of other information about their occupation. But Governor William Browne (HC 1755) of Bermuda, who is known not to have practiced law, though he studied it, is classified in public service, not law.[24] Training in divinity or the earning of an MA is not, however, treated as determinative of a career in the ministry in the absence of other information. Since the careers of ministers are generally known, the graduates who took their MA, or studied divinity, and were never heard from again probably did not enter the ministry. Such individuals are classified under "Unknown".

The second criterion is length of tenure in an occupation. This point is self-explanatory, and Burritt treated it as his major criterion and a proxy for "success."[25] But length of tenure must be carefully balanced against the other criteria, especially the vocation pursued later in life or at the height or culmination of a career. This third criterion is particularly indicative of vocational preference. For example, Gurdon Saltonstall (HC 1684), who left the ministry upon his election as Governor of Connecticut in 1707 and held office until his death in 1724, is classified under "Public Service". Similarly, John Carnes (HC 1742) and Augustine Hibbard (DC 1772) served as ministers for twenty and eleven years respectively,

23. Richard Warch, *School of the Prophets: Yale College, 1701–1740* (New Haven, CT, 1973), p. 270.

24. *Harvard Graduates*, vol. 1, pp. 63–4, 67; vol. 13, p. 551.

25. Burritt, *Professional Distribution*, p. 11.

then left their pulpits and held various public and judicial offices until their deaths some 40 years later. Both are counted under "Public Service."[26] The vocation pursued later in life is particularly determinative if that vocation corresponds to a person's earlier training. Samuel Fowler (YC 1768) studied law and was admitted to practice after graduation; but when the Revolution closed the courts shortly thereafter, he left the bar to become a merchant. He subsequently returned to the law and politics, and was appointed to the judiciary in 1813. He is classified under "Law," for which he originally trained and to which he returned later in life.[27]

The consideration of the vocation pursued later in life is particularly relevant to the classification of college presidents. The difficulty in classifying these individuals is demonstrated by the fact that Burritt included nearly all presidents and rectors in the category of "education," while Morison stated flatly: "All the College presidents except Leverett are counted as clergymen."[28] John Leverett (HC 1680) was educated in divinity and law, chose to leave his legal and public service career to become president of Harvard, and worked there for sixteen years until his death in 1724. He is classified as a college educator on the grounds of this third criterion, as are Eleazar Wheelock (YC 1733), Aaron Burr (YC 1735), and Joseph McKeen (DC 1774), each of whom left their pulpits and served at least seven years as a college president until his death.[29]

If there is reason to think, contrary to Morison, that at least some clergy may be classified as college educators on the basis of choosing a professorship or presidency late in life, there is also the possibility that Burritt may not have looked closely enough at some college presidents who actually preferred the pulpit. Increase Mather (HC 1656), though he became president of Harvard, chose not to leave his prestigious pulpit in Boston and eventually was ousted from the presidency when pressed to choose between the two. He is classified here as a minister. So, too, Samuel Johnson (YC 1714), who went from the ministry to the presidency of King's College in New York and then back to the ministry, is classified under "Theology."[30]

26. George T. Chapman, *Sketches of the Alumni of Dartmouth College from ... 1771 to 1867* (Cambridge, MA, 1867), p. 14; *Harvard Graduates*, vol. 3, pp. 278–81; vol. 11, pp. 137–42. Compare the judgment of McKirdy, for example, who apparently counts Samuel Dana (Harvard 1755) as a clergyman, though he left the ministry and spent his last 20 years in the law. *Harvard Graduates*, vol. 13, pp. 579–85; McKirdy, "Massachusetts Lawyers," p. 335.

27. *Yale Graduates*, vol. 3, pp. 277–8.

28. Burritt, *Professional Distribution*, p. 11; Morison, *Harvard College*, pt. 2, p. 561n.

29. *Harvard Graduates*, vol. 3, pp. 180–98; *Yale Graduates*, vol. 1, pp. 495–6, 531; Chapman, *Sketches ... of Dartmouth College*, p. 16. The same logic holds for college professors. Sylvanus Ripley (DC 1771) and John Smith (DC 1773) studied divinity, were ordained, and then became tutors and subsequently professors at Dartmouth while also holding positions as pastors of the church there until their death. (Chapman, pp. 13, 15–6) Because their pastorates were part of the college, rather than the college being either a part of the pastorates (as with Abraham Pierson, the first rector of Yale, who taught the students in his home) or apart from the pastorates (as with Increase Mather, who retained his prestigious pulpit in Boston), I have classified Ripley and Smith as college educators.

30. *Harvard Graduates*, vol. 1, pp. 410–37; *Yale Graduates*, vol. 1, pp. 124–5.

The fourth criterion is relative status and prestige of the various occupations. This factor applies particularly to teaching school, an occupation that was generally a second-choice or fall-back vocation. Flint Dwight (HC 1724), for example, went to England to be ordained as an Anglican priest, looked unsuccessfully for pulpits in New England and New York, and ended up teaching school in New York until his death in 1745. Similarly, Timothy Minot (HC 1718) preached during the first few years after graduation trying to find a settlement, but gave up and kept the school in Concord, Massachusetts, for the rest of his life.[31]

Medicine, too, was a second-choice or fall-back vocation, but slightly preferred to teaching. Thus, Daniel Witham (HC 1718) taught school in eastern Massachusetts for about 12 years after graduation, then switched to medicine for the rest of his life. And Joseph Baxter (HC 1724), who looked unsuccessfully for a pulpit for several years in Massachusetts, turned to teaching but gave it up in 1731 to become a physician. Baxter's experience demonstrates the fact that theology was especially preferred to either medicine or teaching. Hence, Joseph Marsh (HC 1728) tried and failed first at preaching, next at physic, and finally taught school outside Boston for his life work.[32]

Mindful of this pattern, one must devalue an intermittent or early tenure in teaching or medicine relative to other occupations that were subsequently chosen by the same individual. For example, Samuel Danforth (HC 1715) taught school in Massachusetts from 1715 to 1730, then began to practice medicine and gained some stature in this field. Subsequently, he was named a judge of the Middlesex Court of Common Pleas in 1741, and served in that capacity for 34 years, while also sitting on the Governor's Council. He is classified as under "Public Service."[33]

Danforth's case points to the fact that public service and, to a lesser extent, law – fields that are distinct for reasons described below – were viewed as slightly preferable to teaching and medicine and less preferred than theology. Robert Hale (HC 1686) studied for the ministry after graduation, and preached in Massachusetts and Connecticut. In 1697 poor health forced him to relinquish what he called "the best of employments," and he became a schoolmaster in 1700. Within one year, he left teaching to practice medicine, which he did for the rest of his life while devoting more and more of his time to the public offices of selectman, justice of the peace, and legislative representative. Even more striking is the example of John Sparhawk (HC 1723), who kept school in Plymouth and subsequently worked as a merchant and practiced law in the 1730s. Sparhawk was repeatedly admonished for drunkenness by his church, and in 1740 was dismissed from legal practice for his excesses. He then took up medicine, for which one did not need to obtain a license or survive extensive public scrutiny, as for theology or law. Sparhawk thus remained in this intermediate vocation until his death in 1747.[34]

This fourth criterion must be carefully balanced against the previous three in classifying an individual's vocation. Otherwise, one falls into the circular reasoning that has often plagued categorizations of vocations. Morison and Burritt,

31. *Harvard Graduates*, vol. 7, pp. 333–4; vol. 6, pp. 257–8.
32. *Harvard Graduates*, vol. 6, p. 288; vol. 7, p. 305; vol. 8, p. 448.
33. *Harvard Graduates*, vol. 6, pp. 80–6.
34. *Harvard Graduates*, vol. 3, pp. 362–3; vol. 7, pp. 258–9.

for example, tended to classify all those who ever served in the clergy under "theology" because it was the preferred vocation. But a good part of the evidence for its being preferred is that more graduates chose it. Only by attending to other criteria, as well as the general context, can one begin to account, however imperfectly, for the discontinuities and personal vagaries in vocational choice. Although Gershom Bulkeley (HC 1655) was settled in the pulpit in Wethersfield, Connecticut, until age 41, he left in 1677 to become a physician. He worked in this capacity until his death in 1713; and, in view of the second and third criteria, he is more properly classified as a physician than a minister.[35] Indeed, the fact that a profession generally enjoyed higher status and more social authority may even contribute to its being avoided by an individual. Josiah Cotton (HC 1698) had begun to prepare for the ministry while teaching school after graduation, as was the normal course for a new college graduate. But he decided that writing sermons and preaching were too onerous and accepted the position of schoolmaster in Plymouth instead.[36]

One must therefore balance a set of criteria in making an assessment of an individual's vocation, unless one decides to categorize each individual into several different vocations. This strategy, however, does not really overcome the essential problems of indeterminacy while it introduces the additional problem of emphasizing the choices of some individuals more than others, as described above.

The four criteria have been applied to sort graduates into nine categories of vocational choices, defined as follows.

Theology includes those, whether or not ordained, who engaged primarily in the ministry, whether settled in a pulpit or serving as a missionary or itinerant preacher.

Medicine includes those who engaged primarily in "physic" or "surgery." Almost all colonial "apothecaries" are also counted under "Medicine," but those who established businesses to sell medicines and, unlike in England, did not see patients apart from over-the-counter diagnosis are classified under "Commerce."

Law includes those who engaged primarily in legal practice. Non-lawyers who left other fields, often theology, to work in the government or the judiciary – such as William Stoughton (HC 1650), Peter Bulkley (HC 1660), Joseph Dudley (HC 1665), and Samuel Danforth (HC 1715) – have been classified under "Public service." Burritt tended to classify such individuals as lawyers, but that classification indicates both a lack of understanding about the judiciary in the colonial era and a presentist assumption that since lawyers occupy most judicial and political posts today, then we must call those who did so in the past lawyers as well. On the other hand, someone like Theodore Atkinson (HC 1718), who was admitted to

35. *Harvard Graduates*, vol. 1, pp. 388–401. In contrast to Bulkeley's classification, note that John Bulkley (HC 1642) went to England and served as a minister for about twenty years before being ejected from his pulpit under the 1662 Act of Uniformity. Although he practiced medicine for the rest of his life, he is classified as a minister because he did not choose to leave the ministry, and subsequently was known to administer "natural and spiritual Physick together.... And seldom did he visit his Patients, without reading a Lecture of Divinity to them, and praying with them." *Harvard Graduates*, vol. 1, p. 52.

36. *Harvard Graduates*, vol. 1, pp. 194–208; vol. 2, pp. 68–71, 166–88; vol. 4, pp. 398–401; vol. 6, pp. 80–6.

the bar, practiced law, and then entered government service in New Hampshire, is classified here. So, too, Benjamin Lynde (HC 1718), who studied law, entered government service, and became Chief Justice of Massachusetts, as well as Phineas Lyman (YC 1738), who ended his life in 1774 near Natchez in the present state of Mississippi.[37]

College includes those who worked primarily as a college president, professor, or tutor, except for those who are counted under "Died young."

School includes those who earned their living primarily as schoolmasters, except for those who are classified under "Died young." Note that "School" does not include the office of "Teacher" in the dissenting churches of the seventeenth century. Burritt seems not to have realized that the office of "Teacher" was a ministerial position, for he apparently classified William Ames (HC 1645), the son of the famous dissenting theologian William Ames, as a teacher, rather than a minister, because Ames served the dissenting society in Wrentham, England, for the last 27 years of his life as "Teacher."[38]

Commerce includes those who worked primarily as merchants, financiers, bankers, industrialists, and merchants. Most sea captains, being traders, are counted here as well.

Public service includes those who earned their living (or, being independently wealthy, spent their time) primarily as political, judicial, or military officials. I have followed the practice announced by Burritt and endorsed by others: "those found both in public affairs and in some other profession ... were generally classified in the profession other than public service, in which they were known to have engaged."[39] This point applies particularly to lawyers, such as John Treadwell (YC 1767), who practiced law and then entered politics. Such persons are classified as lawyers. "Law" therefore trumps "Public service," not the reverse. However, in cases where public service is clearly the last of a series of attempted careers, this category holds. Thus, William Brattle (HC 1722), who successively tried preaching, medicine, law, and finally business while continually holding military and political office, is classified here.[40] It should be noted that, because many merchants acquired the means and leisure to occupy political and judicial office, there is a good deal of ambiguity and overlap between "Commerce" and "Public service."

Other includes farmers, innkeepers, tavernkeepers, craftsmen, sailors, gentlemen and all those who do not fit the other categories. Many scholars, ranging from Burritt to Gawalt, have incorporated into "Other" the two categories below.[41] But the distinctions between these last three categories are far more important than attempting to separate, say, farmers from innkeepers or bankers from merchants. "Other" obviously indicates that an individual is known not to fit into any of the foregoing categories, although there is a good deal of ambiguity and overlap between "Other" and "Public service" because gentlemen, who lived on inherited wealth, usually served in some public office.

37. *Harvard Graduates*, vol. 6, pp. 221–30, 250–6; *Yale Graduates*, vol. 1, pp. 605–6.

38. *Harvard Graduates*, vol. 1, pp. 107–9. See Vergil V. Phelps, "The Pastor and Teacher in New England," *Harvard Theological Review*, 4 (1911): 388–99.

39. Burritt, *Professional Distribution*, p. 11; Morison, *Harvard College*, pt. 2, p. 561n.

40. *Yale Graduates*, vol. 3, pp. 247–51; *Harvard Graduates*, vol. 7, pp. 10–23.

41. Burritt, *Professional Distribution*, p. 11; Gawalt, *The Promise of Power*, pp. 141–3.

Unknown always indicates a lack of information rather than a problem of categorization. It is a somewhat neutral category, like "Died young," except that it indicates that the individual probably *did not* become a minister, lawyer, educator, or public servant because these vocations were generally a matter of public record at some point, and graduates in these fields could probably be traced.[42]

Died young includes those individuals who died within about six years of graduation, such as John Oliver (HC 1645), who had begun studying divinity but died in 1646, John Whiting Marsh (YC 1763), who perished on the island of Grenada in 1764, and Nathaniel Huntington (YC 1772), who had begun the study of law but died in 1774 at home.[43] The exception to this general rule covers those individuals who were actively practicing a particular vocation before their death. They are classified in that vocation. Thus, Percival Green (HC 1680) is classified in "Theology" though he died in 1684 one year after beginning his preaching position in Wells, Maine, where he also taught school. Similarly, Stephen Munson (YC 1725), Moses Burr (YC 1734), and Joseph Denison (YC 1763) died within six years of graduation but are counted under "Theology" because they had been licensed and were engaged in preaching in Connecticut. So, too, Augustus Eliot (YC 1740), who died at age 27 after practicing medicine with his father and brother-in-law, is classified in "Medicine."[44]

The exception to the exception covers those individuals who died young while engaged as college tutors or schoolmasters. Since many graduates became school-teachers or college tutors for a few years after graduation while contemplating their vocation, to categorize the graduates who died during these years under "College" or "School" (as all historians mentioned here, except Schneider, have done) would inflate these categories with a number of persons who would not have remained in them. Thus, college tutors, such as Alexander Nowell (HC 1664) who died in 1672, and schoolmasters, such as Joseph Dasset (HC 1687), who died in 1693, and Recompense Wadsworth (HC 1708), who died in 1713, have been counted in the following tables under "Died young."[45]

Like other scholars, Burritt classified these tutors and teachers in "education," except for those whose vocational intentions were supposedly known, such as Joseph Morgan (YC 1723) or Samuel Fisk (YC 1743).[46] I have not followed this

42. Similarly, Overfield concludes that those who are unknown among pre-Reformation university graduates are almost certainly not clergy. In the colonial context, this probability may mean that "Unknown" includes some who properly belong in "Commerce" and especially "Other." James H. Overfield, "University Studies and the Clergy in Pre-reformation Germany," in *Rebirth, Reform and Resilience: Universities in Transition, 1300–1700*, ed. James M. Kittelson and Pamela J. Transue (Columbus, OH, 1984), pp. 259–60.

43. *Harvard Graduates*, vol. 1, p. 105; *Yale Graduates*, vol. 3, pp. 36, 448.

44. *Harvard Graduates*, vol. 3, pp. 208–9; *Yale Graduates*, vol. 1, pp. 316, 506, 647; vol. 3, pp. 17–8.

45. *Harvard Graduates*, vol. 2, pp. 148–9; vol. 3, p. 389; vol. 5, pp. 461–2. If someone taught for a period and then disappears from the records, such as Samuel Campbell (Philadelphia 1762), who served as Tutor at the College of Philadelphia, I have classified him under "Unknown." W. J. Maxwell, *General Alumni Catalogue of the University of Pennsylvania* (Philadelphia, 1917), p. 18; Frazier, *University of Pennsylvania*, pp. 19–20.

46. *Yale Graduates*, vol. 1, pp. 284–5, 735.

practice of classifying graduates who died young according to testimony about their intentions. Many graduates, like those today, expressed a desire to enter one field and then entered another. In view of the unreliability of graduates' early intentions and of testimony about those intentions, I have held to the standard that graduates who died young must have actually begun to practice a particular vocation other than teaching. Samuel Eliot (HC 1660), who served as a Harvard tutor until his death in 1664, is counted under "Died young" even though Cotton Mather described Eliot as "a *Candidate* of the Ministry."[47]

Almost 6 percent (5.98 percent) of the colonial college graduates belong in this category, and this fraction is fairly consistent throughout the period. Schneider is the only scholar that I have found who realized that the failure to factor out this group skews the rest of the data (generally in the direction of an emphasis upon theology and education), and that this category must be considered in any percentages or computed comparisons intended to show the relative preference among professions.[48] Table A2.5 "College graduates sorted by vocation" is therefore adjusted for those who died young. That is to say, the percentages are based upon the total number of graduates minus those who died young and whose career choice is therefore indeterminate.

In conclusion, it may be useful to provide one small illustration of how the following tables offer some instructive contrasts with other partial numerical categorizations that are available. Table A2.1 presents the percentages of clergymen among all college graduates in the classes from 1769 to 1775, as reported in the *Princetonians* volumes, which do not identify their sorting criteria or define their categories.[49]

Based on the criteria and categories defined above, the totals of clergy in the second column would be calculated differently. After eliminating clergymen who left the ministry in preference for another vocation, the fraction for Dartmouth, for example, becomes 64.5 percent (20/31), rather than 74.2 percent (23/31). And even where the totals for clergy do not change – as in the case of the College of Rhode Island – the computed percentages differ because those graduates who died young and whose vocation is therefore indeterminate have not been factored out of the total number of graduates. If one discounts such individuals, then the percentage of clergymen among Rhode Island graduates becomes 35.9 percent (14/39) rather than 31.8 percent (14/44). Table A2.2 presents values corresponding to Table A2.1 but derived from the criteria and definitions proposed here.

Apart from the foregoing arguments concerning criteria and definitions, there are additional reasons to think that Table A2.2 more accurately reflects the numbers of college graduates who pursued a vocation in the ministry. The fact that the overall range of percentages is not quite as broad, (6.0–66.6 percent compared to 4.5–74.2

47. Cotton Mather, *Magnalia Christi Americana; or The Ecclesiastical History of New England* (1702; Hartford, CT, 1855), vol. 2, bk. 4, p. 31. *Harvard Graduates*, vol. 2, p. 61.

48. Schneider, "Education in Colonial American Colleges," p. 203n.

49. *Princetonians*, vol. 2, p. xxviii. *Princetonians* defines clergymen as those who are "ordained," a definition that is both more inclusive and exclusive than the category of "Theology" employed here. Harvard is not included because *Harvard Graduates* currently stops with the class of 1771.

Table A2.1   Percentages of clergymen among college graduates in classes
1769–1775

College	Graduates	Clergy	(%)
Dartmouth	31	23	74.2
New Jersey	150	72	48.0
Yale	188	68	36.2
Rhode Island	44	14	31.8
Queen's	15	2	13.3
Philadelphia	50	6	12.0
King's	44	2	4.5

Source: Princetonians, vol. 2, p. xxviii.

Table A2.2   Recalculated percentages of clergymen among college graduates in
classes 1769–1775

College	Graduates	Clergy	(%)
Queen's	3	2	66.6
Dartmouth	31	20	64.5
New Jersey	142	65	45.8
Yale	177	64	36.2
Rhode Island	39	14	35.9
Philadelphia	62	7	11.3
King's	50	3	6.0

Note: As in the following tables, the number of graduates is adjusted upward to include
Bachelor of Medicine graduates (from Philadelphia and King's Colleges) and down-
ward to exclude those who "died young" and, in the case of Queen's College, those
whose graduation and vocation are unknown.

percent) comports with the relatively uniform educational experience at the colonial
colleges. This narrowing would be slightly more pronounced if Table A2.2 were
based only on BA graduates, as was Table A2.1. The figures for Philadelphia and
King's, the only two colonial colleges that granted MB degrees, would then become
15.2 percent (7/46) and 7.2 percent (4/42) respectively.

More significantly, the percentages of the five explicitly sectarian colleges that
were founded by clergymen in the eighteenth century in order to train ministers for
Calvinist sects are grouped more closely together in Table A2.2 (a range of 35.9–
64.5 percent compared to 13.3–74.2 percent). In particular, the two most recently
founded and enthusiastic of these sectarian colleges, Queen's (1766) and Dartmouth
(1769), are appropriately alligned together at the top of the list, rather than appearing at opposite ends. Meanwhile the two "outliers" – Philadelphia and King's,
which were similarly founded on more secular and pluralistic grounds – are also

grouped more closely together (a range of 6.0–11.3 percent compared to 4.5–12.0 percent) and by themselves, not with Queen's College.

In sum, this small, comparative illustration suggests that the criteria and categories described here may offer an approach to classifying the colonial college graduates by vocation that is more attuned not only to the nature of the available evidence, but also to the historical context. Table A2.1 presents the problem of explaining why the graduates of Dartmouth, Rhode Island, and Queen's – three colleges founded with similar religious missions and similar academic programs within five years of each other – would diverge so radically in choosing to enter the ministry. To be sure, one can think of explanations – geographical, sectarian, and so forth; and part of the reason for attempting to construct such tables is precisely in order to see differences that one did not expect. Nevertheless, when such tables are constructed, as they generally have been in the past, without articulating both how and why the data have been fitted together, such inferred differences may be misleading or unreliable.

The first three of the following tables (Tables A2.3–5) are cumulative, combining the data presented on the subsequent eight tables, each of which addresses an individual colonial college. Table A2.14 lists the names of individuals believed to have attended the College of William and Mary prior to 1777 for at least three years, and these individuals are not incorporated into the cumulative tables. Table A2.3 simply combines the yearly totals from the individual colleges; Table A2.4 compounds the data from the first into four-year, "moving" totals upon which the percentages in Table A2.5 are computed. Percentages are obviously a useful way to evaluate changes in vocational choice, and other categorizations of the vocations of colonial college graduates have reported percentages based upon yearly, three-year or five-year cumulative totals.[50] But such percentages are subject to large fluctuations because the annual number of graduates was relatively small for much of the colonial period. In order to minimize such fluctuations, I have followed the example of J. A. Venn in computing "moving" totals.[51] I have, however, computed four-year, rather than five-year, moving totals because it seemed useful to conform to the quadrennial cycle of generations in the college student population.

50. See, for example, Burritt, *Professional Distribution*, p. 144; McKirdy, "Massachusetts Lawyers," p. 316n.
51. J. A. Venn, *Oxford and Cambridge Matriculations, 1544–1906* (Cambridge, UK, 1908). See, too, Lawrence Stone, "The Educational Revolution in England, 1560–1640," *Past and Present*, 28 (1964): 48–54.

Table A2.3 Cumulative yearly totals of graduates sorted by vocation

	Graduates	Theology	Medicine	Law	College	School	Commerce	Public service	Other	Unknown	Died young
1642	9	5	2	0	0	0	0	0	1	1	0
1643	4	4	0	0	0	0	0	0	0	0	0
1644	0	0	0	0	0	0	0	0	0	0	0
1645	7	4	0	0	0	0	0	0	0	1	2
1646	4	2	2	0	0	0	0	0	0	0	0
1647	7	5	0	0	0	0	0	0	0	2	0
1648	0	0	0	0	0	0	0	0	0	0	0
1649	5	2	0	0	2	0	0	0	2	0	1
1650	9	4	1	0	1	0	0	1	2	0	0
1651	10	4	2	0	0	0	0	0	1	2	1
1652	1	1	0	0	0	0	0	0	0	2	0
1653	17	8	1	0	0	1	0	0	5	2	0
1654	1	0	0	0	0	0	0	0	1	0	0
1655	2	1	1	0	0	0	0	0	0	0	0
1656	8	7	1	0	0	0	0	0	1	0	1
1657	7	4	1	0	0	0	0	0	1	0	0
1658	7	5	0	0	0	1	0	1	0	0	0
1659	10	5	1	0	0	0	0	0	2	2	1
1660	8	2	0	0	0	0	0	1	2	2	0
1661	12	3	2	0	0	1	0	0	1	4	1
1662	6	2	1	0	0	1	0	0	2	0	0
1663	6	2	0	0	0	1	0	0	1	1	1
1664	7	4	0	0	0	0	0	0	1	0	2
1665	8	4	0	0	0	0	0	1	1	0	2

Table A2.3 (Cont'd)

	Graduates	Theology	Medicine	Law	College	School	Commerce	Public service	Other	Unknown	Died young
1666	4	2	1	0	0	0	0	0	1	0	0
1667	7	4	1	0	0	0	0	0	1	1	0
1668	5	3	0	0	0	0	0	0	1	1	0
1669	10	7	1	0	0	1	0	0	0	1	0
1670	4	2	0	0	0	0	0	0	1	0	1
1671	11	7	0	0	0	0	0	0	2	0	2
1672	0	0	0	0	0	0	0	0	0	0	0
1673	4	2	0	0	0	0	0	1	0	1	0
1674	3	0	1	0	0	0	0	0	1	1	0
1675	9	5	1	0	0	1	0	0	1	1	0
1676	3	2	0	0	0	0	0	0	1	0	0
1677	6	4	0	0	0	0	0	0	1	1	0
1678	4	3	0	0	0	0	0	0	0	0	1
1679	4	3	0	0	0	0	0	0	0	0	1
1680	5	3	1	0	1	0	0	0	0	0	0
1681	9	4	1	0	0	0	0	0	1	2	1
1682	0	0	0	0	0	0	0	0	0	0	0
1683	3	3	0	0	0	0	0	0	0	0	0
1684	9	7	0	0	0	0	0	0	1	0	1
1685	14	5	0	1	0	1	0	0	5	0	2
1686	7	2	1	1	0	0	0	0	2	0	1
1687	11	6	1	0	0	0	0	0	1	0	3
1688	0	0	0	0	0	0	0	0	0	0	0
1689	14	6	1	1	1	0	0	0	3	1	2
1690	22	12	0	2	1	0	3	1	0	1	2
1691	8	5	0	0	0	0	0	0	0	1	2

Year											
1692	0	0	1	0	1	0	0	0	0	4	6
1693	0	0	0	0	1	1	1	1	1	10	15
1694	0	0	0	1	2	0	0	0	0	5	8
1695	0	0	0	3	5	0	0	2	3	9	22
1696	0	0	0	0	1	0	0	2	1	5	9
1697	0	0	0	1	1	1	0	1	0	10	14
1698	1	1	1	1	2	1	0	0	1	6	14
1699	1	0	0	3	0	0	0	0	0	8	12
1700	2	0	2	0	1	1	0	0	1	8	15
1701	3	0	1	2	3	2	0	0	0	8	19
1702	0	0	3	2	2	1	0	1	0	5	14
1703	0	1	2	1	0	1	0	0	2	8	15
1704	0	0	0	1	1	0	1	0	0	3	6
1705	3	0	0	0	0	0	1	2	0	9	15
1706	0	0	0	0	1	0	0	0	1	8	10
1707	0	0	4	0	2	1	0	1	1	13	22
1708	2	0	0	1	2	0	0	0	1	10	16
1709	1	1	3	1	2	0	0	0	0	11	19
1710	0	0	0	1	1	1	1	1	0	11	16
1711	2	0	2	2	4	0	0	0	0	5	15
1712	1	2	3	1	2	1	0	1	1	7	19
1713	0	0	1	0	1	1	0	0	0	5	8
1714	2	0	3	1	1	0	0	0	0	13	20
1715	1	0	3	2	2	0	0	0	1	12	21
1716	0	0	2	1	0	1	0	0	1	6	11
1717	0	0	3	0	4	0	0	0	1	14	22
1718	1	0	5	3	1	2	0	4	3	12	32
1719	1	1	1	2	2	0	0	1	2	17	27
1720	3	1	1	0	0	0	0	2	1	23	31
1721	3	1	6	4	5	0	1	2	4	25	51

Table A2.3 (Cont'd)

	Graduates	Theology	Medicine	Law	College	School	Commerce	Public service	Other	Unknown	Died young
1722	39	12	2	2	1	2	6	5	4	3	2
1723	54	24	1	2	0	2	5	5	9	2	4
1724	58	25	5	1	0	4	4	2	9	3	5
1725	54	22	6	1	0	3	7	4	6	2	3
1726	54	17	8	1	0	2	7	3	9	2	5
1727	47	13	1	2	1	1	7	7	8	3	4
1728	54	19	3	4	0	7	4	6	4	6	1
1729	40	21	2	2	0	0	4	4	3	3	1
1730	52	18	4	5	1	2	6	5	6	3	2
1731	47	21	2	4	1	6	3	4	2	1	3
1732	49	19	2	1	1	1	6	7	3	6	3
1733	54	24	3	2	1	7	7	2	4	2	2
1734	41	17	4	3	0	1	1	5	4	2	4
1735	62	21	7	2	1	6	7	4	4	7	3
1736	46	19	4	0	0	2	5	3	8	2	3
1737	58	24	6	2	0	1	2	6	7	5	5
1738	48	18	5	4	0	2	1	7	5	3	3
1739	42	16	5	3	0	2	0	3	8	3	2
1740	43	13	1	5	0	2	4	5	4	5	4
1741	45	25	3	2	0	0	6	4	5	0	0
1742	41	14	3	4	0	0	4	5	5	1	5
1743	55	23	4	4	0	3	3	9	2	2	5
1744	45	13	6	2	1	3	5	6	4	1	4
1745	51	24	5	1	0	0	7	7	4	1	2
1746	24	6	5	2	1	1	3	2	3	0	1
1747	56	19	9	3	0	1	3	7	7	3	4

Year											
1748	6	1	5	7	7	3	1	6	5	25	66
1749	4	2	7	1	3	2	1	2	9	21	52
1750	5	0	4	4	3	0	0	5	9	12	42
1751	2	2	6	10	5	3	0	8	6	25	67
1752	2	0	3	3	3	3	0	6	6	24	50
1753	7	1	7	5	2	0	1	4	7	16	49
1754	5	0	4	1	1	0	1	6	7	30	55
1755	4	1	5	10	2	1	0	9	4	23	60
1756	9	1	12	11	5	3	1	6	8	14	69
1757	2	3	14	6	15	1	0	11	11	31	95
1758	5	6	10	11	9	2	0	11	9	36	99
1759	5	4	8	15	10	4	0	12	9	48	115
1760	2	7	8	12	3	2	0	9	13	28	84
1761	5	8	6	3	10	4	1	17	8	35	97
1762	5	9	10	9	11	3	2	21	17	39	126
1763	4	6	14	5	6	2	1	21	15	37	111
1764	4	1	9	6	11	2	1	9	13	34	90
1765	4	5	26	5	13	10	3	20	14	44	144
1766	7	8	16	14	13	3	0	22	23	25	131
1767	4	2	14	8	10	3	1	14	10	19	85
1768	4	2	8	6	11	1	0	16	27	28	103
1769	6	2	11	4	6	2	2	19	19	37	108
1770	5	7	6	11	4	2	1	17	11	36	100
1771	7	14	12	14	19	5	5	9	26	19	130
1772	7	4	11	12	4	4	1	16	22	32	113
1773	10	13	11	14	13	1	2	12	17	31	124
1774	9	16	11	11	7	3	1	16	17	36	127
1775	6	28	9	14	8	3	0	22	21	41	152
1776	10	16	12	23	6	1	0	19	21	30	138
Total	293	278	507	422	390	157	45	455	541	1,808	4,896

Table A2.4 Four-year "moving" totals of colonial college graduates

	Graduates	Theology	Medicine	Law	College	School	Commerce	Public service	Other	Unknown	Died young
1642–5	20	13	2	0	0	0	0	0	1	2	2
1643–6	15	10	2	0	0	0	0	0	0	1	2
1644–7	18	11	2	0	0	0	0	0	0	3	2
1645–8	18	11	2	0	0	0	0	0	0	3	2
1646–9	16	9	2	0	2	0	0	0	0	2	1
1647–50	21	11	1	0	3	0	0	1	2	2	1
1648–51	24	10	3	0	3	0	0	1	3	2	2
1649–52	25	11	3	0	3	0	0	1	3	2	2
1650–3	37	17	4	0	1	1	0	1	8	4	1
1651–4	29	13	3	0	0	1	0	0	7	4	1
1652–5	21	10	2	0	0	1	0	0	6	2	0
1653–6	28	16	3	0	0	1	0	0	6	2	0
1654–7	18	12	3	0	0	0	0	0	2	0	1
1655–8	24	17	3	0	0	1	0	1	1	0	1
1656–9	32	21	3	0	0	1	0	1	3	2	1
1657–60	32	16	2	0	0	1	0	2	5	4	2
1658–61	37	15	3	0	0	2	0	2	5	8	2
1659–62	36	12	4	0	0	2	0	1	7	8	2
1660–3	32	9	3	0	0	3	0	1	6	7	3
1661–4	31	11	3	0	0	3	0	0	5	5	4
1662–5	27	12	1	0	0	2	0	1	5	1	5
1663–6	25	12	1	0	0	1	0	1	4	1	5
1664–7	26	14	2	0	0	0	0	1	4	1	4
1665–8	24	13	2	0	0	0	0	1	4	2	2

Year											
1666–9	26	16	3	0	0	1	0	0	3	3	0
1667–70	26	16	2	0	0	1	0	0	3	3	1
1668–71	30	19	1	0	0	1	0	0	4	2	3
1669–72	25	16	1	0	0	1	0	0	3	1	3
1670–3	19	11	0	0	0	0	0	1	3	1	3
1671–4	18	9	1	0	0	0	0	1	3	2	2
1672–5	16	7	2	0	0	1	0	1	2	3	0
1673–6	19	9	2	0	0	1	0	1	3	3	0
1674–7	21	11	2	0	0	1	0	0	4	3	0
1675–8	22	14	1	0	0	1	0	0	3	2	1
1676–9	17	12	0	0	0	0	0	0	2	1	2
1677–80	19	13	1	0	0	0	0	0	1	1	2
1678–81	22	13	2	0	0	0	0	0	1	2	3
1679–82	18	10	2	0	0	0	0	0	1	2	2
1680–3	17	10	2	0	0	0	0	0	1	2	1
1681–4	21	14	1	0	1	0	0	0	2	2	2
1682–5	26	15	0	1	1	1	0	0	6	0	3
1683–6	33	17	1	2	1	1	0	0	8	0	4
1684–7	41	20	2	2	1	1	0	0	9	0	7
1685–8	32	13	2	2	1	1	0	0	8	0	6
1686–9	32	14	3	2	0	0	0	0	6	1	6
1687–90	47	24	2	3	1	0	3	0	4	2	7
1688–91	44	23	1	3	1	0	3	1	3	3	6
1689–92	50	27	1	3	1	0	4	1	4	3	6
1690–3	51	31	1	3	2	1	5	1	1	2	4
1691–4	37	24	1	1	1	1	4	1	1	1	2
1692–5	51	28	4	3	1	1	9	4	1	0	0
1693–6	54	29	5	5	1	1	9	4	0	0	0
1694–7	53	29	4	5	0	1	9	5	0	0	0

Table A2.4 (Cont'd)

	Graduates	Theology	Medicine	Law	College	School	Commerce	Public service	Other	Unknown	Died young
1695–8	59	30	5	5	0	2	9	5	1	1	1
1696–9	49	29	2	3	0	2	4	5	1	1	2
1697–1700	55	32	2	1	0	3	4	5	3	1	4
1698–1701	60	30	2	0	0	4	6	6	4	1	7
1699–1702	60	29	1	1	0	4	6	7	6	0	6
1700–3	63	29	3	1	0	5	6	5	8	1	5
1701–4	54	24	2	1	1	4	6	6	6	1	3
1702–5	50	25	2	3	2	2	3	4	5	1	3
1703–6	46	28	3	2	2	1	2	2	2	1	3
1704–7	53	33	2	3	2	1	4	1	4	0	3
1705–8	63	40	3	3	1	1	5	1	4	0	5
1706–9	66	41	3	1	0	1	7	2	7	1	3
1707–10	73	45	2	2	1	2	7	3	7	1	3
1708–11	66	37	1	1	1	1	9	5	5	1	5
1709–12	69	34	1	2	1	2	9	5	8	3	4
1710–3	58	28	1	2	1	3	8	4	6	2	3
1711–4	62	30	1	1	0	2	8	4	9	2	5
1712–5	68	37	2	1	0	2	6	4	10	2	4
1713–6	60	36	2	0	0	2	4	4	9	0	3
1714–7	74	45	3	0	0	1	7	4	11	0	3
1715–8	86	44	6	4	0	3	7	6	13	1	2
1716–9	92	49	7	5	0	3	7	6	11	2	2
1717–20	112	66	7	7	0	2	7	5	10	3	5
1718–21	141	77	10	9	1	2	8	9	13	4	8

Year											
1719–22	9	6	12	11	13	2	2	7	9	77	148
1720–3	12	7	20	14	16	4	2	8	8	84	175
1721–4	14	9	28	16	20	8	2	7	12	86	202
1722–5	14	10	28	16	22	11	1	6	14	83	205
1723–6	17	9	33	14	23	11	0	5	20	88	220
1724–7	17	10	32	16	25	10	1	5	20	77	213
1725–8	13	13	27	20	25	13	1	8	18	71	209
1726–9	11	14	24	20	22	10	1	9	14	70	195
1727–30	8	15	21	22	21	10	2	13	10	71	193
1728–31	7	13	15	19	17	15	2	15	11	79	193
1729–32	9	13	14	20	19	9	3	12	10	79	188
1730–3	10	12	15	18	22	16	4	12	11	82	202
1731–4	12	11	13	18	17	15	3	10	11	81	191
1732–5	12	17	15	18	21	15	3	8	16	81	206
1733–6	12	13	20	14	20	16	2	7	18	81	203
1734–7	15	16	23	18	15	10	1	7	21	81	207
1735–8	14	17	24	20	15	11	1	8	22	82	214
1736–9	13	13	28	19	8	7	0	9	20	77	194
1737–40	14	16	24	21	7	7	0	14	17	71	191
1738–41	9	11	22	19	11	6	0	14	14	72	178
1739–42	11	9	22	17	14	4	0	14	12	68	171
1740–3	14	8	16	23	17	5	1	15	11	75	184
1741–4	14	4	16	24	18	6	1	12	16	75	186
1742–5	16	5	15	27	19	6	2	11	18	74	192
1743–6	12	4	13	24	18	7	2	9	20	66	175
1744–7	11	5	18	22	18	5	2	8	25	62	176
1745–8	13	5	19	23	20	5	2	12	24	74	197
1746–9	15	6	22	17	16	7	3	13	28	71	198
1747–50	19	6	23	19	16	6	2	16	32	77	216

Table A2.4 (Cont'd)

	Graduates	Theology	Medicine	Law	College	School	Commerce	Public service	Other	Unknown	Died young
1748–51	227	83	29	21	2	8	18	22	22	5	17
1749–52	211	82	30	21	1	8	14	18	20	4	13
1750–3	208	77	28	23	0	6	13	22	20	3	16
1751–4	221	95	26	24	1	6	11	19	20	3	16
1752–5	214	93	24	25	2	4	8	19	19	2	18
1753–6	233	83	26	25	2	4	10	27	28	3	25
1754–7	279	98	30	32	3	5	23	28	35	5	20
1755–8	323	104	32	37	2	7	31	38	41	11	20
1756–9	378	129	37	40	1	10	39	43	44	14	21
1757–60	393	143	42	43	1	9	37	44	40	20	14
1758–61	395	147	39	49	1	12	32	41	32	25	17
1759–62	422	150	47	59	3	13	34	39	32	28	17
1760–3	418	139	53	68	4	11	30	29	38	30	16
1761–4	424	145	53	68	5	11	38	23	39	24	18
1762–5	471	154	59	71	7	17	41	25	59	21	17
1763–6	476	140	65	72	5	17	43	30	65	20	19
1764–7	450	122	60	65	5	18	47	33	65	16	19
1765–8	463	116	74	72	4	17	47	33	64	17	19
1766–9	427	109	79	71	3	9	40	32	49	14	21
1767–70	396	120	67	66	4	8	31	29	39	13	19
1768–71	441	120	83	61	8	10	40	35	37	25	22
1769–72	451	124	78	61	9	13	33	41	40	27	25
1770–3	467	118	76	54	9	12	40	51	40	38	29
1771–4	494	118	82	53	9	13	43	51	45	47	33
1772–5	516	140	77	66	4	11	32	51	42	61	32
1773–6	541	138	76	69	3	8	34	62	43	73	35

Table A2.5 College graduates sorted by vocation (derived from four-year "moving" totals adjusted for those who died young)

	Theology (%)	Medicine (%)	Law (%)	College (%)	School (%)	Commerce (%)	Public service (%)	Other (%)	Unknown (%)	Total (%)
1642–5	72.2	11.1	0.0	0.0	0.0	0.0	0.0	5.6	11.1	100.0
1643–6	76.9	15.4	0.0	0.0	0.0	0.0	0.0	0.0	7.7	100.0
1644–7	68.8	12.5	0.0	0.0	0.0	0.0	0.0	0.0	18.8	100.0
1645–8	68.8	12.5	0.0	0.0	0.0	0.0	0.0	0.0	18.8	100.0
1646–9	60.0	13.3	0.0	13.3	0.0	0.0	0.0	0.0	13.3	100.0
1647–50	55.0	5.0	0.0	15.0	0.0	0.0	5.0	10.0	10.0	100.0
1648–51	45.5	13.6	0.0	13.6	0.0	0.0	4.5	13.6	9.1	100.0
1649–52	47.8	13.0	0.0	13.0	0.0	0.0	4.3	13.0	8.7	100.0
1650–3	47.2	11.1	0.0	2.8	2.8	0.0	2.8	22.2	11.1	100.0
1651–4	46.4	10.7	0.0	0.0	3.6	0.0	0.0	25.0	14.3	100.0
1652–5	47.6	9.5	0.0	0.0	4.8	0.0	0.0	28.6	9.5	100.0
1653–6	57.1	10.7	0.0	0.0	3.6	0.0	0.0	21.4	7.1	100.0
1654–7	70.6	17.6	0.0	0.0	0.0	0.0	0.0	11.8	0.0	100.0
1655–8	73.9	13.0	0.0	0.0	4.3	0.0	4.3	4.3	0.0	100.0
1656–9	67.7	9.7	0.0	0.0	3.2	0.0	3.2	9.7	6.5	100.0
1657–60	53.3	6.7	0.0	0.0	3.3	0.0	6.7	16.7	13.3	100.0
1658–61	42.9	8.6	0.0	0.0	5.7	0.0	5.7	14.3	22.9	100.0
1659–62	35.3	11.8	0.0	0.0	5.9	0.0	2.9	20.6	23.5	100.0
1660–3	31.0	10.3	0.0	0.0	10.3	0.0	3.4	20.7	24.1	100.0
1661–4	40.7	11.1	0.0	0.0	11.1	0.0	0.0	18.5	18.5	100.0
1662–5	54.5	4.5	0.0	0.0	9.1	0.0	4.5	22.7	4.5	100.0
1663–6	60.0	5.0	0.0	0.0	5.0	0.0	5.0	20.0	5.0	100.0
1664–7	63.6	9.1	0.0	0.0	0.0	0.0	4.5	18.2	4.5	100.0

Table A2.5 (Cont'd)

	Theology (%)	Medicine (%)	Law (%)	College (%)	School (%)	Commerce (%)	Public service (%)	Other (%)	Unknown (%)	Total (%)
1665–8	59.1	9.1	0.0	0.0	0.0	0.0	4.5	18.2	9.1	100.0
1666–9	61.5	11.5	0.0	0.0	3.8	0.0	0.0	11.5	11.5	100.0
1667–70	64.0	8.0	0.0	0.0	4.0	0.0	0.0	12.0	12.0	100.0
1668–71	70.4	3.7	0.0	0.0	3.7	0.0	0.0	14.8	7.4	100.0
1669–72	72.7	4.5	0.0	0.0	4.5	0.0	0.0	13.6	4.5	100.0
1670–3	68.8	0.0	0.0	0.0	0.0	0.0	6.3	18.8	6.3	100.0
1671–4	56.3	6.3	0.0	0.0	0.0	0.0	6.3	18.8	12.5	100.0
1672–5	43.8	12.5	0.0	0.0	6.3	0.0	6.3	12.5	18.8	100.0
1673–6	47.4	10.5	0.0	0.0	5.3	0.0	5.3	15.8	15.8	100.0
1674–7	52.4	9.5	0.0	0.0	4.8	0.0	0.0	19.0	14.3	100.0
1675–8	66.7	4.8	0.0	0.0	4.8	0.0	0.0	14.3	9.5	100.0
1676–9	80.0	0.0	0.0	0.0	0.0	0.0	0.0	13.3	6.7	100.0
1677–80	76.5	5.9	0.0	5.9	0.0	0.0	0.0	5.9	5.9	100.0
1678–81	68.4	10.5	0.0	5.3	0.0	0.0	0.0	5.3	10.5	100.0
1679–82	62.5	12.5	0.0	6.3	0.0	0.0	0.0	6.3	12.5	100.0
1680–3	62.5	12.5	0.0	6.3	0.0	0.0	0.0	6.3	12.5	100.0
1681–4	73.7	5.3	0.0	0.0	0.0	0.0	0.0	10.5	10.5	100.0
1682–5	65.2	0.0	4.3	0.0	4.3	0.0	0.0	26.1	0.0	100.0
1683–6	58.6	3.4	6.9	0.0	3.4	0.0	0.0	27.6	0.0	100.0
1684–7	58.8	5.9	5.9	0.0	2.9	0.0	0.0	26.5	0.0	100.0
1685–8	50.0	7.7	7.7	0.0	3.8	0.0	0.0	30.8	0.0	100.0
1686–9	53.8	11.5	7.7	0.0	0.0	0.0	0.0	23.1	3.8	100.0
1687–90	60.0	5.0	7.5	2.5	0.0	7.5	2.5	10.0	5.0	100.0

1688–91	60.5	2.6	7.9	2.6	0.0	7.9	2.6	7.9	7.9	100.0
1689–92	61.4	2.3	6.8	2.3	0.0	9.1	2.3	9.1	6.8	100.0
1690–3	66.0	2.1	6.4	4.3	2.1	10.6	2.1	2.1	4.3	100.0
1691–4	68.6	2.9	2.9	2.9	2.9	11.4	2.9	2.9	2.9	100.0
1692–5	54.9	7.8	5.9	2.0	2.0	17.6	7.8	2.0	0.0	100.0
1693–6	53.7	9.3	9.3	1.9	1.9	16.7	7.4	0.0	0.0	100.0
1694–7	54.7	7.5	9.4	0.0	1.9	17.0	9.4	0.0	0.0	100.0
1695–8	51.7	8.6	8.6	0.0	3.4	15.5	8.6	1.7	1.7	100.0
1696–9	61.7	4.3	6.4	0.0	4.3	8.5	10.6	2.1	2.1	100.0
1697–1700	62.7	3.9	2.0	0.0	5.9	7.8	9.8	5.9	2.0	100.0
1698–1701	56.6	3.8	0.0	0.0	7.5	11.3	11.3	7.5	1.9	100.0
1699–1702	53.7	1.9	1.9	0.0	7.4	11.1	13.0	11.1	0.0	100.0
1700–3	50.0	5.2	1.7	0.0	8.6	10.3	8.6	13.8	1.7	100.0
1701–4	47.1	3.9	2.0	2.0	7.8	11.8	11.8	11.8	2.0	100.0
1702–5	53.2	4.3	6.4	4.3	4.3	6.4	8.5	10.6	2.1	100.0
1703–6	65.1	7.0	4.7	4.7	2.3	4.7	4.7	4.7	2.3	100.0
1704–7	66.0	4.0	6.0	4.0	2.0	8.0	2.0	8.0	0.0	100.0
1705–8	69.0	5.2	5.2	1.7	1.7	8.6	1.7	6.9	0.0	100.0
1706–9	65.6	4.7	1.6	0.0	1.6	10.9	3.1	10.9	1.6	100.0
1707–10	64.3	2.9	2.9	1.4	2.9	10.0	4.3	10.0	1.4	100.0
1708–11	60.7	1.6	1.6	1.6	1.6	14.8	8.2	8.2	1.6	100.0
1709–12	52.3	1.5	3.1	1.5	3.1	13.8	7.7	12.3	4.6	100.0
1710–3	50.9	1.8	3.6	1.8	5.5	14.5	7.3	10.9	3.6	100.0
1711–4	52.6	1.8	1.8	0.0	3.5	14.0	7.0	15.8	3.5	100.0
1712–5	57.8	3.1	1.6	0.0	3.1	9.4	6.3	15.6	3.1	100.0
1713–6	63.2	3.5	0.0	0.0	3.5	7.0	7.0	15.8	0.0	100.0
1714–7	63.4	4.2	0.0	0.0	1.4	9.9	5.6	15.5	0.0	100.0
1715–8	52.4	7.1	4.8	0.0	3.6	8.3	7.1	15.5	1.2	100.0
1716–9	54.4	7.8	5.6	0.0	3.3	7.8	6.7	12.2	2.2	100.0
1717–20	61.7	6.5	6.5	0.0	1.9	6.5	4.7	9.3	2.8	100.0

Table A2.5 (Cont'd)

	Theology (%)	Medicine (%)	Law (%)	College (%)	School (%)	Commerce (%)	Public service (%)	Other (%)	Unknown (%)	Total (%)
1718–21	57.9	7.5	6.8	0.8	1.5	6.0	6.8	9.8	3.0	100.0
1719–22	55.4	6.5	5.0	1.4	1.4	9.4	7.9	8.6	4.3	100.0
1720–3	51.5	4.9	4.9	1.2	2.5	9.8	8.6	12.3	4.3	100.0
1721–4	45.7	6.4	3.7	1.1	4.3	10.6	8.5	14.9	4.8	100.0
1722–5	43.5	7.3	3.1	0.5	5.8	11.5	8.4	14.7	5.2	100.0
1723–6	43.3	9.9	2.5	0.0	5.4	11.3	6.9	16.3	4.4	100.0
1724–7	39.3	10.2	2.6	0.5	5.1	12.8	8.2	16.3	5.1	100.0
1725–8	36.2	9.2	4.1	0.5	6.6	12.8	10.2	13.8	6.6	100.0
1726–9	38.0	7.6	4.9	0.5	5.4	12.0	10.9	13.0	7.6	100.0
1727–30	38.4	5.4	7.0	1.1	5.4	11.4	11.9	11.4	8.1	100.0
1728–31	42.5	5.9	8.1	1.1	8.1	9.1	10.2	8.1	7.0	100.0
1729–32	44.1	5.6	6.7	1.7	5.0	10.6	11.2	7.8	7.3	100.0
1730–3	42.7	5.7	6.3	2.1	8.3	11.5	9.4	7.8	6.3	100.0
1731–4	45.3	6.1	5.6	1.7	8.4	9.5	10.1	7.3	6.1	100.0
1732–5	41.8	8.2	4.1	1.5	7.7	10.8	9.3	7.7	8.8	100.0
1733–6	42.4	9.4	3.7	1.0	8.4	10.5	7.3	10.5	6.8	100.0
1734–7	42.2	10.9	3.6	0.5	5.2	7.8	9.4	12.0	8.3	100.0
1735–8	41.0	11.0	4.0	0.5	5.5	7.5	10.0	12.0	8.5	100.0
1736–9	42.5	11.0	5.0	0.0	3.9	4.4	10.5	15.5	7.2	100.0
1737–40	40.1	9.6	7.9	0.0	4.0	4.0	11.9	13.6	9.0	100.0
1738–41	42.6	8.3	8.3	0.0	3.6	6.5	11.2	13.0	6.5	100.0
1739–42	42.5	7.5	8.8	0.0	2.5	8.8	10.6	13.8	5.6	100.0
1740–3	44.1	6.5	8.8	0.0	2.9	10.0	13.5	9.4	4.7	100.0
1741–4	43.6	9.3	7.0	0.6	3.5	10.5	14.0	9.3	2.3	100.0
1742–5	42.0	10.2	6.3	0.6	3.4	10.8	15.3	8.5	2.8	100.0
1743–6	40.5	12.3	5.5	1.2	4.3	11.0	14.7	8.0	2.5	100.0

1744–7	37.6	15.2	4.8	1.2	3.0	10.9	13.3	10.9	3.0	100.0
1745–8	40.2	13.0	6.5	1.1	2.7	10.9	12.5	10.3	2.7	100.0
1746–9	38.8	15.3	7.1	1.6	3.8	8.7	9.3	12.0	3.3	100.0
1747–50	39.1	16.2	8.1	1.0	3.0	8.1	9.6	11.7	3.0	100.0
1748–51	39.5	13.8	10.0	1.0	3.8	8.6	10.5	10.5	2.4	100.0
1749–52	41.4	15.2	10.6	0.5	4.0	7.1	9.1	10.1	2.0	100.0
1750–3	40.1	14.6	12.0	0.0	3.1	6.8	11.5	10.4	1.6	100.0
1751–4	46.3	12.7	11.7	0.5	2.9	5.4	9.3	9.8	1.5	100.0
1752–5	47.4	12.2	12.8	1.0	2.0	4.1	9.7	9.7	1.0	100.0
1753–6	39.9	12.5	12.0	1.0	1.9	4.8	13.0	13.5	1.4	100.0
1754–7	37.8	11.6	12.4	1.2	1.9	8.9	10.8	13.5	1.9	100.0
1755–8	34.3	10.6	12.2	0.7	2.3	10.2	12.5	13.5	3.6	100.0
1756–9	36.1	10.4	11.2	0.3	2.8	10.9	12.0	12.3	3.9	100.0
1757–60	37.7	11.1	11.3	0.3	2.4	9.8	11.6	10.6	5.3	100.0
1758–61	38.9	10.3	13.0	0.3	3.2	8.5	10.8	8.5	6.6	100.0
1759–62	37.0	11.6	14.6	0.7	3.2	8.4	9.6	7.9	6.9	100.0
1760–3	34.6	13.2	16.9	1.0	2.7	7.5	7.2	9.5	7.5	100.0
1761–4	35.7	13.1	16.7	1.2	2.7	9.4	5.7	9.6	5.9	100.0
1762–5	33.9	13.0	15.6	1.5	3.7	9.0	5.5	13.0	4.6	100.0
1763–6	30.6	14.2	15.8	1.1	3.7	9.4	6.6	14.2	4.4	100.0
1764–7	28.3	13.9	15.1	1.2	4.2	10.9	7.7	15.1	3.7	100.0
1765–8	26.1	16.7	16.2	0.9	3.8	10.6	7.4	14.4	3.8	100.0
1766–9	26.8	19.5	17.5	0.7	2.2	9.9	7.9	12.1	3.4	100.0
1767–70	31.8	17.8	17.5	1.1	2.1	8.2	7.7	10.3	3.4	100.0
1768–71	28.6	19.8	14.6	1.9	2.4	9.5	8.4	8.8	6.0	100.0
1769–72	29.1	18.3	14.3	2.1	3.1	7.7	9.6	9.4	6.3	100.0
1770–3	26.9	17.4	12.3	2.1	2.7	9.1	11.6	9.1	8.7	100.0
1771–4	25.6	17.8	11.5	2.0	2.8	9.3	11.1	9.8	10.2	100.0
1772–5	29.7	16.3	14.0	0.8	2.3	6.8	10.8	8.9	10.4	100.0
1773–6	27.9	15.4	14.0	0.6	1.6	6.9	12.6	8.7	12.3	100.0

Note: In the figures for 1772–5 and 1773–6 the 11 graduates of Queen's College, who are classified under "Unknown" in the class of 1775 and whose graduation and vocation are both indeterminate, are discounted as if they had "Died young".

Table A2.6   Graduates of Harvard College sorted by vocation

	Graduates	Theology	Medicine	Law	College	School	Commerce	Public service	Other	Unknown	Died young
1642	9	5	2	0	0	0	0	0	1	1	0
1643	4	4	0	0	0	0	0	0	0	0	0
1644	0	0	0	0	0	0	0	0	0	0	0
1645	7	4	0	0	0	0	0	0	0	1	2
1646	4	2	2	0	0	0	0	0	0	0	0
1647	7	5	0	0	0	0	0	0	0	2	0
1648	0	0	0	0	0	0	0	0	0	0	0
1649	5	2	0	0	2	0	0	0	0	0	1
1650	9	4	1	0	1	0	0	1	2	0	0
1651	10	4	2	0	0	0	0	0	1	2	1
1652	1	1	0	0	0	0	0	0	0	0	0
1653	17	8	1	0	0	1	0	0	5	2	0
1654	1	0	1	0	0	0	0	0	1	0	0
1655	2	1	1	0	0	0	0	0	0	0	0
1656	8	7	1	0	0	0	0	0	0	0	0
1657	7	4	1	0	0	0	0	0	1	0	1
1658	7	5	0	0	0	1	0	1	0	0	0
1659	10	5	1	0	0	0	0	0	2	2	0
1660	8	2	0	0	0	0	0	1	2	2	1
1661	12	3	2	0	0	1	0	0	1	4	1
1662	6	2	1	0	0	1	0	0	2	0	0
1663	6	2	0	0	0	1	0	0	1	1	1
1664	7	4	0	0	0	0	0	0	1	1	0
1665	8	4	0	0	0	0	0	1	1	0	2
1666	4	2	1	0	0	0	0	0	1	0	2
1667	7	4	1	0	0	0	0	0	1	1	0
1668	5	3	0	0	0	0	0	0	1	1	0

Year										
1669	10	7	1	0	1	0	0	0	1	0
1670	4	2	0	0	0	0	0	1	0	1
1671	11	7	0	0	0	0	0	2	0	2
1672	0	0	0	0	0	1	1	0	0	0
1673	4	2	0	0	0	0	0	0	1	0
1674	3	0	1	0	0	0	0	1	1	0
1675	9	5	1	0	1	0	0	1	1	0
1676	3	2	0	0	0	0	0	1	0	0
1677	6	4	0	0	0	0	0	1	1	0
1678	4	3	0	0	0	0	0	0	0	1
1679	4	3	0	1	0	0	0	0	1	1
1680	5	3	1	1	0	0	0	0	0	0
1681	9	4	1	0	0	0	0	1	0	1
1682	0	0	0	0	0	0	0	0	0	0
1683	3	3	0	0	0	0	1	0	2	1
1684	9	7	0	0	0	0	1	0	0	0
1685	14	5	1	0	1	0	0	1	0	0
1686	7	2	1	0	0	0	0	5	0	1
1687	11	6	0	0	0	0	0	2	0	2
1688	0	0	1	3	0	0	1	1	0	1
1689	14	6	0	0	0	0	0	0	0	3
1690	22	12	0	1	0	0	2	3	1	0
1691	8	5	0	1	0	1	0	0	1	2
1692	6	4	1	2	1	3	0	0	1	2
1693	15	10	0	5	0	0	1	1	0	2
1694	8	5	3	1	0	1	2	0	0	0
1695	22	9	1	1	0	1	5	0	0	0
1696	9	5	0	2	1	3	1	0	0	0
1697	14	10	1	0	1	0	1	0	0	0
1698	14	6	0	1	0	0	2	0	0	1
1699	12	8	1	0	1	0	0	1	1	1
1700	15	8	0	0	0	0	1	0	0	2

Table A2.6 (Cont'd)

	Graduates	Theology	Medicine	Law	College	School	Commerce	Public service	Other	Unknown	Died young
1701	19	8	0	0	0	2	3	2	1	0	3
1702	13	4	0	1	0	1	2	2	3	0	0
1703	14	7	2	0	0	1	0	1	2	1	0
1704	3	1	0	0	1	0	1	0	0	0	0
1705	10	5	0	1	1	0	0	0	0	0	3
1706	7	5	1	0	0	0	1	0	0	0	0
1707	17	11	1	1	0	1	1	0	2	0	0
1708	13	8	1	0	0	0	1	1	0	0	2
1709	10	6	0	0	1	0	2	0	0	0	1
1710	14	9	0	1	0	0	1	1	0	1	0
1711	12	4	0	0	0	1	2	1	2	0	2
1712	17	6	1	1	0	0	2	2	2	0	1
1713	5	2	0	0	0	1	1	1	1	2	0
1714	11	7	0	0	0	0	0	0	2	0	1
1715	18	9	1	0	0	0	2	1	3	0	1
1716	8	3	1	0	0	1	0	2	2	0	0
1717	17	9	1	0	0	0	4	1	3	0	0
1718	19	5	2	3	0	2	1	0	2	0	1
1719	23	15	2	0	0	0	2	3	0	1	1
1720	21	17	1	1	0	0	0	2	0	0	2
1721	37	19	3	1	1	2	5	0	3	1	2
1722	31	9	1	2	0	0	6	2	3	0	2
1723	43	19	1	1	1	2	5	5	8	1	2
1724	40	16	4	0	0	4	3	5	6	0	5
1725	45	18	6	1	0	3	5	2	5	1	3
1726	31	8	5	0	0	2	4	3	7	0	3
1727	37	7	0	1	1	1	7	6	8	2	4

Year											
1728	42	15	2	3	0	7	4	5	2	3	1
1729	23	13	2	0	0	0	4	3	1	0	0
1730	34	11	3	3	1	1	4	4	5	0	2
1731	34	14	0	3	1	5	2	4	2	0	3
1732	26	10	1	0	1	1	2	5	2	3	1
1733	38	17	1	2	0	7	5	1	3	0	2
1734	27	9	3	1	0	1	1	5	3	0	4
1735	38	12	4	2	0	5	6	2	3	2	2
1736	27	11	2	0	0	2	2	3	5	0	2
1737	34	16	5	2	0	1	0	1	4	1	4
1738	33	12	3	3	0	1	1	5	3	2	3
1739	32	10	5	2	0	2	0	3	8	1	1
1740	22	6	0	1	0	2	3	4	2	1	3
1741	25	12	2	0	0	0	5	1	5	0	0
1742	24	5	2	0	0	0	3	5	4	0	5
1743	31	11	4	4	0	2	1	5	1	0	3
1744	30	9	4	0	0	3	5	4	2	0	3
1745	24	7	1	0	0	0	6	5	3	1	1
1746	12	2	4	1	0	1	1	0	2	0	1
1747	28	6	5	2	1	1	3	6	3	1	1
1748	24	7	3	2	0	2	4	2	2	0	2
1749	22	5	3	1	0	1	3	0	5	0	3
1750	19	7	2	1	0	0	2	2	3	0	2
1751	35	10	3	6	0	3	2	8	2	0	1
1752	30	15	4	2	1	2	3	1	1	0	2
1753	17	6	2	0	1	0	1	4	1	0	3
1754	20	9	4	1	0	0	0	1	1	0	3
1755	25	7	0	4	0	1	1	7	2	0	2
1756	25	3	4	1	0	2	3	4	6	0	2
1757	25	5	3	5	0	1	4	2	4	0	1
1758	31	14	3	1	0	2	4	3	2	0	2
1759	35	15	3	3	0	2	3	6	0	0	3

Table A2.6 (Cont'd)

	Graduates	Theology	Medicine	Law	College	School	Commerce	Public service	Other	Unknown	Died young
1760	26	8	3	4	0	2	1	2	4	1	1
1761	38	15	4	3	1	2	6	1	4	1	1
1762	47	16	6	9	1	0	5	3	6	0	1
1763	39	10	6	9	1	2	3	4	3	0	1
1764	46	16	7	5	0	2	6	3	6	0	1
1765	54	12	3	7	1	7	10	3	10	0	1
1766	40	4	11	5	0	1	8	7	4	0	1
1767	42	9	6	6	0	3	6	3	4	0	0
1768	42	11	10	7	0	1	6	3	6	0	3
1769	39	13	5	8	0	2	4	4	1	0	2
1770	34	12	5	7	0	1	2	3	4	0	0
1771	63	8	13	4	1	3	10	2	4	0	1
1772	48	7	14	5	0	3	3	9	8	4	3
1773	36	2	5	4	1	3	3	6	6	0	4
1774	48	9	6	6	0	1	6	7	5	2	3
1775	40	6	8	9	0	2	3	5	6	5	6
1776	43	4	10	7	0	1	3	4	3	3	3
							1	8	5	2	5
Total	2,598	950	275	187	24	128	249	244	290	73	178

Sources: Data concerning classes 1642–1771 are from *Harvard Graduates* and *Quinquennial Catalogue of the Officers and Graduates, 1636–1925* (Cambridge, MA, 1925). Concerning the classes 1772–6, I am grateful to Helen Kessler, Edward Hanson, and Conrad E. Wright of the Massachusetts Historical Society for allowing me to examine the Society's files on the members of these classes, which will be included in the next volume of *Harvard Graduates.*[52]

52. Schneider states that he relied on an anonymous source entitled "Brief Manuscript Biographies, 1642–1775" in the Alumni Records of the Harvard University Archives. However, neither the librarians of the archives nor Helen Kessler, who has spent years doing research in the archives, knows of this source. Schneider, "Education in Colonial American Colleges," p. 224.

Table A2.7 Graduates of Yale College sorted by vocation

	Graduates	Theology	Medicine	Law	College	School	Commerce	Public service	Other	Unknown	Died young
1702	1	1	0	0	0	0	0	0	0	0	0
1703	1	1	0	0	0	0	0	0	0	0	0
1704	3	2	0	0	0	0	0	1	0	0	0
1705	5	4	0	1	0	0	0	0	0	0	0
1706	3	3	0	0	0	0	0	0	0	0	0
1707	5	2	0	0	0	0	1	0	2	0	0
1708	3	2	0	0	0	0	1	0	0	0	0
1709	9	5	0	0	0	0	0	1	3	0	0
1710	2	2	0	0	0	0	0	0	0	0	0
1711	3	1	0	0	0	0	0	0	0	0	0
1712	2	1	0	0	0	0	2	0	1	0	0
1713	3	3	0	0	0	0	0	0	0	0	0
1714	9	6	0	0	0	0	1	0	1	0	1
1715	3	3	0	0	0	0	0	0	0	0	0
1716	3	3	0	0	0	0	0	0	0	0	0
1717	5	5	0	0	0	0	0	0	0	0	0
1718	13	7	1	1	0	0	0	0	3	0	0
1719	4	2	0	1	0	0	0	0	1	1	0
1720	10	6	0	1	0	0	0	0	1	0	1
1721	14	6	1	1	0	0	0	2	3	1	1
1722	8	3	1	0	0	0	0	0	1	3	1
1723	11	5	0	1	0	1	1	0	1	1	2
1724	18	9	1	1	0	0	1	0	3	3	0
1725	9	4	0	0	0	0	2	1	1	1	0

Table A2.7 (Cont'd)

	Graduates	Theology	Medicine	Law	College	School	Commerce	Public service	Other	Unknown	Died young
1726	23	9	3	1	0	0	3	1	2	2	2
1727	10	6	1	1	0	0	0	1	0	1	0
1728	12	4	1	1	0	0	0	1	2	3	0
1729	17	8	0	2	0	0	0	1	2	3	1
1730	18	7	1	2	0	1	2	1	1	3	0
1731	13	7	2	1	0	1	1	0	0	1	0
1732	23	9	1	1	0	0	4	2	1	3	2
1733	16	7	2	0	1	0	2	1	1	2	0
1734	14	8	1	2	0	0	0	0	1	2	0
1735	24	9	3	0	1	1	1	2	1	5	1
1736	19	8	2	0	0	0	3	0	3	2	1
1737	24	8	1	0	0	0	2	5	3	4	1
1738	15	6	2	1	0	1	0	2	2	1	0
1739	10	6	0	1	0	0	0	0	0	2	1
1740	21	7	1	4	0	0	1	1	2	4	1
1741	20	13	1	2	0	0	0	3	0	0	0
1742	17	9	1	4	0	0	1	0	1	1	0
1743	24	12	0	0	0	1	2	4	1	2	2
1744	15	4	2	2	1	0	0	2	2	1	1
1745	27	17	4	1	0	0	1	2	1	0	1
1746	12	4	1	1	1	0	2	2	1	0	0
1747	28	13	4	1	0	0	2	2	4	2	0
1748	36	13	2	3	1	1	0	1	3	1	3
1749	23	11	5	1	0	1	3	5	2	1	4
1750	17	2	6	2	0	0	1	1	1	0	1
1751	22	8	1	2	0	0	3	2	4	2	0

Year											
1752	14	5	2	2	0	1	0	2	2	0	0
1753	17	4	4	1	0	0	0	0	4	1	3
1754	16	7	2	2	0	0	1	0	2	0	2
1755	23	10	3	5	0	0	1	1	2	0	1
1756	33	8	3	2	0	1	2	7	5	1	4
1757	40	12	4	4	0	0	6	3	9	1	1
1758	43	15	3	5	0	0	2	6	6	5	1
1759	49	20	4	4	0	0	6	6	8	0	1
1760	33	12	6	4	0	0	1	3	4	2	1
1761	29	12	1	7	0	1	2	1	2	2	1
1762	43	14	7	7	0	1	4	2	3	2	3
1763	42	11	6	8	0	0	2	0	10	2	3
1764	28	10	5	1	1	0	4	2	3	1	1
1765	47	19	5	5	0	0	3	1	13	0	1
1766	37	4	7	5	0	1	3	2	11	0	4
1767	24	7	4	2	0	0	3	1	6	0	1
1768	29	10	4	3	0	0	5	0	5	0	2
1769	26	12	2	2	1	0	0	0	6	0	3
1770	19	8	1	3	0	0	1	5	1	0	0
1771	19	4	3	1	0	1	6	4	0	0	0
1772	23	8	2	6	0	0	0	2	3	0	2
1773	36	10	2	5	0	0	4	2	6	3	4
1774	30	10	5	2	0	0	4	1	4	2	2
1775	35	12	4	4	0	1	4	5	5	0	0
1776	32	9	4	5	0	0	3	4	2	0	5
Total	1,414	554	145	138	7	15	108	107	184	80	76

Note: William Phelps, who received an MA but is not known to have graduated with a BA, is not included in the class of 1776. *Yale Graduates,* vol. 3, p. 630.

Sources: Yale Graduates; George W. Pierson, *A Yale Book of Numbers: Historical Statistics of the College and University, 1701–1976* (New Haven, CT, 1983), pp. 18–9.

Table A2.8 Graduates of the College of New Jersey sorted by vocation

	Graduates	Theology	Medicine	Law	College	School	Commerce	Public service	Other	Unknown	Died young
1748	6	5	0	1	0	0	0	0	0	0	0
1749	7	5	1	0	0	0	0	0	0	1	0
1750	6	3	1	2	0	0	0	0	0	0	0
1751	10	7	2	0	0	0	0	0	0	0	1
1752	6	4	0	2	0	0	0	0	0	0	0
1753	15	6	1	3	0	0	1	1	2	0	1
1754	19	14	1	3	0	0	0	0	1	0	0
1755	12	6	1	0	0	0	0	2	1	1	1
1756	11	3	1	3	0	0	0	0	1	0	3
1757	24	11	3	1	0	0	5	1	1	2	0
1758	18	5	3	3	0	0	3	0	2	0	2
1759	18	8	2	1	0	2	1	2	0	2	0
1760	11	6	2	0	0	0	1	2	0	0	0

1761	14	6	2	2	0	1	1	1	0	0	1
1762	21	6	4	3	1	1	2	1	1	1	1
1763	19	12	2	2	0	0	1	0	1	1	0
1764	14	8	1	1	0	0	1	1	0	0	2
1765	31	10	5	6	0	3	0	1	3	0	2
1766	31	10	4	9	0	1	2	1	1	1	2
1767	11	3	0	2	0	0	0	2	2	2	0
1768	11	5	3	2	1	0	0	0	1	0	0
1769	18	6	1	6	1	0	1	1	1	0	1
1770	22	11	1	5	1	1	1	0	1	0	3
1771	12	2	1	2	0	0	1	1	1	0	0
1772	22	14	1	4	0	1	1	0	2	1	2
1773	29	14	5	2	0	0	3	2	0	2	0
1774	20	8	1	5	0	0	0	3	1	2	1
1775	27	10	5	4	0	0	1	3	1	2	2
1776	27	8	5	5	0	0	1	2	2	4	0
Total	**492**	**216**	**59**	**79**	**3**	**10**	**27**	**27**	**26**	**21**	**24**

Source: Princetonians.

Table A2.9 Graduates of the College of Philadelphia sorted by vocation

	Graduates	Theology	Medicine	Law	College	School	Commerce	Public service	Other	Unknown	Died young
1757	6	3	1	1	1	0	0	0	0	0	0
1758	0	0	0	0	0	0	0	0	0	0	0
1759	11	3	0	4	0	0	0	1	0	2	1
1760	8	1	2	1	0	0	0	2	0	2	0
1761	13	1	1	4	0	0	1	0	0	4	2
1762	6	1	0	1	0	0	0	1	0	3	0
1763	9	4	1	2	0	0	0	0	0	2	0
1764	0	0	0	0	0	0	0	0	0	0	0
1765	7	2	1	0	2	0	0	0	0	2	0
1766	12	6	1	3	0	0	0	0	0	2	0
1767	6	0	0	3	1	0	0	1	0	0	0
1768	15	1	9	3	0	0	1	1	0	1	0
1769	14	3	8	1	0	0	0	0	0	1	0
1770	15	3	4	1	0	0	1	0	0	5	2
1771	18	1	6	0	3	0	1	0	2	5	0
1772	2	0	0	1	0	0	0	0	0	1	0
1773	6	0	1	1	0	0	0	0	0	4	0
1774	1	0	0	0	0	0	0	0	0	0	0
1775	8	0	1	4	0	0	0	0	0	3	0
1776	7	1	1	1	0	0	0	2	0	2	0
Total	164	30	38	31	7	0	4	8	2	39	5

Note: This table includes recipients of the Bachelor of Medicine degree (10 in 1768, 8 in 1769, 1 in 1770, 7 in 1771, 1 in 1773, and 1 in 1774), except for individuals who had previously earned a BA degree (four from New Jersey and one from Philadelphia.)

Sources: [Persifor Frazier et al.], *University of Pennsylvania Biographical Catalogue of the Matriculates of the College ... of Philadelphia ... 1749–1857* (New York, 1894), pp. 1–20; W. J. Maxwell, *General Alumni Catalogue of the University of Pennsylvania* (Philadelphia, 1917, 1921).

Table A2.10   Graduates of King's College sorted by vocation

	Graduates	Theology	Medicine	Law	College	School	Commerce	Public service	Other	Unknown	Died young
1758	7	2	0	2	0	0	0	2	0	1	0
1759	2	2	0	0	0	0	0	0	0	0	0
1760	6	1	0	0	0	0	0	3	0	2	0
1761	3	1	0	1	0	0	0	0	0	1	0
1762	9	2	0	1	0	1	0	2	0	3	0
1763	2	0	0	0	0	0	0	1	0	1	0
1764	2	0	0	2	0	0	0	0	0	0	0
1765	5	1	0	2	0	0	0	0	0	2	1
1766	11	1	0	1	0	0	0	4	0	5	0
1767	2	0	0	1	0	0	0	1	0	0	0
1768	6	1	1	1	0	0	0	1	1	1	1
1769	4	0	2	0	0	0	0	0	0	1	1
1770	6	1	0	0	0	0	0	3	0	1	1
1771	8	0	3	0	0	1	0	0	0	4	0
1772	10	0	4	0	1	0	0	3	0	2	0
1773	6	1	1	0	0	0	0	2	0	1	1
1774	13	1	2	1	0	0	0	2	0	6	1
1775	7	0	1	0	0	0	0	1	0	5	0
1776	7	0	0	0	0	0	0	1	0	6	0
Total	116	14	14	11	1	2	0	26	1	42	5

Note: A medical school was founded at King's College in 1767, and 12 Bachelor of Medicine degrees were awarded between 1769 and 1776. Recipients of these degrees have been incorporated into this table, except for two who were previously awarded BA degrees, one from Yale and one from King's. In the class of 1762, Richard S. Clarke is not counted because he attended Yale and received the BA belatedly. William C. George is included in the class of 1762 because, although Thomas (p. 98) attributes a Yale BA to him, *Yale Graduates* does not corroborate it.

Sources: Catalogue of the Governors, Trustees, and Officers and of the Alumni and other Graduates of Columbia College (Originally King's College) ... from 1754 to 1882 (New York, 1882); *Catalogue of the Officers and Graduates of Columbia University ... from 1754* (New York, 1894, 1906, 1912); Milton H. Thomas, *Columbia University, Officers and Alumni, 1754–1857* (New York, 1936).

Table A2.11   Graduates of the College of Rhode Island sorted by vocation

	Graduates	Theology	Medicine	Law	College	School	Commerce	Public service	Other	Unknown	Died young
1769	7	3	1	2	0	0	0	0	0	0	1
1770	4	1	0	1	0	0	0	1	0	1	0
1771	6	2	0	1	0	0	1	0	0	1	1
1772	6	2	1	0	0	0	0	0	1	1	1
1773	5	1	3	0	0	0	0	0	0	1	0
1774	6	1	2	2	0	0	0	0	0	1	0
1775	10	4	1	0	0	1	0	0	0	2	2
1776	9	5	1	0	0	0	0	1	1	1	0
Total	53	19	9	6	0	1	1	2	2	8	5

Sources: Mary D. Vaughan, comp., *Historical Catalogue of Brown University, 1764–1904* (Providence, RI, 1905); [Louise P. Bates, ed.], *Historical Catalogue of Brown University, 1764–1914* (Providence, RI, 1914); Louise Bauer and William T. Hastings, comps., *The Historical Catalogue of Brown University, 1764–1934* (Providence, RI, 1936).

Table A2.12 Graduates of Dartmouth College sorted by vocation

	Graduates	Theology	Medicine	Law	College	School	Commerce	Public service	Other	Unknown	Died young
1771	4	2	0	1	1	0	0	0	0	0	0
1772	2	1	0	0	0	0	0	1	0	0	0
1773	6	3	0	0	1	0	0	1	0	1	0
1774	8	6	0	0	1	1	0	0	0	0	0
1775	11	8	0	1	0	0	0	1	0	1	0
1776	12	3	0	1	0	0	1	4	2	1	0
Total	43	23	0	3	3	1	1	7	2	3	0

Sources: George T. Chapman, Sketches of the Alumni of Dartmouth College (Cambridge, MA, 1867), pp. 13–8; General Catalogue of Dartmouth College and the Associated Schools, 1769– (Hanover, NH, 1880, 1910, 1940).

Table A2.13 Graduates of Queen's College sorted by vocation

	Graduates	Theology	Medicine	Law	College	School	Commerce	Public service	Other	Unknown	Died young
1774	1	1	0	0	0	0	0	0	0	0	0
1775	14	1	1	0	0	0	0	0	0	12	0
1776	1	0	0	0	0	0	0	1	0	0	0
Total	16	2	1	0	0	0	0	1	0	12	0

Note: Queen's College was chartered in 1766, and instruction began in 1771. Unfortunately, the numbers of graduates in the years before 1781 are unknown because the earliest minute book of the trustees has been lost. It is known that the first graduating class had one student, who became a minister, and that the diploma of Simeon DeWitt was dated in 1776, and he entered public service. Concerning the rest, the historical catalogues merely list 16 "alumni and students" during the years 1774, 1775, and 1776. Demarest states only that there were five or six students in each of the junior and senior classes after the first graduation in 1774, and never makes a claim about how many were graduated. Eells states that 13 students were graduated by 1775, but offers no evidence for this assertion.[53] It does seem reasonable that all these students may have received their degrees in 1775 and 1776 because the college was not occupied until November of 1776 when George Washington led his retreating army through Brunswick. Nevertheless, the 11 "graduates" classified under "Unknown," whose graduation is, in fact, indeterminate, have been discounted in Table 19 as if they had "Died young".

Sources: William H. S. Demarest, *A History of Rutgers College, 1766–1924* (New Brunswick, NJ, 1924), chs. 4, 5; *General Catalogue of Officers and Alumni of Rutgers College, 1766–1916* (New Brunswick, NJ, 1916); [Rutgers University], *Alumni and Students of the Colleges for Men, 1774–1932* (New Brunswick, NJ, 1929).

53. Eells, *Baccalaureate Degrees*, p. 22.

Table A2.14   Individuals believed to have attended the College of William and
Mary for at least three years prior to 1777

1731   John Fox
1735   Thomas Walker
1752   Alexander Champion, Mordecai Cooke, Benjamin Edwards, Francis Fontaine,
        John Ford, Alexander Graeme, John Graeme, Peyton Skipworth, William
        Skipworth
1754   George Plater
1755   Robert Booth Armistead
1756   Lawrence Battaile, Carter Braxton, George Braxton, Daniel Sweeney, Robert
        Wallace
1757   James Armistead, Wilson Miles Cary, Augustine Cooke, John Esten, John Fox,
        Randolph Holt, Charles Mynn Thruston
1758   Mathew [sic] Holt
1760   William Ballard, Peter Bland, John Grymes, Philip Ludwell Grymes, Rodham
        Kenner, Waller Lewis, Daniel McCarty, Philip Smith
1761   Jacquelin Ambler, John Mathews, John Nelson
1762   Hudson Allen, Benjamin Grymes, Charles Grymes, Benjamin Harrison,
        Nathaniel Harrison, John Hubard, William Hubard, James Johnson, Edward
        Hack Moseley, Burgess Smith, John Tazewell
1763   Edward Bland, William Bland, Arthur Emerson, James Emerson, Walter Jones,
        James McClurg, Thomas Massie, John Page, Henry Robinson, John Thompson
1764   Edward Bolling, Beverly Dixon, William Moulston, Edmund Pendleton, John
        Robinson, John Thruston
1765   Bowles Armistead, Archibald Bolling, Nathaniel Burwell, Cole Diggs, John
        Tyler
1766   Austin Moore
1767   Starkey Armistead, John Smith, Charles Tomkies
1768   David Copland, William Marshall, Mann Page, Jr. (son of Mann Page of Rose-
        well), Mann Page, Sr. (son of Hon. J. Page), Thomas Read (Reed?), Benjamin
        Robinson, Edward Champion Travis, Abner Waugh
1769   Walter King Cole, Bernard Moore, Edward Smith
1770   William Leigh, Hugh Nelson, Edward Power
1771   John Byrd, William Byrd Page
1772   Nathaniel Burwell, Thomas Davis, Augustine Tabb
1773   William Dixon, Thomas Hughes, Henry Montfort, Samuel Shield(s?), William
        Shelden Sclater, David Stuart, Christopher Todd
1774   Carter Burwell, John Clayton, John Nelson, Robert Nelson, Thomas Nelson,
        Peyton Randolph
1775   William Boush, Jonathan Calvert, Cole Diggs, Thomas Dixon, John Eustace,
        Walker Maury, Nathaniel Nelson, William Nelson (son of Hon. William Nelson),
        William Nelson (son of Thomas Nelson, Jr.), Thomas Tarpley, William Tarpley,
        John Watson, John Camm White, William Yates
1776   Nathaniel Burwell, George Carter, John Hill Carter, Michael Christian, Joseph
        Eggleston, Daniel Fitzhugh, Theodore Fitzhugh, John Lewis, Carter Page,
        Robert Randolph, Armistead Smith, Thomas Smith, William Steptoe

Note: Dozens of students attended the College of William and Mary during the colonial period. Most of these left without taking a degree, and various dates have been proposed for the granting of the first degree. The College faculty published a catalogue in 1870, which identifies the date of the earliest degree to be 1793, while the second catalogue, published in 1874, indicates the data to be 1783.[54] In 1957 Walter C. Eells made an extensive investigation into the secondary literature and concluded that four degrees were granted before 1776, the first in 1753. However, James A. Servies, the reference librarian of the College in the 1950s informed Eells that the remaining College archives indicate that the earliest BA was awarded in 1772 and pointed out that sources such as the *Dictionary of American Biography*, on which Eells relied, are unreliable in regard to graduates from William and Mary.[55] Meanwhile, in 1941 the College published *A Provisional List of Alumi* ..., which warned against relying on the catalogues of 1870 or 1874.[56]

Staff members of the University Archives, College of William and Mary, assert that a revised list was never prepared, that this provisional list remains the most reliable concerning years of attendance, and that there is no better information concerning degrees. Schneider treated the 1941 list as a list of "graduates" from which he took a random sample, but the 1941 *Provisional List* clearly states: "The term 'alumnus' as used in this list, means any student who attended college even for a year or part of a year."[57] Working from the printed sources referenced here, I have compiled the following list of students who can be said, at least provisionally, to have attended William and Mary for *at least three years* and completed their enrollment prior to 1777. Given the lack and uncertainty of information about most of these individuals and the tentative nature of the list, I have not included this information in the enumeration of college graduates by vocation. The year indicated is the final year of attendance at the College.

54. *The History of the College of William and Mary (including the General Catalogue) from ... 1693, to 1870* (Baltimore, MD, 1870); *The History of the College of William and Mary (including the General Catalogue) from ... 1660, to 1874* (Richmond, VA, 1874), p. 98.

55. Eells, *Baccalaureate Degrees*, pp. 22, 54–5. Servies later produced the bulletin, "Vital Facts: A William and Mary Chronology, 1693–1963," *College of William and Mary Library Contributions*, no. 3, which gave no further insight into this question.

56. *A Provisional List of Alumni, Grammar School Students, Members of the Faculty, and Members of the Board of Visitors of the College of William and Mary in Virginia from 1693 to 1888* (Richmond, VA, 1941), p. 3.

57. Schneider, "Education in Colonial American Colleges," p. 195n.; *A Provisional List*, p. 3. William and Mary archivist Laura F. Parrish has written to me: "The first B.A. degrees of which we have records in the College of William and Mary Archives were awarded in 1772 to James Madison (not the US President, but his cousin the Episcopal Bishop), Nathaniel Burwell, and Thomas Davis. These recipients are listed in the faculty minutes. The next degree of which I am aware is the 1783 BA of Ludwell Lee. John Clopton may have received a degree, but our only mention of it is in the same University of Pennsylvania catalog which you have seen." (Letter of September 10, 1987.) John Clopton, who received an AB from the College of Philadelphia in 1776, is reported to have received an AB from William and Mary in 1773. Frazier, *University of Pennsylvania Biographical Catalogue*, p. 20; Maxwell, *General Alumni Catalogue* (1917), p. 20; Maxwell, *General Alumni Catalogue* (1922), p. 9.

APPENDIX 3

The following is a list of the some fifty-four first editions of dictionaries and lexicons published in the United States before 1861. The list is adapted from Eva Mae Burkett, *American Dictionaries of the English Language before 1861* (1936; Metuchen, NJ, 1979). The dictionaries consulted for generalizations in the text are indicated by an asterisk (*).

[1798]* Samuel Johnson, Jr., *A School Dictionary* (New Haven)

1800* John Elliott and Samuel Johnson, Jr., *A Selected, Pronouncing, and Accented Dictionary ... The whole made Easy and Familiar to Children and Youth and Designed for the Use of Schools in America* (Hartford)

1800* Caleb Alexander, *The Columbian Dictionary of the English Language in which many new words, peculiar to the United States are inserted* (Boston)

1801* William Woodbridge, *A Key to the English Language* (Middletown, CT)

1801* Henry Priest, *The Young Ladies' Pocket Companion, Being a Short Dictionary* (New York)

1804* Daniel Jaudon, Thomas Watson, and Stephen Addington, *The English Orthographical Expositor* (Philadelphia)

1806* Abel Flint, *A Spelling, Pronouncing, and Parsing Dictionary* (Hartford)

1806* Noah Webster, *A Compendious Dictionary of the English Language* (Hartford)

1807* Susanna Rowson, *A Spelling Dictionary ... Selected from Johnson's Dictionary* (Boston)

1807* Noah Webster, *A Dictionary of the English Language; Compiled for Use of the Common Schools in the United States* (New Haven)

1811* Richard Wiggins, *The New York Expositor* (New York)

1813* Richard S. Coxe, *A New Critical Pronouncing Dictionary of the English Language* (Burlington, NJ)

1815* Burgess Allison, *The American Standard of Orthography and Pronounciation and Improved Dictionary* (Burlington, NJ)

1816*	John Pickering, *A Vocabulary, or Collection of Words and Phrases ... Peculiar to the United States* (Boston)
1821*	William Grimshaw, *An Etymological Dictionary or Analysis of the English Language* (Philadelphia)
1822	Jedidiah Kingsbury, *A New Improved Dictionary for Children* (Boston)
1826*	Hezekiah Burhans, *The Nomenclature and Expositor of the English Language* (Philadelphia)
1828*	Lyman Cobb, *Abridgement J. Walker's Critical Pronouncing Dictionary and Expositor of the English Language* (New York)
1828*	Eliza Robbins, *Primary Dictionary ... consisting of nearly Four Thousand Words Adapted to the Comprehension of Children* (New York)
1828*	Noah Webster, *An American Dictionary of the English Language*, 2 vols. (New Haven)
1828*	Joseph E. Worcester, *Johnson's Dictionary, as improved by Todd, and abridged by Chalmers, with Walker's Pronouncing Dictionary Combined* (Boston)
1829*	Noah Webster, *A Dictionary of the English Language, abridged from the American Dictionary for Primary Schools and the Counting House* (New Haven)
1829*	Edward Hazen, *The Speller and Definer ... to Supersede the Necessity of the Use of a Dictionary as a Class-Book* (New York)
1829	William W. Turner, *The School Dictionary* (Hartford)
1829*	William Grimshaw, *The Gentleman's Lexicon or Pocket Dictionary* (Philadelphia) also published under the title *The Ladies' Lexicon, and Parlour Companion* (Philadelphia) and *The Handy Dictionary* (Philadelphia)
1830*	Joseph E. Worcester, *A Comprehensive, Pronouncing and Explanatory Dictionary of the English Language* (Boston)
1831*	Noah J. T. George, *The Gentlemen and Ladies' Pocket Dictionary* (Concord)
1832*	D. J. Browne, *The Etymological Encyclopedia of Technical Words and Phrases* (Boston)
1832*	Lyman Cobb, *A New Dictionary of the English Language* (New York)
1833*	Lyman Cobb, *Expositor or Sequel to the Spelling Book* (New York)
1834	Lyman Cobb, *The Ladies' Reticule Companion, or Little Lexicon of the English Language* (New York)
1835*	Joseph E. Worcester, *Elementary Dictionary* (Boston)
1836*	Rufus Claggett, *The American Expositor, or Intellectual Definer* (Boston, Philadelphia, Providence)
1841*	T. H. Gallaudet and Horace Hooker, *The School and Family Dictionary and Illustrative Definer* (New York)
1841*	Noah Webster, *An American Dictionary of the English Language [revised], First Edition in Octavo* (New Haven)
1846*	Joseph E. Worcester, *A Universal and Critical Dictionary of the English Language* (Boston)
1847*	William Bolles, *An Explanatory and Phonographic Pronouncing Dictionary of the English Language* (New London)

1848* William G. Webster, *A High School Pronouncing Dictionary of the English Language* (New York)

1848* John Russell Bartlett, *Dictionary of Americanisms* (New York)

1850* Noah Webster, *An American Dictionary of the English Language, revised and enlarged by Chauncey A. Goodrich* (Springfield)

1850 William Grimshaw, *A Primary Pronouncing Dictionary*

1850* Joseph E. Worcester, *Primary Dictionary* (Boston)

1851* James H. Martin, *The Orthoepist, Containing a Selection of all Those Words of the English Language Usually Pronounced Improperly* (Cincinnati)

1851 Edward Hazen, *The New Speller and Definer*

1855 "A Public School Teacher", *The Public School Dictionary* (Philadelphia)

1855* Dan S. Smalley and Nathaniel Storrs, *The American Phonetic Dictionary of the English Language* (Cincinnati)

1855* Joseph E. Worcester, *A Pronouncing, Explanatory and Synonymous Dictionary of the English Language* (Boston)

1856* Chauncey A. Goodrich, *Goodrich's Revision and Enlargement of Webster's American Dictionary* (Philadelphia)

1856* William G. Webster, assisted by Chauncey A. Goodrich, *An Explanatory and Pronouncing Dictionary of the English Language* (New York)

1856* Benjamin H. Hall, *A Collection of College Words and Customs* (Cambridge)

1859* Alfred L. Elwyn, *Glossary of Supposed Americanisms* (Philadelphia)

1859 Alexander H. Laidlaw, *An American Pronouncing Dictionary of the English Language* (Philadelphia)

1860* Joseph E. Worcester, *A Dictionary of the English Language* (Boston)

INDEX OF CASES CITED

——

INDEX OF AUTHORS AND SOURCES

___

INDEX OF SUBJECTS

financiers, industrialists, merchants, managers)
career choice to become, 79, 182, 257n., 278n., 280n., 357–86
definition as an occupation and profession, 5, 8, 8–9n., 255–6, 352
economic status of, 55, 167–8, 174, 269
education of (business schools), 228, 249, 255
relationship with: law and lawyers, 166–7, 289–90; learned professions, 167, 256–7, 315–16; science and scientists, 213
social status of, 8, 167, 256–7, 283
see also contract; corporations; economic conditions; industrialization
Butler, Nicholas Murray, 217, 222, 253

Caldwell, David, 97
California, 248, 292, 293; *see also* San Diego; San Francisco
California, University of, 218, 228, 251, 255, 281n.
Callender, Elisha, 66
calling (vocation, *vocatio*), 31–4, 103, 145; *see also* professio; 'profession'
Calvin, John, 19, 27, 41, 49, 87
Calvinism (Calvinists), 22–3, 25–8, 63, 78, 94–5, 115, 301; *see also* architectonic, religious, theological; Baptists; church and state, relationship between; Congregationalists; covenant; dialectic, in theology; Dutch Reformed Church; Presbyterians; Puritan; science, relationship with theology
Cambridge University, 8, 256n.
Campbell, Archibald, 114
Canada, 267; *see also* Nova Scotia
capitalism *see* industrialization; Weber, Max
Carnegie, Andrew, 203, 253, 266, 269
Carnegie Foundation for the Advancement of Teaching, 2, 210, 214, 219, 230, 249n., 252, 260, 266–7, 283, 291, 307, 310
Carr-Saunders, A. M., 1, 3–4, 312, 318, 322, 324
case method of teaching law, 210–11; *see also* lawyers, education and
Catholics (Catholicism, Roman Catholicism), 20n., 22, 25n., 26, 36, 48, 81n., 97, 130, 208, 289
Cattell, J. McKeen, 215, 234, 239, 259, 269
Centenary College, 173

Chandler, Alfred D., Jr, 5, 255n.
Chandler, Asa, 253
Chandler, Thomas, 61
Channing, William Ellery, 187, 195
Charleston (SC), 62, 80; *see also* South Carolina
Charlton, Kenneth, 1, 3
Chase, Samuel, 151
Chauncy, Charles, 79–80
chemistry (chemists), 144, 202, 207, 210, 213, 214, 271; *see also* natural science
Chesapeake region, 52, 60, 116; *see also* Maryland
Chevalier, Michael, 130, 167
Chicago, 216, 241, 245, 247, 273; *see also* Illinois
Chicago, University of, 218, 227, 229, 251, 253, 255, 259, 262, 267, 270, 283, 286, 294, 297
Chillingworth, William, 28, 52
church
attendance and seating at, 51–2
membership of, 47–8
see also buildings, ecclesiastical; church polity
Church of England *see* Anglicans
church polity (ecclesiastical organization), 28, 37–46, 49–50, 129–30; *see also* Congregationalists; dialectic, in church polity; Presbyterians; Puritan
church and state, relationship between, 46–9, 113, 128, 159–60; *see also* Calvinism; clergy, political authority of; Puritan
Cicero, Marcus Tullius, 19
Cincinnati, 144, 146, 163, 180, 247, 257; *see also* Ohio
civil religion *see* church and state, relationship between
Civil War, 107, 139, 160, 171, 190, 191, 193, 194, 196, 200–3, 220, 239, 246, 250, 251, 260, 261, 262, 268, 272, 273, 277, 288, 290
Clark, Jonas G., 253
Clark University, 246, 251
Claxton, Philander P., 218
clergy (ministers, priests), 214n., 322
association of, 42, 44–5, 196–7
career choice to become, 78–9, 180–4, 257n., 280, 286–7, 342–86
economic status of, 54–67, 116–20, 124–5, 169–71, 174, 179, 258–9, 326–38

Michigan, 194, 228
Michigan, University of, 12, 183n., 191,
205, 217, 218, 222, 224–5n., 228, 229,
230, 233, 251
Middle Ages (medieval), 19–20, 54, 97, 99,
108, 192, 212, 322
universities in, 6, 98, 99, 101, 103, 187,
199, 295
middle colonies, 30, 77, 117, 328–41; see
also individual colonies or states
Middlebury College, 183n.
mid-west see western United States
military, 7–8, 212, 322
millennialism, 129
Miller, Perry, 24, 26, 27n., 38, 47, 77, 107,
109, 159
Mills, Jonathan, 65
ministers see clergy
Minnesota, 217, 241
Minnesota, University of, 217, 218, 228,
251, 296
Mississippi, 112, 128, 138n., 150, 158, 175,
245, 289, 292, 352
Missouri, 150, 174, 189, 258, 282; see also
St. Louis
Missouri, University of, 228, 249, 251,
297
Mitchell, David, 78
modern language study (Modern Language
Association), 206, 225, 268, 271–2; see
also humanities
moments in the rhetoric of profession, 16,
199, 304
first, 19–22, 98, 301
second, 30–5, 98, 136, 302
third, 99–102, 136, 302
fourth, 112, 136–49, 192, 302
fifth, 199, 274–7, 295, 303
sixth, 199, 295–7, 303
see also 'learned professions'; 'professed';
'profession'; 'professional'; 'professor';
rhetoric
monastic orders, 19–20, 301
money see economic conditions
Monroe, James, 156
Montana, University of, 218
Montesquieu, Charles Louis ... de, 153
Montgomery, Joseph, 118
Moravians, 25n.
Morgan, Edmund S., 27, 107, 109
Morgan, John Pierpont, 203, 269
Morison, Samuel E., 341–3, 344, 349
Mormons, 111
Munson, Eneas, 78

Murrin, John M., 93
'mystery', 31; see also expertise, functional

Nashville, 167; see also Tennessee
Nashville, University of, 218
National Council of Education, 217, 273;
see also National Education Association
National Education Association (NEA,
National Teachers Association), 190,
193, 214, 223, 230, 232–3, 245, 273;
see also National Council of Education
National Teachers Association see National
Education Association
national university, proposals for a, 160,
245
natural science see astronomy; biology;
botany; chemistry; geology;
mathematics; physics; science
Naval Academy, US, 212
Nebraska, 188, 246, 251
Nebraska, University of, 251
Nevada, 292
Nevin, John W., 156
New England, 57–8, 116, 184, 253
education in, 172, 189, 257n., 339–41
polity, law, lawyers, courts in, 51, 89, 90,
156, 181
religion and clergy in, 22–4, 38, 41–2,
44, 47–8, 51, 52, 66–7, 76–7, 87–90,
116, 119n., 169–71, 180, 185n., 197,
287, 328–38
see also individual states
New Hampshire
polity, law, lawyers, courts in, 74, 85, 93,
128, 135, 352
religion and clergy in, 54–5, 63, 64, 81,
96, 113, 117, 119
New Haven, 30, 43, 47, 73; see also
Connecticut
New Jersey, 253
medicine and physicians in, 83, 184
polity, law, lawyers, courts in, 72, 74–5,
85, 88, 93, 110
religion and clergy in, 6–7, 45, 48, 52,
54, 61, 62, 64, 66, 77, 78, 81n., 96,
101, 117, 118, 145, 169–70
schools and teachers in, 97, 263
New Mexico, 292
New Netherlands, 57, 68–9; see also New
York (colony or state)
New York (colony or state), 57, 58n., 253
polity, law, lawyers, courts in, 73, 75, 86,
93, 111, 137, 146, 150–1, 167, 175–80,
250

Congregationalists; dialectic;
Presbyterians; Quakers; science,
relationship with theology

Quakers (Society of Friends), 21–3, 25n.,
    38, 46, 48, 56, 72, 81, 93, 94, 125
Quincy, Josiah, 161

Randolph, Edward, 30
Randolph-Macon College, 173
Rawson, Grindall, 81
Reinsch, Paul S., 89
religion *see* cultural ideal, of religion
Republicanism (Republicans), 110, 131–2,
    155–6, 160
research, 215–16, 223, 240, 298; *see also*
    cultural ideal, of science and
    education; science, meaning of
Revolution, American, 110, 117, 120, 127,
    131–2, 139–40, 149, 175, 184, 268; *see
    also* Declaration of Independence;
    historiography, about American
    Revolution
Reynolds, Peter, 117
rhetoric, 6, 14–16, 121n., 127–8, 139n.,
    139–40n., 145, 204, 309, 323–5; *see
    also* moments in the rhetoric of
    profession
Rhode Island
    polity, law, lawyers, courts in, 73, 85, 88,
        150, 155
    religion and clergy in, 45, 48, 54, 67,
        81n., 94, 113
    schools and teachers in, 193
Rice, William M., 253
Richardson, Samuel, 141–3
Rochester (NY), 171–2; *see also* New York
    (colony or state)
Rochester, University of, 183n.
Rockefeller, John D., 203, 253, 269
Rodgers, Daniel T., 139–40n.
Rogers, John, 119
Romeyn, Theodore, 82
Roselius, Christian, 209
Rosenberg, Charles E., 237n., 294
Royall, Isaac, 161
Royce, Josiah, 229n.
rule of law *see* jurisprudence, rule of law
    and formal rationalism
rural schools *see* schools, rural
Rush, Benjamin, 101, 121, 130
Rutgers University (Queen's College), 82,
    355–6, 371n., 386

Sage, Henry W., 253
St. Louis (Missouri), 241, 257, 284; *see also*
    Missouri
salary *see* businessmen; clergy; clerks;
    educators; judges; lawyers; physicians;
    presidents; professors; school
    administrators; teachers; tutors
Saltonstall, Gurdon, 51
San Diego, 261, 284; *see also* California
San Francisco, 216, 247, 309; *see also*
    California
San Jose Normal School, 219
Sandemanians, 56
Say, Jean-Baptiste, 164
Sayre, James, 84
Scales, James, 96
Schneider, Donald O., 343–4, 353, 376n.
scholarship about professions, 2–5, 17,
    185–7, 199, 203–4, 222, 308–9, 312n.,
    319–25
    normative shift in, 310–11, 318–19,
        320n.
    theoretical shift in, 311–17, 318–19
school administrators (principals, school
    administration, superintendents),
    217–19, 235
    definition of, 215, 343
    economic status of, 173, 261
    institutional authority of, 241–2, 284n.
    social status of, 284
    see also educators; 'professor', meaning
        school administrator or teacher;
        science, of teaching or education;
        teachers; women
schools
    elementary, 214, 216, 220, 232, 263
    rural, 216, 246, 263, 264n., 277, 284–5
    secondary (high schools), 214, 216, 217,
        220, 232, 234, 247, 250, 282
    system of, 216–17, 224, 242, 243, 247,
        248, 253, 261, 263, 273, 284
    see also buildings, educational; common
        schools; kindergartens; professors,
        involved in schools; vocational
        education
Schurman, Jacob G., 229
science (natural science, physical science,
    scientists), 158, 204–5, 211–12, 230,
    300–1
    Baconian, 158, 204–5, 207, 209
    meaning of, 202, 204–5
    relationship with: jurisprudence,
        209–11, 249, 288, 291–2; medicine,